Handbook of Strategic Enrollment Management

Handbook of Strategic Enrollment Management

Don Hossler
Bob Bontrager
and Associates

JOSSEY-BASS
A Wiley Imprint
www.josseybass.com

AACRAO
Advancing Global Higher Education

Cover Design: Lauryn Tom
Cover Art: © iStockphoto/22926881
John Schuh, Consulting Editor
Copyright © 2015 by American Association of Collegiate Registrars and Admissions Officers. All rights reserved.

Published by Jossey-Bass
A Wiley Brand
One Montgomery Street, Suite 1200, San Francisco, CA 94104-4594—
www.wiley.com

Jossey-Bass books and products are available through most bookstores. To contact Jossey-Bass directly call our Customer Care Department within the U.S. at 800-956-7739, outside the U.S. at 317-572-3986, or fax 317-572-4002.

Wiley publishes in a variety of print and electronic formats and by print-on-demand. Some material included with standard print versions of this book may not be included in e-books or in print-on-demand. If this book refers to media such as a CD or DVD that is not included in the version you purchased, you may download this material at http://booksupport.wiley.com. For more information about Wiley products, visit www.wiley.com.

Library of Congress Cataloging-in-Publication Data

Library of Congress Cataloging-in-Publication Data has been applied for and is on file with the Library of Congress.
ISBN 978-1-118-81948-7 (cloth); ISBN 978-1-118-81953-1 (ebk.); ISBN 978-1-118-81940-1 (ebk.)

Printed in the United States of America
FIRST EDITION

HB Printing   10 9 8 7 6 5 4 3 2

The Jossey-Bass Higher and
Adult Education Series

CONTENTS

PREFACE

Don Hossler and Bob Bontrager

The field of Strategic Enrollment Management (SEM) is arguably the newest major administrative function to emerge at the senior levels of college and university administration. The confluence of competition for students, competition for the prestige associated with college rankings such as the "Best Colleges" rankings published by *US News & World Report*, as well as concerns about retention and graduation rates, and growing investments in campus-based institutional aid to achieve enrollment goals, have resulted in the growing importance of new organizations created with titles such as *Enrollment Services, Enrollment Management, Enrollment Management and Student Affairs*, and so on. Since the 1970s, there has been an exponential increase in research on the topics of student college choice, student retention, and the effects of financial aid on student enrollment behavior.

Part of this evolutionary process has been the naming of this new enterprise. As originally conceived, facing a projected decrease in the number of high school graduates in the mid-1970s, forward-thinking college admissions officers coined the term "enrollment management" to describe a new approach to maintaining the number of new students they enrolled as demand decreased. Early on, the "managing" of enrollments involved examining demographic data, segmenting target groups of students, and ramping up marketing efforts to prospective students in new, more intensive ways. Through the 1980s, enrollment management grew to include other enrollment service functions that proved critical to attracting students, such as financial aid, registration, student records, and fee payment. It grew conceptually as well to focus not just on the number of new students enrolled, but also retention and graduation rates, creating direct ties between institutions' academic and enrollment management efforts. With this comprehensive view of enrollment came more sophisticated financial modeling that linked recruitment and retention rates with institutional revenues. By the late 1980s, the scope of enrollment management had grown into a major strategic component of institutional operations; hence the emergence of the term "Strategic Enrollment Management." It is this comprehensive, advanced understanding of original enrollment management thinking that forms the basis of this book.

As SEM has emerged and grown, what has been lacking is a comprehensive sourcebook on this important administrative function within postsecondary education. Several books and reports have been published on this topic—see, for example, *Enrollment Management: An Integrated Approach* (1984), *Creating Effective Enrollment Management Systems* (1986), *The Strategic Management of College Enrollments* (1990), *Strategic Enrollment Management: Transforming Higher Education (2012)*, *SEM in Canada: Promoting Student and Institutional Success in Canadian Colleges and Universities* (2011), *The Strategic Management of College Enrollments* (1990), *Enrollment Management for the 21st Century: Delivering Institutional Goals, Accountability, and Fiscal Responsibility* (1999), and *A Practical Guide to Strategic Enrollment Management Planning in Higher Education* (2007). None of these publications, however, attempts to provide a comprehensive treatment of relevant research that can inform SEM practices and a thoughtful discussion of the intersection of the economics and finance of higher education and SEM, and none attempts to delineate the leading strategies and administrative functions that define effective SEM organizations. This volume expressly intends to address that void.

Jossey-Bass Publishers, part of the Wiley brand of publications, has a long tradition of publishing extensive handbooks on administrative functions in colleges and universities. Jossey-Bass has already published handbooks in the field of student affairs—*The Handbook of Student Affairs Administration* (3rd Edition, 2009), and *Student Services: A Handbook for the Profession* (5th Edition, 2010). In addition, Wiley has similarly published a compendium on institutional research entitled *The Handbook of Institutional Research* (2012). With the publishing of this book, *Handbook of Strategic Enrollment Management*, Jossey-Bass has added a new volume to its collection of comprehensive source books on the field of higher education.

We hope that this book will be judged useful by the worlds of both practice and research. In this seven-part volume, thirty chapters focus heavily on relevant research, on topics ranging from student college choice, to higher education finance, to considerations regarding how offices such as the registrar or financial aid contribute to SEM. We seek to examine both the *what* and the *why* of SEM. Some practitioners in the field of Strategic Enrollment Management fail to recognize the importance of how research (the why) can inform current practices and provide insights into future directions of the field.

Postsecondary educational institutions find themselves in an era of evidenced-based decision-making. Senior campus policy makers are being asked to demonstrate that they are using research and data to make the best decisions for their institutions. Thus, the increasingly large body of research on topics ranging from the mobility patterns for transfer students, to studies of the effects of campus-based financial aid on access and retention, to research on how colleges organize themselves to increase graduation rates provide a foundation for evidenced-based decision-making. Successful SEM organizations, however, rely not only on evidenced-based decision-making, but they also require successful planning processes, and they need business practices in offices such as admissions, financial aid, and registration and records that use technology to make timely decisions, to support student enrollment patterns, to facilitate access to a range of majors with a myriad of prerequisites, and to identify students whose course-taking patterns might suggest that they are at risk of not graduating. Senior enrollment officers need access to published research, as well as to campus-based SEM-oriented research, in addition to insights into leading practices in SEM organizations that can bolster their requests for resources, the enrollment plans that they implement, and/or the need to reorganize structures within SEM units.

This handbook comprises seven parts and thirty chapters. The seven parts cover the following topical areas.

Part I provides a brief history of the field of Strategic Enrollment Management, as well as an overview of the factors that have shaped the structure of SEM organizations. This is important background, especially for aspiring enrollment managers and other senior campus administrators including provosts, CFOs, student affairs staff, and the president. Having a sense of the history and current structure of SEM units can help inform their thinking of the best ways to structure their Strategic Enrollment Management organization and provides a perspective on what they can expect of SEM units.

In Part II we take a close look at college admissions and recruitment from multiple perspectives. It begins with a research-based examination of what we know about the factors that influence students' enrollment decisions. This is an important contextual chapter that informs and/or influences all of the activities of the remaining chapters in Part II. Other chapters discuss the structure of postsecondary markets in the United States, how institutions market themselves to recruit new students, what enrollment managers should know about transfer students and articulation policies, and how institutions with different missions decide who they will admit.

Moving from admissions and recruitment, Part III takes a closer look at the connections between higher education finance and SEM, including topics of tuition pricing and the economics of using campus-based aid to achieve enrollment goals. These areas have become some of the most important underpinnings of SEM. Indeed, we would argue that a deep understanding of the intersection between higher education finance, tuition pricing, and campus-based financial aid has become one of the most important areas of expertise for senior enrollment professionals. Chapter 11 closely examines the analytical approaches SEM organizations employ to maximize the impact of campus-based aid on achieving institutional enrollment goals.

Part IV moves on to the topic of student retention, persistence, and graduation. Along with college admissions, the topic of student retention and graduation has received a great deal of attention from both researchers and practitioners. This body of literature is so robust that we have organized it around the following themes: theoretical models of student persistence, an overview of the new public policy agenda that considers both retention and persistence as separate outcomes along with graduation, a review of research on traditional age students and the implications for SEM organizations, an overview of what we know about enhancing persistence among students of color, and separate chapters on research on the retention of nontraditional students and students in need of remediation. Part IV ends with a discussion of an understudied area: What do we know about what institutions are doing to enhance student persistence and graduation?

In Part V, we look at an important element of any successful SEM organization: what takes place in the back offices in units such as admissions, financial aid, and the registrar, and the closely associated role of technology. The chapters in Part V are more practice-based than research-based and address functional issues that often are an afterthought in SEM planning, when in fact they are critical to improving recruitment and retention rates. We sought out some of the leading practitioners to provide input on these key areas, and they have delivered thoughtful analyses of intentional structures they have employed.

Part VI addresses several of the strategic areas of SEM, beginning with a discussion of the research structures and data required for effective SEM practices. Chapter 24 links campus-based SEM efforts with policy issues at the state and national levels, recognizing that the achievement of public policy goals ultimately relies on changes at the institutional level. We close this part of the book with two chapters that focus on strategic thinking and planning, offering thoughts and guideposts for transitioning institutions to become more SEM-oriented.

In the final part of this volume, we consider new organizational models for SEM. In Chapter 27, we look at SEM issues and structures for the recruitment of international students and SEM organizations for graduate and professional schools. This is followed by chapters on current trends in SEM and another discussing ethics. We close the final chapter with a summary of the most important topics covered in this volume and recommendations for the future of SEM efforts.

In summary, *Handbook of Strategic Enrollment Management* provides the most complete treatment of SEM that has been attempted. It can be used to help improve the planning and future directions of SEM organizations, and it can help guide future research on various topics related to postsecondary access and success, better to understand the range of postsecondary institutions and to help enhance the health and vitality of colleges and universities.

ABOUT THE EDITORS
AND CONTRIBUTORS

Matt Birnbaum is an associate professor, chair of the Department of Leadership, Policy and Development: Higher Education and P-12 Education at the University of Northern Colorado. He teaches courses on enrollment management, law, public policy, and research design.

Bob Bontrager is Senior Director of Consulting and Strategic Enrollment Management Initiatives for AACRAO and is Editor in Chief of Wiley's *SEM Quarterly* journal. He has written and presented in more than a dozen countries on Strategic Enrollment Management and related topics.

John M. Braxton is a professor of education in Higher Education Leadership at Peabody College, Vanderbilt University. His research centers on the college student experience in general and college student persistence in particular.

Stephen H. Brooks holds a PhD in economics and is the founding president of SHBrooks. He specializes in enrollment management and is one of the nation's foremost experts in applying econometric models to predict and analyze student enrollment.

Guilbert Brown is Vice President for Finance and Administration at Edinboro University of Pennsylvania, serving previously in business officer roles at both public and private universities. He has written and presented internationally on budget models and integrating academic, enrollment, and budget planning.

Marc M. Camille is the Vice President for Enrollment Management and Communications at Loyola University Maryland. He has presented frequently at

AMA's Symposium for the Marketing of Higher Education and AACRAO's Strategic Enrollment Management Conference.

Emily Chung is the Program Director for the USC Center for Enrollment Research, Policy, and Practice at the University of Southern California. She is currently a doctoral student at the USC Rossier School of Education, specializing in higher education administration.

Bruce Clemetsen is Vice President for Student Affairs at Linn-Benton Community College. He has practiced, written, presented, and consulted extensively on Strategic Enrollment Management, student transfer, and institutional partnerships.

Jennifer DeHaemers is Associate Vice Chancellor for Student Affairs and Enrollment Management at the University of Missouri – Kansas City. She has practiced, written, and presented in the areas of Strategic Enrollment Management at two- and four-year institutions.

Afet Dundar is Associate Director of the National Student Clearinghouse Research Center. She plays a leading role in producing the Research Center's Signature Report series of national reports on student access and success and helps to develop the center's research agenda.

Lee Furbeck is the Director of Undergraduate Admissions and Student Transition at Cleveland State University and directs AACRAO's Transfer Conference. She has written and presented extensively on transfer-related topics and student access and equity.

Brent A. Gage is the Associate Provost for Enrollment Management at the University of Alabama at Birmingham (UAB). He is an expert in transforming enrollment management processes.

Tom Green is the Director of Technology Solutions and a Managing Consultant at the AACRAO. He has practiced and published on SEM in the United States and abroad for nearly thirty years.

Jacob P. K. Gross is an assistant professor of Higher Education Administration at the University of Louisville. He works on education policy, particularly policies pertaining to financial aid and finance. His work focuses on educational access and equity for underrepresented students.

Jay W. Goff is Vice President of Enrollment and Retention Management at Saint Louis University. He an author and presenter on Strategic Enrollment Management and has served in advisory roles for ACT, AACRAO's SEM Conference, and the National Student Clearinghouse.

Harold V. Hartley III is Senior Vice President of the Council of Independent Colleges, where he has lead responsibility for CIC's Presidents Institute. He provides leadership for CIC's research and assessment initiatives.

Tom Hayes is chair and professor of Marketing at Xavier University, where he also served as the Director of Institutional Advancement. He has received both CASE's Crystal Apple and Alice Beeman awards for outstanding work in the area of marketing of higher education.

Adam J. Herman is a doctoral student in Higher Education and Student Affairs at Indiana University in Bloomington. His research interests include admissions, marketing, and strategic planning.

Amy S. Hirschy, PhD, is an assistant professor at the University of Louisville. Her research interests focus on theories of college student persistence, organizations, and college student development to identify institutional factors that promote and hinder student learning and success.

Don Hossler is the former Vice-Chancellor of Enrollment Services and currently serves as a professor of higher education at Indiana University Bloomington. He has conducted research and written on college choice, enrollment management, student persistence, and financial aid.

Mary Hutchens is a doctoral candidate at Vanderbilt University, studying Higher Education Leadership and Policy. Her research interests focus on enrollment management and nontraditional students.

Willis A. Jones is an assistant professor of higher education at the University of Kentucky. His research examines various areas related to the study of higher education, including intercollegiate athletic policy, institutional diversity, college student retention, and university prestige.

David Kalsbeek is the Senior Vice President for Enrollment Management and Marketing at DePaul University in Illinois. He has written extensively and given more than 100 presentations and consulted widely on issues related to Strategic Enrollment Management.

Wendy Kilgore is Director of Research and Managing Consultant for the AACRAO. She has more than fifteen years of experience as a higher education administrator and consultant in the United States and Canada.

Jerry Lucido is the Executive Director of the Center for Enrollment Research, Policy, and Practice. He has undertaken research to design and execute effective and principled college admission and enrollment management.

Dawn Lyken-Segosebe is a doctoral candidate in the Higher Education Leadership and Policy Studies program at Vanderbilt University. Her research focuses on faculty (codes of conduct, scholarship, and interaction with students) and the college outcomes of commuter students.

Alicia Moore is Dean of Student and Enrollment Services for Central Oregon Community College. She has presented and written extensively on community colleges, Strategic Enrollment Management, admissions and registrar practices, process redesign, and diversity.

Michelle Mott is Associate Director of Government Relations and Communications at the AACRAO. She also serves as editor of and contributor to the *AACRAO Transcript* e-newsletter.

Eunkyoung Park is an associate research fellow at Korean Educational Development Institute (KEDI). Her research interests include college choice, higher education access and success, quantitative research methods, community colleges, and equity.

Mike Reilly joined AACRAO as Executive Director on June 1, 2012. Prior to coming to AACRAO he served as the Executive Director for the Council of Presidents, an association of the six public baccalaureate degree granting institutions in Washington state.

Michele Sandlin is a Managing Consultant for AACRAO. She has written and presented frequently in the areas of holistic admissions, admissions operations, student transfer, and international admissions.

Dave Sauter is University Registrar at his alma mater, Miami University, having served in similar capacities at two other institutions during a thirty-year career. His contributions to the registrar profession include several AACRAO publications and numerous presentations on a range of topics.

Gabriel Serna is an assistant professor at the University of Northern Colorado. His research interests lie in the areas of higher education economics and finance, enrollment management, and applied econometrics and research design.

Howard Shanken is a Senior Consultant with AACRAO Consulting. He has reviewed policies and processes at a broad spectrum of institutions, including national, international, public, and private universities and colleges.

Douglas T. Shapiro is Executive Research Director at the National Student Clearinghouse. He has fifteen years of experience in research with student-level data at the institutional, state, and national levels.

Monique L. Snowden is the Vice President for Academic and Enrollment Services at Fielding Graduate University. She is a frequent presenter and has conducted research on Strategic Enrollment Management.

Vasti Torres is Dean of the College of Education at the University of South Florida in Tampa. She has worked on community college initiatives including Achieving the Dream, Rural Community College Initiative, and Building Engagement and Attainment for Minority Students.

Darin Wohlgemuth is the Director of Enrollment Research at Iowa State University and leads the university's Enrollment and Research team. He previously served as Director of Budget Research and Analysis in the Provost's office. He contributes often to the SEM profession as an author and presenter.

Mary Ziskin is an assistant professor of educational leadership at the University of Dayton. She conducts research on the enrollment pathways of adult learners and working college students, stratification in postsecondary educational opportunity, and critical research methodologies.

Brian Zucker is the founding director of Human Capital Research Corporation, a higher education research consultancy based in Evanston, Illinois. For nearly three decades, he has served as an economist and policy analyst to industry, government, and the non-profit sector.

ABOUT AACRAO

The American Association of Collegiate Registrars and Admissions Officers, founded in 1910, is a nonprofit, voluntary, professional association of more than 11,000 higher education administrators who represent more than 2,600 institutions and agencies in the United States and in forty countries around the world. From its offices in Washington, DC, AACRAO initiates, interprets, and implements policies and practices for the global educational community. This is accomplished by identifying and promoting standards and leading practices in strategic enrollment management, student services, instructional management, and deployment of information technology. Among its many publications and periodicals, AACRAO produces the *SEM Quarterly* journal published by the Wiley Online Library.

American Association of Collegiate Registrars and Admissions Officers
One Dupont Circle, NW, Suite 520
Washington, DC 20036–1135
Tel: (202) 293–9161
Fax: (202) 872–8857
www.aacrao.org

For a complete listing of AACRAO publications, visit www.aacrao.org/publications.

Handbook of Strategic Enrollment Management

PART ONE

SETTING THE CONTEXT

Part I provides an introduction to Strategic Enrollment Management. Chapter 1 defines SEM and offers a brief history of its emergence and evolution. The chapter discusses several definitions of SEM that collectively point both to organizational structures and research that inform SEM policies and practices. Drawing upon discussions of public management's theory of *new managerialism*, which focuses on the growing use of for-profit business practices in non-profit and public organizations such as postsecondary educational institutions, this chapter helps to frame the rise of SEM in a wider context. It also examines how the combination of demographic trends, public policy shifts, and the emergence of the "Best Colleges" rankings published by *US News & World Report,* plus a growing focus on institutional prestige, has contributed to the attention SEM has garnered from public policy makers and critics of postsecondary education practices.

Chapter 2 more closely examines how public policy shifts toward viewing postsecondary education as a private good has resulted in both public and private postsecondary institutions competing for students in a market model. This, in turn, has resulted in colleges and universities focusing more attention and resources on their ability to attract a sufficient number of tuition-paying students. This chapter also looks at how the changing demographics of traditional-aged students are altering the competitive landscape faced by all postsecondary sectors.

Chapter 3 considers the structure of SEM organizations. The authors examine the variety of university executives to whom senior enrollment officers report and the importance of their ability to work effectively with all senior members of the president's cabinet, particularly the chief financial officer (CFO). The discussion moves on to the importance of campus-based, enrollment-related research and a strong technology infrastructure. Administrative units such as admissions, financial aid, orientation, and others often included within SEM organizations are discussed. The authors also note the dearth of research on the efficacy of different organizational structures for SEM units. This is because success is often dependent upon a complex array of factors that are based on institutional culture, institutional wealth, and the location of the campus, for example. Nevertheless, Chapter 3 helps to establish a common understanding of SEM units.

CHAPTER 1

Origins of Strategic Enrollment Management

Don Hossler

T his chapter presents a brief historical overview of the factors that led
to the rise of Strategic Enrollment Management (SEM). This chapter is
not intended to be a comprehensive history, but instead provides a
context for the chapters that follow, which offer a comprehensive overview
of the organizational structures, processes, types of research, and strategies
that underpin the concept of SEM. This chapter examines the historical roots
of SEM and discusses why demography, governmental trends toward the
privatization of postsecondary education, the role of rankings, and institutional
isomorphism (the tendency of organizations to mimic the structure of similar
organizations) (DiMaggio & Powell, 1983) have created a context in which SEM
will likely not only remain a fixture in postsecondary education, but will grow
in its importance among colleges and universities.

Complete histories have been written on the rise of SEM (for example,
Henderson, 2001; Hossler, 2011). Indeed, SEM has not only emerged as an important managerial function in the United States but also in other parts of the
globe as well. The global trends toward the privatization of tertiary education,
as well as globalization, international rankings of colleges and universities, and
demographic trends in many industrialized nations are making SEM an increasingly common organizational concept in other nation states.

Before providing a historical overview of emergence of SEM, we offer a brief introduction to SEM to set the stage for this chapter. One important caveat is warranted in this introduction: Although some chapters in this handbook may refer to for-profit sector postsecondary institutions as part of the competitive forces that influence the enrollment strategies of non-profit colleges and universities, this volume does not provide an overview of SEM activities and strategies in the for-profit sector. To date, too little is known about the strategies, policies, and practices of the for-profit sector to be included in this book.

Strategic Enrollment Management is perhaps best described by Lee Bolman and Terrence Deal (1991), as a structural framework that can be simultaneously considered as an organizational structure, as a set of processes, and as organizational policies. In this context, SEM is simultaneously a set of processes and policies associated with the recruitment and admission of college students, as well as the retention, academic success, and graduation of students enrolled in postsecondary education. It is also a managerial paradigm for organizations associated with these processes. Typically, SEM organizations include the offices of admissions, financial aid, registration and records, and an enrollment-related institutional research office. In addition, offices such as orientation, academic advising, the bursar, and sometimes offices associated with student affairs and/ or institutional marketing can also be included in SEM organizations.

Bob Bontrager and Christine Kerlin (2004) posited that SEM comprises the following components:

- Characteristics of the institution and the world around it
- Institutional mission and priorities
- Optimal enrollments (number, quality, diversity)
- Student recruitment
- Student fees and financial aid
- Retention
- Institutional marketing
- Career counseling and development
- Academic advising
- Curricular and program development
- Methods of program delivery
- Quality of campus life and facilities

This chapter considers several definitions of SEM, followed by a brief history of its origins—the adoption of for-profit business strategies, demographic trends, and shifts in public policy provide a short historical account. In addition, theoretical frames that have been employed to explain the rise and use of SEM are examined. This chapter ends with a discussion of the future of SEM.

DEFINING STRATEGIC ENROLLMENT MANAGEMENT

A number of definitions for SEM have been advanced since the books and articles first started to appear on this organizational concept. Bontrager (2008) defined SEM as follows: "Strategic Enrollment Management is defined as a co-ordinated set of concepts and processes that enables fulfillment of institutional mission and students' educational goals" (p. 18). Another leading scholar and practitioner in the field, David Kalsbeek (2013), defined SEM as "A comprehensive approach to integrating all of the University's programs, practices, policies, and planning related to achieving the *optimal* recruitment, retention and graduation of students."

Don Hossler and John Bean have proffered the following definition:

> Enrollment management is both an organizational concept as well as a systematic set of activities designed to enable educational institutions to exert more influence over their student enrollments and total net tuition revenue derived from enrolled students. Organized by strategic planning and supported by institutional research, enrollment management activities concern student college choice, transition to college, student attrition and retention, and student outcomes. These processes are studied to guide institutional practices in the areas of new student recruitment and financial aid, student support services, curriculum development and other academic areas that affect enrollments, student persistence, and student outcomes from college (revised in 2001 from Hossler, Bean, & Associates, 1990, p. 5).

This discussion of components and definitions of SEM share a common focus on the systematic integration of the functions of admissions, the relationship between tuition and fees (pricing) and financial aid, and student retention, along with the use of research to inform institutional policies and practices. The importance of curriculum offerings and the quality of the student experience are also recurring themes that are emphasized for the role they play in attracting and retaining students.

A BRIEF HISTORY OF STRATEGIC ENROLLMENT MANAGEMENT

These definitions and the discussion of SEM emphasize the intentional role institutions can play in *shaping the class* and represent key elements of SEM. However, it bears noting that the issues that determine a student's decision to enroll or persist in a college or university (at the undergraduate or graduate level) are far too complex to manage; the real goals are to influence the student's decisions in an ethical manner (assuming that the institution was a good choice for the student in the first place).

This section sets the stage for a brief historical overview of the demographic, societal, institutional, and public policy factors that shaped the emergence of SEM. In successive chapters, the processes, policies, and organizational structures that have been outlined in this introduction will be examined in more detail.

The Impact of Demographic Trends

In the United States, the emergence of SEM can trace its origins to the mid-1970s. At that time a confluence of societal, demographic, and institutional factors created the context for the development of what has arguably become one of the most important administrative functions to emerge at senior levels of college and university administration since the rise of the senior development officer, which emerged in the 1950s (Lasher & Cook, 1996). Collectively, these trends created an institutional environment in which college and university administrators felt the necessity to be more intentional about attracting and retaining students. In addition to their consideration of the demographic and societal trends, campus-based administrators had reason to believe that they had the tools to be more effective in exerting more influence upon their enrollments and their ability to *shape the class.*

To set the stage for the convergence of these trends, it is important to remember that even in the 1950s when the GI Bill had resulted in a dramatic increase in postsecondary participation rates, the foundation for a more competitive admission recruitment environment among postsecondary institutions was being built. The growth of community colleges during the 1950s and 1960s, along with the growth in enrollment at four-year public institutions—especially what we now call *regional public institutions*—had started to place competitive pressures on private colleges that were small, less selective, and less visible—what Alexander Astin and Calvin Lee (1972) called "the invisible colleges." It is important that we not underestimate the impact of the expansion of the postsecondary education system during this time period in the United States (a period that many educational scholars and observers describe as the *Golden Age of Higher Education*), as the number of traditional age high school students declined. Even in 1966, Alden Thresher, in his influential book, *College Admissions and the Public Interest,* reported that many private colleges and universities had found themselves needing to market the institution and recruit students actively in order to maintain enrollment—and the pressures on institutions to maintain their enrollments only intensified. In addition to increasing competition because of the growing number of postsecondary institutions, by the mid-1970s, colleges and universities had additional reasons to focus on competing with each other: They were preparing for a predicted decrease of traditional age college students estimated to be as high as 42 percent (Hossler, 1986). Not surprisingly, increasing competition for a declining pool of traditional age students resulted in campus policy makers placing more emphasis upon the recruitment and retention of students.

The competitive environment that colleges confronted in the 1970s and 1980s were not the only factors that provided the impetus for the emergence of enrollment management. The attitudes of public policy makers toward postsecondary education were also shifting, not just in the United States but around the globe. Historically, the United States has been an outlier; in many countries, postsecondary education had been viewed primarily as a public good and thus it was free, entirely funded by national, state, and/or regional governments. Unlike much of the rest of the world, the United States had a mixed funding model, whereby students and their families paid tuition, even at most public institutions. However, among public sector institutions the *public good* argument had been the rationale for relatively high levels of state subsidies to most public two- and four-year institutions. The fact that college graduates made more money, which enabled them to pay higher taxes; that they were more likely to create new businesses and jobs, to vote, to be involved in community service organizations; and that they were less likely to be unemployed or incarcerated (Bowen, 1980) had resulted in a public policy perspectives that emphasized the societal benefits of expanded postsecondary education opportunities. This was the underlying premise of relatively high levels of support in most states for their public colleges and universities, which helped to keep tuition rates low.

The Emergence of Enrollment/Strategic Enrollment Management

In the United States, the term, and perhaps the concept, of a comprehensive enrollment management system first emerged when Jack Maguire (1976) used the term "enrollment management" to describe his efforts to attract and retain students at Boston College. One of the first times the term formally appeared in public domain literature was in a 1981 *College Board Review* article by Leonard Kreutner and Eric Godfrey (1981) that describes a matrix approach to managing enrollments developed at California State University at Long Beach. Since these early publications, a spate of books, book chapters, monographs, and articles have been published on the topic of enrollment management. However, as a process and set of strategies, SEM, as we have suggested in the first section of this chapter, had been developing for many years. What made the enrollment management concept new when it first appeared was not demographic trends, public policy shifts, the development of new marketing techniques, or new retention strategies; rather, it was the organizational integration of functions such as academic advising, admissions, financial aid, and orientation into a comprehensive institutional approach designed to enable college and university administrators to exert greater influence over the factors that shape their enrollments.

Subsequent to Maguire's coining of the term "enrollment management," professional meetings and additional books and monographs on enrollment management began to appear. Hossler, in a relatively short period of time, authored or co-authored three books on enrollment management including *Enrollment Management: An Integrated Approach* (1984), *Creating Effective Enrollment Management Systems* (1986), and *Managing College Enrollments* (1990). In addition, Frank Kemerer, Victor Baldridge, and Kenneth Green (1982) authored *Strategies for Effective Enrollment Management*. In 1984, Ray Muston published a monograph entitled *Marketing and Enrollment Management in State Universities*. Somewhat later, Michael Dolence (1991, 1996, 1998) also published some influential books and book chapters on SEM.

In addition to these early works, in the 1980s the College Board and Loyola University of Chicago sponsored the first national conferences on enrollment management. Attendance at these conferences was not robust, as the concept was still embryonic. Even so, several core principles were crystallizing that remain key underpinnings of SEM. These include a marketing orientation toward admissions recruitment, an understanding that student retention is as important a part of enrollment efforts as student recruitment, a realization that campus-based financial aid could be used in a systematic fashion to achieve multiple enrollment goals and that SEM depends heavily upon empirical research and data analysis to guide its efforts, and finally an understanding that SEM is a process that has organizational implications and often requires structural change in how various university functions are integrated and organized around efforts to enroll and retain a student body with a desired set of characteristics.

In 1991, the American Association of College Registrars and Admissions Officers (AACRAO) held the first annual Strategic Enrollment Management Conference, and by 2012, this annual conference drew 727 registrants from 300 institutions in nine countries, including Canada, Korea, Mexico, and Saudi Arabia. Although attendees at the early conferences were mostly from tuition-dependent, private, not-for-profit colleges and universities, the attendance now includes flagship and regional public universities, two-year institutions, and a growing international representation. Senior university officers with enrollment management titles and responsibilities are now commonplace. Quickly, the term "enrollment management" became replaced by *Strategic Enrollment Management*. Terms like these are now common throughout both scholarly and professional publications in the field of higher education. Graduate courses and degrees in enrollment management are included in higher education curricula.

Changing Public Policy Priorities

A confluence of factors, including a recession in the United States but also in other developed regions of the world, as well as the growing costs of healthcare services, K–12 education, pension benefits, and other government-funded programs, resulted in declining support for public tertiary education. In the United States, reductions in state and local governments funding between 1987 and 2012 resulted in a reduction of $2,600 of state support per student enrolled after adjusting for inflation (Landy, 2013). In addition, in other nation states such as the United Kingdom or China, there was a push toward *massification*, the expansion of tertiary education, and public policy makers around the globe found that they could no longer afford to provide tertiary education at no cost to the students or their families. Countries ranging from the United Kingdom, to Russia, to China started charging tuition as they moved toward a cost-sharing model for funding postsecondary education (Johnstone & Marcucci, 2010). Public policy makers across the continents started looking for a politically acceptable rationale for declining state support (and rising tuition at public institutions) and emphasized the private benefits of postsecondary education (higher wages, better jobs, more job security, and so on). In addition, neo-liberalism was taking hold in the United States and in many other countries. As a result, public policy makers began to extol the virtues of the market and competition as a way to create better and more efficient publically funded enterprises. Public institutions of higher education were not immune to these trends. Public institutions were expected to compete for faculty, for research dollars, and for students. Thus, colleges and universities, including public institutions, began to recruit students—and their tuition dollars—more actively as a way of recovering revenue lost from government appropriations. Though many state policy makers have decried the rise in college tuition prices, in most instances these increases can be tracked back to declines in state funding (Fethke, 2012).

Theoretical Perspectives on Enrollment Management

Finally, the emergence of enrollment management can be viewed from the lens of three theoretical perspectives drawn from the fields of sociology and public management. We touch briefly on these theoretical perspectives.

Resource Dependency Theory, which was first advanced by Jeffrey Pfeffer and Gerald Salancik (1978), is often used to explain the emergence of SEM (see, for example, Hossler & Hoezee, 2001; Schulz & Lucido, 2011). Resource Dependency Theory posits that organizations respond to changes in the external environment by shifting time, energy, and resources to protect or acquire scarce resources that are central to the health and vitality of the organization. Scott Schulz and Jerome Lucido (2011) drew heavily on the work of Shelia Slaughter and Larry Leslie (1997) and their work on academic capitalism to demonstrate how Resource Dependency Theory has been widely used to explain the shift to the adoption of a market orientation among colleges and universities and the rise of SEM organizations in postsecondary education. Hossler and Hoezee (2001) suggest that during the late 1970s and early 1980s, when there was a precipitous decline in the number of traditional age high school graduates, colleges and universities started to adopt more intentional business-oriented strategies and organizational structures to recruit and enroll students. Subsequently, the rise of the college rankings industry and the growing importance of persistence and graduation rates also resulted in more focus on student success and organizational changes to support these efforts. It is worth noting that these pressures are not unique to North American tertiary institutions. Demographic pressures in parts of Europe and Japan, for example, are causing postsecondary institutions to focus more attention on managing their enrollments, and an increasing number of regional and global rankings have become a global phenomenon that are also fueling the rise of SEM in countries other than the United States.

Institutional theory can also be used to help explain the increasing number of SEM organizations in postsecondary educational institutions, both in North America and in other parts of the world. Paul DiMaggio and Walter Powell (1983) posit that as institutions, and organizations within institutions, seek legitimacy, they often mimic (*mimetic processes*) the organizational patterns and structures of other institutions and organizations deemed to be successful. This can result in a homogenization of organizational structures and patterns within other institutions and organizations that face similar challenges from the external environment. In essence, institutional theory can be thought of as an adaptive strategy whereby institutions mimic the organizational structures of similar organizations that are deemed to be successful. We submit that these processes help to explain the emergence of SEM as a normative organizational structure in many colleges and universities. As deans and provosts move on to become provosts and presidents at other institutions, if their previous college or university had a successful enrollment organization, they assume that it is only natural for them to have similar success at their new institution.

Finally, SEM can be viewed as a manifestation of what scholars of organizational studies in the field of public management scholars have called *new managerialism* (Deem, 1998; Exworthy & Halford, 1998). The term "new managerialism" has been widely used in the study of public sector organizations, and it refers to the adoption of organizational structures, technologies, management practices, and values that are more commonly associated with the private, for-profit business sector. Colleges and universities, many of them public organizations, were not immune from these trends, and the same is true of non-profit private institutions. In the case of SEM, we posit that the adoption of the following techniques are examples of new managerialism: the shift to viewing tertiary education more as a private benefit; the use of business marketing strategies and data analytics to inform strategic enrollment strategies in the areas of admissions recruitment; the use of campus-based financial aid and empirically guided strategies to improve student persistence, success, and college completion; and the growing use of technology such as consumer resource management tools (CRMs), large database student information systems, and so on.

Drawing upon this introduction, we consider in more detail the rise of SEM in the next section.

STRATEGIC ENROLMENT MANAGEMENT: A STRUCTURAL FRAMEWORK

Although all of the factors discussed in the introduction to this chapter played a role in the emergence of SEM in the United States, the single largest factor was the declining number of high school graduates in the 1970s, which accentuated an already competitive environment for the recruitment of traditional age college students. Institutions in other parts of the world, such as China, the United Kingdom, and Russia, began the shift to cost sharing in the late 1980s and continued into the 1990s. This precipitated more focus on student enrollments in many countries where cost sharing became commonplace. As examples of new managerialism, colleges and universities in the United States started devoting more attention to business approaches to strategic planning, admissions marketing, and student retention efforts. For example, in the 1970s, offices of admissions began to use marketing techniques such as improved publication materials, targeted mailing strategies, and telemarketing techniques to attract larger numbers of students. At the same time, senior-level administrators began to utilize strategic planning techniques, also borrowed from business. These new approaches to strategic planning incorporated market research so that organizations could better understand their clients and the institution's position relative to competitors.

The adoption of these new marketing techniques also resulted in admissions officers using tools that enabled them to do a better job of tracking and communicating with prospective students through the use of applied social science analytical techniques and the use of computer and information science–assisted technology. The use of applied social science research methods also resulted in more careful analyses of tuition pricing decisions and the strategic use of campus-based financial aid dollars. Indeed, pricing and the use of campus-based student financial aid have arguably become the most important, as well as one of the most controversial, topics in SEM and are more fully examined in subsequent chapters.

In addition to the increasing use of for-profit business techniques in the areas of admissions and financial aid, student attrition became a widely researched topic in the field of higher education starting in the late 1970s and continuing into the twenty-first century (see, for example, Bean, 1980; Braxton, 2000; Habley, Bloom, & Robbins, 2012; Noel, Levitz, & Saluri, 1985; Pascarella & Terenzini, 2005; College Board, 2011; Tinto, 1993, 2012). This line of inquiry has led to the development of a wide-ranging set of campus-based initiatives to improve student success and college completion. They range from remedial education, intrusive student advising efforts to enhance student engagement and improve student motivation and goal orientation, to the use of campus-based financial aid and CRM tools. Indeed, an entire consulting industry has developed around the area of student retention.

THE FUTURE OF STRATEGIC ENROLLMENT MANAGEMENT

Collectively, the set of converging demographic, public policy, and institutional trends that have been discussed in this chapter provide much of the underlying foundation for the emergence of SEM. However, we have yet to look more carefully at enrollment management and Strategic Enrollment Management, and the organizational structures that have become increasingly commonplace among postsecondary institutions that have implemented some form of SEM.

The rapid expansion and evolution of SEM is well documented elsewhere (Henderson, 2001; Hossler, 2011). At the moment, there seems little doubt that SEM is now, and will continue to be, a fixture and a key function within higher education administration in the United States, and it is likely to become increasingly important in many other countries. The United States has entered a period of another demographic downturn among high school graduates— many of these graduates will come from the families of first-generation recent immigrants who will be less likely to attend college, especially four-year colleges (Western Interstate Commission on Higher Education, 2012). Public institutions continue to see their state funding decline, which makes them increasingly dependent upon student tuition, and thus student enrollment. In addition, in recent years we have seen a dramatic increase in the number of two- and four-year, for-profit institutions. Despite the criticisms of college rankings such as those of *US News & World Report,* the visibility and importance of rankings continues to grow, and many of the metrics associated with rankings are focused on factors such as admissions yield rates, average SAT/ACT scores, and first-year student retention rates. In addition, the accountability movement in higher education has focused heavily on student persistence and graduation rates as indicators of institutional quality. All of these trends and concerns are typically the domain of enrollment management units. Finally, as already noted, DiMaggio and Powell (1983) have described mimetic iso-morphism as the tendency of organizations to imitate another organization's structure because senior managers within the organization come to believe that the structure of peer organization is more effective. As a result, more and more institutions are adopting SEM structures because they have become so common that presidents and provosts believe that this is the best organizational struc-ture for functions such as admissions, financial aid, student retention, and the office of the registrar.

Despite these trends and the rapid adoption of SEM structures across the United States as well as in other countries, SEM is not without its critics. Critics of SEM and college admissions and recruitment practices often infer or suggest that there was a "golden era" when colleges and universities did not com-pete and when most students attended college for the pursuit of knowledge (Quirk, 2005; Thacker, 2005). Critics argue that SEM is a negative example of the winner-takes-all society that has evolved in the United States, with too little thought to the pernicious effects it has on postsecondary educational institu-tions and the students that attend them (Frank, 1999). Although these critiques merit consideration, it is not accurate to suggest that there was ever a "golden era," at least in the United States, when most students attended college because of their love of learning and when colleges and universities did not compete. Historians of postsecondary education in the United States, however, reveal that this was seldom, indeed perhaps never, the case and that the history of postsecondary education is replete with examples of competitive practices and the use of financial aid to provide need-based aid for deserving low-income students and to attract high-performing students from more affluent families (Karabel, 2006; Thelin, 1982; Wilkinson, 2005).

Collectively, these demographic, societal, and political trends suggest that SEM is likely here to stay. Manifestations of SEM may vary according to the institutional mission of a campus, the unique academic programs universities may offer, and the geographical location of a college. However, institutional efforts to exert more influence upon their student enrollments (both matricula-tion and graduation) are unlikely to change. Indeed, in this current competitive environment, the importance of SEM is more likely to intensify than abate. From this perspective, it is fitting to close this brief history of SEM with a quote from Hossler and Kalsbeek (2008):

> But in the spirit of *playfulness*, we would ask this: If enrollment management
> as it has been defined by its critics has such a negative impact on students and
> institutions and the social good, what is the alternative? Should institutions
> not attempt to plan for and manage their enrollments? Should colleges and
> universities just let their enrollments "happen"? Many of the critics of enrollment
> management hint at bygone days where institutional enrollment practices
> exhibited greater integrity and reflected some higher order values. Scholars

who have examined the history of American higher education demonstrate, however, that there is scant evidence to suggest that there was ever a time in the history of American colleges and universities where institutions' leaders were not attempting to exert influence on the numbers and types and mix of students enrolled in order to achieve the institution's mission and goals (pp. 2–9).

In the next two chapters of Part I of this handbook, we more closely examine how the complex interaction of being a public or a non-profit private institution, institutional mission, geographic location, institutional wealth, and state and public policies can influence the SEM strategies and activities on individual campuses. Chapter 2 considers the various organizational structures, range offices, and the uses of technology that have become important elements of SEM organizations.

References

Abrahamson, T. D., & Hossler, D. (1990). Applying marketing strategies in student recruitment. In D. Hossler & J. P. Bean (Eds.), *The Strategic Management of College Enrollments* (pp. 100–118). San Francisco: Jossey-Bass.

Astin, A. W. (1985). *Achieving Educational Excellence*. San Francisco: Jossey-Bass.

Astin, A. W., & Lee, C. (1972). *The Invisible Colleges: A Profile of Small, Private Colleges with Limited Resources*. New York: McGraw-Hill.

Atkinson, R. C. (2001). *Standardized Tests and Access to American Universities*. Washington, DC: Atwell Lecture at American Council on Education, February 18, 2001.

Bean, J. P. (1980). Dropouts and turnover: The synthesis and test of a causal model of student attrition. *Research in Higher Education*, *12*(2), 155–182.

Bean, J. P. (1983). The application of a model of job turnover in work organizations to the student attrition process. *The Review of Higher Education*, *6*(2), 129–148.

Bean, J. P. (1990a). Using retention research in enrollment management. In D. Hossler & J. P. Bean (Eds.), *The Strategic Management of College Enrollments* (pp. 3–20). San Francisco: Jossey-Bass.

Bean, J. P. (1990b). Why students leave: Insights from research. In D.Hossler & J. P. Bean (Eds.), *The Strategic Management of College Enrollments* (pp. 147–169). San Francisco: Jossey-Bass.

Bolman, L. G., & Deal, T. E. (1991). *Reframing Organizations: Artistry, Choice, and Leadership*. San Francisco: Jossey-Bass.

Bontrager, B. (2008). A definition and context for current SEM practice. In B. Bontrager (Ed.), *SEM and Institutional Success: Integrating Enrollment, Finance, and Student Access*. Washington, DC: Association of Collegiate Registrars and Admissions Officers.

Bontrager, B., & Kerlin, C. (2004). *Creating Effective SEM Organizations*. [PowerPoint]. Presented at American Association of Collegiate Registrars and Admissions Officers, Orlando, FL.

Bowen, H. (1980). *The Costs of Higher Education: How Much Do Colleges and Universities Spend per Student and How Much Should They Spend?* San Francisco: Jossey-Bass.

Braxton, J. M. (2000). *Reworking the Student Departure Puzzle.* Nashville, TN: Vanderbilt University Press.

College Board. (2011). *How Four-Year Colleges and Universities Organize Themselves to Promote Student Persistence: The Emerging National Picture.* New York: College Board Advocacy & Policy Center.

Confessore, N. (2003). What makes a college good? *The Atlantic Monthly, 292*(4), 118–126.

Deem, R. (1998). "New managerialism" and higher education: The management of performances and cultures in universities in the United Kingdom. *International Studies in Sociology of Education, 8*(1), 47–70.

DiMaggio, P. J., & Powell, W. W. (1983). The iron cage revisited: Institutional isomorphism and collective rationality in organizational fields. *American Sociological Review, 48*(2), 147–160.

Dolence, M. G. (1991). Setting the Context for Evaluation of Recruitment and Retention Programs. *New Directions for Institutional Research, 1991*(70), 5–19.

Dolence, M. G. (1996). *AACRAO Strategic Enrollment Management Casebook: Cases From the Field.* Washington, DC: American Association of Collegiate Registrars and Admissions Officers.

Dolence, M. G. (1998). Strategic enrollment management. In C. C.Swann & S. E. Henderson (Eds.), *Handbook for the College Admission Profession* (pp. 71–90). Washington, DC: American Association of Collegiate Registrars and Admissions Officers, Greenwood Educators Reference Collection.

Exworthy, M., & Halford, S. (Eds.). (1998). *Professionals and the New Managerialism in the Public Sector.* Philadelphia: Open University Press.

Fethke, D. (2012, April 1). Why does tuition go up? Because taxpayer support goes down. *Chronicle of Higher Education.* (http://chronicle.com/article/Why-Does-Tuition-Go-Up-/131372/)

Frank, R. H. (1999) *Higher education: The ultimate winner-take-all market?* Retrieved from Cornell University, ILR School site, http://digitalcommons.ilr.cornell.edu/cheri/2.

Habley, W. R., Bloom, J. L., & Robbins, S. (2012). *Increasing Persistence: Research-Based Strategies for College Student Success.* San Francisco: Jossey-Bass.

Henderson, S. E. (2001). On the brink of a profession: A history of enrollment management in higher education. In J. Black (Ed.), *The Strategic Enrollment Management Revolution* (pp. 3–36). Washington, DC: American Association of Collegiate Registrars and Admissions Officers.

Hossler, D. (1984). *Enrollment Management: An Integrated Approach.* New York: College Board Publications.

Hossler, D. (1986). *Creating Effective Enrollment Management Systems.* New York: College Entrance Examination Board.

Hossler, D. (2011). From admissions to enrollment management. In F.J.D. MacKinnon & Associates (Eds.), *Rentz's Student Affairs Practice in Higher Education* (4th Edition). Springfield, IL: Charles C. Thomas.

Hossler, D., Bean, J. P., & Associates. (1990). *The Strategic Management of College Enrollments*. San Francisco: Jossey-Bass.

Hossler, D., & Hoezee, L. (2001). Conceptual and theoretical thinking about enrollment management. In J. Black (Ed.), *The Strategic Enrollment Management Revolution* (pp. 57–76). Washington, DC: American Association of Collegiate Registrars and Admissions Officers.

Hossler, D., & Kalsbeek, D. H. (2008). Enrollment management and managing enrollment: Setting the context for dialogue. *College & University*, *83*(4), 2–9.

Hossler, D., Schmit, J., & Vesper, N. (1999). *Going to College: How Social, Economic, and Educational Factors Influence the decisions Students Make*. Baltimore, MD: John Hopkins University Press.

Johnstone, D. B., & Marcucci, P. N. (2010). *Financing Higher Education Worldwide: Who Pays? Who Should Pay?* Baltimore, MD: Johns Hopkins University Press.

Kalsbeek, D. (2013). *A Market-Centered Approach to Strategic Enrollment Management*. [PowerPoint]. Presented at the 2013 ACT Enrollment Planners Conference, Chicago.

Karabel, J. (2006). *The Chosen: The Hidden History of Admission and Exclusion at Harvard, Yale, and Princeton*. Boston: Mariner Books.

Kemerer, F. R., Baldridge, J. V., & Green, K. C. (1982). *Strategies for Effective Enrollment Management*. Washington, DC: American Association of State Colleges and Universities.

Kreutner, L., & Godfrey, E. S. (1981). Enrollment management: A new vehicle for institutional renewal. *College Board Review*, *118*(29), 6–9.

Lasher, W. F., & Cook, W. B. (1996). Toward a theory of fund raising in higher education. *The Review of Higher Education*, *20*(1), 33–51.

Maguire, J. (1976). To the organized, go the students. *Bridge Magazine*, *39*(1), 6–10.

Meyer, J., & Rowan, B. (1977). Institutionalized organizations: Formal structure as myth and ceremony. *The American Journal of Sociology*, *83*(2), 340–363.

Muston, R. (1985). *Marketing and Enrollment Management in State Universities*. Iowa City, IA: ACT.

Noel, L., Levitz, R., Saluri, D., & Associates. (1985). *Increasing Student Retention*. San Francisco: Jossey-Bass.

Pascarella, E. T. (1985). *A program for research and policy development on student persistence at the institutional level*. Paper presented at the Second Annual Chicago Conference on Enrollment Management.

Pascarella, E. T., & Terenzini, P. (2005). *How College Affects Students: A Third Decade of Research*. San Francisco: Jossey Bass.

Pfeffer, J., & Salancik, G. (1978). *The External Control of Organizations: A Resource Dependence Perspective*. Stanford, CA: Stanford University Press.

Quirk, M. (2005). The best class money can buy: The rise of the "enrollment manager" and the cutthroat quest for competitive advantage. The secret weapon: financial-aid leveraging. *The Atlantic.* Retrieved from http://www.theatlantic.com/magazine/archive/2005/11/the-best-class-money-can-buy/304307/.

Rudolph, F. (1962). *The American College and University: A History.* New York: Vintage Books.

Schulz, S. A., & Lucido, J. A. (2011). What enrollment management structures reveal about institutional priorities. *Enrollment Management Journal: Student Access, Finance, and Success in Higher Education, 5*(4), 12–44.

Slaughter, S., & Leslie, L. L. (1997). *Academic Capitalism: Politics, Policies, and the Entrepreneurial University.* Baltimore, MD: The Johns Hopkins University Press.

Swann, C. C. (1998). Admissions officer: A profession and training. In C. Swann & S. Henderson (Eds.), *Handbook for the College Admissions Profession.* Washington, DC: American Association of Collegiate Registrars and Admissions Officers.

Thacker, L. (2005). *College Unranked: Ending the College Admissions Frenzy.* Cambridge, MA: Harvard University Press.

Thelin, J. R. (1982). *Higher Education and Its Useful Past: Applied History in Research and Planning.* Cambridge, MA: Schenkman Publishing Co.

Thresher, B. A. (1966). *College Admissions and the Public Interest.* New York: The College Entrance Examination Board.

Tinto, V. (1993*). Leaving College: Rethinking the Causes and Cures of Student Attrition* (2nd Edition). Chicago: University of Chicago Press.

Tinto, V. (2012). *Completing College: Rethinking Institutional Action.* Chicago: University of Chicago Press.

Western Interstate Commission on Higher Education. (2012). *Knocking at the College Door: Projections of High School Graduates* (8th Edition). Boulder, CO: Western Interstate Commission for Higher Education. Retrieved from http://www.wiche.edu/knocking-8th.

Wilkinson, R. (2005). *Aiding Student, Buying Students: Financial Aid in America.* Nashville, TN: Vanderbilt University Press.

CHAPTER 2

Understanding the Context

Bob Bontrager and
Don Hossler

While Chapter 1 provides a useful exploration of the origins of Strategic Enrollment Management, the current scope of SEM strategies and practices can be best understood in the context of present realities affecting postsecondary student enrollments and the broader enterprise of higher education. The factors highlighted in this chapter focus primarily on the American context. However, we live in an era where most countries have moved toward privatization and the market models for their postsecondary educational systems. Thus, many of the issues discussed in this chapter, and in many successive chapters, parallel issues faced in other countries as well.

This chapter begins by discussing the interplay of postsecondary markets and sectors (four- and two-year non-profit) in shaping which institutions compete for which types of students and how this in turn influences SEM strategy and practice. For instance, SEM has played out differently at community colleges as compared to private four-year institutions. This example also offers insight into the changing nature of SEM. In many states, community colleges have had to raise tuition. Indeed, over the past several decades, community colleges—like virtually all public institutions—have become increasingly tuition-dependent (Katsinas, Tollefson, & Reamey, 2008). From 2007 to 2011 alone, tuition as a percentage of community college revenue increased from 17 percent to 27.7 percent (American Association of Community Colleges, 2009, 2013). Thus, in the current environment, community colleges, like many of their four-year pubic counterparts, have had to rely more on tuition. As a result of these trends, more and more community colleges have become *SEM-conscious.*

This chapter also touches briefly upon public policy as an important factor in enrollment planning and outcomes. This sets the stage for a more complete discussion of the impact of public policy on SEM in Chapter 24.

Finally, the chapter explores the changing characteristics of traditional age students, those 18 to 24 years of age, and the implications for SEM. The trends cited and the conclusions we reach outline the challenges faced by SEM practitioners. These trends are already confronting enrollment managers as they strive to contribute to the success of the students while also assisting the institutions they serve.

THE ROLE OF POSTSECONDARY SECTORS, MARKETS, AND PUBLIC POLICY

The various sectors and market segments within and across postsecondary education in the United States have a significant impact on the challenges confronting SEM organizations. In Chapter 5, we examine postsecondary markets and student enrollment–related marketing in more detail. In this chapter, we set the stage for the chapters that follow. We provide a brief overview of the primary differentiators that can frame the competitive factors that shape the activities of enrollment management organizations.

There is robust literature on markets in postsecondary education (for example, Becker & Toutkoushian, 2013; Brown, 2010; Dill & Soo, 2004; Teixeira, Jongbloed, Dill, & Amaral, 2006). These authors conclude that there is no solitary postsecondary education market, but rather multiple markets. For readers who are interested not only in the applied implications of postsecondary markets, but the underlying factors that influence markets, we recommend reading the sources noted above. However, these more theoretical examinations of tertiary educational markets do not provide sufficient guidance for the strategic admissions marketing decisions that must be made by enrollment managers.

Over the years, Robert Zemsky and the colleagues with whom he has worked have provided important insights into the structure of markets for tertiary education in the United States. Although this body of work focuses on U.S.–based institutions, many of the factors that determine market competition in the United States are similar to those that influence market competition in many developed nations. Underlying the market segmentation work that they have done are the following factors: proximity, tuition cost, size, the extent to which a campus is residential, academic program offerings, mission, wealth, and prestige. We examine these factors in some detail to set the stage for a more complete discussion in Chapter 5.

Proximity is an important factor, because it results in more convenient institutional access. Typically, public institutions in both the two- and four-year public sectors have an advantage, because they are more often located so that they provide easy geographical access to a wide range of students. From research on student college choice (for example Goldrick-Rab, 2007; Hossler, Schmit, & Vesper, 1999; Hoxby, 2007; McDonough, 1997; Perna, 2006), we know that proximity and institutional size are also factors that students consider. Long (2004) reports that high school students were not likely to attend any postsecondary institution after graduation if they had to travel distances greater than 100 miles from home.

In addition to proximity, public institutions often have a market advantage because they have lower tuition rates than private institutions. Public institutions are almost always less expensive (though not always—for instance, BYU-Idaho has a tuition cost of less than $8,000 a year, which makes it less expensive than some regional public institutions). Tuition pricing, however, is not a fixed institutional characteristic. Private and public institutions can manipulate their net price through tuition and financial aid policies that can result in more direct competition between public and private institutions (Allen & Shen, 1999). There are limits to how much most private colleges and universities can lower their costs, however, and in a post–Great Recession environment, the higher costs of private institutions can be a competitive disadvantage. Don Hossler and David Kalsbeek (2013) have noted that the Great Recession resulted in increased cost sensitivity, and more families and students are looking for lower cost alternatives.

Other factors, such as size, residentialness, and special foci on things such as academic programs, religious affiliation, or being a historically black college and university (HBCU), also affect competition and postsecondary market segmentation (Hossler, Braxton, & Coopersmith, 1989; Park & Hossler, Chapter 4). Commuting campuses, by their very nature, draw students whose commuting distances are more convenient. The mission and the profile of the academic offerings also shape the structure of markets. A student interested in education, business, psychology, or history, for example, can consider a wider range of institutions than a student interested in nursing, architecture, or engineering. Some students prefer to attend a small college rather than a large university. For some students, a private institution that is associated with their faith can also be an important factor, just as African American students who have decided to attend a HBCU will have a different competitive set of institutions to consider.

As we have already noted, institutional quality and prestige can also play an important role for some postsecondary market segments. Caroline Hoxby (2007) and Bridget Long (2004) both report that institutional quality and perceived prestige, regardless of whether an institution is public or private, have become more important factors for more affluent families. Institutional wealth, reputation, and admissions selectivity are strongly associated with institutional prestige and rankings not only in the United States but around the globe (Marginson, 2004; Volkwein & Sweitzer, 2006; Winston, 1999). Greater institutional wealth enables tertiary educational institutions to rely less on the number of students paying tuition and thus be more selective. Gordon Winston (1999) stated that "wealth buys prestige and position in the marketplace" (p. 21). Thus, institutional wealth is tightly linked to our discussion of postsecondary markets and where individual institutions are positioned within their market as they compete for students.

In their early work on postsecondary market segments, Robert Zemsky and Penney Oedel (1983) conclude that two- and four-year sectors rarely, if ever, compete with one another for students. The work of Becker and Toutkoushian (2013) also suggests that two- and four-year tertiary institutions are unlikely to compete for the same students. However, this may be changing as a result of increasing price sensitivity coupled with the SEM activities undertaken by community colleges. For example, some community colleges have started honor programs, and many are focusing more attention on articulation and transfer programs (Moltz, 2010). Recent applied market research undertaken by the consulting division of AACRAO has found some competition between institutions in these two sectors. Similarly, two studies conducted by Eduventures (2009, 2013), a research consulting group based in Boston, found that some four-year institutions with modest levels of selectivity had substantial market overlap with regional community colleges. Evidence to date suggests that market competition between two- and four-year colleges is most likely to occur between two-year institutions and open admissions four-year public and private regional colleges and universities. Unfortunately, to date, the paucity of research on the market structures of this sector as well as the for-profit postsecondary sector dictates that most of our attention in this chapter and subsequent chapters will focus upon the non-profit (private and public) four-year institutions. This is an area that merits more applied SEM research in the future.

Before we close this section, it is worth noting that public policy in individual states and in other parts of the world, including Canadian provinces, for example, can also have an impact on competitive forces faced by enrollment managers. Some states offer more generous state financial aid packages for students who attend public institutions. In Michigan (Michigan Department of Treasury, 2013–14), for example, low-income students who start at community colleges receive additional financial aid when they subsequently transfer to a four-year institution. The Canadian province of Manitoba has implemented an incentive for students to stay in Manitoba or to move to the province from other provinces. The Manitoba Tuition Fee Income Tax Rebate provides undergraduate students a 5 percent tax credit advance on tuition fees while they attend school and give graduate students a 60 percent income tax rebate on their eligible tuition fees, to a maximum benefit of $25,000 (Manitoba, 2013). Subsequently, enrollment managers must take into consideration the state or province in which they are located as they determine their enrollment strategies.

THE CHANGING CHARACTERISTICS OF STUDENTS

The current context in which enrollment managers operate reflects continuously evolving environmental factors that have always been integral to SEM practice. This section highlights the demographic and economic characteristics of a student, and how those characteristics interact with institutional priorities and public policy, particularly those related to the access and equity goals espoused by higher education for decades (Bontrager, 2008; Green, 2005; Kalsbeek, 2005; Mortensen, 2012; Whiteside & Mentz, 2003). Colleges and universities face serious challenges as they seek to meet the needs of aspiring students who are increasingly diverse on a range of geographic, ethnic, economic, and educational variables while simultaneously achieving the enrollment goals of the institutions they serve.

Demographics

The demographic characteristics of potential college students and the sheer number of potential college-age students have always had an impact on postsecondary education in the United States. The origin of SEM can be traced to a downturn in American high school graduates that began in 1975. From that point through1993, the number of high school graduates dropped nationally by more than 680,000 students, a decrease of nearly 22 percent (National Center for Educational Statistics, 2012). Thus, with regard to demographics, early SEM development hinged on one overarching question: Are there enough high school graduates to go around? The answer to that question turned to the positive as the number of graduates saw a rapid rise during the period of 1994 to 2010, growing by nearly 950,000 students (Western Interstate Commission for Higher Education, 2012). After a modest decline that ended in 2013, the longer term upward trend is expected through 2024. In the thirty-year period from 1994 to 2024, the number of high school graduates will have grown by more than 1,047,000 students, an increase of 43 percent.

As a single datum, growth in the number of high school graduates would bode well for meeting institutional enrollment goals. However, the overall growth in traditional age students plays out very differently by geographic region, ethnicity, and socioeconomic status, with direct implications for SEM. American states in the South and West have seen, and will continue to see, larger increases in high school graduates than will those in the Midwest and Northeast. While the larger portion of that growth has already occurred, the number of high school graduates in the South will grow by an additional 168,000 students, or 15 percent, from 2014 through 2024. During this same period, the numbers in the West will increase by nearly 70,000 students, or 9 percent. The numbers in Midwestern and Northeastern states will be essentially flat (Western Interstate Commission for Higher Education, 2012).

This significant shift in geographic distribution is accentuated by the radical change in the racial/ethnic composition among high school graduates. The growing diversity in the United States has been well documented; this is also true of high school graduates. During the same period cited for high school graduates, 2014 to 2024, the proportion of public high school graduates for each of the major racial/ethnic groups will change as indicated in Table 2.1.

Though both Asian/Pacific Islanders and Hispanics are expected to grow at comparable rates, Hispanics represent a much larger group. In 2014, Asian/Pacific Islanders are projected to make up just over 6 percent of U.S. public high school graduates, whereas Hispanic students are expected to account for just over 20 percent. By 2024, Asian/Pacific Islander graduates are projected to number 262,000, and Hispanics are expected to total just over 800,000.

Equally vexing is not simply the changing demographic makeup of high school graduates over the next fifteen years, but the postsecondary attendance patterns of Latino students. Much of the growth in Latino high school graduates will comprise low-income, first-generation, recent immigrants from Mexico. There is ample evidence that these students are less likely to attend a postsecondary institution, and among those who do, they are more likely to stay close to home, to commute, and to attend a low-cost community college (Hossler, 2006; Kirsch, Braun, Yamamoto, & Sum, 2007). In some areas, such as the Midwest and the Northeast, the projected number of students is stable *only* because of projected increases in Latino students, which in actuality is likely to translate into fewer potential college attenders. Additionally, many public and private institutions plan to recruit more heavily in the West and Southeast to enroll more nonresident students. The combination of the Great Recession and the large numbers of first-generation Latino students raises serious questions as

Table 2.1: Cumulative percent change in U.S. public high school graduates by race/ethnicity, 2014 to 2024

America Indian/Alaska Native	+24%
Asian/Pacific Islander	+40%
Black, non-Hispanic	+8%
Hispanic	+38
White, non-Hispanic	−4%

Table 2.2: Change in fall enrollment at degree-granting institutions by race/ethnicity, 1980 to 2010

| | Number (thousands) | | | |
	1980	2010	Increase	Percentage
American Indian/Alaskan Native	84	196	112	134.0
Asian/Pacific Islander	286	1,282	996	347.6
Black	1,107	3,039	1,932	174.6
Hispanic	472	2,741	2,270	481.2
White	9,833	12,723	2,890	29.4
Total	11,782	19,981	8,199	69.6

to enrollment difficulties many institutions may face. Indeed, the two most recent postsecondary enrollment reports released by the National Student Clearinghouse Research Center (2012, 2013) indicate a decline in the total number of students enrolled in postsecondary education for both the fall semester of 2012 and the spring semester of 2013.

The implications of these demographic shifts are sobering given the modest track record of American higher education in fostering academic success among diverse populations. On the one hand, racial/ethnic diversity shows up on lists of values and goals for nearly every American college, university, and educational organization, and, to be fair, participation rates among racial/ethnic groups traditionally underserved by higher education have improved. Table 2.2 illustrates comparative increases in participation during the 30-year period from 1980 to 2010 (National Center for Educational Statistics, 2012).

Economics

Although participation is necessary to enhance educational attainment, college completion rates are receiving increased focus (Carnevale & Strohl, 2013; Hauptman, 2012; Lumina Foundation, 2013). This is a critical distinction given the often cited correlation between degree completion and increased lifetime earnings. More recent research on the importance of degree completion has emerged from studies of the effects of the Great Recession. From 2008 to 2010, 5.6 million jobs were lost in the United States; nevertheless, the number of jobs for Americans with at least a bachelor's degree grew by 187,000 during that same time period (Lumina Foundation, 2013, p. 2).

Unfortunately, and especially so given current demographic trends, wide gaps in degree completion rates among racial/ethnic groups have always existed, and they are getting wider. From 1980 to 2000, completion rates increased for persons aged 25 to 64 in each of the major racial/ethnic groups.

Table 2.3: Population 25 years and over with a bachelor's degree by race, 2006–2010 (in percent by persons reporting a single race/ethnicity)

American Indian/ Alaskan Native	8.7
Asian/Pacific Islander	40.4
Black	11.6
Hispanic	8.9
White	18.5
Total population	17.6

However, the increase was significantly greater for white and Asian-American students. In 2000, whites aged 25 to 64 were twice as likely as African Americans to have a bachelor's degree and almost three times as likely as Hispanics/Latinos (National Center for Public Policy and Higher Education, 2005). The most recent census data (U.S. Census Bureau, 2012) regarding bachelor's degree completion is shown in Table 2.3.

The interplay of demographics and the personal finances of students and their families becomes even more significant when cross-referenced with current economic forces at play across higher education—namely, rising college costs, declining federal and state support, and the increasing financial need of students seeking access to higher education. These factors have been reported repeatedly in the higher education literature and will not be reviewed at length here, except to highlight the important relationship between racial/ethnic diversity, family income, and degree completion. As Table 2.4 illustrates, median family income varies significantly among the major racial/ethnic groups. The most recently available data on family income by racial/ethnic groups as reported by the U.S. Census Bureau (2012) are cited in Table 2.4.

Anyone who values diversity and social equity will be concerned about these data. For educators, these findings take on added relevance when considered in light of the relationship between family income and bachelor's degree

Table 2.4: Median family income by race and ethnicity, 2009

Asian/Pacific Islander	$101,097
Black	$52,930
Hispanic	$54,074
White	$81,434

attainment. Data compiled by Tom Mortensen (2012) indicates that persons from the top quartile of family income in the United States are nearly seven times more likely to earn a bachelor's degree, at 71.2 percent, than persons from the lowest quartile, at 10.4 percent.

Taken together, these demographic and economic trends present enormous challenges to all educators, including enrollment managers. The inherent difficulty in effectively addressing those challenges is reflected in the call for improved performance measures and accountability that has become pervasive in the higher education arena (Carnevale & Strohl, 2013; Dickeson 2004; Mortensen, 2012; Lumina Foundation, 2013). As noted previously, this call has been with higher educators for several decades. However, due to the longstanding and worsening nature of the situation, calls to action are becoming more urgent. Indicative of this urgency, the Lumina Foundation's 2013 annual report states, "Put bluntly, this is an intolerable situation. We are all diminished as Americans by an education system that effectively rations postsecondary opportunity based on people's skin color, income or family status" (p. 5).

IMPLICATIONS FOR STRATEGIC ENROLLMENT MANAGERS

Effectively responding to higher education's complex challenges will require a multifaceted response by a wide range of persons both within and outside the institutional setting. That said, SEM practitioners can and should play an important role in leading their institutions to more innovative practices that achieve different outcomes relative to current demographic and economic trends. Strategic enrollment managers can use market research in the context of their missions to help institutions determine whether new academic programs will be attractive to students. They can also help prepare their campuses for changing student characteristics as more Latino and Asian American students matriculate. Furthermore, SEM leaders can help develop student retention initiatives that are based on the changing characteristics of enrolling students.

There are, however, limitations to what SEM leaders can accomplish. They cannot change the geographic location of a campus or alter whether the college or university is public or private. There are limits of the extent to which they can *shape the class*. While some educational observers and seasoned enrollment managers believe that the growth in international students will enable many institutions to weather the current economic and demographic challenges, it remains to be seen as to whether the increasing number of international students will help most institutions get through this period of a declining number of high school graduates and the aftereffects of the Great Recession. Well-developed SEM organizations, as detailed in several other chapters of this book, enable institutions to bring together academics, recruitment, retention, financial aid, and student services in a way that is uniquely suited to addressing student enrollment issues from the required multidimensional perspective. This is not necessarily a matter of organizational structure. Some institutions will find that their enrollment goals are facilitated by organizing a comprehensive set of enrollment-related departments within a single divisional structure, while others will achieve comparable results by creating new avenues for cross-department communication and collaboration.

Whatever the nature of restructuring to achieve SEM purposes, institutions will not simply "get there" on their own. SEM's emerging contribution to the context of higher education is in organizing data—and our associated understandings of the interplay of demographic, economic, and social factors—in new ways to better inform pathways to greater student attainment and fulfillment of institutional enrollment goals. In so doing, strategic enrollment managers can play an important role in responding to the public policy as it relates to student access, persistence, and completion. This is an ambitious agenda that defines the context of SEM practice now and into the future.

References

Allen, R. F., & Shen, J. (1999). Some new evidence of the character of competition among higher education institutions. *Economics of Education Review*, 18(4), 465–470.

American Association of Community Colleges. (2009). *Serving Communities Strengthening the Nation*. Retrieved November 22, 2013, from http://www.aacc.nche.edu/AboutCC/Documents/servingcomms052009.ppt.

American Association of Community Colleges. (2013). 2013 community colleges fast facts. Retrieved from http://www.aacc.nche.edu/AboutCC/Pages/fastfactsfactsheet.aspx.

Becker, W. E., & Toutkoushian, R. K. (2013). On the meaning of markets in higher education. In M. Paulson (Ed.), *Higher Education: Handbook of Theory and Research* (pp. 323–376). The Netherlands: Springer.

Bontrager, B. (2008). A definition and context for current SEM practice. In B. Bontrager (Ed.), *SEM and Institutional Success* (pp. 16–31). Washington, DC: American Association of Collegiate Registrars and Admissions Officers.

Brown, R. (Ed.). (2010). *Higher Education and the Market*. London: Routledge.

Carnevale, A. P., & Strohl, J. (2013). *Separate and unequal: How higher education reinforces the intergenerational reproduction of white racial privilege*. Retrieved July 30, 2013, from http://www9.georgetown.edu/grad/gppi/hpi/cew/pdfs/Separate&Unequal.FR.pdf.

Copeland, T., & Wells, A. (2008). *Enabling SEM: Linking planning and performance*. Unpublished paper, SunGard Higher Education.

Dickeson, R. C. (2004). *Collision Course: Rising College Costs Threaten America's Future and Require Shared Solutions*. Indianapolis: IN: Lumina Foundation for

Education. Retrieved from http://www.luminafoundation.org/publications/
CollisionCourse.pdf.

Dill, D. D., & Soo, M. (2004). Transparency and quality in higher education markets.
In P. Teixeira, B. B. Jongbloed, D. D. Dill, & A. Amaral (Eds.), *Markets in Higher
Education: Rhetoric or Reality?* (pp. 61–85). The Netherlands: Springer.

Eduventures. (2007). *Learning Collaborative for Higher Education.* Enrollment
Management Custom Research Report. Boston: Eduventures

Eduventures. (2009). *Analysis of Enrollment and Retention Overlap for Midwestern
college.* Boston, MA: Eduventures.

Eduventures (2013). *Preference for Institutional Type.* Boston: Eduventures.

Fliegler, C. M. (2006). "Mission creep" or mission possible? *University Business.*
Retrieved May 14, 2008, from http://www.universitybusiness.com/ViewArticle
.aspx?articleid = 70.

Goldrick-Rab, S. (2007). What higher education has to say about the transition to
college. *The Teachers College Record, 109*(10), 2444–2481.

Green, T. (2005). Financial aid, access, and America's social contract with higher
education. *College & University, 80*(3), 9–13.

Hauptman, A. (2012). Redoing Pell. *Inside Higher Education.* Retrieved January 24,
2012, from http://www.insidehighered.com/views/2012/01/24/essay-hauptman-
revise-pell-focus-neediest-students.

Haycock, K. (2006). *Promise Abandoned: How Policy Choices and Institutional Practices
Restrict College Opportunities.* Report by the Education Trust, Washington, DC.

Henderson, S. E. (2001). On the brink of a profession. In J. Black (Ed.), *The SEM
Revolution* (pp. 3–36). Washington, DC: American Association of Collegiate
Registrars and Admissions Officers.

Hossler, D. (2006). Anticipating the future of college admissions. *College Board
Review.*

Hossler, D., Braxton, J., & Coopersmith, G. (1989). Understanding student college
choice. In M. Paulson (Ed.), *Higher Education: Handbook of Theory and Research*
(pp. 231–288). The Netherlands: Springer.

Hossler, D., & Kalsbeek, D. (2013). Enrollment Management and Managing
Enrollments: Revisiting the Context for Institutional Strategy. *Strategic Enrollment
Management Quarterly, 1*(1), 5–25.

Hossler, D., Schmit, J., & Vesper, N. (1999). *Going to College: How Social, Economic,
and Educational Factors Influence the Decisions Students Make.* Baltimore, MD: The
Johns Hopkins University Press.

Hoxby, C. M. (Ed.). (2007). *College Choices: The Economics of Where to Go, When to
Go, and How to Pay for It.* Chicago: University of Chicago Press.

Kalsbeek, D. (2005). *The challenge of access: Structures, strategies, and SEM antics.*
Presentation at the AACRAO Strategic Enrollment Management Conference,
Chicago.

Kalsbeek, D. (2006). Some reflections on SEM structures and strategies (part 1). *College & University.* (*81*)3: 3–10.

Katsinas, S. G., Tollefson, T. A., & Reamey, B. A. (2008). *Funding issues in U.S. community colleges: Findings from a 2007 survey of the National State Directors of Community Colleges.* Report from the American Association of Community Colleges, Washington, DC. Retrieved from http://www.aacc.nche.edu/fundingissues.

Kirsch, I., Braun, H., Yamamoto, K., & Sum, A. (2007). *America's perfect storm: Three forces changing our nation's future.* Policy Information Report of the Educational Testing Service, Princeton, NJ.

Long, B. T. (2004). How have college decisions changed over time? An application of the conditional logistic choice model. *Journal of Econometrics, 121*(1), 271–296.

Lumina Foundation. (2013). *A Stronger Nation through Higher Education: Visualizing data to help us achieve a big goal for college attainment.* Indianapolis, IN: Annual Report from Lumina Foundation for Education. Retrieved July 23, 2013, from http://www.luminafoundation.org/publications/A_stronger_nation_through_higher_education-2013.pdf.

Manitoba government. (2013). Manitoba Tuition Fee Income Tax Rebate. Retrieved November 23, 2013, from http://www.gov.mb.ca/tuition/.

Marginson, S. (2004). National and global competition in higher education. *The Australian Educational Researcher, 31*(2), 1–28.

McDonough, P. M. (1997). *Choosing Colleges: How Social Class and Schools Structure Opportunity.* Albany, NY: State University of New York Press.

Michigan Department of Treasury. (2013). Tuition Incentive Program Fact Sheet: Academic Year 2012–13. Retrieved from http://www.michigan.gov/documents/FactSheetTIP_161201_7.pdf.

Moltz, D. (2010). Two-Year Honors Boom. *Inside Higher Education.* Retrieved February 2, 2010, from http://www.insidehighered.com/news/2010/02/04/honors.

Mortensen, T. (2012). Family income and unequal educational opportunity, 1970–2011. *Postsecondary Education Opportunity, 245*, 1–11.

National Center for Educational Statistics. (2012). *Total fall enrollment in degree-granting institutions, by level of student, sex, attendance status, and race/ethnicity: Selected years, 1976 through 2010.* Retrieved November 25, 2013, from http://nces.ed.gov/programs/digest/d12/tables/dt12_263.asp.

National Center for Public Policy and Higher Education. (2005). *Income of US Workforce Projected to Decline.* Policy Alert. Retrieved from http://www.highereducation.org/reports/pa_decline/pa_decline.pdf.

National Student Clearinghouse Research Center. (2012). *Report: Current Term Enrollment Report—Fall 2012.* Retrieved December 18, 2012, from http://nscresearchcenter.org/currenttermenrollmentestimate-fall2012/.

National Student Clearinghouse Research Center. (2013). *Report: Current Term Enrollment Report—Spring 2013.* Retrieved May 16, 2013, from http://nscresearchcenter.org/currenttermenrollmentestimate-spring2013/.

Ogunwole, S. U., Drewery, M. P., Rios-Vargas, M. (2012). *The Population with a Bachelor's Degree or Higher by Race and Hispanic Origin: 2006–2010*. U.S. Census Bureau, American Community Survey Briefs. Retrieved August 2, 2013, from http://www.census.gov/prod/2012pubs/acsbr10–19.pdf.

Perna, L. W. (2006). Studying college access and choice: A proposed conceptual model. In M.Paulson (Ed.), *Higher Education: Handbook of Theory and Research* (pp. 99–157). The Netherlands: Springer.

Schneider, M., & Kelly, A. P. (2012). *Getting to Graduation: The Completion Agenda in Higher Education*. Baltimore, MD: The Johns Hopkins University Press.

Teixeira, P., Jongbloed, B. B., Dill, D. D., & Amaral, A. (Eds.). (2006). *Markets in Higher Education: Rhetoric or Reality?* The Netherlands: Springer.

Thelin, J. (2004). *A History of American Higher Education*. Baltimore, MD: The Johns Hopkins University Press.

U.S. Census Bureau. (2012). The 2012 Statistical Abstract. *Table 698. Money Income of Families—Distribution by Family Characteristics and Income Level: 2009.* Retrieved August 2, 2013, from http://www.census.gov/compendia/statab/cats/income_expenditures_poverty_wealth/family_income.html.

Volkwein, J. F., & Sweitzer, K. V. (2006). Institutional Prestige and Reputation among Research Universities and Liberal Arts Colleges. *Research in Higher Education*, *47*(2), 129–148.

Western Interstate Commission for Higher Education. (2012). *Knocking at the College Door: Projections of High School Graduates, December 2012*. Retrieved July 12, 2014, from http://www.wiche.edu/pub/knocking-8th-and-supplements.

Whiteside, R., & Mentz, G. (2003). Winds of Change and Enrollment Management: Edu-Trends, College Access and Economic Dynamics. *SEM Source*. Retrieved July 12, 2014, from http://www4.aacrao.org/semsource/sem/indexf861 .html?fa = view&id = 2236.

Winston, G. C. (1999). Subsidies, hierarchy and peers: The awkward economics of higher education. *The Journal of Economic Perspectives*, *13*(1), 13–36.

Zemsky, R., & Oedel, P. (1983). *The Structure of College Choice*. New York: College Entrance Examination Board.

Zemsky, R., Shaman, S., & Shapiro, D. B. (2001). Higher Education as Competitive Enterprise: When Markets Matter. *New Directions for Institutional Research*, (*2001*)111, 1–98.

CHAPTER 3

Successful Strategic Enrollment Management Organizations

Don Hossler,
David H. Kalsbeek,
and Bob Bontrager

Any comprehensive discussion of Strategic Enrollment Management inevitably leads to the configuration and focus of SEM organizations. Michael Porter (1979) notes that one critical ingredient of strategy is the integration of organizational activities and that the structures that organize and integrate those activities are key to sustainable strategic advantage. He also suggests that organizational resources and the activities of the competition should drive the ways that organizations are configured (Porter, 1979).

The current competition for student quality, diversity, and tuition revenue along with organizational isomorphism provide important insights into the structure of SEM organizations. This chapter offers a broad overview of the configuration of SEM organizations, discusses to whom the senior enrollment officer should report, reviews which functions and officers should be included in the SEM organization, and suggests that all of these issues create conditions for successful SEM. Readers should keep in mind that these topics are considered in greater detail in subsequent chapters of this book.

Two key questions are associated with the organizational configuration of enrollment management organizations: To whom should the senior enrollment officer report? What offices and functions should be part of a SEM organization? The first question asks if enrollment management units should be aligned with existing, traditional structures such as student affairs or academic affairs or instead be an entirely separate organization within a college, with its own senior campus leader such as a vice president or associate provost. The second question asks whether offices such as registration and records, orientation, career planning, academic advising, or marketing should be included with admissions and financial aid as part of the enrollment management effort.

Where enrollment units should be located is an interesting and important question but is difficult to answer definitively for several reasons. First, the structural question presupposes that we can answer the basic question, What works best? Don Hossler and David Kalsbeek (2013) note that there is no empirical evidence as to whether the organizational configuration and composition of enrollment units influence their effectiveness, and there are ample examples of successful SEM efforts achieved with a diverse range of organizational models and reporting configurations. They conclude that any organizational models and reporting alignments need to be reflective of the strategies, priorities, organizational culture, and specific mission of an institution.

ORGANIZATIONAL STRUCTURES AND RELATIONSHIPS

Early in the evolution of SEM organizations, there was considerable discussion as to whether enrollment managers were more like directors, coordinators of multiple units or matrix organizations, or oversight providers for all facets of SEM (Kemerer, Baldridge, & Green, 1982). SEM organizations have continued to evolve and take a variety of forms across institutional types and circumstances, as well as within institutions, as they have become more sophisticated in their approach. SEM is now mature enough that in most instances, senior enrollment officers function at the vice president or associate vice presidential level; however, institutional size has a significant impact on the role and responsibilities held by senior enrollment officers (Snowden, 2010). In most small public and private two- and four-year colleges and universities, enrollment functions report to a single individual. Small institutions also permit a more informal management style, and most administrators and faculty know each other; at these institutions, relationships are likely to matter more than positional power. At large institutions, however, the structures are more formal and more political. Some professional schools, for example, may have their own admissions recruitment staff in addition to the traditional undergraduate office of admissions, and all academic units may have endowed scholarships and other forms of financial aid that they administer themselves. Every effort—from setting enrollment goals, to developing marketing strategies, to executing retention efforts, to conducting enrollment research—is complicated by the scale and the multiplicity and independence of schools and colleges within large universities, often leading to the senior enrollment officer operating in more of a matrix model.

Although the organizational culture and mission of an institution are critical factors, an effective SEM effort requires an open systems environment (Hossler, 1986; Snowden, 2010). The factors that influence student enrollment outcomes are too complex for one administrative unit to control and manage; it is a truism that all offices and functions can and do influence student enrollments in some way. The activities of campus marketing and branding efforts, the range of academic offerings, and the quality of student life are all important; however, no one individual or single organizational unit can wholly manage enrollments. Open systems environments encourage the broad sharing of information and decision-making and discourage the creation of organizational silos that operate independently of one another.

In addition to a collaborative and open organizational environment, Hossler and Kalsbeek (2013) offer the following insights regarding the reporting relationships of effective SEM organizations:

- There is a growing realization that enrollment management has become a more complex and consequential enterprise, and that policies and strategies should not be left to the anecdotes that deans and CFOs and faculty and trustees recall from their own experiences of thirty years ago or the recent experiences of their children (who are not likely to be representative of the general population of students).

- Whoever the enrollment management officer reports to needs to be someone who will devote attention to keeping enrollment matters at the forefront of institutional planning and policy. When colleges and universities create a vice-president or vice-provost for enrollment management, that officer will know very clearly that his or her responsibility is to ensure the appropriate primacy of enrollment issues in institutional planning.

- Broad organizational alignments matter; structure and strategy exist and evolve in a continuously, mutually reinforcing process. The pros and cons of various organizational models are many, but what matters is the particular institutional context and idiosyncratic character that dictate how such alignments function and evolve.

Hossler and Kalsbeek (2008, 2013) also emphasize the value of having a senior enrollment officer who sits on the president's cabinet. One of the problems enrollment managers often encounter, as we have already noted, is that to some extent all senior campus administrators see themselves as *experts* on enrollment issues. But at a deeper level, colleges and universities, both private and public, are becoming increasingly tuition-dependent, and a SEM perspective is therefore increasingly relevant to every aspect of institutional strategy and decision-making. This is why the senior enrollment officer's presence in cabinet-level discussions is vital. Additionally, the responsibility to educate institutional leadership on SEM issues does not stop with the executive team; it also extends to the board of trustees. Too often, trustees are not sufficiently aware of the complex factors that influence new student enrollment, the implications of financial aid expenditures, the complexities of improving graduation rates, or the degree to which new academic programs are responsive to market trends, to offer several examples. It is worth noting that most private institutions have board-level committees that focus on SEM issues, while public institutions typically do not have similar committees, even though many public universities now have SEM organizations and have become tuition-dependent to a significant degree.

It is incumbent upon the senior enrollment officer to develop positive working relationships with all members of the president's cabinet. This includes the chief academic officer, the chief student affairs officer, the senior development officer, the senior marketing officer, and the chief financial officer (CFO). It is frequently stated that the chief academic officer is the first among equals on any campus's leadership team, and senior enrollment officers, who often report to provosts, always have as a critical goal to partner effectively with the chief academic officer to ensure that enrollment goals and academic goals are congruent. The task of a SEM unit is not only to enroll and retain a desired number of students overall, but also to ensure that the mix of students across all academic programs is optimal and to minimize the number of specific programs that are undersubscribed. This requires close collaboration and shared priorities between the SEM unit and the academic officers. Additionally, admissions directors have always worked with academic administrators and the faculty on issues related to student recruitment and admissions standards. For SEM organizations that include the registrar's office, the link to academics is even stronger, through engagement with issues such as student academic progress and transfer articulation.

At some institutions, the SEM unit reports to the chief student affairs officer, and at other institutions, student affairs are part of a SEM unit. In either arrangement, there can be tensions between these two units around the following issues: 1) disagreements as to whether units such as orientation or advising should be part of a SEM unit or a student affairs organization; and 2) tensions as to which unit should own the responsibility for overseeing retention efforts on campus.

Senior enrollment officers typically do not work as closely with the senior development officers, but they often do work closely with senior marketing officers. As we note later in this chapter, at many private institutions, the chief marketing officer is increasingly reporting to the senior enrollment officer. Tensions can exist between these two functions. Because admissions and the chief marketing officer are both involved in forms of marketing (admissions to students, campus marketing officers to the media, public officials, alumni, and so forth), there can be clashes as to which unit knows how best to market the institution to prospective students and their parents and tensions in prioritizing which audiences take priority in the marketing strategy. In this volume, we simply note again that structure should follow strategy, and that what works best is when marketing and enrollment officers respect the strengths, mission, and goals of each other's respective units.

We submit, however, that next to the relationship with the president (or the provost if the senior enrollment officer reports to the provost), perhaps the most significant working relationship for a senior enrollment manager is with the CFO. All tuition-dependent private institutions engage in what may be called *enrollment-based budgeting*. By this we mean that the enrollment and net tuition revenue goals of the senior enrollment officers typically start by the CFO determining what is required to balance the budget and fund all personnel costs, benefits, utilities, operations, capital projects, and so on. This phenomenon is not limited to institutions in the private sector. With the reduction of governmental funding for tertiary education, colleges and universities in the United States as well as in many other countries as nations, states, and provinces have become increasingly reliant upon tuition dollars (Johnson, Oliff, & Williams, 2011; Usher & Medow, 2010). To link enrollment and financial outcomes effectively requires frank discussions and shared understandings between the CFO and the enrollment officers about the student marketplace, pricing strategy, and what is achievable with respect to new student enrollment and retention. CFOs also look to senior enrollment officers to provide accurate and timely projections for new student enrollment and often for projected retention rates so that they can develop sound financial plans for the coming academic year.

In addition to institutional budgeting generally, the growing use of tuition dollars to fund campus-based financial aid (tuition discounting) has also brought CFOs and senior enrollment officers into more frequent contact. Too often CFOs view financial aid budgets as fixed, or they place a strong emphasis on minimizing aid expenditures. Senior enrollment officers, however, view the financial aid budget as a percentage of total tuition revenue and a discount to be optimized in producing greater net tuition revenue. Many senior enrollment officers have anecdotes of their CFOs reporting to the board of trustees that financial aid expenditures rose by 14 percent, for example, without simultaneously noting that tuition revenue correspondingly rose by 40 percent. On the other hand, senior enrollment managers may fail to take into consideration the full spectrum of costs—both direct and indirect—incurred with enrolling larger entering classes and how deeply discounted tuition constrains the capacity to hire additional instructors and fund more classroom space to accommodate that enrollment. With an ever-growing share of institutional revenue going to fund institutionally budgeted financial aid, it is essential that the SEM office can accurately track both discounted and endowment dollars being spent and how these expenditures are related to new student enrollment and net tuition revenue. Thus, it is not surprising that strong budget administrative capacity and analytical skills are increasingly seen as critical for SEM practitioners (Schulz & Lucido, 2011a). Several years ago, a highly regarded enrollment manager commented, "When I got into this business I had no idea that I would be spending as much time with the CFO as I have been," reflecting the essential working relationship required between the two offices.

Although there are a wide variety of organizational configurations, some offices and functions are almost always part of an enrollment management organization. But before we discuss the units that are typically part of a strategic enrollment organization, it is important that we consider the overarching skill sets and capacities that the enrollment management organization needs to have in order to be successful (Hossler & Kalsbeek, 2013).

Enrollment management is fueled by a comprehensive research agenda and a need for ongoing "action research" that often is not adequately met by traditional institutional research units. An effective enrollment management organization needs the capacity to conduct ongoing studies and analysis of the admissions process, of the effects of financial aid on matriculation, of student retention, and so on. One of the defining characteristics of SEM is that it is a data-driven, research-dependent process and every successful enrollment management organization has committed resources to supporting that research agenda—either with dedicated research staff or the support of knowledgeable consulting firms.

SEM is increasingly dependent on information systems and technologies; it is very much a technology intensive process and enterprise and the development and management of student data systems is a pivotal part of any enrollment management effort. The enrollment management organization must therefore have the capacity to partner with campus IT divisions in developing, implementing, and managing integrated data systems and web-based strategies and services—and prioritizing among the many competing demands for systems development. The emergence and refinement of data warehouses and data mining strategies that enable deeper and more complex explorations of the nature of institutional enrollment dynamics goes hand-in-hand with the importance of the research agenda mentioned previously. Because virtually all large-scale student information systems link data and services from admissions, financial aid, registration and records, academic advising, and the bursar, many institutions have discovered that there are economies of scale for institutions with respect to staffing and support of these systems if all of these administrative activities are located within a single organizational structure.

The enrollment management organization needs the capacity to help guide and support institutional marketing strategy and tactics. Enrollment management has always employed marketing strategies as part of student recruitment, but increasingly, especially at institutions that are highly tuition-dependent, the overall institutional marketing strategy has to be completely in sync with enrollment goals and objectives. As marketing evolves to include brand marketing, one-to-one relationship marketing, social media marketing, and word-of-mouth marketing, institutional visibility, recognition, brand identity, and competitive market position play an increasingly prevalent role in enrollment success. As a result, the institutional marketing strategy needs to be fully integrated with its core enrollment strategy and vice versa. At a growing number of institutions, the chief enrollment management officer is also the chief marketing officer. The alignment of marketing with enrollment management rather than advancement is becoming more common, particularly at private non-profit institutions. Because the single largest source of revenue at both public and private four-year institutions is student tuition, there is strategic and pragmatic value to this approach.

SEM FUNCTIONS

At most SEM organizations, a set of functions and units are almost always housed within an enrollment management group. These include admissions, financial aid, and registration and records (Schulz & Lucido, 2011a). In addition, as previously noted, SEM units also have an enrollment-related research function, as well as a robust level of IT support that is either manifested through a separate organization or a set of support offices spread across the SEM group. In this section, we discuss the various units found in SEM organizations.

Admissions

Attracting students to apply and matriculate is always part of a SEM organization's activities. Indeed, early in the evolution of SEM it was not uncommon for a president or provost to make the director of admissions the dean or vice president of enrollment management with few, if any, additional changes in their responsibilities. Offices of admissions play an important and complex role in SEM organizations. The task of admissions offices is to identify, recruit, and enroll a desired number of total new students, as well as meet goals associated with the academic quality, gender balance, racial diversity, and socioeconomic mix of the student population. The relative importance and complexity of these efforts varies significantly by the type of institution, differing dramatically between an open admissions community college where the primary goal is often a straightforward desire for enrollment increases, to elite private residential institutions that seek to enroll a precise number of highly qualified new students. For community colleges, local word of mouth, working with local high schools and workforce development centers, along with mass marketing promotions are often the primary forms of outreach, and admissions decision-making is a modest part of the process. Ease of access and proximity are the important factors in the recruitment of new students. For elite private colleges, admissions offices can receive just as much criticism for enrolling too many new students as too few. Admissions units are likely to have specific goals for the number of legacy enrollees, students of color, low income students, national merit scholars, and so forth.

Financial Aid

It is becoming increasingly rare to find a college or university that has not made its financial aid office part of its SEM organization, which says as much about the changing economic and competitive environment for higher education as it does about the evolving nature of enrollment strategy and the place of aid and differential pricing in achieving enrollment goals. Not only is receiving timely communication about offers of federal, state, and institutional financial aid an increasingly critical determinant of students' college choice, but both public and private four-year postsecondary educational institutions are increasingly using campus-funded financial aid to shape their classes. Because financial aid awards can also influence student persistence, financial aid offices also play a role in campus retention efforts.

Like admissions offices, financial aid offices have become very reliant on technology. Federal and state financial aid regulations, the processes governmental bodies employ, and the number of students receiving financial aid have made it virtually impossible to administer financial aid without using software specifically developed to support financial aid administrators. Indeed, a substantial number of financial aid staff members are technology experts who also have subject matter expertise in financial aid policies. This is another factor leading to the organizational integration of admissions and financial aid, since integrated data systems, seamless data processing, and centralized systems support lead naturally to the structural alignment of these offices. The other important role played by knowledgeable financial aid professionals involves keeping their institutions out of legal difficulties, especially with the federal government. Federal regulations require that institutions be audited annually to make sure they are following all federal regulations. Failure to follow these regulations and policies can result in substantial financial penalties levied against the institution.

Registration and Records

Offices of registration and records play important roles within SEM organizations, effectively bridging enrollment management and academic affairs administration. The course registration process is the core business transaction at a tuition-dependent institution; it is where the student's academic interest and the institution's academic offering join, where price is assessed, tuition is paid, and instructional costs are incurred. The most important function of a registrar's office is to enable students to register for classes and to make sure that a sufficient number of courses are being offered at the right time and place. Managing course availability can be a key factor of generating revenue, and cost-effectively balancing instructional resources and ensuring students' timely progress to degree are also key roles for this campus unit. The registrar function is also inextricably connected to academic policy development and implementation; for example, faculty-driven decisions and policies, GPA requirements to keep a student in good standing, or prerequisite course sequencing and admission requirements are implemented through registrar systems and processes and policies. In addition, the registrar function is often engaged in academic space planning, assessing the adequacy of classroom space to accommodate enrollment demand or the capacity of facilities to support new courses or curricula with special space requirements. Finally, it is through the registration process that every student interacts multiple times a year with the institution, and as such it is a critical part of any effort to improve student service and satisfaction with the business of enrolling at the institution.

One reason this function is organized within a SEM organization is to achieve further systems integration and seamless data processing. The registrar's office often has the largest reservoir of professional and support staff who have strong backgrounds in IT and student information systems. Indeed, many registrar's offices are organized in a SEM unit because most new student information systems (SIS) integrate admissions, financial aid, and registration and records, so an integrated, centralized structure is the most cost-effective way to sustain and enhance the capacity of SIS systems (Hossler, 2006). But a corollary benefit is that the student records and registration systems are the source of valuable information and intelligence about student enrollment patterns and outcomes. The institution's capacity to do the longitudinal tracking so critical to retention research depends on the capacities of the student records system. The capacity to support retention initiatives such as early warning systems for students in academic difficulty, early feedback systems from faculty, degree progress and degree audit reports to guide student course selection, and the identification of "high risk" courses with high failure or withdrawal rates all depends on information drawn from student records systems. Patterns of course demand provide marketing insights into students' preferences, which enable faculty to be more responsive to students in the scheduling of courses. Many of the most successful SEM organizations hinge their success on the enrollment intelligence gleaned from ensuring that the student records and registration function does more than just support registration transactions and ensure records management.

SEM RESEARCH

Relying on *Big Data* has become a global phenomenon. Its benefits are touted in fields ranging from medical research, to marketing and advertising, to management. SEM is no different. Increasingly, data from a variety of sources including institutional data, the National Student Clearinghouse, government data sources such as the Integrated Postsecondary Education Data System (IPEDS) and the U.S. Census, and for-profit vendors such as Claritas are all being used for predictive analytics that can drive admissions, financial aid, and retention strategies. The use of quantitative and qualitative research methods to gather data from prospective, current, and prior students has become common to guide SEM strategies. The value of SEM research cannot be overstated. A postsecondary institution can misspend hundreds of thousands of dollars in financial aid or forgo similar amounts of tuition revenue if poorly informed decisions are made related to their position in the tertiary education marketplace.

In addition to SEM being a consumer of data in guiding strategy, the demands on the enrollment management leader to produce data are becoming more intense. Enrollment management officers are called upon to produce information demonstrating student outcomes, placement rates, campus engagement, return-on-investment of marketing initiatives, and evidence of access and affordability. The pressures of accountability and transparency increasingly make knowledge creation, analysis, and dissemination pivotal activities of the senior enrollment officer.

It is now common among large four-year institutions to dedicate a staff of researchers to undertake the types of research described in the previous paragraph, since the demands for enrollment research often exceed the capacity of the typically underfunded institutional research function. Indeed, some large four-year institutions have moved the traditional institutional research function within the SEM organizations better to integrate the institutional research effort with the data-dependent enrollment management process. Regardless, the partnership between institutional research and SEM is critical (Cheslock & Kroc, 2012).

On the other hand, small non-profit public and private institutions often have ongoing relationships with consulting groups that undertake this kind of research. In fact, it is not unusual for institutions of all sizes to seek consultants as they begin major new enrollment-related initiatives or when they believe they have encountered one or more significant enrollment problems that benefits from external expertise and analysis. In both instances, the insights and credibility of an outside expert can be important in shaping SEM decisions.

Traditionally, community colleges have not invested heavily in SEM research. Because they typically focus on local markets only and employ large numbers of adjunct faculty, they can adapt more quickly to shifts in new student enrollments; thus admissions-related research has not been a priority for most community colleges. However, with the growing accountability pressures facing community colleges, especially in the areas of persistence, graduation, and transfer, many community colleges simply have no choice but to invest in more research staff to focus on these important postsecondary outcomes.

ORGANIZING FOR STUDENT RETENTION AND SUCCESS

Student retention, success, and graduation have become significant concerns for all tertiary institutions in the United States, Canada, and many other parts of the world (Fain, 2011; Usher, 2013). However, unlike other functional areas that typically fall within an enrollment management organization, there is no standard organizational approach for efforts to improve student retention and graduation. Some campus retention efforts are led by professionals in academic advising or academic affairs; at other institutions, they are managed by student affairs professionals or are located in SEM organizations. Research efforts between the Project on Academic Success at Indiana University Bloomington and the Center for Enrollment Policy and Practice at the University of Southern California yielded a series of studies at two- and four-year colleges that found that too little organizational focus and coordination is given to campus-based retention efforts (Hossler et al., 2013).

Student retention and success will be discussed later in this volume, so we will not go into further detail in this overview. However, Hossler and Kalsbeek (2013) and Kalsbeek (2013) conclude that if senior campus policy makers are in doubt as to where to locate responsibilities for enhancing student retention, it should be housed within SEM units. They proffer this recommendation because all other major administrative campus offices have multiple foci, and factors affecting student enrollments are only one of many concerns, whereas professionals in SEM are always aware that their task is to enhance institutional performance in all areas related to student enrollment, including improving retention and completion rates.

Variations on a Theme: The Responsibilities of the Senior Enrollment Officer

Several other organizational alignments reflect the evolving nature of SEM organizations. It is not unusual for the entire student affairs organization to be structurally aligned with the SEM unit, with one or the other occasionally managing all of the SEM and student affairs activities depending on institutional history. Until recently, for example, this has been true for all universities in the University of California system.

This is a logical development for many reasons. On some campuses, admissions and financial aid were historically part of student affairs or student services organizations, and the evolution of an enrollment management orientation occurred within that student affairs context. In some cases, as key student services such as registration and financial aid are located in a SEM organization to support enrollment outcomes, the entirety of student services and student affairs functions follow suit to ensure an integrated array of student-facing services and student experiences. In some instances, presidents are reluctant to have too many senior administrators on their campuses and collapse these functions for organizational simplicity. When this happens, the senior officer (typically a vice president, vice-chancellor, or vice-provost) has a strong orientation toward either student affairs or SEM, and the senior officer then appoints a senior associate to balance the attention given to these two broad parts of the administrative portfolio. Regardless, the senior officer must have a strong knowledge base in enrollment management to represent strategic enrollment issues effectively at cabinet meetings.

Another organizational alignment that is becoming increasingly common at the more senior levels is the combination of SEM and institutional marketing. Although no research is yet available on this topic, anecdotal evidence suggests that more and more private colleges are integrating these functions, recognizing that in the context of tuition-dependency, marketing strategy is better tied to the core business of producing tuition revenue than it is if aligned with advancement or an independent marketing and public relations division that is disconnected from the enrollment marketing effort; this puts emphasis first and foremost on audiences and messages and marketing channels that are most influential in shaping enrollment outcomes (Kalsbeek, 2002). At less tuition-dependent institutions such as large public universities or well endowed private institutions, however, it may be less important organizationally to align university marketing with enrollment management, since the marketing agenda is more oriented to policy makers, alumni, or donors.

Many other permutations are possible with regard to the broad organizational alignments of enrollment management. For example, there have been some instances of SEM organizations being organizationally aligned with the Office of Institutional Advancement (Kalsbeek & Montgomery, 2002). The fact remains that structure follows strategy, and the optimal approach is likely the organizational integration and alignment that best fits the institution's particular strategic situation and strategic intentions and its existing strengths, achieving the integration of core activities, which, as Porter (2008) notes, is the key to sustainable competitive advantage. And the prevailing preference for organizational configurations often reflects some underlying core orientations to the nature of the enrollment management enterprise, with some institutions and some institutional leaders leaning naturally toward an academic orientation, versus a student-centered orientation, versus an administrative orientation, or versus a market orientation (Kalsbeek, 2006).

Other Offices Important in SEM

In addition to the standard units that make up a SEM organization, other offices at the senior level are frequently part of SEM organizations. Hossler (2011) notes that new student orientation, academic advising, academic support programs, and career planning offices are often located within SEM organizations (Hossler, 2011; Hossler & Bean, 1990). In addition, increasing numbers of examples of bursar offices are housed within SEM organizations (for example, Purdue University, University of Miami, Southern Illinois University, and the City University of New York). Although there are logical reasons for these organizational structures, there are also substantive arguments against such organizational alignments.

Orientation plays a role in the final steps of recruiting new students, and it has also been identified as an experience that can improve institutional retention, so there are strong arguments for locating orientation with SEM units. At many institutions, orientation is located in student affairs because of all the student activities associated with orientation programs. On the other hand, many senior academic administrators and faculty believe that the most important role for orientation units is to prepare students for academic life, and thus orientation is best aligned with academic affairs. Academic advising and orientation offices often work closely together, so it is not unusual for both offices to be located in academic affairs. However, because academic advising has been proven to be associated with student persistence (Hossler & Bean, 1990), it is also sometimes placed within SEM organizations along with the orientation function.

Bursar offices may be placed within enrollment management organizations often because of the move toward *one-stop services* at many colleges and universities (for example, the University of San Francisco, De Paul University, Drexel University, and the University of Tennessee at Knoxville). When students have a problem associated with registration, for example, it may be because of a problem with their financial aid, or because there is a hold on registration because of unpaid bursar bills. Thus one-stop service centers save students from having to travel to various offices across the campus. There can be economies in staffing by having a service staff cross-trained in all of these areas to field many of the simple, straightforward questions. However, if bursar offices are located in SEM organizations and in a one-stop service center, it is very important with respect to sound financial management to ensure proper separation between the staffing and the processes for packaging and awarding of financial aid and the staffing and processes for collecting tuition and fees. There are many potential conflicts of interest if these offices are fully merged, and yet, although it is important to delineate and manage these as separate functions, the fact is that from the eye of the consumer, these processes are one and the same, and integration in a single service center can dramatically enhance student satisfaction and efficiencies.

One other function that is increasingly better aligned with other SEM units is the career center. The centrality of career and employment outcomes in a college's marketing strategy, the importance of student employment both during and after college in managing their tuition financing, the evolution of the focus of career centers from one of career development to one of career networking, and the connections with area employers as a marketing and boundary spanning process more akin to recruitment than to student service are all reasons why today's career center is more aligned with an enrollment management and marketing orientation than with a strictly student service perspective.

CONCLUSIONS

Every leader and manager prefers certainty to uncertainty and ambiguity (Wolverton, Wolverton, & Gmelch, 1999). Yet research suggests that we lack strong empirical evidence regarding what kind of organizational configuration or individuals are likely to result in a successful SEM unit. Additionally, we would argue that research is unlikely ever to reveal the ideal structure for SEM units. Organizational culture, the preferences of the president and board of trustees, as well as locally situated issues ranging from demographic trends to state policies create a context in which the successful SEM units are likely to be idiosyncratic as they reflect the situation. Repeatedly, literature on the field of SEM indicates that it is a function of the skills of the individual and his or her management team, plus the culture of the organization, that determine the success of SEM efforts on any campus.

Nevertheless, we can reach some normative conclusions, which include the following:

- SEM units are most likely to be successful when the senior enrollment officer sits on the cabinet of the president or in some cases the provost.

- Senior enrollment officers need to form effective working relationships with the president, provost, and CFO, and they must be able to employ SEM-related research to guide enrollment strategies and actions.

- Office of admissions, financial aid, registration and records, and a SEM research unit are critical functions that should be part of any SEM organization.

In the remaining chapters of this volume, we drill down in more detail on the units that make up SEM organizations, the various areas of research and expertise that inform SEM efforts, ranging from marketing, to the effects of financial aid on student college choice and persistence, to a more careful analysis of what we know about student retention and success and how institutions organize themselves to enhance student retention. In the closing chapters, we also examine ethical issues in SEM and the growing demand for well-informed, successful senior enrollment managers.

References

Cheslock, J., & Kroc, R. (2012). Managing enrollments. In R. D.Howard, G. W. McLaughlin, & W. E. Knight (Eds.), *The Handbook of Institutional Research* (pp. 221–236). San Francisco: Jossey-Bass.

DiMaggio, P. J., & Powell, W. W. (1983). The iron cage revisited: Institutional isomorphism and collective rationality in organizational fields. *American Sociological Review*, *48*(2), 147–160.

Dolence, M. G. (1993). *Strategic Enrollment Management: A Primer for Campus Administrators.* Washington, DC: American Association of Collegiate Registrars and Admissions Officers.

Fain, P. (2011). Realistic or radical? *Inside Higher Education*. Retrieved from http://www.insidehighered.com/news/2011/10/24/california-community-college-task-force-pushes-big-changes#sthash.meud22Lt.dpbs.

Hossler, D. (1986). *Creating Effective Enrollment Management Systems*. New York: College Board.

Hossler, D. (2006). Building a Student Information System: Strategies for Success and Implications for Campus Policy Makers. *New Directions for Higher Education*, *2006*(136). San Francisco: Jossey-Bass.

Hossler, D. (2011). From admissions to enrollment management. In F.J.D. MacKinnon & Associates (Eds.), *Rentz's Student Affairs Practice in Higher Education* (4th Edition). Springfield, IL: Charles C. Thomas.

Hossler, D., Bean, J. P., & Associates. (1990). *The Strategic Management of College Enrollments*. San Francisco: Jossey-Bass.

Hossler, D., & Hoezee, L. (2001). Conceptual and theoretical thinking about enrollment management. In. J. Black (Ed.), *The Strategic Enrollment Management Revolution* (pp. 57–76). Washington, DC: American Association of Collegiate Registrars and Admissions Officers.

Hossler, D., & Kalsbeek, D. H. (2008). Enrollment management and managing enrollment: Setting the context for dialogue. *College & University*, *83*(4), 2–9.

Hossler, D., & Kalsbeek, D. H. (2013). Enrollment Management and Managing Enrollments: Revisiting the Context for Institutional Strategy. *Strategic Enrollment Management Quarterly*, *1*(1), 5–25.

Hossler, D., Ziskin, M., Lucido, J., Schulz, S., Dadashova, A., & Zerquera, D. (2011). *How Four-Year Colleges and Universities Organize Themselves to Promote Student Persistence: The Emerging National* Picture. New York: The College Board Advocacy & Policy Center.

Johnson, N., Oliff, P., & Williams, E. (2011). *An Update on State Budget Cuts: At Least 46 States Have Imposed Cuts That Hurt Vulnerable Residents and the Economy*. Washington, DC: Center on Budget and Policy Priorities. Retrieved from http://www.cbpp.org/cms/?fa = view&id = 1214.

Kalsbeek, D. (2002). The Enrollment/Marketing Symbiosis. *Trusteeship*, *10*(2) 14–19.

Kalsbeek, D. (2006). Some reflections on SEM structures and strategies (part 1). *College & University*, *81*(3): 3–10.

Kalsbeek, D. (2013). Reframing Retention Strategy for Institutional Improvement. *New Directions for Higher Education*, *161*, 20–105.

Kalsbeek, D. H., & Montgomery, C. (2002). Changing Places: An alumni relations team joins enrollment management. *Case Currents*, *28*(9), 32–39.

Kemerer, F. R., Baldridge, J. V., & Green, K. C. (1982). *Strategies for Effective Enrollment Management*. Washington, DC: American Association of State Colleges and Universities.

Meyer, J., & Rowan, B. (1977). Institutionalized organizations: Formal structure as myth and ceremony. *The American Journal of Sociology*, *83*(2), 340–363.

Pfeffer, J., & Salancik, G. (1978). *The External Control of Organizations: A Resource Dependence Perspective.*Stanford, CA.: Stanford University Press.

Porter, M. E. (1979). The five competitive forces that shape strategy. *Harvard Business Review* (2008). Retrieved from http://hbr.org/2008/01/the-five-competitive-forces-that-shape-strategy/ar/1.

Porter, M. E. (2008). *On Competition*. Boston: Harvard Business School Press.

Schulz, S. A., & Lucido, J. A. (2011a). What enrollment management structures reveal about institutional priorities. *Enrollment Management Journal: Student Access, Finance, and Success in Higher Education*, *5*(4), 12–44.

Schulz, S. A., & Lucido, J. A. (2011b). Who we are: An in-depth look at the educational backgrounds, career paths and development needs of chief admission officers and enrollment managers. *Journal of College Admission*, *211*, 14–20.

Slaughter, S., & Leslie, L. L. (1997). *Academic Capitalism: Politics, Policies, and the Entrepreneurial University*. Baltimore, MD: The Johns Hopkins University Press.

Snowden, M. L. (2010). *Enrollment Logics and Discourse: Toward Professionalizing Higher Education Enrollment Management*. Unpublished doctoral dissertation, Texas A&M University.

Usher, A. (2013). 70 per cent postsecondary graduation rates, Mr. Trudeau? Check the demographics. *The Globe and Mail*, Toronto, Ontario, April 16, 2013. Retrieved from http://www.theglobeandmail.com/news/national/education/70-per-cent-postsecondary-graduation-rates-mr-trudeau-check-the-demographics/article11239989.

Usher, A., & Medow, J. (2010). *Global Higher Education Rankings 2010. Affordability and Accessibility in Comparative Perspective*. Retrieved from http://www.ireg-observatory.org/pdf/HESA_Global_Higher_EducationRankings2010.pdf.

Wolverton, M., Wolverton, M. L., & Gmelch, W. H. (1999). The impact of role conflict and ambiguity on academic deans. *The Journal of Higher Education*, *70*(1), 80–106.

PART TWO

CHOICE, MARKETS, AND ADMISSIONS

In Part II, we examine relevant research, policies, and practices that are most relevant to the recruitment and admissions functions within Strategic Enrollment Management organizations.

Chapter 5 begins with an overview of research on student college choice. This body of research helps SEM units better understand variations in how students' socioeconomic background, age, gender, ethnicity, and academic performance influence their application and enrollment decisions. It also examines the timing of students' decisions, which can help guide the timing of admissions marketing efforts. Much of this research, though conducted in the United States, is relevant to student decision-making in many other countries.

Chapter 5 also focuses on the structure of postsecondary markets in the United States. David Kalsbeek and Brian Zucker use student enrollment data to build upon previous work of Bob Zemsky and others, who developed models of postsecondary markets using pricing, selectivity, and student choice. The authors employ eleven interrelated measures of publicly available measures of student demand and fiscal strength to develop an empirical model of market positions for both public and private institutions. They also demonstrate that over time there is relatively little institutional movement from one market segment to another.

In Chapter 6, Tom Hayes discusses admissions marketing. He provides an overview of key concepts in postsecondary marketing. He emphasizes the use of service marketing concepts and notes that admissions marketing is the responsibility of the entire institution, not just admissions professionals.

Chapter 7 focuses on factors that influence the enrollment of transfer students. Enrolling new transfer students has become an increasingly important part of SEM efforts at many public and private colleges and universities. Increasingly, states are encouraging students to begin their postsecondary careers at community colleges, and this affects enrollment patterns not only at public and private four-year institutions, but also at two-year institutions. The authors examine vertical transfer (students who transfer from two- to four-year schools) as well as reverse transfers (from four- to two-year institutions), lateral transfers (students who transfer from one community college to another community college), and swirling students (who move back and forth between two- and four-year colleges and universities). They also include a discussion of the role of transfer and articulation agreements on student enrollment behaviors.

In the final chapter of Part II, Jerome Lucido provides a comprehensive overview of the various approaches colleges and universities employ to make admissions decisions. Chapter 8 includes discussions of both the underlying philosophies associated with institutional missions that resulted in taxonomy of the admission decision-making process. The author also examines selectivity models of admissions and includes a discussion of early decision and early action admissions. The chapter also includes a timely discussion of affirmative action and the growing use of noncognitive approaches to college admissions decisions.

In sum, Part II provides a comprehensive overview of research, policies, and practices relevant to college admissions professionals.

CHAPTER 4

Understanding Student College Choice

Eunkyoung Park and
Don Hossler

Strategic Enrollment Management is a field of practice, but increasingly it is informed by research. This research may be institutional based, focusing on factors that predict enrollment or that contribute to student success, or it may focus on the effects of campus-based financial aid on matriculation or graduation. SEM, however, is also informed by what might be called *academic research* and *policy research*. Academic research on student college choice and student retention, perhaps more than any other domain of research in the field of higher education, has expanded dramatically in the last five decades. Much of the impetus for this research was the growing interest among institutional policy makers on how they might influence their student enrollments. Over time, this kind of research became an important part of SEM. For example, research on student college choice has provided invaluable insights into when traditional age students make their decisions about attending college—anywhere—and subsequently decide which institution to attend. Research on student retention has helped enrollment managers better understand how student engagement and intentions to persist influence persistence and graduation rates.

Increasingly, senior enrollment managers are asked to make presentations on the activities of SEM organizations to groups of faculty, boards of trustees, and external groups. Particularly for faculty groups and academic administrators, a manager's ability to contextualize SEM plans within extant theories and research also helps to establish the legitimacy of SEM leaders and their organizations.

This chapter provides an overview of research about college choice that is relevant for professionals in the area of college admissions and SEM. Thus, we focus on the factors that influence students' decisions and the timing of their college choice process. We start with a brief overview of college choice theories and models. Then we describe factors that influence students when they make decisions related to attending college. We also look what are known about the differences between white, African American, Latino, and Asian American students, as well as research on the factors that influence the decisions of nontraditional students. We examine issues of timing—critical junctures when students make important decisions about their postsecondary plans and destinations. Throughout this chapter, we highlight the utility of this body of research for institutional policies and practices. Although these findings can be of use to public policy makers, this audience is not the primary focus of this chapter.

COLLEGE CHOICE THEORIES

An array of theoretical and conceptual models have been used to address student college choice. Theories derived from the disciplines such as economics and sociology have informed much of the academic research on student college choice; however, in the world of practice in which strategic enrollment managers reside, theoretical models often fail to yield sufficient insights into the pragmatic decisions that institutional administrators must make. Thus, this session briefly introduces the three most widely used theoretical models that examine student college choice and then moves on to discuss combined models of college choice (models that draw upon multiple disciplines), which are in a more applied fashion and easily transferable for institutional policies and practices.

We discuss the three theoretical models that frame student college choice: economic, sociological, and information processing approaches. These three approaches emphasize different aspects of factors explaining student college choice. This section briefly introduces the main arguments of these approaches, which serve as a foundation for the combined models of college choice.

Economic Approach

Economists describe college choice as a decision to invest human capital based on the assumption that the lifetime economic benefits will exceed the costs of additional education (Becker, 1993; Ellwood & Kane, 2000; Paulsen, 2001). Human capital theory assumes that individuals calculate the total benefits of attending a college (such as increases in earning, enhancement in social status, enjoyment of the learning experience, better work environments, better health, more informed purchases, lower probability of unemployment, and so on) (Baum & Payea, 2004; Bowen, 1997; Leslie & Brinkman, 1987; Perna, 2006) and compare them with the expected costs (such as a college's price including tuition, fees, room, board, books, and supplies; the price of alternative educational opportunities and/or alternative colleges; financial aid; the opportunity costs of foregone earnings; leisure time; the costs of traveling; and so on) (Becker, 1993; Leslie & Brinkman, 1987). Studies from the economic perspective focus on financial factors such as cost of attendance, financial information, and financial aid policies and practices to explain college choice (see, for example, Avery & Hoxby, 2004; Ellwood & Kane, 2000; Griffith & Rothstein, 2009; Harper & Griffin, 2011; Long, 2004).

Sociological Approach

The sociological approach shares some factors with the economic approach. It, too, describes college choice as a result of the interaction between educational aspirations and constraints. This approach, however, emphasizes the influences of social and cultural capital such as parental education, family income, the extent to which students are taken to museums or read to by parents, and the impact these social interactions have upon students' educational aspirations. In addition, contrary to the economic approach stressing the cost benefit analyses that take place in the later stages of college choice (such as whether and where to enroll), the sociological approach tends to focus more on the earlier stage of college choice (such as academic aspirations and preparation) (Bourdieu, 1986; Hearn, 1988; McDonough, 1997; Terenzini et al., 2001). Focusing on the earlier stage of college choice, the sociological approach explains how an individual's social status shapes his or her educational aspirations and college choice (see, for example Cabrera, La Nasa, & Burkum, 2002; Carnevale & Rose, 2003; Perna, 2006).

Information Processing Approach

The information processing approach focuses on how students gather, process, and make decisions based on information (Huber, 1984; Stinchcombe, 1990). Although the economic approach explains what kind of information students utilize to make a college decision, it does not fully explain the differences in accessing information across students (DesJardins & Toutkoushian, 2005). The information processing perspective, on the other hand, accounts for the differential access to college information as well as the lack of information. According to this approach, primary college information channels are parents and siblings, high school teachers and counselors, college admissions personnel, recruitment materials, college guidebooks, and college fairs (see for example Avery, 2010; Ceja, 2006; Hill & Winston, 2010).

Combined Models of College Choice

In combined models of college choice, the college decision-making process involves multiple stages. For instance, Gregory Jackson (1982) proposed a college choice model with three stages—preference, exclusion, and evaluation—in which students develop their preference for college, then exclude some institutions based on their preference and develop a consideration set, and then evaluate the characteristics of colleges in their consideration set to decide where to attend. Additionally, five-stage models were proposed by Katherine Hanson and Larry Litten (1982) and David Chapman (1984). Hanson and Litten's model includes stages in which students develop their college aspiration, search college information, gather college information, submit a college application, and finally enroll in a college. Chapman's choice model comprises the following stages: pre-search, search, applications, choice, and enrollment.

Based on synthesis and simplification of previous work, Don Hossler and Karen Gallagher (1987) proposed a three-stage model that comprises predisposition, search, and choice. According to this model, students first develop their college aspiration whether they go to college or take other status-attainment paths such as work or military service (*predisposition*). Then, students search and collect college information to learn about specific colleges in their consideration set (*search*). Finally, students apply for several colleges and enroll in a particular institution (*choice*). This is the simplest model and has been widely accepted as a foundation in later studies on college choice (such as DesJardins et al., 2006; Perna, 2006; Institute for Higher Education Policy, 2012).

COLLEGE CHOICE FACTORS

The discipline-based college choice theories and combined college choice models help us understand the process of college choice and serve as a conceptual framework for empirical studies. To date, a large body of empirical studies has explored the factors influencing students' college choice based on these theories and models. The following sections summarize what is known about key predictors of college choice from prior research.

Personal Characteristics

Although most college choice studies include gender as a predicting factor, whether gender influences college choice is open to speculation. Some studies found higher educational expectation for females (Hossler & Stage, 1992), while other studies found higher educational expectation for males (Hao & Bonstead-Bruns, 1998). Hossler and Frances Stage (1992) also found that female students' educational aspirations increased as they discussed college choices with their parents more often, which is not always true for male students. Some studies found higher college attendance rates for females (Perna & Titus, 2004, 2005), but other studies found no significant difference in college attendance rates across gender (Perna, 2000). Research also suggests that college choice processes and outcomes vary across racial/ethnic groups, and this topic is explored later in this chapter.

Family Income

Family income and socioeconomic status have been the strongest predictors of college choice. Family income is reported to influence all the college choice outcomes such as educational aspirations, application behaviors, and enrollment decisions. For instance, low-income students tend to have lower academic aspirations (Kao & Tienda, 1998), are less likely to apply to four-year colleges, tend to submit fewer applications (Avery, 2010; Hill & Winston, 2010; Hurtado et al., 1997), are less likely to enroll in a four-year college, and are more likely to enroll in a two-year, public, and less selective college (Avery, 2010; Ellwood & Kane, 2000; Harper & Griffin, 2011; Hossler et al., 1999; Kane & Rouse, 1999; Winston & Hill, 2005) than their peers from families with high incomes.

Social and Cultural Capital

In addition to family income, social and cultural capital are also closely associated with college choice (Bourdieu, 1986; McDonough, 1997; Terenzini et al., 2001). Parents' educational attainment, parental involvement in their child's education, and parental expectation toward their child are strongly associated with the child's college aspirations, application behaviors, and college enrollment decisions (An, 2012; Harper & Griffin, 2011; Hossler et al., 1999; Hossler & Stage, 1992; Kao & Tienda, 1998; McDonough, 1997; Perna, 2000; Perna & Titus, 2004, 2005; Plank & Jordan, 2001; Rowan-Kenyon et al., 2008). Parents' social networks (Perna & Titus, 2005) and students' peer networks (McDonough, 1997; Hossler & Stage, 1992; Pérez & McDonough, 2008; Person & Rosenbaum, 2006; Valdez, 2008) also influence college choice.

Academic Ability

Higher academic preparation and greater academic achievement are associated with positive college choice outcomes. High academic ability increases the odds that a student will enroll in college preparatory classes in high school, enroll in more math and science classes, take more advanced-placement courses, and graduate with higher grades (ACT, 2005; An, 2012; Hughes et al., 2005; Joensen & Nielsen, 2009; Klopfenstein & Thomas, 2009; Long, Conger, & Iatarola, 2011). Not surprisingly, academic ability also increases the odds of the student's admission to a college or university (DesJardins et al., 2006; Ellwood & Kane, 2000; Horn & Chen, 1998; Hossler, Braxton, & Coopersmith, 1989; Hossler & Stage, 1992; Perna, 2000, 2006; Perna & Titus, 2004, 2005; St. John, 1991). Despite the importance of academic ability in college choice, there are ongoing concerns about the small number of low-income students attending less-selective institutions than the institution they could have attended based on their academic ability (that is, *undermatching*) (Bastedo & Jaquette, 2011; Bowen, Chingos, & McPherson, 2009). Although academic ability is a strong factor influencing college choice, this line of studies implies the existence of other factors that shape college choice in addition to academic ability.

High School Attended

School context also shapes college choice. High school academic quality and affluence, such as teacher qualification, student average academic achievement, student average family income, the availability of advanced courses, college counseling, access to technology, and expenditures per student, are closely related to college choice outcomes (Carnevale & Rose, 2003; Harper & Griffin, 2011; Perna, 2004). Colleges located near the high school the student attended create a college-going atmosphere, expose high school students to higher education, and raise awareness of higher education opportunities, and as a result, they affect high school students' college aspirations and college choices (Avery, 2010; Do, 2004; Griffith & Rothstein, 2009).

Information Sources

Having information sources that can provide accurate college information is also associated with positive college choice outcomes (Martinez, 2013; Stephan & Rosenbaum, 2012). Typical college information providers are parents and siblings, high school teachers and counselors, college admissions personnel, recruitment materials, college guidance and marketing materials, and college fairs and websites (Avery, 2010; Ceja, 2006; Hill & Winston, 2010; Hossler et al., 1999; Kane & Rouse,1999; McDonough, 1997). As students have more access to quality college information (that is, accurate, reliable, and relevant information), such as information distributed from college through marketing materials (such as direct mail, social networking outlets, college guidebooks, college fairs), their chances of applying to and enrolling in a college increase (Hill & Winston, 2010; Wolniak & Engberg, 2007). The availability and the quality of college counseling also influence students' college aspirations and participation (Avery, 2010).

Peer Effects

Peers also affect students' educational outcome through their backgrounds, behaviors, and academic achievement as well as their family background (Sacerdote, 2011). Peers affect a student's academic achievement (mostly measured by test scores) (Hanushek et al., 2003; Hoxby, 2000; Vigdor & Nechyba, 2007) with larger benefits to those who are either at the top or at the bottom of test score distribution (Burke & Sass, 2013; Hoxby & Weingarth, 2005; Lavy, Paserman, & Schlosser,

2007). Regarding college choice, students with many college-bound friends are more likely to apply to colleges (Alvarado & Turley, 2010). More importantly, students who attend high school with more classmates aspiring to college education are more likely to go to college (Fletcher, 2006). Peer college preferences affect students' college choice as it increases the amount of information about specific colleges that the students receive (Bernheim, 1994; Fletcher, 2012).

Costs of Attendance and Financial Aid

Financial factors such as costs of attendance, the availability and the amount of financial aid, and net price affect student college choice to a significant extent. Although oftentimes most students do not know exactly how much they need to pay to attend a college of their choice, the costs of attendance with any measures (such as tuition, net price, sticker price) affect the likelihood of college enrollment and the types of college in which students enroll (Avery & Hoxby, 2004; Ellwood & Kane, 2000; Griffith & Rothstein, 2009; Kane, 1998; Long, 2004). The amount and the type of financial aid also affect student college choice (Alon, 2005; DesJardins et al., 2002; Dowd & Coury, 2006; St. John et al., 2005). Despite the importance of costs and financial aid in their college choice, students oftentimes lack quality information on financial factors. Some scholars found that students having financial information is as important as them having financial aid offers in making a college choice (Harper & Griffin, 2011; Hill & Winston, 2010). Regarding this, a study conducted by Eric Bettinger and his colleagues (2009) proved the importance of simplifying the financial aid application process and providing information by showing that students were more likely to enroll in a college and receive financial aid when they received help with completing the Free Application for Federal Student Aid (FAFSA).

COLLEGE CHOICE BY RACE/ETHNICITY

As mentioned, race/ethnicity is one of the frequently cited factors that shape students' college choice. In this section, we discuss the differences in college choice among students of various races/ethnicities. By providing information on what affects college choice for a specific body of students and what they value most, this section informs colleges and universities that want to attract a specific body of students.

White Students

Studies have found that white students tend to be better off economically, receive better K–12 education, and score higher on standardized tests, which leads them to higher representation at higher education institutions (Carnevale & Strohl, 2013; Kim, 2004; Park, 2013; Perna, 2000). However, it is not an easy task to tease out the individual factors that influence white students. Until recently, most studies of college choice used race as an independent variable but did not focus exclusively on a single racial or ethnic group. To examine white students' college choice, we draw on research that focuses upon white students as well as broader studies for which white students were the majority population.

As described earlier, gender, family income, socioeconomic status, academic achievement, high school attended, college information and guidance, peers, and availability of financial aid affect white students' college choice (Hossler et al., 1999). When they select a college to attend, they consider the availability of programs of study of their interest, costs, financial aid, job placement after graduation, safety, campus environment, distance to home, teacher quality, academic reputation, and so on (Broekemier, 2002; Broekemier & Seshadri, 1999; Canale et al., 1996; Coccari & Javalgi, 1995). In addition, white students are more likely to attend their first-choice institutions than African American, Asian American, and Latino students (Kim, 2004). Studies also found that female white students were less likely to attend their first-choice college than their male counterparts (Kim, 2004). As with other students, white students' college choice is also affected significantly by their academic achievement (Kim, 2004; Park, 2013).

Although white students make up the majority of students in the U.S. higher education system and are considered a successful group in terms of college access, the typical perception about college choice of white students may obscure the barriers and difficulties that first-generation college students or students from low-income families may face. According to Dongbin Kim (2004), among racial/ethnic groups, only white students were more influenced by financial concerns; in fact, white students with greater financial concerns were less likely to attend a college that was their first choice. When white students received financial aid, however, their probability of attending the first-choice college increased (Kim, 2004). Again, this indicates that low-income white students may be disadvantaged from the typical college choice models, which assume that white students usually are more likely to attend college than any other racial/ethnic groups.

African American Students

Over the past decade, the number of African American undergraduates enrolled in colleges and universities nationwide has increased by 75 percent and the number of bachelor's degrees awarded has increased by 55 percent for African Americans (National Center for Education Statistics, 2012, calculation by authors based on Tables 235, 264, and 328). Although more African American students are attending colleges and receiving degrees than ever before, they continue to be underrepresented among both undergraduate enrollees (8 percent) and bachelor's degree recipients (10 percent) relative to their representation in the traditional college-age population (14 percent) (NCES, 2012, calculation by authors based on Tables 235, 264, and 328).

In general, African American students are reported to have high academic aspirations at the early stages of college choice. Their four-year college aspirations are often higher than those of white students and are comparable with those of Asian students (Hurtado et al., 1997). The availability of historically black colleges and universities (HBCUs) is positively related with their high college aspirations (Hurtado et al., 1997). However, many studies have found that African American students' educational attainment is lower than their aspirations (Hearn, 1984; Kim 2004; Perna, 2000; Pitre, 2006).

The discrepancy between educational aspiration and attainment can be explained in several ways. First, as it does for students of other races/ethnicities, academic achievement matters to African American students. Scholars found that African American students' aspirations are not supported by academic achievement in high school (for example, lack of information about postsecondary education, insufficient academic preparation), which might cause negative consequences in college enrollment (Pitre, 2006). Others found that the lack of college information and guidance affects the gap. In other words, African American students are less likely to enroll in a four-year college than Latino or white students with the same educational aspirations, because African American students have lower access to college information and guidance (Perna, 2000). In some cases, African American students hold unrealistic goals and aspirations that are not supported by college behavior or academic achievement (Chen & Volpe, 1998; Perna & Titus, 2005). Parental expectations also matter in African American students' college choice—more than it does for Latino or white students (Hamrick & Stage, 2004).

African American students are more sensitive than other students to costs (such as tuition and financial aid), even after controlling for socioeconomic status and academic ability (Heller, 1997). They are more likely to attend a college when it offers financial aid (Jackson, 1990). With lower access to financial information, African American students are uncertain about their ability to pay and the long-term economic returns of attending college (Perna, 2000). According to some scholars, the discrepancy between educational aspiration and attainment results from the experiences of the student's family and friends, which suggest that educational payoffs in terms of occupation are limited. Thus, when it comes time to decide whether to go to college, the perceived benefits do not outweigh the costs (Mickelson, 1990).

Another thing to note about African American students' college choice is the sizable gender gap. In particular, African American female students are more likely to attend a postsecondary institution than males and tend to outperform male students (Holmes, 2004; Smith & Fleming, 2006). According to Michael

Smith and Michael Fleming (2006), African American parents tend to have different college expectations for their sons and daughters. Parents of daughters think going to a four-year college is the best option for their child's success, with the hope that the college degree will help their daughter achieve personal and financial independence. Unlike Latino parents, African American parents are more willing to send their daughter to college so that she can benefit from all the advantages college has to offer. In contrast, for their sons, they view four-year colleges as only one of several options. According to the researchers' interviews, some African American parents wanted to have their sons near them, with the assumption that their sons are more likely to encounter difficulties once they leave home. Thus, African American males tend to attend colleges and universities closer to home.

Latino Students

Given the rapid increase in the number of Latino high school graduates in the last decade, we examine factors that influence the postsecondary educational decisions in more detail for Latino students than other racial groups in this chapter. Latino students are more likely to be first-generation students (Santiago & Cunningham, 2005; Swail, Cabrera, & Lee, 2004). As a result, they tend to have lower college aspirations and lower high school academic achievement than other students (Wirt, Choy, Rooney, Hussar, Provasnik, & Thompson, 2005; Ingels, Planty, & Bozick, 2005). They also have the lowest expectations for degree attainment and tend to apply to fewer colleges than other students, and this remains true even for high-achieving Latino students (Carter & Wilson, 1992; Hurtado et al., 1997; Ingels et al., 2005). In addition, they are likely to attend two-year institutions or less selective institutions than four-year institutions or more selective institutions (Hurtado et al., 1997; Carter & Wilson, 1992).

Although many Latino parents place great value on education (Ceja, 2004, 2006; Gonzáles, Stoner, & Jovel, 2003), the majority of the Mexican immigrants have little or no college experience in the United States. In addition, many immigrant Latino parents have difficulty in reading and speaking English, which leads them to be reluctant to attend school-sponsored college orientations and contributes to the lack of their child's college knowledge. As a result, despite their high emotional support, many Latino parents provide a lower level of parental involvement than other parents (Perna, 2000). Because their parents have little previous experience with postsecondary education, Latino students seek out college information and guidance from other individuals, such as older siblings and extended family members (cousins, aunts, uncles, and so on) (Ceja, 2006; Perez & McDonough, 2008). Although these information providers are critical and valuable sources of college knowledge, the college guidance from them is not always neutral—in other words, it is "well intended but not without personal bias" (Perez & McDonough, 2008). Studies have found that these information providers propel Latino students to attend low-cost, less-selective institutions, and institutions near home (Kurlaender, 2006; Person & Rosenbaum, 2006; Swail et al., 2004). Also, some studies have reported that the more important the student considers a friend's opinion, the less likely the Latino student will attend his or her first-choice college (Kim, 2004).

Ann Person and James Rosenbaum (2006) explained the importance of family members, peers, and acquaintances in Latino students' college choice using the *chain migration* theory. Basically, chain migration theory can be understood as "movement in which prospective migrants learn of opportunities, are provided with transition and have initial accommodation and employment arranged by means of primary social relationships with previous migrants" (MacDonald & MacDonald, 1964, p. 227). Given Latino students' lack of access to accurate college information, studies have emphasized the importance of other institutional agents, such as teachers, counselors, and college personnel, who can help provide more timely and accurate college information (Ceja, 2006).

Financial concerns also drive Latino students' college choice (Santiago & Cunningham, 2005). With the strong bond within family and relatively high financial difficulties, Latino students tend to prefer colleges near home (Santiago, 2007). Latino students are more likely to limit their college choice first to in-state institutions and second to institutions near home (Pèrez & McDonough, 2008). According to Deborah Santiago (2006), about half of all Latino undergraduates in 2003–04 chose to enroll in the 6 percent of institutions of higher education known as Hispanic-Serving Institutions (HSIs) (that is, public or not-for-profit institutions of higher education that enroll 25 percent or more undergraduate Hispanic full-time equivalent students) (Higher Education Act of 1995 as amended in 1998—see http://www.nrcyd.ou.edu/publication-db/documents/higher-education-act-1965.pdf). The majority of HSIs have open admissions policies (60 percent), are public institutions (70 percent), and are located in communities with large Latino populations (Cunningham, Park, & Engle, 2014). Further, the average tuition and fees at HSIs are lower than those of comparable institutions (Santiago, 2006, 2007). These three factors—access, location, and affordability—may explain why so many Latino students choose to attend such a narrow range of institutions.

Although this section described Latino students' college choice in general, it should be noted that Latino students are diverse in their race and their college experiences vary to a large degree. Postsecondary participation rates and college destinations can be quite different among students from Puerto Rico, Cuba, and Mexico (Bohon, Johnson & Gorman, 2006). For example, Cuban and Puerto Rican students are more likely to enroll in postsecondary education and are not as limited by costs or proximity as other Latino students (Fry, 2002, 2003). Recent studies on Latino students' college choice try to understand these differences (Bohon et al., 2006; Fry, 2002). Thus, although many studies found that Latino students have lower access to higher education, others found that Latino students' college access rates are comparable to or even higher than those of white students after controlling for educational costs, educational aspiration, academic ability, and socioeconomic status (Jackson, 1990; Kane & Spizman, 1994; Kurlaender, 2006; St. John & Noell, 1989), especially among students with high academic ability (Park, 2013).

Asian Students

According to recent data released from the White House Initiative on Asian Americans and Pacific Islanders (2013), the Asian American population grew in the United States by 43 percent between 2000 and 2010 and is projected to grow another 134 percent to more than 35.6 million by 2050. Like Latino students, Asian Americans are a heterogeneous group with different countries of origin: China (22 percent), Philippines (19 percent), India (16 percent), Vietnam (10 percent), Korea (9 percent), Japan (6 percent), and other (18 percent). Although Asian Americans are a growing and diverse population, there is a paucity of research on college choice among Asian American populations, and even that research treats the population as a single group.

The most frequent finding about Asian American students is that they are "the highest-income, best-educated and fastest-growing racial group in the United States" (The Pew Research Center, 2013, p.1). In general, Asian American students show higher academic aspiration and academic achievement, as well as high college attendance rates in terms of both four-year college enrollment and selective college enrollment (Caplan, Choy, & Whitmore, 1991; Hsia, 1988; Hurtado et al., 1997; Park, 2013). In addition, some Asian American students face the same obstacles that other immigrant groups experience, such as economic difficulties and language barriers (Teranishi et al., 2013). Asian American immigrant students' high academic aspirations and achievement and the barriers they face are well reflected in the significant gap in college choice among these students. In other words, the aggregated college choice outcomes emphasize the experiences of only some subgroups with high income and high academic achievement, while others such as Southeast Asian students have significant difficulties in accessing college (National Commission on Asian American and Pacific Islander Research in Education [CARE], 2008).

According to CARE (2008), the proportion of Asian Americans living below the poverty level is higher than that of the total U.S. population. Studies of Southeast Asian students, in particular, show that many live in poverty; when disaggregated, the South Asian, Korean, Japanese, and Chinese populations each have a higher socioeconomic status than that of Southeast Asians (Goyette & Xie, 1999). Japanese and Filipino people have higher incomes than Chinese and Southeast Asian people (Teranishi et al., 2004). In terms of academic backgrounds, South Asian, Japanese, and Korean students' parents had higher levels of education than the parents of other Asian American students and white students (Goyette & Xie, 1999). Korean and Chinese students performed much better on the standardized test than other Asian students and were more likely to take SAT prep courses and submit more applications; however, the gaps between high- and low-income students among the Chinese population are huge (Teranishi et al., 2004). Filipino and Southeast Asian students are more likely to be influenced by relatives and prefer colleges near home more so than Japanese and Korean students (Teranishi et al., 2004). Financial concerns are higher for Southeast Asian and Filipino students than for Chinese, Japanese, and Korean students (Teranishi et al., 2004).

Most successful college access rates are achieved by Chinese, Japanese, and Korean students, compared to Indians, Filipinos, Vietnamese, and other Asian students (Goyette & Xie, 1999). More Chinese and Korean students than Filipino and Southeast Asian students attend highly selective institutions. Even among low-income students, Chinese and Korean students have a greater representation in selective institutions. Chinese, Japanese, and Korean students are also more likely to attend private institutions than Filipino and Southeast Asian students (Teranishi et al., 2004).

With the differences in college choice among Asian American students in mind, the following describes the factors that influence Asian American students' college choice in general. Asian American parents in general show high educational expectations (Chua, 2011; Goyette & Xie, 1999) as well as high involvements (Kim & Gasman, 2011). With many Asian American parents having prior college experience, they also serve as information providers (Wong & Hirschman, 1983). However, not all Asian parents have college education experience and not all of them are highly involved in their children's education. For instance, Asian parents, similar to other immigrant parents, suffer from time constraints, language barriers, and cultural differences (Kim & Gasman, 2011), which can prevent them from collecting and delivering college information to their children.

Asian American parents' high expectations and involvement are frequently borne out by the postsecondary educational experiences of their children. Many Asian American students tend to take attending college for granted and have a sense of responsibility in doing well academically and meeting their parents expectations (Kim & Gasman, 2011), meaning they often attend what the parents deem a "good college" (Yeh et al., 2002). With their high aspirations and expectations, Asian Americans' academic ability is a driving factor when choosing a college (Hurtado et al., 1997). Many academically successful Asian American students value institutions with good academic reputations and prestige and the academic and professional opportunities that colleges provide (Kim & Gasman, 2011). Asians American students also consider future employment and transition to a graduate program important factors when they select a college (Teranishi et al., 2004).

As for financial concerns, Asian Americans' perceived benefits of attending college and attending a prestigious institution outweigh the costs (Kim & Gasman, 2011). Although there is some evidence of debt aversion among Asian American students (Cunningham & Santiago, 2008), financial aid offers, either loans or grants, have a very large impact on students' college choice. Regardless of family income, Asian American parents were willing to pay for their child's education, even if that would mean taking out several loans. In general, Asian American parents seem to put more value on education than on costs of attendance and consider college education a worthwhile investment in their children's future (Kim, 2004). In the same vein, Asian American students were willing to go further to attend their first-choice college or university (Kim & Gasman, 2011). In terms of selective college access, parental income, parental educational levels, U.S. citizenship or permanent resident status, and high school achievement are strongly associated with a student attending a more selective institution (Teranishi et al., 2004).

NONTRADITIONAL STUDENTS

Over the last three decades, the participation of nontraditional students in higher education has increased significantly (Brock, 2010; Seftor & Turner, 2002). According to the U.S. Department of Education, the increase of nontraditional students such as transfer students, part-time students, and adult students will continue in coming years (Snyder, Dillow, & Hoffman, 2007). As their representation grows, nontraditional students' college choices are becoming more important. However, most of the research and data on college choice are limited to first-time, full-time college students, which excludes one-third of the entire college student population such as nontraditional students (Hagelskamp, Schleifer, & DiStasi, 2013). This section briefly discusses the factors that influence nontraditional students' college choice and barriers they may face.

Nontraditional students, unlike traditional students, have multiple responsibilities—managing home, family, work, and study—which set hurdles for them as they try to pursue their education. They also have higher concerns about costs (Bishop & Van Dyk, 1977; Seftor & Turner, 2002), as they must support their own education. Unlike traditional age students, high school graduates who immediately enroll full time, nontraditional students are independent, and they work while attending college and often must raise and care for their children (Choy, 2002). Thus, for them, financial concerns are a major consideration in choosing colleges (Bishop & Van Dyk, 1977; Seftor & Turner, 2002). In effect, changes in availability of federal financial aid were found to have a more significant effect on the enrollment behavior of nontraditional students than on traditional age students (Seftor & Turner, 2002). Nontraditional students' high concentration in community colleges also reflects their concerns about costs (Choy, 2002).

Because of the barriers faced by nontraditional students, the decision to attend college can be more difficult for them than for traditional college age students. Motivations that prompt these nontraditional students to college include desires to have a better job, to make an economic improvement, to advance professionally, to escape from a current situation, to make a career change, to achieve job advancement with a current employer, and to make social friendships, as well as intrinsic motivations such as pure interest in knowledge and satisfaction of obtaining a degree (Bendixen-Noe & Giebelhaus, 1998; Broekemier, 2002; Digilio, 1998; Harju & Eppler, 1997; Richardson & King, 1998; Swenson, 1998).

The barriers and motivations are reflected in nontraditional students' college choices. With all their responsibilities in addition to their own education, non-traditional students tend to limit their college choice set based on geographical range (Levine & Cureton, 1998; Swenson, 1998). Nontraditional students also consider convenience, quality, service, and cost when making a college choice more so than traditional age students, because the nontraditional students' concerns focus on time constraints, childcare, instructional and advising scheduling, and transportation (Broekemier, 2002; Levine & Cureton, 1998; Stone & O'Shea, 2013; Swenson, 1998).

TIMING OF COLLEGE CHOICE

So far, we have described the factors that affect students' college choice with particular focus on race and ethnicity. This section specifically looks at the timing of college choice—when students are making decisions. Although this section includes findings about racial and ethnic differences in the timing of college choice, the body of literature is not sufficiently robust to focus on different racial and ethnic groups with regard to timing.

It is difficult to determine when students first make their decision to attend college, and the timing of the decision varies considerably. Some students make this decision prior to high school enrollment, while other students decide later (Hossler et al., 1999). Most students, however, make their first-choice college decision by the end of ninth grade. Hossler, Jack Schmit, and Nick Vesper (1999) found that the later students developed aspirations and/or applied to college, the less likely they were to enter a college or university, or the more likely they were to attend a two-year college rather than a four-year institution. Decisions made by ninth graders, however, are not firm or serious yet, and thus are not followed by observable actions (such as seeking information or required course taking) (Avery & Kane, 2004; Perna, 2006). By the tenth grade, students with college aspirations start to think more seriously about attending college and seek college information. These students can provide a short list of institutions they are considering and some characteristics that are important to them (Palmer, Park, & Hossler, 2012).

High school juniors with college aspirations become more engaged in seeking college information and take college entrance examinations. Taking the SAT/ACT, which usually occurs in the junior year, is a trigger event that makes the "whole college thing" more concrete (Hossler et al., 1999). Thus, schools can assume that if a student has taken these tests, he or she is more likely to be ready to receive information about going to college or specific colleges. Students also seek more information from external sources outside of family and friends (such as teachers, guidance counselors, administrations personnel, and websites) (Palmer et al., 2012). Students also start to think about majors and detailed characteristics of institutions they are considering (such as size, quality, costs).

High school seniors with college aspirations, of course, pour a considerable amount of time and effort into seeking college information and completing financial aid applications (Palmer et al., 2012). Completing a financial aid application is another trigger event whereby students start to use costs more as a filter for college choice (Hossler et al., 1999). According to a Consortium on Chicago School Research study (Roderick et al., 2008), students who complete a FAFSA and are accepted into a four-year college are much more likely to enroll in college than those who do not. By this time, students think more carefully about the institutions they are considering. Campus visits, college guidance materials, and communications with college personnel play important roles at this stage, as well as high school guidance counselors and teachers (Hill & Winston, 2010; Palmer et al., 2012).

Actually attending a college involves more than just making the decision. As described in the model proposed by Hossler and Gallagher, college choice entails at least three stages: predisposition, search, and choice. Students must successfully complete relevant tasks at each stage to get into a college. For instance, students who do not develop college aspirations soon enough, who do not have sufficient information about colleges available to them, or who do not complete the application process may fail to attend college (Hossler et al., 1999).

The timing of college choice and the completion of tasks at each stage vary by income and racial groups, and the differences are apparent as early as the beginning of high school (Berkener & Chavez, 1997; Kao & Tienda, 1998). Studies found that low-income and first-generation students tend to have lower academic aspirations, request college information later, and apply later for college and for financial aid than high-income and non-first-generation students

(Hossler et al., 1999). Also, low-income students are less likely to maintain their college aspirations throughout the college choice process, compared to their high-income peers (Avery & Kane, 2004). Thus, the gap in college aspirations across income groups is larger as the students progress to college enrollment (Klasik, 2012). Interestingly, the gap between tenth grade and twelfth grade college aspirations are tightened when students visit their college counselors or meet with a college representative (Klasik, 2012).

By race, the gaps in educational aspirations have nearly closed to a significant degree (Roderick et al., 2008), with the only notable difference found for Asian Americans students and parents, who tend to think about going to college earlier than others (Kim & Gasman, 2011). In most cases, the differences among racial and income groups are smaller in early stages and grow larger as students progress toward college enrollment (Klasik, 2012; Berkener & Chavez, 1997). As far as selective colleges are concerned, educational aspirations are developed or discouraged the most during the predisposition stage, mostly based on students' academic preparation (Park, 2013).

Even for students who have college aspirations, students must complete a number of tasks to enroll in college at the search and choice stages, which include, but are not limited to, taking the PSAT or college entrance exam, meeting with college counselors, visiting colleges, submitting applications, and applying for financial aid (Avery & Kane, 2004; Klasik, 2012). These are all important factors. However, many students with four-year college aspirations (more than half of them) do not take the necessary steps to go to college (such as collecting college information, applying for colleges, and enrolling in a college) (Roderick et al., 2008). Not surprisingly, students from high-income demographics are more likely to complete those tasks than students from low-income demographics. By race, Latino students are the least likely to apply to a four-year college and complete a FAFSA (Avery & Kane, 2004).

IMPLICATIONS FOR INSTITUTIONAL POLICIES AND PRACTICES

Our primary goal in this chapter is to provide an overview of college choice for enrollment managers as well as professionals working in admissions and financial aid. However, it will also be of use to readers involved in public policy, so we address all of these audiences with an emphasis on institutional policy makers in this section.

As will be evident in Chapters 5, 6, and 8, admissions professionals are increasingly using market research to target their recruitment efforts, both in terms of timing and the types of information provided, and to make admissions decisions. Research on college choice can help guide these efforts. Understanding the differences parents play in the college choice process among white, Hispanic, and

African American students, for example, should lead to different recruitment strategies. When a policy maker knows the approximate time frame in which high school students begin narrowing the list of colleges and universities they are considering attending, admissions officials can make admissions outreach activities more effective. Contacting high school students before they are ready for information on college costs, for example, is a waste of scarce admissions resources. But these insights are relevant not only for institutional policy makers, given that both federal and state policy makers are also trying to increase the number of students entering and completing postsecondary education.

This literature review makes it clear that the factors that influence students' postsecondary aspirations and their matriculation decisions are complex and varied. Differences among racial groups are mediated by family income and educational background, student academic ability, the quality of schools, and the habitus (the norms, values, and number of students aspiring to pursue secondary education) of schools and communities in which students reside. Geographical proximity, federal and state financial aid programs, and timely access to college information also impact student college choice. It is also evident that recent high school graduates are more likely to be receptive to information and recruitment efforts of institutions at different times during their junior and senior years. For nontraditional students, proximity, cost, and convenience are their most important considerations. However, it is worth noting that many students choose higher cost private institutions because these schools make their course offerings more convenient.

These complexities lead us to conclusions that were identified by Litten (1982) more than thirty years ago: that different students and different institutions operate in different markets (see Chapters 5 and 6 for more discussion on this topic). This is consistent with the work of Robert Zemsky and colleagues (Zemsky, Shaman, & Iannozzi, 2001; Zemsky, Shaman, & Shapiro, 2001; Zemsky, Wegner, & Massy, 2005), which are referenced several times in chapters by Hossler, David Kalsbeek, and Brian Zucker in this volume. Enrollment and admissions professionals need to have a clear sense of where they fall in the postsecondary education marketplace and the types of students who are most likely to be interested in their recruitment efforts. As Kalsbeek and Hossler (2009) have pointed out in some respects, the tuition discount rates that schools must employ to achieve their enrollment goals are good indirect indicators of where they stand in the student marketplace.

References

ACT. (2005). *Crisis at the Core: Preparing All Students for College and Work*. Iowa City, IA: ACT. Retrieved from https://www.act.org/research/policymakers/pdf/crisis_report.pdf.

Alon, S. (2005). Model misspecification in assessing the impact of financial aid on academic outcomes. *Research in Higher Education*, *46*(1), 109–125.

Alvarado, S. E., & Turley, R. N. (2010). *College Bound Friends: A Study of Racial and Ethnic Differences.* Paper presented at the American Sociological Association Annual Meeting, Atlanta, GA, Aug 14, 2010. Retrieved from http://www .allacademic.com/meta/p408412_index.html.

An, B. (2012). The impact of dual enrollment on college degree attainment: Do low-SES students benefit? *Educational Evaluation and Policy Analysis*, *35*(1), 57–75.

Avery, C. (2010). *The Effects of College Counseling on High-Achieving, Low-Income Students.* NBER Working Paper No. 16359. Cambridge, MA: National Bureau of Economic Research. Retrieved from http://www.nber.org/papers/w16359.

Avery, C., & Hoxby, C. M. (2004). Do and should financial aid packages affect students' college choices? In C. M. Hoxby (Ed.), *College Choices: The Economics of Where to Go, When to Go, and How to Pay for It* (pp. 239–302). Chicago: University of Chicago Press.

Avery, C., & Kane, T. (2004). Student perceptions of college opportunities: The Boston COACH program. In C. M. Hoxby (Ed.), *College Choices: The Economics of Where to Go, When to Go, and How to Pay for It* (pp. 355–391). Chicago: University of Chicago Press.

Bastedo, M. N., & Jaquette, O. (2011). Running in place: Low-income students and the dynamics of higher education stratification. *Educational Evaluation and Policy Analysis*, *33*(3), 318–339.

Baum, S., & Payea, K. (2004). *Education Pays 2004: The Benefits of Higher Education for Individuals and Society.* New York: College Entrance Examination Board.

Becker, G. S. (1993). *Human Capital: A Theoretical and Empirical Analysis with Special Reference to Education* (3rd Edition). Chicago: University of Chicago Press.

Bendixen-Noe, M. K., & Giebelhaus, C. (1998). Nontraditional students in higher education: Meeting their needs as learners. *Mid-Western Educational Researcher*, *11*(2), 27–31.

Berkener, L., & Chavez, L. (1997). *Access to Postsecondary Education for the 1992 High School Graduates.* Washington, DC: US Department of Education, Office of Educational Research and Improvement, National Center for Education Statistics. Retrieved from http://nces.ed.gov/pubsearch/pubsinfo.asp?pubid = 98105.

Bernheim, B. D. (1994). A theory of conformity. *Journal of Political Economics*, *102*(5), 841–877.

Bettinger, E. P., Long, B. T., Oreopoulos, P., & Sanbonmatsu, L. (2009). *The Role of Simplification and Information in College Decisions: Results from the H&R Block FAFSA Experiment.* NBER Working Paper No. 15361. Cambridge, MA: National Bureau of Economic Research. Retrieved from http://www.nber.org/papers/ w15361.

Bishop, J., & Van Dyk, J. (1977). Can adults be hooked on college? Some determinants of adult college attendance. *Journal of Higher Education*, *48*(1), 39–62.

Bohon, S. A., Johnson, M. K., & Gorman, B. K. (2006). College aspirations and expectations among Latino adolescents in the United States. *Social Problems*, *53*(2), 207–225.

Bourdieu, P. (1986). The forms of capital. In J. G. Richardson (Ed.), *Handbook of Theory and Research for the Sociology of Education* (pp. 241–258). New York: Greenwood Press.

Bowen, H. R. (1997). *Investment in Learning: The Individual and Social Value of American Higher Education*. Baltimore: The Johns Hopkins University Press.

Bowen, W. G., Chingos, M. M., & McPherson, M. S. (2009). *Crossing the Finish Line: Completing College at America's Public Universities*. Princeton, NJ: Princeton University Press.

Brock, T. (2010). Young adults and higher education: Barriers and breakthroughs to success. *The Future of Children*, *20*(1), 109–132.

Broekemier, G. M. (2002). A comparison of two-year and four-year adult students: Motivations to attend college and the importance of choice criteria. *Journal of Marketing for Higher Education*, *12*(1), 31–48.

Broekemier, G. M., & Seshadri, S. (1999). Differences in college choice criteria between deciding students and their parents. *Journal of Marketing for Higher Education*, *9*(3), 1–13.

Burke, M. A., & Sass, T. R. (2013). Classroom peer effects and student achievement. *Journal of Labor Economics*, *31*(1), 51–82.

Cabrera, A. F., La Nasa, S. M., & Burkum, K. R. (2002). Pathways to college: What affects lowest-SES students' decisions to transfer to a four-year institution. In A. Seidman (Ed.), *College Student Retention: A Formula for Success* (pp. 155–214). Lanham, MD: Rowman & Littlefield Publishers, Inc.

Canale, J. R., Dunlap, L., Britt, M., & Donahue, T. (1996). The relative importance of various college characteristics to students in influencing their choice of a college. *College Student Journal*, *30*(2), 214–216.

Caplan, N., Whitmore, J. K., & Choy, M. H. (1989). *The Boat People and Achievement in America: A Study of Family Life, Hard Work, and Cultural Values*. Ann Arbor: The University of Michigan Press.

Caplan, N. S., Choy, M. H., & Whitmore, J. K. (1991). *Children of the Boat People: A Study of Educational Success*. Ann Arbor: University of Michigan Press.

Carnevale, A. P., & Rose, S. J. (2003). *Socioeconomic Status, Race/Ethnicity, and Selective College Admissions*. New York: Century Foundation.

Carnevale, A. P., & Strohl, J. (2013). *Separate and Unequal: How Higher Education Reinforces the Intergenerational Reproduction of White Racial Privilege*. Washington, DC: Georgetown University Center on Education and the Workforce.

Carter, D., & Wilson, R. (1992). *Tenth Annual Status Report on Minorities in Higher Education*. Washington, DC: American Council on Education.

Ceja, M. (2004). Chicana college aspirations and the role of parents: Developing educational resiliency. *Journal of Hispanic Higher Education*, *3*(4), 1–25.

Ceja, M. (2006). Understanding the role of parents and siblings as information sources in the college choice process of Chicana students. *Journal of College Student Development, 47*(1), 87–104.

Chapman, D. (1984). *Toward a Theory of College Choice: A Model of College Search and Choice Behavior.* Alberta, Canada: University of Alberta Press.

Chen, H., & Volpe, R. P. (1998). An analysis of personal financial literacy among college students. *Financial Services Review, 7*(2), 107–128.

Choy, S. P. (2002). *Access & Persistence: Findings from 10 Years of Longitudinal Research on Students.* Washington, DC: American Council on Education Center for Policy Analysis.

Chua, A. (2011). *Battle Hymn of the Tiger Mother.* New York: The Penguin Press.

Coccari, R. L., & Javalgi, R. G. (1995). Analysis of students' needs in selecting a college or university in a changing environment. *Journal of Marketing for Higher Education, 6*(2), 27–39.

Cunningham, A. F., Park, E., & Engle, J. (2014). *Minority-Serving Institutions: Doing More with Less.* Washington, DC: Institute for Higher Education Policy.

Cunningham, A. F., & Santiago, D. A. (2008). *Student Aversion to Borrowing: Who Borrows and Who Doesn't.* Washington, DC: Institute for Higher Education Policy and Excellencia in Education.

DesJardins, S. L., Ahlburg, D. A., & McCall, B. P. (2002). Simulating the longitudinal effects of changes in financial aid on student departure from college. *Journal of Human Resources, 37*(3), 653–679.

DesJardins, S. L., Ahlburg, D. A., & McCall, B. P. (2006). An integrated model of application, admission, enrollment, and financial aid. *The Journal of Higher Education, 77*(3), 381–429.

DesJardins, S. L., & Toutkoushian, R. K. (2005). Are students really rational? The development of rational thought and its application to student choice. In M. Paulson (Ed.), *Higher Education: Handbook of Theory and Research* (pp. 191–240). The Netherlands: Springer.

Digilio, A. H. (1998). Web-based instruction adjusts. *Journal of Instruction Delivery Systems, 12*(4), 26–28.

Do, C. (2004). The effects of local colleges on the quality of college attended. *Economics of Education Review, 23*, 249–257.

Dowd, A. C., & Coury, T. (2006). The effect of loans on the persistence and attainment of community college students. *Research in Higher Education, 47*(1), 33–62.

Ellwood, D. T., & Kane, T. J. (2000). Who is getting a college education? Family background and the growing gaps in enrollment. In S. Danziger & J. Waldfogel (Eds.), *Securing the Future: Investing in Children from Birth to College* (pp. 283–324). New York: Russell Sage Foundation.

Fletcher, J. M. (2006). *Social Interactions in College Choice: The Interplay of Information, Preferences, Social Norms, and Individual Characteristics in Predicting College Choice.* Retrieved from http://theop.princeton.edu/reports/wp/Fletcher%20THEOP.pdf.

Fletcher, J. M. (2012). Similarity in peer college preferences: New evidence from Texas. *Social Science Research, 41*(2), 321–330.

Fry, R. (2002). *Latinos in Higher Education: Many Enroll, Too Few Graduate.* Washington, DC: Pew Hispanic Center.

Fry, R. (2003). *Hispanics in College: Participation and Degree Attainment.* New York: ERIC Clearinghouse on Urban Education, Institute for Urban and Minority Education.

González, K. P., Stoner, C., & Jovel, J. (2003). Examining the role of social capital in access to college for Latinas: Toward a college opportunity framework. *Journal of Hispanic Higher Education, 2*(2), 146–170.

Goyette, K., & Xie, Y. (1999). Educational expectations of Asian American youths: Determinants and ethnic differences. *Sociology of Education, 72*(1), 22–36.

Griffith, A. L., & Rothstein, D. S. (2009). Can't get there from here: The decision to apply to a selective college. *Economics of Education Review, 28*(5), 620–628.

Hagelskamp, C., Schleifer, D., & DiStasi, C. (2013). *Is College Worth It for Me? How Adults Without Degrees Think about Going (Back) to School.* New York: Public Agenda.

Hamrick, F. A., & Stage, F. K. (2004). College predisposition at high-minority enrollment, low-income schools. *The Review of Higher Education, 27*(2), 151–168.

Hanson, K., & Litten, L. (1982). Mapping the road to academia: A review of research on women, men, and the college selection process. In P. Perun (Ed.), *The Undergraduate Woman: ISSUES in Educational Equity.* Lexington, MA: Lexington Books.

Hanushek, E. A., Kain, J. F., Markman, J. M., & Rivkin, S. G. (2003). Does peer ability affect student achievement? *Journal of Applied Econometrics, 18*(5), 527–544.

Hao, L., & Bonstead-Bruns, M. (1998). Parent-child differences in educational expectations and the academic achievement of immigrant and native students. *Sociology of Education, 71*(3), 175–198.

Harju, B. L., & Eppler, M. A. (1997). Achievement motivation, flow and irrational beliefs in traditional and adult college students. *Journal of Instructional Psychology, 24*(3), 147–157.

Harper, S. R., & Griffin, K. A. (2011). Opportunity beyond affirmative action: How low-income and working-class Black male achievers access highly selective, high-cost colleges and universities. *Harvard Journal of African American Public Policy, 17*(1), 43–60.

Hearn, J. C. (1984). The relative roles of academic, ascribed, and socioeconomic characteristics in college destinations. *Sociology of Education, 57*(1), 22–30.

Hearn, J. C. (1988). Attendance at higher-cost colleges: Ascribed, socioeconomic, and academic influences on student enrollment patterns. *Economics of Education Review, 7*(1), 65–76.

Heller, D. E. (1997). Student price responses in higher education: An update to Leslie and Brinkman. *The Journal of Higher Education, 68*(6), 624–659.

Hill, C. B., & Winston, G. C. (2010). Low-income students and highly selective private colleges: Geography, searching, and recruiting. *Economics of Education Review, 29*(4), 495–503.

Holmes, M. (2004). Howard seeks to close its gender gap. *The Hilltop*. Retrieved from http://www.thehilltoponline.com/news/howard-seeks-to-close-its-gender-gap-1.469898#.UqFJXcRDuPs.

Horn, L. J. & Carroll, C. D. (1997). *Confronting the Odds: Students At Risk and the Pipeline to Higher Education*. Washington, DC: U.S. Department of Education, Office of Educational Research and Improvement. Retrieved from http://nces.ed.gov/pubs98/web/98094.asp.

Horn, L.J., and Chen, X. (1998). *Toward Resiliency: At-Risk Students Who Make It to College.* Office of Educational Research and Improvement. Washington, DC: U.S. Department of Education.

Hossler, D., Braxton, D., & Coopersmith, G. (1989). Understanding student college choice. In M. Paulson (Ed.), *Higher Education: Handbook of Theory and Research* (pp. 231–288). The Netherlands: Springer.

Hossler, D., & Gallagher, K. (1987). Studying college choice: A three-phase model and the implication for policy makers. *College and University*, *62*(3), 207–221.

Hossler, D., Schmit, J., & Vesper, N. (1999). *Going to College: How Social, Economic, and Educational Factors Influence the Decisions Students Make*. Baltimore, MD: The Johns Hopkins University Press.

Hossler, D., & Stage, F. (1992). Family and high school experience influences on the postsecondary plans of ninth grade students: A structural model of predisposition to college. *American Educational Research Journal*, *29*(2), 425–451.

Hoxby, C. M. (2000). *Peer effects in the classroom: Learning from gender and race variation*. NBER Working Paper No. 7867. Cambridge, MA: National Bureau of Economic Research. Retrieved from http://www.nber.org/papers/w7867.

Hoxby, C. M., & Weingarth, G. (2005). *Taking Race out of the Equation: School Reassignment and the Structure of Peer Effects*. Retrieved from http://citeseerx.ist.psu.edu/viewdoc/download?doi = 10.1.1.75.4661&rep = rep1&type = pdf.

Hsia, J. (1988) *Asian Americans in Higher Education and at Work*. Hillsdale, NJ: Lawrence Erlbaum Associates.

Huber, G. (1984). The Nature and Design of Post-Industrial Organizations. *Management Science*, *30*(8), 928–951.

Hughes, K. L., Karp, M. M., Fermin, B. J., & Bailey, T. R. (2005). *Pathways to College Access and Success*. Washington, DC: U.S. Department of Education, Office of Vocational and Adult Education.

Hurtado, S., Inkelas, K. K., Briggs, C., & Rhee, B. (1997). Differences in college access and choice among racial/ethnic groups: Identifying continuing barriers. *Research in Higher Education*, *38*(1), 43–75.

Iatarola, P., Conger, D., & Long, M. C. (2011). Determinants of high schools' advanced course offerings. *Educational Evaluation and Policy Analysis*, *33*(3), 340–359.

Ingels, S. J., Planty, M., & Bozick, R. (2005). *A Profile of the American High School Senior in 2004: A First Look. Initial Results From the First Follow-Up of the Education*

Longitudinal Study of 2002. Washington, DC: U.S. Department of Education, National Center for Education Statistics.

Institute for Higher Education Policy. (2012). *Supporting First-Generation College Students Through Classroom-Based Practices*. Washington, DC: Institute for Higher Education Policy.

Jackson, C. K. (2010). A little now for a lot later: A look at a Texas advanced placement incentive program. *Journal of Human Resources, 45*(3), 591–639.

Jackson, G. A. (1982). Public efficiency and private choice in higher education. *Educational Evaluation and Policy Analysis, 4*(2), 237–247.

Jackson, G. A. (1990). Financial aid, college entry, and affirmative action. *American Journal of Education, 98*(4), 523–550.

Joensen, J. S., & Nielsen, H. S. (2009). Is there a causal effect of high school math on labor market outcomes? *Journal of Human Resources, 44*(1), 171–219.

Kalsbeek, D. H., & Hossler, D. (2009). Enrollment management: A market-centered perspective. *College & University, 84*(3), 2–11.

Kane, J., & Spizman, L. M. (1994). Race, financial aid awards and college attendance. *American Journal of Economics and Sociology, 53*(1), 85–96.

Kane, T. J. (1998). *The Price of Admission: Rethinking How Americans Pay for College.* Washington, DC: Brookings Institution Press.

Kane, T. J., & Rouse, C. E. (1999). The community college: Educating students at the margin between college and work. *The Journal of Economic Perspectives, 13*(1), 63–84.

Kao, G., & Tienda, M. (1998). Educational aspirations of minority youth. *American Journal of Education, 106*(3), 349–384.

Kim, D. (2004). The effect of financial aid on students' college choice: Differences by racial groups. *Research in Higher Education, 45*(1), 43–70.

Kim, J. K., & Gasman, M. (2011). In search of a "good college": Decisions and determinations behind Asian American students' college choice. *Journal of College Student Development, 52*(6), 706–728.

Klasik, D. (2012). The college application gauntlet: A systematic analysis of the steps to four-year college enrollment. *Research in Higher Education, 53*(5), 506–549.

Klopfenstein, K., & Thomas, M. (2009). The link between advanced placement experience and early college success. *Southern Economic Journal, 75*(3), 873–891.

Kurlaender, M. (2006). Choosing community college: Factors affecting Latino college choice. *New Directions for Community Colleges, (2006)*133, 7–16.

Lavy, V., Paserman, M. D., & Schlosser, A. (2007). *Inside the Black of Box of Ability Peer Effects: Evidence from Variation in the Proportion of Low Achievers in the Classroom*. NBER Working Paper No 14415. Cambridge, MA: National Bureau of Economic Research. Retrieved from http://www.nber.org/papers/w14415.

Leslie, L. L., & Brinkman, P. T. (1987). Institutional factors and access student price response in higher education: The student demand studies. *The Journal of Higher Education, 58*(2), 181–204.

Levine, A., & Cureton, J. S. (1998). What we know about today's college students. *About Campus*, *3*(1), 4–9.

Litten, L. H. (1982). Different strokes in the applicant pool: Some refinements in a model of student college choice. *The Journal of Higher Education*, *53*(4), 383–402.

Long, B. T. (2004). How have college decisions changed over time? An application of the conditional logistic choice model. *Journal of Econometrics*, *121*, 271–296.

MacDonald, J. S., & MacDonald, L. D. (1964). Chain migration, ethnic neighborhood formation, and social networks. *Milbank Memorial Fund Quarterly*, *42*(1), 82–97.

Martinez, M. A. (2013). Helping Latina/o students navigate the college choice process: Considerations for secondary school counselors. *Journal of School Counseling*, *11*(1).

McDonough, P. M. (1997). *Choosing Colleges: How Social Class and Schools Structure Opportunity*. Albany, NY: State University of New York Press.

Mickelson, R. A. (1990). The attitude-achievement paradox among black adolescents. *Sociology of Education*, *63*(1), 44–61.

National Center for Education Statistics. (2013). *Digest of Education Statistics: 2012*. Washington, DC: US Department of Education, Institute of Education Sciences. Retrieved from http://nces.ed.gov/programs/digest/d12/.

National Commission on Asian American and Pacific Islander Research in Education (CARE). (2008). *Asian Americans and Pacific Islander: Facts, Not Fiction: Setting the Record Straight*. New York: The College Board.

Palmer, M., Park, E., & Hossler, D. (2012). Why understand research on college choice? In National Association for College Admission Counseling (Eds.), *Fundamentals of College Admissions Counseling: A Textbook for Graduate Students and Practicing Counselors* (3rd Edition) (pp. 105–120). Dubuque, IA: Kendall/Hunt.

Park, E. (2013). *Low-income students' access to selective higher education*. PhD dissertation, Indiana University. Retrieved from ProQuest Dissertations & Theses. (Publication number 3602806).

Paulsen, M. B. (2001). The economics of human capital and investment in higher education. In M. B. Paulsen, & J. C. Smart (Eds.), *The Finance of Higher Education: Theory, Research, Policy, and Practice* (pp. 55–94). New York: Agathon Press.

Pérez, P. A., & McDonough, P. M. (2008). Understanding Latina and Latino college choice: A social capital and chain migration analysis. *Journal of Hispanic Higher Education*, *7*(3), 249–265.

Perna, L. W. (2000). Differences in the decision to attend college among African Americans, Hispanics, and Whites. *The Journal of Higher Education*, *71*(2), 117–141.

Perna, L. W. (2004). The key to college access: A college preparatory curriculum. In W. G. Tierney, Z. B. Corwin, & J. E. Colyar (Eds.), *Preparing for College: Nine Elements of Effective Outreach* (pp. 113–134). Albany, NY: State University of New York Press.

Perna, L. W. (2006). Studying college access and choice: A proposed conceptual model. In J. C. Smart (Ed.), *Higher Education: Handbook of Theory and Research*, Vol. 21, (pp. 99–157). The Netherlands: Springer.

Perna, L. W., & Titus, M. (2004). Understanding differences in the choice of college attended: The role of state public policies. *Review of Higher Education*, *27*(4), 501–525.

Perna, L. W., & Titus, M. (2005). The relationship between parental involvement as social capital and college enrollment: An examination of racial/ethnic group differences. *The Journal of Higher Education*, *76*(5), 485–518.

Person, A. E., & Rosenbaum, J. E. (2006). Chain enrollment and college enclaves: Benefits and drawbacks of Latino college students' enrollment decisions. *New Directions for Community Colleges*, *133*, 51–60.

Pew Research Center. (2013). *The Rise of Asian Americans*. Washington, DC: Pew Research Center.

Pitre, P. E. (2006). College choice: A study of African American and White student aspirations and perceptions related to college attendance. *College Student Journal*, *40*(3), 562–574.

Plank, S. B., & Jordan, W. J. (2001). Effects of information, guidance, and actions on postsecondary destinations: A study of talent loss. *American Educational Research Journal*, *38*(4), 947–979.

Richardson, J. T., & King, E. (1998). Adult students in higher education. *The Journal of Higher Education*, *69*(1), 65–88.

Roderick, M., Nagaoka, J., Coca, V., Moeller, E., Roddie, K., Gilliam, J., & Patton, D. (2008). *From High School to the Future: Potholes on the Road to College*. Chicago: Consortium on Chicago School Research at the University of Chicago.

Rowan-Kenyon, H. T., Bell, A. D., & Perna, L. W. (2008). Contextual influences on parental involvement in college going: Variations by socioeconomic class. *The Journal of Higher Education*, *79*(5), 564–486.

Sacerdote, B. (2011). Peer effects in education: How might they work, how big are they and how much do we know thus far? In E. A. Hanushek, S. Machin, & L. Woessmann (Eds.), *Handbook of the Economics of Education*, Vol. 3 (249–277). San Diego, CA: North Holland.

Santiago, D. A. (2006). *Inventing Hispanic-Serving Institutions (HSIs): The Basics*. Washington, DC: Excelencia in Education.

Santiago, D. A. (2007). *Choosing Hispanic-Serving Institutions (HSIs): A Closer Look at Latino Students' College Choices*. Washington, DC: Excelencia in Education.

Santiago, D. A., & Cunningham, A. (2005). *How Latinos Pay for College: Patterns of Financial Aid for 2003–04*. Washington, DC: Excelencia in Education and the Institute for Higher Education Policy.

Seftor, N. S., & Turner, S. E. (2002). Back to school: Federal student aid policy and adult college enrollment. *The Journal of Human Resources*, *37*(2), 336–352.

Smith, M. J., & Fleming, M. K. (2006). African American parents in the search stage of college choice: Unintentional contributions to the female to male college enrollment gap. *Urban Education*, *41*(1), 71–100.

Snyder, T. D., Dillow, S. A., & Hoffman, C. M. (2007). *Digest of education statistics 2006*. Washington, DC: US Department of Education, National Center for Education Statistics.

St. John, E. P. (1991). What really influences minority student attendance? An analysis of the high school and beyond sophomore cohort. *Research in Higher Education, 31*(2), 161–176.

St. John, E. P., & Noell, J. (1989). The effects of student financial aid on access to higher education: An analysis of progress with special consideration of minority enrollments. *Research in Higher Education, 30*(6), 563–581.

St. John, E. P., Paulsen, M. B., & Carter, D. F. (2005). Diversity, college costs, and postsecondary opportunity: An examination of the college choice-persistence nexus for African Americans and Whites. *The Journal of Higher Education, 76*(5), 545–569.

Stage, F. K., & Hamrick, F. A. (1998). High minority enrollment, high school lunch-rates: Predisposition to college. *The Review of Higher Education, 21*(4), 343–357.

Stephan, J. L., & Rosenbaum, J. E. (2012). Can high schools reduce college enrollment gaps with a new counseling model? *Educational Evaluation and Policy Analysis, 35*(2), 200–219.

Stinchcombe, A. (1990). *Information and Organizations*. Berkeley: University of California Press.

Stone, C., & O'Shea, S. E. (2013). Time, money, leisure and guilt: The gendered challenges of higher education for mature-age students. *Australian Journal of Adult Learning, 53*(1), 95–116.

Swail, W. S., Cabrera, A .F., & Lee, C. (2004). *Latino Youth and the Pathway to College*. Washington DC: Educational Policy Institute.

Swenson, C. (1998). Customers and markets: The cuss words of academe. *Change, 30*(5), 34–39.

Teranishi, R., Lok, L., & Nguyen, B.M.D. (2013). *iCount: A Data Quality Movement for Asian Americans and Pacific Islanders in higher education*. National Commission on Asian American and Pacific Islander Research in Education (CARE).

Teranishi, R. T., Ceja, M., Antonio, A. L., & Allen, W. R. (2004). The college-choice process for Asian Pacific Americans: Ethnicity and socioeconomic class in context. *The Review of Higher Education, 27*(4), 527–551.

Terenzini, P. T., Cabrera, A. F., & Bernal, E. M. (2001). *Swimming Against the Tide: The Poor in American Higher Education*. College Board Research Report No. 2001–1. New York: College Entrance Examination Board.

Valdez, J. R. (2008). Shaping the educational decisions of Mexican immigrant high school students. *American Educational Research Journal, 45*, 834–860.

Vigdor. J. L., & Nechyba, T. S. (2007). Peer effects in North Carolina public schools. In L.Woessmann, & P. E. Peterson (Eds.), *Schools and the Equal Opportunity Problem* (pp. 73–101). Cambridge, MA: MIT Press.

White House Initiative on Asian Americans and Pacific Islanders. (2013). The AAPI community: Demographics chart. Retrieved from http://www.whitehouse.gov/sites/default/files/docs/infographic_1.pdf.

Winston, G. C., & Hill, C. B. (2005). *Access to the Most Selective Private Colleges by High-Ability, Low-Income Students: Are They Out There?* Williamstown, MA: Williams Project on the Economics of Higher Education, Williams College.

Wirt, J., Choy, S., Rooney, P., Hussar, W., Provasnik, S., & Hampden-Thompson, G. (2005). The Condition of Education. National Center for Education Statistics Report 2005–094. Retrieved from http://eric.ed.gov/?id = ED492631.

Wolniak, G. C., & Engberg, M. E. (2007). The effects of high school feeder networks on college enrollment. *Review of Higher Education, 31*(1), 27–53.

Wong, M. G., & Hirschman, C. (1983). The new Asian immigrants. In W. C. McCready (Ed.), *Culture, Ethnicity, and Identity: Current Issues in Research* (pp. 381–403). New York: Academic Press.

Yeh, T. L. (2002). Asian American college students who are educationally at risk. *New Directions for Student Services, 2002*(97), 61–72.

Zemsky, R., Shaman, S., & Iannozzi, M. (1997). In search of a strategic perspective: A tool for mapping the market in post-secondary education. *Change, 29*(6), 23–8.

Zemsky, R., Shaman, S., & Shapiro, D. B. (2001). Higher education as competitive enterprise: When markets matter. *New Directions for Institutional Research, 2001*(111), 1–98.

Zemsky, R., Wegner, G., & Massy, W. F. (2005). *Remaking the American University: Market-Smart and Mission-Centered.* New Brunswick, NJ: Rutgers University Press.

CHAPTER 5

Markets and Market Niches

David H. Kalsbeek and
Brian Zucker

On a Friday morning at Alpha University, members of the board of trustees have identified the following topics that will be explored in various committees and then discussed as a committee of the whole at an upcoming meeting. After committee business, each of the committee chairpersons addresses his or her committee's respective agenda topics:

- The Academic Committee is interested in having the provost present the outlook for next year's applicant pool, with the expectation that Alpha will be in a position to raise its selectivity and thereby improve student quality and the institution's academic profile as reported in the national rankings.

- The Finance Committee, in collaboration with the CFO, wants to focus upon Alpha's steadily rising tuition discount rate, which they believe must be reduced in the next fiscal year—even as tuition and fees are expected to increase—based on a perception that discount is eroding institutional revenue needed for faculty pay raises and to fund capital improvements.

- The Student Affairs Committee wants Alpha to improve student retention and degree completion rates, so that the university can be first among its peer group in cohort four-year graduation rates.

- The Mission Committee wants to focus on increasing access and opportunity to achieve a greater representation of low-income and first-generation students and elevate Alpha's overall diversity.

- The Advancement Committee has received a report from the Alumni Association indicating that Alpha must improve its US News & World Report "Best Colleges" ranking to elevate the university's prestige as a key to expanding alumni support.

None of these agenda items is atypical for a trustee meeting at any campus. Each committee is addressing a goal related to its charge, and each presumes the university can improve its performance with respect to a particular enrollment-related metric—be it demand, acceptance rates, net revenue, access, attainment, or prestige. For most colleges and universities, none of these objectives, independent of one another, would be regarded as unrealistic or unreasonable.

The challenge Alpha faces, however, lies in the fact that these issues are addressed through a partitioned committee structure that is typical of most boards. As a result, each topic is addressed independently, when in fact they are all closely interrelated and interdependent. To achieve the envisioned goal Alpha has for each topic, they must be explored, understood, and addressed collectively.

At a strategic level, Alpha's institutional goals, and ultimately their outcomes, are deeply seated in the underlying reality of its market position—Alpha's place in a systemic, stratified, and structured marketplace of higher education institutions. Thus, it is the market structure and Alpha's position in it that frames and, to a great extent, dictates the range of outcomes to which its board committees can realistically aspire. Alpha's place in this market structure has significant bearing on the interdependencies of its board's various objectives; insofar as it defines the inherent tensions, tradeoffs, and points of mutual leverage between and among Alpha's various enrollment goals, it creates a market-centered context for Strategic Enrollment Management. Exploring that challenge is the focus of this chapter.

FINDING CONTEXT

As institutional boards of trustees nationwide engage in discussions similar to those of Alpha's board, these deliberations, in most instances, are shaped by a deepening concern for the efficacy and sustainability of current prevailing practices in higher education. Repeated negative outlooks and a rising number of downgrades from credit rating agencies focus on how all but a few privileged institutions face declining marginal net tuition revenue, stagnant family incomes and declining earnings for recent graduates, and rising student debt and loan delinquencies and defaults, all in the context of an inexorable expansion of expenses. Add to that the growing concern by government and the public as to the relative value and return of a college education, the rapid development of new modes of educational delivery, and the rising competitive prominence of for-profit providers, and it's understandable that board meetings at many institutions focus as much on survival as ascent.

Naturally, this discourse by boards often acknowledges (sometimes obliquely and sometimes explicitly) the hierarchical structure of the higher education market. References to *US News & World Report*'s "Best Colleges"—or more abstractly, the "pecking order"—bring with them a host of assumptions about the relative value and comparative qualities of institutions and spawn a seemingly relentless fixation on institutional prestige. Whether the pursuit of rankings and institutional prestige is hidden behind other issues or front and center, this is the context of many board deliberations and the terrain in which SEM leaders must navigate. Although the particular issues will ebb and flow over time and vary across institutions, the broader market environment remains the persistent and pervasive reality through which SEM is conceived, practiced, and evaluated.

The purpose of this chapter is to illustrate a way to bring form and focus to the assumptions about the underlying structure of the marketplace of colleges and universities, and to introduce and quantify the notion of institutional "market position" as an underlying context for SEM. We emphasize the sector of the broader higher education arena that is composed of four-year colleges and universities in the United States—both private and public. Two-year colleges, for-profit and largely online institutions, and institutions outside the United States are bracketed off from this analysis and discussion. We have made this choice because, comparatively, there is less publicly accessible data available, and the analytic foundations for this discussion would by necessity be significantly different than for four-year U.S. institutions. Although the overarching concept of a structured market and institutional market position has meaning, relevance, and implications for all classes of institutions across the globe, those considerations are beyond the scope of this chapter.

ZEMSKY'S FOUNDATIONAL WORK

A rich literature on higher education markets constitutes a foundation for market-centered SEM, but here we focus on only one strand of that literature. We draw on the following works of Robert Zemsky and his colleagues: *The Structure of College Choice* (Zemsky & Oedel, 1983), which offers an empirical exploration of the structure of the higher education marketplace through a lens of pricing, selectivity, and student choice; and "Higher Education as Competitive Enterprise: When Markets Matter" (Zemsky, Shaman, & Shapiro, 2001) and the earlier "In Search of a Strategic Perspective: A Tool for Mapping the Market in Post-Secondary Education" (Zemsky, Shaman, & Iannozzi, 1997), which provide a scheme for sorting and segmenting the market for postsecondary education.

There are, of course, many ways by which we typically classify colleges and universities; for example, we use Carnegie classifications to distinguish research universities from comprehensive universities and liberal arts colleges. We cluster schools by control, such as public or private non-profit and for-profit, or by affiliation and mission, such as Catholic colleges or historically black institutions. Hierarchical rankings of institutions can also be used to classify institutions. Zemsky and his colleagues, however, suggest that these rankings are not typically adequate to explain or account for differences observed in many national studies regarding student outcomes, and that a construct of institutional position in a stratified, systemically structured market continuum is most helpful in accounting for these differences.

Toward that end, the taxonomy developed by Zemsky, Shaman, and Iannozzi (1997) reveals how institutional and educational outcomes are integrally related to the structure and stratification of the postsecondary market. It is a market structure within which students compare, consider, and choose among their higher education options and opportunities and which is the context for the competitive maneuvering between colleges and universities in pursuit of their goals and aspirations. It is, in short, a context for SEM.

The Zemsky model (1997) segments colleges and universities on an empirically derived continuum intended to avoid a hierarchical ranking by its horizontal presentation. That continuum includes at one extreme those institutions that have enrollment profiles marked by great demand and high selectivity, with expensive tuition, large residential capacity, high academic profiles, and wide geographic draw. They are highly capitalized with large net assets, and high expenditures on instruction and faculty. They enjoy broad brand recognition and high levels of prestige.

At the opposite extreme of this continuum are colleges and universities with enrollment profiles characterized by part-time, adult, and intermittently enrolled and non-degree students; these institutions have less demand, and are less selective and less expensive. From a financial profile, they have fewer assets per student, they spend less on instruction, and have more part-time and adjunct faculty. They don't enjoy great prestige and place a priority on being accessible and affordable to a local market.

In Zemsky's scheme, the majority of institutions occupy a vast middle market of institutions that seek to straddle these two extremes. These institutions pursue greater name recognition, higher academic profile and selectivity, and greater price points while simultaneously needing to cater to the part-time, adult, commuter, and convenience markets. This middle market is highly competitive as colleges seek to balance these market dynamics and tensions.

Using this construct for inspiration as much as information, in the following section we present an empirical index of market position to illustrate more fully how the structures, symmetries, and segmentation of the market of

U.S. four-year colleges and universities create an important context for the practice of SEM.

DEFINING MARKET STRUCTURES AND POSITION

We commence this illustration of market structure and position by advancing two primary, defining dimensions. One is demand itself, as manifested in the strength in numbers and profile of the students who apply and matriculate. The other concerns the financial wherewithal of the institution, as manifested in its capitalization and capacity to contribute and exert its financial influence both in the education marketplace and the economy at large.

We acknowledge at the outset that ultimately what these two dimensions share in common is the accumulation of social capital and wealth. Whether it be the standardized test scores and the socioeconomic status of the incoming freshman class, the stature of its alumni or the prominence of faculty, the size of the library and archival holdings, or the grandeur of the physical plant, virtually all facets of an institution's market position point to the long-term accumulation of human talent and dollars—and the attendant benefits that both together bring to the learning enterprise. This is a point to which we return in our concluding comments.

We begin by considering indicators of enrollment demand and financial capitalization that can readily serve to index the comparative place where four-year undergraduate institutions stand in the marketplace relative to one another. To construct an empirical measure of position that is within reach, both conceptually and operationally, and considering the availability and limitations of public domain information, our approach begins with a set of eleven distinct but interrelated measures of enrollment demand and institutional fiscal strength. These measures are then integrated into a single composite index reflecting market position. In practice, this index serves as a simple, powerful, and instructive approach for mapping institutional market position, exploring the similarities and proximities of institutions in the competitive landscape, and identifying the interdependencies and intercorrelations of institutional characteristics and attributes that underlie market structure (Zucker, 2011). As evidenced across a wide array of metrics, the market position index maintains a high degree of acuity and reliability as a consistent predictor of institutional operating characteristics and outcomes—including a host of metrics commonly considered performance indicators within the SEM practice.

The Profile-Demand Dimension

Among the universe of widely available enrollment performance measures that speak to strength of demand, five stand out in particular at the freshmen stage of enrollment: acceptance rates, enrollment yield, ratio of applicants to enrolled; entering student standardized test scores, and the incidence of freshmen who attend without institutional grant assistance—weighted by published tuition and fees—controlling for sector. Independently, but especially in combination, these five measures capture the most salient aspects of demand, and more generally constitute focal points of college admissions for the majority of four-year colleges and universities in the United States.

Figure 5.1 shows the national percentile rankings for each of these five measures by sector (public and private non-profit) for fiscal 2012, based on

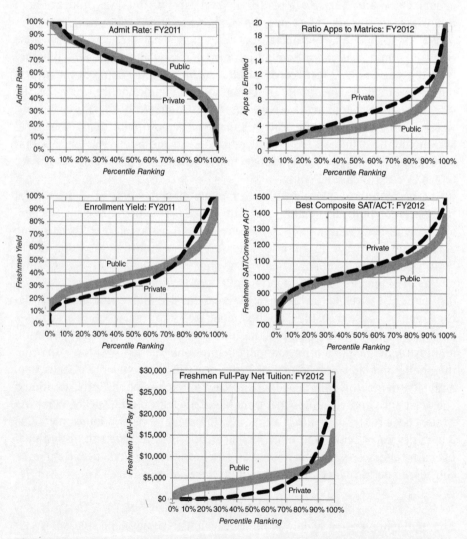

Figure 5.1 Cumulative distribution of selected enrollment demand metrics by sector

a sample of approximately 1,620 four-year institutions. Each of these five exhibits shows the relative ranking of schools based on these various enrollment demand metrics. Among other implications, these exhibits reveal that the variance in values for schools that operate in the broad middle ranges is relatively small, but as institutions approach about the 80th percentile for any of the five measures, the variance rises exponentially. In some respects, this suggests that traversing the competitive territory between the 50th and the 80th percentile constitutes a smaller numerical ascent, per se, than rising from the 80th to the 85th percentile.

The Institutional Wealth Dimension

The wealth dimension consists of six metrics that, in combination, define an institution's investment in academic product, its overall capitalization, and, more generally, its fiscal strength and economic wherewithal. For purposes of this analysis, our six measures of wealth consist of: current fund expenditures per full-time equivalent (FTE) student for direct instruction, academic support and student services, net assets per FTE student, an adjusted instruction-based student-faculty ratio, and compensation of professors, normalized on a nine-month contractual basis. Figure 5.2 shows the national percentile rankings for each of the six measures by sector for fiscal 2011 (the most recent year for which data are publically available) based on the same sample of approximately 1,620 four-year U.S. institutions used for the profile-demand measures. Inasmuch as these measures speak directly to institutional wealth and capitalization, it is important to recognize that they do not necessarily reflect an institution's operating margin—which can vary as widely within a given tier of wealth as across wealth tiers.

At first glance, the distribution patterns of the wealth measures appear similar to the profile-demand metrics, but upon closer examination, you'll notice a number of important distinctions. To begin, net assets per FTE student, which reflects endowment as well as the book value of a school's physical plant and equipment (among other assets), is highly skewed. To a greater extent than any of the profile-demand measures, the skew in net assets reveals the extent to which the operating assets of higher education are largely concentrated among a remarkably small number of institutions. In fiscal 2011, for instance, the sixty-five wealthiest private colleges and universities in America (less than 3 percent of all private non-profits) accounted for a full two-thirds of the sector's aggregate wealth, and more than 70 percent of the increase in net assets over the last decade. Although the other metrics reveal a skew as well, the disparities are not nearly as great.

When integrated together, the five profile-demand metrics in combination with the six wealth measures provide a single market position index that allows for arraying and classifying colleges and universities in ways that go beyond

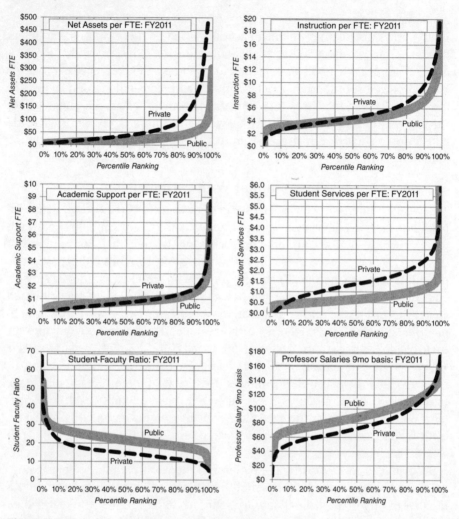

Figure 5.2 Cumulative distribution of selected finance metrics by sector

what we might otherwise glean about market position from any of these eleven components alone. This index thereby brings a more holistic and comprehensive depiction of a school's current situation and its future outlook. In turn, this single index of market position readily lends itself to the exploration and contextualization of a wide variety of other institutional characteristics and attributes—with potential bearing on virtually every aspect of the academy—from first-year retention, to cohort loan default rates, to alumni giving. In short, it grounds SEM in a market context.

Consider, for example, Figure 5.3, which shows freshman cohort six-year graduation rates by market position based on the index, for both public and

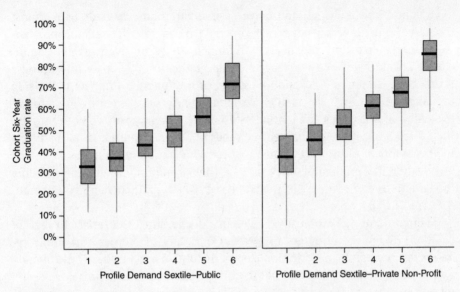

Figure 5.3 Six-year graduation rates by market position sextiles: public and private non-profit institutions

private institutions. In this and subsequent exhibits in this chapter, our universe of 1,600 four-year institutions has been grouped into six tiers based on the market index. Each tier, or sextile, accounts for approximately one-sixth of new entering freshmen enrollment at four-year public and private non-profit institutions nationally, with the weakest positioned schools represented by the first sextile, and the strongest positioned by the sixth.

As evidenced by this simple box plot, cohort graduation rates array in a near perfect correlation with institution market position. In fact, the relationship between retention and degree outcomes and institution market position stands among the most predictable of all enrollment outcome measures. David Kalsbeek and Brian Zucker (2013) argued that since retention and completion rates are so intertwined with all other factors defining an institution's place in the stratified higher education marketplace, graduation rates are more an *attribute* of market position than an institutional *achievement*. Some institutions do, of course, surpass and some fall short of their expected graduation rate, given their market position. That may, in fact, reflect greater or lesser learning productivity or a superior institutional strategy, and it is certainly possible for institutions to see some movement in completion rates due to institutional effort. But, for the most part, as evidenced by Figure 5.3, the variance in graduation rates by market position makes clear the general potentiality of a school given its market position.

In light of the growing importance of graduation rates as perhaps the most definitive and universal education outcome measures, the relationship between market position and degree attainment takes on even greater significance. Consider, for example, the role that graduation rates play in shaping a prospective student's perception of value, or the long-term impact that rising or falling rates can have on the size and affinity of an institution's alumni base. In both instances, graduation rates shape market position, both through their direct impact on the learner outcomes of a given cohort and indirectly on the behaviors of future and former cohorts. This notion underscores Zemsky's observation that graduation rates are of particular importance in understanding the structures and contours of the higher education market (Zemsky, Shaman, & Shapiro, 2001).

Though hardly an exhaustive inventory of measures that relate to market position, Figure 5.4 through 5.7 present a variety of metrics commonly regarded as integral to an institution's enrollment plan and profile. These include published tuition and fees and net tuition revenue, student financial need, the relative quality of aid packages, tuition discount rates, and reliance on student-parent debt expressed as a percent of institutional net tuition. The chart set also includes selected measures of student background, including a representation of African American and Asian students as a share of the freshman class, a geographic diversity measure and proportion of non–traditional age students, the proportion of students attending part-time, as well as overall size of the entering freshmen class. Figure 5.4 and 5.5 show these various measures arrayed by market position sextile for the universe of private non-profit institutions nationally; Figure 5.6 and 5.7 provide the same information for public four-year institutions.

This chart series on enrollment and college finance metrics contrasts and juxtaposes the operating conditions and potentiality that exist from one market tier to the next. As a starting point, consider the share of freshmen who are African American or Asian descendants, respectively, representing the two major ethnic racial groups with the lowest and highest levels of college participation and parent education. Compared side-by-side, these two ethnic groups provide a striking contrast in the social background of students who attend one tier of institution versus another. Ultimately, these differences in background reflect a world of difference in the experiences and circumstances that students may face years before reaching college age—many of which tie directly and indirectly to a student's likelihood of college success and to the demand on institutional resources necessary to support attainment.

A similar contrast and juxtaposition by market tier is found in the second pair of exhibits that show, respectively, the proportion of non–traditional age freshmen side-by-side with the proportion of students from out of state. As with the prior pair of exhibits, these two figures reveal not only the extent

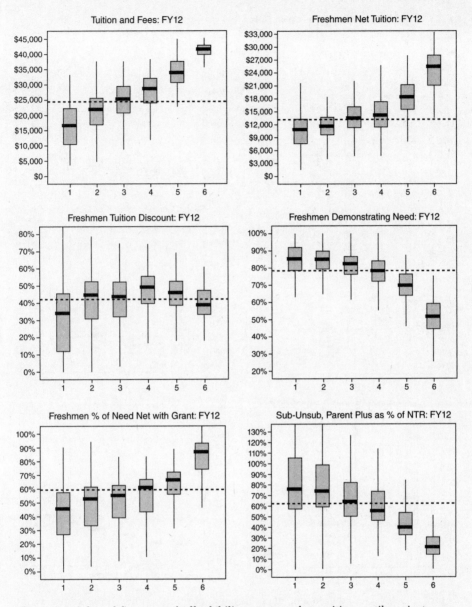

Figure 5.4 Selected finance and affordability measures by position sextile: private non-profit institutions

to which compositional differences in student population by position tier go well beyond direct measures of academic profile, but also embody sometimes widely different circumstances that various student groups bring with their attendance—differences that ultimately serve either to reinforce or detract from an institution's standing within the marketplace.

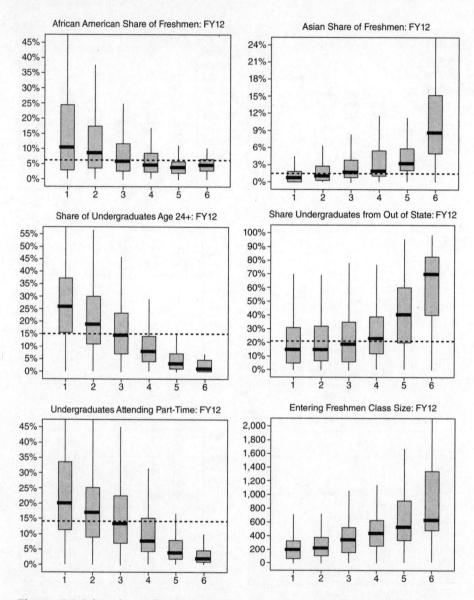

Figure 5.5 Selected enrollment measures by position sextile: private non-profit institutions

For instance, adult (so-called nontraditional) students are more likely to face competing responsibilities while attending college (not the least of which are employment and dependents) and are more likely to take less than a full-time class load. As a result, these students tend to exhibit far more complex enrollment flow patterns than is observed for traditional age full-time students, often resulting in higher levels of attrition, prolonged time to completion, and, in many instances, greater economic volatility for the institution. The greater

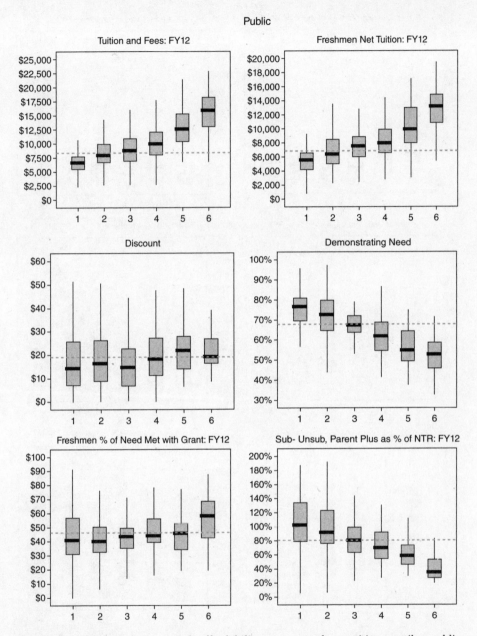

Figure 5.6 Selected finance and affordability measures by position sextile: public institutions

reliance upon and enrollment of these student populations relates directly to market position. Conversely, market position is intertwined with the proportion of the freshmen who are nonresident (out of state) students. In general, stronger position schools demonstrate a broader market range and greater geographic diversity, while lower-tiered schools almost invariably are tied to

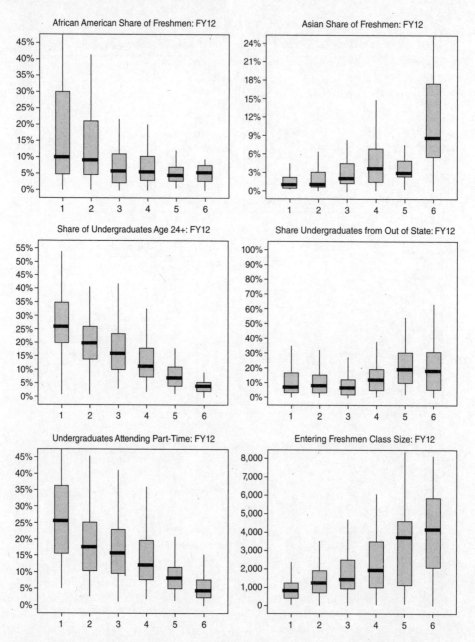

Figure 5.7 Selected enrollment measures by position sextile: public institutions

a more localized or regional territory. Among other implications, these differences in market reach and geographic representation directly and indirectly place lower-tiered institutions in a more vulnerable position with respect to cyclical downturns and/or demographic shifts—with the overall effect, again of reinforcing an institution's standing in the marketplace.

Distinctions in market position are also clearly manifested in differences in institution pricing policies and financial aid awarding practices. As evidenced by the second set of exhibits, it becomes readily apparent that for the most part, price follows position as opposed to the other way around. By the same token, it is also apparent that an institution's position is highly correlated with the socioeconomic profile of the families it serves. Taken together, these six price–aid–related exhibits reveal not only how far reaching the differences in socioeconomic background of students are from one tier to the next, but also how it is possible for stronger positioned institutions to provide significantly higher quality aid packages to needy students and still maintain a moderate tuition discount rate and significantly higher levels of net tuition than their weaker-positioned counterparts. Similar contrasts to the dozen enrollment and financial aid metrics presented here can be found across a wide array of other student and institutional characteristics—many of which speak directly to the comparative advantages and disadvantages that come with market position, and many of which tend to operate in tandem with one another—setting in motion an array of cascading effects that accrue back to position. Although we would not go so far as to suggest that the structure of the four-year higher education market is a caste system in which the destiny of each and every institution has been set, we would nonetheless suggest that the confluence of factors with bearing on position suggests that the likelihood of significant ascent, while not impossible, remains the least probable of outcomes.

Drawing on multiple years of data, we are able to explore the dynamics of market position over time. When we consider shifts in position, it is important to acknowledge that a school's place in the market and its relative ranking are based on the prevailing market conditions, circumstances, and metrics of all institutions in a given academic year. Because market conditions change from year to year, all of our eleven defining metrics can be regarded as moving targets; private sector enrollment yields, for example, have fallen more than 10 points in the last decade, while net assets have risen by more than 60 percent. As a result, even when the operating characteristics of a given institution remain largely constant, it is nearly certain that its position will change due to the shifts experienced by all other institutions—and for many institutions, given the dynamics of the market writ large, this has essentially translated into an ever greater effort merely to sustain one's position.

To help put this into perspective, consider the following set of benchmarks. For the period from fiscal 2003 to 2012, annual position rankings based on the criteria discussed earlier are available for 1,180 four-year public and private non-profit colleges and universities, representing approximately 73 percent of the 1,620 school universe that served as the basis for the analysis presented in this chapter. Of that number, a mere 4.3 percent experienced a sustained gain in position equivalent to a 15-point or more increase in their percentile ranking while 2.5 percent of all schools showed a decline in excess of 15 points or

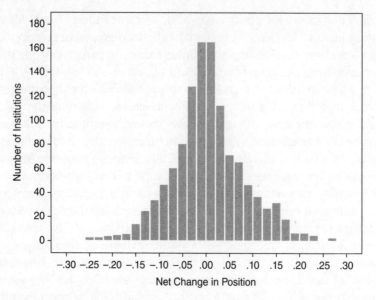

Figure 5.8 Distribution of public and private non-profit four-year institutions by change in market position, 2003 to 2012

more—making for fewer than one in fourteen posting an appreciable shift in position over the past decade, and fewer than one in twenty-three experiencing an appreciable gain. Figure 5.8 shows the distribution of the 1,180 school sample by net change in position ranking from 2003 to 2012.

Some implications of these insights gleaned from this approach to defining and mapping the terrain in which SEM operates are offered in the final section of this chapter.

IMPLICATIONS FOR ALPHA COLLEGE

A deeper understanding of institutional market position and the ways by which it provides a context for institutional planning has many implications for the practice of SEM and for SEM leadership. If we circle back to the opening vignette of Alpha's board meetings, how can this market-centered perspective reframe their discussions and help map institutional decisions about preferred directions?

First, the Academic Committee at Alpha is addressing questions of applicant demand as a reflection of institutional quality, and the trustees may pressure the administration to invest in expanding its applicant pool to elevate measures of selectivity, thereby presumably improving prestige. There is evidence in the analysis of market position that admissions selectivity and measures of student quality correlate with nearly every other SEM performance metric, suggesting that as legitimate growth in demand translates into greater selectivity and thereby improved quality, it can solidify and even elevate institutional market position. But selectivity is meaningful as a measure of market position only to the degree that it is not artificially manipulated. Selectivity improves market position only to the extent that it actually contributes to enhanced academic performance; otherwise, it is merely symbolic of position.

The SEM industry (Schultz & Lucido, 2011) offers institutions many tactical approaches to expanding the number of applicants for admission (such as online fast-apps, waiver of application fees, elimination of essay requirements, and so on), but depending on the tactic, such efforts may give rise to an applicant pool with little or no affinity for the institution—and therefore a low likelihood of enrolling—that, at best, creates the appearance of greater market demand. In fact, elevated application volume and manipulated acceptance rates can translate into lower enrollment yields, thereby working directly against the intended objective of market ascendance. Regardless of dubious long-term outcomes, such tactics too often prove to have little sustainable value and limited strategic impact; they can be costly and can distract energy and resources from more promising strategies with real enrollment impact. A market-centered perspective can help the SEM officer meaningfully place the drivers of demand in the context of Alpha's underlying market objectives and thereby lead to a deeper consideration of more authentic ways to improve demand, selectivity, and quality rather than simple shortcuts.

Alpha's Finance Committee is deliberating next year's tuition and financial aid budget. Although the board's insistence on lowering that discount rate is a predictable response to an industry-wide trend in which financial aid budgets in aggregate are increasing at a faster rate than tuition revenue, resulting in declining marginal income (the share of that tuition increase that institutions ultimately realize), they may not fully appreciate the tradeoffs that potentially come with reductions in discount and/or above average increases in tuition.

To begin, it is essential that Alpha's trustees understand the drivers underlying the changes in its discount rate. Among other possibilities, Alpha's rise in discount may reflect a diminished capacity on the part of families to finance their education without additional grant aid to keep the cost of attendance within reach. It may result from reductions in federal and/or state grant aid that must be offset with institutional aid to sustain affordability. Alpha's rising discount rates may also reflect a diminished willingness among its prospective students to pay the same level of tuition as in prior years given the attractiveness of competing alternatives.

Within the context of a market-centered framework, a board directive simply to lower the discount rate implicitly assumes that Alpha is either currently offering a net price lower than its market position can actually support or that Alpha students are sufficiently price inelastic and thereby willing and able to absorb an increase in cost. Given what was demonstrated in the earlier analysis of the relationship of price to position, and how net price is both a function and a reflection of position, and of the intertwined nature of discount rates, percent of students aided, students' academic profile, and students' financial need profile, any discussion at the Finance Committee concerning tuition and discount without due consideration of the many position-centered tradeoffs constitutes at best a short-term view of the problem. Without that consideration, the development of a pricing/aid strategy will be a response that more likely exacerbates the symptoms of diminished demand than addresses the root causes that underlie declining marginal revenue.

Understanding these tradeoffs is at the very heart of SEM analysis and practice—and the more one can consider the implications of these choices with respect to their collateral effects on and interrelatedness with market position, the more comprehensive and strategic the institution's approach to enrollment planning becomes. In fact, a market-centered perspective compels the Finance and the Academic Committees of Alpha's board to work together, insofar as they really share the same agenda, knowingly or not. That agenda is the quintessential SEM challenge: How can Alpha meaningfully, substantively, and strategically solidify its position in the market so that it can effectively and simultaneously respond to the challenge of increasing demand, selectivity, and quality while increasing net revenue. This requires seeing these outcomes for what they are: institutional indicators of one reality—namely Alpha's market position—not independent variables that can be considered and pursued independently. It is the underlying framework of market position that helps lay the common ground for these strategic conversations to occur.

At the same time, the Student Affairs Committee is addressing retention and degree completion, with an expectation that retention and graduation rates can be elevated to be on par with a set of peer institutions Alpha defines as "aspirational." In all likelihood, those so-called "aspirational" peers are regarded as such in part because they demonstrate notably higher retention and completion rates, which is more likely attributable to differences in market position than to having developed and implemented an array of effective retention initiatives and interventions.

Campus retention discussions are frequently framed with an interventionist orientation, often focused on responding to students defined as "at risk" or trying to accommodate or work around obstacles to student success. A market-centered perspective, to the contrary, prompts Alpha's conversation about retention strategy to begin with an understanding of how retention and completion rates are highly predictable in light of Alpha's student and market profile (Kalsbeek & Zucker, 2013). A market-centered perspective can help Alpha embrace that student profile as a necessary starting point and an integral part of the retention strategy rather than bracketing it off as something to be accommodated. It would, in short, connect retention with the balance of the enrollment management goals shaping the new student profile (Cortes & Kalsbeek, 2012).

Retention, too, then becomes a shared, inseparable agenda with the prior board committees. Overall, a market-centered perspective encourages Alpha to begin its retention efforts by first establishing goals and objectives in a context meaningfully framed by the entirety of its own distinct and definable position. This reorients the SEM strategy to move beyond only implementing a set of tactical interventions aimed narrowly at preventing attrition, and to understand how institution-wide strategies rooted in this concept of market position have significant bearing on long-term institutional outcomes, including rates of retention and degree completion.

Alpha's Mission Committee is concerned with access and diversity, and increasing Alpha's enrollments of minority, low-income, and first-generation students in particular. Naturally, the foundational drivers of these dynamics are tied to forces that are only partially within Alpha's control—not the least of which is its so-called footprint and the underlying sociodemographic makeup of the specific territories that constitute Alpha's core market territory. Effectively and strategically framing diversity and access goals therefore presents challenges that emanate from the inextricable linkages between a college and its market geography, alumni presence, and longstanding patterns of community and high school relationships.

That discussion also surfaces the inevitable interconnections—if not tensions—that exist between access and diversity and the entire array of other enrollment performance metrics under consideration by Alpha's other board committees: selectivity, academic profile, net price and affordability, retention, and completion. The underlying and systemic interdependencies related to market position bring access and diversity onto the same agenda as all other dimensions of institutional aspiration and strategy. In fact, some institutions find that embedding these mission-focused conversations in a market-centered perspective so effectively surfaces the tensions and tradeoffs that the institutional values and mission-based priorities come into stark relief, become more energized, and certainly become more than ambiguous rhetoric (Kalsbeek, 2009).

Finally, Alpha's Advancement Committee is focusing on improving Alpha's rankings, responding to alumni pressure to elevate Alpha's prestige and thereby the value of the diplomas on their walls; this, too, is not an uncommon point of discussion and concern among trustees at campuses nationwide. Sometimes, such concern prompts the development of marketing campaigns with the intent to improve the peer ratings in surveys or to raise alumni giving rates or any number of other extent metrics that are suggestive of enhanced position, including selectivity, retention, geographic diversity, or class size.

Despite a growing chorus of voices on the national stage bemoaning the pernicious consequences of a rankings-obsessed industry, many schools continue to face enrollment agenda shaped at the trustee level with the primary intent to elevate their institution's rankings and prestige as directly and expeditiously as possible and as an end unto itself rather than seeking such gains as an outcome of deeper, more lasting achievements and transformations. What the SEM leader can do is bring a market-centered perspective to this discussion, showing that, as Zemsky and others have argued (Zemsky, Shaman, & Shapiro, 2001), such rankings are really reflections of underlying, systemic market dynamics and should be treated as such. Doing so then sets this topic squarely on the same board agenda as the prior committees, integrated inseparably with the other discussions of institutional strategy, and not something that can be meaningfully addressed independently.

With a market-centered perspective, a SEM leader can reframe and perhaps redirect the board's questions:

- Academic Committee: How does Alpha's applicant pool—in its size and profile—compare to institutions with a similar market position? In the context of Alpha's position and its academic and financial profile, what opportunities exist for expanding demand in markets within Alpha's current footprint?

- Finance Committee: Given Alpha's market position, which students can afford to enroll in light of Alpha's net price, and which students can Alpha afford to enroll in terms of net revenue? If the correlates of market position suggest that Alpha's current price and net price are in an appropriate range, what cost-containment strategies or what value-enhancing strategies can be developed and implemented that can improve the net revenue per student and relieve pressure to raise discount?

- Student Affairs Committee: Are Alpha's rates of retention and degree completion better, worse, or on par with what would be predicted from all of the other measures of its market position? What's the likely range of outcomes that would be expected, given Alpha's profile and position? How can Alpha's enrollment profile be shaped to improve these outcomes?

- Mission Committee: Which students can and do have access to an Alpha education in light of its current market position and, conversely, which students can Alpha access in its enrollment strategy? How are mission-based enrollment aspirations regarding diversity and access defined and specified in the full context of market profile and of the demonstrable correlates with other stated enrollment goals? And like the Finance

Committee's agenda, which students can afford to enroll at Alpha and which can Alpha afford to enroll?

- Advancement Committee: Which are the component parts of the ranking calculations where Alpha's metrics are in line with the correlates of its overall academic and financial market position? Which can be improved within the range of those correlates?

A market-centered perspective on SEM can effectively envelope nearly all of the key performance metrics of any enrollment plan and accentuate their inter-dependencies by embedding them definitionally, conceptually, and empirically in the notion of market position. That unifying framework and perspective may be what is missing at Alpha College. As the leadership team at Alpha prepares for its full board meeting, a valuable exercise would be a candid exposition and exploration of the market landscape, Alpha's market position within that con-text, and all of the correlates, interdependencies, and comparative outcomes related to that position. By showing how the independent agenda of the various committees dynamically and empirically interrelate and overlap, Alpha can perhaps forge a greater convergence of interest and a more informed outlook as it maps out its aspirations, intentions, and priorities. And that is what makes enrollment management strategic.

PUTTING THE "S" IN STRATEGIC ENROLLMENT MANAGEMENT

In the 1990s, enrollment management began to be described as *Strategic* Enroll-ment Management (Henderson, 2012; Dolence, 1993) for a number of reasons. Kalsbeek (2003), however, emphasized that what puts the "strategic" in SEM is an external and market orientation in which the focus shifts from internal proc-esses and tactical activities toward external realities, environmental dynamics, and competitive conditions. In this sense, SEM becomes strategic as it actively integrates the activities and priorities in the formal enrollment management units with the institution's strategic thinking and planning. Embracing a market-centered perspective is an important means for achieving that linkage. The rest of this chapter addresses a few ways by which the notion of institutional mar-ket position brings this strategic orientation to SEM.

Creative Tension

In Peter Senge's explorations of the requisite conditions for complex organiza-tions to change strategically and to advance in ways that achieve and sustain a strategic and competitive advantage, he noted the importance of a shared vision of the future, an organization-wide agreement on the preferred strategic directions to be pursued (Senge, Scharmer, Jaworski, & Flowers, 2005). It is not at all uncommon for universities to invest considerable time and energy in crafting noble and inspiring statements of the levels of institutional attainment to which they collectively aspire. But Senge et al., noted that for systemic change to occur, it is also important to have an accurate understanding of the current reality. He noted that an accurate and informed understanding of an organization's current situation provides an essential context and an empowering mooring that brings that shared vision to life through a creative tension.

There may perhaps be no better way by which the SEM leader can contribute to the strategic thinking at an institution than to use this notion of market structures and market position and all of the key performance indicators that are inextricably related to it as a way to help institutional leaders appreciate the institution's current reality. This type of market sensibility can not only embed leaders' understanding of the institution's situation in the systemic and stratified marketplace, but it also can embolden their visions for the future by placing meaningful parameters on the many metrics of institutional performance, showing the likely range of what is possible and both the payoffs and tradeoffs of doing so.

Benchmarking

Benchmarking is a common component of institutional strategic thinking and planning. It typically refers to the process of comparing particular business processes or performance metrics to industry "best practices." By comparing results or process metrics, institutions can evaluate opportunities for improvement or adopt specific practices to improve certain outcomes. Benchmarking can also entail placing institutional performance metrics in a comparative context against industry averages or plotting them against peer groups. Benchmarking is another means by which one brings an external orientation to institutional planning and evaluation, and it can be a key part of introducing more strategic thinking.

A market construct such as the one described here can be extremely valuable in such an exercise. It certainly provides a meaningful framework for placing institutional performance measures into comparative context. But more importantly, starting with a market perspective keeps institutional leaders from making inappropriate comparisons of specific metrics between institutions that are not similarly positioned. Every SEM leader has experienced trustees, presidents, or faculties inclined to compare graduation rates or net prices between their school and another that might be similar in some respects (for example, geographic proximity, same religious affiliation) but which occupies such a dramatically different market position that one cannot meaningfully compare their performance outcomes. Using a market framework, one can more clearly see that if one institution is significantly different than another on the core academic and financial indices, it isn't likely appropriate to benchmark on more specific metrics.

Long-Term Planning

Perhaps the most important implication of this market-centered approach for strategic enrollment planning is drawn from the realization that very few institutions have significantly changed market position over the years. Granted, there can be notable improvements in specific metrics, though the above analysis suggests that those improvements are likely to be bounded by a high and a low end of likely outcomes given the institution's market position. Nonetheless, those improvements still can be significant and highly impactful; for example, improving 3 percentage points in degree completion rate, yield rate, or discount rate is no small change, though still within an expected range given a school's market position.

But in the context of long-term strategic planning, the underlying systemic interrelationships that define the market structure show the challenge of advancing the institution's fundamental and relative market position to any significant degree within the horizon of most institutions' strategic planning time frames. Trustees, presidents, and provosts often express intentions to position or reposition the institution to achieve a presumably more advantageous, prestigious, or sustainable competitive situation; it is far easier said than done.

In this sense, perhaps the most strategic insight to keep in mind is that the word "position" is more a noun than a verb. Drawing on the brand marketing field, it is often noted that the brand of a university and the position it holds is something that exists only in the mind of key audiences; in that sense, the institution does not and cannot unilaterally brand or position itself, since it in fact is situated in a perceived position by certain audiences as they weigh its relative value and attributes compared to other institutions. Nevertheless, it is common for institutional plans to address how to brand and position the institution competitively. Such language unfortunately implies that an institution's position can be advanced in a relatively short time frame, and the conversation about how to do so too often focuses either on tactics such as brand messaging, advertising, and other marketing communications, or it focuses on changing specific performance metrics (such as increasing applicant demand, lowering net price, and so on) as if that alters the deeper underlying construct.

What this suggests to the SEM leader is that the five- to ten-year planning horizons that characterize most institutions' strategic plans are not time frames within which a significant advancement of market position is likely to occur, despite the rhetorical flourish that may characterize such plans. What is also clear is that advancing market position is not an objective that can be attained only through enrollment management and marketing strategies. The market construct discussed here is grounded in such fundamental academic and financial realities that enrollment strategies, tactics, and initiatives may be necessary but are not sufficient leverage for advancement. However, although it may be difficult to advance, an institution can certainly lose ground in market position through the erosion of financial resources and diminished academic quality and demand.

Effective SEM practices can and do help secure market position, and ineffective SEM practices can and do certainly contribute to an eroding position.

It is in that light that a market-centered definition of SEM has merit. The premise is that what puts the "S" in SEM, what makes it strategic, is shifting from internally oriented perspectives to externally oriented perspectives, keeping the institution's market position and market context as the touchstone in all enrollment planning. If the focus of SEM is the institution's competitive market position, then the foundation of SEM is the development of a research-based definition of the current and the desired or preferred strategic market position relative to key competitors. The function of SEM, then, is a comprehensive approach to informing and integrating the institution's plans, priorities, processes, and practices either to strengthen or shift its market position in pursuit of the institution's mission, and its optimal enrollment, academic, and financial profile (Kalsbeek, 2003).

CONCLUSION

In the aftermath of the 2008 financial crisis, a growing number of institutions are seeing greater fragility and instability in their core financial and academic indices and are questioning the sustainability of their current position and business model. Credit rating agencies see it, too (Bogaty, 2013), not just for individual institutions but for the entire higher education sector. There are growing pressures on managing enrollment as all sectors become more tuition dependent, and enrollment management is increasingly appreciated as a necessary element in the sustainability of the institution. For many institutions, simply securing and sustaining their current market position is success. Although an effective enrollment strategy is a necessary ingredient in doing this, it is not sufficient, insofar as the current demographic, economic, and competitive realities require a strategic approach to more than enrollment outcomes.

Most importantly, this new reality may finally bring caution and common sense to what has been a relentless pursuit across all of higher education of upward ascent in this market construct. The much maligned "arms race" between colleges and universities, accompanied by extreme investments in prestige-enhancing facilities, programs, and amenities, is all a reflection of the potency and pervasiveness of this market construct. The pursuit of upward movement has consumed precious resources, typically at the students' expense and at the expense of the academic enterprise.

But the implications and consequences of this market-centered view of higher education's obsessions go well beyond the futures and fortunes of individual institutions. As noted earlier, the distribution of institutional wealth and advantage reflects the accumulation and amassing of all forms of social capital, and the inequitable access to that social capital provides and perpetuates "advantage for the advantaged" in the United States. The obsession by institutions on elevating their relative position and society's similar fixation on the prestige associated with that position has only exacerbated the nation's socioeconomic inequities. As columnist David Brooks noted in a provocative op-ed piece in *The New York Times*, "Let's say you work at a university or a college. You are a cog in the one of the great inequality producing machines this country has known. What are you doing to change that?" (2005, paragraph 1).

References

Bogaty, E. (2013). 2014 *Outlook—US Higher Education, Not-for-Profits and Independent Schools.* Report No. 160659. New York: Moody's Investors Service.

Brooks, D. (2005). The education gap. *The New York Times*, New York, September, 25, 2005. Retrieved from http://query.nytimes.com/gst/fullpage.html?res = 9B03E1DA1 430F936A1575AC0A9639C8B63.

Cortes, C. M., & Kalsbeek, D. (2012). *Linking Admission Strategies to Student Retention.* Paper presented at the National Symposium on Student Retention Conference, New Orleans.

Dolence, M. (1993). *Strategic Enrollment Management: A Primer for Campus Administrators.* Washington, DC: American Association of Collegiate Registrars and Admissions Officers.

Henderson, S. E. (2012). Integrating evolving perspectives: The roots and wings of enrollment management. In B. Bontrager (Ed.), *Strategic Enrollment Management: Transforming Higher Education* (pp. 1–21). Washington DC: American Association of Collegiate Registrars and Admissions Officers.

Kalsbeek, D. (2003). *Redefining SEM: New perspectives and new priorities.* Keynote presentation at American Association of Collegiate Registrars and Admissions Officers SEM XIII National Conference, Boston.

Kalsbeek, D. (2009). *Balancing Market and Mission: Enrollment Management Strategies in Catholic Higher Education.* 2009 Balancing Market and Mission symposium proceedings. Chicago: DePaul University.

Kalsbeek, D., & Zucker, B. (2013). Reframing retention strategy: A focus on profile. In D.Kalsbeek (Ed.), Reframing Retention Strategy for Institutional Improvement. *New Directions for Higher Education, 2013*(161).

Schultz, S., & Lucido, J. (2011). *Enrollment Management, Inc.: External Influences on Our Practice.* Los Angeles: USC Center for Enrollment Research, Policy, and Practice.

Senge, P. M. (1990). *The Fifth Discipline: The Art & Practice of the Learning Organization.* New York: Currency Doubleday.

Senge, P. M., Scharmer, C. O., Jaworski, J., & Flowers, B. S. (2005). *Presence: An Exploration of Profound Change in People, Organizations, and Society.* New York: Random House.

Zemsky, R., & Oedel, P. (1983). *The Structure of College Choice*. New York: College Entrance Examination Board.

Zemsky, R., Shaman, S., & Iannozzi, M. (1997). In search of a strategic perspective: A tool for mapping the market in post-secondary education. *Change, 29*(6), 23–38.

Zemsky, R., Shaman, S., & Shapiro, B. D. (2001). Higher Education as Competitive Enterprise: When Markets Matter. *New Directions for Institutional Research, 2001*(111), 1–98.

Zemsky, R., Wegner, R. G., & Massy, W. F. (2005). *Remaking the American University: Market-Smart and Mission-Centered*. Piscataway, NJ: Rutgers University Press.

Zucker, B. (2011). *Exploring enrollment management metrics in the context of institutional market position*. Research paper presented at Human Capital Research Symposium, Chicago.

CHAPTER 6

Admissions and Recruitment Marketing

Tom Hayes

Marketing is a tool that, when combined with the other tools and disciplines discussed in this book, enhances and strengthens Strategic Enrollment Management efforts. This chapter begins by defining marketing and explains how the marketing of services such as education is different from marketing of physical goods. It develops the important concepts of customer satisfaction, marketing research, and understanding the needs of the potential student as the foundation of effective marketing for education. The last third of the chapter articulates what is known as the *seven P's of marketing* as the basis of executing marketing strategy in the enrollment process.

WHAT IS MARKETING?

Marketing is easily one of the most misunderstood disciplines both inside and outside the university environment. Furthermore, in many cases, the importance and contribution of marketing is given little credence in the academy. This chapter describes how marketing should be an integral part of the admissions and recruitment efforts within universities and colleges.

Most people who have not studied marketing believe it to be related to advertising or sales. But marketing can be defined in a variety of ways. Some definitions are formal and known within the field. One of the most established definitions comes from the American Marketing Association (2013), which states, "Marketing is the activity, set of institutions, and processes for creating, communicating, delivering, and exchanging offerings that have value for customers, clients, partners, and society at large."

The idea that marketing is "the activity, set of institutions, and processes" implies that the responsibility of marketing goes well beyond an individual or department with "marketing" in its title. In some universities, marketing is a part of university relations; in others, it may be a part of enrollment management, and increasingly it is a freestanding department or division. Regardless of where marketing is found in an organizational chart, it is imperative that marketing is integrated with all other functions of a university. It is just as important as good financial management, strategic planning, and strong human resources.

The concept that marketing creates and delivers value to customers is based on the principle that the institution has effectively identified potential consumers it seeks to attract. In an academic setting, and for the purposes of this book, these consumers are potential students. Marketing plays an important role in helping to identify who those students might be, but invariably the mission, vision, and values of the institution take precedence. Once a potential student population is identified, marketing efforts seek to understand that population's values and to create roadmap to determine how best to deliver what the students need and want. As you will learn in this chapter, this process goes well beyond advertising and sales.

If marketing benefits the organization and its stakeholders, the role and definition of marketing must be viewed from the perspective of an exchange process.

MARKETING AS AN EXCHANGE PROCESS

Perhaps the simplest way to understand marketing is to think of it as the *facilitator of exchange*. An institution of higher learning is challenged to provide a service to its customers—students—in exchange for something of value—a college education and the experiences that accompany the education. As indicated earlier, the institution's first marketing step is to identify the student population it wants to attract. Once this has been accomplished, the institution uses marketing to identify what that student group is looking for in the exchange and then to set about creating, delivering, and promoting these things to attract the targeted students. Marketing research is the tool employed by the institution both to identify what the student population is seeking in the exchange as well as the students' satisfaction in what the institution has delivered.

What a student population values depends on who the students are. It is relatively easy to understand that the educational experiences that would attract an adult, nontraditional student may be different than the experiences attractive to a traditional eighteen-year-old freshman. Understanding the students' divergent needs, wants, and desired outcomes is part of the marketing process.

As noted, the exchange principle is based on providing something of value for something of value. In this exchange the institution requires something of its student population as well. Obviously, the first requirement that comes to mind is money, in the form of tuition. All institutions, whether public, private, not-for-profit, or profit—require balanced budgets and hopefully a surplus in order to survive. However, they may also want to be the recipients of their students' energy and positive publicity via word of mouth.

A successful exchange process *must be equitable*. If students do not receive what they want in the educational experience, they will not enroll, or, if they do enroll, they are not likely to stay. This results in negative word of mouth and poor retention, which leads to financial difficulties for the institution. If the institution does not receive the necessary financial inflow and student support, its long-term prospects are diminished. Lack of equity in the relationship typically stems from the institution not understanding what its targeted student population is looking for or a failure to deliver the experience in a consistent, quality manner.

Once again, successful marketing begins with identifying and understanding the target population. Institutions must understand what their student populations seek and whether these populations possess the willingness and capability of delivering their end of the exchange process. It is entirely possible that although a targeted student population is willing to enroll in a college, the population base is not large enough to provide the necessary financial support. In these instances, marketing processes may help identify new and more financially viable student market segments. This could come in the form of something as simple as new majors or programs or as large as a shift in the institution's mission and vision.

THE UNIVERSITY AS A SERVICE INSTITUTION

Misunderstanding the marketing process goes well beyond its definition, role, and scope within the academic institution. Misunderstanding is often a result of the lack of differentiation between marketing a physical good and marketing a service. Ironically, the basis of this misunderstanding is often found within our institutions' teaching of the subject: Any college that offers marketing as a major or teaches a principles of marketing course may inadvertently be contributing to this misunderstanding. Introductory marketing textbooks are focused primarily on the consumer product arena. In an effort to maintain the students' interest, examples of marketing throughout the textbook are more likely than not to be about products of interest to that student population. As a result, companies such as Nike, Apple, and the latest game software companies are the focus of the marketing materials. A review of the top-selling principles of marketing textbooks demonstrates that there are, on average, twenty chapters in each book. At most, only one of these chapters, and more likely half a chapter, is focused on the marketing of services. What makes this particularly unfortunate is that more than 80 percent of the Gross Domestic Product (GDP) of the United States, and most developed nations, is made up of services rather than physical goods, according to the International Monetary Fund (2012). As is developed by Thomas Hayes (2009), universities and colleges are included in this service sector. Therefore, to market educational institutions properly, the institution must know how to market a service.

At universities, what is offered—what is "sold"—is education. It is at the core of what universities do and represents their central mission. Prospective students are asked to make one of the biggest and most expensive decisions of their lives by enrolling in the institution. And they must make this decision without the opportunity to inspect the offered service in a detailed manner. If a consumer wants to buy a car, a computer, or a pair of athletic shoes, he or she can simply inspect and objectively evaluate the quality and features of the product. Services, as will be explained in the following paragraphs, are by nature intangible. A service cannot be touched, viewed, or evaluated in any meaningful way before its use. In fact, the consumer does not know how good the service is until *after* it is used. Students can never be assured of the quality of their education until after they experience it. They are first asked to commit their money and energy, trusting that they will find the educational experience worth the expense.

As Parsu Parasuraman, Valerie Zeithaml, and Len Berry established (1985), the marketing of services differs from the marketing of physical goods along four basic dimensions: intangibility, inseparability, variability, and perishability.

Intangibility

The *intangibility* of the service offered means it cannot be seen, tasted, felt, heard, or smelled before it is purchased. Students cannot hold education in their hands and inspect the merchandise. By merely visiting a campus, a student cannot determine the quality of education the institution offers or know how the university experience might benefit him or her in the future. As a result, students and their parents look for signals for indications of quality. They may judge the quality of education by what they can see and touch. The beauty, cleanliness, and upkeep of the campus facilities, the quality of printed materials, and their interactions with college representatives all may become the basis of further judgment about the quality of the institution. Furthermore, in absence of physical indicators, prospects will look to the experiences and opinions of others to make their judgment; universities must realize that potential students trust their friends more than they trust university officials. The resulting implications of intangibility means that the physical evidence found on the campus must be satisfactory, and the institution must make every effort to build, enhance, and protect its reputation.

Inseparability

Inseparability means that the quality of the service is only as good as the person who delivers it. On college campuses, the core service of education is inseparable from the staff and faculty's ability to organize and communicate its content. Indeed, across campuses, each of the services provided are inseparable from those delivering them. The quality of counseling, for example, is based on the knowledge and skills of the counselors. The quality of student life is directly influenced by the capabilities of the professionals in that department.

The prospective student forms his or her impressions based upon interactions with others during their college search. So, for example, when a student makes a phone call to a university, whoever answers the phone is representing the institution and has the ability to make a positive or negative impression. When students first visit a campus, the security guards or grounds personnel may be the first people they meet. How students are treated by these campus representatives can affect their decision to attend. The resulting implication of inseparability is that the institution must give a great deal of thought to each and every person hired. Furthermore, implementing training and reward systems across campus must be in line with the goal of providing a quality educational experience to the student population.

Variability

Unfortunately, one of the other characteristics of services is that they are by nature variable. This *variability* is a direct result of inseparability. Unlike machines, people have bad days and may find it difficult to perform consistently in a way that satisfies the needs of prospective students. The fact that no one is capable of always working at the highest level creates special problems within service institutions and, by extension, universities. When prospective students experience inconsistencies, their faith and trust with regard to promises of a quality education can be diminished. When prospective students experience inconsistencies in service or information, they will project their level of doubt to the bigger issue of the university's ability to provide the level of education they require. In short, variability destroys trust. A student's lack of trust in what is said and promised will diminish the institution's ability to attract and retain students. The implications of variability demand that systems and processes be created to minimize its occurrence. Variability further highlights the importance of hiring, training, and rewarding employees for jobs well done.

Perishability

In services, performance sells. Universities cannot store an excellent campus tour or an inspirational, in-person class lecture for future use; each of these elements is ephemeral and *perishable*. Every new interaction with a prospective student requires the same level of consistency and quality of those that came before. The focus of every interaction must be on what's happening now. A prospective student may have had a wonderful campus visit or interview with an admissions counselor, but once those experiences are over, it is imperative that the next experience be just as positive, if not better.

THE IMPORTANCE AND ROLE OF CUSTOMER SATISFACTION IN THE RECRUITMENT PROCESS

With services, the most important metric indicative of future success is that of customer satisfaction. To survive in a highly competitive environment, service organizations must satisfy their customers better than what is offered by their competitors. To set the institution apart from competitors, a university must strive to exceed students' expectations. As a result, each time a student has had his or her expectations exceeded and has experienced a new level of service, that new level becomes the new bar at which expectations are set. To make university competition even more challenging, a student's expectations may be affected by an experience with another institution in a completely different market. For example, if an appliance store can use your cell phone to provide a thirty-minute window before delivering your new purchase, why do cable companies still require a four-hour window, making it necessary for the consumer to sit at home waiting? If Disney has mastered the art of "waiting in line," why can't the TSA?

This "cross-fertilization of expectations" has a particularly strong impact on the institution with regard to competing for new students. The core service is education, yet most universities and colleges offer many different types of services in an attempt to enhance the students' college experience.

Students' expectations and eventual level of satisfaction are greatly determined by their experiences outside campus. For example, universities that provide housing are also in the hospitality business, and the expectations of students who live in university housing may be affected by the arrangements they had at home. Based upon current demographics, many freshmen have never shared a bedroom, yet at the university they may be housed with one or two other students in a space half the size of their bedroom at home. Universities are also in the food business, and to make the experience more acceptable to students, dining halls may look more like mall food courts than cafeterias.

Universities also provide healthcare, financing, entertainment, and academic support. Students will compare the quality of all of these service functions to similar services outside the university environment. In short, the institution's ability to satisfy its students is not determined simply by what other colleges may be doing, but also by other life experiences outside the university.

MARKETING IS EVERYONE'S RESPONSIBILITY

Admissions centers are the institution's "front doors," and admissions counselors are the frontline employees. The admissions and enrollment staff shoulders the responsibility for "bringing in the class." Obviously, admissions and enrollment staff should be educated and trained in the field of marketing. That said, by now the reader must realize that the marketing of the institution and its role in the admissions and enrollment process is everyone's responsibility. Every point of contact or impression experienced by a potential student at the institution becomes a moment of truth in his or her decision process. Every employee of the college must understand that he or she has an influence and makes a difference in attracting, enrolling, and retaining students. Whether it's the security guard who greets a family on their first visit to campus, the faculty member who holds open the door or answers a question, or the smile on the face of an employee in the dining hall—everyone provides the cues and indicators of a quality educational experience. The faculty and staff of a university *are* the university. Their actions and behaviors provide a tangible representation of the promises made in the enrollment process.

A WORD ABOUT MARKET RESEARCH

The use of research will be further developed in Part VI of this book, where we will discuss the use of internal data and environmental analysis. At this point, however, it is important that you understand the role of market research in the marketing process. In fact, it is often stated that without market research, true marketing cannot be applied. Market research is vitally important in university decision-making and enrollment.

One of the ironies in a university environment is that a strong research agenda is encouraged and rewarded for faculty. However, although research is a bedrock of business analysis, decision-making, and strategic planning, use of market research to inform a university's decision-making process regarding course offerings and other student enticements is typically lacking (Hayes, 2009). Market research funding is difficult to obtain, and the value of research is not only underappreciated, but often not even considered. Simply put, what is taught in the classroom about the role of marketing is not being used within the institution itself.

As the education market becomes more competitive, universities can no longer afford to base their decisions on assumptions and personal judgments, regardless of the decision-makers' experience. Well-crafted, accurate, and timely research is indispensable to a successful enrollment strategy. This is true for two reasons: first, the university is not the customer, and second, everything changes.

Shifts in the marketplace necessitate a consistent revisiting of the perceptions of the target market and the institution's place in the competitive field. Every time an institution's strategies and tactics are successful and a target group of students is enrolled, the marketplace changes. One institution's successes lead to other institutions' failures, and as an institution redoubles its efforts to attract students, the competition with other institutions intensifies. One institution's changes can impact the decisions and subsequent strategies of competing institutions. The result is an ever-changing and shifting of student expectations and institutional tactics to attract them.

Market research comprises two methods: qualitative research and quantitative research.

Qualitative research is typically used in the exploratory stage of a research project. Almost all qualitative efforts employ open-ended questions and a discussion format to explore the thoughts, feelings, and perceptions of the target student population. The most typical qualitative research used in enrollment strategies is the *focus group*: a group of students from the target population are asked to attend a meeting, in person or online, to discuss a given topic in an informal manner. The information provided in this type of research can be used to accomplish a range of goals:

- Probe deeply into potential students' underlying needs, perceptions, and preferences.
- Gain a better understanding of past strategic efforts.
- Develop ideas and marketing strategies that can be further tested using quantitative research.
- Search for potential new services that may be desired by potential students (Hayes, 2009).

Qualitative research is perceived as easy to employ and inexpensive to finance. Unfortunately, however, it is the most misused type of research in the enrollment process. Trained moderators who understand group dynamics are rarely used on college campuses. In addition, the number and nature of participants in qualitative research does not lend itself to extrapolation. For these reasons, qualitative research should never be used as a basis for marketing strategy; instead, quantitative research is necessary.

Quantitative research is designed to collect and analyze data in such a way that it can be projected to a larger population. In this form of research, surveys (usually online) are administered to a random sample of the target population. To be used effectively, surveys must be designed to achieve very specific and clear objectives, constructed in an unbiased manner and executed on a consistent basis. The resulting information is statistically sound and can be confidently applied when making strategic decisions.

Many different types of market research studies, such as the following, can enhance enrollment efforts:

- Perception or image studies can investigate how the institution is viewed by its targeted student population.

- Competitive positioning studies can enable the institution to be compared to other institutions within the competitive landscape.

- Performance studies enable the institution to identify attributes that are important to the target population with regard to an educational experience, and to measure how well the institution and its competitors are perceived to perform along these dimensions.

- Pricing studies can determine the impact of incremental tuition increases on enrollment.

Most universities do not have the resources or skills to conduct such research. As a result, they rely on outside market research consultants to assist them in these efforts. However, outside consultants can be costly, and unless the institution already appreciates the value of market research, securing funding for this type of research can be a challenge. If decision-makers view research as an investment rather than a cost, securing funding and support is less difficult.

One way to overcome objections to the cost of market research is to introduce the concept of the "lifetime value of a customer." This concept measures the profitability a student can achieve for the institution over his or her lifetime. This would entail counting the profit margins the student contributes to the university based on his or her four years of attendance, potential room and board, and average alumni donations after graduation. For some institutions, this is not typically calculated, yet it should be. The resulting figure can then be used to determine how many additional student enrollments would be required to effectively pay for the research. When this technique is employed, it quickly becomes apparent that market research is worth the expense, as supported by Robert Shaw and Melvin Stone (1988).

Market research is key to the institution's understanding of the student decision process when they choose a college. This includes understanding when students begin to see college as something to pursue, how and where they go about looking for information to facilitate their choice, what processes they use to make the final choice, and any changes to their perspective after a choice is made.

CREATING MARKETING STRATEGY: THE SEVEN P'S OF ENROLLMENT AND ADMISSION EFFORTS

Pick up a principles of marketing textbook and you may discover that marketing strategy is built upon *uncontrollable* and *controllable variables.* Uncontrollable variables include competitors' tactics, changes in the legal or economic environment, socioeconomic or demographic shifts, and technological innovations. Although marketers have little or no influence on uncontrollable variables, these variables must be carefully monitored. Understanding the shifting patterns of these variables and their implications on marketing strategy is an important component of strategic marketing planning.

In this chapter, the focus is on controllable variables. In traditional marketing texts, the controllable variables are typically referred to as *the four P's*, made famous by Jerome E. McCarthy (1960): *product, price, place,* and *promotion.* Education, however, is a service and not a physical good. As such, marketing services differ from marketing athletic shoes or smart phones, so with regard to education, three more P's were added by Bernard H. Booms and Mary Jo Bitner (1981): *physical evidence, processes,* and *people.* The resulting *seven P's* are created and integrated in line with the targeted student population's desires in an educational experience. A key word here and throughout this chapter is "integration." Just as marketing must be integrated with all the other managerial functions within a college, the controllable variables of marketing must be integrated as well.

Product

The core product or service of colleges and universities is education. As part of the total education experience, services are provided, such as hospitality, food service, financing, entertainment, and healthcare, to name a few. The key to how the institution provides these services is understanding the *why* and *what* the targeted student population hopes to achieve with their education. Are students enrolling for the mere sake of learning? Are they enrolling to increase their job opportunities or because of the prestige in competitive position the university provides? Knowing the answers to these questions helps the university shape its strategy and manipulation of the seven P's. Answers to these questions come from market research and understanding the consumer decision-making process.

Two of the most important components of the university product, however, are the academic majors provided and the institutional *brand*. The enrollment office may be able to provide insight and recommendations to the types of majors and fields of study that students are seeking. As the division of the university closest to the target market, enrollment staff are in the best position to understand shifts in consumer demand. In some colleges, the responsibility for branding lies within the enrollment division; in others, it may be the responsibility of university relations or an independent marketing division.

Branding can have many definitions. Some define it as the promise the institution makes to its constituents. Others think of it as the sum total of all the good and bad impressions the marketplace has about the institution. For the purposes of this chapter, it is defined as a consistency of message and action over time. This definition implies that the institution has control over its brand; unfortunately, although all institutions have a brand, many do not manage it well. The key to any strong brand is ensuring that it is relevant, distinctive, and true. Figure 6.1 shows the "brand triangles," which represent this concept.

In the three brand triangles in Figure 6.1, the upper-right triangle represents what the institution does well. Information included in this triangle is a result of interviews with administrators, faculty, and staff across campus. It represents a consensus of what is believed to be unique and distinctive about the institution. The problem is, however, that what an internal staff member believes to be unique and distinctive may be meaningless to the external market. For this reason, internal perceptions must be evaluated through the eyes of

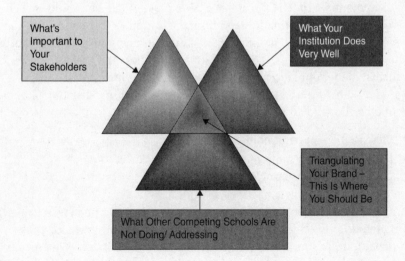

Figure 6.1 The brand triangle

Source: SimpsonScarborough. Used with permission.

external stakeholders. This involves marketing research based on quantitative surveys. The objective is to identify that which is true about the institution and relevant to the targeted student population. To do this, the institution can compare the internal brand position to that which exists in the marketplace. If a direct competitor already "owns" a given brand position, for example, focusing on the same brand space will not be effective.

Finding the intersection of the three brand triangles represents the ideal brand position for the institution. Once the brand is identified, all further marketing strategies, communication activities, and institutional initiatives must refer to this brand position. Given that a strong brand is truly a consistency of message and action over time, the integration and execution of the brand position must be found in everything the university does.

Price

The economics of tuition and other expenses and the implications on university strategy are developed fully in Part III of this book. Understanding the scientific implications of pricing theory and practice is vitally important to a strong enrollment effort. This is clearly explained in upcoming chapters. In this section, we emphasize the psychology of pricing, in particular the price-value relationship.

When students, or their parents, think of the price of a college education, it is not uncommon for them to gravitate to the financial, or dollar, cost that will be required. In reality, however, nonmonetary costs can be as great or greater than the dollar amount spent. The basis for establishing a price-value relationship in a potential student's mind can be expressed like so: Value = Benefits – Costs. A dearth of information and research examines this concept. Although this expression is simple, its implications are extremely important in an institution's strategic decisions. The institution that offers the greatest value to its intended student population provides the highest ratio of benefits to costs.

Based on this formula, there are only three ways to increase the value of an institution's educational offering:

- Increase benefits and hold costs constant.
- Hold benefits constant and decrease costs.
- Increase benefits and reduce costs.

Any of these approaches will result in a net increase in perceived value. The key, therefore, is to understand what constitutes a *benefit* and a *cost*.

A *benefit*, in its simplest terms, is a solution to a problem. This means understanding why a potential student is seeking an education in the first place. What does the student hope to achieve by attending the university? Helping students reach their goals and solving their "problems" should be the goals of the university. Once again, market research is the tool used to identify the benefits potential students are seeking.

The *cost* side of the equation is far more complicated than the outlay of dollars. The following nonmonetary costs all influence a student's decision to attend and/or remain at a university:

- Times/convenience costs: Are classes held at a convenient time and location? How many years will it take to complete the program? Ensuring that students are not wasting their time has a major impact on their decision process.

- Hassle costs: Does the university make it easy for students to take care of necessary business? Does a centralized location allow students a "one-stop shopping" experience? Can students register and pay for classes within the same building? Do online services offer a simple and seamless experience for completing business tasks? Students should not be sent on a scavenger hunt across campus to enroll in class or complete other tasks.

- Physical costs: Is the campus located in a major city? Does the campus, regardless of location, have ample lighting on sidewalks and does it provide late night escorts for students? Market research demonstrates that safety is one of the most important variables in an educational experience for women and parents. Helping potential students feel safe is therefore vitally important. Increasing the perception of a safe and secure campus is best achieved by providing a clean and well cared for physical environment.

- Sensory costs: Are classroom chairs comfortable? Is the air temperature properly regulated? Is adequate space available to meet and socialize with fellow students? Does the university offer appropriate technology to enhance the educational experience? Ensuring that students are physically comfortable is important to reducing this cost.

- Psychological costs: What are the odds of being admitted, and if not admitted what will people think? Will the college be a good fit? When making a high-risk decision, such as choosing a university, major, and classes, students can experience anxiety. Institutions can reinforce students by addressing these risks, anticipating questions, and having answers ready. By helping to reduce student anxiety, the university can reassure potential students that their choice in the institution is the best decision.

- Social costs: Is this considered a *good college* for students like me? Will there be students from similar backgrounds? Choosing a college is a very personal decision. The image and brand strength of the institution reflects back on the student who is enrolled there, and for traditional age students, it also reflects upon their parents. Enhancing and protecting the institutions brand is key to reducing social costs.

By reducing nonmonetary costs, the institution not only increases customer perceptions of the value it offers, but it also encourages prospective students and parents that these added values are worth the monetary costs required to attend the university. In short, the university's attention to nonmonetary cost reductions to enhance the value proposition must be front and center in any integrated marketing effort.

Place

Within the university setting, *place* typically relates to the institution's physical location, geographic markets served, and points of access. Most institutions have been physically located in the same place for decades, at least. The institution may have expanded its physical footprint, but the essential location remains the same. From a marketing perspective, the university must find a way to make its location an asset rather than a liability. The implication is that the college must embrace its locale and promote this in the best possible light. If the university is located in the middle of an urban environment, for example, it might highlight access to internships, jobs, and social opportunities. If the university is located in a rural environment, the comfortable pace and sense of community may serve as an important drawing card. If the university is located on a hill overlooking the ocean, or is five minutes from a ski resort, highlighting the benefits of the locale is easy.

In addition to the permanent physical location, satellite campuses may increase the institution's ability to react to demographic shifts and market opportunities. The choice of new facilities must be in line with projected long-term growth and not in reaction to a short-term market development.

Some institutions provide online courses in an attempt to overcoming geographic restrictions. Although online education opens the door to national and international markets, it also opens the door to national and international competition. A strong academic brand and program will help the institution compete effectively. Technology in general, and on the Internet in particular, allows potential students to access services when and how they want, twenty-four hours a day, seven days a week. Appropriating this technology, however, does not guarantee success. The worst possible scenario is that the institution opens the door to new markets but is not properly prepared to provide service to those who attempt to access it.

Promotion

Earlier in the chapter, it was purported that most people believe marketing and promotion are one and the same. By now, you should understand that promotion is but one part of an integrated marketing effort. Additionally, it is important to understand that successful promotion is dependent on integrated marketing communications (IMC).

Integrated marketing communications has been best defined by Robert Sevier and Robert Johnson (1999) as "a comprehensive, coordinated institution wide effort to communicate mission-critical values and messages in a way the target audiences notice, understand and respond to" (p. 5). This approach focuses on data-driven segmentation, message integration, and evaluation, with the goal of coordinating all of the institution's messages—all should have a common look, sound, and feel across different media and audience segments.

As with many topics in this book, the topic of IMC could fill an entire text. For now, the dimensions of effective communication strategy will be developed briefly, while emphasizing some of the more important communication tactics for enrollment strategies.

The university's communications mix, also known as the promotional mix, consists of five tools that are well accepted in the industry: *advertising, personal selling, public relations, sales promotions,* and *direct marketing.* These tools are discussed next.

Advertising. Advertising is any paid form of non-personal presentation that uses mass media by an identified sponsor. Television, radio, billboards, magazines (including viewbooks), and newspapers are all examples of advertising. Advertising is typically characterized as the most expensive communication format, but it is also capable of reaching the largest audience. Due to advertising expense, the institution should be especially careful to make sure its use is reflective of clear objectives and consistent execution. Understanding the return on investment is especially important here as a result. Measuring the effectiveness and efficiency of advertising is an important strategic step.

Personal Selling. Personal selling is any form of personal presentation by representatives of an institution for the purpose of making sales or building customer relationships. In the enrollment process, personal selling is mostly represented through the work of admissions counselors at college fairs and high school visits or through campus tours. To a prospective student, the admissions counselor *is* the university. His or her knowledge, enthusiasm, and charisma reflect directly on the image and brand of the university. Prospective students and their parents must place their trust in these individuals. To be effective, admission counselors must know a little about every academic program offered, the city and neighborhood, extracurricular and entertainment options, and so much more. Clearly, these staff members are very important in the institution's recruitment success. Students who are chosen to be tour leaders on campus similarly represent their institution to potential students and their families. Effective marketing strategies require that admission counselors and campus tour leaders must be carefully hired, properly trained, and rewarded to optimize their communication effectiveness.

Public Relations. The purpose of public relations is to create positive impressions about the institution within the marketplace. This could mean planning, designing, and obtaining favorable publicity about the institution in the media. Like any other part of the marketing strategy, good public relations is built on market research and strategic planning. It is far easier to obtain favorable media coverage when what you are sharing is of interest and relevant to a particular media outlets market.

Sales Promotions. Sales promotions are short-term incentives intended to encourage a targeted action. The objective of any sales promotion is to attract the attention of a targeted audience and serve as an inducement to pay attention— for example, giving away Frisbees or USB flash drives as part of a social media campaign, or handing out bobble heads at an athletic event. In both cases, the promotion is used to attract the attention of the targeted student population so that other forms of communication or experiences may be more readily introduced.

Direct Marketing. Direct communication with a carefully targeted audience can be used to obtain an immediate result. Mail, telephone, social media, and email are the most commonly used direct marketing tools. The key to effective direct marketing is to ensure that the message being delivered is tailored to the target audience. The effective use of technology and databases allow colleges and universities to communicate to prospective students about what they care about in an individual manner. Being personable, yet authentic, is important. Increasing social engagement is a big part of this effort. The explosion of the Internet and the use of social media tools to engage in conversations has had a major impact on the communications mix. Posting timely information, listening for feedback, engaging in conversations, and understanding social metrics create a continuous responsibility for any enrollment office. Those who are not seriously considering the importance or speed of social media are missing out on considerable encounters with prospective students.

It is commonly stated that the goal of all communication is to inform, persuade, or remind. In other words, the institution's messages should disperse important information to target audiences that is relevant to the students' interests and needs, should be persuasive in nature so that the potential student is more likely to choose the university, and should help prospective students stay continually aware of what the university offers. To this list of goals it is important to add the word "engage." With the advent of social media (Facebook, Twitter, Instagram, and so on), a form of direct marketing, the importance of creating a dialog with potential students is paramount. Communication, by definition, is a two-way street, and social media demonstrates this more than any other form of communication. Students use social media to interact and communicate with their peers. To get their attention, institutions must communicate with them on their terms—this means not only sending texts but inviting them into a conversation. As such, developing and executing a strong social media platform means 24/7 monitoring, creating valuable content, and actively engaging in dialogue with prospective students.

Physical Evidence

As a part of the service sector, education is intangible—that is, it's impossible for a potential student to "see" a quality educational experience. Because of this, the student will look for other cues to help determine the strength of an institution's educational offerings. Reputation represents one of these cues, and physical evidence is another. In other words, potential students will look to the physical components of the college campus as an indication of the quality of education. In short, a clean, well-kept college campus will have a much more positive impact on a potential student's decision process than a campus that has experienced years of deferred maintenance. Like everything else in integrated marketing strategy, the facility exterior, interior, and other tangibles must be managed and coordinated in thought and practice to communicate a consistent positive message.

Mary Jo Bitner (1997) studied the impact of physical evidence on consumer decision-making in the service sector. She classifies physical evidence into three broad categories:

- Facility exterior
- Facility interior
- Other tangibles

The following list demonstrates what might fit into these categories on a college campus:

Facility maintenance	Admissions office
Neighborhood	Admissions lobby
Campus tour stops	Décor
Signage	Business dress
Layout	Furnishings
Viewbooks	Business cards
Entrance road	University websites
Parking availability	Available technology
Landscaping	Classrooms

These aspects of the institution's physical appearance are just a small part of what affects a potential student's visual perception of a college campus. It is easy to imagine a student's and his or her parents' first impressions as they drive onto campus. In the waiting room of the admissions office, they may have time to look around and get "a feel" for the place. No doubt they will be looking for information to help them make a college decision, and what they see goes a long way toward helping them make that decision. (I recall a college visit with my daughter that was cut short based on the impression of the college biology and chemistry labs. They appeared to be of the 1950s era and held little promise for the needs of an aspiring medical doctor. Think, for instance, of the facilities of the typical feeder high schools. The facilities must be minimally the same but likely much better than the student's current setting. Going backward is not an option for most students.)

The institution is asking potential students to stay four years. Many universities are also asking students to live on campus. Without a doubt, the student's perception of the institution is affected by what he or she sees in front of them.

When considering the physical appearance of the campus, institutions must ask the following questions:

- Is the campus signage confusing?
- Does the campus appear safe?
- Do classrooms employ the latest technology?
- Do the residence halls appear warm and inviting?
- Are spaces available that invite and encourage student socialization?
- Does the university have "curb appeal"?
- What does the physical evidence say about the campus?
- Does the marketing research ask your potential students the same questions?

Processes

This sixth "P" is also a result of managing and marketing the educational experience from a services perspective. We have already established that variability is innate in any service system. At the same time, variability destroys the trust and confidence a student must have to make an important decision regarding enrolling in a college. The university's job is to make that decision as easy as possible. Its processes should be designed and executed so that the student's decision to enroll is seamless and anxiety-free.

Two areas may be of particular importance in aiding, or hindering, a student's decision to enroll: service systems and cycle times.

Service systems refer to the processes that increase customer satisfaction or reduce unnecessary expenditures of time and money. Reducing and removing barriers to student inquiry should be the goal of every admissions process. Service systems should be designed so that they work for both the institution and the targeted student population. College online applications or telephone registration, for example, can streamline service systems. Although online applications simplify the work for the admissions staff, the telephone may be more convenient for potential students' parents, who may be more comfortable with a direct conversation. Service systems could also include the provision of iPads to connect to self-directed campus stores when staff is not available or the admissions office is closed, or GPS-activated videos at selected campus locations that explain and highlight what the student is observing.

Managing and coordinating the entire admissions process, from the time the student customer initially makes contact with the university either online or in person, to their interactions with admissions counselors over the phone or in person, to visiting the campus and having face-to-face meetings and a campus tour, to the follow-up thank you notes and calls, should be seamless and well crafted.

Cycle times refer to the amount of time it takes to complete a process. As a rule, shorter cycle times are better than longer ones. In today's high-tech culture of immediacy, some processes can be quick or even instantaneous. Imagine the impact of a long cycle time between a student applying for admission and the subsequent notification of acceptance. Unnecessary delays in processing student applications and follow-up communications lead to perceptions of disinterest and/or inefficiencies at the college. Long cycle times in the admission process also increase the chances that the potential student will choose a competing institution in the interim. Cycle times also affect the amount of time it may take a student to graduate from an institution. Assuring the student and his or her parents that a degree can be achieved in four years is not only important but can provide a competitive edge. Some programs even offer a combination four-year undergraduate and master's track, thereby enhancing the attractiveness of its competitive offering. For universities whose market is primarily adult and part-time students, the time to complete a degree is often the most important factor in the decision to enroll.

People

Although people are not typically considered a "controllable variable," in this case, the people in focus are the targeted students and the employees at the college or university. Processes and systems help reduce variability among service employees, but these can only go so far. The emphasis on this variable regards controlling the student market targeted by the institution and the hiring decisions it makes.

A university's brand position is created with a particular target audience in mind. A strong position attracts as well as deflects, providing the signal to potential students that this institution is "for people like you." If a college reaches out to multiple target audiences, it must be assured that all audiences "mix well." For example, combining traditional full-time students with part-time adult students in the same classroom does not always work. The two segments may have different life experiences, motivations for attending school, and expectations for the classes and degrees. At the graduate MBA level, for example, combining full-time millennial students with part-time working students can also be problematic. The MBA is very much an applied degree. Students obtaining their MBA straight from an undergraduate program without work experience may be seen as detrimental to the educational experience by part-time students who are also working professionals. The pressures of "filling a class" may cause enrollment officers to combine student segments that in the long run causes more harm than good.

The SEM office, in particular, and the university as a whole, must also be selective in its hiring processes. Because services are inseparable from the people who deliver them, the institution must take care to hire individuals with a service inclination. Imagine the negative impact a disengaged tour guide or an apathetic administrative assistant can have on the enrollment process. Hiring, and by extension, the training and rewarding of admission employees, must be in line with the marketing strategy of the institution and the ability to provide superior customer service.

CONCLUSION

Hopefully, this chapter has demonstrated that marketing is an integral part of any successful SEM process. Marketing helps identify potential student populations, is integral to understanding what students are looking for in the educational experience, helps articulate when and how the targeted student population should be contacted, and outlines the strategy to ensure that they not only enroll, but matriculate. Although much of the chapter focused on marketing strategies and tactics within enrollment offices, this should be but a small part of the institution's overall marketing strategy. Every decision made by the institution should incorporate a marketing-oriented filter. Although the admissions office represents the university's front door, the institution's ultimate success in "bringing in the class" lies within how well marketing is integrated and executed across the campus.

References

American Marketing Association. (2014). Definition of marketing. Retrieved from http://www.marketingpower.com/AboutAMA/Pages/DefinitionofMarketing.aspx.

Bitner, M. J. (1997). Servicescapes: The impact of physical surroundings on customers and employees. *Journal of Marketing*, (56), 57–71

Booms, B. H., & Bitner, M. J. (1981). Marketing strategies and organization structures for service firms. In J. Donnelly & W. R. George (Eds.), *Marketing of Services*. Chicago: American Marketing Association.

Hayes, T. J. (2009). *Marketing Colleges and Universities: A Services Approach*. New York: Council for Advancement and Support of Education (CASE).

International Monetary Fund. (2012). World Economic Outlook Database, April 2012: Nominal GDP list of countries. Retrieved from http://www.imf.org/external/pubs/ft/weo/data/changes.htm.

Keefe, L. (2008). Marketing defined. *Marketing News*, January 15, 2008, 28–29.

McCarthy, E. J. (1960). *Basic Marketing: A Managerial Approach*. Homewood, IL: Richard D. Irwin.

Parasuraman, A., Zeithaml, V. A., & Berry L. L. (1985). A conceptual model of service quality and its implications for future research. *Journal of Marketing*, (49), 41–50.

Sevier, R. A., & Johnson, R. E. (1999). *Integrated marketing communications*. New York: Council for Advancement and Support of Education (CASE).

Shaw, R., & Stone, M. (1988). *Database Marketing*. London: Gower.

SimpsonScarborough, LLC. Alexandria, VA.

CHAPTER 7

Understanding Transfer and Articulation

Implications for Enrolling Transfer Students

Bruce Clemetsen, Lee Furbeck,
and Alicia Moore

Thus far in Part II we have focused upon recruitment and the market structure for traditional age students. In this chapter we shift our focus to transfer students. Facing pressure by federal or state government and by private foundations, colleges and universities in the United States face an ever-growing challenge to increase the number of students completing a certificate or degree. At the same time, however, research indicates that nearly 33 percent of all U.S. college or university students transfer prior to reaching this academic milestone (Hossler et al., 2012a) and, unfortunately, the nation's primary database tracking student completion—the Integrated Postsecondary Education Database System (IPEDS)—wholly ignores transfer students in its metrics. The combination creates significant challenges for institutions actively engaged in Strategic Enrollment Management. If an institution is to be successful with its SEM work, then it must actively research transfer student enrollment patterns, build strategic relationships with partner institutions, and develop programs and services to support degree completion for its most mobile student population.

In support of comprehensive SEM planning, this chapter addresses multiple topics related to student transfer. Following a review of current research about student transfer, the authors describe specific enrollment patterns, including the concept of "student swirl." The second section summarizes state and institutional level transfer student support services, including institutional partnerships, credit transfer policies, and technology. As a whole, this chapter provides

SEM leaders with a broad overview from which to understand current trends and efforts, enabling them to be strategic in working with the transfer student population at community colleges and universities.

TRANSFER STUDENT RESEARCH

Higher education professionals frequently make broad-based assumptions about transfer students. Among these are that students transfer due to poor academic performance at their first institution, part-time students transfer more frequently than full-time students, transfer students are undecided as to academic and career plans, and similar statements. Recent research by the National Student Clearinghouse Research Center (NSCRC) (Hossler et al., 2012a) and Noel-Levitz (2011) both uphold and dispel these and other common assumptions about transfers, illustrating the futility of ascribing a single set of characteristics to all students. Highlights from these reports include the following.

- Forty percent of all transfer students did not complete Algebra II while in high school.
- Transfer students are typically traditional age students.
- Thirty-two percent of all transfer students earned more than twenty credits prior to their first year of transfer.
- Transfer students are less engaged with and experience a lower sense of belonging at their transfer institution than other students.
- Fifty-three percent of all transfer students, regardless of destination of transfer, indicate that financial reasons will interfere with their ability to finish.
- Transfer students typically seek out assistance with academic advising at their transfer institution at a rate higher than other students.

These characteristics paint a complex picture but also provide clues as to how SEM leaders may strategically adjust services and strategies. A more complete understanding of transfer students and transfer patterns—including rate, timing, frequency, and destination—provides SEM leaders with the information they need to understand and support this population.

Rate, Timing, and Frequency

In 2012, the NSCRC conducted three in-depth examinations of transfer student enrollment patterns. The first of these reports, *Transfer & Mobility: A National View of Pre-Degree Student Movement in Postsecondary Institutions* (Hossler et al., 2012a), reviewed data on 2.8 million first-time students whose enrollment information was submitted to the NSCRC for fall 2006, following these students through summer 2011. Of the 2.8 million students, 33.1 percent of all students transferred at some point in their academic career, with the largest percentage of students transferring during their second year (37 percent); surprisingly, 22.2 percent of students transferred in years four and five. Nearly 75 percent of students transferred only once, and approximately 8 percent did so three or more times. Transfer rates of students starting at two-year or four-year, public or private not-for-profit institutions were relatively similar, ranging from 32.1 percent to 34.4 percent. In contrast, an average of only 17.9 percent of those who started at for-profit institutions transferred out (Hossler et al., 2012a).

Destination

According to the NSCRC (Hossler et al., 2012a), the most common transfer destination was two-year public institutions, regardless of the student's institution of origin. Of the transfer students who began their academic careers at four-year public institutions, more than 85 percent transferred to two- or four-year public institutions. However, the transfer destinations for students who began at four-year private institutions are distributed relatively evenly between public and private institutions.

It is important to note that transfer students also frequently cross state boundaries. According to research by Cliff Adelman and the U.S. Department of Education (1999), 40 percent of students who transferred enrolled at an institution in another state. More recently, NSCRC (Hossler et al., 2012a) data indicate that 27 percent of all transfer students cross state lines to enroll. Regardless of the number, this data raises compelling questions regarding the value of in-state course and program partnerships and demonstrates the limitations of state-specific reporting metrics (National Student Clearinghouse Research Center, 2012).

Vertical Transfer

Two recent studies from ACT and the NSCRC (ACT, 2013; NSCRC, 2012) provide insight into community college students who later transfer to a university in pursuit of a bachelor's degree. The ACT report indicates that 11 percent of undergraduates in the 2011 ACT cohort had co-enrolled and another 41 percent attended more than one institution. Furthermore, 29 percent of those who began at a community college transferred, and 14 percent of those who began at a four-year institution transferred to a two-year institution. A 2012 NSCRC study revealed that 45 percent of all 2010 bachelor degree–earning students previously attended a community college. Of these, 40 percent attended a community college for one or two terms, 19 percent for three or four, and 12 percent for at least ten terms. Although some variation exists among the findings, the magnitude of transfer behavior underscores the need for SEM professionals to analyze student enrollment patterns to understand the behavior of this population and to determine how to recognize factors leading to transfer student success.

Predictors of Transfer

An understanding of the factors that led to transfer and to transfer student success provides crucial information for enrollment planners. Luke Wood, Carlos Nevarez, and Adriel Hilton (2012) explored which community college student characteristics may predict whether a student transfers. Their findings echoed past studies: Students who were younger, had a higher high school GPA (Pascarella & Terenzini, 2005), were not first-generation students (Goldrick-Rab & Pfeffer, 2009), and were enrolled full-time (Dougherty & Kienzl, 2006) were more likely to transfer than other students. Additionally, students who were engaged with faculty outside of class, met with an academic advisor, or partici-pated in study groups, student clubs, or sports (competitive or not) were more likely to transfer. These variables intersect with qualitative research findings documenting an intimidation factor linked to transferring from a community college to a four-year institution. Students active on campus and others with support networks were more likely to overcome their fears and transfer (Chin-Newman & Shaw, 2013). Other research indicates that being single and not having children positively affect student transfer (Dougherty & Kienzl, 2006; Roska, 2006; Wang, 2009) and that increased credit loads and continuous en-rollment also influence student transfer and post-transfer success (Doyle, 2009; Li, 2010). Additional findings of the NSCRC (Hossler et al., 2012a) indicate that full-time students transferred at nearly the same rate as part-time students. De-spite this similarity in percentages, it is important to recognize that "full-time transfer students transferred earlier in their careers than part-time students did" (Hossler et al., 2012a, p. 24), suggesting that the number of accumulated credits *may* influence student transfer.

Limitations of Transfer Student Completion Data

IPEDS is the primary national instrument that determines student completion rates and is often relied upon by regulatory agencies, the media, and other sourc-es to indicate low rates of completion for U.S. colleges and universities. However, this data set tracks only those students who are full-time, first-time, freshman; it fully ignores transfer students. Such limited accounting shortchanges both the initial and transfer institution(s) in regards to student completion data.

Given the increasing volume of transfer students and multiple patterns of transfer, a recent NSCRC report (Hossler et al., 2012a) noted that "a new view may prove useful, one in which students are the unit of analysis and institutions are viewed as stepping stones along a diverse set of educational paths" (p. 8). Therefore, a skilled SEM professional must develop institution-specific mechanisms to understand transfer student data (both those who transfer out *and* those who transfer in), which can then support development of institutional completion goals. Several institutions are now tracking each fall cohort over a six-year period to determine whether each student is still enrolled, graduated from their home institution, is enrolled at another institution, graduated from another institution, or is no longer enrolled without completing. Such knowledge provides SEM professionals with the data needed to manage and support students.

STUDENT SWIRL AND TRANSFER PATTERNS

Alfredo de los Santos and Irene Wright (1990) studied the enrollment patterns of students attending the Maricopa Community College System (Arizona) and coined the phrase "student swirl" to describe the enrollment patterns of nearly 33 percent of Arizona State University graduates who attend MCCS. In a later study, Alexander McCormick (2003) expanded upon the definition of student swirl and identified six different types of transfer students: trial enrollers, supplemental enrollers, consolidated enrollers, special program enrollers, serial transfers, and non-degree students. More recent studies of transfer attendance patterns have examined the impact of swirl on departures from and returns to an individual institution (Johnson & Muse, 2012), swirl as a pathway for academically dismissed students (Yan & Tom, 2009), and lateral transfer between community colleges (Bahr, 2012). Because each of these transfer patterns calls for different SEM strategies, SEM leaders must understand the transfer behavior of students moving in and out of their institution. This section describes these transfer patterns and offers suggestions for working with each type of student.

Trial and Supplemental Enrollers

The first two of McCormick's (2003) patterns are *trial enrollers,* who take a few courses to explore the possibility of transferring, and *supplemental enrollers,* who enroll in few courses with the purpose of accelerating progress to degree by taking courses during break periods. Creating internal mechanisms to identify students and monitoring credits transferred to the "home" institution allows the institution to improve engagement with and support for this population. By providing clear, accessible transfer equivalency information, informed advisors, and a mechanism for pre-approval of outside coursework—all of which are key elements of targeted SEM planning—the home institution benefits by keeping students on track for graduation; the supplemental institution benefits from additional tuition revenue.

Consolidated and Special Program Enrollers

From the student perspective, the lines between community colleges and universities are often blurred, and as such, many choose what practitioners would call "nontraditional enrollment patterns." McCormick (2003) identified this population as *consolidated enrollers,* who intentionally select courses at a variety of institutions to complete a degree program at a home institution; variations include students who alternate enrollment at two institutions or enroll simultaneously at two or more institutions. Those interested in opportunities not offered by their home school may engage in *special program enrollment* to take advantage of courses not offered by the home institution. Although these populations may not be large nationally, individual institutions may see greater numbers, especially those with multiple institutions in close geographic proximity. Skilled SEM leaders will identify such enrollment behaviors and develop clear pathways to assist in student degree completion.

Serial Transfers

In contrast to the purposefulness of consolidated and special program enrollers, other students do not find a fit, and as a consequence they may move from institution to institution as *serial transfers*. These students frequently move between institutional types because of poor grades, financial constraints, lack of clear goals, family pressure, or a misunderstanding of how to navigate higher education. Identifying these students and providing the necessary support are keys to success for the individuals and the institutions involved.

For serial enrollers who begin at community colleges, early identification and achieving milestones can end the school-to-school-to-school transfer cycle. According to the NSCRC (Hossler et al., 2012a), only one in five community college students transfer to a four-year institution. Of those, 60 percent earn a bachelor's degree within four years. However, the percentage of bachelor's degree earners jumps to 71 percent for students who complete an associate degree prior to transferring. Populations most likely to begin at a community college with the intent of transferring include students of color, first-generation students, recent immigrants, students who work while attending school, single parents, and nontraditional students.

SEM leaders who identify vertical transfer behavior have several tools to help these students reach these milestones. Agreements allowing for reverse transfer of credit from a four-year to a two-year institution can assist by providing credentials to a student who left a two-year institution before earning a degree, while also boosting the community college's completion rate. "Recruit back" programs identify students who left an institution without earning a degree and provide support services to get these students re-engaged in their education. Financial counseling can also assist students with making wise decisions about borrowing and enrolling, putting them back on the path toward graduation.

Non-Degree Students

McCormick (2003) labeled students who take courses for personal or professional benefits without intent to earn a credential as *non-degree students*. SEM leaders should be aware of the demographics, enrollment patterns, and motives of these populations. Each year, hundreds of colleges and universities offer free or substantially reduced tuition for senior citizens who enroll in courses on traditional campuses; similar opportunities also exist for high school students. When non-degree offerings and programs are managed correctly, institutions can benefit from such arrangements, as older students can contribute real-world examples in the classroom, inspire traditional age students to continue pursuing their education goals, while remaining intellectually active.

Simple Transfer Patterns

In the absence of swirl, descriptors of transfer behavior have focused on the characteristics of the sending and receiving institutions. As a result, students are often described as *reverse transfers* (who transfer from a four-year to a two-year institution), *lateral transfers* (who transfer between two-year institutions), and *vertical transfers* (who transfer from a two-year to a four-year institution).

Frequently, reverse transfer students behave similarly to McCormick's (2003) supplemental enrollers. According to the NSCRC (Hossler et al., 2012b) completion rates at the four-year institution can be predicted based on when and how long the reverse transfer student is enrolled at the two-year institution, as well as by supplemental enrollment behavior. For example, although nearly 81 percent of summer-only course takers returned to their original institution, only 16.6 percent of students who took community college classes at other times of the year returned to their original institution. Reverse transfer students who took a community college class during summer term had completion rates of nearly 78 percent at the four-year institution, as compared to 58 percent of students who never enrolled in a summer class at a community college (Hossler et al., 2012b). Summer attendance seems to be predictive of success and creates an opportunity for partnerships between institutions.

Lateral transfer students, on the other hand, transfer between the same institutional types. The reasons for transferring from one four-year institution to another vary widely and include financial considerations, fit, programs offered, personal circumstances, and more. According to Peter Bahr (2009), the number of lateral two-year transfer students is second only to students engaged in vertical transfer, with estimates suggesting that two of every fifteen community college students transfer to another community college at some point in their academic careers. Bahr identifies those students most engaged with two-year lateral transfer activity as male, traditional age, African-American or Asian-American, or those with less grant aid, confirming the findings of other researchers (Nora & Rendón, 1990; Wood, Nevarez, & Hilton, 2011).

As recent research and the variety of transfer patterns suggest, transfer students are not one size fits all. Managing variation in transfer behavior and transfer motives and demographics demands an analysis of the patterns associated with a particular institution's transfer population. Only by understanding these patterns can SEM leaders manage enrollment by providing key services that match the needs of the transfer population.

CREATING A TRANSFER CULTURE

For students who are working toward their educational goal via transfer or enrolling at multiple institutions, there exists a need for appropriate support services and transfer-friendly policies (Ellis, 2013; Goldrick-Rab & Roska, 2008; Hagedorn, 2004). Although the list of programs and services supporting transfer students is extensive, the following sections highlight many best practices regarding recruitment, advising, transfer credit practices, articulation agreements, and state-level agreements, among others. Such foundational work creates a campus culture supportive of transfer students; provides the foundation needed to attract, enroll, and support this population; and is integral to any successful SEM planning process.

Transfer Student Recruitment

A key element of any successful SEM planning process is understanding an institution's "enrollment funnel," or the number of students at each step of the pre-enrollment process, from inquiry through first-day attendance. For vertical transfer students, the enrollment funnel operates differently from the typical first-year student funnel and follows a different timeline. The first-year funnel has traditionally been wide at the prospect stage, narrowing from inquiry to application. The transfer funnel is much narrower with a substantial number of applicants for whom the original source is the application itself (oftentimes referred to as "stealth applicants"). Given the smaller volume, a more comprehensive, personalized approach to recruiting transfer students is recommended. Table 7.1 reveals that large number of transfer students who apply, are admitted, and pay their deposit matriculate.

Table 7.1: 2010 Admissions funnel benchmarks for four-year and two-year institutions

	Application to admit (all applications)	Application to admit (complete applications)	Admit to enroll (yield)	Deposit/ confirmed to enroll
Public universities	64 percent	88 percent	66 percent	88 percent
Private colleges and universities	56 percent	90 percent	53 percent	86 percent

Source: Adapted from Noel-Levitz (2010)

A successful transfer recruitment plan must be specific to the transfer population and must consider the enrollment motivations of transfer students. Although no two transfer students are the same, they generally have three major motivations when deciding where to enroll. The first is applicability of transfer credits towards degree requirements; flexibility in how credits apply and communicating this information at the earliest possible point in the funnel is critical to helping transfer students make enrollment decisions. Second, institutions must provide admissions or academic advisors who can best guide transfer students on their options. Finally, although traditional, college-savvy students tend to be interested in the college experience, transfer students tend to be more concerned about attainment of degree goals, building pathways to a successful career, or admission to graduate/professional school (Noel-Levitz, 2010).

Successful transfer student recruitment depends on the following strategies (Engle, 2010):

- Create a specific recruitment plan for transfer students.
- Build and track a separate transfer inquiry pool.
- Communicate directly with transfer students.
- Have staff who can cater to the needs of transfer students.
- Create new articulation agreements and strengthen existing ones.

The first three strategies speak to differentiating the mode and message for transfer students; the fourth speaks to the advising component. Transfer recruiters must be able to answer the key questions of how credits transfer and apply to a degree. The fifth speaks to partnerships. With a population of many stealth applicants making decisions prior to applying, building relationships with those in a position to influence student behavior at the community college is crucial. By including transfer students as part of recruitment planning and tailoring communications directly to their needs, both two- and four-year schools can achieve recruitment success.

Transfer Centers

The question of who is responsible for advising a transfer student is a difficult one. Should it be the home institution? The destination institution? Surprisingly, several studies found that neither institution does enough in this capacity and instead, the student frequently relies on his or her ability to advocate and/or investigate on their own or seeks out advice from friends and family (Flaga, 2006; Gard, Paton, & Gosselin, 2012; Townsend, 1995). That aside, best practices do exist in terms of serving transfer students, especially with regard to advising and advising-like activities both before and after transfer.

A key tenet of core SEM elements is to have the right staff, with the right training, connecting with students at the right time. To this end, universities wanting to court community college transfer students actively will not only build strong working relationships with their community college partners (the right training), but will also hold frequent admissions sessions at the community colleges. The "best of the best" will not only provide this information via admissions staff, but will include university advisors to provide students with on-the-spot guidance toward university course requirements (the right staff). Moreover, an increasing number of community colleges and/or universities are offering transfer seminar courses, which familiarize students with transfer options, services at destination colleges or universities, and guidance to help insure course transferability before transfer (the right time).

Transfer Credit Practices

The types of credits earned by students who swirl challenge institutional transfer credit policies through various programs that accelerate traditional models of credit accumulation. Often coined *prior learning assessment*, this form of college credit is growing in importance for higher education professionals. Students under the prior learning assessment umbrella will often include high school graduates with enough credits to earn an associate degree, students with Advanced Placement (AP) or College Level Examination Program (CLEP) credits, adults with military or job-training credentials, and successful completers of "massively open online courses," or MOOCs. Although many accreditation agencies require that institutions publish transfer credit policies, institutions truly wishing to cater to transfer students must expand their scope of thinking to include all nontraditional means of earning credit and actively develop *and promote* policies to support these students.

Articulation Agreements

Prior research indicates that the transfer of credits between institutions is a serious challenge facing most transfer students (Ellis, 2013; Glass & Bunn, 1998). To increase opportunities for the successful transfer of credits, community colleges and universities often will enter into formal agreements regarding specific courses or degrees. The intent of these partnerships, referred to as *articulation agreements*, are to ease a student's transfer between institutions and guarantee transfer of credits toward the receiving institution's general education or major requirements (Gutierrez, 2004). In recent years, several researchers have tackled the question of effectiveness of these types of agreements. Two recent in-depth reports found that state-level articulation agreements do not impact student transfer rates (Anderson, Sun, & Alfonso, 2006; Gross, & Goldhaber, 2009). So why do these articulation agreements fail? Too often, articulation agreements are entered into purely for the sake of publicity, or they are not adhered to, especially when mandated. To create a functional and effective articulation agreement, both institutions must following the key tenets of the agreement, the tenets must have specific outcomes geared toward student completion, the agreements must be available and understandable, and enough students must be available to benefit from the intended outcomes. Even in the case of state and system policies, utility depends on these elements (Bers, 2013). Without these pieces, an articulation agreement is worth little to students and has minimal impact on student success.

In the absence of articulation agreements, students with career and technical coursework often do not receive university-level credit for courses determined to be "non-academic" in nature. For this reason, articulation for students enrolled in career and technical programs occurs on several levels ranging from high school to the baccalaureate. Program-to-program articulation between a two-year institution and a similar program at the four-year school in areas such as agriculture is one example. Specialized bachelor's degrees designed especially for applied degree recipients such as the bachelor of applied technology or the bachelor of applied science are another manifestation. Finally, some states and individual four-year institutions have policies in place allowing career and technical courses to count as elective credit.

State-Level Agreements

There are different approaches to crafting state-level transfer and articulation agreements. In this section we examine these approaches.

Common Course Numbering. Many states, higher education systems, and institutional consortia have adopted *common course numbering systems* that create a more transparent and seamless system of articulation. Common course numbering often appears as actual shared numbering systems but may also refer to course crosswalks or databases using a common number to illustrate course equivalency across institutions. Transferability is ensured as all courses map to the same name and number, which will transfer to the receiving institution on a one-to-one basis with the equivalent courses. As an example, the state of North Dakota facilitates common course numbering among its public and private colleges and universities (including tribal colleges) by having courses with common, transferable content share the same number, the same name, and the same course description (www.ndus.nodak.edu). One of the most robust systems, with 110 institutions participating voluntarily, is the Texas Common Course Numbering System (TCCNS), which features a mix of institutions using either a uniform course designation or other numbering systems but mapping courses to the common designator. Students can use the TCCNS website to verify how courses from one institution map to the common numbering system or select two institutions and compare their courses to the common course matrix (www.tccns.org). Others with shared course designations include systems in Florida, Montana, Nevada, and Utah (McGill, 2010). Several community college systems such as those in Washington, Colorado, and Iowa also share course numbering and course descriptions.

Although common course numbering can be helpful for students, it can also be difficult to implement, it does not eliminate the potential that a student may take unneeded courses, and it does not guarantee that the credits earned will apply to a specific degree program (McGill, 2010). Applied literally, common course numbering may entail modifying information systems at multiple institutions and maintaining dual numbering systems for some time—a time-consuming and expensive process. Common course numbering often applies only to lower division courses and may include only a subset of those, such as courses transferred most frequently or courses that are part of a general education curriculum.

Common Core Requirements. In the United States, community college and university degrees typically require a core component of introductory courses in writing, math, and communications, as well as a minimum number of credit requirements in science, social sciences, and humanities/arts. Referred to as the "common core" or a "general education core," these courses are typically the same across degrees but may vary among degree types. For example, a bachelor of arts degree from institution "A" will have a general education core regardless of the student's major, while the bachelor of science degree will most likely have a slightly different general education core; in both circumstances, the core will remain the same regardless of the student's major.

In attempting to address transferability of credits, several states have adopted common general education requirements shared by *all* public community colleges and universities in that state. Jan Ignash and Barbara Townsend (2001) conducted a survey in 2001 to determine state transfer and articulation practices; results indicated that as many as twenty-four states maintained a general education core curriculum. A Western Interstate Commission for Higher Education (WICHE) survey indicated that fifteen states did so (not all states responded) (Hezel Associates, 2010). Regardless of the numbers, the intent of a common core is to guarantee that the general education portion of a degree—not the major-specific requirements—will be the same as any other institution in the state, thereby making student mobility between institutions more seamless.

Finally, state-level policies that simplify the transfer process can also assist in creating streamlined paths between institutions. Such policies can increase transfer rates (Anderson, Sun, & Alfonso, 2006) and prevent the loss of credits (Ellis, 2013; Roska & Keith, 2008). Such statewide policies have implications for SEM practitioners at two levels. First, it is imperative that SEM practitioners provide the appropriate supports, services, and information to students so that students are aware of common core requirements and their applicability within their current institution and as the student considers transfer. Second, such statewide efforts demonstrate how SEM practitioners can engage outside of their institution to promote student access and success at a broader level by advocating for seamless pathways needed by our increasingly mobile student population.

Block Transfer Degrees. Facilitating transfer of students between institutions, and the associated transfer of credit, has become a focus for many state legislators and higher education leaders. To this end, many states have established *block transfer* agreements and/or degrees, a promising and prevalent practice supporting student transition between the community colleges and universities. Block transfer *agreements* provide students assurance that all credits will be accepted by the receiving institution, fulfilling certain established degree requirements, typically general education requirements. Block transfer *degrees*, on the other hand, not only guarantee transfer of credits, but typically provide an admitted student with junior status at the institution to which the student is transferring and completion of university general education requirements. It is important to note that unless major-specific articulation agreements exist, block transfer degrees do not guarantee junior status within a program of study. According to WICHE (Hezel Associates, 2010), twenty states report having some level of block transfer agreements and thirty-one states have a block transfer degree.

Although the practice of block transfer agreements and degrees has become more popular in recent years, research on their impact on student transfer is scarce. An exception is a four-state study by the Center for the Study of Community Colleges (CSCC) (Kisker, Wagoner, & Cohen, 2011) that examines the alignment between transfer degree policy goals and system efficiencies. The authors identify seven curricula and policy factors that can be used to understand the purpose of transfer degrees: 1) establishing a common general education core; 2) establishing common curricular pre-major and early-major pathways; 3) improving credit applicability; 4) establishing junior status at point of transfer; 5) promoting guaranteed and/or priority four-year institution admission; 6) managing transfer within associate and bachelor's degree credit limits; and 7) developing an acceptance policy for upper division credits. The CCSC report concluded that in the four states included in the study, outcomes data supported the notion that transfer degrees enhance system efficiency and produce cost savings for students.

SEM professionals are in an excellent position to support the development and evaluation of block credit and transfer degrees. This work requires collaboration between sending and receiving institutions and an improvement of the understanding of the transfer process as it relates to students and institutional goals. Moreover, assessment regarding effectiveness of the agreements can identify curricular alignments, as well as where potential new efforts may be needed. Effective block credit programs facilitate student and institutional outcome goals, making them important elements of SEM at two-year and four-year institutions.

Admission and Enrollment Partnership Models

A core element of any successful SEM plan is knowing one's students, albeit demographic characteristics, academic preparedness, or programs of study; most certainly, it also includes knowing student enrollment patterns to include origins and destination of transfer students and providing support services that align with these patterns. Although the range of services can be vast, an emerging best practice focuses on creating institutional partnerships to support student mobility. Such partnerships make visible and support the bridge between the community college and university and hold promise for supporting degree completion. The two-year/four-year partnership continuum (Clemetsen, 2009) provides a model delineating institutional relationships for supporting vertical student transfer, which is often labeled "dual- or co-enrollment" programs. Katharin Peter, Emily Cataldi, and C. Dennis Carroll (2005) reported that "Students who began in public two-year institutions who had co-enrolled had higher rates of bachelor's degree attainments and persistence at four-year institutions than their counterparts who did not co-enroll" (p. 19). Figure 7.1 provides an overview of the range of two-year and four-year college partnerships.

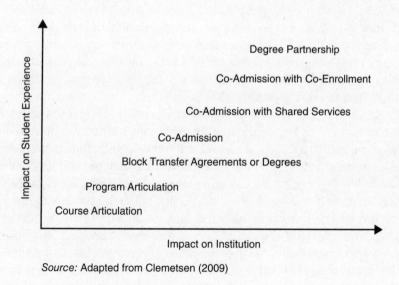

Source: Adapted from Clemetsen (2009)

Figure 7.1 Two-year/four-year partnership continuum

The initial partnership level to support student transfer is grounded in the need for strong academic articulation. The more advanced levels of institutional partnership allow students to create the educational experience they believe best meets their needs, using the resources of more than one institution to accomplish their educational goal.

Strong articulation supports is the foundation for the two-year/four-year partnership continuum; the next level of the partnership extends to developing co-admission programs (or dual enrollment), which may include shared services and guaranteed admission. These programs connect the student with the university early in the transfer process, creating the opportunity for students to make pre-matriculation connections with advisers and, in turn, providing improved course planning.

To illustrate this type of partnership, the Northern Virginia Community Colleges (NOVA) and George Mason University initiated Pathway to the Baccalaureate, which supports student transition from high school to the community college, and then from NOVA to George Mason, allowing students to participate in campus life and early dual enrollment opportunities at both institutions. Admission to George Mason is guaranteed upon completion of a NOVA associate degree and a minimum GPA. Research indicates that students in the program have a first- to second-semester retention rate of 90 percent and a degree completion rate nearly double the overall NOVA rate, as well as positive gains for traditionally underserved populations (Whitmire & Esch, 2010).

A program between the University of Texas at Austin (UTA) and Austin Community College (ACC) called Path to Admission through Co-Enrollment (PACE) targets students who were eligible for automatic admission to UTA based on high school class rank but not admitted due to enrollment caps (University of Texas at Austin, 2013). The program standardizes the existing transfer pathway from ACC to UTA and allows students to access advising and student services at both campuses. Satisfactory completion of the PACE program qualifies students for automatic transfer admission to UTA.

The last levels of two-year/four-year partnerships involve co-admission, co-enrollment, and even coordinated financial aid. Institutions that establish partnerships that coordinate academic, enrollment, and student life actually facilitate student vertical and reverse transfer. Partnerships with extensive coordination and have been developing in Oregon since 1999, for example. The partnership between Oregon State University and Linn-Benton Community College involves co-admission, co-enrollment, acceptance of block transfer degrees, shared housing, buses, student programs, support services, and financial aid. Program data indicate that approximately 40 percent of students who participate in the program complete a bachelor's degree, with graduates averaging nineteen fewer credits than other transfer student graduates (Linn-Benton Community College, 2013).

To date, most of the extant research indicates that transfer students appear to be following unpredictable enrollment patterns. Additionally, these patterns place them at risk of not completing a degree due to a lack of structure for choosing courses and experiences. Institutional partnerships, however, such as those described in this section, offer institutions an opportunity to establish structures to guide and support a student in utilizing resources at multiple institutions in a manner that supports completion.

Reverse Transfer Degrees

Though not a new phenomenon, there is a growing need to factor the "reverse" of the traditional transfer pattern into SEM planning at universities and community colleges. Reverse transfer, first described by Burton Clark (1960) in his report on California junior colleges, is a phenomenon of growing interest as SEM leaders look to improve student transfer and completion. Barbara Townsend and John Dever (1999) described undergraduate reverse transfers as students who started at four-year institutions and transferred to a two-year college for a period of time, and then transferred back to a four-year institution. The review of the research by these authors supported the need for institutional leaders to consider why students move between institutions and that studying reverse transfers offers a new perspective on institutional roles in supporting student achievement. A NSCRC report (Hossler et al., 2012b) substantiates Townsend and Dever's position, finding that 14.4 percent of first-time students who began at a four-year institution enrolled at two-year institutions during the traditional academic year, and 5.4 percent enrolled during a summer period only. Students who were part-time and students who were at public institutions had the greatest percentage transferring to two-year institutions.

Another type of reverse transfer involves the moving of credits from a university back to a community college to award the former community college student an associate's degree. The structured approach for this type of reverse transfer, developed between the University of Texas-El Paso (UTEP) and El Paso Community College (EPCC), has served as a leading model of this type of reverse transfer program. UTEP electronically sends quarterly lower division credits and grades of all current UTEP students who formerly attended EPCC. EPCC then uses its degree audit system to determine whether or not the student has earned an associate degree, contacting the student with updated information as to their progress (Ekal & Krebs, 2011). The program has increased both the graduation rate at the community college and the retention rate at the university. Moreover, early data indicate that students who earn an associate degree through the reverse transfer program are more likely to graduate from UTEP than those who do not (Ekal, personal communication, September 19, 2011).

To scale-up the success of programs such as those described in this chapter, five national foundations are supporting reverse transfer degrees through the

Kresge Foundation's "Credit When It's Due: Recognizing the Value of Quality Associates Degrees" program (Kresge Foundation, 2012). The purpose of the program is to benefit students, and to "fairly credit community colleges for their work in preparing transfer students; clarify the value of sub-baccalaureate degrees by awarding them consistently; and promote efforts to more clearly define the learning outcomes inherent in all associate degrees" (p. 1).

Technology Tools for Transfer

The marriage of technology and student transfer is an important element for SEM. Technology has played two main roles in facilitating transfer. For the transfer student, knowing how credit will move from one institution to another is crucial. Recent technologies have made obtaining this knowledge faster and easier, and receiving institutions providing this service are more popular transfer destinations. Historically, transfer credit evaluation entailed manual course look-up in paper catalogs or microfiche. Today, transfer credit evaluation is automated at most institutions through the use of online systems for researching course information, transfer credit evaluation workflow tools, and national transfer networks providing on-demand equivalencies, some of which are provided by vendors, some through homegrown systems, and others through a combination of the two. The most robust include multiple components that allow users to integrate an extensive library of online catalogs and course descriptions with degree audit, transfer articulation systems, and academic planning tools. Such integration enables students to track how their credits transfer to fulfill various degree requirements, thus answering key questions on course transferability and remaining course requirements. Arizona State University, for example, combines a vendor-supplied product with a homegrown forward-facing system that enables students to enter coursework and instantly see how courses transfer to ASU (https://transfer.asu.edu/credits). University of Northern Iowa's (UNI) Transfer Plan-It program, on the other hand, is a homegrown system that allows prospective students to enter their completed and in-progress coursework, select a UNI major, and receive an instant summary of how courses apply to the major and the remaining requirements (http://uni .edu/admissions/transfer).

Technology tools are utilized also at the state level to facilitate transfer within a single state or system. In late 2009, WICHE and the WICHE Cooperative for Educational Technologies (WCET) conducted a national research project to identify how states use web-based tools to guide transfer students. WCET reviewed twenty-four state transfer credit portals, all of which went beyond simple text and links. Such portals provide a current presentation of transfer information and can be a catalyst for increased inter-institutional cooperation. Although some portals have been in place for almost twenty years, more than half were launched since 2005 (McGill, 2010).

Statewide portals utilize a variety of delivery methods and provide a variety of features. Whether vendor products or homegrown, the portals can include such features as personal accounts for users, customizable views of course and program information, admissions applications, transcript request services, prior learning assessment tools, and transfer appeals mechanisms (McGill, 2010). In Arizona, the state's Academic Program Articulation Steering Committee provides technology tools on its AZTransfer website, where students can research the transferability of their courses, including Advanced Placement and International Baccalaureate credit, and develop a customized academic plan or pathway. The Arizona State System for Information on Student Transfer (ASSIST) enables community colleges to track persistence, time to degree, and other factors. Universities can generate reports related to transfers throughout the system, and the state can track enrollment patterns and success rates (Arizona Board of Regents and Arizona Community Colleges, 2012). Additional examples of state portals include Alabama's STARS (Statewide Transfer and Articulation Reporting System), Florida's FACTS (Florida's Advising, Counseling, and Tracking for Students), Illinois's iTransfer, Minnesota's Transfer, and the University of Texas System's Transfer 101.

Yet another tool allowing for increased efficiency is the electronic transcript and corresponding software that enables automated download of course information at the receiving institution. Electronic transcript exchange services save institutions and students both time and money. As with portals, electronic transcript services are increasingly becoming system-wide services—and sometimes state-funded or even created—with institutions aligned to send and receive via a single product.

The Future of Transfer Student Services

The recent rise and rapid expansion of massive open online courses (MOOCs) is testing assumptions about institutional practices in awarding college credit. Heralded by some as a harbinger of unprecedented change in higher education, MOOCs and other experiments with online pedagogy are beginning to thrive as students seek cost-effective access and convenient delivery. Coursera (https://coursera.org), an online clearinghouse for MOOCs, already has 4.5 million users from around the world and offers courses from eighty-five leading colleges and universities. Although most MOOCs are offered as noncredit courses, the American Council on Education determined that some MOOCs are similar enough to traditional college courses and have sufficient controls in place that they should be eligible for transfer credit (Kolowich, 2013). As the debate gears up, MOOCs and similar iterations are poised to be big players in student transfer.

Although no one can predict the future, it is extremely likely that transfer will continue to be an important issue in higher education as the sources of credit continue to diversify. In the last few years, an explosion in the number of students presenting credit from multiple sources is changing the definition of what constitutes (or should constitute) "learning."

CONCLUSION

Student transfer and mobility is a part of the educational landscape for which SEM leaders must be cognizant. Students are developing educational pathways that do not necessarily follow institutionally structured and preferred progression. The motivation of students to create educational pathways that meet their needs requires that institutions focus their attention on this population. As the diversity of educational options accessed by students grows, it will be imperative for institutions to study student enrollment patterns and to understand the motivations that draw students to these options.

Institutional efforts to meet national calls for accountability regarding degree completion require that institutions make fundamental changes. One distinct avenue within the umbrella of potential changes is an intentional focus on transfer student pathways, programs, and services, and the recognition of transfer as a regular component of student progression. Many institutions have already moved down this pathway, deploying new programs and services and developing institutional partnership all in the name of transfer student success. However, even with all the activity, WICHE president David Longanecker noted that, "while we can identify 'promising practices,' there is so little evidence of what actually works that we still must rely to a great extent on hunches" (2010b, p. vi, WICHE). Regardless, SEM leaders are no longer simply being asked to "improve" practices, but are instead mandated to create greater and greater opportunities for students to succeed; indeed, many institutions face funding streams that focus solely on students reaching specific success metrics. Viewing transfer students services as a key strategy in the race for better completion numbers is an area more than worthy of attention. As this chapter was being written, an article in *The Chronicle of Higher Education* noted that the millions of students who are swirling through higher education are waiting to see if the system will be configured to support their success (Selingo, 2013).

Much of the focus of SEM professionals is too often concerning students enrolled in four-year institutions, forgetting about students enrolled in two-year and certificate programs, and not thinking strategically about serving transfer students. Enrollment professionals need to be informed consumers of the transfer student research and must be engaged in their institution's data so as to reveal the various student pathways. This knowledge allows the institutions to create transparent and appropriately supported pathways that increase the student learning outcome attainment and improve institutional effectiveness in meeting student and institutional goals. In the next chapter, we discuss how admissions decisions are made, which involves much less complexity regarding the admissions decisions of transfer students.

References

ACT. (2013). *The Reality of College Readiness 2013*. Iowa City, IA: ACT. Retrieved from http://www.act.org/readinessreality/13/pdf/Reality-of-College-Readiness-2013.pdf.

Adelman, C. (1999). Answers in the Tool Box: Academic Intensity, Attendance Patterns, and Bachelor's Degree Attainment. Retrieved from http://www2.ed.gov/pubs/Toolbox/index.html.

Adelman, C. (2008). *Turning nomads into transfers*. Washington, DC: American Association of Collegiate Registrars and Admissions Officers. [PowerPoint] Retrieved from http://www.aacrao.org/transfer/Cliff_Adelman.pdf.

Anderson, G., Sun, J., and Alfonso, M. (2006). Effectiveness of statewide articulation agreements on the probability of transfer: A preliminary policy analysis. *The Review of Higher Education*, *29*(3), 261–291.

Arizona Board of Regents and Arizona Community Colleges. (2012). *Articulation and Transfer for Arizona Postsecondary Education*. Tempe, AZ: Academic Program Articulation Steering Committee.

Bahr, P. R. (2009). College hopping: Exploring the occurrence, frequency, and consequences of lateral transfer. *Community College Review*, *36*(4), 271–298.

Bahr, P. R. (2012). Student Flow Between Community Colleges: Investigating Lateral Transfer. *Research In Higher Education*, *53*(1), 94–121.

Bers, T. H. (2013). Deciphering Articulation and State/System Policies and Agreements. *New Directions for Higher Education*, *2013*(162), 17–26.

Chin-Newman, C. S., & Shaw, S. T. (2013). The Anxiety of Change: How New Transfer Students Overcome Challenges. *Journal of College Admission*, (221), 14–21.

Clark, B. C. (1960). The "cooling-out" function in higher education. *American Journal of Sociology*, *65*(6), 569–576.

Clemetsen, B. (2009). Building effective community college/university partnerships. In B. Bontrager & B. Clemetsen (Eds.), *Applying SEM at the Community College*. Washington, DC: American Association of Collegiate Registrars and Admission Officers.

De los Santos, A., Jr., & Wright, I. (1990). Maricopa's swirling students: Earning one-third of Arizona state's bachelor's degrees. *Community, Technical, and Junior College Journal*, *60*(6), 32–34.

Dougherty, K. J., & Kienzl, G. S. (2006). It's not enough to get through the open door: Inequalities by social background in transfer from community colleges to four-year colleges. *Teachers College Record*, *108*(3) 452–487.

Doyle, W. R. (2009). Impact of Increased Academic Intensity on Transfer Rates: An Application of Matching Estimators to Student-Unit Record Data. *Research in Higher Education*, *50*(1), 52–72.

Ekal, D., & Krebs, P. M. (2011). Reverse-Transfer Programs Reward Students and Colleges Alike. *The Chronicle of Higher Education*. Retrieved from http://chronicle.com/article/Reverse-Transfer-Programs/127942.

Ellis, M. M. (2013). Successful community college transfer students speak out. *Community College Journal of Research and Practice, 37*(2), 73–84.

Engel, C.(2011). *Understanding enrollment motives of college transfer students*. Retrieved from http://blog.noellevitz.com/2011/08/25/understanding-enrollment-motives-college-transfer-students/.

Flaga, C. T. (2006). The process of transition for community college transfer students. *Community College Journal of Research and Practice, 30*(1), 3–19.

Gard, D. R., Paton, V., & Gosselin, K. (2012). Student perceptions of factors contributing to community college-to-university transfer success. *Community College Journal of Research and Practice, 36*(11), 833–848.

Glass, J. C., & Bunn, C. E. (1998). Length of time required to graduation for community college students transferring to senior institutions. *Community College Journal of Research and Practice, 22*(3), 239–261.

Goldrick-Rab, S. (2010). Challenges and opportunities for improving community college student success. *Review of Educational Research, 80*(3), 437–469.

Goldrick-Rab, S., & Pfeffer, F. T. (2009). Beyond access: Explaining socioeconomic differences in college transfer. *Sociology of Education, 82*(2), 101–125

Goldrick-Rab, S., & Roska, J. (2008). *A Federal Agenda for Promoting Student Success and Degree Completion*. Washington, DC: Center for American Progress.

Gross, B., & Goldhaber, D. (2009). *Community College Transfer and Articulation Policies: Looking Beneath the Surface*. Seattle: Center on Reinventing Public Education, University of Washington.

Gutierrez, D. A. (2004). Articulation agreements that foster a transfer mentality. In B. C. Jacobs (Ed.), *The College Transfer Student in America: The Forgotten Student*. Washington, DC: American Association of Collegiate Registrars and Admissions Officers.

Hagedorn, L. S. (2004). Traveling Successfully on the Community College Pathway: TRUCCS: The research findings of Transfer and Retention of Urban Community College Students project. Los Angeles: University of Southern California.

Hezel Associates. (2010). *Promising Practices in Statewide Transfer and Articulation Systems*. Boulder, CO: Western Interstate Commission for Higher Education.

Hossler, D., Shapiro, D., Dundar, A., Ziskin, M., Chen, J., Zerquera, D., & Torres, V. (2012a). *Transfer & Mobility: A National View of Pre-Degree Student Movement in Postsecondary Institutions*. Retrieved from http://www.studentclearinghouse.info/signature/2/NSC_Signature_Report_2.pdf.

Hossler, D., Shapiro, D., Dundar, A., Ziskin, M., Chen, J., Zerquera, D., & Torres, V. (2012b). *Reverse Transfer: A National View of Student Mobility from Four-Year to Two-Year Institutions*. Retrieved from http://www.studentclearinghouse.info/signature/3/.

Ignash, J. M., & Townsend, B. K. (2001). Statewide transfer and articulation policies: Current practices and emerging issues. In B. K. Townsend & S. B. Twombly (Eds.), *Community Colleges: Policy in Future Context* (pp. 172–192). Westport, CT: Ablex Publishing.

Johnson, I., & Muse, W. (2012). Student Swirl at a Single Institution: The Role of Timing and Student Characteristics. *Research In Higher Education, 53*(2), 152–181.

Kisker, C. B, Wagoner, R. L., & Cohen, A. M. (2011). *Implementing Statewide Transfer and Articulation Reform: An Analysis of Transfer Associate Degrees in Four States.* Oak Park, CA: Center for the Study of Community Colleges.

Kolowich, S. (2013). American Council on Education Recommends 5 MOOCs for Credit. *The Chronicle of Higher Education.* Retrieved from http://chronicle.com/article/American-Council-on-Education/137155/.

Kresge Foundation. (2012). Kresge and Lumina offer grants to ensure community college transfer students get "credit when it's due" [Press release]. Retrieved from http://kresge.org/news/kresge-and-lumina-offer-grants-ensure-community-college-transfer-students-get-%E2%80%98credit-when-it%E2%80%99s.

Li, D. (2010). They need help: Transfer students from four-year to four-year institutions. *The Review of Higher Education, 33*(2), 207–238.

Linn-Benton Community College. (2013). Degree Partnerships. Retrieved from http://linnbenton.edu/go/degree-partnership.

McCormick, A. (2003). Swirling and Double-Dipping: New Patterns of Student Attendance and Their Implications for Higher Education. *New Directions for Higher Education, 2003*(121), 13–24.

McGill, M. (2010). *Higher Education Web Portals: Serving State and Transfer Needs.* Boulder, CO: Western Interstate Commission for Higher Education.

National Student Clearinghouse Research Center (NSCRC). (2012). *The Role of Two-Year Institutions in Four-Year Success.* Retrieved from http://nscresearchcenter.org/wp-content/uploads/SnapshotReport6-TwoYearContributions.pdf.

Noel-Levitz. (2010). *2010 Admissions Funnel Benchmarks for Four-Year Public and Private Institutions.* Retrieved from https://www.noellevitz.com/documents/shared/Papers_and_Research/2010/2010AdmissionsFunnelReport.pdf.

Noel-Levitz. (2013). *The Attitudes of Second-Year College Students.* Retrieved from https://www.noellevitz.com/papers-research-higher-education/2013/2013-report-the-attitudes-of-second-year-college-students.

Nora, A., & Rendón, L. I. (1990). Determinants of predisposition to transfer among community college students: A structural model. *Research in Higher Education, 31*(3), 235–255.

Pascarella, E. T., & Terenzini, P. T. (2005). *How College Affects Students: A Third Decade of Research.* San Francisco: Jossey-Bass.

Peter, K., Cataldi, E. F., & Carroll, C. D. (2005). *The Road Less Traveled? Students Who Enroll in Multiple Institutions.* Washington, DC: National Center for Education Statistics.

Roska, J. (2006). Does the vocational focus of community colleges hinder students' education attainment? *The Review of Higher Education, 29*(4), 499–526.

Roska, J., & Keith, B. (2008). Credits, time, and attainment: Articulation policies and success after transfer. *Educational Evaluation and Policy Analysis, 30*(3), 236–254.

Selingo, J. J. (2013). The new, nonlinear path through college. *The Chronicle of Higher Education.* Retrieved from http://chronicle.com/article/The-New-Lifelong-Nonlinear/141867/?cid = at&utm_source = at&utm_medium = en.

Townsend, B. K. (1995). Community college transfers students: A case study of survival. *The Review of Higher Education, 18*(2), 175–193.

Townsend, B. K., & Dever, J. T. (1999). What do we know about reverse transfer students? In B. K. Townsend (Ed.), *Understanding the Impact of Reverse Transfer Students on Community Colleges*, New Directions for Community Colleges, *1999*(106), 5–14.

University of Texas at Austin (2013). *Path to Admission Through Co-Enrollment.* Retrieved on September 2, 2013, from http://www.utexas.edu/enrollment-management/programs/pace.

Wang, X. (2009). Baccalaureate attainment and college persistence of community college transfer students at four-year institutions. *Research in Higher Education, 50*(6), 570–588

Wang, X. (2012). Factors contributing to the upward transfer of baccalaureate aspirants beginning at community colleges. *The Journal of Higher Education, 83*(6), 851–875.

Western Interstate Commission for Higher Education (WICHE). (2010). *Promising Practices in Statewide Articulation and Transfer Systems.* Boulder, CO: WICHE.

Whitmire, R., & Esch, C. (2010). *Pathway to the Baccalaureate: How one community college is helping underprepared students succeed.* New America Foundation. Retrieved from http://education.newamerica.net/sites/newamerica.net/files/policydocs/NOVA_Report_Final_2.pdf.

Wood, J. L., Nevarez, C., Hilton, A. A. (2011). Creating a culture of transfer in the community college. *Making Connections, 13*(1), 54–61

Wood, J. L., Nevarez, C., Hilton, A. A. (2012). Determinants of transfer among community college students. *Journal of Applied Research in the Community College, 19*(2), 64–69.

Yan, W., & Tom, P. (2009). Understanding Student Swirl: The Role of Environmental Factors and Retention Efforts in the Later Academic Success of Suspended Students. *Journal of College Student Retention: Research, Theory & Practice, 11*(2), 211–226.

CHAPTER 8

How Admission Decisions Get Made

Jerome A. Lucido

It is the business of a university to provide that atmosphere which is most conducive to speculation, experiment, and creation. It is an atmosphere in which there prevail "the four essential freedoms" of a university—to determine for itself on academic grounds who may teach, what may be taught, how it shall be taught, and who may be admitted to study.

Justice Felix Frankfurter (*Sweezy v. New Hampshire*, 1957, p. 263)

Of the "four essential freedoms" so clearly and forcefully outlined by Justice Frankfurter in *Sweezy v. New Hampshire*, the freedoms this chapter addresses are how colleges and universities determine "who may be admitted to study." What are the "academic grounds" on which this freedom rests and how are they determined and identified? What other factors come into play and for whom? And, finally, how do these factors differ based on the mission, wealth, and prestige of institutions within higher education?

This final chapter of Part II begins this analysis with a few essential points that place the admissions decision in needed perspective. First, as B. Alden Thresher (1966) observed in the seminal monograph, *College Admissions and the Public Interest*, most college admission decisions occur outside the office of admissions, not within it. Although Thresher wrote in 1966, what he said then is still true today: "the process of admission to college is more sociologically than academically driven" (p. 1). When low-income students attend college, they most often enroll at community colleges, career and technical colleges, or local and regional state-assisted colleges and universities (Bastedo & Jaquette, 2011). The opportunity to acquire the advanced collegiate preparation and savvy needed to compete at more selective colleges and universities is more frequently fostered in selective magnet schools, well-resourced suburban schools, and private independent day and boarding schools, where the family income and other social capital needed to gain access to these opportunities are often prerequisites. Moreover, state-based student aid programs and institutional financial assistance programs alike have steadily moved away from awards based upon financial need to awards based upon some form of merit (Heller, 2008). This latter trend takes viable educational options out of reach for many low-income students as subsidies go to students who already have the ability to pay all or a substantial portion of college tuition. As a result of these conditions, a comparatively small subset of students in the United States annually go through the highly competitive admission process that is so often characterized as normative in the popular press.

Further, an examination of how admission decisions are made must reach below the surface of how, technically, an admissions officer evaluates a student's credentials. To understand how admission decisions are made, one must look at three distinct perspectives—those of the student, those of the institution, and those of the society in which the student and institution operate. As we will find, all three have a bearing on how admission policies are constructed, how they are carried out, who benefits from them, and why. Finally, admission policy and practice should be viewed within the overall context of the strategic enrollment goals of the campus. How each institution defines its mission and trajectory is at the foundation of this discussion. Indeed, student, institutional, and societal benefits are mediated through institutional mission and methodology, including the size and mix of students, the blend of academic programs, and the contribution of campus culture to learning and personal development.

PHILOSOPHY AND MISSION IN STUDENT SELECTION

The term "admission," as James Jump (2004) reminded us, is derived from Latin roots and can be translated as "toward the mission" (p. 16). Institutional missions are formulated out of a variety of factors, including locus of control (public versus private), educational classification (two-year, four-year, master's granting, doctoral granting, or research intensive), and educational focus (technical and career, transfer, liberal arts, professional education, STEM (science, technology, engineering, and mathematics), fine and professional arts, comprehensive university, and so on). The philosophy underpinning admission policy, then, is often rooted in one or more of these classifications. Land grant institutions will differ in purpose from an Ivy League school, which will differ in purpose from a community college, which will differ from a regional public university. Decisions about whom to admit and what criteria to use depend on the societal role the institution is required, is compelled, or chooses to pursue (Perfetto & College Entrance Examination Board, 1999).

The devil, they say, is in the details, and how each institution translates its unique mission and purpose can result in a confusing and sometimes conflicting mixture of goals that include academic excellence, access to underrepresented sectors of society, identification and development of talent, sustenance of institutional traditions, and campus financial viability. In an effort to clarify and illuminate the many admission models in practice across the country, the College Board gathered approximately fifty admission deans and directors from American four-year institutions for four "admission models" summits throughout the years of 1998 and 1999. One key outcome of these meetings was the development of a taxonomy of the admission decision-making process—a conceptual model for understanding "the different approaches and challenges implicit in admission selection" (Perfetto & College Entrance Examination Board, 1999, p. 3).

When the taxonomy first appeared, it was clear that two fundamental models of admission were in operation. The first, the eligibility model, depended upon publicly stated admission criteria, usually a pattern of coursework and minimum grade point averages or test scores. In this case, eligibility equaled admission; students who met the eligibility criteria were automatically admitted. The second model, the selectivity model, differed in that students were not evaluated against a static standard but were evaluated relative to others within the applicant pool. In this model, students were considered for admission using a variety of factors. When publicly stated standards existed, those standards acted fundamentally as minimums to be achieved. In other words, whatever means the institutions used to determine eligibility, students were chosen from among those deemed as eligible for admission using factors beyond the minimums. Although both eligibility and selectivity models continue to exist, financial constraints have placed pressure on the number of available spaces across the nation. As a result, even those schools with eligibility models find themselves unable to admit all students who meet stated criteria (Krieger, 2008). Therefore, most institutions use some form of selectivity model.

With this as background, it is important to explore the philosophical underpinnings of admission policy. What is its intent? What mission or missions is it designed to serve? The taxonomy serves this purpose by providing a useful compendium of constructs that undergird existing policies and practices. Viewing the information in this chapter through the following lenses will broaden one's understanding of the elements of the admission decision-making process. Indeed, most colleges and universities draw from several of these theoretical foundations to align their policies and practices with their missions.

PHILOSOPHICAL BASES FOR ADMISSIONS DECISION-MAKING

The real value in spending time with the following nine categories is in the elucidation and evaluation of admission criteria and decision-making processes (Perfetto & College Entrance Examination Board, 1999). Which of these philosophical constructs operate at the institution? Which are most reflective of the mission? Which are in play due to factors beyond the campus, such as financial conditions? How can these constructs lead to better alignment of admission practices with institutional mission? As this analysis turns to admission criteria and how they ultimately come together in decision-making, readers are asked to consider the questions offered here in light of how they bear on individual campuses and how the system operates as a whole.

Eligibility-Based Models

- **Entitlement:** Higher education is an inalienable right and should be made available to everyone.

- **Open Access:** College is a natural progression after high school and should be made available to everyone who is qualified.

Performance Based Models

- **Meritocracy:** Access to higher education is a reward for those who have been most academically successful.

- **Character:** Access to higher education is a reward for personal virtue, dedication, perseverance, community service, and hard work.

Student Capacity to Benefit Models

- **Enhancement:** The goal of higher education is to seek out and nurture talent.

- **Mobilization:** Higher education is the "great equalizer" and must promote social and economic mobility.

Student Capacity to Contribute Models

- **Investment:** Access to higher education should promote the greater good and further the development of society.

- **Environmental/Institutional**: The admissions selection process is designed to meet the enrollment goals and unique organizational needs of the admitting institution while promoting the overall quality of students' educational experience.

- **Fiduciary:** Higher education is a business, and access must first preserve the institution's fiscal integrity (Perfetto & College Entrance Examination Board, 1999, p. 5–7).

Admission Criteria

Unless an institution is fully open—for example, without criteria for admission—some level of academic achievement is needed for consideration for admission. Nearly all post-secondary educational options, by definition, require completion of high school and proof of graduation in the form of high school transcripts. Beyond this, the array of criteria most frequently used for initial entry (freshman/first term admission) may include all or some of the following: rigor of high school coursework completed; grades earned and grade point average; rank-in-class; standardized test scores (SAT, ACT); scholastic and extracurricular honors, awards, accomplishments, and participation; personal statements and essays; and letters of recommendation (Blackburn, 1990; Camara & Kimmel, 2005; Ciompi, 1993). For students transferring from one college to another, a review of all previous college work completed and grades received are the usual criteria.

In the United States, admissions officers focus heavy attention on freshman/first-year admission, so a closer look at the criteria most frequently considered and their role in the admission decision are discussed in the following sections. Together, these factors provide the foundational information on which the admission decision rests. Other factors, including student interviews in some segments of the private college sector, also contribute.

As readers begin their progression through the criterion most frequently considered, however, it is important to state at the outset that admission decision-makers should conduct regular validity studies to understand the contribution of the elements that they use in decision-making to the prediction of grade point average and persistence on the campus. Some elements will contribute more to predictions of success than will others, and these elements may vary from campus to campus and over time (Young & Kobrin, 2001). Finally, it is equally important to state that some elements may be difficult to capture quantitatively, but this does not mean that they are not valuable. New research on non-cognitive variables, for example, demonstrates their promise in predicting persistence in college and effectiveness in the workplace (Kyllonen, 2008).

High School Coursework The bedrock of college admission decisions is the depth and breadth of the high school curriculum attempted and completed. Indeed, movements to make educational curricula across states more uniform and rigorous are responses to broadening college access through better preparation. (For example, see Common Core's State Standard Initiative website, "Preparing America's students for success," at http://www.corestandards.org.) Statewide standards at public universities typically outline a pattern of courses that include a number of years of study in designated subject matter areas.

Although the number of years of study and the requirements in each subject area may vary, a typical array of such standards is as follows:

- Four years of English
- Three or four years of mathematics, including Algebra I and Algebra II
- Three years of science, including one year of laboratory science
- Two years of social studies, including American history and government
- Two years of foreign language (taken in the same language)
- One or two years of fine arts (not always required)
- One or more years of electives from the above subject areas

The A–G requirements in California, for example, are an array of such requirements. Generally, students who attempt and complete a pattern of coursework such as A–G or the preceding list are considered prepared for college-level coursework (University of California, 2013). Nonetheless, selective colleges often expect greater numbers of years of study within the subject matter areas and coursework at higher levels such as honors or Advanced Placement courses. Further, particular majors may specify additional coursework or require flexibility in the pattern of coursework. For example, engineering schools may require physics and advanced mathematics, while music schools will expect years of music study that may deter students from taking the full array of coursework in the preceding list.

Grades and Grade Point Average The grades earned in each course, typically beginning in the ninth grade, are reviewed in admission decision-making for both eligibility (in the case that a C grade or better is required, for example) and for competitiveness. Grades are most useful to determine the extent to which a student has met the expectations of the teacher and requirements of the course within each school's context. Grades have limitations in that they do not tell admission officers about the particular strengths and weaknesses of a student within a course; rather, they are an overall indicator of achievement through the duration of the course. The grade point averages for a particular grading period, an academic year, and a high school career are fundamental indicators of student achievement over time. Therefore, they provide a useful comparative indicator of student competitiveness over an academic career. Patterns, weaknesses, trends, and consistency are noted in the admission review.

Rank-in-Class Rank-in-class is a mathematical calculation of a student's academic achievement relative to other students in the class. In eligibility models such as those used to specify minimum requirements at public universities, class rank, for example ranking in the top half or top quarter of the class, is sometimes used as a threshold requirement. In the selectivity model, when

colleges evaluate student credentials within the context of their pool of applicants, a traditional way to compare applicants is to consider how well they
have performed against their current set of peers. Class rank is a useful indicator of this construct. However, this has become more difficult to ascertain in
recent years as many secondary schools, in the belief that providing class rank
disadvantages some of their students in the admission process, have ceased to
provide class rank on high school transcripts. As a result, a recent poll of the
National Association of College Admission Counseling (NACAC) showed that
the influence of class rank on admission decisions has been diminishing in
importance (Clinedinst, Hurley, & Hawkins, 2011).

Standardized Testing National measures of aptitude, reasoning skill, and content mastery, including the SAT, ACT, and SAT Subject Tests, are utilized widely
in college admissions. Given the vast variation in high school opportunity,
curriculum offerings, standards within courses, and grading practices, these assessments measure student achievement on educationally relevant constructs
and place them on a national score distribution. Standardized tests are useful
for the purpose noted here, but they are not without complexity and controversy. Indeed, there is widespread misuse of scores, including overreliance on
them as measures of student quality on campus, in national rankings, and
in comparing campuses. Space does not permit a longer discussion of these
and other issues, but ample literature is available for investigation. Additional
discussion of standardized testing can be found later in the section, "Equity,
Fairness, and the Place of Race as a Consideration."

Application Information The information and manner in which students
present themselves on the application for admission provide numerous additional opportunities to evaluate the skills, level of engagement, and personal
qualities of students. Academic honors and awards, school and community
involvement, leadership positions held, work and volunteer experience, and
more provide admission decision-makers with valuable insight into what, how,
where, and how deeply students are engaged in pursuits outside the classroom
(Blackburn, 1990; Ciompi, 1993).

Essays Essays and short-answer questions are elements of many selective admission processes. What students write, and how well they write it, is assessed
by admission evaluators to gain insight into how students think, what they are
passionate about, and how well they express themselves.

Recommendations Counselor and teacher recommendations provide insight
into a student's academic and personal strengths, contributions to school and
community, and personal qualities, and they can explain irregularities that may

be evident in an academic record. Recommendations are a valuable asset in understanding the student's role in the school setting and in gaining a comprehensive understanding of the student.

OUTSIDE THE LINES: SPECIAL CONSIDERATIONS AND CLAIMS ON ADMISSION SPACES

Foundational factors are important in making admission decisions, but they are supplemented based upon a variety of factors including institutional educational objectives, financial considerations, and external influences on the campus. Indeed, there are many claims on admission spaces at a given college or university. A brief look at some of these factors is needed prior to addressing how the many factors contribute to decision-making.

Special Talent

Among the objectives of colleges and universities is the nurturance of special talent. As a result, students who possess exceptional talent in areas such as music, art, theatre, dance, and creative writing may, and often do, receive consideration for their talent as they populate the programs designed to nurture them.

Athletics

Athletics could be included in the special talent area—there is special talent nurtured and demonstrated in this arena to be sure. However, it is primarily extracurricular programs rather than academic ones that nurture this set of talents, and student athletes enroll in programs across the curriculum. Special consideration is applied to the applications of prospective student athletes to fill the rosters of athletic programs for reasons that include student athlete development, school pride and affiliation, competitive stature, alumni engagement, fundraising, and student recruitment.

Diversity

The educational value of student diversity has been established in U.S. Supreme Court cases (such as *Regents of the University of California v. Bakke*, 1978), educational research, and university mission and purpose statements; Bowen & Bok, 1998; Milem, 2003). Although a topic of national debate, considerations of student diversity are part of admission decision-making in the selective admission model. These considerations include family income, first-generation college students, geographic diversity, and cultural diversity. Consideration of race in the admission process has been before the Supreme Court in four cases to date (one is under consideration as this chapter is being written). In general, these cases were brought by white students who claimed that they had been denied admission even though their test scores and grades were better than those of minority students who had been admitted. In each case, the consideration of race as one factor among many in the admission process has been affirmed by the courts (*Regents of the University of California v. Bakke,*1978; *Grutter v. Bollinger,* 2013) or left unchanged and sent back to lower courts for further review (Fisher, 2013). A more thorough discussion of the courts and race-conscious admission follows.

Globalization/Internationalization

The United States is a prime destination for higher education across the globe (Fischer, 2013). Further, globalization has emerged as an educational goal in American higher education (Lucido, 2000). Additionally, U.S. institutions of higher education have increasingly viewed international students as a source of tuition revenue (Stephens, 2013). Accordingly, international students are afforded places on campus as an essential resource to foster cross-cultural understanding, based on their academic ability and their ability to contribute to financial stability and sustainability. Therefore, although international students add to the cultural and educational diversity of a campus, they are sought for reasons that extend beyond diversity.

Alumni/Legacy

In the selectivity model, students with a history of family enrollment at a given institution are often given additional consideration. This preference can be substantial in highly selective universities (Bowen & Bok, 1998). Moreover, it is a staple of private college culture and occurs in some selective public campuses as well. (Hemel, 2007; Kahlenberg, 2010a). The practice, however, is not without critics; it has been attacked as "affirmative action for the rich." Indeed, legacy admission is cited as benefiting more students than race-conscious affirmative action policies and disproportionately benefiting wealthy white students (Kahlenberg, 2010b).

Influence of Donors/Legislators/and Other Pressure Points

An analysis of admission factors would be incomplete without mention of pressure points that can be placed on admission decisions. These include the influence of donors and legislators that hold the purse strings that support higher education. Here, the press has revealed legislative intervention (Cohen, 2013), and others have documented that children and relations of prominent and potential donors can receive a leg up in college admission (Golden, 2006).

Financial Considerations: Full Payers and Net Tuition Revenue

Being aware of student and family financial resources is not a new phenomenon in college admission. However, as public sources of support for higher education have become a smaller share of institutional revenue, colleges and universities have become more tuition-dependent. Increasingly, admission recruitment strategies target students who can pay all or a substantial part of their full college costs. Accordingly, family resources have become an increasing factor in college admission selection. Need-blind admission, where admission decision-makers are unaware of family resources, is practiced only among a very well-resourced tier of institutions (Kiley, 2012). Being need-aware, when family resources can be considered in decision-making, is the normative practice.

EQUITY, FAIRNESS, AND THE PLACE OF RACE AS A CONSIDERATION

This discussion has presented numerous factors that are used in various weights and ways to arrive at admission decisions. It has not, however, yet arrived at methods in which the interplay of these factors result, or should result, in choices of students. It is the complex nature of this process that makes arriving at a summary so difficult. Indeed, some of the factors discussed so far, perhaps all of the factors, can be richly debated as to their educational value, fairness, and objectivity. College admission is one place where the meritocratic and the egalitarian impulses of the American character play out in both competing and complementary ways.

What is meritorious today? Is merit represented in academic brilliance and talent, or is it represented in a promising low-income student who works to keep the family afloat? Is it in having more physicians who return to practice in Latino neighborhoods where health care is poor, or is it in nurturing the national winners in speech and debate—our next legislators? The answer, of course, is yes to all of the above. But when there are not enough spaces for all of them, how does one decide? Moreover, how can these decisions be made using equitable means and measures?

To consider this, I draw upon egalitarian impulses, those that posit that students should have an equal opportunity to compete for spaces on their merits and by taking advantage of the opportunities presented to them. What is it that permits an examination of highly accomplished students who attend schools with an enriched curriculum of Advanced Placement courses to be conducted alongside those students with more modest accomplishments but who rise above their peers in a setting where few go on to college? One can begin by asking if the objective measures in play are truly objective.

Limitations and Considerations of Equity in Objective Criteria

High school grades, class rank, and standardized test scores are the most ubiq-
uitous of objective criteria. Each provides numbers that can easily be compared.
However, grade inflation and alternative methods of weighting grades have rendered grade point averages difficult to compare from school to school. Indeed,
college admission units may calculate their own grade point average or develop
a local rating schema for grades achieved in order to evaluate classroom performance across the applicant pool on a reasonably comparable scale. Further, admission decision-makers attempt to be aware of the grading patterns in each
school, doing so through the examination of the school profile, which contains
courses offered, grade distributions, and profiles of the community served.

Standardized test scores have the advantage of being a common assessment
and therefore a common performance measure. However, study after study
has confirmed that test score achievement is positively correlated to the family
income of students (Camara & Schmidt, 1999). Students with high family
incomes attend better-resourced schools with stronger teachers and curricular
offerings, and they perform better on these measures. Such students also
have more opportunity to avail themselves of test preparation courses than do
low-income students. As a result, standardized test scores are not necessarily
indicative of the relative merit of one student to another. Indeed, it can be
argued that strict use of test score criteria is not objective at all. Rather, it is
disadvantageous to low-income populations that do not have the curricular
offerings and other educational opportunities to compete on a level playing
field (Soares, 2012). In other words, the arena of standardized testing tilts
toward wealth. It is important, then, that admission decision-makers use test
scores to understand the constructs being tested rather than as strict measures
of student merit.

Evaluating in Context: Toward Giving All Applicants Their Best Chance

As we were reminded by Thresher (1966) earlier in the chapter, admission
is more sociologically than academically determined. Given unequal educational opportunity, it is incumbent upon admission evaluators to strive to
understand the conditions under which each applicant has performed and to
make judgments based on the context of those conditions. The high school
profile provides critical school data, and the application for admission can reveal important details about the level of educational attainment in the family,
family occupation and income, and the student responsibilities outside of the
school. As judgments are made, understanding performance in the context of
opportunity is a critical component of equitable decision-making in the college
admission process.

On Race-Conscious and Race-Neutral Alternatives:
The Courts and Student Selection

Colleges and universities may wish to consider race as a factor in student admissions for a number of reasons. They may wish to reflect the community or the state in which they reside; they may seek to nurture talent and develop leadership and skill in populations that have been historically underrepresented in higher education; and they may seek to enhance student learning and cross-cultural competence by adding diverse perspectives in the classroom and throughout the campus (La Noue, 2003; Milem, 2003). The most direct route to accomplish a campus that is racially diverse is to use race as a factor in the admission decision (Tienda, 2013). Indeed, race-conscious policies are defined as "those that involve explicit racial classifications . . . where race is (*sic*) an express factor used in evaluating applicants" (Coleman, Palmer, & Winnick, 2008, p. 4). As noted earlier, the Supreme Court has heretofore upheld the use of race as a factor in college admission, but colleges and universities are by no means able to admit students solely because of their race. In the Bakke case in 1978, the Court ruled that use of race was a compelling state interest, yet it also ruled that racial quotas were not permissible. In June 2003, in the case of *Grutter v. Bollinger*, the Court ruled that the University of Michigan Law School could give preferential treatment to minorities in the admission process. However, also in June 2003, in the case of *Gratz v. Bollinger*, the court struck down a race-conscious admission policy that gave specific weight to minority applicants that was used in undergraduate admissions at the University of Michigan. Shortly thereafter, the Court ruled that race can be used in university admission programs but that it cannot be an exclusive factor. In other words, race can be used as one factor among many in a comprehensive review of student files.

Although the use of race as a factor in college admission continues to be the law of the land, a number of states have passed voter referenda to prevent this practice in public institutions, including Michigan, Washington, and California. In 1999, Florida Governor Jeb Bush announced an executive order that eliminated the use of race in admissions at public universities within the state as part of his One Florida initiative. In these and other states where it is impermissible to use race in college admission at public universities, efforts to increase racial diversity on public campuses must be achieved using race-neutral means. Indeed, race-neutral policies, by definition, are "those that, with respect to both operation . . . and intent, are neutral" (Coleman et al., 2008). Race, in these cases, is not a factor in the admission process.

Whether racial diversity can be achieved through race-neutral means is an open question. In Texas, the use of race in admissions was halted in 1996 by order of the state's attorney general. Minority enrollment at the University of Texas at Austin plummeted immediately thereafter (Arnold & Wertheimer, 2002). As a result, and as a substitute for race-conscious admissions, a plan known as *House Bill 588* was enacted. Commonly known as the "Top Ten Percent Rule," the bill guaranteed admission at all Texas public universities for each high school student in the state who graduated in the top 10 percent of the high school class (Ryan, 2013). Many observers pointed to the irony of this plan, which relied upon racially segregated high schools to produce diversity on college campuses (Powell, 2011). Yet, UT-Austin returned to previous levels of diversity after implementing the rule (Wilgoren, 1999). A more recent study, however, took into account growth and application trends over the period that the rule was exclusively in effect (1998–2003). Evidence from the study demonstrates that African American and Hispanic students in Texas actually lost more ground to their white and Asian counterparts than they would have if a race-conscious policy had remained in place. To put it more succinctly, the study showed that these groups would have gained substantially in representation had they retained the share of admits they had when affirmative action was in place (Harris & Tienda, 2010).

The University of Texas reinstituted race as a factor for applicants below the top 10 percent in 2003. In 2008, Abigail Fisher sued the university, claiming the use of race worked against her. In 2013, the Supreme Court remanded the case back to the Fifth Circuit Court of Appeals for further review as this book was being written. It is clear that courtroom battles over the use of race in college admissions are not over. In the meantime, in the eyes of the Supreme Court, and when not otherwise prevented through referenda or executive order, the use of race remains permissible as one factor among many in comprehensive review. It is also clear that the exploration and evaluation of race-neutral alternatives remain important, as the use of race may yet be overturned or judged as permissible only if race-neutral alternatives are demonstrated to be ineffective (Lipper & Coleman, 2013).

The Role of Financial Need in Admissions

The matters of need-blind and need-aware admission plans were briefly discussed earlier in the section, "Financial Considerations: Full Payers and Net Tuition Revenue," and this issue, as well as many others here, would benefit from the treatment of a full chapter on its own. Given space limitations, it is important to reiterate that financial considerations play an increasingly important role in college admission decisions. Ideally, students would not be turned away because they do not have the resources to pay for college. This remains true in a very small percentage of institutions, particularly those that are not highly dependent on tuition for resources—that is, institutions with large endowments. Most institutions, however, derive a large portion of student aid from the tuition revenue that they generate. In these cases, student aid competes with faculty salaries, new campus initiatives, and campus maintenance for tuition revenue dollars. These campuses, then, are limited in the number of students to which they can provide financial assistance. As a result, the ability to pay becomes a consideration in admission decisions for a portion, and at times a substantial portion, of their decisions.

About Merit

Returning to the philosophical constructs of the taxonomy for the moment and reflecting on the many considerations that may enter into an admission decision, what are the underpinnings of how merit should be defined? Merit, no matter what the temptation or the ubiquity of practice, is not a narrowly defined concept that is easily determined by a grade point average or a test score. There is merit in providing equitable opportunity. There is merit in rewarding academic achievement. There is merit in developing talent among populations that are historically underrepresented. There is merit in students with means and in students without means. There is merit in personal virtue, in courage, and in conscientiousness, and in empathy. There is merit in building great educational institutions. There is merit in building a better society.

Admission policy directed "toward the mission" should be a reflection of institutional purpose, but it should also be a reflection of a commitment to educate students and a commitment to benefit society. As this discussion turns to how admission decisions are made, it is important to see how students, institutions, and society are served. Our definitions of merit, as reflected in admission decisions, may be relatively simply expressed or they may be quite complicated indeed (see the taxonomy presented earlier).

HOW DECISIONS GET MADE: SELECTION PROCESSES

For actual admissions decisions to be made, admission philosophy, institutional mission, case law, views of merit, and the many possible considerations noted in this chapter must be operationalized. Two fundamental methods are employed to help decision makers: *open admission and eligibility models* and *selectivity models*. Both lead to final admissions decisions.

Open Admission and Eligibility Models

Eligibility models are the clearest and most direct expressions of admission. In open admissions, all who can benefit are admitted. This includes programs in community colleges for adult and community education and those that provide the high school equivalency diploma, the GED. In other programs, a high school diploma or a GED, along with an application for admission, are the only credentials needed to enroll. Increasingly, however, community colleges find that demand exceeds their capacity in particular programs of study. These programs will require additional high school or community college coursework and higher levels of demonstrated achievement. (For examples of institutions that base admissions policies on this model, see the Columbus State Community College website at http://www.cscc.edu/admissions/open_enrollment. shtml and the Colorado Department of Higher Education website at http://highered.colorado.gov/Academics/Admissions/.)

In public four-year systems of higher education, eligibility requirements are openly stated and typically specify (1) high school graduation, (2) a required pattern of coursework, and (3) a threshold level of performance such as a designated grade point average, test scores, or an index that takes into account both grade point average and test scores. In these models, students are often guaranteed admission to a campus within a university system, though not always to a particular campus. Campuses with excess demand in particular programs or for the campus generally require higher levels of academic achievement. For examples, compare the following programs at Northern Arizona University, http://nau.edu/Admissions/Getting-Started/Requirements/Freshmen/; at University of North Carolina, http://www.northcarolina.edu/aa/admissions/requirements.htm; and at California State University, https://secure.csumentor.edu/planning/high_school/.

Eligibility models can be transformed into selectivity models, discussed next, when campuses experience student demand that exceeds the spaces available. This is the case on public university campuses across the country, where comprehensive and individualized review of credentials is performed to arrive at admission decision (the Texas Top Ten Percent Rule is an example). It is also the case at private colleges and universities, where individualized review has historically been the normative practice. Like their public counterparts, most private colleges will publicize their admission criteria, though in less specific form than public university eligibility requirements. In other words, it will be made clear that a rigorous pattern of high school coursework must be pursued, that competitive grades and test scores (when required) must be presented, and that personal statements and essays will be reviewed alongside counselor and teacher recommendations and extracurricular accomplishments. These are the foundations of the selective models.

Selectivity Models: Comprehensive/ Individualized/Holistic Review

These interchangeable terms represent admission selection processes that are based upon a combination of academic and personal qualities. For the purpose of this discussion, the term "individualized review" is used to describe this process.

Academic credentials are given the greatest weight in most selective admission models, though the academic record is supplemented with personal factors that are illuminated by supplementary admission credentials such as recommendations and personal statements. Each institution defines desired personal qualities rather differently according to its mission, though many institutions value leadership, intellectual curiosity, contributions to school and community, special talent, and other background characteristics such as socioeconomic status, racial/ethnic identity, and gender (Rigol, 2004).

Inside the Black Box of Selective Admissions For years, selective admission processes have been the topic of newspaper articles, books, magazines, student anxiety, and parental frenzy (Golden, 2006; Steinberg, 2002; Abrams, 2013; *US News & World Report*, 2013). How the many factors of an individualized selection process are brought together in decision-making appears as a mysterious black box to students and families. Indeed, calls for greater transparency have existed since the beginning of the millennium and are not abating (Lucido, 2011; Rigol, 2004).

A brief outline of decision-making processes in the selectivity model follows. No single model can capture the many iterations that are used; the reasons for choosing one process over another are rooted in the philosophy and the proclivities of the campuses. However, understanding that these are variations on a theme, one can examine how the models operate.

File Review *Individualized review* generally means just that: each application is reviewed and evaluated individually and, in many cases, by more than one reader. The approaches of public and private institutions are similar, though public universities tend to have stated minimum eligibility standards and more highly structured processes (Rigol, 2004).

Ratings and rubrics guide the reader in file evaluation. The curriculum completed, the grades achieved, academic honors and awards, teacher and counselor recommendations, and essays and personal statements may all receive an individual rating. In some cases, elements of the individual ratings will be rolled into an overall academic rating. Similarly, extracurricular activities and personal characteristics will also receive ratings. These may include depth of involvement, leadership, service, and ability to overcome disadvantaged circumstances or other indicators of drive and determination. Ultimately, a reader will assign an overall rating to a dossier or will make a preliminary judgment to admit, deny, or assign a student to the waitlist or a future review pending new information such as senior year grades or test scores.

Application reading assignments are made in a number of ways. Some institutions have staff members read by expertise, which may mean reading all applications from a particular recruitment territory or all applications to a particular program (engineering, for example). Other institutions prefer to have applications for admission assigned to readers randomly. As the applications move forward in the process, a second reader may read the application "blind," or without knowing the evaluation of the first reader, and then assign a second set of ratings. Alternatively, a second reader may "read behind" a first reader to validate the ratings and make a second judgment. Should readers vary in their judgments, a senior reader or an admission committee will make a judgment on the file. Other decision mechanisms include bringing all rated files to a full committee review, where a staff or a team of readers can vote on the file.

The decisions rendered on an application by a first reader, a second reader, a senior reader, or a committee may or may not be the final decision rendered and received by the student. Based upon all the factors noted in this chapter, selective campuses shape the class that they believe most meets their mission, their goals, and their financial realities.

The Final Decision No recent research has examined the final decision-making processes at selective colleges and universities. Given the need to manage the intersection of academic quality, tuition revenue, diversity in its many forms, and the sustenance of academic and athletic programs, it is clear that final reviews of admission decisions are conducted by teams of senior managers or by the deans and directors themselves, and that decisions are finalized at this stage. Some of these final decisions are more readily discerned than others. Academic programs will be filled, orchestras will be kept whole, and athletic rosters will be completed. On the other hand, the final decision-makers must take into account who is likely to enroll and from where, how much revenue will be generated and how much student aid expended, whether adequate diversity will be represented, and whether the whole of the class will advance the mission of the institution. Moreover, pressure on admission leaders to push institutions up the rankings ladder, up the test score scales, and down in the percentage of applicants admitted reduces their degrees of freedom to provide broader access to campus (Wegner, Thacker, Lucido, & Schulz, 2011).

Given this complex calculus, there is no doubt that some of the decisions made by readers and committees are overturned in the final decision-making process. Much is made of the responsibility of students and colleges to make a good match in their respective duties in the college admission process. The difficulty for students is that a match from the college perspective is made on many more grounds than the student can control.

THE ROLE AND EFFECT OF COLLEGE ADMISSION PLANS IN SELECTION

Admission decisions take place with the context of the admission plans offered within colleges and universities. In open admission plans, students can sometimes simultaneously apply, be admitted, and enroll (Ancrum, 1992). Other plans, however, can have an impact on admission decisions.

Rolling Admission Plans

In rolling admission plans, students are considered at the time that their application for admission becomes complete, and the applicant is immediately notified. Practiced in institutions at a variety of selectivity levels, students are admitted on a rolling basis as long as space is available (Ancrum, 1992). Many schools that practice rolling admission have priority deadlines. Among the prominent schools currently using rolling admission are Penn State University, Purdue University, the University of Pittsburgh, Rutgers University, and Michigan State University (Haynie, 2013).

Regular Admission/Competitive Pooling

Under regular admission plans, applications for admission are pooled so that readers can weigh the credentials of students alongside others in the applicant pool. These plans usually have a winter application deadline (often in January or February) and students are notified of their decisions in early spring (usually in early April). Colleges employing the selectivity models described earlier in the chapter utilize regular admission plans.

Early Decision Plans

Early decision plans supplement regular admission plans at many colleges and universities. These plans are designed to allow students who have a clear first choice an opportunity to apply for admission and to receive an admission decision early. For example, most early decision plans require an application by November 1 and will notify applicants of a decision on their application sometime between mid-December and mid-January (Ancrum, 1992). Since students who apply through early decision plans are declaring their first choice, they are permitted to apply to the early decision plan of only one institution, and they are pledged to enroll there if admitted. If admission results, the process for the student is then completed early, as the program's name suggests. Students may be admitted, denied, or deferred to the regular admission pool under early decision plans.

Of the variety of admission plans, early decision has the most impact on decision-making within the admission office. Admission rates for students applying early decision are most often higher, sometimes much higher, than admission rates for students applying through the same college's regular decision plan (*US News & World Report*, 2009). Several reasons may account for this: Better applicants may be applying early decision—though there is little evidence to support this. It is far more likely that applicants with greater financial means and more alumni children are applying early decision and that student athletes and other students with special talent and connections are applying early (Avery, Fairbanks, & Zeckhauser, 2003). Finally, colleges and universities could be admitting more early applicants because they demonstrate more interest and are more likely to enroll. Indeed, in *The Early Admission Game*, a five-year study of the impact of early admission plans, Christopher Avery and his colleagues found that applying early decision was a decided advantage in the admission process, that students and their counselors believed it to be true, and that a greater degree of sophistication on the part of applicants was required to participate (Avery, Fairbanks, & Zeckhauser, 2003). Although a much longer discussion of the impact of early decision is required to unpack the many issues attendant to it, it is clear that early decision plans have a decided impact on and outcome of the decision calculus discussed.

Early Action Plans

Two early actions plans are now predominant in American colleges and universities: a nonbinding early action plan and a single-choice, non-binding early action plan. Under the first plan, students may apply early under much the same admission calendar as discussed with early decision. They receive an early answer from the admissions office, but they are not bound to attend the school and can make a decision later in the academic year, usually by the May 1 universal decision date. Unlike early decision, students may apply to as many early decision programs as they wish. Under early decision–single choice, the plan is the same in each respect, with the exception that students are asked to apply to one school only. Space does not allow a thorough discussion of both plans. However, like early decision, though to a lesser degree, early action plans offer an advantage to students who apply (Avery, Fairbanks, & Zeckhauser, 2003). Finally, and returning to Avery's point that sophisticated knowledge of these processes is required to take advantage of them, it is important to note that these and the early decision plans exacerbate inequalities that exist as a result of a lack of counseling and college-going experience in low-income areas.

TOWARD THE FUTURE: NONCOGNITIVE FACTORS AND TWENTY-FIRST CENTURY SKILLS

Educational trends outside of the admissions office may soon have an impact within it. As noted earlier, a number of factors contribute to the admission decision and reveal evidence of personal qualities. These include what scholars describe as *moral* and *performance character*. Evidence of moral character includes traits such as honesty, empathy, compassion, and integrity, while evidence of performance character includes zest, grit, optimism, and conscientiousness (Kyllonen, 2008). Increasingly, employers are identifying personal traits as critical to workplace performance, and scholars are identifying these, and other traits, as twenty-first century skills and attributes.

According to the National Academy of Sciences and the National Research Council, the skills needed for success in the twenty-first century consist of cognitive, interpersonal (social), and intrapersonal (emotional) skills. Cognitive skills include critical thinking, systems thinking, problem solving, study skills, adaptability, creativity, and meta-cognitive skills. Interpersonal skills include complex communication, emotional and social intelligence, teamwork and collaboration, leadership, and cultural sensitivity. Intrapersonal skills include self-efficacy, self-concept, work ethic, persistence, organization, time management, and lifelong learning (Kyllonen, 2012).

Indeed, such skills are rated highly by employers of both high school and college graduates and a good number are rated above traditionally taught subject areas (Educational Testing Service, 2014). Moreover, more traditional measures are limited and reinforce social divisions based on racial/ethnic, gender, and socioeconomic status. Although useful for all students, these non-cognitive or meta-cognitive variables are particularly critical for low-income and other underrepresented students as standardized tests and prior grades may provide only a limited view of their potential.

As a result, an emerging frontier in college admissions may be the identification of these factors in the admission process. Indeed, given research by the Educational Testing Service (ETS), it is possible that the assessment of these variables in college admissions can supplement grades and standardized test scores for admission decisions, may increase validity, and may have less adverse impact on underrepresented populations.

Medical, Law, and Graduate School Admission

Medical, law, and graduate school admissions provide additional evidence of this trend. Studies have found, for example, that competent doctors exhibit traits including empathy, resiliency, altruism, reliability, integrity, compassion, and communication skills. Medical school admission, however, relies primarily upon cognitive measures including the MCAT score. This makes sense, since the MCAT has been shown to be valid for academic performance; on the other hand, research also demonstrates that it is not valid for clinical competence (McGaghie, 1999). As a result, the Association of American Medical Colleges is leading the effort to include non-cognitive variables in the medical school review process (Albanese, Snow, Skochelak, Huggett, & Farrell, 2003).

Similarly, in a study conducted at the University of California at Berkeley, researchers found that the undergraduate grade point average, the LSAT, and the academic index used heavily in law school admission were not useful for determining performance on many critical factors identified as effective "lawyering" (Shultz & Zedeck, 2011). Finally, some graduate admission operations are now including the Personal Performance Index, a non-cognitive assessment designed by ETS, as a supplement to the GRE. In sum, while non-cognitive assessments must yet be validated for use more widely, they show promise in broadening the characteristics valued in the admission processes across the spectrum of higher education.

THE NATIONAL ATTAINMENT AGENDA, TRANSFER ADMISSION, AND THE SWIRLING STUDENT

This analysis has concentrated on freshman or first-year admission to America's colleges and universities. Although admission directly to community colleges has been touched upon briefly, transfer admission from two-year to four-year institutions has not been covered. Space limitations do not permit a thorough-going discussion; however, it is critically important to note that the community college transfer function is an increasingly important part of college and university effort and enrollment plans (Jaschik, 2013). This is particularly important as ambitious national educational attainment goals have been established by President Obama, the College Board, and the Lumina Foundation (College Board, 2008; The White House, 2013). Transfer from two-year to four-year institutions is a critical component of these goals.

Although transfer admission is relatively straightforward, it is not without challenges. Typically, an application for admission and transcripts of all previous colleges attended are required for review by four-year institutions. Additionally, some four-year schools will require high school records and standardized test scores in addition to transcripts of prior college coursework. Some programs of study will also require the completion of prerequisite courses and threshold grade point averages for direct entry. Helping to facilitate the transfer function are transfer articulation agreements and, more recently, state initiatives such as *Senate Bill 440* in California, which guarantees admission to the California State University at junior level to those students who complete "transfer model curriculum-aligned associate degrees" (*Senate Bill 440*: California Senate, 2013). Moreover, the state of Florida has a longstanding policy of standard course numbering systems and transfer regulations designed to facilitate student mobility (Florida Department of Education, 2013).

CONCLUSION

"In the broad context of the general welfare, the overwhelming obligation of higher education is the provision of education for all capable of realizing its benefits and feeding those back in multiplied vigor into the general polity" (Thresher, 1966, p. 23).

This chapter began with Justice Frankfurter's clear and forceful statement of the "essential freedoms of a university, one of which is to determine for itself on academic grounds . . . who may be admitted to study." This precedent has resulted in substantial judicial deference in the affairs of universities ever since (Higginbotham & Bergen, 2003). Admission decisions, we have seen, however, are not without constraints, and they are not always made on academic grounds. Voters, governors, and attorneys general have restricted the consideration of race in some states; donors, legislators, and alumni retain considerable influence; and financial conditions have squeezed opportunity for low- and middle-income students as colleges increasingly seek and admit full payers who do not need financial assistance. Indeed, the issue of finance has seen even the prestigious University of California admit more out-of-state and international students to bolster its budgets (Gordon, 2011). It appears that the degrees of freedom available to pursue decisions "toward the mission" are diminishing.

An argument can be made that each of the constraints noted here can be tangentially tied to mission attainment. However, admission policies and practices that are limited in their ability to pursue the twin objectives of equity and merit as described here may well serve institutions, but they do not serve the long-term interests of students and the wider society. It appears wise for admission decision-makers and their academic leaders to examine policies and practices in light of institutional mission and purpose, to clarify as much as possible how admission decisions are made, to set forth plans to balance powerful influences against equity, and to provide evidence of the educational value of their decision-making. The latter point may be most important if continued deference is to be granted in the courts.

Thresher (1966) reminded people that "the general welfare" is an obligation of admission policy and practice in American higher education. As noted here, there are numerous ways that student aptitudes, proclivities, and character traits can be identified and contribute to admission decisions, and numerous methodologies can be employed to arrive at admission determinations. Therefore, it is the responsibility of admission policy-makers and campus leaders to devise policies that are well-researched in the national and local contexts, equitable and fair, mindful that talent and preparation come in many forms and from many people and places, and that permit institutions to be at their educational best in meeting their respective missions.

For the admission practitioner, it is imperative to have deep knowledge of the factors and influences included in this chapter. Responsible admission programs are thoughtful about the tradeoffs inherent in selecting one student over another or in using one set of criteria over another. In sum, they are thoughtful about the societal consequences of their policies, their practices, and, ultimately, of their decisions. Increasingly, the American dream is mediated through the decisions made in the admissions office. To be an admission expert, then, is to be an educational leader in the admissions office, on the campus, and in the wider community.

References

Abrams, T. (2013). Colleges report 2013 admission yields and wait-list offers. *The Choice: Getting into College and Paying for It. The New York Times.* Retrieved from http://thechoice.blogs.nytimes.com/category/admissions-data/.

Albanese, M. A., Snow, M., Skochelak, S., Huggett, K., & Farrell, P. M. (2003). Matriculating student perceptions of changes to the admissions interview process at the University of Wisconsin Medical School: A prospective, controlled comparison. *WMJ-MADISON, 102*(2), 30–33.

Ancrum, R. (1992). *The College Application and Admission Process.* New York: College Entrance Examination Board.

Arnold, E., & Wertheimer, L. (2002). Post affirmative action. [Radio broadcast episode]. Washington, DC: National Public Radio.

Association of Medical Colleges. (n.d.). *Holistic Review.* Retrieved from https://www.aamc.org/initiatives/holisticreview/#.UreMT6Xzi5c.

Avery, C., Fairbanks, A., & Zeckhauser, R. (2003). *The Early Admissions Game: Joining the Elite.* Cambridge, MA: Harvard University Press.

Bastedo, M. N., & Jaquette, O. (2011). Running in place: Low-income students and the dynamics of higher education stratification. *Educational Evaluation and Policy Analysis, 33*(3), 318–339.

Blackburn, J. A. (1990). *Assessment and Evaluation in Admission.* New York: College Entrance Examination Board.

Bowen, W. G., & Bok, D. C. (1998). *The Shape of the River: Long-Term Consequences of Considering Race in College and University Admissions.* Princeton, NJ: Princeton University Press.

California Senate. *Public postsecondary education: Student Transfer Achievement Reform Act.* 2013–2014 Session. S.B. 440. Retrieved December 22, 2013, from http://leginfo.legislature.ca.gov/faces/billNavClient.xhtml?bill_id=201320140SB440.

Camara, W. J., & Kimmel, E. W. (2005). *Choosing Students: Higher Education Admissions Tools for the 21st Century.* Mahwah, NJ: L. Erlbaum Associates.

Camara, W. J., & Schmidt, A. E. (1999). *Group Differences in Standardized Testing and Social Stratification.* New York: College Entrance Examination Board.

Chang, M. J. (2011). *Quality matters: Achieving Benefits Associated with Racial Diversity.* Report commissioned by the Kirwan Institute for the Study of Race and Ethnicity, The Ohio State University Democratic Merit Project.

Ciompi, K. (1993). *How Colleges Choose Students.* New York: College Entrance Examination Board.

Clinedinst, M. E.; Hurley, S. F.; Hawkins, D. A. (2011). *2011 State of College Admission*. Alexandria, VA: National Association for College Admission Counseling.

Cohen, J. (2013). U. of I. tracking attempts to influence admissions. *Chicago Tribune*. Retrieved from http://articles.chicagotribune.com/2013–12–27/news/ct-met-university-of-illinois-admissions-log-20131226_1_admissions-representative-connected-applicants-log.

Coleman, A., Palmer, S., & Winnick, S. (2008). *Race-Neutral Policies in Higher Education: From Theory to Action*. New York: College Board.

College Board. (2008). *Coming to Our Senses: Education and the American Future*. New York: College Board Advocacy.

College Entrance Examination Board. (2002). *Best Practices in Admissions Decisions: A Report on the Third College Board Conference on Admission Models*. New York: College Board.

Educational Testing Service. (2014). Educational Testing Service website. Retrieved from http://www.ets.org.

Fischer, K. (2013). U.S. Will Be Fastest-Growing Foreign-Student Destination, Report Predicts. *The Chronicle of Higher Education*. Retrieved from http://chronicle.com/article/US-Will-Be-Fastest-Growing/142191/.

Fisher v. University of Texas at Austin, 570 U.S., 133. (2013).

Florida Department of Education. (2013). Statewide Course Numbering System. Retrieved December 22, 2013, from http://scns.fldoe.org/scns/public/pb_index.jsp.

Golden, D. (2006). *The Price of Admission: How America's Ruling Class Buys Its Way into Elite Colleges—and Who Gets Left Outside the Gates*. New York: Three Rivers Press.

Gordon, L. (2011). University of California enrolls more out-of-state freshmen. *Los Angeles Times*. Retrieved from http://articles.latimes.com/2011/jul/01/local/la-me-uc-admit-20110630.

Gratz v. Bollinger, 539 U.S. 244 (2003).

Grutter v. Bollinger, 539 U.S. 306 (2003).

Harris, A., & Tienda, M. (2010). Minority higher education pipeline: Consequences of changes in college admissions policy in Texas. *The Annals of the American Academy of Political and Social Science*, *627*(1), 60–81.

Haynie, D. (2013). Highest-ranked universities with rolling admissions. *US News & World Report*. Retrieved from http://www.usnews.com/education/best-colleges/the-short-list-college/articles/2013/11/05/highest-ranked-universities-with-rolling-admissions.

Heller, D. (2008). *Financial Aid and Admission: Tuition Discounting, Merit Aid, & Need-aware Admission*. Seattle: National Association for College Admission Counseling White Paper. Retrieved from http://www.usc.edu/programs/cerpp/docs/Heller.pdf.

Hemel, D. (2007). Leave Behind (a) Legacy. *The Harvard Crimson*. Retrieved from http://www.thecrimson.com/article/2007/6/6/leave-behind-a-legacy-at-harvards/.

Higgenbotham, F. M., & Bergen, K. A. (2003). The Court Has Granted Wide Deference to Colleges. *The Chronicle Review (The Chronicle of Higher Education)*, 49(29), B11.

Jaschik, S. (2013). Feeling the Heat: The 2013 Survey of College and University Admissions Directors. *Inside Higher Ed.* Retrieved from http://www.insidehighered .com/news/survey/feeling-heat-2013-survey college-and-university-admissions-directors.

Jump, J. (2004). Admission, Heal Thyself: A Prescription for Reclaiming College Admission as a Profession. *Journal of College Admission*, (184), 12–17.

Kahlenberg, R. D. (2010a). *Affirmative Action for the Rich: Legacy Preferences in College Admissions.* New York: The Century Foundation Press.

Kahlenberg, R. D. (2010b). *Rewarding Strivers: Helping Low-Income Students Succeed in College.* New York: Century Foundation Press.

Kiley, K. (2012). Need and Want. *Inside Higher Ed.* Retrieved from http://www. insidehighered.com/news/2012/10/30/colleges-rethink-need-blind-admissions-favor-meeting-need.

Krieger, L. (2008). CSU chancellor: System to turn away 10,000 eligible freshmen in 2009. *San Jose Mercury News.* Retrieved from http://www.mercurynews.com/ ci_11006451?source = rss.

Kyllonen, P. (2008). *The Research Behind the ETS Personal Potential Index (PPI).* Background paper, Educational Testing Service.

Kyllonen, P. (2012). *Measurement of 21st Century Skills Within the Common Core State Standards.* Invitational Research Symposium on Technology Enhanced Assessments, May 2012.

La Noue, G. (2003). *Diversity in College Admissions: Issues for Trustees.* Washington, DC: Institute for Effective Governance. Retrieved from http://www.goacta.org/ images/download/diversity_in_college_admissions.pdf.

Lipper, K. L., & Coleman, A. (2013). *Diversity in the Balance, Part II: Key Steps for Higher Education Institutions to Consider in Preparation for the U.S. Supreme Court's Decision in Fisher v.* University of Texas. New York: College Board.

Loeb, J. W. (1992). *Academic Standards in Higher Education.* New York: College Entrance Examination Board.

Lucido, J. A. (2000). *Managing Academe: The AAU Provosts.* Unpublished doctoral dissertation, University of Arizona.

Lumina Foundation. (n.d.). Lumina Foundation Strategic Plan 2013–2016. Retrieved from http://www.luminafoundation.org/goal_2025.html.

McGaghie, W. (1999). Perspectives on medical school admissions. *Academic Medicine,* 65(3), 136–139.

McPherson, M. S., & Schapiro, M. O. (1990). *Selective Admission and the Public Interest.* New York: College Entrance Examination Board.

Milem, J. F. (2003). The educational benefits of diversity: Evidence from multiple sectors. In M. Chang, D. Witt, J. Jones, & K. Hakuta (Eds.), *Compelling Interest:*

Examining the Evidence on Racial Dynamics in Higher Education. Palo Alto, CA: Stanford University Press.

Perfetto, G., & College Entrance Examination Board. (1999). *Toward a taxonomy of the admissions decision-making process: A public document based on the first and second College Board conferences on admissions models*. New York: The College Board.

Powell, J. A. (2011). *The Many Faces of Affirmative Action*. Retrieved from http://diversity.berkeley.edu/many-faces-affirmative-action.

Regents of the University of California v. Bakke, 438 U.S. 265 (1978).

Rigol, G. W. (2004). *Selection Through Individualized Review: A Report on Phase IV of the Admissions Models Project*. New York: College Entrance Examination Board.

Rigol, G. W., & College Entrance Examination Board. (2003). *Admissions Decision-Making Models: How U.S. Institutions of Higher Education Select Undergraduate Students*. New York: College Entrance Examination Board.

Ryan, E. (2013). Race and Admissions: The University of Texas' Long History. NPR. Retrieved from http://www.npr.org/2013/05/31/187573418/race- and-admissions-the-university-of-texas-long-history.

Shultz, M., & Zedeck, S. (2011). Predicting lawyer effectiveness: Broadening the basis for law school admission decisions. *Law and Social Inquiry*, *36*(3), 620–661.

Soares, J. (2012). *SAT Wars: The Case for Test Optional College Admissions.* New York: Teachers College Press.

Steinberg, J. (2002). *The Gatekeepers: Inside the Admissions Process of a Premier College.* New York: Penguin Books

Stephens, Paul (2013, October). International students: Separate but profitable. Washington Monthly. (http://www.washingtonmonthly.com/magazine/september_october_2013/features/international_students_separat046454.php?page = all)

Sweezy v. New Hampshire, 354 U.S. 234 (1957).

Thresher, B. A. (1966). *College Admissions and the Public Interest*. New York: College Entrance Examination Board.

Tienda, M. (2013). A race-conscious holistic approach. *The New York Times*. Retrieved from http://www.nytimes.com/roomfordebate/2013/05/13/can-diversity-survive-without-affirmative-action/a-race-conscious-holistic-approach-to-college-admissions.

University of California. (2013). *A–G Subject Requirements.* Retrieved December 28, 2013, from http://www.ucop.edu/agguide/a-g-requirements/.

US News & World Report. (2009). Colleges where applying early action helps. Retrieved from http://www.usnews.com/education/best-colleges/applying/applying-101/articles/2009/09/30/colleges-where-applying-early-action-helps.

US News & World Report. (2013). Best colleges. Retrieved from http://colleges.usnews.rankingsandreviews.com/best-colleges.

Wegner, G., Thacker, L., Lucido, J., & Schulz, S. (2011). *The Case for Change in College Admissions: A Call for Individual and Collective Leadership*. Center for Enrollment Research, Policy, and Practice, University of Southern California in Los Angeles.

The White House. (2013). Higher Education. Retrieved from http://www.whitehouse. gov/issues/education/higher-education.

Wilgoren, J. (1999). New law in texas preserves racial mix in state's colleges. *The New York Times*. Retrieved from http://www.nytimes.com/1999/11/24/us/new-law-in-texas-preserves-racial-mix-in-state-s-colleges.html.

Young, J., & Kobrin, J. (2001). *Differential Validity, Differential Prediction, and College Admission Testing: A Comprehensive Review and Analysis*. New York: College Entrance Examination Board.

PART THREE

PRICING AND FINANCIAL AID

In this part of the handbook, we discuss the relationships and connections among pricing, budgets, enrollments, and financial aid. These elements of Strategic Enrollment Management cannot be separated; they exist in a sometimes complex and overlapping web in which change in one area has implications for the others. For example, an increase in offers of institutional aid can reduce tuition price and will likely increase enrollments, but it may negatively impact institutional budgets. As with the rest of the volume, the focus of the following chapters is on delineating key concepts—many of which may be intuitive to SEM professionals—and then applying them to the field of practice.

Chapter 9, by Gabriel Serna and Matthew Birnbaum, provides an introduction to economic concepts embedded in the work of enrollment managers, including supply and demand, elasticity, and consumer choice. Although seasoned SEM professionals may intuitively understand aspects of economic theory, the goal of this chapter is to provide a clear explanation of essential ideas along with examples of their application to the field. Building from this discussion, Jacob Gross's Chapter 10 helps contextualize the use of institutional financial aid within the broader context of higher education finance, with a focus on financial aid coming from state, federal, and private sources. Trends in higher education policy affecting enrollment management are reviewed, including satisfactory academic progress, state merit-based aid, performance funding, and more.

With the context and concepts laid out, the last two chapters in this part get to the heart of using financial aid strategically to recruit the desired profile of students to meet academic and budgetary goals. In Chapter 11, Stephen Brooks, an economist and seasoned enrollment consultant, reviews the different uses of institutional financial aid to accomplish various goals. Included are varied examples of and models for leveraging aid. Part III ends with a chapter by Guilbert Brown and Jacob Gross, which completes the picture of SEM and the use of financial aid by drawing out the relationships among budgets, enrollment, and aid. It includes a discussion of the business model of higher education, drawing distinctions between it and models used by other industries (particularly those that are for-profit). The chapter concludes with a discussion of the changing nature of higher education finance and its effects on institutional budgets.

In Part IV, this volume shifts to examine student retention and graduation.

CHAPTER 9

Economic Perspectives on Pricing and What It Means for SEM

Gabriel R. Serna and Matthew Birnbaum

Growing competition, constrained resources, and increasing public scrutiny of tuition and fee levels have come to characterize the higher education marketplace. Within this context, enrollment managers are tasked with developing tuition, fees, and aid policies designed to increase net revenues and admit an academically prepared and diverse student body (Bontrager, 2007; Hossler, 2004, 2008). Because institutional pricing strategies often influence the choices enrollment managers make, they play a central role in an institution's position in the higher education market. Moreover, pricing decisions impact institutional budgets and, by extension, the ability of decision-makers to fund strategic priorities. It is in this context that economic theory can help enrollment managers appreciate and understand how market competition and pricing behaviors intersect with practice (Cheslock & Kroc, 2012; Hillman, 2012).

As the field of enrollment management has matured over the past twenty years, so, too, have the expectations of enrollment professionals (Bontrager, 2008; Henderson, 2001; Serna, in press). Although seasoned enrollment management professionals may have an intuitive understanding of economic principles, it is increasingly important that they are able to discuss these principles with presidents, board members, faculty, and the general public. Enrollment managers, who are often a part of the executive leadership, supervise large staffs and budgets and must navigate presidential/board expectations, faculty and athletic demands, and changing external policies and pressures (Hossler, 2008). The ability to articulate specific strategies in economic terms conveys a sense of professionalism and understanding of the marketplace. It also provides a set of basic principles that can be discussed in the abstract or related to institution-specific cases. It is with this in mind that we present a set of economic theories that can aid enrollment managers in both decision-making around pricing options and the communication of possible alternatives.

CONTEXT

The price of attending college has received attention from higher education researchers and strategic enrollment managers for more than thirty years (Archibald & Feldman, 2011; Bontrager, 2007; Bowen, Chingos, & McPherson, 2009; Cheslock & Kroc, 2012; Hearn & Longanecker, 1985; Heller, 2008, 2011; Hossler, 2004, 2008; Hossler, Bean, & Associates, 1990; Rusk & Leslie, 1978). Tuition and fees, which often serve as a proxy for price, occupy a central position in policy and research debates (Winston, 2003) because they are the most easily quantifiable figures tied to college attendance and an institution's perceived ability to generate revenue. Although generating revenue often serves as a primary basis for pricing decisions, institutions also tie it to access, diversity, and public perceptions. It is within this context that enrollment managers must provide rationales for developing pricing policies.

This chapter introduces basic economic theories useful to those charged with Strategic Enrollment Management and provides some possible implications associated with pricing decisions. We start with an introduction to demand and supply, elasticity, consumer choice theory, and marginalism. We then apply these principles to institutional pricing strategies and relate them to the implications that arise for enrollment management practice.

BASICS OF SUPPLY AND DEMAND

The supply of, and demand for, higher education has been a perennial interest to those concerned with institutional level decision-making and student (consumer) behavior based on the perceived associated costs and benefits (G. Becker, 1993; W. Becker, 1990; Hopkins, 1990; Paulsen, 2001a, 2001b). On the supply side, questions about college and university decisions are primarily driven by researchers' desire to understand how institutions develop price policy and allocate resources to key priorities in a complex market environment characterized by increasing competition for enrollments (Bontrager, 2008; Brown, 2008; Hossler, 2008; Kalsbeek & Hossler, 2008; Serna, in press). On the demand side, attention has focused on students' responsiveness to changes in price and its relationship to enrollments (Heller, 1997; Hossler, 2000, 2008; Leslie & Brink-man, 1987; McPherson & Schapiro, 1998; Perna, 2010; Serna, in press).

Supply and demand principles provide enrollment managers a foundation for decision-making, especially as regards pricing (DesJardins & Bell, 2006). For example, Figure 9.1 presents two models illustrating internal (endogenous) changes and external (exogenous) changes. The first model illustrates a change in *quantity demanded* (e_1-e_0) where an institution raises its tuition (P_0-P_1). Points B and A represent consumer demand in relationship to the number of enrollments an institution can or is willing to offer at particular price points, assuming there is a relatively fixed supply of enrollment spaces. In other words, tuition decisions and changes in enrollments are reflected as a movement along the same curve, much like price changes in other markets. In this case, the price faced by the students rises from P_0 to P_1 and revenues went from being equal to area P_0, A, e_0, 0, to area P_1, B, e_0, e_1. Simple multiplication of P along Q provides institutional leaders a sense for how revenue will change as a result of tuition increases and changes in the quantity of enrollments demanded. This model provides a guide for making decisions about price based on internal changes in tuition and fee levels.

The second model in Figure 9.1 illustrates the influence of an external or environmental change on the *demand* for a particular institution. In this scenario, something other than changing tuition effects consumer demand and creates an entirely new demand curve that can shift to the left (drop) or right (increase) based on the specifics of the external change. For example, if the federal government suddenly changed aid policy so that many more individuals qualified for grants, this would increase the number of potential enrollments in the market for higher education and result in an entirely new demand curve. Hence, this increase in demand has effectively increased revenues (this is shown by comparing area P_0, A, e_0, 0 to area P_1, B, e_0, 0). In other words, the shift in demand has increased tuition and fee revenues without decreasing enrollments.

Because enrollment managers have limited control over the external environment, the first model in model one is a better representation of the impacts of pricing decisions made by enrollment managers when they can exercise control over these decisions. Nonetheless, the basic distinction between changes in *quantity demanded* and shifts in *demand* illustrate why enrollment managers should be aware of their institution's external environment and develop "what if" plans based on various scenarios. Even if enrollment managers do not necessarily control the published level of tuition and fees, they nonetheless can exert some control over the effective price faced by students because of tuition discounts. This process works in much the same way theoretically, because, especially in the case of public institutions where these decisions are made system-wide, pricing choices made by enrollment managers around net price are pricing decisions. In other words, the same analysis regarding price

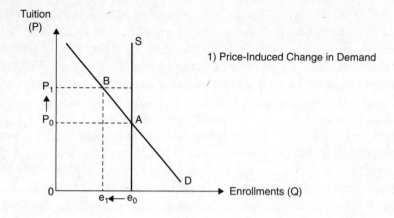

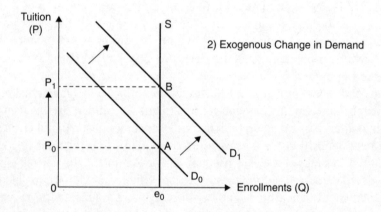

Figure 9.1 Basic distinction between a change in *quantity demanded* and a change in *demand* for higher education

Source: Adapted from Toutkoushian & Shafiq (2010, p. 43) and Serna (2013, pp. 98–99)

and quantity can be carried out whether based on published price or net prices. This would mean that regardless of whether at the system or institutional level, the theoretical considerations remain the same.

PRACTICAL CONSIDERATIONS: DEMAND AND SUPPLY IN MULTIPLE PRICING CONTEXTS

The relationship between supply and demand offers a framework for thinking about an institution's pricing decisions, assuming applicants are able to assess objectively the utility of obtaining a college education. Because the relationships outlined by economic theory can be limited, the job of enrollment managers goes well beyond simply suggesting pricing strategies for producing the desired number of enrollments and net revenues. For example, external factors such as a local economic downturn or changes in students' preferences may shift demand left or right. Moreover, changes in the policies of one or more of an institution's competitors can influence an institution's demand curve. Similarly, internal choices or policies can adversely impact the quantity of enrollments demanded by students and by extension net revenues. For example, an institution may lower tuition and fees when faced with enrollment shortfalls. However, this may or may not be an appropriate course of action given the context in which the decision is being made. In fact, lowering tuition and fees without a more comprehensive understanding of the market forces at play could result in decreased net revenues even as enrollments rise. Another important consideration exists when the institution does control its own pricing decisions. For example, many states make decisions system-wide, which renders comprehensive strategic pricing decisions difficult. However, the managers can still focus on the use of tuition discounts to help make a class.

Enrollment managers may also use the supply and demand principles to achieve institutional goals, such as increasing selectivity, an important component to some ranking measures. For example, an institution may keep enrollment spaces at a lower quantity than can be supplied. In this approach, an institution retains a surplus of spaces and forgoes tuition revenue in order to increase selectivity.

To illustrate how supply concerns can vary depending on institution, we consider two institutions with different missions. The first institution's mission is linked to an open-access philosophy and the second is highly selective. Both face enrollment demand well above available supply. Although each has a distinct mission focus, both have physical limitations on the number of enrollments they can support in the short term (Serna, 2013), even though price and enrollment philosophy vary substantially between institutions. As DesJardins & Bell (2006) note, although mission may help determine pricing approaches, physical plant limits can serve as the primary limit on enrollments. For both of these institutions, tradeoffs between pricing decisions, mission fidelity, and revenue generation play a role in their strategic management of enrollments, albeit in distinct ways. In both instances, supply and demand theories can provide a starting point for decision-making regarding price even as institutional mission foci differ.

ELASTICITIES

Elasticity, a concept closely related to supply and demand, is the measure of the percentage change in one variable based on the percentage change in another variable. In higher education, its primary use is for understanding the effects of pricing choices. It serves as a "what if" tool for analysis when multiple price points are being considered and can help enrollment managers estimate the price responsiveness of student subgroups. Elasticities are particularly useful because they are not dependent upon units of measurement but instead provide unit-less estimates of changes even when prices and quantity are measured differently[1] (DesJardins & Bell, 2006). For the sake of completeness, it should be noted that elasticities that are greater than one in absolute terms are considered elastic, indicating that enrollments are very responsive to changes in price; those equal to one are unit elastic, indicating that enrollment changes are proportional to price changes; and those less than one are inelastic, indicating that enrollments are less sensitive to price changes.[2]

We again consider two different institutions with distinct demand curves and demand elasticities. For the first institution, let us assume a relatively inelastic demand curve, whereas the second institution has a relatively elastic demand curve. A pricing decision taken where tuition rises by an equal amount at both institutions would be related to a comparatively small decrease in enrollments for the first institution as compared to the second. This is where an understanding of elasticities is exceptionally useful (Paulsen & Pesau, 1989) given that pricing choices should account for student demand for enrollments, especially if the demographic served by the institution is price sensitive.

The intuition behind the use of elasticities in SEM is that they show how an equal price change, implemented by institutions that share dissimilar enrollment demand levels, can have drastically different effects for net revenues. In the case where demand is linear, as in Figure 9.2, price changes at particular points along the curve can increase, decrease, or leave unchanged total revenues if pricing changes occur in the elastic, inelastic, or unit elastic portion of the curve (DesJardins, & Bell, 2006; Parkin, 2010). In other words, net revenues may increase, decrease, or remain unchanged even as enrollments rise based on both the elasticity of the curve and the point at which the institution sits when the decision is made.

The analysis in Figure 9.2 extends to diversity goals as well. For example, elasticities can tell us how subgroups of students are likely to respond to price changes. Because price-sensitive student responses are a concern for nearly every institution of higher education, the insight underlying elasticity is again evident. It can help guide pricing policy that integrates differential responses by combining revenue generation and diversity goals into a process undergirded by sound theory and institution-specific context.

Figure 9.3 illustrates how changes in the demand for goods or services that share a consumption relationship, often referred to as cross-elasticities, with higher education might impact enrollments. Let us assume that we are examining the situation from the perspective of our own institution. In our example, we first show what a price change in a complement does for demand at our institution. Here the price of campus housing first increases and then decreases.

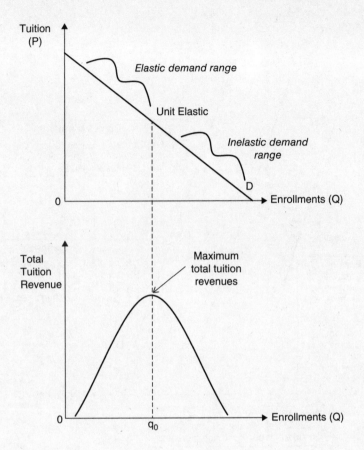

Figure 9.2 Graphical illustration of the relationship between total tuition, revenues, and elasticity

Source: Adapted from DesJardins & Bell (2006, p. 64) and Parkin (2010, p. 90)

This means that the total costs faced by the student have increased/decreased, and as a result demand for the institution's enrollment spaces shifted; first rightward (an increase to D_1), and then leftward (a decrease to D_2). The same model shows what happens when price changes occur for substitute goods or services. Suppose a competitor institution raises its price. If students consider both institutions to be similar, then the demand for enrollment spaces at our institution will shift rightward (an increase to D_1). If our competitor institution decreases its prices and students consider our institutions to be similar, then enrollment demand for our institution will shift leftward (a decrease to D_2). This basic analysis shows how competitive pricing decisions, market differentiation, and information provided can affect student enrollment choices. In a market where institutions are facing increasing competition, knowing how

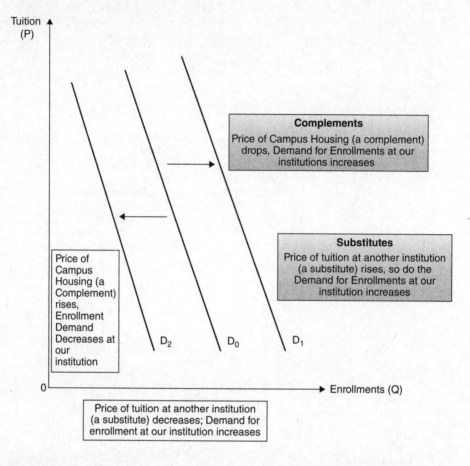

Figure 9.3 Graphical relationship of higher education consumption with substitutes and complements

Source: Adapted from Parkin (2010, p. 61)

pricing decisions affect demand, in addition to other prices in other campus areas at both your own and competitor institutions, is valuable for establishing recruitment and marketing materials.

PRACTICAL CONSIDERATIONS: PRICING RESPONSIVENESS AND REVENUE IMPACTS

Elasticities provide decision-makers a model for predicting enrollment responses to price changes; it is clear, however, that institutional type matters when developing pricing policy. To illustrate, let us again consider institutions with differing missions, as presented earlier. The first institution is a large research university serving students from across the country. The second is a regional institution serving students primarily from the local geographic area. Based on the position each institution occupies in the higher education market, tuition increases could result in significant financial strain/gain and an inability/ability to meet enrollment projections. For the research institution, a price increase might have little impact on the demand for enrollment spaces and result in increased net revenues. At the regional institution, a price increase might result in more students enrolling at a community college, resulting in lower net revenue. Therefore, elasticity as a concept can help enrollment managers anticipate— based upon mission focus, institutional type, and market position—how enrollments, net revenues, and class makeup will be impacted when choosing pricing and aid policies, even if only at a theoretical level. However, institutions heavily reliant upon tuition and fees as budgetary resources, and who occupy a middling position in the higher education hierarchy, must remain cognizant of responsiveness to price of the consumers they serve (Curs & Singell, 2010; DesJardins & Bell, 2006; Goldstein, 2012).

Critics of higher education observe that the cost of obtaining a college degree has become unaffordable to many families. Because demand for enrollment spaces has been shown to be generally inelastic for the market as a whole, this aggregate measure fails to account for populations of students who cannot afford the often high price tag attached to obtaining a college degree. Student price sensitivities are of special concern for institutions, especially because many price-sensitive students tend to come from unrepresented backgrounds (Archibald & Feldman, 2011; Bowen, Chingos & McPherson, 2009; Leslie & Brinkman, 1987; Hearn & Longanecker, 1985; Heller, 1997). In this context, it is possible for enrollment managers to consider from an intuitive perspective how different populations might respond to a price change. It also provides a basis for understanding the role aid plays for certain student populations when price concerns remain a barrier to access. Finally, it relates the institutions' pricing decisions to net revenue requirements by providing guidance for decisions around price changes and enrollments.

As stated previously, the interaction between enrollment demand and internal policy choices regarding price is highlighted in economic theory in a number of ways. In this instance, responsiveness to price changes is understood in at least two ways: 1) SEM can more carefully consider the impacts of price changes on student demand from multiple populations and 2) SEM can help develop a more nuanced understanding of the relationship between price and net revenue generation based on specific institutional characteristics and contexts while recognizing that the increased enrollments are not always related to increased net revenues, and vice versa.

The relationship of the prices of other goods, or the prices of competitor services, should also be of importance to enrollment managers. A goal in practice should be to consider the impact of substitute and complementary goods on the choices students make with limited budgets, as outlined in the upcoming section on consumer choice theory. A number of campus amenities, such as housing and meal plans, share a consumption relationship with enrollment. Therefore, pricing policies should not just consider the response of students to a change in tuition and fee levels, but also the prices of other campus resources. Moreover, institutions who serve students that are geographically bound may find that changes in the price of related goods and services may deter students from choosing their institution or accessing higher education.

The influence of competitor prices is also of concern to enrollment managers. If we consider an institution serving a primarily local population and another that serves a national population, price could serve as the primary choice driver. At national institutions, it is less likely that the price of competitor institutions will play a large role in the decision-making process for students seeking a certain level of prestige—though this is not to suggest that price does not matter at all. Conversely, institutions that compete primarily in the local region are more susceptible to the possibility that students view multiple local institutions as close substitutes for one another, and hence price plays a central role in the choice process.

Finally, the use of institutional aid is also a way to help students distinguish between institutions that might be considered competitors. In this context, the use of aid can establish a sufficient degree of differentiation so that institutions that are competitors are viewed as distinct by students. Once more, the role of SEM is to manage the message so that students can make better decisions in the allocation of often limited resources. Its role also extends to the use of institutional resources, and the balance that is sought among net revenue generation, prestige, and diversity.

CONSUMER CHOICE THEORY

Consumer choice theory considers a "typical" student's reaction to price changes based upon a few assumptions. For those seeking to examine the relationship of tradeoffs between higher education and All Other Goods[3] (AOGs), consumer choice theory provides a solid foundation. In this theoretical model, economists often assume that students face a budget constraint, and that they are making consumption decisions between higher education and AOGs based on the bundles of available choices mapped by a curve. This curve shows us the bundles of AOGs and higher education among which the student is indifferent (indifference curve)[4]. In other words, the indifference curve provides an analytical tool for understanding how much of the AOGs student population is willing to give up in order to obtain more units of higher education while accounting for budget constraint. However, because a student wishes to maximize the benefits she obtains, the goal is to move to a point on the budget constraint where she has spent all of her money and obtained the highest levels of higher education and AOGs possible. This point is indicated by the consumer optimum. At any point other than the consumer optimum, the outcome is suboptimal. That is, total benefits or satisfaction have not been achieved.

Let us now consider the impact of a price increase for higher education on the consumption choices of a "typical" student. If we assume that consumer income remains the same when a price increase occurs for either higher education or AOGs, then the budget becomes tighter and the consumer must make do with less AOGs and purchase less higher education as well. The price increase has effectively decreased total utility (benefits) for the student. The implication of this theoretical construct for enrollment managers making pricing decisions is that there are material effects on students when tuition is increased. Though this analysis might not hold for every student, we know that price sensitivity is a real concern for many institutions and students (Bowen, Chingos, & McPherson, 2009). Hence, consumer choice theory provides a basic foundation for understanding the consequences of pricing decisions on college attendance and choice.

In a related vein, both public and private institutions rely on subsidies to offset tuition and make higher education more attractive to various student populations. Figure 9.4 illustrates the role subsidies play in higher education. Without subsidies, all students would pay price P_0. In the case of public institutions, state

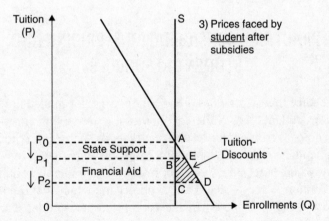

Figure 9.4 The role of subsidies in Strategic Enrollment Management

Source: Adapted from Toutkoushian & Shafiq (2010, p. 44) and Serna (2013, pp. 98–99)

support helps lower the price to P_1. Institutional, state, and federal aid lowers the price at both types of institutions to P_2. Subsidies reduce tuition costs and promote access, especially among price-sensitive individuals, to higher education (Baum, Lapovsky & Ma, 2010; Baum, Ma, & Payea, 2010; Hearn & Longanecker, 1985; Hillman, 2012; Hossler, 2000; Toutkoushian & Hillman, 2012). In terms of consumer choice theory, subsidies serve to increase students' budget constraints, thus allowing students to consume more higher education and AOGs.

From an institutional perspective, enrollment managers must also consider how institutional aid or student subsidies impacts net revenues. Total revenues increase proportionately with increased state and federal subsidies, while institutional aid directly decreases net revenues—in this case, indicated by the striped area (B, E, C, D) in Figure 9.4. The area represented by B, E, C, D underscores SEM's need to weigh fiscal concerns with academic and diversity goals often accomplished with tuition discounts. If B, E, C, D becomes too large, it will not be sustainable.

Another important theoretical concept related to both subsidies and pricing decisions is the notion of "corner solutions." A corner solution in economic theory is a solution in which the consumer is either unwilling or incapable of making tradeoffs between two goods. In higher education, this would mean that a student may or may not be willing or able to trade consumption between education and AOGs. This often occurs when at least one optimal consumption point is equal to a negative quantity or zero. When this arises, one of two things is expected to happen: using our higher education example, either a student will consume only higher education or they will consume only AOGs. This type of analysis is especially useful for understanding the behavior of students who will attend the institution no matter what and those who will not attend regardless of institutional efforts.

PRACTICAL CONSIDERATIONS: PRICING AND STUDENT RESOURCES

Consumer choice theory provides a basic framework for modeling the impacts of pricing on students with different financial resources. In practical terms, consumer choice theory demonstrates the tradeoffs that occur when the price of college attendance increases without a commensurate rise in income. Before determining whether to attend college, prospective students evaluate attendance costs (tuition + fees − all aid and support) and which institution provides the best cost/benefit. As noted in the case of corner solutions, irrespective of institutional efforts, some students will enroll and others will not. For the enrollment manager, the goal should be to focus resources on students somewhere in the middle of these two extremes. Allocation of limited resources should be concentrated on students for which marginal differences in aid can help the institution craft a class (Cheslock & Kroc, 2012).

Regardless of institutional prestige or mission, consumer choice theory suggest that as the price of higher education increases, individuals with limited budgets must make tradeoffs in other consumption areas or decide not to attend college (Archibald & Feldman, 2011; Bowen et al., 2009). It also offers a rationale for providing institutional aid to those who most need it, though there remains a need to balance net revenue generation with aid. It also offers a powerful analytic tool for formulating aid policy since budget constraints can be shifted by the inclusion of intuitional aid, though this also necessitates a decrease in net revenues (see Figure 9.4). Institutions should also consider the role of complements and substitutes when developing pricing policy, especially at institutions enrolling many lower income students. Consumer choice theory reminds us that students with limited budgets must make tradeoffs about which amenities can be purchased for less elsewhere as they undertake the implicit calculus of the college-going and choice process (Paulsen & Pesau, 1989).

MARGINALISM

Marginalism identifies the cost associated with producing one additional unit of a good and is helpful for understanding the economic implications of an incremental change such as admitting an additional student to an entering class. Marginal analysis suggests that production decisions should be couched in the costs and benefits associated with the addition or subtraction of incremental units from a particular activity or resource. For example, marginalism identifies the cost of each additional bed when designing a new residence hall. Say, for example, that the average cost to build beds 1–100 is always high, because it requires creating the initial infrastructure. However, the cost to create bed 101 is usually much smaller, because the foundation, roof, and plumbing are already in place. John Cheslock (2006) notes, "Economists regularly exhort people to think at the margin" (p.28), because it challenges us to consider established rationales for decisions such as class sizes.

The usefulness of marginalism in pricing is found in its applicability to the cost and revenue impacts of enrollment changes as well as for the information provided in the college-going and choice process for students (Cheslock, 2006; Paulsen, 2001a; Paulsen & Pesau, 1989). For example, from a revenue standpoint, marginal revenue measures how a change in total revenue is related to incremental or one-unit changes in enrollments. In terms of marginal cost, enrollment managers are often tasked with determining whether increased enrollments are a good idea based on the required additional expenditures. Paul Brinkman (2006) states that "in contemplating the value of increased enrollment, it is worth asking whether marginal costs will equal or exceed the revenue gained per additional student enrolled" (p. 51). In other words, does the additional (marginal) revenue generated by enrolling an additional student at a particular price point equal or exceed the additional (marginal) costs associated with enrolling each new student? In theory, the goal is to increase enrollments in one-unit increments until marginal benefit equals marginal cost. However, the data requirements for the calculation of marginal revenues and costs are very high. Still, they provide a number of fruitful approaches to doing so. (See Brinkman, 2006, and Cheslock, 2006, for a detailed analysis and treatment of the topic.)

Another important component of marginalism is related to student choices based on the marginal costs and benefits they face. In SEM, information regarding prospective students' choice behaviors plays a key role in the accuracy of enrollment forecasts. Students' choice behaviors and the "intuitive calculus" (Paulsen & Pesau, 1989, p. 9) that accompanies the college choice process influence the likelihood that enrollment forecasts will be accurate. These choice behaviors are associated with the information students receive regarding the expected marginal costs and benefits, both explicit and implicit, associated with a college degree (Paulsen, 2001a; Paulsen & Pesau, 1989). Michael Paulsen (2001a) indicates that students attempt to examine the costs and benefits of a particular institutional choice based in large part on the earnings differential they expect as a result of earning a degree from the institution as well as what they deem to be an appropriate fit. For SEM to be effective, a primary concern should be making appropriate decisions regarding the direct costs (tuition and fee) students face, in addition to considering how institutional subsidies impact both the academic and fiscal profile of the institution.

PRACTICAL CONSIDERATIONS: PRICING AND DECISION-MAKING

Because most enrollment managers rely on average revenues and costs to determine the number of enrollments to offer and the price necessary to meet budget requirements, an understanding of marginalism provides pricing and enrollment guidance. For example, Brinkman (2006) and Cheslock (2006) both suggest that the use of average costs and revenues is inappropriate because they can differ importantly from their marginal counterparts. Moreover, the use of institutional aid as a prestige-enhancing or recruitment tool can benefit significantly from an understanding of marginalism. Enrollment managers can make better resource allocation decisions based the marginal benefits and costs associated with a particular aid policy; these decisions can materially impact an institution's net revenues and class composition.

From a student perspective, investment in a college education takes on many of the same decision-making criteria as those employed in SEM: students are expected to make choices based upon the marginal benefits and costs associated with investment in a college education (Paulsen, 2001a). As noted previously, institutional aid practices and pricing decisions flow directly into the student's decision-making process. Even a basic understanding of marginalism provides a student with foundational perspective for understanding the ways in which incremental changes surrounding pricing impact institutional finances in addition to the choices he or she must make based on the marginal benefits and costs associated with attending college altogether or a particular institution.

Enrollment managers must communicate the benefits and costs associated with earning a degree from their specific institution to students and, increasingly, parents. In other words, managing the price message is almost as important as the price itself, especially when the sticker price does not reflect the true cost of attendance. It is here that institutional aid can be leveraged to raise the profile of the institutions, to generate net revenues, and to help diversify campuses, in addition to creating more equitable access opportunities (Bontrager, 2007). The basic tenets of marginalism suggest that strategic enrollment managers can manage the message about price while simultaneously helping students grasp more completely the direct costs they will actually face. It is also an important recruitment tool, because implicit costs are considered part of the equation—that is, institutional fit and campus climate are part of the implicit calculations undertaken in the college-going and choice process. Because SEM offices often house recruitment efforts, they are in a prime position to provide the needed information that is central to the student's decision-making process and that can help provide more information regarding the marginal benefits and costs of attending a particular institution.

In this context, marginalism provides a rationale for providing more information regarding the costs and benefits of attending a specific institution and for college-going in general. For SEM on the whole, the goal should be to focus this energy during the recruitment process. The information that students receive during the college selection process informs the decision to attend college and at which institution.

CONCLUSION

In this chapter we have outlined several basic economic theories that can help in the SEM process when considering pricing decisions. Because economic theory provides a formalized approach to the analysis of price, these serve as a foundation for both developing and understanding the rationales that accompany pricing choices. Although these theories are closely related to one another, each provides a lens for thinking about pricing policy. Enrollment managers should have enough familiarity with these concepts to explain them to various campus constituents and apply them to the institutions. Given the complex and professionalized nature of the SEM function, useful tools for guiding decisions around price are required to make more informed choices.

Endnotes

1. A useful method for overcoming the difficulties introduced by percentage changes is to take the average elasticity over a particular area of the demand curve using the midpoint method (see Parkin, 2010, pp.88–89 for a basic treatment of the subject).

2. See DesJardins & Bell (2006) or Parkin (2010) for both graphical and mathematical expositions of this concept.

3. AOGs are also known as composite goods. We employ this "good" to help ease analysis and to isolate the impacts of pricing decisions on the tradeoffs consumers have to make between higher education and other consumption choices.

4. A number of assumptions accompany the use of consumer choice theory as explained here. For the current analysis, we assume that both AOG and higher education are normal goods, in that we assume that as an individual's income increases, they want to consume more of both goods.

References

Archibald, R., & Feldman, D. (2011). *Why Does College Cost so Much?* New York: Oxford University Press.

Baum, S., Lapovsky, L., & Ma, J. (2010). *Tuition discounting: Institutional aid patterns at public and private colleges and universities, 2001-01 to 2008-09.* New York: College Board.

Baum, S., Ma, J., & Payea, K. (2010). *Education pays: The benefits of higher education for individuals and society.* New York: College Board.

Becker, G. (1993). *Human Capital: A Theoretical and Empirical Analysis with Special Reference to Education* (3rd Edition). Chicago: The University of Chicago Press.

Becker, W. (1990). The demand for higher education. In S. Hoenack & E. Collins (Eds.), *The Economics of American Universities: Management, Operations, and Fiscal Environment* (pp. 155–188). Albany, NY: State University of New York Press.

Bontrager, B. (2007). The brave new world of Strategic Enrollment Management. *College & University*, *82*(2), 3–6.

Bontrager, B. (2008). A definition and context for current SEM practice. In B. Bontrager (Ed.), *SEM and Institutional Success: Integrating Enrollment, Finance, and Student Access* (pp. 15–31). Washington, DC: American Association of Collegiate Registrars and Admissions Officers.

Bowen, W., Chingos, M., & McPherson, M. (2009). *Crossing the Finish Line: Completing College at America's Public Universities*. Princeton, NJ: Princeton University Press.

Brinkman, P. (2006). Using economic concepts in institutional research on higher education costs. *New Directions for Institutional Research, 2006*(132), 43–58.

Brown, B. (2008). Higher education costs and the role of tuition. In B. Bontrager, *SEM and Institutional Success: Integrating Enrollment, Finance, and Student Access* (pp. 33–46). Washington, DC: AACRAO.

Cheslock, J., & Kroc, R. (2012). Managing college enrollments. In R. Howard, G. McLaughlin, W. Knight, & Associates, *The Handbook of Institutional Research* (pp. 221–236). San Francisco: Jossey-Bass.

Curs, B., & Singell, L. (2010). Aim high or go low? Pricing strategies and enrollment effects when the net price elasticity varies with need and ability. *The Journal of Higher Education, 81*(4), 515–543.

DesJardins, S., & Bell, A. (2006). Using Economic Concepts to Inform Enrollment Management. *New Directions for Institutional Research*, (132), 59–74.

Goldstein, L. (2012). *A Guide to College & University Budgeting: Foundations for Institutional Effectiveness* (4th Edition). Washington, DC: National Association of College and University Budget Officers.

Griswold, C., & Marine, G. (1996). Political influences on state policy: Higher tuition, higher-aid, and the real world. *The Review of Higher Education, 19*(4), 361–389.

Hearn, J., & Longanecker, D. (1985). Enrollment effects of alternative postsecondary pricing policies. *The Journal of Higher Education, 56*(5), 485–508.

Heller, D. (1997). Student price response in higher education: An update to Leslie and Brinkman. *The Journal of Higher Education, 68*(6), 624-659.

Heller, D. (2008). *Financial Aid and Admission: Tuition Discounting, Merit Aid and Need-aware Admission*. Arlington, VA: National Association for College Admission Counseling.

Heller, D. (2011). Trends in the affordability of public colleges and universities: The contradiction of increasing prices and increasing enrollment. In D. Heller (Ed.), *The States and Public Higher Education Policy: Affordability, Access, and Accountability*. Baltimore, MD: The Johns Hopkins University Press.

Henderson, S. (2001). On the brink of a profession. In J. Black (Ed.), *The Strategic Enrollment Management Revolution* (pp. 3–36). Washington, DC: AACRAO.

Hillman, N. (2012). Tuition discounting for revenue management. *Research in Higher Education, 53*(3), 263–281.

Hopkins, D. (1990). The higher education production function: Theoretical foundations and empirical findings. In S. Hoenack & E. Collins (Eds.), *The Economics of American Universities: Management, Operations, and Fiscal Environment* (pp. 11–32). Albany, NY: State University of New York Press.

Hossler, D. (2000). The Role of Financial Aid in Enrollment Management. *New Directions for Student Services*, (89), 77–90.

Hossler, D. (2004). Refinancing public universities: Student enrollments, incentive-based budgeting, and incremental revenue. In E. St. John & M. Parsons (Eds.), *Public Funding of Higher Education: Changing Contexts and New Rationales*. Baltimore, MD: The Johns Hopkins University Press.

Hossler, D. (2008). The public policy landscape: Financing higher education in America. In B. Bontrager (Ed.), *SEM and Institutional Success: Integrating Enrollment, Finance, and Student Access* (pp. 1–13). Washington, DC: American Association of Collegiate Registrars and Admissions Officers.

Hossler, D., Bean, J. P., & Associates. (1990). *The Strategic Management of College Enrollments*. San Francisco: Jossey-Bass.

Kalsbeek, D., & Hossler, D. (2008c). Enrollment management a market-center perspective. *College & University*, *84*(3), 2–11.

Leslie, L., & Brinkman, P. (1987). Student price response in higher education: The student demand studies. *The Journal of Higher Education*, *58*(2), 181–204.

McPherson, M., & Schapiro, M. (1998). *The Student Aid Game: Meeting Need and Rewarding Talent in American Higher Education*. Princeton, NJ: Princeton University Press.

Neill, C. (2009). Tuition fees and the demand for university places. *Economics of Education Review*, *28*(5), 561–570.

Parkin, M. (2010). *Microeconomics* (9th Edition). Boston: Addison-Wesley.

Paulsen, M. (2001a). The economics of human capital and investment in higher education. In M. Paulsen & J. Smart (Eds.), *The Finance of Higher Education: Theory, Research, Policy & Practice* (pp. 55–94). New York: Agathon Press.

Paulsen, M. (2001b). The economics of the public sector. In M. Paulsen & J. Smart (Eds.), *The Finance of Higher Education: Theory, Research, Policy & Practice* (pp. 95–132). New York: Agathon Press.

Paulsen, M., & Pesau, B. (1989). Ten essential economic concepts every administrator should know. *Journal for Higher Education Management*, *5*(1), 9–17.

Perna, L. (2010). Toward a more complete understanding of the role of financial aid in promoting college enrollment: The importance of context. In J. C. Smart (Ed.), *Higher Education: Handbook of Theory and Research*, (25), 129–179. New York: Springer.

Rusk, J., & Leslie, L. (1978). The setting of tuition in public higher education. *The Journal of Higher Education*, *49*(6), 531–547.

Serna, G. (2013). Understanding the effects of state oversight and fiscal policy on university revenues: Considerations for financial planning. *Planning for Higher Education Journal*, *41*(2), 1–16.

Serna, G. (in press). Enrollment management in higher education. In D. Brewer & L. Picus (Eds.), *The Encyclopedia of Education Economics and Finance*. San Francisco: Jossey-Bass.

Toutkoushian, R., & Hillman, N. (2012). The impacts of state appropriations and grants on access to higher education and outmigration. *The Review of Higher Education*, *36*(1), 51–90.

Toutkoushian, R., & Shafiq, M. (2010). A conceptual analysis of state support for higher education: Appropriations versus need-based financial aid. *Research in Higher Education, 51*(1), 40–64.

Winston, G. (2003). *Toward a Theory of Tuition: Prices, Peer Wages, and Competition in Higher Education*. Williamstown, MA: Williams Project on the Economics of Higher Education.

CHAPTER 10

Understanding Financial Aid and Its Effects on Student Enrollments and Institutional Finance

Jacob P. K. Gross

Strategic Enrollment Management considers the impact of net price (that is, total cost of attendance less all subsidies) on students' enrollment decisions. Ostensibly, the goal is to maximize the probability of a student enrolling by reducing the net price, while simultaneously minimizing cost to the institution, thereby enabling the institution to maximize multiple goals (such as balancing budgets, attracting a diverse class, enhancing institutional prestige). However, institutional pricing is but one part of a complex tapestry of financial aid in the United States. Ultimately, net price is affected by federal, state, local, and private sources of aid in addition to what is offered by an institution.

Federal, state, and institutional aid policies, therefore, play an important role in determining the enrollment strategies of institutions. Moreover, the effects of these policies may vary depending on context (for example, state, type of institution). For example, a state with strong need-based aid policies may enable an institution to focus its attention on merit-based aid. As another example, federal loan policies, such as the recent shift to a three-year period for calculating cohort default rates, may have a more pronounced impact on enrollment strategies of historically black colleges and universities (HBCUs), proprietary institutions, and community colleges.

With this in mind, this chapter examines financial aid policies to help enrollment managers consider the impacts of these policies on their institutional strategies. To begin, this chapter relied on work by Robert E. Martin (2004) to introduce the concept of opportunity cost as it relates to sources of financial aid. This provides a framework for SEM professionals to evaluate the use of institutional resources in setting net price for students. Next, a brief overview is provided of the varied sources of aid that impact the price a student pays to attend college. The chapter concludes by considering major policy shifts in financial aid of which SEM professionals should be particularly aware.

CONCEPTUAL FRAMEWORK

In economics, every resource (such as personnel, equipment, financial aid, buildings) has an opportunity cost. Simply put, the *opportunity cost* of a resource is the value of forgone opportunities to use that resource in a different way (Henderson, 2008). In using a resource for one purpose, you cannot simultaneously use the resource for another purpose. For example, a student who decides to take a course on enrollment management spends her time (that is, the resource) in a classroom. The opportunity cost of that time includes the other activities the student could be doing during that class (such as paid work, time with family, sleeping). Another (and perhaps all too familiar) example would be the opportunity cost of (yet again) attending a meeting for a busy enrollment manager. The opportunity cost of the time spent in that meeting is the value of the other things the manager could be doing with the time.

This is an important concept, because to estimate the true costs of decisions (such as whether or not to provide an institutional scholarship), we must calculate the pecuniary (that is, financial) as well as opportunity costs. For example, when a student decides whether or not to attend college, the true cost of the decision includes not only the net price paid in tuition, but also the opportunity cost of foregone income while the student is enrolled. As David R. Henderson (2008) illustrates, if a student pays $4,000 to attend college while the state provides an $8,000 a year subsidy, it may seem that the cost of attendance is $12,000. However, to figure the true cost of attendance, we would have to include the foregone income for the student. If we estimate that at $20,000 for a recent high school graduate, then the true cost of attendance for the student is $32,000. We can extend this concept to types of financial aid by considering the source of aid.

The source of a financial aid dollar affects its opportunity cost from an institutional perspective. To elaborate, Martin (2004) discusses funded and unfunded scholarships from internal and external sources. External (that is, outside the institution) sources of financial aid for students have no opportunity cost, because they cannot be spent any other way by the institution. For example, Pell Grant dollars can be utilized only for financial aid. The same is true of private scholarships (such as Kiwanis), state merit grants, or state need-based grants, as a few examples. By contrast, internal scholarships (those provided by the institution) may have an associated opportunity cost depending on whether they are funded or unfunded. Funded internal scholarships come from endowed funds and are restricted to financial aid purposes (Martin, 2004). Unfunded internal scholarships represent true tuition discounting (Breneman, 1994). Examples here include institutional grants or tuition waivers that do not come from endowed funds. These are institutional dollars that could be spent for other purposes at the institution and therefore have an opportunity cost. From an economic perspective, enrollment managers should seek to maximize use of external and funded scholarships (which have no opportunity cost) and minimize use of internal, unfunded dollars (which could be spent for other institutional purposes, such as instruction) (Martin, 2004).

SOURCES OF AID

During the 2012–2013 academic year, $247 billion in student aid was used to finance postsecondary education, including aid from all sources (such as private, employer, private loans, institutional grants, tax benefits) according to data from the College Board's Annual Survey of Colleges (ASC) (Baum & Payea, 2013). Of this amount, the largest single source was federal loans (see Figure 10.1),

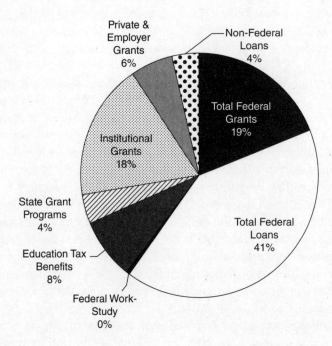

Figure 10.1 Proportion of total aid by type

Source: Author's analysis, Table 1, College Board Trends in Student Aid, 2012–2013

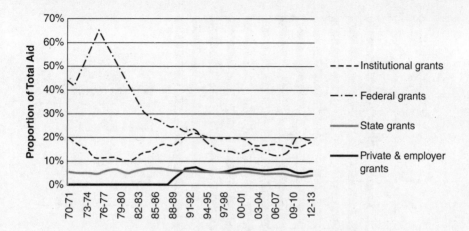

Figure 10.2 Grant aid from all sources as proportion of total aid, 1971–2013

Source: Author's analysis, Table 1, College Board Trends in Student Aid, 2012–2013

constituting about 41 percent. In total, the student aid provided by the federal government as a proportion of total aid has grown over the past decade. In 2002–2003, the federal government provided about 68 percent of all student aid. By comparison, in 2012–2012 the proportion was 71 percent (in constant 2012 dollars) (Baum & Payea, 2013).

Since 1971, there has been a shift with respect to sources of grant aid to students. In 1975–76, grant aid from the federal government made up about 65 percent of all financial aid to students, compared to about 11 percent of all aid coming from institutional grants that same year (see Figure 10.2) (Baum & Payea, 2013). Although the amount of money given to students in the form of federal and institutional grant aid increased between 2002–2003 and 2012–2013, federal grant aid represented a smaller slice of the student aid pie overall (20 percent of all aid given to students) (Baum & Payea, 2013).

Institutional grant aid has shifted as well over the past decade. A higher proportion of institutional grant aid at both public and private four-year institutions is being awarded to meet the need. In 2012–2013 about 51 percent of institutional aid at public institutions was awarded to meet financial need, compared to 31 percent in 2001–2002 (see Figure 10.3).

By comparison, at four-year private institutions, about 72 percent of institutional aid was awarded to meet financial need in 2012–2013 compared to 68 percent in 2001–2002 (see Figure 10.4). Overall, institutions appear to be using their financial aid in ways that support students with need. However, data from the College Board's ASC do not distinguish how institutions define need and to what extent, if at all, need corresponds to income. Data from the National Post-secondary Student Aid Study (NPSAS) further illuminates the ways in which institutions are using their financial aid dollars.

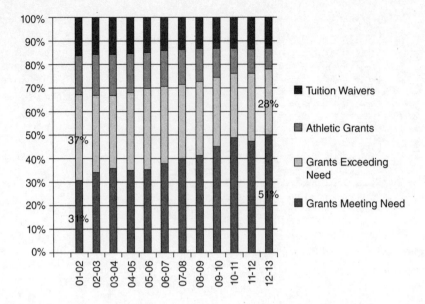

Figure 10.3 Average institutional grant aid per FTE student at four-year public institutions

Source: Figure 20A, College Board Trends in Student Aid, 2012–2013

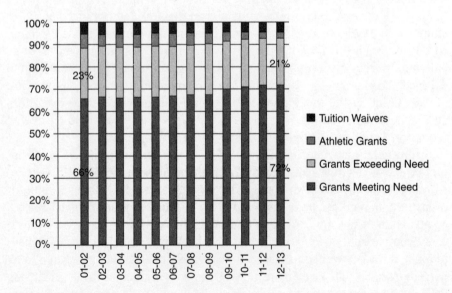

Figure 10.4 Average institutional grant aid per FTE student at four-year private, non-profit institutions

Source: Figure 20B, College Board Trends in Student Aid, 2012–2013

Table 10.1: Institutional need- and merit-based grants by income quartile (for full-time, full-year, one institution's dependent undergraduates)

	Income	Institutional grants total	Institutional need-based grants	Total merit-only grants	Net price after grants as % of income
Income quartile			Median amount		
Less than $30,000	$ 18,559.00	$4,616.00	$2,950.00	$4,600.00	78
$30,000–64,999	$ 45,838.00	$6,000.00	$3,500.00	$5,000.00	34
$65,000–105,999	$ 84,000.00	$7,000.00	$3,700.00	$6,000.00	24
$106,000 or more	$144,681.00	$8,084.00	$5,000.00	$6,100.00	16

Source: Author's analysis, U.S. Department of Education, National Center for Education Statistics, 2011–2012, National Postsecondary Student Aid Study (NPSAS, 2012).

Table 10.1 illustrates uses of institutional aid by income quartiles. These are the median amounts of institutional aid from the sample. We see that, overall, it is the highest income students (those whose families earn more than $106,000 per year) who receive the most money in institutional grants, both merit-only and need-based. In fact, students in the highest income quartile receive almost twice as much ($8,084) in institutional grants compared to their low-income (families that earn less than $30,000) peers. A comparison of the proportion of family income necessary to pay the net price of attendance *after all forms of grants* depicts the affordability problem low-income families face in the United States. The net price of attending college (after all other grants have been applied) for a family earning less than $30,000 is 78 percent of that family's annual income. This compares to 16 percent of annual income for the highest income families.

Although additional analysis is needed, the preceding data suggests that institutional spending on financial aid may further disadvantage low-income students. Whether this has shifted historically is a matter of empirical debate. One study (Doyle, 2010) uses national data spanning four full-time, under-graduate cohorts from 1992–1993 to 2003–2004 to ascertain whether institutions have shifted criteria for awarding aid from need to a merit basis. Overall, Will Doyle (2010) found that across all sectors (non-profit public or private, doctoral or non-doctoral institutions) institutions have become more responsive to academic measures in awarding aid and less responsive to income. The only exception to this trend was at public four-year doctoral institutions. Doyle (2010) found that these institutions have been consistent in providing institutional aid relative to financial need. Interestingly, his results also indicate that institutional aid in this sector has been particularly responsive to tuition. He hypothesized that these four-year public doctoral institutions "recycle" tuition, reallocating tuition dollars paid to lower income students. Interestingly, the relationship between state grant aid and institutional aid was positive, but not highly significant. An increase in state grant aid in most sectors was associated with a modest increase in institutional aid, controlling for all else.

FINANCIAL AID POLICY

The administration of financial aid, perhaps more so than most areas of postsecondary education, is closely connected to federal and state policy. The reasons for this become clear when we consider the preceding data about the sources of financial aid for students: Around 75 percent of financial aid to students comes from non-institutional sources (although, as is discussed next, aid from endowments and private sources has been on the rise and merits consideration as well). SEM professionals, particularly financial aid directors, must stay well versed in and well informed of the ever-shifting regulatory landscape in the United States. Some policy debates (for example, methods for measuring financial need) persist, but others may prove to be fleeting (such as financial aid shopping sheets). Although it is outside the scope of this chapter to detail the entirety of the financial aid policy landscape, it is valuable to consider some of the major policy trends of which SEM professionals should be aware. These are discussed next, specifically the overall policy climate for financial aid, changes in student loan default policies, and shifts in the criteria states use to ration state grant aid.

The Policy Climate

As context for considering trends in financial aid policy, the federal policy climate for postsecondary education is impacted by ongoing disagreement about balancing the budget as well as increased calls for accountability for all sectors of postsecondary education. Regarding the budget, since 2011, continuing bipartisan disagreement about spending and borrowing at the federal level have led to a form of brinksmanship that included a sixteen-day shutdown of the U.S. government in the fall of 2013. The political nuances of these disagreements are far too complex to discuss here, but the tangible effects of the federal fiscal climate include cuts in mandatory and discretionary spending on financial aid for students. As part of the mandatory cuts enacted by the federal budget sequestration, some programs (such as the Teacher Education Assistance for College and Higher Education [TEACH] Grant) have seen across-the-board cuts, while others (such as the Pell Grant) remain untouched. For the time being, the fiscal climate remains characterized by uncertainty and partisanship, contributing to the challenges faced by SEM professionals. Debates in 2012 about interest rates on Stafford loans are indicative of the (perhaps increased) politicization of federal aid policies.

In the summer of 2012, just prior to the U.S. presidential election, the U.S. Congress found itself in a polarized debate about the expected doubling of interest rates on Stafford loans. Legislation holding rates at 3.4 percent was set to expire, doubling the rate to 6.8 percent, costing borrowers about $1,000 more over the life of an average loan, or $6 per month, according to an analysis conducted by Mark Kantrowitz and Lynn O'Shaughnessy (2012). The extent to which this was politically engineered to become an election issue is unclear. Certainly, polls from the time suggest that allowing the rates to double was politically unpopular, and ostensibly neither Democrats nor Republicans wanted to allow it. However, as has been pointed out (Kantrowitz & O'Shaughnessy, 2012), the need to renew policies such as those that lowered interest rates are not typically a surprise and can be anticipated by policy makers. Whatever the motive, the ensuing debate over whether or not to continue low rates became entangled in broader issues such as the Affordable Care Act and federal subsidies to oil producers.

Within this fiscal, economic, and political context, national and state governments are paying increased attention to performance and accountability metrics for institutions as well as students. Although a full discussion of this is outside the scope of this chapter, several aspects merit mention. I focus on institutions first; nevertheless, accountability and performance metrics at the institution and student level often overlap and interweave, as is discussed later in the case of Satisfactory Academic Progress (SAP) policies as well as changes in the availability of Pell Grants.

In the fall of 2013, President Obama revealed his College Affordability Plan that consists of (a) paying for performance; (b) promoting innovation and completion; and (c) ensuring student debt remains affordable. In sum, the plan attempts to address the entirety of the postsecondary pipeline (that is, going, staying, and graduating) through market mechanisms such as tying aid to performance, ensuring that consumers have as much information as possible in their shopping process, and providing flexible student loan repayment options. Whatever the outcome of the proposal, it is indicative of a climate in which performance metrics (however imperfect) are used to ration scarce federal financial resources.

Another aspect of increased attention to institutional accountability metrics, occurring at the state level, is the rise in performance funding. At its core, performance funding ties states' direct appropriations to colleges and universities to pre-established performance metrics (such as graduation rates, completion for low-income students). Contrasted with traditional funding formulas (which were typically based on enrollment numbers), the philosophy of performance funding is to shift to output- rather than input-based appropriations. Evidence for the efficacy of these funding formulas is mixed (Dougherty & Reddy, 2013), yet they are politically popular and have seen resurgence through the support of private philanthropy.

Illustrative of policies that blur the lines between institutional and student accountability is the debate over Gainful Employment (GE) as well as standards for Satisfactory Academic Progress (SAP). Although still in negotiated rulemaking, gainful employment regulations passed in 2011 (but put on hold by a federal court) established three initial criteria (a federal student loan repayment rate of at least 35 percent, a debt-to-income ratio of less than 12 percent, or a debt-to-discretionary-income ratio of less than 30 percent) for institutions to meet in order to continue qualifying as Title IV eligible institution. Although all sectors and types of institutions would be subject to the criteria, proprietary (or for-profit) institutions disproportionately failed to meet the criteria according to initial data released in June 2012. Prior to and after the release of these initial data, advocates for the proprietary sector argued that default and income were largely a function of the students they served (low-income, underrepresented). Proponents of the legislation pointed to the fact the non-profit institutions with comparable student demographics fared better under the proposed GE policies, suggesting the proprietary institutions needed to be held more accountable.

Federal policies pegging satisfactory academic progress to continued student (rather than institutional) eligibility for financial aid were enacted in July 2011. SAP policies dictate that in order to continue receiving federal financial aid, students must make continued, satisfactory, and timely progress toward a degree. Students are held accountable for their performance. However, institutions must also have in place the necessary monitoring and advising infrastructure. To remain eligible for Title IV funds, each institution must have a clear, written policy, available to students, although institutions have some discretion to set standards for qualitative performance and adequate pace, for example.

Increasingly, SEM professionals need to remain abreast of education policy debates at the state and federal levels. The current environment of increased accountability for outcomes, coupled with increased oversight, contributes to an environment of shrinking autonomy for professionals. Moreover, SEM professionals can expect that uncertainty around external sources of aid for their students will continue, and, at the same time, the ways in which institutions spend their financial aid dollars will fall under increasing scrutiny. This suggests that SEM professionals must pay even greater attention to the strategic use of unfunded institutional aid as the opportunity costs of such aid may increase, given ambiguities in the financial aid policy climate. It is within this context that I turn next to two particularly important areas of financial aid and financial aid policy: student loan debt and merit aid.

Student Debt and Loan Default

Passage of the 2008 Higher Education Opportunity Act (HEOA) (Public Law 110-315, a reauthorization of the Higher Education Act of 1965) changed the way student loan default was defined, with implications for SEM. Previously, a loan was considered in default if the borrower had not made a payment on a loan in 180 days once it entered repayment. HEOA changed the number of days to 270. This extended the window of time during which a loan would *count* toward an institution's cohort default rate. A cohort default rate (CDR) represents the ratio of borrowers who are in default to the total number of borrowers who entered repayment in a given year. The federal government uses a combination of carrots (benefits) and sticks (sanctions) to encourage institutions to keep default low.

The primary benefits include greater freedom for an institutional to disburse federal aid to students. For example, institutions with a CDR less than 5 percent that are eligible home institutions can disburse loans to students studying abroad in a single installment (giving the students greater freedom to use the loan for travel and living expenses perhaps), regardless of the students' loan period (U.S. Department of Education, 2013). In sum, the assumption is that institutions that have been successful in working with borrowers to keep defaults low can be granted greater autonomy in administering loans for students.

The sticks (sanctions) can be substantial. Under the most current legislation, if an institution's default rate is equal to or greater than 25 percent for the most recent three years or exceeds 40 percent in a given year, the institution may lose its eligibility to receive student loans as well as Pell Grants for up to three years. Institutions can appeal sanctions for a number of reasons (such as incorrect data, demonstrating it serves a high number of low-income students and has high completion rates) (U.S. Department of Education, 2013).

The implications of this policy shift remain unclear. The perception of a *default problem* will be distributed differently across institution types and sectors. The proprietary sector saw the greatest increase in its published CDR, with an almost 9-point (or nearly 70 percent) increase under the three-year window compared to the two-year window (see Table 10.2). Historically black colleges and universities (HBCUs) saw an increase in their default rates as well. In fiscal year 2011–12, no institutions exceeded the permissible CDR under the two-year window. By comparison, for fiscal year 2010–11 (the most current year of available data), fourteen institutions (representing 13.9 percent of all HBCUs) had exceeded the federal threshold.

Beyond the ways in which institutions are perceived, we have yet to know whether more institutions will be sanctioned. The transition period built into HEOA allowed that no institution would receive sanctions based on the three-year

Table 10.2:   Comparison of cohort default rate by definition and institutional type, 2010 fiscal year

Institution type	2-year (percent)	3-year (percent)	Point increase	Percent increase
Public	8.3	13.0	4.70	57
Less than 2 yrs	10.0	16.5	6.50	65
2–3 yrs	13.4	20.9	7.50	56
4 yrs (+)	6.0	9.3	3.30	55
Private	5.2	8.2	3.00	58
Less than 2 yrs	13.6	21.8	8.20	60
2–3 yrs	8.5	14.2	5.70	67
4 yrs (+)	5.1	8.0	2.90	57
Proprietary	12.9	21.8	8.90	69
Less than 2 yrs	11.8	20.9	9.10	77
2–3 yrs	12.0	21.4	9.40	78
4 yrs (+)	13.6	22.1	8.50	63
Foreign	2.9	4.6	1.70	59
Total	9.1	14.7	5.60	62

Source: U.S. Department of Education (2013), Cohort Default Rate Guide, 2- and 3-Year Rates

CDR until three annual rates are published, which occurs in 2014 with the release of the 2011 fiscal year official cohort default rates. In 2012, the first year in which published three-year default rates were available from fiscal year 2009, a number of schools were subject to monitoring. There were 218 schools that had a three-year CDR of 30 percent or more in a given year. These schools had to establish default prevention task forces and submit default management plans to the U.S. Department of Education. Thirty-seven schools had a three-year CDR over 40 percent for a single year (U.S. Department of Education, 2012). This represents 4.3 percent of institutions that participated in Title IV programs.

From a SEM perspective, student loan default policies may impact the public perception of the institution as well as its business operations if eligibility for federal aid is lost. Given that less than 5 percent of institutions were subject to monitoring following the release of the fiscal year 2009 official three-year CDR, it is difficult to argue that SEM professionals will be widely impacted with respect to sanctions and their potential impacts on business operations. Rather, the more pressing issue is likely to be the perception of an institution's default problem. The so-called "student loan default crisis" has been widely reported in the media, leading to proposals to hold institutions more accountable for the default of their students (even though most institutions have relatively low rates of default).

SEM managers will have a role to play in responding to growing public concerns about loan default. First, enrollment management units may be tasked with monitoring default rates and, if necessary, implementing default management plans. Even for institutions that are not required to have management plans in place as a result of federal sanctions, the perception of a default problem may prompt implementation of risk mitigation programs that include entrance and exit counseling or ongoing monitoring of student repayment behaviors. These are yet another set of responsibilities SEM professionals must undertake and balance.

In addition, at those institutions where default is likely to be a greater concern because of the populations served (e.g., such as low income) or poor academic outcomes (such as completing a degree, finding post-graduate employment), SEM professionals may consider limiting institutional risk by rationing admittance or foregoing use of federal loans altogether (as has happened at community colleges in some cases).

It is beyond the scope of this chapter to evaluate either of these strategies, but caution is warranted as each may have unintended consequences, such as limiting access or contributing to mission drift. A review (Gross, Cekic, Hossler, & Hillman, 2009) of the empirical research points toward additional areas of strategy that may be fruitful for SEM professionals:

- Students who earn a credential are less likely to default, controlling for other factors (such as race/ethnicity, income);
- Students who borrow less are not as likely to default as their peers who take on greater debt overall;
- Graduates who are employed are less likely to default, controlling for all else.

The preceding areas are certainly much broader than a typical SEM office's day-to-day mission, yet they are demonstrative of the scope necessary to understand and address student loan default. SEM professionals can play a role in stimulating institution-wide conversations and strategies around this important policy area.

Finally, it is important to consider the role of loans within the conceptual framework of this chapter. Student loans have no accompanying opportunity cost in terms of financial aid. They come from an external source, travel with students, and can be used only for financial aid. Nonetheless, the preceding discussion demonstrates that other forms of opportunity cost accompany institutional use of student loans. Proprietary institutions, which have been under increased scrutiny because of their disproportionate reliance on student loans, have faced significant opportunity costs in the form of litigation, lobbying, and public relations to respond to critiques.

Shifting Criteria for Rationing State Aid

To date, thirty states have implemented broad-based merit aid scholarship programs, many of them modeled after what is considered to be the grandparent program, Georgia's Helping Outstanding Pupils Excel (HOPE) Scholarship, implemented in 1993. As is discussed next, the use of merit criteria in rationing aid is well established, although the current iteration is distinct in a number of ways. This movement toward merit rationing of financial aid has important implications for the practice of SEM.

Merit scholarship policies are certainly not new in the sphere of postsecondary education. Civic organizations, local governments, churches, states, and even private individuals have programs whereby meritorious achievement is defined and rewarded (Allan, 1988; Dynarski, 2002). The National Defense Act of 1958 awarded aid based on interests of national defense and encouraging high academic achievers to attend a postsecondary institution (Baum & Schwartz, 1988). It was not until passage of the Higher Education Act in 1965 that a shift in thinking began to occur that posited financial need and equal opportunity as the twin yardsticks by which to dole out scholarship money in the form of both grants and guaranteed loans.

As the primary locus of support for postsecondary institutions, states have long been in the business of awarding merit aid. Susan Dynarski (2002) argued that states, in one sense, award merit aid to students via tuition subsidization for in-state residents. Institutions define and award merit on the basis of admission for study, according to this logic. Once admitted, students are granted equal opportunity to pursue an education.

Awarding of general state support as a form of merit aid aside, states have historically focused resources on their most academically talented students. Earlier merit policies, however, were not intended to influence choice (in terms of both attendance versus non-attendance and which institution) or access. These ancestors to today's much broader policies were designed to award the exceptionally high academic achievement of those who were already likely committed to pursuing tertiary education (Dynarski, 2002).

By contrast, broad-based state merit scholarship policies have the goals of encouraging high academic achievement at the high school level, promoting pursuit of tertiary education, encouraging students to remain in state for their education, and in some cases broadening access. Such policies have relatively lower thresholds for achievement, which are often met by as much as 30 percent of graduating seniors (Dynarski 2002). It is the combination of the broader policy scope and the intended outcomes that differentiate the policies of interest in this analysis from other merit aid policies. Although the majority of state aid is still awarded based solely on need, the trend has been increasingly to use merit criteria (alone or in combination with need) to ration aid (see Table 10.3). Since the mid-1990s, state spending on merit-based financial aid programs has increased at a faster rate than for need-based aid programs (Heller, 2002).

Table 10.3: Comparison of state aid awarded based on need or merit criteria

Criteria	Academic year 2003–2004	2011–2012
	Proportion of total state aid*	
Need-only	51.1	47.0
Merit-only	17.1	19.1
Need and merit	16.2	20.0

* Note: Figures do not equal 100 percent. Special purpose aid constitutes the remainder of state aid.

Sources: Table 8, National Association of Student Grant and Aid Programs (NASSGAP) 43rd Annual Survey Report, 2011–2012; Table 8, NASSGAP 35th Annual Survey Report, 2003–2004

The state shift toward use of merit criteria in awarding aid has important implication for SEM professionals. As discussed in Chapter 12, the last chapter in Part III, the pricing of colleges has been the subject of vigorous scholarly and public policy debate. A key aspect of the debate is the relationship between state appropriations (direct to institutions and for students) and institutional behaviors. Institutional responses to state policies using broad merit criteria to ration aid can include increasing the price charged to recoup external dollars or shifting institutional resources to focus on other priorities (such as more need-based aid), as two examples.

Some evidence suggests that institutions may respond to state merit-based aid programs by increasing costs in order to capture more of the state subsidy (particularly in the face of declining direct appropriations from states). For example, a study (Long, 2004) of the state of Georgia's HOPE Scholarship found some evidence that institutions raised prices in response to increased state merit scholarships. Specifically, public institutions in Georgia appeared to increase room and board costs, while private institutions (with more autonomy to set prices than public institutions) increased tuition. The magnitude of price increase was about 10 cents in additional room and board charges for every HOPE dollar at public institutions and about 30 cents in additional tuition for every HOPE dollar at private institutions (in 2000 dollars). In the case of Georgia, we lack evidence as to how institutions used the additional revenue and whether, for example, institutional aid dollars were reallocated. Some evidence suggests that the state aid programs affect the overall enrollment decisions of students, which is important to consider from a SEM perspective, as is discussed next.

The mix of merit- and need-based aid within a state affects students' enrollment decisions and patterns, with consequences for SEM professionals. For example, Laura Perna and Marvin Titus (2004) found that increases in state need-based aid were associated with the increased likelihood of a student enrolling in a four-year public or private institution in state. However, Robert Toutkoushian and Nick Hillman (2012) found that merit-based aid programs had a larger statewide impact than need-based programs.

This suggests that an institution's SEM approach should take into consideration the effects of state aid programs. For example, in states with relatively strong merit and need aid programs, institutional resources might be reallocated to focus on enrolling more out-of-state students given that strong state financial aid may induce more students to enroll, particularly in-state. Alternatively, in states where need-based aid has declined at the expense of merit-based aid, institutions might focus institutional aid on need-based aid. Evidence (Curs, 2008) suggests that wealthier students are more responsive to merit-based aid than lower income students. Moreover, the growing use of merit criteria in rationing aid for students may come at the expense of programs that support access for underrepresented students (such as, low-income, students of color) (Heller & Marin, 2004). Institutions must evaluate the effects of state merit aid programs on the composition of their applicant pool and determine what, if anything, should be done to ensure optimal levels of diversity (defined broadly).

Certainly, state merit aid that accompanies high-achieving students is desirable from an institutional perspective, as it represents an external source of financial aid with no opportunity cost in terms of financial aid dollars (the money cannot be spent any other way). However, it remains unclear whether institutions are using state merit aid to magnify efforts to climb the prestige ladder or whether state merit aid frees up other institutional resources to focus on need-based or need-rationed aid.

CONCLUSION

Perhaps more so than any other area of higher education, financial aid administration intersects with a complex web of institutional priorities, social needs, and governmental policy. Increasingly, SEM professionals are at the nexus of this intersection, requiring an ever-expanding skill set. I conclude this chapter with suggestions about specific resources that may be particularly important in staying informed of the ever-shifting financial aid landscape.

Foremost among these resources are the professional associations of which SEM professionals are a part. Organizations such as the American Association of Collegiate Registrars and Admissions Officers (AACRAO) and the National Association of Student Financial Aid Administrators (NASFAA) employ full-time policy analysis professionals who provide members with key information about existing and anticipated changes to the policy environment. Moreover, these associations serve as a conduit for policy change in that they are involved in the policy-making process. NASFAA, as one example, has been involved in financial aid policy making since its founding almost fifty years ago.

In addition to professional associations, a number of annual reports provide current data about the state of postsecondary financial aid. Each year since 1983, the College Board has published its "Trends in Student Aid" report, drawing on a variety of data sources, including primary data collected through its Annual Survey of Colleges. Another valuable resource is the National Center for Education Statistics' (NCES) annual *Digest of Education Statistics.* This comprehensive compendium of education data is longitudinal and includes all levels (primary, secondary, tertiary) and sectors (public, private, proprietary) of education. Of particular relevance to SEM professionals in the NCES digest are the data under "Student Charges" in Chapter 3 (Postsecondary Education), which include average tuition charges, aid awards, costs of attendance, and more.

Finally, for more fine-grained analysis, NCES also has a variety of tools (such as the Integrated Postsecondary Education Data System, or IPEDS) that allow for more specific comparison of trends at the institutional level. The National Postsecondary Student Aid Study (NPSAS) is another data resource that can provide national data to a great level of detail (such as number of hours a student worked off campus at a public, four-year institution). If pulling and analyzing data from sources such as NCES proves to be too cumbersome, your own institutional research office should be familiar with these data sources and should have the capacity to pull data by request.

In the next chapter, Steve Brooks provides an overview of how institutions use econometric techniques to determine how they will spend their financial aid dollars and the tradeoffs between net-tuition revenue and other campus priorities.

References

Allan, G. (1988). No need for no-need. *Journal of College Admission*, 120, 23–26.

Baum, S., & Payea, K. (2013). *Trends in Student Aid: 2013.* Retrieved from http://trends.collegeboard.org/sites/default/files/student-aid-2013-full-report.pdf.

Baum, S. R., & Schwartz, S. (1988). Merit aid to college students. *Economics of Education Review*, 7(1), 127–134.

Breneman, D. W. (1994). *Liberal Arts Colleges: Thriving, Surviving, or Endangered?* Washington, DC: The Brookings Institution.

Curs, B. R. (2008). The Effects of Institutional Merit-Based Aid on the Enrollment Decisions of Needy Students. *Enrollment Management Journal*, 2(1), 10–31.

Dougherty, K. J., & Reddy, V. (2013). *Performance Funding for Higher Education: What Are the Mechanisms? What Are the Impacts?* San Francisco: Jossey-Bass.

Doyle, W. R. (2010). Changes in institutional aid, 1992–2003: The evolving role of merit aid. *Research in Higher Education*, 51(8), 789–810.

Dynarski, S. (2002). *The consequences of merit aid*. JCPR Working Paper. Chicago, IL: Joint Center for Poverty Research.

Gross, J. P., Cekic, O., Hossler, D., & Hillman, N. (2009). What matters in student loan default: A review of the research literature. *Journal of Student Financial Aid*, *39*(1), 19–29.

Heller, D. E. (2002). The policy shift in state financial aid programs. In J. C. Smart (Ed.), *Higher Education: Handbook of Theory and Research* (pp. 221–261). New York: Agathon Press.

Heller, D. E., & Marin, P. (Eds.). (2004). *State Merit Scholarship Programs and Racial Inequality*. Cambridge, MA: The Civil Rights Project at Harvard University.

Henderson, D. R. (2008) Opportunity cost. *The Concise Encyclopedia of Economics*. Retrieved from http://www.econlib.org/library/Enc/OpportunityCost.html

Kantrowitz, M., & O'Shaughnessy, L. (2012). Much ado about double or nothing. *The New York Times*. Retrieved from http://www.nytimes.com/2012/05/10/opinion/much-ado-about-students-loans.html

Long, B. T. (2004). How do financial aid policies affect colleges? The institutional impact of the Georgia HOPE scholarship. *Journal of Human Resources*, *39*(4), 1045–1066.

Martin, R. E. (2004). Tuition discounting without tears. *Economics of Education Review*, *23*(2), 177–189.

Perna, L. W., & Titus, M. A. (2004). Understanding differences in the choice of college attended: The role of state public policies. *The Review of Higher Education*, *27*(4), 501–525.

Toutkoushian, R. K., & Hillman, N. W. (2012). The impact of state appropriations and grants on access to higher education and outmigration. *The Review of Higher Education*, *36*(1), 51–90.

U.S. Department of Education. (2012). First official three-year student loan default rates published. Department continues efforts to help students better manage their debt. Retrieved from http://www.ed.gov/news/press-releases/first-official-three-year-student-loan-default-rates-published

U.S. Department of Education. (2013). Cohort default guide. Retrieved from http://ifap.ed.gov/DefaultManagement/guide/attachments/CDRMasterFile.pdf

CHAPTER 11

Using Campus-Based Financial Aid Strategically

Stephen Brooks

O ver the years, the goals of campus-based aid has been designed around four fairly simple and straightforward goals: broaden access, provide equity, redistribute income (Wilkinson, 2005), and reward talent (academic merit, athletic talent, musical talent, and so on). The financial situation of each student and family was evaluated to determine their ability to contribute to the cost of education. Students were offered admission regardless of their ability to pay, and, given a more-or-less uniform method for evaluating the family's ability to pay, the aid offers were uniform as well. Students could make their college-choice decision exclusively on the merits of a college (program, selectivity, stature, and other intangibles) and not its cost (Bamberger & Carlton, 2004). Indeed for many years, a large group of selective institutions would meet and determine the level and distribution of aid to be offered each student by each of the participating institutions.

The goal of this effort, of course, was to insure that each student could make a college-selection decision without regard to its cost. The practical outcome was that the most selective colleges were able to play an extremely strong hand. They could attract talented students without fear that a less-selective competitor would offer their admitted students more generous and attractive aid packages and thereby cut into their yields.

This began to change in the late 1980s and early 1990s when the U.S. Justice Department began their "price-fixing" challenge to the practice (Bamberger & Carlton, 2004). Shortly thereafter, the overlap group, as it was

213

called, was more or less disbanded and the practice (once referred to as "benevolent collusion") stopped. It is probably fair to date this period as the start of what has now become a much more complicated and diverse financial-aid environment in higher education. In addition, over these twenty or so years, the rapidly rising cost of higher education, combined with declining real value of federal and state aid, has meant that financial aid offered by the institutions themselves plays a much bigger role in enrollment decisions than it did in the early 1990s.

Today, at a minimum, the following additional goals to the four goals of financial aid can be added:

- Maintain or increase class size.
- Increase ethnic diversity.
- Improve academic profile.
- Increase net tuition revenue.
- Lower the tuition discount rate.
- Strengthen weak academic programs.
- Maximize the return on strong academic programs.
- Support athletic or other specialized programs on campus.

The overwhelming challenge for enrollment officers is to achieve the proper balance for their institution among these often conflicting set of goals.

This chapter addresses issues of defining need for the purposes of financial aid awards as well as the various approaches to packaging financial aid. Next, it discusses how enrollment databases can be coupled with econometric tools to accomplish various enrollment and budgetary goals. Finally, it provides a brief overview of the types of questions an institution can answer using these econometric tools and their own institutional data.

DIFFERENT APPROACHES TO FINANCIAL AID

The most selective colleges that made up the core of the overlap group still more-or-less stick to the historical financial aid approach of (1) admitting students without regard to their financial need and (2) meeting the full "demonstrated" (that is, proven through the family's Free Application For Federal Student Aid [FAFSA] filing) need of the admitted student. But this need-blind, meet-full-need approach is becoming more and more rare. Moreover, according to the standard codes of enrollment behavior, a need-blind institution is allowed to call itself need-blind while being need-aware in wait-list decisions (at the end of the enrollment cycle) and with international admits. These are potentially significant opportunities to move away slightly from need-blind without actually stating it.

In addition, the fact that an institution meets the full demonstrated need of an admitted applicant does not speak to anything about how that need ends up being packaged. The mix of grants (free institutional gift aid), loans, and work study could be different across institutions and within institutions, depending on the desirability of the admitted applicant.

Finally, there are a seemingly infinite number of ways to calculate the full demonstrated need of an admitted applicant. Virtually all meet-full-need institutions use institutional needs-analysis methodologies that, although having a common core, will often have different adjustments depending on the handling of business income, home equity, non–custodial-parent contributions, local and regional price differentials, professional judgment, and so on.

Being Need Aware

The first step back from the meet-full-need approach is usually to become "need-aware" in admission. This means that, although each student's financial need is fully met, admission decisions are, to a lesser or greater degree, made depending on the financial well-being of the family. In all instances, the use of a need-aware approach is limited only to a relatively small subset of the less-able or less-desirable admission applicants. The most able applicants or the most desirable applicants (based on some other criteria) at a typical need-aware institution are admitted without regard to need.

But meeting full need (whether admission is need-blind or need-aware) does not limit an institution from offering financial aid packages in excess of need (or to those who don't apply for financial aid). Today, most private colleges and universities offer some sort of "merit" scholarships that are not need-based and that are not in any way based on the resources of the student and his or her family.

Meeting Less Than Full Need

Ironically, institutions who do not claim to meet full need often end up being far more need-blind than those that do meet full need. The key difference is that, because they don't have to meet full need, these institutions are able to admit any student who meets admission criteria regardless of the student's need, because the institution will offer that student only as much aid as its budget or packaging rules will allow.

Institutions that meet less than full need will typically use the "federal methodology," which relies on the needs analysis determined by the U.S. Department of Education based on the student's submission of a FAFSA.

DEFINITIONS OF NEED

Determining the "true" need of a student is one of the most vexing problems facing enrollment managers, who recognize their responsibility to provide financial aid at least in part on the basis of the student's family resources. Although enrollment managers may rely on either the federal methodology or perhaps differently complex versions of the institutional methodology, there is absolutely no clear sense that they have got the number right except in the most general possible sense. Judging the need of international students for whom there are no federal estimates is an even harder, more uncertain process.

I recently completed a research task for one client wanting to move from the federal methodology to one of the institutional-methodology variants. The task was to determine how much need would change for individual students as a result of the changed methodology. One of the surprising findings was that roughly 20 percent of their aid-requesting students would have had a change in their need (either up or down) of more than $10,000. Of these, 7 percent would have a change of more than $20,000.

Averaged over a large number of admitted aid requesters, the institutional methodology typically returns need around $2,000 less than those returned by the federal methodology. But individually, the differences can vary widely (both up and down). This distressing lack of precision, especially in an age when families are reported to seek methods actively to reduce their demonstrated need, makes it hard to have too much confidence in any single student's calculated need. This uncertainty gives rise to stories of financial-aid directors using online tools to check estimated home values and car ownership to assess the accuracy of a family's measured need.

Thus, one finds reasonably frequent adjustments and revisions to the needs-analysis methodologies, especially for those meeting full need. For the overwhelming bulk of those institutions that don't promise to meet full need, the complications (and cost to the families) of the institutional methodology don't make much sense and so most rely on the federal methodology.

PACKAGING OF INSTITUTIONAL GIFT AID

If there is increasing uncertainty and variation surrounding estimates of need, there are even greater complexities surrounding how that aid is actually packaged as grant (free gift aid from all sources), loan, or work study. Two examples pretty much span the range of possible variations in the packaging of institutional grant aid. Both are actual examples drawn from awards offered to

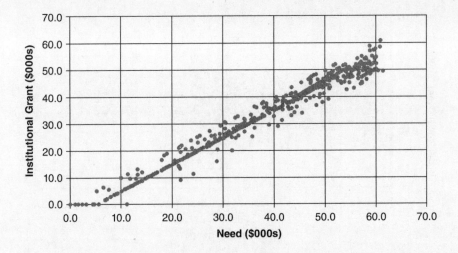

Figure 11.1 Need-grant scatter—need-blind, meet-full-need, fall 2013

admitted financial aid requesters applying for admission in the fall of 2013 by two different institutions.

The figures that follow represent scatter diagrams, where each dot is a single admitted aid requester. The horizontal axis captures the student's need (as measured by that institution). The vertical axis captures the size of the *institutional* gift aid (or grant) from all sources including merit- and need-based aid. Moreover, this measure of grant is completely independent of the source of the funds for those grants. The source could be either endowed funds or pure tuition discount.

Figure 11.1 represents the classical need-blind, meet-full-need example. Figure 11.1 displays a "hockey-stick" pattern, where the first $5,000 or $6,000 in need is met with "self-help" consisting of Stafford loans and work study. This is the flat portion on the left-hand side of the hockey stick. No institutional grants are offered to families with needs at or below that value. After that level of need is reached, students with needs above that amount have their remaining need met dollar-for-dollar. The upward sloping section of the hockey stick has a slope of 1.0.

Certain awards fall slightly off that line (either above or below) because of appeals, the existence of outside grant dollars (federal, state, or other private sources), and so on. But generally the dots are very closely grouped along that 45-degree line. The gift or grant aid from this institution is determined almost exclusively by the student's demonstrated need.

Figure 11.2 represents an institution with differentially packaged gift aid.

This school provides aggressive merit scholarships to a great number of its admitted applicants. Those merit amounts can be seen, most clearly, in two

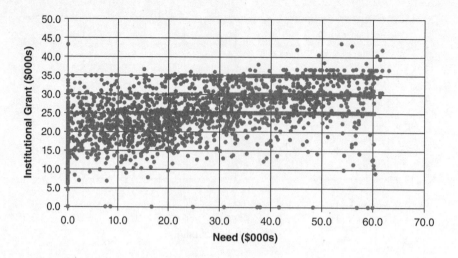

Figure 11.2 Need-grant scatter, differentially packaged grant aid, fall 2013

areas: first, along the vertical axis (where all the students have no need) each of the dots represents a merit scholarship; and, second, any award that lies above the 45-degree line starting at the origin and moving upward to the right carries with it some non-zero merit amount.

There seem to be three horizontal lines at about $25,000, $30,000, and $35,000. These are capped merit awards, where the student receives those amounts regardless of need. Although they appear to be solid lines, that is simply an artifact of the number of dots on those ranges. They actually all represent individual students.

If one studies the dots closely, one can make out a hazy upward-to-the-right pattern of dots in the range of about $15,000 of need to roughly $35,000 of need. But it is not very distinct, certainly not like the pattern of dots in Figure 11.1. This is about the only way to infer from the figure that need plays any role in the packaging of grants from this institution.

The other striking feature of Figure 11.2 (particularly when compared with Figure 11.1) is that above about $40,000 in need, there is an increasing gap between the student's need and the amount of gift aid offered by this institution. On the other hand, the yield of those admitted aid requesters with need above $40,000 is essentially identical to their overall yield.

The pattern shown in Figure 11.2 reflects an institution aggressively and generously targeting its most desirable admitted applicants with merit- and need-based aid. But, lacking strong endowment resources and being largely tuition-driven, the institution is unable to provide enough aid to meet the full needs of their neediest students.

There is a strong sense that, for the bulk of private colleges and universities, actual packaging of aid lands somewhere between Figures 11.1 and 11.2 but probably tending slightly more toward Figure 11.2.

At this point, the reader may have the sense that anything goes, or that there are few common best practices when it comes to awarding financial aid. Indeed, the current financial aid landscape in the United States is one of conflicting enrollment goals, uncertain measures of financial need, and vastly different packaging strategies.

HOW IS AVAILABILITY OF AID COMMUNICATED TO PROSPECTIVE APPLICANTS?

There is a distinction in higher education between those schools that, on the one hand, are able to select a limited number of able admits from a large applicant pool and, on the other, must actively market and recruit every single admitted student to meet their enrollment goals.

In the first group (which would include the institution whose packaging of aid is shown in Figure 11.1) are well-established, highly selective schools with formidable market positions, very large endowments, and a long history of enrollment successes. They make it clear in all of their communication materials that they meet the full need of their admitted applicants. This is a major selling point and an opportunity for the institution to claim the high moral ground. Many have eliminated loans for lower-income families, and this feature of their aid package is also communicated directly and clearly to prospects by their enrollment professionals. Many have merit programs. They may require scholarship days on campus for interviewing, testing, and selection. This would be clearly spelled out in communication materials (including invitations to apply for the scholarships) and on their websites.

But most colleges and universities do not enjoy such luxuries. For the rest, especially private institutions facing strong competition from public options, there is a perceived need to make sure applicants are aware that the high sticker price for a private institution can be largely offset with generous financial aid including merit scholarships. Most institutions will provide guidance as to the range of aid offered for different merit scholarships. Students can compare their GPA and test scores with the scholarship criteria and get a good sense of what their award will likely be. Some schools will even guarantee specific dollar amounts if GPA and class rank and/or test scores fall within certain bands. The chief concern with this approach is that efforts to appear more affordable will be perceived as aggressive attempts to "buy" students. Institutions would like to be thought of as the best because of their academic stature and program strength, not because of their cheap cost.

The introduction of mandated net-price calculators (NPCs) has expanded the options for families to tally the likely cost of attendance at individual institutions based on a student's grades, scores and family need. The student data are self-reported, so there are lots of opportunities for error. The general sense is that the NPCs are not used very frequently. The Institute for College Access & Success (Cheng, Asher, Abernathy, Cochrane, & Thompson, 2012) found that although improvements have been made since they were first required, most NPCs are still hard to find, cumbersome to use, and not easily compared due to differences in net-price calculations. There are only a few instances of families complaining that the NPC provided an estimated grant amount that was greater than what they were actually offered. Anecdotally, when it does occur, the difference is often because of errors in the reporting of family income and need information.

UNDERSTANDING ENROLLMENT BEHAVIOR

Regardless of the overarching admission and aid philosophies of any given institution, there remains an underlying need to know how financial aid will affect its admitted students. Whether need-blind, need-aware, meeting full need, or none of the above, enrollment managers, must have a working notion of the relationship between aid offered to a student and the likelihood that the student will enroll. Even schools that are need-blind and meeting full need have to worry about the fraction of the need that is being met with grants as compared to loans and work study. Institutions with merit awards must have a sense of whether their merit scholarships are targeted at the right groups of students and whether they are the right amounts. Those who package awards differentially on the basis of ability, program, or other factors clearly need to know what impact to expect from any changes in their packaging rules. However, enrollment managers should have a working tool of some sort to explain enrollment behavior. They must have a way to estimate what happens when there is an increase or decrease of aid to this or that population of admitted students.

What Is the Impact of Financial Aid?

There are a number of alternative techniques to arrive at a working sense of how changes in aid will affect admitted applicants. Most are, alas, retrospective: looking at recent enrollment outcomes to see how students have responded to aid in the past. The only non-retrospective technique would be to poll students and their families to ask how they would respond to different prices, financial aid packages, and net costs. Although this technique has value, the responses would be subjective and not likely to be available in real time in the face of a rapidly changing competitive environment. Moreover, it's unlikely that such a survey could, at a reasonable cost, have sample sizes large enough to be of value when looking at all the relevant subgroups of the accepted-student pool by gender, ethnicity, program of interest, distance from campus, family income and need, and so on.

Broadly speaking, there are two retrospective approaches for projecting next year's yields. The first is to make a simple estimate based on last year's yield or the trend in the last several years' yields. The second is econometric, which will be discussed in turn.

Projecting Using Historical Yields

Of course, there are many variants of this basic technique, ranging from the simple to the complex. At the simple end, one can consider the class as a whole and base the estimates on the recent trend in the yield of all admitted applicants. Here is a typical example. Figure 11.3 shows the recent history of first-year yields at a representative institution.

Despite some ups and downs, yields have been averaging around 30 percent with no discernible trend. This fall's yield would then be estimated to lie somewhere between the six-year average and last year's yield.

At the more complex end, consider discrete "slices" of the class, perhaps dividing up the admitted applicants by an admission rating and the amount of institutional dollars offered. Projected yields for this year are then based on trend yields of students in similar "slices" of the class. Table 11.1 shows an example from another institution. Across the top of the table, the admits are grouped by their financial-aid status (no aid requested; no aid requested,

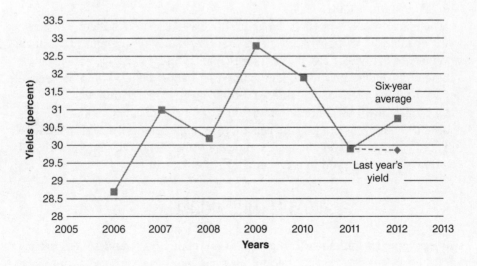

Figure 11.3 First-year yields

Table 11.1: Yields by financial aid status and ability

Yields (percent)	No aid requested	Aid requested (grants in dollars)			
	No grant	Merit award	0–5,000	5,000–10,000	10,000 +
SAT: 0–800	29	n/a	27	43	65
SAT: 805–1000	28	50	42	62	57
SAT:1005–1200	26	50	34	48	43
SAT:1205–1600	15	29	24	31	31

but merit dollars awarded; aid requested, offered grant less than $5,000; and so on). Down the side of the table, they are grouped by their ability (using the college's admission rating system). The table shows a single-year's results, but data from prior years could be analyzed similarly. For this year, all the admits would be placed in their proper group depending on their rating and grant. The prediction for the coming fall's yield would then be based on the number of admitted students in each of the cells and the yields in those cells.

If the institution is limited to using one of these approaches, the second approach is much preferred to the first. In the first, the institution would be shooting blind, ignoring all information about the admitted students. But the second also has some very serious limitations. What makes someone think that this (or any other more or less arbitrary scheme) is the correct way to classify the admitted students? Was this tested statistically to see whether these groupings are the most important?

There are countless ways to break up the class based on student characteristics or interests. Suppose that yields are systematically different for women and men, or that yields are different for Hispanics and Asians, or that yields are different depending on the student's proposed major. Tables would be needed for women and men, or for different ethnic groups, or for different majors—each broken down by admission rating and grant size. That is a lot of different tables. Ultimately, as the process gets more complex, the cell sizes become too small to provide any confidence that they are truly robust and representative of the underlying true yield in each cell.

ECONOMETRIC MODELING

The econometric approach (using regression modeling) is preferred to simply projecting historical yields no matter how complex a variant of that approach used. It calculates the independent effect on yield of each student characteristic (college aid, ability, classroom performance, ethnicity, geographic origin, expected major, and so on). It allows the institution to test statistically whether or not a particular characteristic "matters" in determining yield. It produces a direct estimate of the probability of each student's matriculation. It can estimate the effect on matriculation probabilities of changes in institutional aid awards. It does all of this entirely with admission and financial aid data. It provides clear estimates of student price sensitivity (including by subgroups of the admit pool). It provides estimates of whether or not any of the specific majors or programs have greater or less-than-normal drawing power.

Problems and Concerns with the Econometric Approach

Data accuracy and consistency is probably the single biggest concern for any institution undertaking econometric modeling of enrollment behavior. The models can only be as good as the data on which they are built. Although that is true of any approach requiring the use of historical data to help predict the future, it is more critical for econometric techniques, because of the possibility that coefficient estimates (particularly the coefficient associated with the institutional grant awards) can be inaccurately estimated.

The following set of concerns should be considered when approaching the use of historical data either to build econometric models or to provide a more general understanding of an institution's competitive enrollment market.

Are the Data Complete? One needs to be sure that there is usable accurate data for both enrolling and non-enrolling students across all the variables intended for use. Of these, the most important of the "Data-complete?" questions concerns the availability of financial aid awards for the non-enrolling admitted applicants. One will certainly have all the award information for enrolling students, but if there is no similar information for non-enrolling admits, there will be no way to estimate econometrically the impact of differences in awards on enrollment. The most important parameters in the models are those reflecting the change in enrollment probability associated with a change in institutional grant offers. That parameter cannot be estimated without seeing how differences in awards are associated with differences in enrollment outcomes across the admit pool.

Are Enough Data Available? Moderately large sample sizes are critical to ensure that one's estimation data set will have enough power to find and accurately measure the factors most important in determining the enrollment probability of accepted applicants.

Are the Data Biased? There are very serious potential problems resulting from measurement error. Anyone using enrollment data must be wary of problems working with "home-grown" institutional data. Are the data clean and do they properly capture the factors that they appear to? If they do not, the models will produce inaccurate coefficient estimates and inferences about causal influence derived from the model's structure, and coefficients will likely be inaccurate. Similarly, any change in the process used to produce the enrollment data must be accounted for in a systematic way or the models will be inaccurate. If those responsible for creating, updating, and maintaining the enrollment data are doing things differently for enrolling students and non-enrolling students, then there is a very strong possibility of introducing inaccuracies into the structure and coefficient values in the models. Here's an example drawn from experiences working with enrollment data: Suppose there is a supplement process to gather or (if already gathered in paper files) enter into the enrollment database information concerning the "legacy" status of enrolled students. In that case, the legacy variable will be extraordinarily significant and positively related to enrollment in the econometric models. Similar problems can occur over a wide range of variables.

Have Any Variables Been Omitted? In any real-time work with enrollment data, enrollment staff will rarely or completely know one of the most important pieces of information in understanding why a student either does or does not enroll at the institution: how much aid he or she is being offered from competitor institutions. Those who appeal for more generous financial aid will often provide offers from other institutions to which they have been accepted. But appealers are, typically, only a relatively small subset of the class and, by appealing, they have immediately set themselves apart from the remainder of the accepted-student pool. It is important that models include variables that can be considered proxies for what the student is being offered by competitors. The most frequently used of such a proxy is simply the student's ability as captured by high school classroom performance, results from standardized tests, interview results, and so on. But problems with omitted variables go beyond just this most obvious one. One must know what makes the institution different from its competitors, know what characteristics or actions of applicants make them more or less likely to enroll, and then be sure that one's models capture those factors in the most complete and accurate way possible.

Have Too Many Variables Been Included in the Model? There is a strong temptation to include any variable that is even marginally significant in the model. The significance of each variable should be tested in randomly selected subsamples of the data to make sure that a variable's statistical significance is not just an artifact of the particular data set one is working with. Do the coefficient estimates make sense? What sort of inferences can be drawn from them concerning the student's responsiveness to financial aid?

Do Models Reflect the Past, Rather than the Future? Recognize that the models are retrospective. If there is a clear and obvious change in the competitive environment that will impact the enrollment (competitors' awards being the most important), realize and adjust for the fact that your model predictions are not going to be taking that into account. Another example would be a significant new change or initiative in marketing or recruiting efforts. Use reasonable common sense and judgment in evaluating the impact of both internal and external changes that the models have not seen in their historical data.

Modeling Approaches

Without digging deep into econometric issues, here are a few thoughts on modeling approaches. One should plan to use a "limited-dependent variable" regression estimation technique (either Probit or Logit) to estimate model parameters. We recommend estimating alternative models using different time spans of history to capture longer term trends as well as the last year's activity. This can be especially important when the enrollment environment seems to be shifting. One should have a model that is built on just the last year's data. But given that events can be transitory, predictions from models built over longer history (two, three, or four years of data) can smooth out some of the impermanent blips in the data. In working with multiple years of data, dollar values (aid amounts, need, income, and so on) should be deflated to a common year's "real" value.

USING MODELS IN ENROLLMENT ANALYSIS

The most pervasive and open-ended question asked by virtually all enrollment managers is, "How can I package financial aid that helps meet the enrollment goals of our institution and is consistent with our underlying mission to provide an affordable, high-quality educational experience for the broadest and most diverse possible community of learners?" Embedded in that question are two very important threads: first, the enrollment goals of the institution; second, the institutional mission through which those goals have been determined. Each institution must determine what it wants to be and what, given constraints, it realistically can be.

A successful financial aid system helps achieve enrollment goals and supports the institution's mission. The models themselves can be ideal tools for exploring the range of financial-aid options available to an institution constrained by limited resources in an increasingly competitive marketplace. How can this process be used in practice? What questions can it answer?

The models are designed to return a measure of the enrollment probability of each student with values ranging from 0 to 1. For a given set of students, the average of those estimated probabilities is the best model prediction of the yield for that group of students. The sum of all the enrollment probabilities is the best model prediction of the total number of enrolled students.

Model users can simulate alternative amounts of institutional aid offered to a selected group of students to see how the probabilities of individual students change with higher or lower aid amounts. Those individual changes in enrollment probability can be translated into predicted changes in yield or enrollment counts. Moreover, with some additional work, it is possible to evaluate changes in revenue associated with the changes in institutional grant offers. With this process up and running, users can evaluate the model-estimated changes in enrollment, net tuition revenue, academic profile, ethnic mix, and any other relevant enrollment-related variable resulting from changes in aid offers.

Following are some examples of how econometric models of enrollment probability can be used, drawn from our experiences working with higher education clients.

- **We have a set of merit scholarships of varying amounts.** Can we achieve a better result by changing the amounts of those scholarships? Can we improve our outcomes by changing the groups of admitted applicants offered those scholarships?

- **We need to reduce our tuition discount rate.** Should we reduce the value of our merit scholarships or limit need-based grant-in-aid? And depending on which of these alternatives we choose, what are the likely impacts on overall enrollment, ethnic diversity, academic profile, net revenue, and so on, of our enrolled first-year class?

- **We are currently need-aware in our admission decisions**. How much would it cost us in lost net tuition revenue if we became need-blind? How would the characteristics of our incoming class differ? How much could we improve the academic profile or diversity of our class by being need-blind?

- **We would like to change our needs analysis**. What will be the outcome from using our existing packaging rules applied to the new measures of estimated family contributions (EFC) and need? How would we change our packaging rules to remain enrollment-neutral from the change, and how would we limit any unwanted impact of the change in needs analysis on specific subgroups of the class?

- **Yield fell this past fall.** What were the main factors contributing to the decline in yield? Was it a change in the academic profile of our admitted students? Less generous financial aid? Increasing competitiveness from key overlap competitors? Can we identify pockets of weakness where additional financial aid could help offset the yield decline at the smallest possible cost in net tuition revenue?

This is a relatively small, but representative, set of the questions that the models of enrollment probability can help answer within the context of a well-developed and well-maintained enrollment data system that helps support research and analysis needs of enrollment management.

CONCLUSION

Beware the total reliance on financial aid. It cannot be the magic pill that solves all the problems and moves an institution from where it is now to where it hopes to be in the future. Nevertheless, one must be aware of the need for and ability of financial aid packaging to *support* movement toward those goals. If there are institutional options to do so, one must be willing to experiment and learn more about the enrollment behavior of the admitted applicants. And one must recognize that, in the ever-changing enrollment environment, what one learns this year may very well change next year. The final chapter in Part III addresses these trade-offs and their impacts on institutional budgets. The models can help point individuals in key directions and offer suggestions of things that are likely to work and help—but nothing can replace the hard truth of actual enrollment outcomes.

References

Bamberger, G., & Carlton, D. (2004). Antitrust and higher education: MIT financial aid. In J. Kwoka & L. White (Eds.), *The Antitrust Revolution: Economics, Competition, and Policy.* New York: Oxford University Press.

Cheng, D., Asher, L., Abernathy, P., Cochrane, D., & Thompson J. (2012). *Adding it all up 2012: Are college net price calculators easy to find, use, and compare?* The Institute for College Access & Success. Retrieved from http://www.ticas.org/files/pub/Adding_It_All_Up_2012.pdf.

Wilkinson, R. (2005). *Aiding Students, Buying Students: Financial Aid in America.* Nashville, TN: Vanderbilt University Press.

CHAPTER 12

Budgets, Aid, and Enrollments

Guilbert L. Brown and Jacob P. K. Gross

Tight linkages exist between pricing, institutional aid, and campus budgeting practices. In many ways, these three prongs of finance are inseparable and exert a strong influence on the health and vitality of postsecondary institutions. This chapter considers the following: (a) higher education's business model in the context of basic economic attributes of colleges and universities; (b) how higher education financing has changed in recent decades and is likely to change in the future; and (c) how Strategic Enrollment Management practitioners can effectually support student and institutional success through the use of pricing and financial aid strategies. The fiscal health of higher education institutions will increasingly depend on utilizing the tools and techniques of SEM. In addition, it is essential that senior enrollment officers understand higher education finance. Many of their discussions with other senior campus policy makers will revolve around campus financial issues. If a senior enrollment officer does not understand these issues, he or she is poorly positioned to influence the outcomes of those discussions.

In the context of SEM, financial aid facilitates paying the bills for both students and the institutions they attend. Without financial aid, many students could not afford to attend college or would choose to attend a lower cost institution. Similarly, without the enrollment revenues provided by the same students, many colleges and universities could not afford to pay employee salaries and other operating costs. For enrollment managers, financial aid is one of the most useful mechanisms available to influence students' enrollment decisions.

From the perspective of institutional budgeting, financial aid programs are fundamental to financing both private and public institutions of higher education. Budgets for most public and private colleges and universities in the United States are dependent on tuition from enrollments, financed via financial aid, and provide the cash flows needed to fund operating costs. We turn next to a discussion of the higher education business model, including a summary of the competing theories about increasing college costs.

THE BUSINESS MODEL OF HIGHER EDUCATION

Before we delve into the relationship between pricing, financial aid, and budgets, it is constructive to consider the question, "Is higher education a business?" Robert Zemsky, Gregory Wegner, and William Massy (2005) noted that the tension between markets (higher education as a business) and mission (higher education as a social institution) is as old as higher education itself in the United States. This is evident in the very structures and diversity of our institutions. Compare the core missions of our liberal arts institutions (for example, broaden knowledge, cultivate humanity) with our land grant institutions (train the people in practical skills), for example. For the purposes of this chapter, we focus on the non-profit rather than for-profit business model for higher education. The majority of students nationally enroll in non-profit institutions, which make up the majority of total institutions. Although business-like in some respect, higher education differs from businesses in a number of important ways.

First, the business model of higher education does not seek to maximize profits, but rather prestige. A fundamental difference between for-profit and non-profit educational firms is that non-profits face a non-distribution constraint—that is, operating profits cannot be redistributed among owners or shareholders (in fact, there are no owners or shareholders of a non-profit educational firm (Hansmann, 1981). Rather, revenues in excess of expenditures can only be reinvested in the mission of the non-profit. College and universities, like all non-profits, derive revenue from two sources: donations and the sale of good or services (Winston, 1999). Therefore, colleges and universities follow a donative-commercial model (Hansmann, 1981; Winston, 1999), deriving revenue from alumni donations, legislative appropriations, or other charitable gifts alongside revenue generated from tuition, patents, technical assistance, consulting, and more.

A second important way in which higher education's business model differs is that it relies on a customer-input technology (Winston, 1999). Arguably, the most important input (or technology) in education is the student who is being educated. Students are both inputs in and recipients of the education production process, with the quality of education often being a function of the students. From this perspective, students pay a fee for service (tuition) but are also paid to be inputs (such as merit scholarships). Therefore, a function of SEM is to use pricing to attract the inputs (students) deemed necessary to create the product (education) desired by the higher education institution. For example, Berea College in Kentucky has a long history as an institution serving low-income students. Overall, 100 percent of its students received some form of financial aid in 2011–2012, with 87 percent receiving Pell Grants. With its nearly $1 billion endowment, Berea College can reduce net price through institutional scholarships to attract low-income students (their input), thereby creating the overall product (education) for which it was established.

The donative-commercial model and the reliance on customer-input technology are key aspects of the higher education business model. With this business model in mind, we can disentangle the relationships among budgets, aid, and enrollments, better understanding how each relates to the others. To understand budgets, we next turn to a discussion of costs, a major driver in establishing institutional budgets and setting prices (no institution can survive long if its costs exceed revenues).

BUDGETS AND COSTS IN HIGHER EDUCATION

There is no single answer to the often-asked question, "Why does college cost so much?" This is a heavily debated topic, with divergent opinions politically and empirically. A challenge in attempting to answer the question is that there are different ways to conceptualize cost. Winston (1999) describes cost as the sum of the price paid by students plus external subsidies; "cost" is thus what institutions expend to provide services, which is greater than what students pay ("price," the commercial component) by the amount of subsidy (the donative component). Bruce Johnstone (2001) identifies four different definitions of cost:

- **Production cost:** This represents the underlying cost of instruction, including costs of salaries, benefits, facilities, and more.
- **Tuition or sticker price:** This is the published price of tuition, which often excludes fees and associated costs (such as room and board, books, travel).
- **Total cost:** This includes tuition, fees, books, room and board, and all other associated costs. In most cases, tuition makes up less than the majority of the total cost of attendance.
- **Net price or net cost:** This is the total cost of attendance less all financial assistance received. In some cases, loans may be subtracted

from the total cost of attendance to arrive at a net price (as is the case with many net price calculators now required by the federal government). Whether loans represent a reduction in total cost (with interest, they represent an increase in cost actually) is a matter of debate.

As Johnstone (2001) noted, it is often sticker price that receives the most attention in popular reports decrying the rise in college costs. Penelope Wang (2008) identified the "Chivas Regal anomaly," whereby institutions attempt to use higher prices as a means of differentiating (higher) quality in the perception of higher education consumers. As SEM professionals know, net price often differs from sticker price for students. Yet, the question remains regarding why college seems to be so expensive. Multiple rationales have been proposed (for example, see Getz & Siegfried, 1991) to explain cost increases; however, we focus on the two major theories: the Revenue Theory of Costs and the Cost Disease theory.

An important contribution to the debate about these theories (and costs in general) comes from the empirical work of two economists, Robert B. Archibald and David H. Feldman (2008). Using time-series and cross-sectional data, they compared higher education as an industry to others in the economy to determine to what extent the cost curves are similar. Overall, they found that higher education costs rise in ways that mirror other labor-intensive industries, lending support for the Cost Disease theory. Archibald and Feldman (2008) wrote, "In our view, the correct way to view past experience is to recognize that higher education behaves much the same way as other personal service industries that use highly educated labor" (p. 289). Their work suggests that the Revenue Theory of Cost should be viewed with skepticism. They go on to conclude that personal service industries (such as education) have not benefited from growth in productivity that has been enjoyed in manufacturing industries. Productivity increases that do not lower quality, therefore, may be the appropriate focus of institutions of higher education concerned about costs increases. On the whole, however, higher education has not seen cost increases that are significantly different from other personal service industries.

Revenue Theory of Cost

Howard Bowen's Revenue Theory of Costs (sometimes called Bowen's Law) suggests that unit costs vary to such a large degree at institutions because costs are a function of revenue (Bowen, 1980). In part due to the non-distribution constraint imposed on non-profits, institutions of higher education reinvest all the revenue they generate in their missions. Therefore, costs are less a function of the underlying production expenses and more a result of the revenue raising aspirations of the institution, according to Bowen's theory. In short, the only limit on institutional costs is revenue. This theory was famously invoked by the former U.S. Secretary of Education William J. Bennett in his February 18, 1987, opinion-editorial in *The New York Times*, titled "Our Greedy Colleges." Offered in part as a defense of the continuing cuts to higher education spending by the Reagan administration, Bennett suggested we in higher education are "under-accountable and under-productive."

Cost Disease Theory

The Cost Disease theory, offered by William J. Baumol and William G. Bowen (1966), claims that costs are driven by inherent limitations on the efficiency of higher education as a labor-intensive undertaking, where economies of scale cannot be realized past a certain point without adversely impacting quality. In sum, there is only so much you can do toward increasing productivity (and lowering costs) through technological innovations in higher education. Over time, according to the Cost Disease theory, the cost of personnel services must rise and so, too, will the underlying costs of instruction.

Other Theories of Cost

In terms of other theories that have been offered to explain rising costs, Massy and Zemsky (1994) pointed to increasing levels of administrative specialization resulting in increasingly complex and expensive higher education delivery and support systems. A number of commentators have pointed to market and commercial forces as increasing revenue-generation demands through the corporatization of higher education (Bok, 2003; Washburn, 2005). As will be discussed later in this chapter, some scholars (such as Slaughter & Rhoades, 2004) identify revenue-generating practices such as SEM among the key drivers in higher education costs.

As should be clear from the preceding discussion, debates about costs (which are a major driver of budgets) in higher education need to be approached thoughtfully and with some skepticism. To simply say that institutions are greedy and revenue-maximizing overlooks important aspects of our production model (that is, we need instructors to educate students) and has little empirical support. Moreover, as we discuss next, the financing models for higher education have been in flux for several decades, affecting the ways in which institutions plan strategically in their budgeting, awarding of aid, and in enrolling students.

THE CHANGING MODEL OF HIGHER EDUCATION FINANCE

Through the last quarter of the twentieth century and beginning decade of the twenty-first, major sectors of the U.S. economy have experienced fundamental transformations ranging from significant automation (and overseas exportation) of manufacturing, to the Internet as a primary means of advertising and delivering goods and services. For public higher education institutions, these transformations have included reductions to public funds supporting instruction, changes to federal policies impacting cost reimbursements for research and medical training, the shifting of student aid programs to emphasize loans over grants, and a shifting of the burden for paying for higher education from governmental support to students and their families (College Board, 1999; State Higher Education Executive Officers, 2013). Concurrent with these changes is a significant emphasis on entrepreneurial initiatives in public colleges and universities that hold as their objective the generation of revenue to support the mission-critical institutional programs of instruction, public service, discovery or creation, and subsequent dissemination of new knowledge (Rhoades & Slaughter, 1997).

Enrollment managers occupy a unique role where institutional programs and finances intersect with student attendance decisions that in turn involve individual financial matters. Financial aid is an essential tool for enrollment managers to achieve institutional and individual student goals simultaneously. With increased tuition dependency, American higher education's evolving business model depends on effective combinations of pricing and financial aid strategies. Economically, pricing, financial aid, and enrollments are interrelated. Changing one can directly impact the others. For example, when prices increase, the need for aid increases. Enrollment changes can prompt changes in pricing and financial aid strategies. And financial aid strategies can impact both enrollments and pricing. All three—pricing, aid, and enrollments—impact budgets. For budgeting, as for enrollment management, finding the right combination of pricing and financial aid to support institutional objectives depends on a host of factors that vary from one institution to the next. The enrollment management professional is in a unique organizational position to inform institutional discussions and strategies regarding pricing and aid decisions and their impacts on enrollments—and, consequently, on budgets.

The following series of tables illustrates the dynamics of these interrelationships. For both public institutions receiving state appropriations and private institutions subsidized with gift or endowment funds, the relationships among tuition, enrollments, costs, and subsidies are similar. In the following examples, averages from public institutions are used to show how changes to costs, enrollments, and subsidies impact the average net price per student (shown as "Average Student Tuition") that must be realized to balance the budget given the other assumptions in each model.

Assume that an institution enrolls 1,000 students and charges $5,189 tuition per student, the national average for public institutions in 2012 (SHEEO, 2013). In addition, the institution receives a $5,906 per student subsidy from its state, also the national average amount for 2012 (SHEEO, 2013). Assume further that

Table 12.1: Steady state institutional finances—1,000 students

Item	Year one	Year two	Change	Percent change
Revenue				
Tuition	$5,189,000	$5,344,670	$155,670	3.0
State support	$5,906,000	$6,083,180	$177,180	3.0
Total revenue	$11,095,000	$11,427,850	$332,850	3.0
Expense				
Salaries	$8,876,000	$9,142,280	$266,280	3.0
All other expenses	$2,219,000	$2,285,570	$66,570	3.0
Total expense	$11,095,000	$11,427,850	$332,850	3.0
Total # of students	1,000	1,000	—	—
Avg. student tuition	$5,189	$5,344	$155	3.0
Cost per student	$11,095	$11,428	$333	3.0

all revenues and expenses are increasing by 3 percent and enrollments are level—that is, not increasing or decreasing. Approximately 80 percent of expenses are for salaries. The resulting two-year finances for the institution might resemble the figures shown in Table 12.1.

Table 12.1 illustrates how, in a uniform steady state condition—with no increases or decreases to enrollments, and all revenue sources and expenses growing together—tuition increases, salary increases, and total spending (cost) per student would increase at comparable rates based on uniform cost and price inflation. Although simple, the mathematical relationships in this model make intuitive sense and represent a commonsense understanding of how tuition might be expected to increase over time. With enrollments remaining constant and revenues and expenses increasing 3 percent, the average tuition charge also increases by 3 percent. Both students and faculty benefit directly from the increased subsidies as average costs per student increase by $333, funded primarily through increased subsidies ($178) and only partially by increased tuition ($155), and faculty receive salary increases for teaching the same numbers of students.

Conversely, when subsidies do not keep pace with increased enrollments, both students and faculty pay the consequences. Average postsecondary state appropriations per student peaked in 2001 and since then have declined by 31.9 percent after adjustments for inflation; during the same period, tuition increased by 44.3 percent in real terms (SHEEO, 2013). As a result, and when combined with enrollment growth, funding per student from the combination of tuition and state appropriations actually *declined* by 9.6 percent from $12,267 in 2001 to $11,095 in 2012 (SHEEO, 2013) when adjusted for inflation. The long-term trends of declining subsidies combined with enrollment growth result in significant tuition increases without corresponding increases to spending per student.

Even without adjustments to inflation, as subsidies fail to keep up with enrollment growth, Cost Disease results in dramatic increases to tuition rates without corresponding increases in per-student spending. Average annual changes to enrollments and state support from 2001 to 2012 are illustrated in Table 12.2. In this one-year period, public enrollments grew by 3.3 percent (the average annual increase to public enrollments since 2001) and state appropriations per student declined by 2.9 percent. Changing only these assumptions in the second year of the previous example, overall support from the state increases only slightly, while the increase in enrollments and total tuition revenue must increase by over twice the rate of expense increases to balance the budget. Even if no additional costs associated with the increased enrollments are assumed, for example, hiring additional faculty, tuition revenue must increase by 6.1 percent. Of the increased tuition, the new enrollments (volume) would account for about 3.3 percent of the revenue increase, and average tuition charges per student (rate) would need to increase by 2.7 percent.

For continuing students, annual tuition increases may exacerbate financial pressures to the point of a student having to withdraw from school, increase borrowing, or increase work hours. Despite the 2.7 percent tuition rate increase, the institution will be spending less per student than during the prior

Table 12.2: Increasing enrollments and declining state support

Item	Year one	Year two	Change	Percent change
Revenue				
Tuition	$5,189,000	$5,503,878	$314,878	6.1
State support	$5,906,000	$5,923,972	$17,972	< 0.1
Total revenue	$11,095,000	$11,427,850	$332,850	3.0
Expense				
Salaries	$8,876,000	$9,142,280	$266,280	3.0
All other expenses	$2,219,000	$2,285,570	$66,570	3.0
Total expense	$11,095,000	$11,427,850	$332,850	3.0
Total # of students	1,000	1,033	33	3.3
Avg. student tuition	$5,189	$5,328	$171	2.7
Cost per student	$11,095	$11,063	($32)	(0.3)

year, as part of the tuition increase is funding a portion of the average cost for new students that would otherwise be provided by increased subsidies (state support). As a result. continuing students pay an additional $171 on average with nothing more spent on their educations. Similarly for the faculty, 3 percent salary increases leave no funds available to increase the size of the faculty, so with enrollment growth, classes will be larger and demands for grading, office hours, advising, and other instruction-related activities will increase (by about 3.0 percent, the size of the enrollment growth).

During the past twenty-five years, public college and university tuition has increased by 100.5 percent, while state appropriations per student have decreased 30.5 percent and enrollments have increased by 62.1 percent (SHEEO, 2013). The combination of increased enrollments and decreased subsidies has resulted in students paying a greater share of educational costs—and incurring increasing levels of debt—and colleges spending less per student in real terms. However, in 2012, public college enrollments declined for the first time since the late 1990s (SHEEO, 2013). The combination of decreasing enrollments and declining state support places even greater pressures on tuition as a revenue stream to support operations.

Table 12.3, using average one-year change factors for all U.S. public colleges and universities in 2012, illustrates the impact on tuition rates for the hypothetical 1,000 student college in Tables 12.1 and 12.2. Again, operating costs are assumed to increase by 3.0 percent, requiring a 3.0 percent revenue increase. Enrollments decrease by 0.7 percent, the actual 2012 public institution

Table 12.3: Decreasing enrollments and declining state support

Item	Year one	Year two	Change	Percent change
Revenue				
Tuition	$5,189,000	$5,733,267	$ 544,267	10.5
State support	$5,906,000	$5,694,583	($ 211,417)	(3.6)
Total revenue	$11,095,000	$11,427,850	$ 332,850	3.0
Expense				
Salaries	$8,876,000	$9,142,280	$ 266,280	3.0
All other expenses	$2,219,000	$2,285,570	$ 66,570	3.0
Total expense	$11,095,000	$11,427,850	$ 332,850	3.0
Total # of students	1,000	993	(7)	(0.7)
Avg. student tuition	$5,189	$5,774	$ 585	11.3
Cost per student	$11,095	$11,508	$ 413	3.7

enrollment decrease factor, and state support per student decreases by about 2.9 percent, as in the preceding examples. What results from these assumptions is that a tuition increase of 11.3 percent is required to fund the 3.0 percent expense inflation, with total tuition revenue increasing by 10.5 percent and the cost per student increasing by 3.7 percent as a function of both increased operating expense and decreased enrollments.

Tables 12.1, 12.2, and 12.3 illustrate how the economic structure of colleges and universities can, in the context of decreasing subsidies, simultaneously reflect rapidly escalating prices in the form of tuition increases, modest increases to the overall expenditure base, decreased spending on a per-student basis, and increased workload from a faculty perspective. As these exhibits illustrate, given salary costs in the range of 80 percent, subsidies in the range of 60 percent, and modest changes to both variables combined with enrollment growth result in a tuition rate increase by multiples of the base cost inflation. The simple reality is that public higher education has been expanding enrollments at the same time that subsidies on a per student basis have declined. Increased enrollments without corresponding increases to instructional programs reduces course availability, program quality, and affordability. Institutions are called upon to provide extracurricular (non-instructional) support services to an expanded student body. Despite increasing at nearly twice the rate of expense growth, the tuition rate increases illustrated in Table 12.2 result in *less* spending per student while creating new financial barriers to access based on price.

Table 12.4 posits the same enrollment and external subsidy reduction assumptions as the preceding table but attempts to maintain the same nominal level of spending per student through cost reductions. Table 12.4 makes a simplifying assumption that costs could be decreased by the same percentage as the change to enrollments. In fact, the extent to which costs are variable (subject to change based on volume) rather than fixed (do no change with volume) can vary significantly among different types of institutions. What is notable in Table 12.4 is that *only* tuition is increasing as other revenues and costs decrease. In this case, average tuition per student must increase by several percentage points simply to maintain the same level of spending per student. Because reductions to personnel and non-personnel expenses can seldom be made across-the-board, in this situation the institution would be required to identify savings beyond the outright expense reductions; for example, the costs of many contracted goods and services inflate annually. Similarly, to retain key faculty, the institution may need to offer targeted salary increases, potentially resulting in staffing reductions beyond what the level of decreased spending would suggest. Depending on the institution, any reduction to faculty could necessitate program reductions or eliminations.

The preceding examples, though fictitious, model the economic and financial dynamics faced by both public and private colleges and universities as

Table 12.4:   Decreasing enrollments, declining state support, and cost reductions

Item	Year one	Year two	Change	Percent change
Revenue				
Tuition	$ 5,189,000	$ 5,322,752	$133,752	2.6
State support	$ 5,906,000	$ 5,694,583	($211,417)	(3.6)
Total revenue	$11,095,000	$11,017,335	($77,665)	(0.7)
Expense				
Salaries	$ 8,876,000	$ 8,813,868	($62,132)	(0.7)
All other expenses	$ 2,219,000	$ 2,203,467	($15,533)	(0.7)
Total expense	$11,095,000	$11,017,335	($77,665)	(0.7)
Total # of students	1,000	93	(7)	(0.7)
Avg. student tuition	$ 5,189	$ 5,360	$171	3.3
Cost per student	$ 1,095	$ 1,095	—	—

endowment or state support decreases, enrollments increase or decrease, and costs inflate. How institutions fare in the marketplace of student demand and tuition is a significant revenue variable that makes budget balancing and institutional success possible. Faced with the difficult challenge to realize sufficient revenues to maintain or enhance program quality, while at the same time increasing access through more affordable pricing structures, public higher education institutions have invested in, and turned to, pricing and aid strategies informed by enrollment management practices. Untangling the tuition pricing implications of increased operating expenses in environments of increasing enrollments and decreasing subsidies is not a simple matter. In contrast to a commercial environment, where increasing volume might be expected to result in lower per-unit costs, in labor-intensive colleges and universities, increased numbers of students without corresponding increases in external subsidies gives rise to escalating per-student costs. Lower prices would be realized under the historical funding model, whereby external subsidies provided directly to institutions increased with enrollments and program offerings. On the revenue side, SEM strategies establish differential pricing achieved in part through the use of financial aid (or "discount," or "leveraging") strategies both to achieve lower prices for students who otherwise cannot afford to attend and higher prices for students willing and able to pay. SEM strategies address the tuition rate compounding of the Baumol Effect by selectively increasing the *average* tuition price. At its highest level, Winston's higher education economic model compares average price to average cost and finds price to be lower, on average, by the amount of the average subsidy. Yet some students pay more than the average price and even more than the average cost of their educations. SEM and the blending of financial aid, scholarship, and recruitment strategies is specifically concerned with how a broad range of institutional goals as described by Bob Bontrager (2008) can be simultaneously addressed.

On the cost side, the extent to which revenue-generating infrastructure in the forms of personnel, marketing, consulting, and other costs add to the overall cost base can be readily identified. The extent to which that infrastructure provides critical support to the public mission of colleges and universities (for example, through the equitable distribution of opportunity via tuition discounting) is more difficult to establish. Comparisons of need- and merit-based aid trends beyond the student level do not readily capture the net revenue consequences of discounting the highest tuition prices paid by students by large percentages or amounts, for example. At many public institutions, the resident tuition price does not cover average costs, while the nonresident price is significantly higher than the average cost. Providing merit aid to nonresident students still yields net revenue that serves to subsidize resident students. The financial reporting structures of colleges and universities do not readily facilitate combining this student level analysis with cost accounting for the overhead related to the administration of SEM. Furthermore, to the extent SEM plays a role in equitably distributing the scarce commodity of postsecondary educational opportunity among prospective students, the costs of enrollment management may serve public institutional missions beyond the generation of net revenues and recruitment of qualified students. As the preceding discussion shows, increasing enrollments without increasing subsidies—a circumstance many public higher education institutions assume will be the "new normal" for years to come—creates substantial budgetary pressures on current programs and services. With this context in mind, we turn now to the role of SEM professionals in supporting institutional and student success through budgets, aid, and enrollment.

THE ROLE OF SEM IN SUPPORTING INSTITUTIONAL AND STUDENT SUCCESS

This final chapter in Part III bring to a close our discussion of economic perspectives that provide a deep understanding of economic concepts that inform the SEM professionals on interplay between tuition, financial, net price, and student demand for postsecondary education. Part III has also looked in detail at how econometric techniques can be used to analyze the effects of financial aid, and, finally, we have examined the relationships between enrollments, financial aid, and institutional budgeting.

Enrollment management strategies have grown in scope and sophistication over the past several decades to include in their objectives the realization of both institutional mission and students' educational goals (Bontrager, 2008). The core principles elucidated by Leonard Kreutner and Eric Godfrey (1981)— marketing, enrollment, retention, and research (to improve on subsequent marketing, enrollment, and retention activities)—continue to be reflected in outcome-driven Strategic Enrollment Management activities (Hossler, Bean, & Associates, 1990). Whether enrollment management leads to the realization of institutional mission and students' educational goals as Bob Bontrager argued, or to the further stratification of educational opportunity as Slaughter and Rhodes (2004) suggested, there is little question that the practices of enrollment management lead to increased costs for merit-based financial aid (Davis, 2003) and that the institutions engaging most frequently in those strategies, private research universities, have experienced the most significant growth in tuition prices fueled largely by competition for prestige, high-profile students, and resources (Clotfelter, 1996; Wellman, 2006; Winston, 2001).

The resulting higher education business model described as "academic capitalism" (Rhoades and Slaughter, 1997) necessitates new organizational structures and processes to support revenue generation. These structures consume significant financial resources, the argument continues, and instill regulatory and bureaucratic cultures that reduce the efficiency of mission-critical activities. For Slaughter and Rhoades (2004), SEM is an example of this more generalized trend, focusing "on maximizing yield rates and quality, and minimizing tuition discounts and financial aid. This approach has become the focus of annual meetings and several publications sponsored by the American Association of Collegiate Registrars and Admissions Officers (AACRAO). It has also become "a cottage consulting industry" (pp. 295–6). Numerous studies suggest that the leveraging strategies of SEM provide the greatest financial benefit to students who could otherwise afford to pay, while driving up costs in a recruiting "arms race" to enroll the "best and brightest" students.

In contrast to this characterization, in his examination of selective liberal arts colleges, David Breneman (1994) described how institutions that could otherwise act to maximize revenues by admitting only those capable of paying undiscounted tuition rates instead elected to discount tuition to attract students of diverse backgrounds and abilities. SEM practitioners would argue that tuition discounting and financial aid are tools used not only to recruit high-profile students, but also to realize socioeconomic, gender, and ethnic diversity in the student body, and that the tuition revenue gains from the practice of SEM facilitate increased levels of institutional financial aid to traditionally underrepresented groups (Bontrager, 2004). Even the use of merit aid to drive net-revenue–producing enrollments can advance goals of affordability and access. Applying SEM principles in public institution settings frequently results in using merit aid to recruit nonresident students who pay significantly more than their own costs of education, in effect supplementing or supplanting subsidies (and making possible lower tuition rates, and thus diminished financial need) for resident students (Bontrager, 2008).

What is clear is that limited revenue sources are available to fund higher education costs. If the cost is not borne by public subsidies, private philanthropy, other income streams such as indirect cost recovery for research or auxiliary enterprise sales and services, the funds required to balance the budget will come from tuition charges. To the extent revenue-generating infrastructure actually succeeds in generating new revenues, as opposed to consuming revenues that could be allocated to new programs or other mission-critical activities, diverting resources away from that infrastructure might erode revenues. The challenge for SEM practitioners is to demonstrate in both general and specific manners how their activities cost-effectively support and enhance their institutions' missions in comparison to alternative uses for funds invested in SEM-related activities including financial aid. We conclude this chapter with a brief overview of strategies SEM professionals might employ.

- Become knowledgeable about institutional revenue and expense trends and the critical role of tuition, subsidies, and financial aid in financing program costs.

- Help to craft institutional net revenue strategies that leverage financial aid to yield sufficient net revenue for the institution to fund its programs adequately while facilitating students' ability to pay.

- Help increase pathways toward degrees via increased use of community colleges, transfer, and high school programs for college credit (reduces overall student and family costs).

- Change the conversation regarding college costs—for example, housing and dining costs have nothing to do with tuition inflation. Monitor and control recruitment costs. Work with colleagues to define and communicate institutional cost drivers.

- In managing the enrollment function, be an example of efficient management and use of institutional resources.

- Enrollment management is a support function—albeit a critical one—for the academic enterprise. Cultivate a culture of committed service among enrollment management staff, dedicated both to student and institutional success.

- Service does not equate to servitude at the behest of others: enrollment managers are professionals who are uniquely situated to help their institutions thrive both financially and in the fulfillment of their nonfinancial missions.

- Student and institutional success are complementary, not competing, goals. Find and promote the appropriate balance between them.

References

Allan, G. (1988). No need for no-need. *Journal of College Admission*, 120, 23–26.

Archibald, R. B., & Feldman, D. H. (2008). Explaining increases in higher education costs. *The Journal of Higher Education*, *79*(3), 268–295.

Baum, S. & Lapovsky, L. (2006). *Tuition Discounting: Not Just a Private College Practice*. New York: College Board.

Baumol, W. J., & Bowen, W. G. (1966). *Performing Arts: The Economic Dilemma*. New York: The Twentieth Century Fund.

Bennett, W. J. (1987). Our greedy colleges. *The New York Times*. February 18, 1987. Retrieved from http://www.nytimes.com/1987/02/18/opinion/our-greedy-colleges.htm.

Bok, D. C. (2003). *Universities in the Marketplace: The Commercialization of Higher Education*. Princeton, NJ: Princeton University Press.

Bontrager, B. (2004). Strategic enrollment management: Core strategies and best practices. *College & University*, *79*(4), 9–15.

Bontrager, B. (Ed.). (2008). *SEM and Institutional Success: Integrating Enrollment, Finance, and Student Access*. Washington, DC: American Association of Collegiate Registrars and Admissions Officers.

Bowen, H. (1980). *The Costs of Higher Education: How Much Do Colleges and Universities Spend per Student and How Much Should They Spend?* San Francisco: Jossey-Bass.

Bowen, W. G. (1967). *The Economics of the Major Private Research Universities*. Berkeley, CA: Carnegie Commission on Higher Education.

Breneman, D. W. (1994). *Liberal Arts Colleges: Thriving, Surviving, or Endangered?* Washington, DC: The Brookings Institution.

Brittan, G. G., Jr. (2003). Public goods, private benefits, and the university. *The Montana Professor*, *13*(1).

Clotfelter, C. T. (1996). *Buying the Best: Cost Escalation in Elite Higher Education*. Princeton, NJ: Princeton University Press.

College Board. (1999). *Trends in Student Aid*. Washington, DC: College Board.

Davis, J. S. (2003). Unintended Consequences of Tuition Discounting. *Lumina Foundation for Education New Agenda Series*, *5*(1). Retrieved from http://www.luminafoundation.org/publications/Tuitiondiscounting.pdf.

Delta Project on Postsecondary Education Costs, Productivity, and Accountability. (2009). *Issue Brief #2: Metrics for Improving Cost Accountability.* Retrieved from http://www.deltacostproject.org/resources/pdf/issuebrief_02.pdf.

Dill, D. D. (2003). An institutional perspective on higher education policy: The case of academic quality assurance. In J. C. Smart (Ed.), *Higher Education: Handbook of Theory and Research XVIII*, 669–699. Dordrecht, The Netherlands: Kluwer.

Ehrenberg, R. G. (2006) *Tuition Rising: Why College Costs So Much.* Cambridge, MA: Harvard University Press.

Getz, M., & Siegfried, J. J. (1991). Cost and productivity in American colleges and universities. In C. Clotfelter, R. Ehrenberg, M. Getz, & J. J. Siegfried (Eds.), *Economic Challenges in Higher Education* (pp. 261–392). Chicago: University of Chicago Press.

Hansmann, H. (1981). The rationale for exempting nonprofit organizations from corporate income taxation. *The Yale Law Journal, 91*(1), 54–100.

Harvey, J. (1998). *Straight Talk about College Costs and Prices: Report of the National Commission on the Cost of Higher Education.* Phoenix, AZ: National Commission on the Cost of Higher Education, American Council on Education.

Hossler, D. (1990). *The Strategic Management of College Enrollments.* San Francisco: Jossey-Bass.

Hossler, D. (2004). Refinancing public universities: Student enrollments, incentive-based budgeting, and incremental revenue. In E. St. John & M. Parsons (Eds.), *Public Funding of Higher Education: Changing Contexts and New Rationales.* Baltimore, MD: The Johns Hopkins University Press.

Immerwahr, J., & Johnson, J. (2010). Squeeze play: How Parents and the Public Look at Higher Education Today. National Center for Public Policy and Higher Education. Retrieved from http://www.highereducation.org/reports/squeeze_play/squeeze_play.pdf.

Johnstone, D. B. (2001). Higher education and those "out of control costs." In P. G. Altbach, P. J. Gumport, & D. B. Johnstone (Eds.), *In Defense of American Higher Education* (pp. 144–180). Baltimore, MD: The Johns Hopkins University Press.

Kreutner, L., & Godfrey, E. S. (1981). Enrollment management: A new vehicle for institutional renewal. *College Board Review, 118*(29), 6–9.

Lingenfelter, P. E. (2008). The financing of public colleges and universities in the United States. In H. F. Ladd & E. B. Fiske (Eds.), *Handbook of Research in Education Finance and Policy.* New York and London: Routledge.

Mabry, T. N. (1987). Enrollment management. Los Angeles: ERIC Clearinghouse for Junior Colleges. Retrieved from http://www.ericdigests.org/pre-926/management.htm.

Massy, W. F., & Zemsky, R. (1994). Faculty Discretionary Time: Departments and the "Academic Ratchet." *The Journal of Higher Education, 65*(1), 1–22.

Middaugh, M. F. (2005). Understanding higher education costs. *Planning for Higher Education 33*(3), 5–18.

National Center for Education Statistics (NCES). (2010). *The Condition of Education 2010*. Retrieved June 5, 2010, from http://nces.ed.gov/pubsearch/pubsinfo.asp?pubid = 2010028.

Office of Management and Budget. (2000). The White House. Circular No. A-21: Cost principles for educational institutions. Retrieved from http://www.whitehouse.gov/omb/rewrite/circulars/a021/a021.html.

Rhoades, G., & Slaughter, S. (1997). Academic capitalism, managed professionals and supply-side higher education. *Social Text 51*(2), 9–38.

Slaughter, S., & Rhoades, G. (2004). *Academic Capitalism and the New Economy: Markets, State, and Higher Education*. Baltimore, MD: The Johns Hopkins University Press.

State Higher Education Executive Officers (SHEEO). (2010). State Higher Education Finance FY 2009. Retrieved from http://www.sheeo.org/finance/shef/SHEF_FY_2009.pdf.

State Higher Education Executive Officers (SHEEO). (2013). State Higher Education Finance FY 2013. Retrieved from http://www.sheeo.org/sites/default/files/publications/SHEF_FY13_04292014.pdf.

Wang, P. (2008). Is college still worth the price? *Money Magazine*. Retrieved from http://money.cnn.com/2008/08/20/pf/college/college_price.moneymag.

Washburn, J. (2005). *University Inc.: The Corporate Corruption of Higher Education*. Cambridge, MA: Basic Books.

Wellman, J. (2006). *Costs, Prices and Affordability: A Background Paper for the Secretary's Commission on the Future of Higher Education*. Thirteenth in a series of Issue Papers released at the request of Chairman Charles Miller. Retrieved from http://www2.ed.gov/about/bdscomm/list/hiedfuture/reports/wellman.pdf.

Winston, G. C. (1999). Subsidies, hierarchy and peers: The awkward economics of higher education. *The Journal of Economic Perspectives, 13*(1), 13–36.

Winston, G. C. (2001). *"Grow" the College? Why Bigger May be Far from Better*. Williams Project on the Economics of Higher Education. Retrieved from http://www.williams.edu/wpehe/DPs/DP-60.pdf.

Zemsky, R. (2003). Have we lost the "public" in higher education? *The Chronicle of Higher Education*, B20.

Zemsky, R., Wegner, R. G., & Massy, W. F. (2005). *Remaking the American University: Market-Smart and Mission-Centered*. Piscataway, NJ: Rutgers University Press.

PART FOUR

STUDENT RETENTION, PERSISTENCE, AND SUCCESS

In a 2012 report, the American College Testing Program reported that 66.5 percent of first-year students return to their college of initial enrollment for their second year. This aggregated retention rate varies by institutional type with PhD granting private universities attaining the highest rate (80.2 percent) to a low of 55.5 percent for both public and private two-year colleges (American College Testing Program, 2012). These rates vary across individual colleges and universities. Because an institution's student retention rate affects both its financial resources and reputation, enrollment managers should hold keen interest in their college's or university's rate of student retention.

The following chapters address various topics pertinent to student retention. Although the words "persistence" and "retention" are often used interchangeably in the literature and in practice, we use the term "retention" because the chapters of this part hold relevance to institutional efforts to increase their rates of student retention. Hagedorn (2005) states that "institutions retain students and students persist" (p.92).

In Chapter 13, Afet Dundar and Doug Shapiro assert that traditional measures of retention and graduation rates typically used by enrollment managers must give way to new metrics for measuring the educational pathways of students who attend multiple institutions. As a consequence, enrollment managers must work to develop metrics and institutional policies and practices that will lead to the success of such students. Thus, enrollment managers must shift their focus, from retaining and graduating students who initially enrolled at their college or university, to ensuring the success of students even if attending other colleges and universities best meets their needs. Put differently, Dundar and Shapiro argue that enrollment managers must embrace an institutional obligation to safeguard the welfare of students as clients, even if safeguarding their welfare means that students attend other colleges and universities.

In Chapter 14, Amy Hirschy offers enrollment mangers a set of concerns for the selection of theories or combination of theories to guide their practice. In this chapter, she discusses such matters as deterrents to using theoretically derived models, considerations for the use of such models, and approaches to using theoretically derived models in practice. As an aid to enrollment managers, Hirschy, in Table 14.1, arrays selected theories of student success by their population of emphasis, their level, context, and the disciplinary perspective that underlies the selected theories. She also offers a set of recommendations for the selection of theoretically derived models by enrollment managers.

John Braxton, Harold Hartley, and Dawn Lyken-Segosebe present in Chapter 15 what they call a "continuous vigilance system" to identify students at risk for departure from both residential and commuter colleges and universities. The authors label it a continuous vigilance system because such dimensions of these profiles require attention throughout an academic year, rather than as an early warning at the start of a semester. The authors present separate profiles for at-risk students in residential and in commuter colleges and universities. They developed these separate profiles using theoretically based empirical research. The authors place academic advising at the center of such a vigilance system by outlining the range of actions advisors can take to reduce the possibilities of the departure of at-risk students. They also present the institutional arrangements needed for such a continuous vigilance system sustained by student academic advisors.

Willis Jones, in Chapter 16, presents a range of topics pertinent to the persistence of students of color. These topics include a statistical summary of institutional retention and graduation rates by race and ethnicity, a description of theoretical frameworks developed to explain the persistence of students of color, and an overview of empirically based factors significant for the retention of students of color. Jones presents such empirically based factors for American Indian/Alaskan Natives, Asian/Pacific Islander, Hispanics, and African American students. This chapter also advances recommendations for enrollment managers to increase the retention of students of color by creating a campus culture that affirms the cultural origins of these students.

In Chapter 17, author Mary Hutchens calls attention to the need for enrollment managers to be attentive to the needs of this population of students. She points out that 73 percent of students enrolled in United States postsecondary institutions are nontraditional in some way, and that the persistence rates of such students are typically lower than those of traditional college and university students. Hutchens describes seven student characteristics that define a student as nontraditional. She points out that these seven characteristics provide the basis of a continuum of nontraditionality that ranges from minimally to highly nontraditional. In this chapter, Hutchens also presents challenges that nontraditional students face that include their decision to enroll, financial aid, and other matters such as having to work while attending college and being responsible for members of their families. Hutchens closes the chapter by outlining six principles of practice for enrollment managers to guide their efforts to improve the persistence of nontraditional students

In the eighteenth and last chapter of this part, Mary Ziskin, Jerome Lucido, Jacob Gross, Donald Hossler, Emily Chung, and Vasti Torres describe the results of three studies that focus on the organizational arrangements and efforts of institutions to improve their student retention rates. Accordingly, this chapter aptly bears the title "The Institutional Role in Student Retention: Thinking Beyond Student Characteristics." In addition to describing these three studies, the authors offer four lessons learned from these studies concerning the implementation of institutional efforts to ensure student success. The authors also put forth guiding principles regarding institutional structures and practices designed to increase institutional retention rates.

Enrollment managers may choose to read and use the chapters of this part of the handbook selectively. Enrollment managers seeking guidance on the design and implementation of policies and practices to increase their institution's student retention rate will find Chapters 13–17 particularly useful. For institutions that enroll large numbers of nontraditional students and students of color, Chapters 16 and 17 will be particularly useful to enrollment managers in their design and implementation of institutional efforts to increase the retention of such students. Enrollment managers in colleges and universities that note multi-institutional attendance patterns of their students will find value in the advice on new metrics to assess student success in such institutions by Dundar and Shapiro in Chapter 13.

Scholars assert that many institutions are not engaged in institutional research that seeks to understand student persistence at their particular college or university (Braxton et al., 2006; Patton et al., 2006). As a consequence, Jones and Braxton (2009) recommend that colleges and universities conduct methodologically rigorous studies of student persistence at their institutions. I add that theory should guide such institutional research. Accordingly, enrollment mangers heeding this advice will find Chapter 14 particularly useful, as Hirschy provides a guide to the selection of theory. Enrollment managers in colleges and universities in which the retention of students of color and nontraditional students looms problematic will find Chapters 16 and 17 valuable to them in requesting and understanding the findings of institutional research designed to understand student persistence at their college or university.

Enrollment managers should use the findings of such institutional research to guide their development of institutional efforts to increase their institution's retention rates.

To sum up, the six chapters in Part IV provide various perspectives on college student retention. These chapters address significant issues, and enrollment managers will find them variable in their usefulness to their work; some chapters will be of greater use than others. However, as a group, these chapters offer perspectives of much importance to enrollment management.

References

American College Testing Program. (2012). *National Collegiate Retention and Persistence to Degree Rates.* Retrieved from http://act.org/research/policymakers/pdf/retain_2012.pdf.

Braxton, J. M., McKinney, J. S. & and Reynolds, P. J. (2006). Cataloguing institutional efforts to understand and reduce college student departure. In E. P. St. John (Ed.), *Reframing Persistence Research to Improve Academic Success. New Directions for Institutional Research, 2006*(130), 25–32.

Hagedorn, L. S. (2005). How to define retention: A new look at an old problem. In A.Seidman (Ed.), *College Student Retention: Formula for Student Success.* Westport, CT: American Council on Education and Praeger Publishers.

Jones, W. A., & Braxton, J. M. (2009). Cataloging and comparing institutional efforts to increase student retention rates. *Journal of College Student Retention: Research, Theory & Practice, 11*(1), 123–139.

Patton, L., Morelon, C., Whitehead, D., & Hossler, D. (2006). Campus-based retention initiatives: Does the emperor have clothes? In E. P. St. John (Ed.), *Reframing Persistence Research to Improve Academic Success. New Directions for Institutional Research, 2006*(130), 9–24.

CHAPTER 13

New Context for Retention
and Persistence

Doug Shapiro and Afet Dundar

Traditional measures of retention and graduation for first-time, full-time entering student cohorts give us only limited understanding of postsecondary students and their varied pathways to success. As students embrace mobility and multi-institution pathways, new national policy goals, institutional performance standards, and accountability measures are emerging to reflect students' changed enrollment behaviors and expectations. As a result, the existing literature on retention and the metrics that support it now fall short in terms of the tools and methods that strategic enrollment managers need to drive institutional improvement. Using national trends and specific institutional examples, this chapter shows how new metrics that examine complete student pathways can lead to higher institutional effectiveness and a more informed institutional commitment to the success of all students.

THE HISTORICAL ROOTS OF INSTITUTIONAL RETENTION

American higher education went through significant changes in 1960s and 1970s. This was an era of movement toward providing mass access to higher education—an era that witnessed an expansion of community colleges, emergence of for-profit higher education, as well as growth in private and public colleges (Thelin, 2011). Increase in the number of enrollments during this period clearly shows the massive expansion. Although total student enrollments were

2.7 million in 1949–1950, the number increased to 3.6 million in 1960 and doubled over a decade, reaching 7.9 million in 1970 (Thelin, 2011). This massive expansion brought up a need for systematic information on how higher education institutions functioned in order to assist them in planning.

To meet this need, Carnegie Commission on Higher Education and later Carnegie Council on Policy Studies were established, which published a series of research reports. The need for systematic information also led the federal government to help develop the Higher Education General Information Survey (HEGIS) to collect standardized data from all colleges and universities. Later this survey was renamed Integrated Postsecondary Education Data Systems, or IPEDS. The dramatic increase in enrollments also brought in a new concern about undergraduate students: their retention and degree completion. Institutions implemented various practices such as advising, teaching, and learning centers to assist students to persist and graduate. The focus on access and institutional attrition stayed unchanged until recent years. Postsecondary institutions have clear incentives to focus on student retention. Because of the large cost of undergraduate instruction, campuses are interested in analyzing student departure, as every student retained is one less student to be recruited in successive classes.

The Policy Shift to College Completion

Research shows that increased enrollments in the last few decades have not been followed by similar increases in college completion (Bound, Lovenheim, & Turner, 2010; Perna, 2013; Reason, 2009). Large disparities remain in college completion rates among ethnic groups as well as between traditional and nontraditional students (Radford, Berkner, Wheeless, & Shepherd, 2010). Publications by international organizations also revealed that although the United States had the world's highest rate of higher education participation (Organisation for Economic Cooperation and Development [OECD], 2012), other nations have outperformed the U.S. higher education system in degree completion (National Center for Public Policy and Higher Education, 2008). One possible reason for this could be the difference in what various countries include in degree completion. However, it is no secret that many students who enter postsecondary education with high hopes for a college degree fail to graduate. Taking into account the current degree production and population growth, Patrick Kelly (2010) estimated that the U.S. degree production needs to increase by 4.2 percent annually through 2020 in order for the nation to close the attainment gap with leading OECD countries. Emphasizing the link between college attainment figures and economic competitiveness, education policy makers across the nation have started focusing higher education policy on the college completion agenda.

The Obama administration has also contributed to this shift in public policy making. President Obama's first budget proposal included a five-year, $2.5 billion

Access and Completion Incentive Fund to support state efforts to help low-income students complete their college education. Citing growing concerns regarding the U.S. position in the global economy in his 2009 address to congress, President Obama established a new goal: "By 2020, America will once again have the highest proportion of college graduates in the world" (Obama, 2009).

A wide range of organizations across the United States have also launched initiatives in support of the college completion agenda, which also reflects the growing concern that the nation's declining economic competitiveness is related to inadequate levels of educational attainment in the nation's workforce. The broad goal of these diverse initiatives is the same: to increase significantly the number of adults in the United States with a postsecondary credential. The College Board, for example, seeks to increase the prevalence of college-educated adults from the current level of 39 percent to 55 percent by 2025 (Lee et al., 2011), while the postsecondary success goal of the Bill and Melinda Gates Foundation (2009) is to help the nation double the number of low-income students enrolled in a postsecondary institution by age twenty six. Lumina Foundation's Strategic Plan for 2013–2016 set a new vision to achieve the previously announced goal of increasing the percentage of Americans with high-quality degrees and credentials from the current 39 percent to 60 percent by 2025. The strategic plan focuses on mobilizing action at the local, state, and national levels that includes not only promoting relevant state and federal policies to increase the attainment, but also involving employers, metro areas, and regions as well as higher education itself in achieving this goal.

Recent years have also seen substantive development in the implementation of performance-based or outcomes-based funding at the state level, with more than a quarter of the states implementing outcomes-based funding in at least one institutional sector, including ten states that use it across all sectors (Jones, 2013). States that use outcomes-based funding use completed credit hours as opposed to the enrolled credit hours for their funding models and incorporate quality metrics into their allocation models. Outcomes-based funding strategies also include focus on productivity and efficiency often measured by the number of degree awards per FTE (Jones, 2013).

Accountability Measures Revisited

These state developments are just the beginning. The increased attention to student outcomes and degree attainment at the state, national, and international levels will undoubtedly lead to even more new accountability measures for postsecondary institutions, and many of these will look at the outcomes of all students, including nontraditional students who enroll part-time, transfer in, transfer out, and stop out, as opposed to only the first-time, full-time cohorts that institutions are used to tracking. The important work of Clifford Adelman (2006) pointed the way for this shift by emphasizing the growing numbers of students who successfully complete degrees outside of the traditional single-institution pathway. Already, hundreds of institutions are publicizing their performance on expanded outcome measures that take account of student success and progress beyond the starting institution, through the Voluntary System of Accountability (VSA) for four-year institutions and the Voluntary Framework of Accountability (VFA) for two-year institutions. These institutions recognize that today's students are increasingly attending multiple institutions, both sequentially and concurrently, and thus analyzing a student's enrollment only at a single institution, through traditional retention and graduation rates, has serious limitations. *Persistence,* on the other hand, expands the notion of retention to include students who transfer to another institution. Because it requires tracking student information across institutions, persistence is considered a student measure and not an institutional measure (Adelman, 2006; Hagedorn, 2012). More fundamentally, persistence can be viewed as a student behavior, the continued pursuit of educational goals irrespective of institutional locale, while retention is more aptly an institutional behavior, the act of keeping a student enrolled at the starting place (Hagedorn, 2012).

INSTITUTIONAL SUCCESS VERSUS STUDENT SUCCESS

Institutional researchers and strategic enrollment managers are rightly focused on institutional measures of success. After all, those measures define their occupational imperatives. But institutional success and student success are increasingly different concepts, even within the context of student outcomes. This is because growing numbers of students today have fundamentally different views of education from those of the institutions they attend, and SEM practitioners who ignore these students will increasingly find themselves focused on the success of smaller and smaller shares of their enrollment base.

Institutional measures of success that focus only on the outcomes at the starting institution constrain the view of students into the narrow window of single campus or the time frame of a single academic program. The institution is the home, where students are intended to start and finish and everything in between. However, the institution often does not see what happened before or after the student walks through its gates. Students, on the other hand, based on their observable enrollment behaviors, increasingly view education as a pathway, as a career, as something that happens in many institutions at many times, and often in different institutions at the same time. They stop in and out for employment, or family, or life, taking courses online, across town, or in another state. The institution often becomes a stepping stone rather than a home to them: a place where you stay for a time to make progress toward your goals, or to refine or revise your goals, and then continue on the path (Adelman,

2005, Hossler et al., 2012a). Thus, the kind of measures that are important to institutional success, which is often derived from the various reporting and accountability requirements imposed on institutions, are typically those that pertain to students' successful attainment of goals during that narrow window on each campus: access, cost, engagement, retention, and graduation rates. The kind of measures that are important to student success, on the other hand, are those that inform us about the pathways, and the relative success rates of different behavioral patterns along those pathways, not necessarily within a single window.

As long as the official metrics on which they are ranked and rewarded continue to be based upon the former, institutional policy makers must continue to keep their eye very squarely upon them, but they ignore the latter at their peril for two important reasons. First, the institutional measures are changing. As noted, the growing policy focus on student attainment and success will lead to more institutional accountability that is based upon student measures. This means that institutions are increasingly going to be able to recognize the contributions they made to a student graduating elsewhere, because those students will likely be included in the official measures. Student persistence and graduation at a subsequent institution, for example, is becoming easier and more reliable for the starting institution to track, and may thus become a measured outcome (as in many cases it already is, particularly for accreditation purposes, if the institution has a transfer mission). There are several other possibilities as well. One is that separate persistence and completion rates will be tracked and measured for students who transfer into an institution. Another is that institutions will be able to measure and report credits awarded toward the degrees earned by successful students, even if those students neither start nor finish there, but simply pass through along an educational pathway comprising several institutions. Yet another example is the tracking and measuring of student completion rates over longer time frames, better to capture students who enroll part time and/or who stop out and return, taking more than the standard 150 percent of program time to earn their degree or credential. As it becomes increasingly likely that institutional accountability metrics will encompass specific student outcomes, there is little reason to imagine that institutions would want the student who successfully transfers and graduates elsewhere to be indistinguishable in those metrics from the one who simply drops out.

The astute institutions will grasp this quickly and get ahead of the new rules of the game, perhaps even positioning their institutions for an active role in the development of the new measures to ensure that they are in sync with institutional missions. To be sure, it is not yet clear whether the new metrics will apply to all institutions or only to certain types of colleges and universities. As with any change, there will be some that stand to benefit more than others. For many institutions, particularly those with open admissions and the largest numbers of transfer students, the new metrics will paint a much more positive picture of their efforts to support all of their students successfully. For others, such as highly selective institutions, there may be good reason to insist that the traditional metrics, under which they look best, still matter. Either way, the increasingly wider adoption of institutional measures that take into account complete student pathways is well under way, and this shift will change not only the conversation about student success, but also the incentive structures for many institutions. Enrollment managers and their institutions will increasingly be measured and recognized for what they do, or do not do, to serve mobile students.

This leads to the second reason why enrollment managers should not ignore the new measures of student-focused outcomes to higher education: regardless of what the new official metrics will eventually come to capture, all institutions can benefit from becoming familiar with the emerging metrics and learning to use them to their advantage wherever possible. Perhaps the clearest illustration of this is that institutions that continue to focus only upon traditional measures of success risk losing sight of the growing numbers of mobile students who are not counted. These students are undoubtedly already on campus and likely having significant effects, whether positively or negatively, on enrollment, tuition revenue, and brand value. Tracking their progress and measuring their outcomes is essential to understanding their needs, serving them better, and maximizing their impacts on the institution. In the following sections of this chapter, we discuss in more detail why these measures have immediate relevance for institutional policy makers, and we provide examples from recent national trends of how important, actionable insights can be drawn from them at the institution level.

WHAT IS MISSING IN THE PERSISTENCE AND COMPLETION LITERATURE

Research on retention in postsecondary education (remaining enrolled at the institution where students began) has garnered a great deal of attention from academic researchers and public policy makers since the 1970s (Tinto, 2006). Working with Tinto's theory of student integration (Tinto, 1975, 1994), derived from Durkheim's sociological theory of suicide, and later with Bean's Job-Turnover Model of Student Attrition (Bean, 1980), a large number of studies have examined how student background characteristics interact with the attributes of institutions and social and academic experiences at the institution of enrollment. These theories were focused on individual institutions. Consequently, in many studies that came afterward, student success was defined as the commitment to the institution of origin. Student departure from the starting institution was a failure of the student to form meaningful interactions or to engage with the culture of that institution. Although student departure can happen because of such a failure, student success does not have to be limited to the commitment to the starting institution. Students who complete a degree or a certificate beyond their starting institutions serve as good evidence to this (Shapiro et al., 2012).

Single institution perspective being an essential part of IPEDS data and definitions also makes viewing the institutional success from the perspective of the student less attractive to the institutions. However, unlike the time when IPEDS was initially established, reliance on definitions that tell a story from the perspective of the starting institution does not reflect the changing characteristics of today's student population, which also means that nontraditional pathways that include attendance at multiple institutions or attainment rates of adult learners and students who attend at less than full-time status are not captured correctly. As more students attend multiple institutions throughout their academic career and enroll at less-than-full-time-status, relying on retention and graduation rates at the institution of origin only will increasingly understate student success rates.

Although the single institution perspective prevailed in much of higher education research, some researchers drew attention to mobile students. For example, Adelman (2006) and Robert Reason (2009) called for greater focus on persistence rates as a broad measure of students' continued enrollment within higher education as well as a better understanding of factors that influence persistence to graduation. Adelman (2006) argued that the language of "retention" leads institutions "to hold on to students, keeping them in places that may be unproductive, at all costs, and for the sake of their public ratings," whereas using the language of persistence would lead to a view of mobility in a more positive light, under which students benefit from "the opportunities offered by institutions so as both to discover true interests and reach productive ends" (p.138). Such an approach, however, requires institutions to create structures of opportunities that are relevant to those on different pathways, making support services for students who transferred in or intend to transfer out as important as those for incoming first-time freshmen. Ultimately, this will require institutions to develop a new perspective toward students, embracing a commitment to each student's success irrespective of his or her possible intentions, or indeed needs, to transfer out in pursuit of it.

In this framework, the institution's commitment to student welfare emerges as one of the key factors contributing to student persistence. In *Rethinking College Student Retention* (2013), John Braxton and his colleagues define this client-like commitment as "an abiding concern for the growth and development of its students by a given college or university" (p. 174). Valuing students, respect for students as individuals, and the equitable treatment of students are all important dimensions. The authors also identify the following potential sources of influence that can positively affect student perceptions of the commitment of their institution to student welfare: the organizational behavior of fairness in the administration of rules and regulations, faculty interest in students, and student-reported good teaching by faculty members. Their analysis shows that the more students perceive that their institution is committed to the welfare of its students, the greater their degree of subsequent commitment to that institution.

DEVELOPING AND USING NEW METRICS WITH MORE COMPREHENSIVE DATA

The current focus of practitioners on the single-institution measures of success has some important effects, perhaps the most important of which is that campuses quickly lose sight of students who are not going to contribute to the measures. A student who transfers in does not become part of "the cohort" of first-time, full-time students who make up the denominator of the standard retention and graduation rates. This student literally does not count, and therefore receives less attention and support from the student success office or enrollment management team that is tasked with raising those rates. A student who transfers out, on the other hand, perhaps to complete her degree at the second or even third institution in her path, looks like just another failure to the first institution, even if that institution laid the academic groundwork for her success, helped her to clarify her goal and the pathway by which she would attain it, and accelerated her progress along that path. If the institution is focused only on increasing its own retention and graduation rates, it is likely to fail to serve this student well, and, moreover, once it labels her a "failure," it is likely to deny itself the opportunity of any continuing positive relationship with her, even if she felt positive about the institution's role in helping her attain her ultimate goal. How does a college preserve this relationship? How does it measure its contribution to a student's education when the chief result of that contribution is a higher aspiration, an elevated goal, or a new pathway leading elsewhere? How does it craft policies and practices that support students along their educational pathways as they really are, rather than as tradition says they should be?

Finding the answers to these questions is not easy, but it starts with analyzing data about complete student pathways, and with using those data to increase understanding of the goals and needs of all the students who cross the threshold. These data are necessarily detailed at the student level and describe many different student characteristics, goals, and behavior patterns. They are longitudinal and multidimensional. Only the rare enrollment management shop will have the capacity to analyze them fully without significant commitments from institutional researchers and possibly faculty members as well. We suggest some basic approaches and some specific examples in the following discussion, but each institution will want to address distinct concerns related to its own mission and student population.

To begin with, our current focus on institutional measures, rather than student measures, may mean that many enrollment managers do not even know how many students they are missing in the traditional metrics. How many students are mobile? It depends on what you mean by "student." Among all undergraduate students who began college in the United States in fall 2006, one in three were mobile, meaning they enrolled at a different institution, via formal transfer or other type of mobility, within five years and before earning a degree or certificate (Hossler et al., 2012a). This one-third proportion comes from measuring unique students, however, whereas what walks into each campus registrar's office is an enrolled student, and each mobile student by definition enrolls in two (and sometimes more) different institutions over time. This means that on average one-half, not one-third, of all the enrollees seen by the typical institution are students who have either come from, or are going to, another postsecondary institution on their way to their first undergraduate degree or certificate. These are students who are not coming straight from high school and not staying straight through from admissions through graduation. Institutions will serve these students better when they understand the whole educational pathway they travel, including what institutions they arrive from, what institutions they leave for, and why.

Table 13.1 shows the breakdowns for six different institutional categories, for each of the 914,447 students who entered postsecondary education in fall 2006 and transferred or enrolled elsewhere within five years. As shown, two-year institutions not only are common institutions of origin for students arriving at four-year institutions, they are also surprisingly common destination institutions for students leaving any kind of institution, according to National Student Clearinghouse Research Center data. In fact, among all students who began college at a four-year institution in fall 2006 and later transferred or enrolled elsewhere, about half had headed to a two-year institution. This type of "reverse transfer" behavior encompasses several important student pathways described in detail in the Clearinghouse's third Signature Report on reverse transfer students (Hossler et al., 2012b), that strategic enrollment managers can benefit from understanding. For example, the Clearinghouse's study of the reverse transfer pathway found that about one-quarter of these students were enrolling in the community college only during summer terms, while three-quarters enrolled at the community college for at least one term during the regular academic year (see Table 13.2).

Table 13.1: Origins and destinations of first instance of transfer or mobility through spring 2011, by sector and control of origin and destination institutions; fall 2006 starting cohort

| | Destination institution | | | | | | |
| | Two-year | | | Four-year | | | |
	Public	Private non-profit	Private for-profit	Public	Private non-profit	Private for-profit	Total for origin
Origin inst.							
2-year public	158,537	1,107	5,750	173,883	59,763	23,002	422,042
2-year private non-profit	1,221	17	15	628	532	102	2,516
2-year private for-profit	4,516	16	951	1,049	623	2,082	9,238
4-year public	168,582	562	1,695	111,930	33,044	8,925	324,738
4-year private non-profit	57,009	490	393	48,708	27,890	3,328	137,819
4-year private for-profit	7,936	41	511	2,809	2,427	4,372	18,095
Total for dest.	397,801	2,233	9,314	339,008	124,279	41,812	914,447

Source: Hossler et al., 2012a

Looking at subsequent enrollments, and tracking the outcomes for these students up to six years, the Clearinghouse data revealed that this summer versus regular term enrollment behavior was an indicator of very different educational pathways (see Table 13.3).

Students who left a four-year institution to enroll in a community college only during summer terms were mostly headed back to their starting institution. More

Table 13.2: Enrollment at two-year institutions by students who began at four-year institutions

	Count	Percent of all fall 2005 four-year enrollees (n = 1,244,349)
Reverse transfer students	178,846	14.4
Summer session course takers	67,231	5.4
Total	246,078	19.8

Source: Hossler et al., 2012b.

Table 13.3:   Subsequent enrollment outcomes for reverse transfer students and summer session course takers after first enrollment at two-year institution

	Returned to four-year sector at institution of origin		Returned to four-year sector at different institution		Did not return to four-year sector		Row total	
	Count	Percent	Count	Percent	Count	Percent	Count	Percent
Reverse transfer students	29,683	16.60	50,686	28.34	98,477	55.06	178,846	100.00
Summer session course takers	54,252	80.70	9,723	14.46	3,256	4.84	67,231	100.00

Source: Hossler et al., 2012b

than 80 percent of them returned, in fact, compared to only 17 percent of the students who spent at least one regular term at a community college. Perhaps more strikingly, these 80 percent who returned went on to become even more successful at their starting institutions than their classmates who had never left. These "superchargers" were clearly taking advantage of curricular opportunities at the two-year colleges to accelerate their progress to a degree at their starting institution. Within six years, 77 percent of them had graduated from their starting institution, compared to around 60 percent of those who had never left (56 percent of those at public four-year institutions; 64 percent at private non-profits). Students pursuing this particular pathway might easily escape the notice of the four-year institutions, but a strategic enrollment manager at a community college may want to look for ways to identify them, track their subsequent enrollment or degree completion outcomes, and tell an important story of institutional value-added that might otherwise go unrecognized. Are these students perhaps local high school graduates, coming home for the summer and checking off basic course requirements or saving money on credits at the state flagship? Are they older students from the local university who don't need summer jobs, but find more convenient class times (and lower tuition) at the community college?

At the same time, enrollment managers at four-year institutions, who may be trained to think that any course taken elsewhere by a native student is merely lost tuition revenue, might reconsider this view when the tradeoff is higher traditional graduation rates. Those who can identify these trends may want to recognize the existing pathways, highlight their value to strong students, and perhaps even encourage more students to make informed choices about which specific courses and institutions are most beneficial.

By contrast, students who returned to their original institution after just a single regular-term enrollment at a community college were much less likely to complete a bachelor's degree, both when compared to the superchargers who took a summer course and to those who never left the starting institution. Only about 40 percent of these students were successful at their starting institution within six years. Analyzing the data to understand why could provide critical insights to the way different programs are serving specific types of students. It may, for example, enable a strategic enrollment manager to identify students in a particular major who transfer to a community college during a regular term as more likely to be struggling and looking to regain their footing, either along their original pathway or perhaps along a new educational pathway. Understanding the chances of success that similar students experienced by pursuing these pathways might better prepare such students, and their advisers, for the choices they make along the way. Empowering students to make wiser choices could lead to higher levels of both student success and institutional success.

In fact, in the Clearinghouse study, the students who made regular term transfers to community colleges were more likely to return to the four-year sector at a different institution (if they returned at all) than they were to return to their original institution. About 28 percent of them returned to some other four-year college, compared to the 17 percent who returned to their starting institution. These students may be thought of as "rechargers," switching gears but then re-entering their original pathway at a college that offers a better fit. They are likely to have struggled academically at their original institution and to have picked up important study skills, goal awareness, motivation, or even remedial coursework while at the community college. Strategic enrollment managers at both two-year institutions and four-year destination institutions might want to single out this type of student among their incoming transfers for special attention.

Yet another group of reverse transfer students never return to the four-year sector at all, but stay in two-year institutions, either earning a degree there, or in some cases dropping out of postsecondary education altogether. These "rebooters," who are likely to have experienced a dramatic reset of their educational goals and pathways, represent the majority (55 percent) of those who left their four-year starting institution during a regular term. They are clearly a set of students that strategic enrollment managers at two-year institutions would want to watch for, and perhaps probe more deeply for ways to make sure that they find successful outcomes within their new pathways. These students might represent a significant contribution to the institution's degree awards even if, under cohort definition standards that look only at "first-time" beginning students, they would not count toward an institutional graduation rate for IPEDS, or for state accountability measures.

Findings also showed pathways other than much talked about traditional or reverse transfer. Particularly since the recession, to reduce costs, students seeking bachelor's degrees are increasingly looking to start their postsecondary careers at two-year institutions and transfer to four-year colleges. But among the one-third of students who changed institutions in the Clearinghouse mobility study, this traditional transfer pathway is only the beginning of the story. Of the 505,000 students who began college in fall 2006 and later transferred into a four-year institution, only about half (262,000) arrived at the four-year destination from an initial enrollment at a two-year institution. The rest came from another four-year institution.

Strategic enrollment managers at both two-year and four-year institutions would also benefit from studying the local and national data on students who follow the traditional transfer path of beginning at a two-year institution with the intention of transferring to a four-year institution. Many may be surprised by the different degree completion rates for students who transfer at different stages of progress and at different types of institutions. For example, Clearinghouse data show that, nationally, students are more likely to transfer without first earning an associate's degree, even though the chances of completing a bachelor's degree within six years at the destination institution are higher for students who do earn the associate's first (Hossler et al., 2012a; Shapiro et al., 2012). Practitioners at four-year institutions may view community colleges as merely providing easier and cheaper courses for weaker students, and the less time spent there the better (for one recent example, see Fain, 2013). But, in fact, students who transfer after having completed four to six terms at the two-year institution have higher bachelor's completion rates nationally than those who stayed at the two-year level for fewer terms, and this is true regardless of whether or not they had actually earned an associate's degree.

It is not hard to see how practitioners can use these kinds of insights to help students at either the original or the destination institutions to provide better information for students trying to plan when and how best to make the transfer, or to provide better-tailored programs and services at the destination institution to meet the needs of students when they arrive. A first response, after analyzing institution-level data on transfer and success patterns and comparing it to the national results, might be to revisit transfer or articulation policies with key feeder institutions. At a deeper level, analysis of student-level data could identify specific correlates of success, perhaps for students in certain majors or with specific demographic characteristics that would further inform policy changes and add substance to conversations with feeder institutions. If the policy changes are likely to result in a significant shift in enrollment or revenue patterns, clarifying the offsetting benefits in student success rates or degree production might empower the institution to emphasize other programs or courses with higher comparative advantage and value added.

Research using Clearinghouse data also showed that students who transfer to a public four-year institution are more likely to complete a bachelor's degree within six years of transferring than those who transfer to a private non-profit (Shapiro et al., 2013). This is just the opposite of what one would expect from merely looking at the IPEDS graduation rates of first-time, full-time students who start (and finish) at public versus private four-year institutions. The higher completion rate of transfer students at four-year public institutions may be related to the number of credits students were able to transfer in because of articulation agreements in place in many states. It could also be related to more established partnerships between particular four-year public institutions and their local community colleges that may likewise smooth the transition for transfer students. Either way, these are important insights for strategic enrollment managers and those who are tasked with advising and supporting the students who are following these pathways. Under new student success metrics, institutions will no longer be able to ignore these students who transfer in. Tracking their success will become yet another indicator of institutional quality. Understanding how to enhance their success will allow enrollment managers to get ahead of the curve and prepare their institutions for how they will look under the new measures.

WHAT SHOULD INSTITUTIONAL RESEARCHERS AND ENROLLMENT MANAGERS BE DOING DIFFERENTLY?

Institutional researchers can easily obtain the information presented here for the entire starting cohort in a particular year for students transferring to and from their own institution, and compare it to the national benchmark for their institutional category. The basic shape of this information can be obtained by tracking the prior and subsequent enrollments of current and former students, to learn about the pathways simply from the numbers of terms and types of origin and destination institutions. Further details, and much richer institutional insights about where and why students transfer, emerges when these data are merged with student-level information at the institution about student demographics, academic preparation and performance, major or degree program, and more. Equipped with these kinds of data, strategic enrollment managers can begin to better understand their students' complete educational pathways, and to devise and implement policies that lead to more valuable institutional supports and, ultimately, more successful students. Closely examining the pathways of their own students, institutions may also gain a better understanding of them and design support programs that fit those students' needs. For example, many enrollment managers at four-year institutions may incorrectly assume that the students who transfer in from other four-year institutions are recovering from a poor start academically or a poor fit for any number of other reasons, and thus need special transition programs similar to those offered to freshmen. Indeed, most institutions now have specific orientation programs focused on transfers that offer these supports. But many transfer students may also be looking for more intellectual challenge or a specific program offering, and they may be well on their way to accelerated progress. Transfer orientation programs should work toward identifying such students so that academic advisors can suggest intellectually challenging courses or specific academic programs.

One four-year institution that studied its own transfer-out students found that they were typically not those who were struggling academically, as many faculty members had assumed, but rather students who were among the most promising. When the institutional researchers examined Clearinghouse data on the transfer destinations of second- and third-year students who had left their institution, they found that the students were typically going to more demanding and not less demanding institutions. These insights were used to focus internal attention on enhancing the programs that the students were transferring out of, to insure that top students were finding sufficient academic challenge. The findings are a good example of how these kinds of insights can become a motivation to look more closely at the characteristics and prior academic experiences of similar students who were transferring *into* the institution from similar four-year colleges who might be in the same situation.

Strategic enrollment managers should also examine assumptions about the types of students who arrive from previous enrollments at two-year institutions. It is easy to accept uncritically the "traditional wisdom" that often emerges, for example, of struggling transfer students arriving from the local community college under-prepared for the rigorous courses at the four-year institution. One institutional research office that studied the data, however, found a wide range of patterns among students with prior enrollments at a key feeder community college. Students who entered social science majors at this four-year institution, for example, did quite well, while those entering biological and physical science majors had struggled. Students transferring from the community college who had previously enrolled at yet another four-year institution—that is, for whom the two-year institution was but one step on a longer educational pathway—turned out to be much stronger academically than expected and much clearer in their academic goals and expectations than other transfer students. These types of insights represent more than anecdote when they emerge from analyses of both institutional data on student progress and linked external data such as the Clearinghouse's on the prior and subsequent enrollments along student educational pathways. In this example, admissions officers were empowered by the data to work more closely with advisers and students from the community college to set appropriate expectations, and students pursuing this transfer pathway were able to form more realistic plans based on the actual experiences of similar students who had preceded them.

CONCLUSION

The growing policy focus on mobile students will inevitably lead to new measures for institutional performance and accountability that take into account more of the complete student pathway, including students who transfer in, transfer out, and persist to graduation at any institution. Already, state performance funding models, the Voluntary System of Accountability, and Voluntary Framework of Accountability are moving institutions in the direction of counting, or in some sense taking credit for, all of their contributions to student success regardless of where along the student's pathway that contribution occurs. The methodologies for measuring these contributions are far from settled, however, and institutions will need to consider carefully how their experience with their own students, and their own data analyses, might contribute to the development of more general measures that would be appropriate for similar institutions or for policy makers concerned with them.

In the meantime, enrollment managers will find that traditional retention and graduation rate measures apply only to a shrinking percentage of their students—those who enter as first-time, full-time students. To understand how best to serve all their students, they must first find ways to measure their students' complete educational pathways and identify the patterns, practices, and policies that can lead to enhanced likelihoods of success. In most cases, however, identifying and understanding these practices will not be sufficient without a significant change in organizational culture to apply what they learn, impartially, to the interests of their students. This change amounts to the development of an institutional obligation, embraced by faculty and administrators alike, to safeguarding the welfare of their students as clients, even when that welfare may lead the student clients to other programs on other campuses.

Institutions must be prepared to keep students informed of the multiple pathways to success so they can better make informed choices, goals, and plans. For some students, merely knowing that nontraditional and multi-institution pathways to degrees exist and can be successful will be empowering all by itself. For other students, arming them with specific information about the likelihood of success when following the different available pathways, both early in their careers and at key junctures along their pathway, can help them to make informed choices that match their circumstances.

Institutions should also strive to keep policy makers and practitioners informed of local and national trends in student educational pathways and of how those trends play out with their own students. Those who can inform policy makers, and link public policy with institutional policy on what counts for a successful institution, will be best positioned to benefit from the changing environment. Only by understanding the whole student pathways, including where students arrive from and where they leave for, and why, can they devise and implement policies that lead to more successful students and improved institutional effectiveness.

References

Adelman, C. (2005). *Moving into Town—and Moving On: The Community College in the Lives of Traditional-Age Students*. Washington, DC: U.S. Department of Education.

Adelman, C. (2006). *The Toolbox Revisited: Paths to Degree Completion from High School Through College*. Washington, DC: U.S. Department of Education.

Bean, J. (1980). Dropouts and turnover: The synthesis and test of a causal model of student attrition. *Research in Higher Education, 12*(2), 155–187.

Bill and Melinda Gates Foundation. (2009). *Postsecondary Success: Strategy Overview.* Retrieved from http://www.gatesfoundation.org/postsecondaryeducation.

Bound, J., Lovenheim, M., & Turner, S. (2010). Why have college completion rates declined? An analysis of changing student preparation and collegiate resources. *American Economic Journal: Applied Economics, 2*(3), 129–157.

Braxton, J. M. (Ed.). (2000). *Reworking the Student Departure Puzzle*. Nashville, TN: Vanderbilt University Press.

Braxton, J. M., Doyle, W. R., Hartley III, H. V., Hirschy, A. S., Jones, W. A., & McLendon, M. K. (2013). *Rethinking College Student Retention*. San Francisco: Jossey-Bass.

Cabrera, A. F., Burkum, K. R., & La Nasa, S. M. (2005). Pathways to a four-year degree: Determinants of transfer and degree completion. In A. Seidman (Ed.), *College Student Retention: Formula for Student Success* (pp. 155–214). Westport, CT: Praeger Publishers.

Cabrera, A. F., Nora, A., & Castenada, M. B. (1993). College persistence: Structural equation modeling test of an integrated model of student retention. *The Journal of Higher Education, 64*(2), 123–139.

Dundar, A., Hossler, D., Shapiro, D., Chen, J., Martin, S., Torres, V., Zerquera, D., & Ziskin, M. (2011). *National Postsecondary Enrollment Trends: Before, During, and After the Great Recession*. Washington, DC: National Student Clearinghouse Research Center.

Fain, P. (2013). What Goes into a Degree? *Inside Higher Ed*. Retrieved from http://www.insidehighered.com/news/2013/11/21/controversy-and-important-questions-around-uconns-proposal-limit-outside-credits#ixzz2lfRkodYX.

Hagedorn, L. S. (2012). How to define retention: A new look at an old problem. In A. Seidman (Ed.), *College Student Retention: A Formula for Success* (pp. 81–100). Lanham, MD: Rowman & Littlefield Publishers, Inc.

Hossler, D., Shapiro, D., Dundar, A., Ziskin, M., Chen, J., Zerquera, D., & Torres, V. (2012a). *Transfer and Mobility: A National View of Pre-Degree Student Movement in Postsecondary Institutions*. Herndon, VA: National Student Clearinghouse Research Center.

Hossler, D., Shapiro, D., Dundar, A., Ziskin, M., Chen, J., Zerquera, D., & Torres, V. (2012b). *Reverse Transfer: A National View of Student Mobility from Four-Year to Two-Year Institutions*. Herndon, VA: National Student Clearinghouse Research Center.

Jones, D. P. (2013). *Outcomes-Based Funding: The Wave of Implementation*. Retrieved from http://completecollege.org/pdfs/Outcomes-Based-Funding-Report-Final.pdf.

Kelly, P. (2010). *Closing the College Attainment Gap Between the U.S. and Most Educated Countries, and the Contributions to be Made by the States*. Retrieved from http://www.nchems.org/pubs/docs/Closing%20the%20U%20S%20%20Degree%20Gap%20NCHEMS%20Final.pdf.

Kuh, G. D, Kinzie, J., Buckley, J. A., Bridges, B. K., & Hayek, J. C. (2007). Piecing together the student success puzzle: Research, propositions and recommendations. *ASHE-ERIC Higher Education Report*, *32*(5). San Francisco: Jossey-Bass.

Lee, Jr., J. M., Edwards, K., Menson, R., & Rawls, A. (2011). *The College Completion Agenda: 2011 Progress Report*. New York: College Board Advocacy and Policy Center.

Lumina Foundation for Education. (2013). Strategic Plan 2013 to 2016. Retrieved from http://www.luminafoundation.org/advantage/document/goal_2025/2013-Lumina_Strategic_Plan.pdf.

National Center for Public Policy and Higher Education (NCPPHE). (2008). *Measuring up 2008. The National Report Card on Higher Education*.

Obama, B. (2009). Remarks of President Barack Obama—Address to joint session of Congress, February 24, 2009. Retrieved from http://www.whitehouse.gov/the_press_office/Remarks-of-President-Barack-Obama-Address-to-Joint-Session-of-Congress/.

Organisation for Economic Co-operation and Development (OECD). (2012) Education at a Glance 2012: OECD Indicators. OECD Publishing. Retrieved from http://dx.doi.org/10.1787/eag-2012-en.

Pascarella, E. T., & Terenzini, P. T. (1991). *How College Affects Students: A Third Decade of Research*. San Francisco: Jossey-Bass.

Perna, L. W. (2013). Improving college, persistence, and completion: Lessons learned. In L. W. Perna & A. P. Jones (Eds.), *The State of College Access and Completion: Improving College Success for Students from Underrepresented Groups* (pp. 208–224). New York: Routledge.

Radford, A. W., Berkner, L., Wheeless, S. C., & Shepherd, B. (2010). *Persistence and Attainment of 2003–04 Beginning Postsecondary Students: After 6 Years*. Washington, DC: National Center for Education Statistics.

Reason, R. D. (2009). An examination of persistence research through the lens of a comprehensive conceptual framework. *Journal of College Student Development*, *50*(6), 659–682.

Rendón, L. I., Jalomo, Jr., R., & Nora, A. (2000). Theoretical considerations in the study of minority student retention in higher education. In J. M. Braxton (Ed.), *Reworking the Student Departure Puzzle* (pp. 127–156). Nashville, TN: Vanderbilt University Press.

Shapiro, D., Dundar, A., Chen, J., Ziskin, M., Park, E., Torres, V., & Chiang, Y. (2012). *Completing college: A National View of Student Attainment Rates*. Herndon, VA: National Student Clearinghouse Research Center.

Shapiro, D., Dundar, A., Ziskin, M., Chiang, Y., Chen, J., Harrell, A., & Torres, V. (2013). *Baccalaureate Attainment: A National View of the Postsecondary Outcomes of Students Who Transfer from Two-Year to Four-Year Institutions*. Herndon, VA: National Student Clearinghouse Research Center.

St. John, E. P., Paulsen, M. B., & Starkey, J. B. (1996). The nexus between college choice and persistence. *Research in Higher Education, 7*(2), 175–220.

Thelin, J. R. (2011). *A History of American Higher Education*. Baltimore, MD: The Johns Hopkins University Press.

Tinto, V. (1975). Dropout from higher education: A theoretical synthesis of recent research. *Review of Educational Research, 45*(1), 89–125.

Tinto, V. (1994). *Leaving College: Rethinking the Causes and Cures of Student Departure*. Chicago: University of Chicago Press.

Tinto, V. (2006). Research and practice of student retention: What next? *Journal of Student Retention, 8*(1), 1–19.

CHAPTER 14

Models of Student Retention and Persistence

Amy S. Hirschy

Problems facing university administrators eighty years ago concerned student enrollments, educational costs, university publicity, and the widening scope of university work (Lindsay & Holland, 1930, p. 562). Although these issues remain contemporary, approaches to addressing them have evolved considerably. One such movement is the development of the Strategic Enrollment Management profession. SEM is a "complex of concepts and processes that enables the fulfillment of institutional mission and students' educational goals" (Bontrager, 2004, p. 12). SEM leaders view the student experience through a wide-angled lens (Hossler & Bean, 1990). Among the identified core concepts of SEM is to promote academic success by improving student access, transition, persistence, and graduation (Bontrager, 2004; Bontrager & Green, 2012).

A large number of theoretically derived models have been advanced to help explain the student college choice process and student persistence decisions in postsecondary institutions. Professional literature provides ample overviews of the history and development of such models (for recent reviews, see Bergerson, 2009; Braxton & Hirschy, 2005; Braxton, et al., 2013; Habley, Bloom, & Robbins, 2012; Perna & Thomas, 2008), to the point that college administrators face the overwhelming tasks of managing complex daily roles and responsibilities while trying to stay current with the latest research developments, make sense of them, and translate them into useful tools in their work. The purpose of this chapter is to consider ways in which SEM professionals might assess the relevance and utility of various student success models for their particular contexts. Acknowledging that no perfect, universal model exists for every situation, a key part of this discernment process relies on the expert knowledge and professional judgment of the SEM staff members.

SEM leaders competent in applying research-based models to their practice can ask their institutional research office to conduct a retention study in a very informed way and collaborate with faculty and student affairs staff members in targeted, effective approaches to enhance student success. Understanding such models may reveal new possibilities to partner with high school counselors, administrators, and families of prospective new students.

The chapter begins with definitions of relevant terms, then explores the limitations and strengths of applying empirically based models, and follows with some brief examples that aim to guide SEM professionals in how to select suitable models in their work. The chapter concludes with recommendations for practitioners and researchers.

DEFINITIONS OF TERMS

A mutual understanding of the terms often used in how, what, and who studies college student success may be helpful for readers of this chapter, even if consensus does not exist among the community. For example, *student success* definitions vary by educational stakeholders (Davenport, Martinez-Saenz, & Rhine, 2012). Students may evaluate success as the achievement of an educational goal (Braxton, 2003). Faculty and administrators may consider student learning, development, and engagement as indicators of success, whereas institutions and the state may define success outcomes as retention or completion rates.

Student success models often reference overlapping constructs. *Retention* focuses on the goal of a focal institution to keep students enrolled from one term of study to the next until completion of a credential. *Persistence* refers to students maintaining or completing their enrollment at any college or university in the postsecondary system. Put differently, institutions *retain* and students *persist* (Hagedorn, 2005). *Completion* focuses on students' attainment of a degree or other credential (U.S. Department of Education, 2013). *Attrition* indicates a decrease in student enrollment at the individual, institution, or system level (Hirschy, Bremer, & Castellano, 2011).

Not surprisingly, scholars also do not agree on a single definition of *theory*. Michael Bastedo (2012) suggested that "theory must, at its heart, convey the causal logic of social explanation" (p. 336), explaining through a narrative why the constructs or concepts are important, and how and why they are related. Positivist theories attempt to explain, predict, or control a phenomenon (Bess

& Dee, 2008). Social constructivist theories allow for multiple perspectives or frames of reference about reality, and post-positivist perspectives critique the assumptions of power and privilege that may undergird existing theories (Bess & Dee, 2008). Although beyond the scope of this chapter, extended examinations of the state of theory in the field of higher education exist (see Bess & Dee, 2008; Kezar, 2006).

Theoretically derived models may not meet the criteria of a formal theory, but they rely on empirically grounded research findings that are informed by theory. In other words, the variables and their proposed interrelationships emanate from structured, quantitative, and/or qualitative inquiries that draw on one or more theories. A *conceptual model* shows the relationships among variables that are derived from a body of research (Perna & Thomas, 2008). The terms "conceptual," "empirically based," and "theoretically derived" models are used inconsistently within the academic community in general and in the scholarship pertaining to student success in particular. This chapter will focus on depictions of interrelated variables that spring from research findings.

THEORY AND PRACTICE

Professional and research literature focused on student success theories abounds. For instance, SEM leaders share decades of history of empirically based models focused on student college choice (Hossler, Braxton, & Coopersmith, 1989; Hossler & Gallagher, 1987), and nearly twenty-five years ago, John Bean (1990a, 1990b) summarized insights from retention research and theoretical models in enrollment management. Vincent Tinto's (1975, 2012) contributions to understanding voluntary student departure span more than thirty-five years. Subsequent research on these topics both supports and critiques the earlier scholarship. Yet for a variety of reasons, some administrators eschew using theoretically derived models in their practice. The following sections identify reasons that incorporating such models into practice presents challenges to time-strapped SEM practitioners, offer a rationale for making the effort to use empirically based models, and provide criteria to assist in selecting apt student success models.

Deterrents to Using Theoretically Derived Models

Postsecondary administrators "increasingly find the academic study of organizations distant from their problems, concerns, and leadership aspirations" (Bastedo, 2012, p. 9). Even in higher education, an applied field, many academics who publish in scholarly journals and other professional publications fail to adequately consider practitioners as knowledge partners in their work. The theoretical concepts described may be arcane, confusing readers who may not share the knowledge of the ideas that undergird the model. Narrative descriptions articulating the implications of findings for practitioners can be absent, vague, or untethered to the realities of the practice. Not all scholarship has equal value, yet it remains difficult to assess the relevance and import of findings without knowing the quality of the research review process, and some research articles provide insufficient detail for readers to interpret or evaluate the results reported (Valentine et al., 2011). As a consequence, models may be poorly validated or tested, measures used to evaluate the models may be suspect, or methodologies may be weak.

The nature of theory building is that it involves generating, testing, and refining concepts over time (Wallace, 1971). As such, many models evolve to reflect new understandings—some are supported, partially supported, revised, and some are refuted. Others are developed and published but then lie dormant if no subsequent studies follow. Administrators who have the academic and/ or professional training to evaluate and decipher the meaning of published research findings may lack the time or interest to follow the volume of professional and scholarly publications that address college student success. With new research activity that produces oft-conflicting findings, dead ends, uneven quality, and unclear relevance, no wonder some practitioners are reluctant to adopt theoretical models in their work. So why bother? What compelling case can possibly be made to take the time to sift through the noise and confusion?

Considerations in Using Theoretically Derived Models

Competing interests from various community stakeholders can pull away focus from the institutional mission and students' best interests (Bontrager, 2008), and theory adds coherence and order to interrelated ideas (Kezar, 2006). Theories (and by extension, models) "become sources of awareness to us, ways of organizing our thinking about our students, suggestions of areas for exploration, and keys to insights about possible courses of action" (Parker, Widick, & Knefelkamp, 1978, p. xiv). To reduce rates of student departure, Tinto (2012) recommended applying a coherent framework for institutional action. John Braxton, et al. (2013) added that such a framework "optimally emerges from empirical research guided by theory" (p. 3). Institutional practices informed by theoretically based research findings benefit from the explanatory power of empirically tested theory. A comprehensive understanding of the basis for institutional choices guides decision-making and ensures fidelity of the actions selected. Further, an understanding of theoretically based empirical findings can inform any adjustments that need to be made when implementing a recommended policy or program (Braxton et al., 2013).

Employing empirically based models can be useful in identifying how institutional levers (such as programs and policies) can be used more effectively in helping students achieve their educational goals, and practitioners seek efficient, effective ways to target limited resources to help students succeed (Hirschy, Bremer, & Castellano, 2011). It is likely that an administrator prefers a theory over another (or chooses whether to use theory at all) based on an amalgam of one's professional experiences (Nidiffer, 2000). Professional judgment informs how well individual theories or models "square" with the goals at hand and how they may be applied effectively.

Professional Judgment Formal and informal theories "make the many complex facets of experience manageable, understandable, meaningful, and consistent rather than random" (McEwen, 2003, p. 154). Some practitioners may mistrust formal theories because they are often forced to subscribe to them, discounting their own informal theories that are based on personal and professional experiences (Love, 2012). What some may call intuition, hunches, and gut instincts can be considered theories-in-use (Argyris, 1976), informal theories (Love, 2012), or the "internal or implicit rules that people apply in a given situation" (Nidiffer, 2000, p. 65). Practical knowledge is acquired through experience, informing professionals about how to recognize assumptions, identify courses of actions, and respond effectively to new situations. Often professionals who rely on this internalized approach do not cite particular formal theories, but they have captured practical knowledge about understanding and addressing complex issues in the work setting.

Quoting Aristotle, Jon C. Dalton (2002) suggested that "wisdom is the most finished form of knowledge," and practical wisdom is the result of three kinds of learning: "academic study, accumulated professional experience, and mentoring with colleagues in the profession" (pp. 6–7). More recently, Gregory Blimling (2011) offered that theory and practice intersect to form professional judgment. Using student affairs administration as the context, he identifies theories as the body of work that helps "describe, understand, and engage students in college" experience as the accumulated knowledge learned throughout a career, and practice as the "application of theory and experience to student affairs work" (p. 43). Professional judgment integrates lessons from professional practice, theories, research findings, discussions with colleagues, readings, and other forms of professional engagement (Blimling, 2011). In other words, blending formal and informal theories through professional judgment enhances effective administrative practice.

Though professionals tend to use approaches to organizational change that are familiar or popular (Kezar, 2001), they should consider several criteria when appraising the use of student success models. First, SEM practitioners can assess critically which models or theories most directly address their campus concerns, applying professional judgment to a careful review of what is empirically known to support student success. Prioritizing the particular campus context and student population profiles is paramount in determining the relevance of existing student success models. Second, understanding the intended level and corresponding context of the model is necessary to evaluate a fit for selection. Finally, the theoretical lens or lenses on which the model is based signals perspectives and assumptions of the model, and empirical grounding lends credibility. Descriptions of these factors for selecting student success models follow. Table 14.1 displays some examples of theoretically derived, empirically based student success models and how they can be classified according to the selection criteria.

Level and Context Theories can be classified by levels (Merton, 1968). Grand theories explain broad, large-scale topics that are universally applied to all types of organizations throughout societies. Examples of grand theories are Alexander Astin's (1984) theory of student involvement, Tinto's Interactionalist Theory (1993), and Alberto Cabrera, Amaury Nora, and Maria Castañeda's (1993) integrated model of student retention. Theories of the middle-range are more limited in scope than grand theories, but they can be applied to more than one setting. Middle-range theories can be applied to groups that share characteristics, such as minority or low-income students (see Chapter 16) or residential institutions (see Chapter 15). Another theory of the middle-range is John Bean and Barbara Metzner's (1985) conceptual model for nontraditional undergraduate students. Low-level theories explain behavior in an even more limited, specific context, such as a particular student population within a specific institutional setting. Two such conceptual models include Eddie Comeaux and Keith Harrison's (2011) model for Division 1 student athlete success and Lawrence Jenicke, Monica Holmes, and Michael Pisani's (2013) model for university business students. Middle-range and low-level theories are more relevant for practitioners' work than grand theories (Kezar, 2006), because they permit empirical testing (Merton, 1968) and allow—in fact, *require*—sensitivity to the context of interest. Put differently, theories concerning student success are context dependent and not universal in nature—no theory or model will work in every kind of institution or for all students.

To elaborate, Tinto's Interactionalist Theory (1975, 1987) can be considered a grand theory, as it was intended to apply to college students in various institutional types. Based on voluminous empirical testing, Tinto revised his work (1993) to include a broader swath of individual student and institutional characteristics. After appraising the empirical tests of Tinto's theory, Braxton and colleagues (2013) proffered a revision of Tinto's theory that addresses student departure from residential colleges and universities and a separate theory that considers students attending commuter institutions. Because they target narrower contexts, the latter two are considered theories of the middle-range. More tapered yet are low-level theories. An example of a low-level conceptual model is one that focuses on community college students pursuing a career-related

Table 14.1: Comparison of selected theory derived, empirically based student success models

Model	Population of Emphasis	Level	Context	Theoretical Lenses	Selected Key Concepts
Astin (1984)	College students	Grand	Colleges and universities	Psychological	Student involvement
Bean (1980)	College students	Grand	Colleges and universities	Organizational	Work turnover model applied to student attrition—students leave college for reasons similar to those that cause employees to resign
Bean & Eaton (2000)	College students	Grand	Colleges and universities	Psychological	Personal characteristics (e.g., coping strategies, personality, motivations, self-efficacy) affect the ways students interact with the institutional environment
Bean & Metzner (1985)	Non-traditional college students	Middle-range	Colleges and universities	Sociological Psychological	Student interactions with academic and external environment influence academic and psychological outcomes
Berger (2000)	First generation college students	Middle-range	Colleges and universities	Sociological	Social class and cultural capital; individual and institutional levels
Braxton, et al. (2013)	Residential college students	Middle-range	Residential colleges and universities	Economic Organizational Psychological Sociological	Student interactions with campus environment; antecedents to social integration

(continued)

Table 14.1: (*Continued*)

Model	Population of Emphasis	Level	Context	Theoretical Lenses	Selected Key Concepts
Cabrera, Nora, & Castañeda (1992)	College students	Middle-range	Large, public, urban universities	Economic Sociological	Student perceptions and attitudes of finances influence social and academic processes
Cabrera, Nora, & Castañeda (1993)	College students	Grand	Colleges and universities	Economic Sociological	Integrates multiple models; includes individual, environmental, and institutional factors.
Comeaux & Harrison (2011)	College student athletes	Low-range	Division 1 colleges and universities	Sociological Organizational	Student interaction with campus and sport environment; sport commitment, Scholar-Baller Paradigm
Braxton, et al. (2013)	Commuter college students	Middle-range	Commuter colleges and universities	Economic Organizational Psychological Sociological	Student interactions with campus and external environment
Hirschy, Bremer, & Castellano (2011)	Career and technical college students	Low-range	Community colleges	Economic Organizational Psychological Sociological	Student interactions with campus and external environment; career integration
Jenicke, Holms, & Pisani (2013-2014)	College business students	Low-range	Colleges and universities	Organizational	Quality improvement methodology: Six Sigma
Kuh, Kinzie, Schuh, Whitt, & Assoc. (2005)	College students	Grand	Colleges and universities	Organizational Psychological	Student engagement

Model	Population of Emphasis	Level	Context	Theoretical Lenses	Selected Key Concepts
Kuh & Love (2000)	College students	Middle-range	Colleges and universities	Sociological	Cultural
Perna & Thomas (2008)	Precollege and college students	Grand	4 layers of context that inform college access, choice, and success	Sociological Educational Psychological Economic	Core layer is the individual student; then family; school; and finally, the broader social, economic, and policy context
Reason (2009)	College students	Grand	Colleges and universities	Organizational Psychological Sociological	Interactions between the individual and campus environment
Strange & Banning (2001)	Campus community	Middle-range	Colleges and universities	Cultural Organizational	Educational environment
St. John, Paulsen, & Carter (2005)	African American and White precollege and college students	Middle-range	Colleges and universities	Economic Sociological	Ability to pay and perceptions of debt influence college choice and persistence decisions
Tinto (1993)	College students	Grand	Colleges and universities	Sociological	Interactions between the individual and campus environment; academic and social integration, goal and institutional commitments

credential, such as a certificate or associate degree. This limited context allows for an examination of a particular student population within academic and career integration programs distinct from the students enrolled at the same institution who pursue general education programs intending to transfer to a four-year institution (see Hirschy, Bremer, & Castellano, 2011). Applying a grand theory for this targeted population may mask important nuances of their experiences.

Theoretical Lens and Empirical Support Investigating the details of how a model was developed will provide important considerations to determine its usefulness. On what population(s) is the model based? To what extent can it be generalized to the focal context? Is the model supported by research findings? Braxton (2000b) recommends revising existing theories by including constructs grounded in empirical findings, meeting a higher standard than ideas that are proposed through reasoning alone. What disciplinary perspective(s) does a theory reflect? Examples of disciplinary lenses on student success problems include anthropology, economics, education, history, organizations, philosophy, political science, psychology, and sociology (Braxton, 2000a; McEwen, 2003; Tinto, 1993).

The underlying objectives of theoretical perspectives differ. Brief explanations of the four dominant theoretical lenses in studies of student persistence follow. Models with an economic perspective consider how a college student weighs the costs and benefits of attending against the costs and benefits associated with not being in school. The student's ability to pay (as well as perceptions of financial issues) and the institution's cost and financial policies reflect economic concerns in student choice and retention decisions (see St. John, Paulson, & Carter, 2005; Cabrera, Nora, & Castañeda, 1993). Organizational perspectives in retention models look at the role of organizational structure and behavior. Ways in which institutions are organized and the effectiveness of various processes (such as admission, academic advising, registration, and financial aid policies) can influence student success (see conceptual model for identifying and addressing problems experienced by university business students by Jenicke, Holmes, and Pisani, 2013). How institutional leaders communicate with students and provide meaningful ways for student participation also represent organizational aspects of student success models (see work turnover approach to student persistence by Bean, 1980). Individual student characteristics such as personality traits, motivational states, and academic aptitudes reveal elements of a psychological perspective in understanding student departure. For instance, John Bean and Shevawn Eaton's (2000) psychological model of college student retention acknowledges that personal aspects of the individual student's characteristics at entry (such as personality, self-efficacy, normative beliefs, and skills and abilities) influence the student's interactions with the institution and his or her subsequent persistence decisions. Finally, the sociological perspective shows the influence of social structures and social forces on college student success. Variables such as the influences of family responsibilities (see Bean & Metzner, 1985), anticipatory socialization for college, and cultural capital (see Berger, 2000) demonstrate a sociological perspective. Additionally, social forces such as the student's culture of origin and interactions with college student peers and faculty can be included in the sociological perspective (see Kuh & Love, 2000).

Laura Perna and Scott Thomas's conceptual model (2008) is based on an extensive review of research from four disciplines (sociology, education, psychology, and economics). Updating Perna's earlier model of student access and choice (2006), Perna and Thomas (2008) created a deep, multilayered conceptual model of student success. The model is based on six assumptions:

- The relative contribution of different disciplinary and area perspectives to student success varies.
- When considered together, multiple theoretical approaches yield more comprehensive understandings of student success.
- Student success is shaped by multiple levels of context.
- Student success processes vary across groups.
- Multiple methodological approaches contribute to knowledge of student success.
- Student success is a longitudinal process (p. 30).

Perna and Thomas's conceptual model (2008) recognized four layers of context. The first, core layer is the internal context of the student. The next layer comprises family context. The next layer represents the school context, which includes primary, secondary, and postsecondary levels of educational institutions. Finally, the fourth layer of context recognizes the social, economic, and policy context. Practitioners may find this model useful in thinking about how the four layers of context (and the four disciplinary perspectives within each layer) might look different for various groups of students. For example, starting at the outer context layer, some federal policies vary for international students, those who serve or have served in the U.S. military, and students with disabilities. Regarding the third layer, the school context, college knowledge and preparation programs in primary and secondary school systems may not be available or well-developed for students from low-income neighborhoods, affecting college access and choice (McDonough, 1997; Perna & Kurban, 2013). Closer to home in the family context layer, first-generation college students may have high educational aspirations but inherit insufficient cultural capital (Bourdieu & Passeron, 1977) from their families to help them understand the mores of navigating various complex institutional systems, such as applying for admission and financial aid, registering for courses, and selecting an academic major.

As for the core, internal layer, how students manage their responsibilities—at school, work, and home—can affect their persistence. Students with high levels of motivation and self-efficacy (Perna & Thomas, 2008) have higher persistence rates, for example. Meanwhile, students with significant responsibilities at home may be less likely to persist if they perceive that their enrollment negatively affects their family (Braxton et al., 2013).

By considering the layers of context for a particular subgroup of students, SEM administrators acknowledge that students have diverse backgrounds and may need differing supports from their institution compared to their peers. Perna and Thomas's conceptual model (2008) provided a framework for considering the diverse challenges that may hinder students from reaching their educational goals.

Whole or Parts? Should a model be used only in its original, complete form? Can parts of different models be combined and used to construct a model for a given college or university? In short, SEM leaders must rely on professional judgment to determine what might be the best fit given the context and the goals of the inquiry. This may mean using an entire, single model. Alternatively, SEM practitioners may use selected parts of a model because the institutional leaders' focus is on only one aspect, such as improving the learning environment on campus. In this case, some institutions may draw solely on Tinto's (1993) student's academic integration construct and its link to subsequent commitment to the institution. In another case, a campus may use an approach of combining aspects of several models. The charge is to match the most relevant theories or parts of theories with the challenge presented. An understanding of various models provides a SEM professional an increased awareness of options to consider.

In an example, Robert Reason's conceptual model (2009) is based on persistence research findings. The framework includes a broader array of influences on college success than many earlier persistence models, taking into account interrelated student, faculty, and institutional factors. The model of student learning and persistence proposed by Reason (2009) considered the influence of precollege characteristics and experiences, the organizational context of the institution, and individual student experiences with the curriculum and among peers. Precollege student characteristics include socio-demographic traits, academic preparation and performance, and student dispositions. The college experience includes organizational factors (such as institutional size, type, and institutional behavior and context), the student peer environment (such as campus racial climate and academic norms), and individual student curricular, classroom, and co-curricular experiences. Reason (2009) argued that examination of multiple interactions between the individual and the college environment leads to a more nuanced understanding of student persistence.

Compared to Perna and Thomas's model (2008), Reason's model (2009) focused more specifically on the student experience within the college environment.

Campus leaders who want to target the student learning environment on campus would likely find Reason's model (2009) appealing, and they could supplement their inquiry by considering academic and social integration (Tinto, 1993), student engagement (Kuh, Kinzie, Schuh, Whitt, & Associates, 2005), and C. Carney Strange and James Banning's (2001) educating by design framework. The student engagement concept proposed by George Kuh et al. (2005) involved two related components that influence student success outcomes. First, the amount of time and energy that students devote to educationally purposeful activities is related to learning and personal development. Second, the ways that the institution organizes and supports student learning opportunities and services contribute to the effort students exert to participate in such activities. The authors propose an intentional, institution-wide effort to promote student engagement. Strange and Banning's (2001) framework assessed the campus learning environment by considering four components: "the physical condition, design, and layout; the characteristics of the people who inhabit them; organizational structure related to their purposes and goals; and the inhabitants' collective perceptions or constructions of the context and culture of the setting" (p. 5). Examining the campus environment through these four perspectives (physical, aggregate, organizational, and constructed) may provide insights to the SEM leader in creating an action plan to study and improve the learning environment on campus. By combining aspects of several models, SEM leaders can create a useful, relevant framework to examine the kinds of intentional educational opportunities students experience both in and outside the classroom. Drawing on multiple disciplinary lenses may offer a more complex analysis and help create innovative interventions for improved practice. Phrased differently, facets of several models could contribute elements that may be meaningful to the goals of examining and improving a particular campus's learning environment. The intent of most SEM leaders is to improve practice at their institutions, not to empirically test and provide validity to a given theory. Accordingly, using facets of several models is appropriate.

EXAMPLES OF THEORY TO PRACTICE APPROACHES

This chapter emphasizes that using theoretically derived models can buttress student success efforts if they are judiciously evaluated and applied by SEM professionals. The process of selecting among models is one step in enacting strategic organizational improvement. The next section presents two comprehensive approaches to applying theory in practice with suggested revisions (noted in italics) to consider theoretically derived models.

First, Edward St. John, Jeffrey McKinney, and Tina Tuttle (2006) recommended a five-step approach to addressing critical challenges in higher education. After defining the critical issue, the first step is to build an understanding of the challenge by assessing why it exists and what efforts have been made to address it in the past and reviewing those results. The second is to look internally and externally for solutions. In this step, SEM leaders should seek insights from various sources—talk with people on campus to gather their ideas, scan best practices in the field, *and gather information on theoretically derived models with potential relevance.* Third, assess possible solutions and resources. Fourth, develop action plans that include designing a pilot test. Finally, implement a pilot test, evaluate the results, and complete the learning cycle by continuing to build on the understanding of the challenge.

Second, the Practice to Theory to Practice (PTP) approach is adapted from L. Lee Knefelkamp's recommendations on applying student development theory to student affairs practice (1984, as cited in Evans et al., 2010, and Upcraft, 1994). The ten steps follow:

1. Identify issues that need to be addressed.

2. Determine desired goal and outcomes.

3. Analyze relevant student and environmental characteristics.

4. Investigate available student success models that may be useful in understanding the issues and meeting the desired goals. Determine which models or aspects of models may fit best. Some models may address specific populations or types of institutions more effectively. Consider multi-disciplinary perspectives.

5. Reexamine goals and outcomes in light of the analysis. Modify if needed.

6. Design the interventions/initiatives/action plan using methods that will encourage achieving the goals.

7. Implement the action plan.

8. Monitor and evaluate the plan.

9. Redesign the plan if necessary. Consider alternatives and make adjustments.

10. Revise or confirm the model based on its utility in practice.

RECOMMENDATIONS FOR SELECTING STUDENT SUCCESS MODELS

To improve student access, transition, persistence, and graduation rates, practitioners and scholars can consider ways to use theoretically derived student success models. Recommendations for each of the selection criteria follow.

Professional Judgment

- Use professional judgment and wisdom throughout the process of assessing the fit of student success models, giving credence to informal theory based on experiences gained in professional roles. Paying attention to what model or components resonate with what one knows about the institutional characteristics, such as the values of the community, can assist in discerning what models (or parts of models) offer the best potential to inform strategic action.

Level and Context of Model

- Institution, know thyself. Understanding relevant student and environmental characteristics will assist SEM leaders to make data-informed judgments about assessing the applicability of theoretically derived models.

- Develop and maintain close partnerships with those who have access to institutional data. "Just as there is nothing so good as a good theory, there is no substitute for well-conceived and adequately presented institutional research" (Julius, Baldridge, & Pfeffer, 2000, p. 52).

- Consider both the strengths and limitations of selecting grand, middle-range, and low-level models given the institutional challenge at hand.

- Consider models that examine key enrollment indicators (KEI): Student attributes and institutional attributes (Bontrager & Green, 2012). Student attributes include academic ability, academic program interest, special skills (athletics, fine arts, leadership), race/ethnicity, undergraduate/graduate/certificate, financial means, and geographic origin. Institutional attributes include program and facilities capacities and course delivery modes (on-campus, satellite campus, online).

Theoretical Lens and Empirical Support

- Read professional and research literature widely, and select carefully. Recognize the disciplinary approach(es) the models represent and consider looking at the challenge at hand through multiple theoretical lenses.

- Understand the empirical basis of various models to determine their relative merit. Consider models that are grounded in theory and research to guide decision-making.

- After selecting a model, evaluate results and share insights about what works, what does not, and what is missing from existing student success models and theories. Practitioners and scholars must work in concert to improve the development, testing, and revision of theories and communicate results in meaningful ways (Broido, 2011). Theorists from various academic disciplines must understand the context of higher education as an organization for their contributions to be most relevant and valuable, and SEM leaders provide such expertise.

Whole or Parts?
- Be flexible and use what is likely to best align with the needs, priorities, and characteristics of the institution.
- Consider both the strengths and limitations of using a single, comprehensive model or a combination of models given the institutional challenge at hand.

CONCLUSION

Several of the models presented in this handbook represent updated versions of previous models (see Chapter 15). Such revisions represent the changing nature of reliable knowledge in the field, a potential source of both hope and frustration for those challenged to keep current on these important matters of student success. Likewise, the landscape of higher education continually shifts. Internal and external environments change—student demographics; senior campus leadership; institutional, state, and federal policies and priorities; technology; competition; and public expectations, to name a few. Investing the time and resources to stay apprised of such changes may contribute to competitive advantages not possible otherwise.

Increasing collaboration among departments across the campus to support enrollment goals is one of the purposes of SEM (Bontrager & Green, 2012), and organizational silos sometimes create unintentional barriers to student success. Given the multiple perspectives on how to define student success (Davenport, Martinez-Saenz, & Rhine, 2012), the process of determining which (or what aspects of) empirically based models may be relevant could assist academic communities in clarifying the goals and outcomes of student success, even if no consensus results (see Davenport, Martinez-Saenz, & Rhine, 2012, for their insightful elaboration on the "student success conundrum"). Effective leaders are capable of creating meaningful dialogue and connecting perspectives that seem divergent, yet that share underlying values (Kezar, 2014). Discussing the various viewpoints of stakeholders can elevate understanding that may lead to new and creative approaches to long-standing issues. For example, models that reflect multiple disciplinary lenses may provide opportunities for stakeholders to recognize a more integrated, holistic perspective to promote student successes in access, transition, persistence, and graduation. More specifically, models that are rooted in the interest of the welfare of students (Braxton & Hirschy,

2005) may offer various constituents a common language and focus to discuss collaborative approaches to the student success puzzle. Campus leaders who are informed by both current research and valuable professional wisdom may be best positioned to enhance and advocate for their strategic approaches to support college student success.

References

Argyris, C. (1976). Theories of action that inhibit individual learning. *American Psychologist, 31*, 638–654.

Astin, A. W. (1984). Student involvement: A developmental theory for higher education. *Journal of College Student Personnel, 25*, 297–308.

Bastedo, M. N. (2012). Organizing higher education: A manifesto. In M. N. Bastedo (Ed.), *The Organization of Higher Education: Managing Colleges for a New Era*. Baltimore, MD: The Johns Hopkins University Press.

Bean, J. P. (1980). Dropouts and turnover: The synthesis and test of a causal model of student attrition. *Research in Higher Education, 12*, 155–187.

Bean, J. P. (1990a). Why students leave: Insights from research. In D. Hossler, J. P. Bean, & Associates (Eds.), *The Strategic Management of College Enrollments* (pp. 147–169). San Francisco: Jossey-Bass.

Bean, J. P. (1990b). Using retention research in enrollment management. In D. Hossler, J. P. Bean, & Associates (Eds.), *The Strategic Management of College Enrollments* (pp. 170–185). San Francisco: Jossey-Bass.

Bean, J. P., & Eaton, S. (2000). A psychological model of college student retention. In J. M. Braxton (Ed.), *Reworking the Student Departure Puzzle* (pp. 48–61). Nashville, TN: Vanderbilt University Press.

Bean, J. P., & Metzner, B. S. (1985). A conceptual model of nontraditional student attrition. *Review of Educational Research, 55*, 485–540.

Berger, J. B. (2000). Optimizing capital, social reproduction, and undergraduate persistence: A sociological perspective. In J. M. Braxton (Ed.), *Reworking the Student Departure Puzzle* (pp. 95–124). Nashville, TN: Vanderbilt University Press.

Bergerson, A. A. (2009). College choice and access to college: Moving policy, research, and practice to the 21st century. *ASHE Higher Education Report, 35*(4). San Francisco: Jossey-Bass.

Bess, J. L., & Dee, J. R. (2008). *Understanding College and University Organization: Theories for Effective Policy and Practice, Volume I: The State of the System*. Sterling, VA: Stylus Publishing.

Blimling, G. S. (2011). Developing professional judgment. In P. M. Magolda & M. B. Baxter Magolda (Eds.), *Contested Issues in Student Affairs: Diverse Perspectives and Respectful Dialogue* (pp. 42–53). Sterling, VA: Stylus Publishing.

Bontrager, B. (2004). Enrollment management: An introduction to concepts and structures. *College & University, 79*(3), 11–16.

Bontrager, B. (2008). A definition and context for current SEM practice. In B. Bontrager (Ed.), *SEM and Institutional Success: Integrating Enrollment, Finance, and Student Access* (pp. 15–32). Washington, DC: American Association of Collegiate Registrars and Admissions Officers.

Bontrager, B., & Green, T. (2012). A structure for SEM planning. In B. Bontrager, D. Ingersoll, & R. Ingersoll (Eds.), *Strategic Enrollment Management: Transforming Higher Education* (pp. 271–284). Washington, DC: American Association of Collegiate Registrars and Admissions Officers.

Bourdieu, P., & Passeron, J. (1977). *Reproduction in Education, Society, and Culture*. London: Sage Publications.

Broido, E. M. (2011). Moving beyond dichotomies: Integrating theory, scholarship, experience, and practice. In P. M. Magolda & M. B. Baxter Magolda (Eds.), *Contested Issues in Student Affairs: Diverse Perspectives and Respectful Dialogue* (pp. 54–59). Sterling, VA: Stylus Publishing.

Braxton, J. M. (Ed.). (2000a). *Reworking the Student Departure Puzzle*. Nashville, TN: Vanderbilt University Press.

Braxton, J. M. (2000b). Conclusion: Reinvigorating theory and research on the departure puzzle. In J. M. Braxton (Ed.), *Reworking the Student Departure Puzzle* (pp. 257–274). Nashville, TN: Vanderbilt University Press.

Braxton, J. M. (2003). Student success. In S. R. Komives, D. B. Woodard, Jr., & Associates (Eds.), *Student Services: A Handbook for the Profession* (4th Edition), (pp. 317–335). San Francisco: Jossey-Bass.

Braxton, J. M., Doyle, W. R., Hartley, H. V., III, Hirschy, A. S., Jones, W. A., & McLendon, M. K. (2013). *Rethinking College Student Retention*. San Francisco: Jossey-Bass.

Braxton, J. M., & Hirschy, A. S. (2005). Theoretical developments in the study of college student departure. In A. Seidman (Ed.), *College Student Retention: Formula for Student Success* (pp. 61–87). Westport, CT: Praeger Publishers.

Braxton, J. M., Hirschy, A. S., & McClendon, S. A. (2004). Understanding and reducing college student departure. *ASHE-ERIC Higher Education Research Report Series*, *30*(3). San Francisco: Jossey-Bass.

Braxton, J. M., Sullivan, A. S., & Johnson, R. M., Jr. (1997). Appraising Tinto's theory of college student departure. In J. Smart (Ed.), *Higher Education: Handbook of Theory and Research*, Vol. 12 (pp. 107–164). New York: Agathon.

Cabrera, A. F., Nora, A., & Castañeda, M. B. (1992). The role of finances in the persistence process: A structural model. *Research in Higher Education*, *33*, 571–593.

Cabrera, A. F., Nora, A., & Castañeda, M. B. (1993). College persistence: Structural equations modeling test of an integrated model of student retention. *The Journal of Higher Education*, *64*, 123–139.

Comeaux, E., & Harrison, C. K. (2011). A conceptual model of academic success for student-athletes. *Educational Researcher*, *40*, 235–245.

Dalton, J. C. (2002). The art and practical wisdom of student affairs leadership. In J. C. Dalton & M. McClinton (Eds.), *The Art and Practical Wisdom of Student Affairs Leadership* (pp. 3–9). New Directions for Student Services, (98).

Davenport, Z., Martinez-Saenz, M., & Rhine, L. (2012). The student success conundrum. In B. Bontrager, D. Ingersoll, & R. Ingersoll (Eds.), *Strategic Enrollment Management: Transforming Higher Education* (pp. 25–50). Washington, DC: American Association of Collegiate Registrars and Admissions Officers.

Evans, N. J., Forney, D. S., Guido-DiBrito, F. M., Patton, L. D., & Renn, K. A. (2010). *Student Development in College: Theory, Research, and Practice.* San Francisco: Jossey-Bass.

Habley, W. R., Bloom, J. L., & Robbins, S. (2012). *Increasing Persistence: Research-Based Strategies for Student Success.* San Francisco: Jossey-Bass.

Hagedorn, L. S. (2005). How to define retention: A new look at an old problem. In A. Seidman, (Ed.), *College Student Retention: Formula for Student Success* (pp. 89–105). Westport, CT: Praeger Publishers.

Hirschy, A. S., Bremer, C. D., & Castellano, M. (2011). Career and technical education (CTE) student success in community colleges: A conceptual model. *Community College Review*, *39*(3), 296–318.

Hossler, D., & Bean, J. P. (1990). Principles and objectives. In D. Hossler, J. P. Bean, & Associates (Eds.), *The Strategic Management of College Enrollments* (pp. 3–20). San Francisco: Jossey-Bass.

Hossler, D., Braxton, J. M., & Coopersmith, G. (1989). Understanding student college choice. In J. C. Smart (Ed.), *Higher Education: Handbook of Theory and Research*, Vol. 5. New York: Agathon Press.

Hossler, D., & Gallagher, K. (1987). Studying student college choice: A three-phase model and the implications for policymakers. *College & University*, *2*(3), 207–221.

Jenicke, L. O., Holmes, M. C., & Pisani, M. C. (2013). Approaching the challenge of student retention through the lens of quality control: A conceptual model of university business student retention utilizing Six Sigma. *Journal of College Student Retention*, *15*, 193–214.

Julius, D. J., Baldridge, V. J., & Pfeffer, J. (2000). A memorandum from Machiavelli on the principled use of power in the academy. In A. M. Hoffman & R. W. Summers (Eds.), *Managing Colleges and Universities: Issues for Leadership* (pp. 23–62). Westport, CT: Bergin & Garvey.

Kezar, A. (2001). Understanding and facilitating organizational change in the 21st century: Recent research and conceptualizations. *ASHE Higher Education Report*, *28*(4). San Francisco: Jossey-Bass.

Kezar, A. (2006). To use or not to use theory: Is that the question? In J. C. Smart (Ed.), *Higher Education: Handbook of Theory and Research*, Vol. XXI (pp. 283–344). Dordrecht, The Netherlands: Springer.

Kezar, A. (2014). *How Colleges Change: Understanding, Leading, and Enacting Change.* New York: Routledge.

Knefelkamp, L. L. (1984). *A workbook for the practice to theory to practice model.* Unpublished manuscript, University of Maryland, College Park.

Kuh, G. D., Kinzie, J., Schuh, J. H., Whitt, E. J., & Associates. (2005). *Student Success in College: Creating Conditions That Matter.* San Francisco: Jossey-Bass.

Kuh, G. D., & Love, P. G. (2000). A cultural perspective on student departure. In J. M. Braxton (Ed.), *Reworking the Student Departure Puzzle* (pp. 196–212). Nashville, TN: Vanderbilt University Press.

Lindsay, E. E., & Holland, E. O. (1930). *College and University Administration.* New York: MacMillan.

Love, P. G. (2012). Informal theory: The ignored link in theory-to-practice. *Journal of College Student Development, 53,* 177–191.

McDonough, P. M. (1997). *Choosing Colleges: How Social Class and Schools Structure Opportunity.* Albany, NY: State University of New York Press.

McEwen, M. K. (2003). The nature and uses of theory. In S. R. Komives, D. B. Woodard, Jr., & Associates (Eds.), *Student Services: A Handbook for the Profession* (4th Edition), (pp. 153–178). San Francisco: Jossey-Bass.

Merton, R. K. (1968). *Social Theory and Social Structure.* New York: The Free Press.

Nidiffer, J. (2000). Higher education management in theory and practice. In A. M. Hoffman & R. W. Summers (Eds.), *Managing Colleges and Universities: Issues for Leadership* (pp. 63–73). Westport, CT: Bergin & Garvey.

Parker, C. A., Widick, C., & Knefelkamp, L. (1978) Why bother with theory? In L. Knefelkamp, C. Widick, C. A. Parker, & others, *Applying new developmental findings* (pp. vii–xvi). *New Directions for Student Services,* (4).

Perna, L. W. (2006). Studying college choice: A proposed conceptual model. In J. C. Smart (Ed.), *Higher Education: Handbook of Theory and Research,* Vol. XXI (pp. 99–157). Dordrecht, The Netherlands: Springer.

Perna, L. W., & Kurban, E. R. (2013). Improving college access and choice. In L. W. Perna and A. P. Jones (Eds.), *The State of College Access and Completion: Improving College Success for Students from Underrepresented Groups* (pp.10–33). New York: Routledge.

Perna, L. W., & Thomas, S. L. (2008). Theoretical perspectives on student success. *ASHE Higher Education Report, 34*(1). Hoboken, NJ: Wiley.

Reason, R. D. (2009). An examination of persistence research through the lens of a comprehensive conceptual framework. *Journal of College Student Development, 50,* 659–682.

St. John, E. P., Cabrera, A. F., Nora, A., & Asker, E. H. (2000). Economic influences on persistence reconsidered: How can finance research inform the reconceptualization of persistence models? In J. M. Braxton (Ed.), *Reworking the Student Departure Puzzle* (pp. 29–47). Nashville, TN: Vanderbilt University Press.

St. John, E. P., McKinney, J. S., & Tuttle, T. (2006). Using action inquiry to address critical challenges. In E. P. St. John & M. Wilkerson (Eds.), Reframing persistence research to improve academic success. *New Directions for Institutional Research*, 130, 63–76.

St. John, E. P., Paulsen, M. B., & Carter, D. F. (2005). Diversity, college costs, and postsecondary opportunity: An examination of the college choice-persistence nexus for African Americans and Whites. *The Journal of Higher Education, 76*(5), 545–69.

St. John, E. P., Paulson, M. B., & Starkey, J. B. (1996). The nexus between college choice and persistence. *Research in Higher Education, 37*, 175–220.

Strange, C. C., & Banning, J. H. (2001). *Educating by Design: Creating Campus Learning Environments That Work.* San Francisco: Jossey-Bass.

Tinto, V. (1975). Dropout from higher education: A theoretical synthesis of recent research. *Review of Educational Research, 45*(1), 89–125.

Tinto, V. (1987). *Leaving College: Rethinking the Causes and Cures of Student Attrition.* Chicago: University of Chicago Press.

Tinto, V. (1993). *Leaving College: Rethinking the Causes and Cures of Student Attrition.* (2nd Edition). Chicago: University of Chicago Press.

Tinto, V. (2012). *Completing College: Rethinking Institutional Action.* Chicago: University of Chicago Press.

Upcraft, M. L. (1994). The dilemmas of translating theory to practice. *Journal of College Student Development, 35*, 438–443.

U.S. Department of Education. (2013). *Integrated postsecondary education data system glossary.* Washington, DC: National Center for Education Statistics. Retrieved from http://nces.ed.gov/ipeds/glossary/?charindex = C.

Valentine, J. C., Hirschy, A. S., Bremer, C. D., Novillo, W., Castellano, M., & Banister, A. (2011). Keeping at-risk students in school: A systematic review of college retention programs. *Educational Evaluation and Policy Analysis, 33*, 214–234.

Wallace, W. (1971). *The Logic of Science in Sociology.* Chicago: Aldine-Atherton.

CHAPTER 15

Students at Risk in Residential and Commuter Colleges and Universities

John M. Braxton,
Harold V. Hartley III, and
Dawn Lyken-Segosebe

Success in college requires persistence to graduation. Progression from the first to the second year of college stands as an important milestone toward ensuring that students obtain a college degree. Yet, according to the College Board, as of 2010, first-year to second-year retention rates ranged from 59.9 percent of first-time, full-time, degree- or certificate-seeking students at public two-year colleges to 80 percent of first-time, full-time, degree-seeking students at private not-for-profit colleges and universities. Retention rates are even lower among part-time students (College Board, 2012). Unnecessary student departure thwarts the aspirations of students who seek to earn a college degree, it undermines national objectives to dramatically increase college degree attainment, and it is costly to colleges and universities. As such, early departure constitutes a concern of enrollment managers who are responsible for student retention and also a concern of faculty members and student affairs professionals who advise and support students in their academic progress. Because of their keen interest in college completion rates, policy makers are also concerned about student departure (Braxton et al., 2014; Goldrick-Rab & Roksa, 2008; Turner, 2004).

This chapter examines findings from recent research that is theoretically grounded in order to present recommendations for institutional action that have a likelihood of increasing college student persistence. Identifying students who are at risk of premature departure from college and developing strategies to promote their persistence to degree are essential institutional objectives and can ensure that the investments made to recruit and successfully enroll these students are not squandered. Building on the success of early warning systems, we put forth a more comprehensive continuous vigilance system for at-risk students enrolled in four-year commuter and residential colleges and universities.

Early warning systems constitute a common practice of colleges and universities seeking to increase their college student retention rates, especially those rates for first-year students. Wesley Habley, Mike Valiga, Randy McClanahan, and Kurt Burkum (2010) report that a substantial majority of institutions that responded to a survey administered by the American College Testing Program indicate that they have an early warning system. More specifically, 74 percent of four-year public institutions, 78 percent of four-year private institutions, and 68 percent of two-year institutions have such a system (Habley et al., 2010; Habley, Bloom, & Robbins, 2012). The early identification of students enables the institution to make use of various actions designed to reduce unnecessary student departure.

"Early warning," "early-alert," and "early intervention" are just some of the terminology used within the research literature to refer to systems that strive to identify students at risk for departure from the institution early in an academic term. Joe Cuseo (2011) defines an early-alert system as "a formal, proactive, feedback system though which students and student-support agents are alerted to early manifestations of poor academic performance (e.g., low in-progress grades) or academic disengagement (high rates of absenteeism)" (p. 1).

Early warning systems exist in two general forms. Colleges and universities may implement systems that predict students at the greatest risk of dropping out and/or systems that track student progress once they are already in college (Spradlin, Burroughs, Rutkowski, Lang, & Hardesty, 2010). The first set of systems is proactive in nature and relies on students' high school data, attitudes, and behaviors. Institutions may rely on predictors of persistence such as high school class rank and grades and ACT and SAT scores as well as noncognitive factors (Beck & Davidson, 2001). Colleges and universities use such predictors to identify students who are performing poorly academically early in a semester.

Alternatively or in conjunction with predictive systems, institutions may choose to rely on actual student behavior once the student is already in college rather than potential behavior inferred from demographic, pre-college, and self-reported data using assessment instruments (Cuseo, 2011). This second set of early warning systems is reactive in nature and utilizes midterm grades/alerts and pre-midterm alert systems to identify at-risk students and rely on reports from faculty members. Such forms of alerts fit within the notion of continuous vigilance.

Although early warning systems focused on the identification of students at risk for academic failure play a necessary part in increasing institutional rates of retention, such systems also fail to capture many students with high probabilities of departing. Vincent Tinto (1993) contends that less than 25 percent of students who depart do so because of academic difficulties. Thus, the vast majority of students depart voluntarily. Accordingly, early warning systems need to take into account factors other than poor academic performance.

Although we view the reduction of unnecessary student departure as a worthy institutional goal, we also readily acknowledge that in some cases a student's departure may serve the best interests of either the student or the institution (Tinto, 1982). With this proviso in place, we assert that more comprehensive systems to alert institutional leaders of students at risk of voluntary departure must rest on a foundation of findings from theoretically driven empirical studies. Theoretically driven studies model the complexity of the process of voluntary student departure. As a consequence, early warning systems must also account for the complexity of voluntary student departure. To convey such complexity fully, we describe profiles of students likely to depart that are grounded in theoretically driven empirical research. Profiles allow us to give a nuanced picture of such students. Moreover, some students at risk for departure defy early detection as the factors that lead to their departure emerge during the course of their first year of college rather than during the first few weeks of an academic term. Although some aspects of the profiles we offer in this chapter suggest the need for early warnings, our profiles also suggest the need for continuous vigilance during the course of an academic year. Hence, we prefer to call the alerts systems that these profiles serve a "continuous vigilance system for at-risk students."

We describe separate profiles of students at risk for first-year departure from four commuter colleges and universities and from four-year residential colleges and universities. We offer two distinct profiles of at-risk students because of the fundamental differences between these two types of collegiate institutions. These differences involve the role of the external environment and the characteristics of social communities. In contrast to residential institutions, commuter colleges and universities lack well-defined and structured social communities in which students may develop relationships with other students (Braxton, Hirschy, & McClendon, 2004). The external environment also plays an important part in the student experience in commuter colleges and universities. Commuter students typically experience conflicts among their obligations to family, work, and college (Tinto, 1993). Their work and family obligations greatly determine their daily activities (Webb, 1990).

Given all of the interest in college completion at community colleges, we note the importance of being able to extend research on at-risk students enrolled in two-year community colleges. Unfortunately, we are unable to extend our findings from the research undertaken for this chapter to community colleges, because the empirical basis for the development of this profile emerged from a test of the theory of student persistence in four-year commuter colleges and universities (Braxton, Hirschy, & McClendon, 2004; Braxton et al., 2014). Nevertheless there is a need for two-year institutions to develop empirically derived profiles for students who are at risk for departure as well as accompanying continuous vigilance systems. The construction of such a profile would require the testing of the theory of commuter college student persistence in community colleges. John Braxton, Amy Hirschy, and Shederick McClendon (2004) assert that this theory is suitable for testing in two-year colleges when using a sample of degree-seeking students.

In the following section, we offer a profile of students at risk for first-year departure from four-year commuter colleges and universities. We also delineate mechanisms for maintaining a continuous vigilance of the experiences of such students as well as some recommendations for institutional action to prevent their unnecessary departure.

PROFILE OF STUDENTS AT RISK FOR DEPARTURE FROM FOUR-YEAR COMMUTER COLLEGES AND UNIVERSITIES

As previously indicated, we use theoretically based research findings to construct the profile of students at risk for first-year departure from commuter colleges and universities that we offer in this section of the chapter. We obtained these findings from the book *Rethinking College Student Retention* by John Braxton, William Doyle, Harold Hartley, Amy Hirschy, Willis Jones, and Michael McLendon (2014), which reports the results of an empirical test of the theory of student persistence in commuter colleges and universities. The test of this theory used a longitudinal panel design of 714 students enrolled at five publicly supported commuter colleges and universities who have completed two or fewer semesters at their college or university and who live at home with their parents, with their spouse or partner, or by themselves. We refer readers interested in more details about this theory and the testing of it to *Rethinking College Student Retention*. We list findings that support the elements of the following profile of at-risk students along with the theoretical constructs on which the findings are based in Table 15.1.

Categories of At-Risk Students

We divide the elements of the profile of at-risk students in commuter colleges and universities into two categories. One category includes student entry characteristics as well as their enrollment status. The other category consists of elements that pertain to aspects of the student's experience while attending a commuter college or university.

Table 15.1: Research grounding for the profile of at-risk students for departure from commuter colleges and universities

Profile elements	Research grounding for profile elements
Entry characteristics	
Male students	Male students have lower levels of academic and intellectual development. Academic development positively influences subsequent institutional commitment, which in turn positively influences student persistence. Thus, male students are at risk for departure.
Students of color	Students of color have lower levels of subsequent institutional commitment. Subsequent institutional commitment positively influences student persistence. Thus, students of color are at risk for departure.
Higher educational level of parents	Students whose parents have higher levels of education have lower degrees of subsequent institutional commitment. Subsequent institutional commitment positively influences student persistence. Thus, students whose parents have higher levels of education are at risk for departure.
Higher levels of high school academic achievement	Students with higher levels of high school academic achievement have lower levels of subsequent institutional commitment. Subsequent institutional commitment positively influences student persistence. Thus, students with higher levels of high school academic achievement are at risk for departure.
Part-time attendance	Students attending part-time have lower levels of subsequent institutional commitment and are also less likely to persist. Thus, students attending part-time are at risk for departure.
Attendance unsupported by significant others	Students who feel less supported in their college attendance by significant others have lower levels of subsequent institutional commitment. Subsequent institutional commitment positively influences student persistence. Thus, students who feel unsupported in their college attendance by significant others are at risk for departure.

Profile elements	Research grounding for profile elements
Student's college experience	
Low levels of academic and intellectual development	Students with lower levels of academic and intellectual development have lower levels of subsequent institutional commitment which, in turn, positively influences student persistence. Thus, students with lower levels of academic and intellectual development are at risk for departure.
Institution perceived as uncommitted to the welfare of its students	Students who perceive that their institution is uncommitted to the welfare of its students have lower levels of academic and intellectual development. Academic development positively influences subsequent institutional commitment, which in turn positively influences student persistence. Thus, students who perceive that their institution is uncommitted to the welfare of its students are at risk for departure.
Decisions and actions of institution are believed to be incongruent with institution's goals and mission	Students who perceive that the decisions and actions of their institution are incongruent with the institution's goals and mission have lower levels of both academic and intellectual development and subsequent institutional commitment. Subsequent institutional commitment positively influences student persistence. Thus, students who perceive that the decisions and actions of their institution are incongruent with the institution's goals and mission are at risk for departure.

Source: Research findings derived from Chapter 9 and from Table C.5 in *Rethinking College Student Retention* (Braxton, Doyle, Hartley, Hirschy, Jones, & McLendon, 2004).

Student Entry Characteristics/Enrollment Status Following are the entry characteristics and enrollment status of students at commuter colleges and universities who are at risk of early departure as reported by Braxton et al. (2014):

- Male students
- Students of color
- Students whose parents have higher levels of education
- Students with higher levels of academic achievement in high school

- Students who attend college on a part-time basis
- Students who feel that their college attendance is unsupported by their spouse or life partner, family members, or close friends

Gender, race/ethnicity, high school academic records, and the educational level of parents represent types of information typically available at the time of enrollment. As such, these elements lend themselves for use in an early warning part of a continuous vigilance system. Use of proactive warning systems ensures timely attention to at-risk students. Student perceptions of the support for their college attendance by spouses or life partners, family members, and close friends should be an item added to forms completed by students at entrance. Hall Beck and William Davidson (2001) suggest that an early warning system would enable counselors, faculty, and student personnel specialists to be aware of students with serious problems before these problems jeopardized their college careers.

Using such information available at entrance, professional advisors, faculty advisors, and student affairs professionals can recommend, for example, that male students and students attending part-time should enroll in a learning community. Learning communities are block-scheduled courses organized around a particular theme (Braxton et al., 2014; Tinto, 2000). Another strategy is to encourage at-risk students to enroll in courses taught by faculty members who are known to exhibit effective teaching practices, such as displaying a genuine interest in students, being well organized and prepared for class, and explaining course material clearly. Because at-risk students tend to report lower levels of academic and intellectual development, encouraging them to enroll in learning communities and courses taught by faculty members who exhibit effective teaching practices will likely yield academic success (Braxton et al., 2014).

Moreover, students of color, students whose parents have higher levels of education, students with higher levels of high school academic achievement, and students who feel unsupported in their college attendance by their spouse/life partner, family members, or close friends tend to experience less commitment to their college or university after matriculation (Braxton et al., 2014). Academic advisors should also encourage students with these at-risk characteristics to enroll in learning communities and courses taught by faculty members who exhibit effective teaching practices, because students who take such courses tend to experience greater degrees of academic and intellectual development that, in turn, positively influences their level of subsequent institutional commitment (Braxton et al., 2014). Both academic and intellectual development and subsequent institutional commitment play important roles in the departure of students from commuter colleges and universities (Braxton et al., 2014).

Tinto (1993) suggests that early intervention should happen within the first six weeks of the student entering college. However, we urge that such intervention take place even earlier, during first-year student orientation. First-year orientation provides an optimum opportunity for advisors to make such recommendations to those students determined to beat risk for departure because of their entry characteristics or enrollment status. Such orientation programs should occur before the start of classes for the focal academic term. The schedule for the first-year orientation program should include time for students to meet with their academic advisors. Attendance at a first-year orientation program in general and at the scheduled meeting with the student's advisor should be mandatory for all full- and part-time, first-year students. Academic advising that equips students for academic success has been found to play a positive role in the persistence of students in commuter colleges or universities (Braxton et al., 2014). In addition, the orientation program material should encourage the attendance and participation of spouses or life partners and parents, as such encouragement tends to increase the support for college attendance by significant others, and thus provides a positive effect on persistence (Braxton et al., 2014).

The Student's College Experience Following are the college experiences of students at commuter colleges and universities who are at risk of early departure as found by Braxton et al. (2014):

- Students who perceive that they are not developing academically and intellectually because of their college attendance
- Students who perceive that their college or university is uncommitted to the growth and development of its students, to placing a high value on students, and to treating students equitably and with respect as individuals
- Students who perceive that decisions and actions of the administration, faculty, and staff of their college are incongruent with the institution's goals and mission
- Students who feel that their college attendance is unsupported by their spouse or life partner, family members, or close friends

These profile elements pose challenges to the identification of students possessing one or more of them because of their perceptual nature. However, advising affords a mechanism of vigilance. Although advisors should schedule a meeting with their advisees prior to midterm grade reporting, the reporting of midterm grades can prompt at-risk students to seek advice from their academic advisor at a critical period in the semester.

Beyond advising sessions prompted by midterm grade reports, professional advisors, faculty advisors, peer advisors, and student affairs professionals can all play a part in the identification of students at risk because of their collegiate experiences. In their interactions with first-year students over the course of the academic year, such advisors should ask students about their perceptions of their own academic and intellectual development, how committed they perceive the college or university to be to their welfare as a student, and how congruent they perceive the decisions and actions of the administration, faculty, and staff of their college to be with their college or university's goals and mission. Support from family, friends, and partners is an important aspect of an early warning system, and advisors to all first-year students should remain vigilant about ensuring that students have support and should schedule frequent face-to-face meetings with the student during the course of the academic year. Part-time students require particular attention. For example, Braxton et al. (2014) recommend that at matriculation to the institution, all part-time students should be assigned an advisor. They also stress that all part-time students should meet periodically with their assigned advisor, at times convenient for the student, during the course of an academic year (Braxton et al., 2014). Such periodic advisory sessions are an important mechanism of a system of continuous vigilance.

For those students identified as at risk through such advising interactions, advisors can take a range of actions. Although we present these actions for at-risk students, all students would benefit from these actions. One set of actions involves providing information about institutional practices that affect commuter students. For example, advisors should tell students about the availability of on-campus parking for commuting students; about the convenient times such university offices as financial aid, counseling, and the registrar are open to serve students who work while attending school; and about the availability of general use computers with Internet access throughout the campus. The more students perceive that such practices exist, the more favorable they perceive their institution's integrity as well as the level of commitment of their college or university to the welfare of its students (Braxton et al., 2014).

Other actions that advisors can take to assist at-risk students involve recommendations for course selection. Unfortunately, these recommendations involve course selections for subsequent, but not the current, terms of enrollment. These recommendations for course selection include enrolling the student in a learning community, and enrolling the student in a course or courses from faculty members who exhibit the following types of effective teaching practices: expressing a genuine interest in students, being well-prepared and organized in their teaching, being clear in their instruction, and making use of active learning practices in their courses. Research has found that students who take such courses tend to experience greater degrees of academic and intellectual development (Braxton et al., 2014). Moreover, students who take courses from faculty known as genuinely interested in students, faculty who students perceive as well-prepared and organized in their teaching, and faculty who students perceive as being clear in their instruction tend to view their institution's commitment to the welfare of its students as well as its level of institutional integrity in a more positive light (Braxton et al., 2014).

ASSUMPTIONS AND RECOMMENDATIONS FOR THE CONTINUOUS VIGILANCE OF AT-RISK STUDENTS IN FOUR-YEAR COMMUTER COLLEGES AND UNIVERSITIES

The actions outlined in the last section of this chapter make the following key assumptions about the existence of supporting institutional arrangements:

1. The institution makes available information about students for use by advisors. Such information should be available during first-year orientation for advising purposes. Advisors must maintain strict confidentiality about the particulars of such information in general and in particular for students designated as at risk for voluntary departure because they match one or more of the elements of the at-risk profile for students in commuter colleges and universities.

2. All full- and part-time students are assigned an academic advisor. Braxton et al. (2014) recommends that at matriculation to a commuter college or university, all students be assigned an advisor. Students should enter the institution knowing the name and contact information of their academic advisor.

3. All full- and part-time first-year students are required to participate in orientation programs for first-year students at the start of each academic term. Such orientation programs inform students of administrative and academic regulations, various available student organizations and activities, the availability of various student services, degree requirements, and opportunities for selecting courses for their first semester (Pascarella, Terenzini, & Wolfe, 1986). Ernest Pascarella, Patrick Terenzini, and Lee Wolfe (1986) contend that orientation functions as a mechanism of anticipatory socialization. Anticipatory socialization pertains to the process through which individuals seeking membership in an organization take on the attitudes, values, and behaviors of that organization or group (Merton, 1957). For individuals who successfully anticipate these attitudes, values, and behaviors, their adjustment to the organization or group is facilitated. Thus, the various activities of orientation help first-year students learn the attitudes, values, and behaviors needed for success in their college or university of enrollment.

4. Students and their advisors meet during the orientation program prior to the start of the academic year and at regular intervals during the academic year.

5. Information about faculty and the courses they teach is readily available to advisors. Such information includes the level of interest each faculty member shows in students, the frequency of their use of active learning practices in their courses, and their student course ratings of their instructional clarity and their degree of organization and preparation. Institutions can meet this particular assumption by collecting such information on individual faculty members and making it readily available to academic advisors. Items could be included on student course rating instruments to gather such information.

6. The institution offers an array of credit-bearing learning communities for first-year students.

7. The institution has the following commuter-student–centered services: ample parking, office hours convenient for working students, and available general-use computers with Internet access throughout the campus.

PROFILE OF STUDENTS AT RISK FOR DEPARTURE FROM FOUR-YEAR RESIDENTIAL COLLEGES AND UNIVERSITIES

In this section, we construct a profile of students at risk for first-year departure from residential colleges and universities. Like our profile for students at risk of departure from commuter colleges and universities, we use theoretically based research findings to build the profile of students at risk for first-year departure from residential colleges and universities. We obtained these findings from an empirical test of the revised theory of student persistence in residential colleges and universities (Braxton, Hirschy, & McClendon, 2004) using a longitudinal panel design of 408 first-time, full-time, first-year students in eight residential and religiously affiliated colleges and universities (Braxton et al., 2014). We exhibit the findings that support the elements of the following profile of at-risk students, along with the theoretical constructs upon which the findings are based, in Table 15.2.

Categories of At-Risk Students

The profile of at-risk students in residential colleges and universities includes two categories. One category consists of student entry characteristics or enrollment status, whereas the other category includes those elements that

Table 15.2: Research grounding for the profile of at-risk students for departure from residential colleges and universities

Profile elements	Research grounding for profile elements
Entry characteristics	
Students of color	Students of color have lower levels of social integration. Social integration positively influences subsequent institutional commitment, which in turn positively influences student persistence. Thus, students of color are at risk for departure.
Parents with lower incomes	Students with parents having lower levels of income have lower levels of psychosocial engagement. Psychosocial engagement positively influences social integration. Social integration positively influences subsequent institutional commitment, which in turn positively influences student persistence. Thus, student with parents with lower income levels are at risk for departure.
Lower levels of cultural capital	Students with lower levels of cultural capital have lower levels of psychosocial engagement. Psychosocial engagement positively influences social integration. Social integration positively influences subsequent institutional commitment, which in turn positively influences student persistence. Thus, students with lower levels of cultural capital are at risk for departure.
Live off campus	Students who live off campus during their first year have lower degrees of social integration. Social integration positively influences subsequent institutional commitment, which in turn positively influences student persistence. Thus, students who live off campus during their first year are at risk for departure.
Not attending first-choice college	Students who are not attending their first-choice college have lower degrees of subsequent institutional commitment and are more likely to depart. Thus, students who are not attending their first-choice college are at risk for departure.

Profile elements	Research grounding for profile elements

Student's college experience

Unable to find subgroup of students with similar values, beliefs, & goals	Students who perceive that they are unable to find a subgroup of students with similar values, beliefs, and goals have lower levels of psychosocial engagement. Psychosocial engagement positively influences social integration. Social integration positively influences subsequent institutional commitment, which in turn positively influences student persistence. Thus, students who perceive that they are unable to find a subgroup of students with similar values, beliefs, and goals are at risk for departure.
Have not made any close friends at college	Students who have not made any close friends at college have lower levels of social integration. Social integration positively influences subsequent institutional commitment, which in turn positively influences student persistence. Thus, students who have not made close friends at college are at risk for departure.
Do not perceive themselves as members of their residence hall floor community	Students who do not perceive themselves as members of the community of their residence hall floor have lower levels of psychosocial engagement. Psychosocial engagement positively influences social integration. Social integration positively influences subsequent institutional commitment, which in turn positively influences student persistence. Thus, students who do not perceive themselves as members of the community of their residence hall floor are at risk for departure.
Do not frequently interact face-to-face with students on their residence hall floor	Students who do not frequently interact face-to-face with students on their residence hall floor have lower levels of psychosocial engagement. Psychosocial engagement positively influences social integration. Social integration positively influences subsequent institutional commitment, which in turn positively influences student persistence. Thus, students who do not frequently interact face-to-face with students on their residence hall floor are at risk for departure.

(continued)

Table 15.2: *(Continued)*

Profile elements	Research grounding for profile elements
Institution perceived as uncommitted to the welfare of its students	Students who perceive that their institution is uncommitted to the welfare of its students have lower levels of both social integration and subsequent institutional commitment. Subsequent institutional commitment positively influences student persistence. Thus, students who perceive that their institution is uncommitted to the welfare of its students are at risk for departure.
Decisions and actions of the institution are perceived as incongruent with the institution's goals and mission	Students who perceive that decisions and actions of the institution are incongruent with the institution's goals and mission have lower degrees of social integration. Social integration positively influences subsequent institutional commitment, which in turn positively influences student persistence. Thus, students who perceive that decisions and actions of the institution are incongruent with the institution's goals and missions are at risk for departure.

relate to aspects of the student's experience with attending a residential college or university.

Student Entry Characteristics/Enrollment Status Following are the entry characteristics and enrollment status of students at residential colleges and universities who are at risk of early departure as found by Braxton et al. (2014):

- Students of color
- Students from lower income homes
- Students with lower levels of involvement during their last year in high school in various cultural activities that require cultural knowledge, such as visiting an art museum, attending a symphony concert, or traveling abroad (that is, cultural capital)
- Students who do not live on campus
- Students who indicate that the college was not their first choice of attendance (that is, not their initial institutional commitment)

Residential colleges and universities should have information on students with one or more of these profile elements readily available for use in an early warning part of a continuous vigilance system. Information forms for students to complete upon their matriculation should contain items that tap the student's level of cultural capital and their level of initial institutional commitment. To assess the level of cultural capital, such forms should include items that ask students to indicate their levels of involvement during their last year in high school in various cultural activities, such as visiting an art museum, attending a symphony concert, or traveling abroad. To assess their level of initial institutional commitment, such forms should also ask students if the college of enrollment was their first, second, third, or fourth choice of a college or university to attend.

Residential colleges and universities using early warning systems should develop profiles of all entering first-year students using the at-risk elements specified previously. Faculty advisors and professional advisors who advise first-year students should receive such profiles for each of the first-year students that they advise and should have the profiles available for use during the orientation period for new first-year students. As previously indicated, orientation programs function as mechanisms of anticipatory socialization, a process important to students acquiring the norms, attitudes, values, and behaviors needed for success in their chosen college or university.

First-year orientation programs should include time periods allotted for advisors to meet individually with their advisees. Although advisors should meet with all first-year students during such time periods during the first-year orientation program, advisors should give special attention to their advisees who match one or more of the elements of the at-risk profile during this period.

The findings shown in Table 15.2 indicate that students of color, students who are not attending their first-choice college, and students living off campus have difficulties achieving social integration. Social integration refers to the student's perception of their degree of social affiliation with others and their degree of congruency with the attitudes, beliefs, norms, and values of the social communities of a college or university (Braxton, Hirschy, & McClendon, 2004; Tinto, 1975). Advisors should recommend that at-risk students join various clubs and organizations in order to meet other students with similar interests and values. Advisors might also suggest that at-risk students strive to talk with or discuss course content with other students outside of class, make an effort to study or socialize with other students, and attend campus movies, plays, concerts, or recitals. Through these forms of psychosocial engagement, greater degrees of social integration for such students become more likely. Additionally, advisors should make similar recommendations to low-income students and students who enter with lower levels of cultural capital, because their degree of social integration depends to some extent on their level of psychosocial engagement (Braxton et al., 2014).

In addition to these recommendations, course selections also provide opportunities for at-risk students to meet other students with similar attitudes and values. Advising sessions during first-year student orientation typically involve the selection of courses for the fall semester. Learning community courses and courses that emphasize active learning foster the development of small social communities within the classroom (Braxton, Hirschy, & McClendon, 2004; Tinto, 2000). Active learning prompts student thinking about course content (Bonwell & Eison, 1991) through the use of such activities as debates, role-playing, discussion, and group and pair work. Opportunities for social interaction among class members occur because of these active learning activities (Braxton, Hirschy, & McClendon, 2004). Likewise, participation in a learning community creates opportunities for social interaction among class members. As previously stated, learning communities involve the block scheduling of courses, so that the same group of students takes a set of courses together (Tinto, 2000). Because the same group of students takes a set of courses together, there are greater opportunities for social interaction among members of these courses. The opportunities for social interaction created by active learning and learning communities may result in student friendships which, in turn, lead to psychosocial engagement and social integration for those students identified as at risk for early departure.

Advisors should make the recommendations we outlined previously at their meeting with at-risk students during the first-year orientation program. In making such recommendations, advisors should be careful to point out that taking these actions will enable at-risk students to benefit more fully from their collegiate experience given our proviso at the beginning of this chapter.

The Student's College Experience Following are the college experiences of students at residential colleges and universities who are at risk of early departure as found by Braxton et al. (2014):

- Students who feel that they are unable to find a subgroup of students within the various communities of their college or university that hold values, beliefs, and goals similar to their own (that is, communal potential)

- Students who feel that they have not made any close friends at the college (that is, social integration)

- Students who do not perceive themselves as members of the community in their residence hall

- Students who do not frequently interact face-to-face with students on their residence hall floor

- Students who perceive that their college or university is uncommitted to the growth and development of its students, to placing a high value on students, and to treating students equitably and with respect as individuals (that is, institutional commitment to student welfare)

- Students who perceive that decisions and actions of the administration, faculty, and staff of their college are incongruent with the institution's goals and mission (that is, institutional integrity)

Because these profile elements reflect the perceptions of students, they require continuous vigilance. Some of these at-risk elements may not manifest themselves until late in the first semester or during the second semester of the student's first year of attendance. Advisors may learn of such student perceptions during advising sessions scheduled throughout the academic year. Consequently, advisors should ask their advisees if they have been able to find a subgroup of students that holds values, beliefs, and goals similar to their own; if they have made any close friends at college; if they feel that the institution demonstrates a commitment to the welfare of its students; and how congruent they perceive the decisions and actions of the administration, faculty, and staff of their college to be with their college or university's goals and mission.

For students who indicate that they have not been able to find a subgroup of students similar to themselves or who have been unable to make friends, advisors should recommend that they join clubs and organizations to meet other students with similar interests and values. Advisors might also suggest that such at-risk students discuss course content with other students outside of class, make an effort to study or socialize with other students, and attend campus movies, plays, concerts, or recitals. Through such forms of psychosocial engagement, a greater degree of social integration becomes more likely for students at risk, which in turn yields a greater likelihood of persistence.

Advising sessions focused on course selection for subsequent academic terms also present opportunities for advisors to make recommendations for students at risk of early departure. Advisors should recommend enrollment in learning community courses or in courses in which faculty make use of active learning practices. As outlined earlier, such courses provide opportunities for greater social interaction among class members. From such social interactions, friendships with students with similar attitudes and values may develop, resulting in a greater sense of communal potential and greater degree of social integration for the at-risk student.

Advisors who learn that some of their advisees are at risk because they perceive that the institution does not demonstrate a commitment to the welfare of its students, and who feel that the decisions and actions of the administration, faculty, and staff of their college are incongruent with its goals and mission, should also make recommendations regarding the selection of courses in subsequent academic terms. For example, such students should be advised to take courses offered by faculty known for their genuine interest in students. By taking courses from such faculty, at-risk students may come to view the institution as both concerned about the welfare of its students and as having institutional integrity (Braxton et al., 2014).

In addition to professional advisors and faculty advisors, residence hall staff members also play an important part in attending to the needs of students at risk for voluntary departure from residential colleges and universities. Residence hall staff members include student affairs professionals (residence hall professionals) and student resident advisors (RAs). Unlike academic advisors, residence hall professionals and student resident advisors interact with students in their residence halls on a frequent basis. Because of their frequent contact with students in general and with at-risk students in particular, such individuals occupy an important place in the front lines of a continuous vigilance system for at-risk students. In particular, student resident advisors assigned to a floor of a residence hall hold a prominent place given the likelihood of their near daily face-to-face interactions with students on their residence hall floor. Such frequent day-to-day interactions enable RAs to identify students on their floor who appear not to have made any friends, who seldom or never interact face-to-face with other students on the floor, and who do not participate in floor activities. RAs should meet individually with at-risk students to learn of their interests, attitudes, and values as well as problems they may be having with their adjustment to college.

The actions of RAs who identify such at-risk students include suggesting clubs and organizations that might interest the students and enabling them to meet other students with similar interests, attitudes, and values. RAs might also suggest the names of other students on the floor who share similar interests. In addition, RAs might personally invite at-risk students to participate in activities of the floor or ask them to join a planning committee for floor activities for the semester or academic year.

ASSUMPTIONS AND RECOMMENDATIONS FOR THE CONTINUOUS VIGILANCE OF AT-RISK STUDENTS IN RESIDENTIAL COLLEGES AND UNIVERSITIES

The actions we have described in this chapter make crucial assumptions about the presence of supporting institutional arrangements. We have advanced many of these assumptions regarding institutional arrangements in commuter colleges and universities. However, we repeat them here to stress their importance and relevance to residential colleges and universities. These assumptions include the following:

1. The institution makes available information about students for use by advisors. Such information should be available during first-year

orientation for advising purposes. Advisors must maintain strict confidentiality about the particulars of such information in general and in particular for students designated as at risk for voluntary departure because they match one or more of the elements of the at-risk profile for students in residential colleges and universities. Student resident advisors, in particular, must pledge the maintenance of strict confidentiality given their student-peer relationships with at-risk students.

2. All full- and part-time students are assigned an academic advisor. Students enter the institution knowing the name and contact information for their academic advisor.

3. All full- and part-time first-year students are required to participate in orientation programs for first-year students at the start of the fall academic term. For first-year students attending a residential college or university who live off campus, their participation in the orientation program looms particularly important.

4. Students and their advisors meet at a designated time during the orientation program and at regular intervals during the academic year.

5. Information about faculty and the courses they teach is readily available to advisors. Such information includes the level of interest each faculty member shows in students and the frequency of their use of active learning practices in their courses. Institutions meet this particular assumption by collecting such information on individual faculty members and making it readily available to academic advisors. Items included on student course rating instruments are used to gather such information.

6. The institution offers an array of credit-bearing learning communities for first-year students.

7. Student Resident Advisors are provided with training to orient them to the needs of at-risk students related to residence hall living. Such training concentrates on approaches to identifying students who match one or more of the at-risk profile elements pertaining to the student's college experience. This training also focuses on the actions RAs can take regarding students they identify as at risk for voluntary departure.

8. Residence hall staff members develop programs for each floor or living unit that foster a sense of community among students through frequent face-to-face interactions among residents of the floor and through such weekly social activities as pizza night or game night. Residence hall staff members also present opportunities for students to work together

to solve problems of the residence hall floor such as establishing and maintaining quiet hours for studying (Braxton et al., 2014).

CONCLUSION

In this chapter, we presented an array of recommendations that professional and faculty advisors might offer to students who are at risk for voluntary departure from both commuter and residential colleges and universities. We also presented recommendations and actions that student residence hall advisors might make regarding residence hall students who they identify as being at risk for voluntary departure.

In proposing these recommendations and actions, we embrace the important underlying assumption that such recommendations and actions will improve the college experience of at-risk students if the student follows the advice given. By improving their college experience, at-risk students will persist in their enrollment at the focal college or university. The tenability of this important assumption depends to some degree on adherence to three indispensable conditions of institutions that seek to improve their institutional retention rates. First, such colleges and universities should employ each supporting institutional arrangement as we described. Second, professional advisors, academic advisors, and other designated individuals should shoulder responsibility for improving the college experience of at-risk students by taking the actions and making the recommendations that we put forth in this chapter. Third, the institution supports the first two conditions by enacting various institutional policies and practices recommended by such scholars as Tinto (2012), Habley et al. (2010), and Braxton et al. (2014). Enrollment managers in colleges and universities charged with the task of developing policies and programs designed to increase their institution's student retention rate should review the extensive recommendations made by these scholars to identify recommendations for enactment by their institution.

Consistent with our emphases in this chapter, in the last chapter in Part IV Ziskin, Lucido, Gross, Hossler, Chung, and Torres suggest a fourth indispensable condition as they assert that institutional policies and practice require focus and intensity in their implementation. To ensure the focus and intensity that we emphasize in this chapter, Ziskin et al. emphasize the importance of organizational structures that demonstrate commitment, including retention coordinators and visible camps committees that should have budgetary authority to initiate retention-oriented programs and to enact campus policies and practices to enhance student persistence.

In closing, we reiterate our perspective that the reduction of unnecessary student departure constitutes a worthy institutional goal. However, it is not an end in itself. Its value stems from the importance of student retention to the attainment of other markers of student success, such as student course learning, acquisition of general education, development of academic competence (such as writing and speaking in a clear manner), development of cognitive skills and intellectual dispositions, occupational attainment, preparation for adulthood and citizenship, personal accomplishments (such as work on the college newspaper, election to student office), and personal development (Braxton, 2008). The achievement of such markers of student success resonates more fully with the value preferences of professional advisors, faculty advisors, and student affairs professionals who advise at-risk students than merely the reduction of unnecessary student departure.

References

Beck, H. P., & Davidson, W. D. (2001). Establishing an early warning system: Predicting low grades in college students from survey of academic orientations scores. *Research in Higher Education, 42*(6), 709–723.

Bonwell, C., & Eison, J. (1991). Active Learning: Creating Excitement in the Classroom. *AAHE-ERIC Higher Education Report, 1.* Washington, DC: The George Washington University, School of Education and Human Development.

Braxton, J. M. (2008). Toward a theory of faculty professional choice in teaching that fosters college student success. In J. C. Smart (Ed), *Higher Education: Handbook of Theory and Research,* Vol. XXIII (pp.181–207). Dordrecht, The Netherlands: Springer.

Braxton J., Doyle, W., Hartley, H., Hirschy, A., Jones, W., & McLendon, M. (2014). *Rethinking College Student Retention.* San Francisco: Jossey-Bass.

Braxton, J. M., Hirschy, A. S., & McClendon, S. A. (2004). Understanding and reducing college student departure. *ASHE-ERIC Higher Education Report, 30*(3).

College Board. (2012). Recommendation nine: Dramatically increase college completion rates. In *The College Completion Agenda.* Retrieved November 10, 2013, from http://completionagenda.collegeboard.org/recommendations/nine?qt-recomm endation = 1&indicator = 37.

Cuseo, J. (2011). *Early Alert: Developing a Program that Maximizes Student Engagement and Success.* Webinar sponsored by Innovative Educators, Boulder, CO.

Goldrick-Rab, S., & Roksa, J. (2008). *A Federal Agenda for Promoting Student Success and Degree Completion.* Washington, DC: Center of American Progress. Retrieved from http://www.americanprogress.org/issues/labor/report/2008/08/12/4810/a-federal-agenda-for-promoting-student-success-and-degree-completion/.

Habley, W. R., Bloom, J. L., & Robbins, S. (2012). *Increasing Persistence: Research-Based Strategies for College Student Success.* San Francisco: Jossey-Bass.

Habley, W., Valiga, M., McClanahan, R., & Burkum, K. (2010). *What Works in Student Retention? Report for All Colleges and Universities.* Iowa City, IA: ACT, Inc.

Merton, R. K. (1957). *Social Theory and Social Structure.* New York: The Free Press.

Pascarella, E. T., Terenzini, P. T., & Wolfe, L. (1986). Orientation to college and anticipatory socialization: Indirect effects on freshman year persistence. *The Journal of Higher Education, 57,* 155–175.

Spradlin, T. E., Burroughs, N. A., Rutkowski, D. J., Lang, J. R., & Hardesty. J. W. (2010). College persistence and completion strategies: Opportunities for scaling up. *Education Policy Brief, 8*(4), 1–16. Bloomington, IN: Center for Evaluation & Education Policy.

Turner, J. (2004). Language as academic purpose. *Journal of English for Academic Purposes,* 3(2), 95–109.

Tinto, V. (1975). Dropout from higher education: A theoretical synthesis of recent research. *Review of Educational Research, 45*(1), 89–125.

Tinto, V. (1982). Limits of theory and practice in student attrition. *The Journal of Higher Education, 5*(6), 687–700.

Tinto, V. (1993). *Leaving College: Rethinking the Causes of Student Attrition* (2nd Edition). Chicago: University of Chicago Press.

Tinto, V. (1997). Classrooms as communities: Exploring the educational character of student persistence. *The Journal of Higher Education, 68,* 599–623.

Tinto, V. (1998). Colleges as communities: Taking research on student persistence seriously. *The Review of Higher Education, 21,* 167–177.

Tinto, V. (2000). Linking learning and leaving: Exploring the role of the college classroom in student departure. In J. M. Braxton (Ed.), *Reworking the Student Departure Puzzle.* Nashville, TN: Vanderbilt University Press.

Tinto, V. (2012). *Completing College: Rethinking Institutional Action.* Chicago: University of Chicago Press.

Webb, M. W., II. (1990). *Development and testing of a theoretical model for predicting student degree persistence at four-year commuter colleges.* Paper presented at a meeting of the American Educational Research Association, April 1990, Boston.

Ziskin, M., Lucido, J., Gross, J., Hossler, D., Chung, E., & Torres, V. (in press). The Institutional role in student retention: Extending the discussion beyond student characteristics. In D. Hossler & R. Bontrager (Eds.), *Handbook of Strategic Enrollment Management.* San Francisco: Jossey-Bass.

CHAPTER 16

The Persistence of Students of Color

Willis A. Jones

O ver the past twenty years, federal, state, and institutional policies designed
to increase the college enrollment of students of color have been fairly
successful. By nearly any metric, today's college campuses are more diverse
than ever before. In absolute terms, students of color (defined as individuals
identifying as African American, Hispanic/Latino, Asian/Pacific Islander, or
American Indian/Alaska native) undergraduate enrollment in degree-granting
colleges and universities increased from 2.5 million in 1990 to 3.9 million in
2000. By 2010, 6.4 million students of color were enrolled in degree-granting
colleges and universities. In terms of percentage distribution, in 1990 just
20.6 percent of undergraduates were students of color. In 2000, that number had
increased to 29.5 percent. In 2010, 37.5 percent of undergraduate students were
students of color. The percentage of 18- to 24-year-old individuals of color in
college has also increased. In 1990, 25.4 percent of African Americans between
the ages of 18 and 24 were enrolled in degree-granting institutions of higher
education. That number increased to 30.5 percent in 2000 and 38.4 percent
in 2010. Hispanic enrollment as a percentage of all 18- to 24-year-olds also
increased from 15.8 percent to 21.7 percent and 31.9 percent in 1990, 2000, and
2010, respectively (National Center for Education Statistics, 2012).

Although enrollment numbers have increased, the persistence rates of students of color continue to be a concern for enrollment managers. Students of
color (especially African American, Hispanic, and American Indian students)
graduate at a significantly lower rate than white students (Roach, 2013). As

institutions work to reduce this persistence gap, it is important that administrators and practitioners have an understanding of the factors associated with the departure of students of color and what they can do to improve their retention and graduation rates. This chapter reviews theory and research related to the persistence of students of color in higher education. It begins with a statistical summary of institutional retention and graduation rates disaggregated by race/ethnicity. This is followed by a description of theoretical frameworks that have been forwarded to help explain the persistence decisions of students of color. Research addressing the various factors influential in the persistence decisions of students of color is then summarized. The chapter concludes with recommendations of institutional practices and policies that can help institutions increase the retention and graduation rates of students of color.

STATISTICS ON THE GRADUATION RATES OF STUDENTS OF COLOR

Although student retention has become a major topic of discussion within higher education, only a few sources are available for calculating graduation rates at a national level (Cook & Pullaro, 2010). Each has its advantages and disadvantages. For purposes of this chapter, data were collected from the Integrated Postsecondary Education Data System (IPEDS), which is housed by the U.S. Department of Education's National Center for Educational Statistics. IPEDS is the only survey of graduation rates that mandates participation by all institutions receiving Title IV funds. This ensures broad representation of institutions from a variety of sectors. IPEDS also allows for the disaggregation of graduation rates by race/ethnicity and gender. The first cohort in which student graduation rate data were collected from IPEDS was 1996 (Cook & Pullaro, 2010). At the time this chapter was written, data from the 2004 cohort were the most recent available.

Figure 16.1 displays the percentage of first-time, full-time degree-seeking students who graduated within six years of entering higher education by race/ethnicity. This chart highlights several often discussed concerns related to the persistence of students of color. Numerous reports and scholarly papers have been written about the graduation gap between students of color and white students. Figure 16.1 shows that indeed white students graduate at a higher rate than most subpopulations of students of color. Data from the 2004 cohort shows that the graduation rate of white students was 61.5 percent. For African American students, the graduation rate was 39.5 percent. Hispanic students, with a graduation rate of 50.1 percent and American Indian/Pacific Islander students, with a graduation rate of 39.4 percent also persisted at a

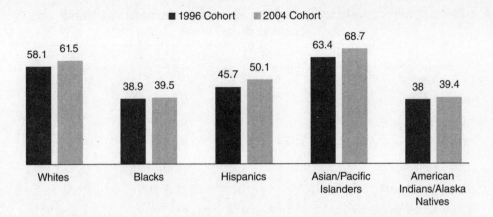

Figure 16.1 Six-year graduation rates of first-time, full-time degree seeking undergraduates by race/ethnicity and cohort

lower rate than white students. Asian students, however, had a graduation rate (68.7 percent) that is higher than that of white students. When members of the higher education community discuss the graduation gap between white students and students of color, it is important to highlight the variations within the subpopulations of students of color.

Figure 16.1 also highlights the slow rate at which graduate rates of students of color have increased over the past several years. This is especially true among African American students and American Indian/Alaska native students. The graduation rate of African American students in the 2004 cohort was only 0.06 percent higher than the graduation rates of African American students in the 1996 cohort. For American Indian/Alaska native students, the graduation rate of the 2004 cohort was just 1.4 percent higher in comparison to the 1996 cohort. Other students of color have seen steeper increases in their graduation rates. Asian student graduation rates increased 5.5 percent from the 1996 cohort to the 2004 cohort. Hispanic student graduation rates increased 4.4 percent from the 1996 cohort to the 2004 cohort.

The gender gap with regard to student graduation rates also has been the subject of much discussion in the higher education community (DiPrete & Buchmann, 2013; Strauss, 2010). Table 16.1 displays the percentage of first-time, full-time degree-seeking students who graduated within six years of entering higher education by race/ethnicity and gender. Among every racial/ethnic group, graduation rates among men were lower than graduation rates among women. This gap was especially pronounced among African American and Hispanic students. The African American male graduation rate in the 1996 cohort was 32.8 percent. The African American female graduation rate

Table 16.1: Six-year graduation rates of first-time, full-time degree-seeking undergraduates by race/ethnicity, gender, and cohort

	1996 cohort	2004 cohort
White men	54.8	58.8
White women	60.9	63.8
African American men	32.8	34.2
African American women	43	43.1
Hispanic men	41.3	45.6
Hispanic women	49.1	53.4
Asian/Pacific Islander men	59.5	65.7
Asian/Pacific Islander women	66.8	71.3
American Indian/Alaska native men	36.2	37.5
American Indian/Alaska native women	39.5	40.9

in the 1996 cohort was 43 percent. This gap remained significant in the 2004 cohort, where African American males had a graduation rate of 34.2 percent, while African American females had a graduation rate of 43.1 percent. Among Hispanic students, men graduated at a rate that was 8.2 percent below that of Hispanic women in the 1996 cohort. In the 2004 cohort, Hispanic men graduated at a rate 7.8 percent below that of Hispanic women.

Table 16.2 displays the percentage of first-time, full-time degree-seeking students who graduated within six years of entering higher education disaggregated by race and institutional type. Given that typically private, non-profit institutions are smaller, are more selective, and have fewer transfer students, we would expect that those institutions would have higher student graduation rates in comparison to other institutional types, and this was shown to be true in the data. Across races and within both cohorts, private not-for-profit institutions had the highest graduation rates. The data also show that private for-profit institutions consistently had the lowest graduation rates among major institutional types. Within the 2004 cohort, only 21.3 percent of African American students, 28.9 percent of Hispanic students, and 19.2 percent of American Indian/Alaska native students who started at for-profit institutions went on to earn their degrees from those institutions.

Although national graduation rate data are publicly available, data on student graduation rates by major or area of study are more difficult to obtain (Selingo, 2013). None of the major graduation rate databases provide institutional level retention and graduation rate data disaggregated by student major. Therefore,

Table 16.2: Six-year graduation rates of first-time, full-time degree-seeking undergraduates by race/ethnicity, institutional type, and cohort

	1996 cohort	2004 cohort
White students—public institutions	54.3	58.9
White students—private institutions, non-profit	65.7	67.9
White students—private institutions, for-profit	33.2	35.3
Black students—public institutions	36.8	38.3
Black students—private institutions, non-profit	44.6	44.9
Black students—private institutions, for-profit	19.2	21.3
Hispanic students—public institutions	42.1	47.8
Hispanic students—private institutions, non-profit	55.7	60.5
Hispanic students—private institutions, for-profit	24.6	28.9
Asian/Pacific Islanders—public institutions	59.5	66.2
Asian/Pacific Islanders—private institutions, non-profit	73.5	76.2
Asian/Pacific Islanders—private institutions, for-profit	28.9	38.9
AmerInd/Alaska Nat—public institutions	35.3	37.0
AmerInd/Alaska Nat—private institutions, non-profit	48.1	50.7
AmerInd/Alaska Nat—private institutions, for-profit	23.1	19.2

estimates are often obtained from research reports on smaller subsets of colleges and universities. Many of these reports in recent years have focused on Science, Technology, Engineering, and Math (STEM) majors. Two reports have found that African American, Hispanic, and Native American students have lower undergraduate STEM degree completion rates in comparison to white and Asian students. Gary Huang, Nebiyu Taddese, and Elizabeth Walter (2000) found that 26.8 percent of African American, Hispanic, and Native American STEM majors completed their STEM degree within five years of initial enrollment. White and Asian student STEM majors completed their degrees at a rate of 46 percent. The Center for Institutional Data Exchange and Analysis (2001) found very similar numbers in their study of STEM majors from the 1993 cohort. The center found that 23 percent of African American, Hispanic, and Native American student STEM majors earned a STEM bachelor's degree within six years of initial enrollment as compared to a 41 percent STEM completion rate for white and Asian students.

Most recently, Silvia Hurtado, Kevin Eagan, and Mitch Chang (2010) used data from the 2004 Cooperative Institutional Research Program (CIRP) freshmen survey along with data from the National Student Clearinghouse to calculate completion rates among 62,115 students who reported plans to major in a STEM field upon entering college. The study found that 42 percent of white students and 46 percent of Asian STEM majors earned a bachelor's degree in any discipline within four years. Each of these figures was higher than those of African American students, Hispanic students, and American Indian students. Around 30 percent of Hispanic STEM majors, 23 percent of African American STEM majors, and 28 percent of Native American STEM majors completed a bachelor's degree in any field within four years.

These numbers become more interesting when compared to those of students who entered college as non-STEM majors. Hurtado et al. (2010) found that across all races, the overall completion rates of students who start in STEM disciplines compared to their counterparts who entered college in non-STEM disciplines was much lower. In other words, "students who initially enter undergraduate STEM programs have substantially lower degree completion rates than their same-race peers who enter other academic disciplines" (p. 3). This finding is somewhat surprising given that STEM majors often have stronger incoming academic credentials than their counterparts in non-science majors (Arcidiacono, Aucejo, & Hotz, 2013).

The data presented in this section highlight the need for enrollment managers to be concerned about the persistence of students of color. The "Age of Structure" within Strategic Enrollment Management, which focused on increasing student enrollment through enhanced recruiting models, financial aid, and leveraging, has helped colleges become more racially diversity (Black, 2001). Many of these students of color, however, never earn their baccalaureate degrees. As SEM moves into "The Age of Academic Context," characterized by enrollment management's branching out into the academic side of the university, greater emphasis is being placed on promoting student success and completion (Black, 2001; Henderson, 2005). Therefore, it is important that institutions be cognizant of programs and policies that could help increase the graduation rates of students of color. The next two sections discuss theoretical frameworks that have been used to help understand the departure decision of students of color and research examining the factors most strongly associated with student departure.

THEORIES OF MINORITY STUDENT DEPARTURE

As college student departure has become of greater concern within the higher education community, a number of theoretical frameworks from a variety of disciplinary backgrounds have been proposed to help better understand this *ill-structured problem* (Braxton & Hirschy, 2005). Recently, a number of these frameworks have focused primarily on students of color. Much of the impetus for the development of models specific to the experiences of students of color has been the perceived limitations of Vincent Tinto's (1987, 1993) Interactionalist Theory of College Student Departure. Tinto's theory has been the most studied, tested, and cited framework on college student departure (Braxton & Hirschy, 2005). Tinto's theory has also been the most criticized student departure framework, especially among those interested in the study of racial minority students. These criticisms were articulated by Laura Rendón, Romero Jalomo, and Amaury Nora (2000) in their book chapter titled "Theoretical Considerations in the Study of Minority Student Retention in Higher Education."

Rendón et al. (2000) focused criticism on two important aspects of Tinto's (1993) framework. The first is Tinto's reliance on the concepts of separation and transition in the student departure theory. Tinto's (1993) departure theory is grounded in the work of Arnold Van Gennep (1960). Van Gennep proposed that an individual's transition from youth to adulthood occurs in three phases: separation, transition, and incorporation. Separation involves disassociating with previous communities of membership. Transition involves an individual beginning to interact in new ways with members of the new community in which he or she is becoming part of. During this process, an individual begins to acquire the knowledge, skills, and behavior patterns of the new group. At the third phase, incorporation, an individual has taken on the patterns necessary to become a competent member of the new group. Communication and interaction with previous membership groups are engaged in only from the perspective of their new group membership.

Tinto (1993) argued that the process of student persistence is similar to the process of becoming incorporated into a human community. Therefore, Tinto (1993) argued, a student's likelihood of persisting in college is positively correlated with his or her ability to incorporate fully, both socially and academically, into the life of their institution. This process of incorporation is facilitated by a student's ability to separate from his or her previous communities. Tinto notes that "in order to become fully incorporated in the life of the college, [students] have to physically as well as socially dissociate themselves from the communities of the past" (1993, p. 93).

Rendón et al. (2000) noted an important assumption within the concept of separation that is problematic when understanding the departure decisions of students of color. The separation idea assumes that "an individual's values and beliefs rooted in his or her cultural background must be abandoned to successfully incorporate the values and beliefs not only of the institution but of the majority population upon which they are based" (p. 132). The authors discussed two concepts that challenge this assumption: biculturalism and dual socialization. Biculturalism proposes that, throughout their lives, individuals of color are simultaneously socialized into two different cultures. In other words, racial minorities have the ability to step in and out of the rules and traditions of two cultures (their own culture and the culture of the white majority) perceived to be distinct and separate. Dual socialization argues that for most majority and minority cultures, there is overlap with regard to shared values and norms. When this is the case, an individual of color has the ability to "understand and predict successfully two cultural environments and adjust his or her behavior according to the norms of each culture" (Rendón et al., 2000, p. 102). So at colleges and universities where some overlap exists between the campus culture and the cultural backgrounds of students of color, duel socialization skills can be utilized. Rendón et al. argued that biculturalism and duel socialization seriously challenge the assumption that students of color must separate from their home culture to increase their likelihood of persisting in college.

The second aspect of Tinto's (1993) student departure framework that concerned Rendón et al. (2000) was the ideas of social and academic integration. As noted earlier, Tinto believed that student persistence requires that individuals become incorporated into the ongoing social and intellectual life of a college. This integration is argued to occur as a result of the continual interaction of students and institutions in a variety of formal and informal situations. Rendón et al. believed this integration framework makes a number of assumptions and ignores the realities faced by many students of color. One is the assumptions that students of color will find it relatively easy to gain membership within the culture of a college or university. Rendón and her associates, however, suggest that many students of color enter college cultures that lack acceptance of racial/ethnic minorities. This creates stress and tension. As a result, students of color, even those who abandon their cultural heritage and adopt the cultural codes/values of the campus community, may not find acceptance and therefore could not become fully incorporated in the life of the college. Rendón et al. also criticize Tinto's (1993) integration framework for its focus on the individual student rather than the institution as being responsible for departure decisions, the framework's lack of acknowledgement of the various constraints on the institutional involvement of students of color, and the framework's focus on the negative impact of the external community on student involvement.

So although a number of theories of college student departure, led by Tinto's (1993) Interactionalist Theory, have been postulated over the years (Braxton & Hirschy, 2005), the application of these theories to students of color has been questioned. In an effort to address these shortcomings, several scholars have proposed departure frameworks grounded in the experiences of students of color. Four of these models can be described as culturally based perspectives on the retention of students of color. Rendón (1994) introduced a validation theory of student success with particular application to underrepresented students in higher education, which she developed based on qualitative interviews with 132 first-year students from a variety of colleges and universities.

Rendón conceptualized validation as the intentional, proactive affirmation of students by agents of the college/university. This theory contains six elements. The first states that initial contact with students should be the responsibility of institutional agents such as faculty, advisers, and administrators. The second element notes that when validation is present, students feel capable of learning and have a greater sense of self-worth. The third element states that validation is a prerequisite for student development. The fourth element states that validation can occur in and out of class. Element five states that validation should not be viewed as an end, but rather as a developmental process that begins earlier and is continuous. The final element of Rendón's validation theory stated that because underrepresented students can benefit from early validating experiences and positive interactions in college, validation is most critical when administered early in the college experience, especially during the first few weeks of students' freshmen year. Colleges and universities, she argued, must create a culture that works to validate all students, not just "traditional" students. Rendón, Laura Linares, and Susana Muñoz (2011) highlighted theoretical and empirical support for this validation framework.

William Tierney (1999) proposed a theoretical model of student departure centered on the concepts of cultural integrity, capital, and habitus. Tierney believed that instead of assuming that students of color must commit a form of cultural suicide to increase their likelihood of persisting, colleges and universities should work to engage the cultural backgrounds of these students in a manner that is affirming and honoring. By doing this (which enhances the cultural integrity of students of color), the habitus of students of color who often lack economic or cultural capital becomes less deterministic in their college success. This model suggests that if postsecondary institutions make concerted and meaningful efforts to affirm the cultural identities of students of color, persistence rates will increase.

George Kuh and Patrick Love (2000) also proposed a culturally based conceptualization of student departure. The authors proposed eight propositions consistent with student departure as interpreted through culture lenses. Though Kuh and Love pointed out that their propositions do not constitute a theory (p. 200), the propositions do provide a framework for understanding how overlapping cultures, cultural distance, cultural stress, and cultural connections can work together to influence departure decisions. These cultural propositions, however, remain in need of research supporting their validity and utility (Reason, 2009).

A third culturally based perspective on the retention of students of color was presented by Douglas Guiffrida (2006). Guiffrida argued that several changes to Tinto's (1993) departure framework must occur if the model is to be truly applicable to students of color. The changes proposed by Guiffrida include the recognition of the potential of families and friends from home to support students once they arrive at college, greater attention to the relationship between succeeding at college and maintaining connections to cultural heritages and traditions, and greater attention to the ability of home systems and college social systems to shape and fulfill the salient needs of students. The changes would, Guiffrida argued, move "Tinto's theory away from an integrationist perspective that emphasizes student adaptation to the majority culture to one that values diversity and encourages colleges and universities to affirm and honor diverse student cultures" (p. 458).The viability of the proposed changes to Tinto's theory, Guiffrida stated, is supported by research examining the relationships among motivational orientation, cultural orientation, and academic achievement and persistence.

A fifth theoretical response to the retention concerns of students of color focuses less on culture and would best be described as an interactionist framework. Watson Swail's Geometric Model of Student Persistence and Achievement emphasized the relationship between college/university practices and students' attributes (Swail, Redd, & Perna, 2003). Swail argued that the college student experience is influenced by three forces:. Cognitive forces are the academic strengths and weaknesses of a student. Social forces are a student's ability to interact with others, maturity, attitudes toward others, and cultural history. Institutional forces are the practices, strategies, and culture of a college or university that in both intended and unintended ways impact student experiences. Students who are able to obtain equilibrium among these three factors, Swail argued, are more likely to persist. Achieving equilibrium, however, does not necessary mean that each of these three forces has to exert an equal effect on a student. Swail et al. (2003) noted that "the individuality of the student necessitates that the model must shift and sway and evolve in a variety of ways and still provide a model of stability" (p. 82). Therefore, students with weak cognitive skills but with very strong social skills and institutional support can reach a state of equilibrium. Students with strong cognitive and social forces at an institution with few resources can also reach equilibrium. The utility of the Swail model to students of color was its emphasis on the institution's responsibility to identify, understand, and support the various needs of these students. As opposed to requiring that students of color adjust or assimilate to the institution, Swail argued that institutions must work proactively to provide a menu of programs that can make up for the social or academic concerns of students of color.

This summary of theoretical frameworks that have been proposed better to address the persistence of students of color provides enrollment managers with a review of how the higher education community has attempted to conceptualize departure among underrepresented students. Although this type of review often unknowingly omits some frameworks, most major conceptual models of students of color college persistence are covered. These theories differ from

Tinto's popular model of student departure in two ways: One, they emphasize the importance of the cultural backgrounds of students of color and argue that retaining connections with these cultural roots can increase a student's likelihood of persistence. Two, theories of departure from the perspective of students of color highlight the institution's responsibility in creating an atmosphere that supports the unique needs and challenges of these students. Although some of these frameworks have been empirically supported by research, more work is needed to validate persistence frameworks with an emphasis on the experiences of students of color.

FACTORS RELATED TO THE RETENTION OF STUDENTS OF COLOR

The proliferation of theoretical frameworks related to the departure decisions of students of color has coincided with an increase in empirical research on the topic. The following section surveys this literature and highlights the factors that have been identified as most significant in the retention of students of color.

American Indian/Alaska Native Student Retention

Despite the well-documented high departure rates of Native American college students, uncertainty remains about the factors that influence their departure decisions. This is due largely to a dearth of research on Native American students (Larimore & McClellan, 2005). The few studies that had examined the persistence rates of Native American students before 2005 were reviewed by Jim Larimore and George McClellan (2005). Among the individual factors identified as being influential in student persistence were family support, an individual's level of institutional commitment, personal commitment to obtaining a degree, and connections to homeland and culture. Obstacles to the persistence of Native American students were found to include inadequate academic preparation, vague educational goals, lack of finances, and the experience of prejudice and social isolation on college campuses.

Since 2005, other studies have explored the persistence decisions of Native American students and found similar results to those summarized by Larimore and McClellan (2005). Heather J. Shotton, E. Star Oosahwe, and Rosa Cintrón (2007) examined a peer-mentoring program at a midsized, Midwestern university and found that the program played a positive role in the retention of American Indian students. Raphael M. Guillory and Mimi Wolverton (2008) interviewed thirty Native American students at three universities to better understand their persistence decisions. The conceptual frameworks used in this study were Tinto's (1993) model of attrition, Alexander Astin's (1985) theory of involvement, and Ernest Pascarella's (1985) general model of effecting change. The authors also utilized the Family Education Model (FEM) as a framework for interpreting their work. Factors found to be positively associated with persistence were a desire to give back to their tribal community and involvement with on-campus support organizations. Factors negatively correlated with persistence were single parenthood, inadequate financial resources, and a lack of academic preparation for college. Family was found to be both positively and negatively correlated with persistence and was an important source of motivation for many of the Native American students interviewed. Many students noted that they often "felt the pull from their families to come home, especially in situations where family members were dependent upon them for financial and emotional support" (p. 77). This paradox of family being both a positive and negative factor in retention decisions was a great source of frustration for the students interviewed.

The relationship among family, finances, and persistence was also evident in a study by Junghee Lee, William Donlan, and Eddie Brown (2011) of American Indian/Alaska native students. Using various forms of data from students at three campus sites of a large university in a metropolitan area, the researchers asked what factors were associated with American Indian/Alaska native undergraduate student attrition from the institution. Family obligations, financial difficulty, and the interaction between the two were most strongly associated with attrition. The authors noted that American Indian/Alaska native students "appeared to perceive a greater degree of family obligation, which when experienced in the context of family financial difficulty appeared to conflict with, and pose a threat to, their academic performance" and subsequent persistence (p. 268). Tinto's (1993) model of attrition was the conceptual framework used in this study.

Jesse P. Mendez, Pilar Mendoza, and Zaria Malcolm (2011) looked at the impact of various forms of financial aid on the persistence of Native American students using multiyear state-level data from Oklahoma. Among the many findings presented in the paper was the fact that different types of aid packages impact retention differently based on student gender, income, and grade point average (GPA). For the most part, however, higher income Native American students with any form of financial aid had higher retention rates than lower income Native Americans with similar financial aid packages. Although not entirely surprising, the study does highlight the importance of financial resources in the persistence decision of Native Americans.

Stephen Flynn, Kelly Duncan, and Maribeth Jorgensen (2012) engaged in a phenomenological study of American Indian undergraduate students at four public institutions in South Dakota. Their intention was to better understand the factors that promote the transition and persistence of these students in higher education. Ten themes emerged from their study. Two of these themes were the antecedents of college completion/retention and the antecedent for college dropout/academic probation. The events that set the stage for college retention according to the study participants were family expectations, motivation to complete college, strategizing for success, and pride in the ability to be a high achiever. The common factors that set the stage for departure were a lack of institutional investment, a lack or student mentorship, feelings of inferiority, lack of independence, and isolation.

To summarize, a number of factors have been found to correlate both positively and negatively with the attrition of American Indian/Alaska native students. Factors encouraging persistence include on-campus support through peer mentoring and student organizations, the desire to give back to their community, and family support and motivation. The factors found to hinder retention include a lack of financial support, the pressures of family obligations, and experiences of social isolation on campus.

Asian Student/Pacific Islander Retention

Due in large part to the "model minority" stereotype often attached to Asian/Pacific Islander students, research on the persistence of these students has been sparse (Museus, 2009; Yeh, 2004). Though limited in scale, the research has shown compelling evidence to suggest that although in the aggregate Asian students enjoy relatively high persistence rates, certain subgroups face significant hurtles in their efforts to persist through graduation. Theresa Yeh (2004) summarized research on the issues of persistence faced by Asian and Asian Pacific American college students. The review focuses specifically on research documenting the individual and institutional challenges facing Southeast Asian students (mainly Vietnamese, Cambodian, Laotian, and Hmong). Many of these groups, Yeh highlighted, immigrated to the United States after 1975. Therefore, although most Southeast Asian students are U.S. citizens by birth, they face many of the same persistence challenges immigrants face. These included academic under-preparedness, first-generation status, language barriers, financial difficulties, and family obligations. Yeh also found that institutional factors such as marginalization on campus, discrimination on campus, cultural barriers, and the model minority stereotype make persistence challenging for Southeast Asian students.

Recent research on the persistence of Asian students in higher education has focused largely on issues of institutional climate and sense of belonging. Vichet Chhuon and Cynthia Hudley (2008), guided by the retention frameworks of Tinto (1993) and Guiffrida (2006), interviewed ten Cambodian American students from one Southern California university. They found four factors to be significant in supporting the college persistence of these students: academic support services, positive faculty contact, campus social organizations for Cambodian students, and emotional/social support from their previous communities.

Samuel Museus and Dina Maramba (2010) engaged in a quantitative examination of the correlation between Filipino students' cultural relationships and their sense of belonging on campus. Sense of belonging, conceptualized as students' sense of cohesion with the campus community, has become a popular alternative to Tinto's (1993) concept of integration of membership (Hausmann, Schofield, & Woods, 2007; Hurtado & Carter, 1997) for predicting student persistence. In addition to the concept of sense of belonging, Museus and Maramba grounded their study in the frameworks of Kuh and Love (2000) and Tierney (1999). The authors found that "pressure to commit cultural suicide and connections to cultural heritages significantly and indirectly influenced sense of belonging via their impact on cultural adjustment" (p. 251). These results, the authors argued, indicated that for Filipino students, retaining strong cultural connections can facilitate successful transition to university life and subsequent persistence.

In 2012, a second study exploring the antecedents of Filipino students' sense of belonging was published by Maramba and Museus (2012–2013). In this study, the researchers again used Structural Equation Modeling to explore how three variables (campus racial culture, ethnic group cohesion, and cross-cultural interactions) influence Filipino American students' sense of belonging. Each of the variables was found to have a direct effect on sense of belonging. Greater cross-cultural interactions, a more positive perception of the campus racial climate, and a stronger connection to their own ethnic group positively correlated with sense of belonging of Filipino students.

In sum, limited research has explored the persistence challenges of Asian/Pacific Islander students in higher education. A review of this research reveals that social support from home cultures and a sense of cohesion with the campus community strongly correlated with the retention of these students. The "model minority myth" has been found to be a detriment to the persistence of Asian/Pacific Islander students.

Hispanic Student Retention

Given the population growth and increased presence of Hispanic/Latino students on college campuses throughout the United States, it is not surprising to see a large and growing body of literature that explores the persistence of Hispanic/Latino students. This literature has been comprehensively surveyed by a number of scholars (Hernandez & Lopez, 2004; Hurtado & Kamimura, 2003; Oseguera, Locks, & Vega, 2009; Padilla, 2007).

Hernandez and Lopez (2004) reviewed retention literature in an attempt to summarize the factors that impact the persistence of Latino students and provide recommendations for appropriate institutional responses to these persistence factors. The researchers began their review by highlighting the inefficiency of grades and test scores as predictors of retention. They noted that "it would appear unwise for college admissions offices to continue to rely exclusively on high school grade point average and test scores because the predictive power (in relation to student retention) of these traditional assessments is modest" (p. 40) for Latino students. Hernandez and Lopez recommended a focus on personal non-cognitive factors as predictors of Latino student retention. The non-cognitive factors evidence supported as determinates of Latino student persistence were academic self-concept, family support and encouragement, and financial assistance. The authors also found research supporting the contention that the college environment plays a key role in the retention of Latino students. A positive racial climate on campus reduced feelings of isolation among Latino students. Research also found that the presence of an ethnic community on campus, which was developed through the enrollment of a critical mass of Latino students, helped combat feelings of marginalization. Campus involvement factors such as faculty-student interactions, mentorship, and membership in student organizations were also predictors of Latino student retention. The final set of retention factors the authors discuss are sociocultural factors. These included immigration status (which could impact a Latino student's educational aspirations) and community orientations (specifically membership in external communities).

Oseguera et al. (2009) reviewed research on Latino student persistence published since 1995. As with Hernandez and Lopez (2004), Oseguera et al. highlighted the fact that research has shown little correlation between standardized assessment of students' academic ability and their withdrawal decisions. If anything, the authors noted, the overreliance on standardized test scores has been found to correlate with lower academic self-concepts among Latino students and makes them more vulnerable to stereotype threat.

Oseguera et al. (2009) went on to discuss other institutional variables that have been shown to impact the persistence decisions of Latino students. With regard to campus culture and ethnic identity, the authors noted that "the common thread in the research highlights institutional responsibility to establish inclusive campus climates and, perhaps more encouraging, that the effects of these institutional commitments are real" (p. 36). With regard to diversity among university faculty and staff, the authors state that "Latina/o faculty and administrator presence on campuses has been proven to have a positive effect on student retention. Latina/o faculty members and administrators are key players in institutional retention efforts because their presence sends a message of inclusivity" (p. 37). In the area of finances, the authors stated that "financial aid is an important factor for Latino college student retention, both in the college choice process and during college" (p. 38). The relationship between financial aid and Latino student success, however, can be complicated. The researchers cited several articles noting that the type of aid received is key when considered against Latino student retention. Need-based aid in the form of grants was particularly important to helping retain Latino students. The review concluded with a presentation of national, state, and local programs that have shown to be effective at increasing the retention rate of Latino students.

Both the Hernandez and Lopez (2004) and Oseguera et al. (2009) literature reviews highlighted important factors found to be related to the retention of Hispanic students. Campus variables such as a positive and inclusive campus culture and the enrollment/employment of a diverse student body/faculty have been shown to correlate positively with the retention of Hispanic students. Family encouragement and need-based financial aid were also associated with retention.

African American Student Retention

A voluminous amount of literature on the persistence of African American college students has evolved over the years. Comprehensively surveying this literature would be beyond the scope of this review. It is possible, however, to point out the variables that have been correlated with the persistence decisions of African American students. Many of these factors are similar to those related to the persistence of other racial minority groups. Sense of belonging among African American students, especially first-year students, has been shown to be correlated with intentions to persist (Hausmann, Schofield, & Woods, 2007; Hausmann, Ye, Schofield, & Woods, 2009). Discrimination and microagressions (defined as subtle, innocuous, preconscious, or unconscious degradations and putdowns) on campus have also been found to correlate strongly with the persistence decisions of students. Successful African American students, particularly African American males, are often forced to overcome stereotyping, marginalization, and low expectations on college campuses (Harper, 2009; Smith, Allen, & Danley, 2007).

The negative impact of a hostile campus climate on African American students' persistence may be mediated by student organizations. Several studies have found that student organizations and cultural centers can be critical tools for helping facilitate African American students' cultural adjustment and subsequent retention (Guiffrida, 2003; Jones & Williams, 2006; Museus, 2008; Patton Davis, 2006; Strayhorn, Terrell, Redmond, & Walton, 2012). Other forms of engagement, such as involvement in extracurricular activities, may also reduce the negative impact of a hostile campus on retention (Fischer, 2007; Kuh, Cruce, Shoup, Kinzie, & Gonyea, 2008).

As with other racial/ethnic groups, family has been shown both to hinder and support the persistence of African American students. Guiffrida (2005) found that African American college persistent students saw their family as an important source of emotional and financial support. Those students who departed, however, described the emotional strain resulting from extenuating family circumstances as contributing to their attrition. Leavers also felt guilty for being away from home and/or for lacking the ability to support their families.

RECOMMENDATIONS FOR ENROLLMENT MANAGERS

It is impossible to adequately address the broad array of factors that are identified as predictors of retention among students of color. Previous research, however, suggests that enrollment managers and other administrators may have the ability to reduce the departure of students of color by addressing their unique needs and challenges. Both theory and research suggest that colleges and universities should work to create a campus culture that affirms the cultural background and traditions of students of color (Chhuon & Hudley, 2008; Guillory & Wolverton, 2008; Oseguera et al., 2009; Smith et al., 2007). This starts in the admissions office. Enrollment managers must work to create a racially diverse student body on their respective campuses. This could be accomplished through targeted recruitment efforts with specialized marketing materials, outreach to high schools and junior high schools with large numbers of students of color, and the employment of recruiters knowledgeable in working in communities of color. The enrollment of a critical mass of racial minorities will help create a campus culture that overlaps the cultural backgrounds of students of color. The creation of a diverse student body also increases the ability of students of color to develop the kind of supports systems (such as student organizations or peer mentoring) that help reduce departure.

Simply enrolling a more diverse student body, however, is not sufficient. Higher education diversity scholars have noted that institutions must enact policies and practices that facilitate interactions among diverse students if the hope is to make campus culture more inclusive (Gurin, Dey, Hurtado, & Gurin, 2002; Milem, 2003). Enrollment managers could aid in this task by working with student affairs divisions to promote student engagement. Given that enrollment managers are often the first point of contact for students, enrollment managers could leverage their relationships with students to help encourage their active involvement on campus. Although it would be difficult for overworked enrollment management professionals to follow up with students after their enrollment, this practice could have great payoffs in student retention.

Encouraging interactions with diverse students could help address several factors that have shown to reduce the persistence of students of color. Research suggest that increasing student interactions with diverse others would likely lead to reduced prejudice and discrimination on campus, which would subsequently increase the sense of belonging and academic self-concept of students of color.

Institutions should work to engage the families of students of color into their college experiences. Family has, for the most part, been found to be an important source of support for students of color. To encourage family involvement, institutions could offer opportunities for families to participate in first-year student orientations and increase the number of parent weekends during the academic year. Parent newsletters about campus happenings could also increase the families' ability of to support students of color. Faculty could support retention efforts by allowing students of color to make up assignments missed when the need to address family issues results in missed class time. Again, given the relationships enrollment managers build with families during the recruitment process, they may have the ability to facilitate campus initiatives to address the importance of family contact and support in the lives of students of color.

Another recommendation based on this review is that enrollment managers commission studies on the persistence of students of color using the theoretical constructs of Rendón (1994); Tierney (1999); Kuh & Love (2000); Swail, Redd, & Perna (2003); and Guiffrida (2006). Many of these frameworks are in need of empirical validation, which would help the higher education community transition the ideas and propositions put forward by these authors into institutional action.

Increasing the retention and graduation rates of students of color will continue to be a priority of colleges and universities for years to come. By better understanding the theory and research addressing this complicated issue, enrollment managers can be equipped with the knowledge they need to be proactive in reducing the number of students of color who leave campus due to issues that could have been addressed.

References

Arcidiacono, P., Aucejo, E. M., & Hotz, V. J. (2013). *University Differences in the Graduation of Minorities in STEM Fields: Evidence from California.* National Bureau of Economic Research Working Paper No. 18799.

Astin, A. W. (1985). *Achieving Educational Excellence: A Critical Assessment for Priorities and Practices in Higher Education.* San Francisco: Jossey-Bass.

Black, J. (2001). *Strategic Enrollment Management Revolution.* Washington, DC: American Association of Collegiate Registrars and Admissions Officers.

Braxton, J., & Hirschy, A. S. (2005). Theoretical developments in the study of college student departure. In A. Seidman (Ed.), *College Student Retention: Formula for Student Success* (pp. 61–87). Westport, CT: Praeger Publishers.

Braxton, J., & Mundy, M. (2001). Powerful institutional levers to reduce college student departure. *Journal of College Student Retention, 3*(1), 91–118.

Center for Institutional Data Exchange and Analysis. (2001). 1999–2000 SMET retention report. Norman, OK: University of Oklahoma.

Chhuon, V., & Hudley, C. (2008). Factors supporting Cambodian American students' successful adjustment into the university. *Journal of College Student Development, 49*(1), 15–30.

Cook, B., & Pullaro, N. (2010). *College Graduation Rates: Behind the Numbers.* Washington, DC: American Council on Education.

DiPrete, T. A., & Buchmann, C. (2013). *The Rise of Women: The Growing Gender Gap in Education and What It Means for American Schools.* New York: Russell Sage Foundation.

Fischer, M. J. (2007). Settling into campus life: Differences by race/ethnicity in college involvement and outcomes. *The Journal of Higher Education, 78*(2), 125–156.

Flynn, S. V., Duncan, K., & Jorgensen, M. F. (2012). An emergent phenomenon of American indian postsecondary transition and retention. *Journal of Counseling and Development, 90*(4), 437–449.

Guiffrida, D. A. (2003). African American student organizations as agents of social integration. *Journal of College Student Development, 44*(3), 304–319.

Guiffrida, D. A. (2005). To break away or strengthen ties to home: A complex issue for African American college students attending a predominantly white institution. *Equity & Excellence in Education, 38*(1), 49–60.

Guiffrida, D. A. (2006). Toward a cultural advancement of Tinto's theory. *The Review of Higher Education, 29*(4), 451–472.

Guillory, R. M., & Wolverton, M. (2008). It's about family: Native American student persistence in higher education. *The Journal of Higher Education, 79*(1), 58–87.

Gurin, P., Dey, E., Hurtado, S., & Gurin, G. (2002). Diversity and higher education: Theory and impact on educational outcomes. *Harvard Educational Review, 72*, 330–366.

Harper, S. R. (2009). Niggers no more: A critical race counternarrative on black male student achievement at predominantly white colleges and universities. *International Journal of Qualitative Studies in Education, 22*(6), 697–712.

Hausmann, L., Schofield, J. W., & Woods, R. L. (2007). Sense of belonging as a predictor of intentions to persist among African American and white first-year College Students. *Research in Higher Education, 48*(7), 803–839.

Hausmann, L., Ye, F., Schofield, J., & Woods, R. (2009). Sense of belonging and persistence in white and African American first-year students. *Research in Higher Education, 50*(7), 649–669.

Henderson, S. E. (2005). Refocusing enrollment management: Losing structure and finding the academic context. *College & University, 80*(3), 3–8.

Hernandez, J. C., & Lopez, M. A. (2004). Leaking Pipeline: Issues Impacting Latino/a College Student Retention. *Journal of College Student Retention: Research, Theory and Practice, 6*(1), 37–60.

Huang, G., Taddese, N., & Walter, E. (2000). *Entry and Persistence of Women and Minorities in College Science and Engineering Education.* Washington, DC: National Center for Education Statistics.

Hurtado, S., & Carter, D. (1997). Effects of college transition and perceptions of the campus racial climate on Latino college students' sense of belonging. *Sociology of Education, 70*(4), 324–345.

Hurtado, S., Eagan, K., & Chang, M. (2010). *Degrees of Success: Bachelor's Degree Completion Rates among Initial STEM Majors.* Los Angeles: Higher Education Research Institute, UCLA.

Hurtado, S., & Kamimura, M. (2003). Latina/o retention in four-year institutions. In J. Castellanos & L.Jones (Eds.), *The Majority in the Minority: Expanding the Representation of Latina/o Faculty, Administrators, and Students in Higher Education* (pp. 139–150). Sterling, VA: Stylus.

Jones, J. D., & Williams, M. (2006). The African American student center and black student retention at a Pacific Northwest PWI. *The Western Journal of Black Studies, 30*(4), 24–34.

Kuh, G., Cruce, T. M., Shoup, R., Kinzie, J., & Gonyea, R .M. (2008). Unmasking the effects of student engagement on first-year college grades and persistence. *The Journal of Higher Education, 79*(5), 540–563.

Kuh, G., & Love, P. (2000). A cultural perspective on student departure. In J. Braxton (Ed.), *Reworking the Student Departure Puzzle* (pp. 196–212). Nashville, TN: Vanderbilt University Press.

Larimore, J. A., & McClellan, G. S. (2005). Native American Student Retention in U.S. Postsecondary Education. *New Directions for Student Services, 2005*(109), 17–32.

Lee, J., Donlan, W., & Brown, E. F. (2011). American Indian/Alaskan native undergraduate retention at predominantly white institutions: An elaboration of Tinto's theory of college student departure. *Journal of College Student Retention: Research, Theory and Practice, 12*(3), 257–276.

Maramba, D. C., & Museus, S. D. (2012–2013). Examining the effects of campus climate, ethnic group cohesion, and cross-cultural interaction on Filipino American students' sense of belonging in college. *Journal of College Student Retention: Research, Theory and Practice, 14*(4), 495–522.

Mendez, J. P., Mendoza, P., & Malcolm, Z. (2011). The impact of financial aid on Native American students. *Journal of Diversity in Higher Education, 4*(1), 12–25.

Milem, J. (2003). The educational benefits of diversity: Evidence from multiple sectors. In M. Chang, D. Witt, J. Jones, & K. Hakuta (Eds.), *Compelling Interest: Examining the Evidence on Racial Dynamics in Colleges and Universities* (pp. 126–169). Palo Alto, CA: Stanford University Press.

Museus, S. D. (2008). The role of ethnic student organizations in fostering African American and Asian American students' cultural adjustment and membership at predominantly white institutions. *Journal of College Student Development, 49*(6), 568–586.

Museus, S. D. (2009). A critical analysis of the exclusion of Asian Americans from higher education research and discourse. In L. Zahn (Ed.), *Asian American Voices: Engaging, Empowering, Enabling.* New York: NLN Press.

Museus, S. D., & Maramba, D. C. (2010). The impact of culture on Filipino American students' sense of belonging. *The Review of Higher Education, 34*(2), 231–258.

National Center for Education Statistics. (2012). Digest of education statistics. Retrieved from http://nces.ed.gov/programs/digest/2012menu_tables.asp.

Oseguera, L., Locks, A.M., & Vega, I.I. (2009). Increasing Latina/o students' baccalaureate attainment a focus on retention. *Journal of Hispanic Higher Education*, 8(1), 23–53.

Padilla, R. (2007). *Camino a la Universidad: The Road to College.* Indianapolis, IN: Lumina Foundation for Education.

Pascarella, E. T. (1985). College environmental influences on learning and cognitive development: A critical review and synthesis. In J. Smart (Ed.), *Higher Education: Handbook of Theory and Research* (pp. 1–61). New York: Agathon.

Patton Davis, L. (2006). The voice of reason: A qualitative examination of black student perceptions of their black culture center. *Journal of College Student Development*, 47(6), 628–646.

Reason, R. D. (2009). An examination of persistence research through the lens of a comprehensive conceptual framework. *Journal of College Student Development*, 50(6), 659–682.

Rendón, L. (1994). Validating culturally diverse students: Toward a new model of learning and student development. *Innovative Higher Education*, 19(1), 33–51.

Rendón, L., Jalomo, R., & Nora, A. (2000). Theoretical considerations in the study of minority student retention in higher education. In J. Braxton (Ed.), *Reworking the Student Departure Puzzle* (pp. 127–156). Nashville, TN: Vanderbilt University Press.

Rendón, L., Linares, L., & Muñoz, S. (2011). Revisiting validation theory: Theoretical foundations, applications, and extensions. *Enrollment Management Journal: Student Access, Finance, and Success in Higher Education*, 5(2), 12–33.

Roach, R. (2013). Steady College Enrollment Growth for Underrepresented Minorities, College Completion Rates Increasing More Slowly. *Diverse: Issues in Higher Education.* Retrieved from http://diverseeducation.com/article/54837/#.

Selingo, J. (2013). Graduation rates: Flawed as a measure of colleges, but still useful. *Chronicle of Higher Education.* Retrieved from http://chronicle.com/blogs/next/2013/05/19/graduation-rates-flawed-as-a-measure-of-colleges-but-still-useful/.

Shotton, H. J., Oosahwe, E.S.L., & Cintrón, R. (2007). Stories of success: Experiences of American Indian students in a peer-mentoring retention program. *The Review of Higher Education*, 31(1), 81–107.

Smith, W. A., Allen, W. R., & Danley, L. L. (2007). "Assume the position . . . you fit the description." Psychosocial Experiences and Racial Battle Fatigue Among African American Male College Students. *American Behavioral Scientist*, 51(4), 551–578.

Strauss, V. (2010). Gender gap in higher education growing—report. *The Washington Post.* Retrieved from http://voices.washingtonpost.com/answer-sheet/higher-education/gender-gap-in-higher-education.html.

Strayhorn, T. L., Terrell, M. C., Redmond, J. S., & Walton, C. N. (2012). A home away from home. In T. L. Strayhorn & M. C. Terrell (Eds.), *The Evolving Challenges of Black College Students: New Insights for Policy, Practice, and Research* (pp. 122–137). Sterling, VA: Stylus.

Swail, W., Redd, K., & Perna, L. (2003). *Retaining Minority Students in Higher Education: A Framework for Success.* San Francisco: Jossey-Bass.

Tierney, W. G. (1999). Models of minority college-going and retention: Cultural integrity versus cultural suicide. *Journal of Negro Education, 68*(1), 80–91.

Tinto, V. (1987). *Leaving College: Rethinking the Causes and Cures of Student Attrition.* Chicago: University of Chicago Press.

Tinto, V. (1993). *Leaving College: Rethinking the Causes and Cures of Student Attrition* (2nd Edition). Chicago: University of Chicago Press.

Van Gennep, A. (1960). *The Rites of Passage.* London: Routledge.

Yeh, T. L. (2004). Issues of college persistence between Asian and Asian Pacific American students. *Journal of College Student Retention: Research, Theory and Practice, 6*(1), 81–96.

CHAPTER 17

Nontraditional Students and Student Persistence

Mary K. Hutchens

The term "nontraditional students" encompasses a large and heterogeneous group of college students in the United States. This term can and has referred to adult students, students who delay their entry into college, students with children, students who are married, students attending part-time, students working full time, students who are financially independent, students who lack a high school diploma, and the variety of student groups that are traditionally underrepresented in higher education (including first-generation and minority students). First-generation and minority students have already warranted considerable attention in other studies and are not included in this analysis, although students who fulfill the other criteria mentioned above are much more likely to be first-generation or minority students than their "traditional" peers (Horn & Carroll, 1996). In colleges today, minority and first-generation students remain underrepresented, and nontraditional students matching the other descriptors are actually the norm (Kim, 2002). Therefore, a discussion of underrepresented students (first-generation and minority students) should be separated from a discussion of those students who are more than adequately represented on college campuses yet also being underserved.

This chapter focuses on an important aspect of enrollment management: student persistence, as it relates to nontraditional college students. This text defines the population of nontraditional students of interest, discusses the particular challenges faced by nontraditional students, and considers why examining persistence among these particular students is important for enrollment managers. Additionally, a review of the existing literature in this area is presented, and based on these findings, recommendations are presented for enrollment managers.

MULTIPLE IDENTIFIERS OF NONTRADITIONALITY

In her report for the U.S. Department of Education (USDE), Susan Choy (2002) defines *nontraditional* students in opposition to *traditional* undergraduates. Traditional undergraduates are characterized as those who earn a high school diploma, enroll immediately after high school, attend full time, are financially dependent, and do not work full time. These students are the exception, however, rather than the rule. Just 27 percent of college students enrolled today meet these "traditional" criteria (Choy, 2002). The USDE has identified the following seven characteristics as defining nontraditional status (the following is from Choy's 2002 report):

- Delays enrollment (does not enter postsecondary education in the same calendar year that he or she finishes high school)
- Attends part-time for at least part of the academic year
- Works full time (35 hours or more per week) while enrolled
- Is considered financially independent for purposes of determining eligibility for financial aid
- Has dependents other than a spouse (usually children, but sometimes others)
- Is a single parent (either not married or married but separated and has dependents
- Does not have a high school diploma (completed high school with a GED or other high school completion certificate or did not finish high school)

The difference between a student who has only one of the above characteristics and a student who has all of them is likely to be stark. For this reason, an earlier USDE report created a continuum of nontraditionality wherein students are considered "minimally" nontraditional if they can be described using only one of the preceding characteristics, "moderately" nontraditional if they can be described using two or three, and "highly" nontraditional if they can be described using four or more (Horn & Carroll, 1996).

HOW MANY NONTRADITIONAL STUDENTS ARE THERE?

All in all, 73 percent of students enrolled in U.S. postsecondary institutions are nontraditional in some way. Utilizing the continuum of nontraditionality described previously, we know that 17 percent of all college students are minimally nontraditional (possessing only one nontraditional characteristic), 28 percent are moderately nontraditional, and 28 percent are highly nontraditional (Choy, 2002). These statistics are especially striking when one considers that more students are highly nontraditional (possessing four or more nontraditional characteristics) than are considered traditional undergraduates.

Common Characteristics

While nontraditional students are a heterogeneous group, varying in age, socioeconomic status, ethnicity, family background, and motivation, they tend to share a number of common traits. Among these commonalities are lower rates of persistence, a tendency to fill multiple roles simultaneously, a focus on vocational education, and academic performance that is, on average, better than that of traditional students. The following section delves more deeply into each of these characteristics.

Limited Persistence The most troubling characteristic shared by the diverse students that fall under the "nontraditional" heading is that they do not complete or persist at the same rates as do their more traditional peers (Cavote & Kopera-Frye, 2006). Typically, when nontraditional students do earn degrees, it takes them longer to do so because they are more likely to be enrolled part-time or to take a break, and the education they receive ends up costing them significantly more over time (Capps, 2012; Horn & Carroll, 1996). Potentially related to this, nontraditional students are much more likely to doubt their ability to succeed, perhaps because they have attempted and failed before or perhaps because their life experiences have led them to conclude that things frequently do not work out (Chartrand, 1990; Klein, 1990).

Multiple Life Roles Another challenging characteristic shared by many students in this group is that they are almost always juggling multiple roles and responsibilities outside of their role as "student" (Backels & Meashey, 1997; Chartrand, 1990; Donaldson & Graham, 1999; Eppler & Harju, 1997; Fairchild, 2003; Gerson, 1985; Jacobs & King, 2002; Jacoby, 1989; Kasworm & Pike, 1994; Lucas, 2009; Morris, Brooks, & May, 2003; Edwards & Person, 1997; Roksa & Velez, 2012; White, 2002). These multiple roles include spouse, parent, caretaker, and employee and frequently take precedence over the student role

(Deutsch & Schmertz, 2011). One quantitative study demonstrated that being required to perform multiple roles had a negative impact on students, whether those multiple roles were required of them before or after enrollment (Roksa & Velez, 2012). However, some researchers assert that the multitasking required in their daily lives leads nontraditional students to be more successful in their academic endeavors, because they have developed coping mechanisms that more sheltered traditional undergraduates have not been required to develop (Fairchild, 2003; Morris et al., 2003).

Many nontraditional students are working while enrolled in college, and for them work is often the highest priority (Berker, Horn, & Carroll, 2003; Donaldson & Graham, 1999; Kerka, 1995). This creates a very different experience for these students. Berker, Horn, and Carroll referred to "employees who study" and compared them to "students who work." They found that most nontraditional students are employees who study, considering work their main activity, while traditional students who happen to have jobs consider themselves students who work. A number of challenges are inherent to the employee who studies, especially the difficulty in acquiring financial aid due to the student employee's part-time enrollment and full-time employment status. Part-time students are un-likely to qualify for aid, and even if they attend full time, the amount or aid they qualify for can be lower due to the income they receive from their job (Hart, 2003). These employees who study are likely to attend community colleges, aim-ing for an associate's degree and majoring in vocational and technical fields such as computer science and business (Berker, Horn, & Carroll, 2003; Compton & Cox, 2006). The Berker, Horn, & Carroll (2003) study showed that these students are also far more likely to drop out, especially within the first year of enrollment.

Choice of Vocational Track Because of the importance of work in their lives, many nontraditional students are most likely to pursue a vocational track (Compton & Cox, 2006). Their motivation is different from that of tradi-tional undergraduates, and there is often a close connection between their particular educational goals and their careers (Chao & Good, 2004; Eppler & Harju, 1997). Because there is such a close connection between what they learn and their work experience, they tend to emphasize learning goals over performance goals such as grades and grade point averages (Chao & Good, 2004; Eppler & Harju, 1997; Jacoby, 2000b; Klein, 1990; Morris et al., 2003; Shields, 1993; Whitt, 1994; Wolfgang & Dowling, 1981). Although being pulled in so many directions leads to more negative strain for nontraditional students, it can also lead to significantly more gratification from their aca-demic experience (Gerson, 1985).

Academic Performance This increased gratification might be due in part to the fact that nontraditional students perform better in school than do their traditional counterparts, especially when it comes to traditional measures of academic success such as grades and grade point averages (Capps, 2012; Forbus, Newbold, & Mehta, 2010; Graham, 1998; Hagedorn, 2005; Kasworm, 2005; Morris et al., 2003). Research has shown that nontraditional students tend to be of low socioeconomic status, academically underprepared, and less involved on campus, which would lead traditional models of academic success to suggest that they should perform less well academically, but this has not been shown to be the case. Although pre-college characteristics are poor indicators of future academic success for nontraditional students, marital status and income in adult students explain variability in grades more accurately for this group (Kasworm, 2005). The adult students' improved performance over their traditionally aged peers might be explained by their comparative wealth in personal and work experiences. Applicability of knowledge has been shown to be important to learning, and students with work, life, and family experiences outside of school have an advantage in that area. Being better able to connect classroom learning to real-world scenarios may be the reason that adult students can overcome other deficits and outperform traditional undergraduates (Chao & Good, 2004; Graham, 1998). Research has found that things that are traditionally detrimental to student success, such as first-generation status, can actually be tempered if the student is also an adult returning to school (Gerson, 1985).

Personal Characteristics Other characteristics shared by students in this group include independence, maturity, clear goals, and a lack of participation on campus (Backels & Meashey, 1997; Kerka, 1995). Nontraditional undergraduates exhibit strong ties to their career culture but limited ties to the academic culture of their institution (Kerka, 1995). Social integration at the institutional level is unimportant to them, but the classroom experience is highly salient for this group, and when social integration is measured at the classroom level instead of the institutional level, it has a significant positive effect on nontraditional student retention (Ashar & Skenes, 1993; Kerka, 1995). These findings serve to demonstrate that an understanding of positive and negative factors in the success of traditional undergraduates cannot be applied to the understanding of nontraditional student success.

PERSISTENCE AND GRADUATION OUTCOMES FOR TRADITIONAL VERSUS NONTRADITIONAL STUDENTS

The sheer number of nontraditional students is impressive, but more compelling is how these students fare in comparison to their traditional counterparts. Students with any nontraditional characteristics are far less likely than traditional students to achieve their educational goals (Capps, 2012; Cavote & Kopera-Frye, 2006; Horn & Carroll, 1996). Among students whose stated goal is to obtain a bachelor's degree, 54 percent of traditional students will do so within five years. In comparison, 31 percent of nontraditional students will achieve that goal, and 11 percent of highly nontraditional students will do so. When it comes to leaving college before their degree is complete, 19 percent of traditional students do so within five years, compared to 42 percent of nontraditional students (Choy, 2002). It is important to understand these differences in outcomes.

WHY FOCUS ON NONTRADITIONAL STUDENTS?

We cannot understand nontraditional students by applying to them what we know about traditional students. Quite simply, things that work to improve the success of traditional student do not work for nontraditional students, by and large. Social integration is not nearly as salient a concern for students whose lives are not centered on their college campus (Bean & Metzner, 1985; Chartrand, 1990; Forbus, Newbold, & Mehta, 2010). Researchers do not agree on what *retention* means for these students because their educational goals tend to vary widely and do not always include a credential of any kind (Fincher, 2010). Although research largely agrees about the importance of the first-year experience for traditional undergraduates, there is considerable disagreement in whether that experience is important to nontraditional students at all (Cavote & Kopera-Frye, 2006).

Many of the same factors contribute to success or failure for both types of students, but the relationships between background characteristics and academic outcomes are different, and sometimes opposite. Research shows that pre-college characteristics, so important to predicting success for traditional college students, do not accurately predict outcomes among nontraditional students (Kasworm, 2005). Even the personal and economic benefits of college are not the same across these two groups. Social development is not an important outcome of the nontraditional student experience (Wolfgang & Dowling, 1981). Additionally, the financial benefits of college attendance are much smaller for those who attend later in life (Monks, 1997). Because the two groups are essentially incomparable, a separate understanding must be established for the way in which nontraditional students experience college and make persistence decisions.

Distinct Challenges for Nontraditional Students

Nontraditional students face a variety of challenges that traditional students do not have to conquer. For example, they deal with a time crunch and financial strain that is unique to their situation (Forbus, Newbold, & Mehta, 2010). Additionally, nontraditional students have largely been neglected in American higher education, made to feel invisible and marginalized, and denied the resources they need to succeed (Sissel, Hansman, & Kasworm, 2001). They are moving against the prevailing social norms (dictating that school precedes work over the course of an individual's life) in their decision to return to school, even if those social norms have eased slightly, and they are doing so in an institution designed to facilitate the success of another kind of student entirely—the traditional student (Hagedorn, 2005). Moreover, even though the numbers of nontraditional students are overwhelming, the system is unlikely to change easily or quickly to accommodate them because the residential model of college-going is so intrinsic to higher education in the United States (Jacoby, 2000a). These challenges can be a lot to overcome. Additionally, nontraditional students face challenges that are of particular interest to enrollment managers, specifically those regarding the decision to enroll, receipt of financial aid, and persistence decisions.

The Decision to Enroll Most commonly, research has found that nontraditional college students choose to enroll in school at or immediately following major transitions in their lives (Bers & Smith, 1987; Bradburn, Moen, & Dempster-McClain, 1995; Chao & Good, 2004; Compton & Cox, 2006; Fairchild, 2003; Graham, 1998; Hagedorn, 2005; Phillip & Iris, 1997; Roksa & Velez, 2012; White, 2002). Whereas for traditional undergraduates, enrolling in college is the primary life transition, nontraditional students are typically experiencing at least two significant life events at the same time. This is likely to make the decision to enroll more difficult for the nontraditional student, as well as making college an even greater challenge. One study exploring the negative impact of delayed entry—students who delay are 78 percent less likely to achieve their educational goals than those who enroll on time—found that life course transitions such as widowhood, divorce, and job loss, when introduced as explanatory variables, explain the significant negative impact of delay on degree completion (Roksa & Velez, 2012). Clearly, the intersection of these significant events and college enrollment are important factors in the success or failure of nontraditional students.

Financial Aid Perhaps the most overwhelming challenge faced by nontraditional students is related to finances and financial aid. The financial strain on nontraditional students is significant, and considerably more intense than that placed on traditional college students. Nontraditional students are responsible for their tuition, fees, books, supplies, rent, car or other commuting costs, childcare, and other unavoidable expenses, while traditional undergraduates usually do not experience such extensive financial demands and many receive financial aid (Forbus, Newbold, & Mehta, 2010). Nontraditional students' financial independence contributes directly to the challenges they face related to financial aid. Because nontraditional college students file for financial aid as independent adults, for the most part, limited financial aid funding is available to them. The financial aid for which they qualify is further limited by nontraditional students' existing debts, with which traditional students are far less likely to be burdened (Hart, 2003).

The different attendance patterns of nontraditional students, namely part-time attendance, mean that these students often do not qualify for any financial aid at all (Forbus, Newbold, & Mehta, 2010; Hart, 2003). Nontraditional students' financial responsibilities often extend beyond those of most traditional students. They are responsible for educational expenses and transportation expenses, also while frequently supporting multiple family members and other dependents. This means that they must find a way to pay everything expected of a traditional student in addition to paying for their existing financial commitments, and they must do it with less assistance than traditional students often receive (Hart, 2003).

Additionally, financial aid offices at most colleges and universities are ill equipped to deal with issues that are specific to nontraditional students. Nontraditional students might be divorced, estranged from parents or spouses, recently unemployed, or have multiple dependents draining their personal financial resources. These are complicated issues not faced by most traditional students, and many financial aid officers and counselors frequently do not have the knowledge or training to assist students in dealing with these complications (Hart, 2003). On top of this, financial aid policies that are currently in place at the institutional, state, and federal levels are designed with the traditional college student in mind and rarely make allowances for the life circumstances of nontraditional students (Hagedorn, 2005; Hart, 2003). It is very difficult for nontraditional students to secure the funding they need to ease the burden of college tuition.

Other Challenges Although some assume that it is lack of academic ability that leads nontraditional students to depart from college, multiple studies have found that we cannot attribute higher departure rates to academic performance, because nontraditional students' academic performance does not differ significantly from that of traditional students who are departing with much less frequency (Choy, 2002; Eppler & Harju, 1997; Forbus, Newbold, & Mehta, 2010; Jacoby, 2000a, 2000b). In addition, it appears that nontraditional students' long-term educational goals bear little relationship to short-term persistence decisions (Chartrand, 1992). Moreover, nontraditional students lead complex lives outside of school and having significant external commitments, contributing to increased financial sensitivity and social isolation.

Nontraditional students often have families for which they are responsible, and any number of family dynamics could lead them to suspend their education. The stress and guilt of leaving families, especially children, can lead nontraditional students to conclude that pursuing an education simply is not worth it. When they are in school, nontraditional students are often unable to work as much as they did previously, putting strain on family finances, which compounds the strain also placed there by tuition, book costs, and other fees. These realities of the lives of nontraditional students are certainly responsible for some decisions to leave school (Deutsch & Schmertz, 2011; Phillip & Iris, 1997). Affordability of school is of significant concern to these students, and their sensitivity to financial concerns is considerably greater than that of many traditional students. The typical financial aid model offers built-in incentives to maintain a solid grade point average and to complete one's degree in a timely manner. However, as mentioned, financial aid is largely unavailable to nontraditional students, so those incentives do not exist for them. Additionally, nontraditional students have more significant financial burdens than traditional students, so a lack of financial aid can be detrimental to their pursuit of a college degree (Forbus, Newbold, & Mehta, 2010; Hart, 2003; Taniguchi & Kaufman, 2005).

An additional explanation that has been offered by recent research is the social isolation of nontraditional students (Jacoby, 2000a, 2000b; Taniguchi & Kaufman, 2005; Laird & Cruce, 2009). These findings seem to be in opposition to John Bean and Barbara Metzner's (1985) assertion that social integration factors should have only small influence on the departure of nontraditional students. Social integration apparently has a significant negative relationship with departure; adults in college are more likely to persist if they feel socially tied to their campus's social community (Ashar & Skenes, 1993; Kerka, 1995). Nonetheless, recent research has found that the fact that nontraditional students are essentially limited to classroom interactions negatively effects their degree completion (Taniguchi & Kaufman, 2005). These students' external commitments to jobs and family also play a large part in isolating them amidst their peers, which can lead to the decision to leave school (Hagedorn, 2005; Kasworm, 2010).

A particularly apt metaphor for nontraditional students' college experience is that of a trip to the supermarket. Nontraditional students often feel that they come to their college or university to get what they need and leave as soon as they have it—much like a run to the supermarket. Contributing to this feeling is the fact that most four-year college campuses are physically unwelcoming to students who do not live there (Jacoby, 1989, 2000a, 2000b). Few campuses have places for nonresidential students to store their personal belongings throughout the day, lounges or study areas where they can comfortably spend significant periods of time between classes, convenient parking, or other amenities to make a nontraditional students' time on campus more comfortable. Nontraditional students do not feel welcome on campuses that serve mostly residential students (Spanard, 1990; Graham, 1998).

CONCLUSIONS AND PRINCIPLES OF PRACTICE: HOW ENROLLMENT MANAGERS CAN PROMOTE NONTRADITIONAL STUDENT PERSISTENCE

Studies of the nontraditional student population have increased in frequency and depth, and although there is still much we do not know, practitioners in higher education have a variety of options when it comes to helping these students meet their goals. This section of the chapter describes six principles of practice for enrollment managers to follow in their efforts to promote the persistence of nontraditional students enrolled in their college or university.

Recognize the Reality of Student Demographics

The first step to addressing an issue successfully is recognizing that the issue exists. As stated earlier, 73 percent of college students in the United States are nontraditional in some way (Choy, 2002). One of the best things enrollment managers can do to improve persistence among these students is simply to be aware of this fact. Ernest Pascarella and Patrick Terenzini (1998) put it succinctly when they said we must recognize that "our college campuses are no longer predominantly populated by the students described" in most research (p. 152). Financial aid policies, orientation programs, recruitment efforts, student services, and retention programs are, for the most part, targeted to residential college students, aged 18–24, who are dependent on their parents and attend their college or university full time (Pascarella & Terenzini, 1998). Yet many institutions have yet to make real changes in response to the fact that only 27 percent of college students enrolled today fit that description. It is important to note that many of the challenges faced by nontraditional students are out of institutional control, though institutions can take several to ease the path to success (Capps, 2012).

It is important not only that institutions acknowledge the presence of nontraditional students on campus, but that institutions recognize the singular and separate needs and issues specific to these students (Backels & Meashey, 1997; Chao & Good, 2004). It is not adequate to use programs and approaches designed for traditional students and merely direct them at nontraditional undergraduates (Backels & Meashey, 1997). Much of the work done on college campuses to improve retention today focuses on increased involvement and techniques designed to tie a student to the campus community. This is not an appropriate tool for improving nontraditional student outcomes, because adult and commuter students spend minimal time on campus and are unable to dedicate more time due to external responsibilities and constraints (Graham, 1998).

Be Aware of the Student's Educational Goals

Although it is true that part of an enrollment manager's job is to promote persistence and completion for all enrolled students, this can be a complicated endeavor when it comes to nontraditional students. We cannot assume that every nontraditional student who enrolls is doing so in an effort to earn a credential of some kind (Fincher, 2010). Nontraditional students enroll for a variety of reasons, frequently related to their existing jobs, and although, for many, a credential is what they need to move up in their job, some need only to acquire a new skill, which can be accomplished by enrolling in one or two courses (Chao & Good, 2004; Deutsch & Schmertz, 2011; Phillip & Iris, 1997). If enrollment managers define success for these students as "persistence to degree," they are dooming to failure those students for whom this is not the goal. Clarity is key here. Enrollment managers must communicate clearly with nontraditional students upon their decision to enroll and discuss their educational goals. Additionally, since nontraditional students' lives have many moving parts, enrollment professionals should continue to check in with them throughout their enrollment to determine whether their goals have changed. It is only through this clarity and understanding that enrollment managers can set accurate goals for their institutions' retention rates and help ensure that students accomplish the goals they set for themselves.

Make School Feel Less Like a Supermarket

A key aspect of the nontraditional college experience is the "supermarket" feel it engenders, caused, in part, by the limited interaction between nontraditional students and other campus community members (Laird & Cruce, 2009). A number of commitments outside of school demand the time and attention of nontraditional students, who often have little time to spend on campus outside of required activities—generally classes. Whereas traditional students live their lives on campus, with the luxury of attending additional study sessions, lectures, and social events, nontraditional students lack exposure to such primary agents of socialization at the college or university (Bean and Metzner 1985).

To combat this, enrollment managers can help to make a nontraditional student's trip to campus feel less like a visit to the supermarket and more like a trip to the office or some other place where the student belongs, is productive, and has space to work. This can be accomplished in a variety of ways, which would likely vary by campus. For instance, to counter nontraditional students' sense of being unwelcome visitors, campuses could provide secure places for students to store their belongings, study areas dedicated to commuter students, lounges or break rooms where students could warm up and eat lunches brought to campus. Facilitating increased contact with other community members is a more difficult endeavor, but a start might be to incorporate these spaces designed for nonresidential students into the spaces utilized by other students and faculty members. Creating space for these students but isolating them in an area of campus where they encounter only other nontraditional students would likely be counterproductive.

Focus on the Classroom

When nontraditional students are on campus, they are generally attending a class, but the classroom can be a difficult place for them (Chao & Good, 2004; Taniguchi & Kaufman, 2005). Generally, nontraditional students feel that they do not fit in with other students because of their different lifestyles, priorities, experiences, and life stages. Also, many nontraditional students believe that a stereotype attributed to them paints them as unmotivated, uninvolved, lazy, and uncaring (Jacoby, 2000a, 2000b; Ogren, 2003). In a classroom setting, as elsewhere on campus, many nontraditional students feel that they are on the outside looking in. Moreover, nontraditional students can be especially self-conscious in a mixed-age classroom and report significant anxiety about appearing conspicuously older than their peers (Hagedorn, 2005). Nontraditional students report that classes with more traditional students can be an unpleasant experience, especially socially. Because social relationships formed outside of class are likely to carry over into the classroom, nontraditional students have difficulty inserting themselves into class discussions, finding partners for class projects, and utilizing peer support for difficult material. Nontraditional students say that this makes them feel disenfranchised and confirms for them what they already feared: that they do not belong in school (Kasworm, 2010).

For these reasons, teaching faculty must be brought in to the conversation about nontraditional student persistence. The classroom is an important place for nontraditional students because it is where they spend the majority of their time on campus, and the only interactions taking place in the classroom occur between student and classmates and student and instructor. Because nontraditional students often feel disenfranchised by their classmates, the relationships developed with faculty members in the classroom are likely to be very influential. Enrollment management is a campus-wide endeavor and enrollment managers can work to involve faculty members, especially where nontraditional students are concerned. Information can be powerful here: enrollment managers can inform teaching faculty of the importance of the classroom to nontraditional students, the importance of faculty relationships, and the challenges nontraditional students face. Faculty relationships have been found to be the most significant campus relationships for nontraditional students

(Kasworm, 2010; Tan & Pope, 2007), and facilitating these relationships can be a step toward improving outcomes for these students (Jacoby, 2000b; Laird & Cruce, 2009).

Alter Standard Programs to Benefit Nontraditional Students

Considerable challenges are involved in restructuring institutional offerings for a population of students with different needs, goals, and priorities, and doing so will require vast systemic changes over the long term. However, smaller changes can be made to some existing programs to promote persistence and completion that will make them more beneficial to nontraditional students. As discussed, the choice to enroll in college often coincides with other major life events for nontraditional students (Bers & Smith, 1987; Bradburn, Moen, & Dempster-McClain, 1995; Chao & Good, 2004; Compton & Cox, 2006; Fairchild, 2003; Graham, 1998; Hagedorn, 2005; Phillip & Iris, 1997; Roksa & Velez, 2012; White, 2002). Student life staff are already very closely attuned to the stressors experienced by traditional students enrolling in college, but it would be beneficial if these staff members were more aware of and engaged in the struggles faced by nontraditional students choosing to start or continue their college education.

First-year experience courses or orientation programs should be offered or altered to meet the specific needs of nontraditional students. One study examined the impact of a traditional first-year experience course on the persistence of nontraditional students and found the course to be ineffective at improving the persistence of nontraditional students (Cavote & Kopera-Frye, 2007). In order for these types of courses or orientations better to serve nontraditional students, and thereby institutions through increased retention rates, they need to be tailored to nontraditional student needs and concerns. It would be beneficial to include money management, time management, study skills, and other concerns of importance to nontraditional students, because it is often these stressors that lead nontraditional students to depart. As discussed, nontraditional students often have money concerns above and beyond those of their traditional peers; they typically have more demands on their time in the form of dependents and full-time jobs; and, for many, it has been years since they were students, so the skills required to succeed may be rusty (Cavote & Kopera-Frye, 2007; Hart, 2003). Additionally, involving nontraditional students' families in the orientations in some way could help to bridge the gap between the students' two worlds and teach their families how best to offer support in a difficult and stressful period (Chao & Good, 2004; Deutsch & Schmertz, 2011).

Improve Financial Aid Services to Nontraditional Students

Difficulties with financial aid have a significant impact on whether nontraditional students persist (Hart, 2003; Taniguchi & Kaufman, 2005). Hart makes many suggestions for improved financial aid practices. Among these suggestions for institutions is the early availability of financial awards. This will give non-traditional students time to determine how much they will receive, what they will owe, and how they will make up the difference without a lot of rush or pressure. Also, continuing students should get timely information about the next year's awards so that they are able to register in advance and secure the classes they want or need. When account statements are issued, financial aid should be reflected on them. This will require business offices and financial aid offices to coordinate their schedules, but it will be helpful in reducing the stress level of nontraditional students and will decrease the likelihood that a student will leave because of inaccurate information. This may seem fairly basic, but response rates to inquiries made of the financial aid office should be higher than they currently are and the process should be streamlined so that fewer questions are required when filling out financial aid forms (Hart, 2003).

Finally, colleges and universities should keep in mind that many nontraditional students are taking on the expense of college while also being responsible for significant personal expenses and dependents. Moreover, because of their complicated lives off campus, many nontraditional students are forced to enroll part-time (Taniguchi & Kaufman, 2005). In addition, nontraditional students are less likely to receive the financial aid they need (Berker, Horn, & Carroll, 2003). Institutions interested in increasing the persistence of these students should consider offering aid to students who attend part-time, or offering aid that helps students defray expenses beyond tuition. Before implementing full-scale changes of this kind, institutions might benefit from offering this type of aid on a limited basis and tracking the results. All of these suggestions for institutions seek to eliminate the situation in which a nontraditional student leaves school due to avoidable financial aid snafus (Hart, 2003).

CONCLUSION

The term "nontraditional" seems inaccurate to describe a group of students who make up the vast majority of the American student population and have been present in American higher education for a significant period of time (Ogren, 2003). Despite their ubiquity, these students are generally underserved in their postsecondary endeavors. They struggle to enroll, to pay for school, and to accomplish their educational goals. Although many of the factors impacting their success are related to their lives off campus, there are things enrollment managers can do to promote persistence and goal attainment for nontraditional students. Small steps on individual campuses have the potential to make real differences in the education nontraditional students receive.

References

Ashar, H., & Skenes, R. (1993). Can Tinto's student departure model be applied to nontraditional students? *Adult Education Quarterly, 43*(2), 90–100.

Backels, S., & Meashey, L. E. (1997). Anxiety, depression and the 4.0: Brief therapy with high-achieving, nontraditional female students. *Journal of College Student Psychotherapy, 12*(1), 45–56.

Bean, J. P., & Metzner, B. S. (1985). A conceptual model of nontraditional undergraduate student attrition. *Review of Educational Research, 55*(4), 485–540.

Berker, A., & Horn, L., & Carroll, C. D. (2003). *Work First, Study Second: Adult Undergraduates Who Combine Employment and Postsecondary Enrollment.* Postsecondary Educational Descriptive Analysis Reports, U.S. Department of Education National Center for Education Statistics.

Bers, T., & Smith, K. (1987). College choice and the nontraditional student. *Community College Review, 15*, 39–45.

Bradburn, E. M., Moen, P., & Dempster-McClain, D. (1995). Women's return to school following the transition to motherhood. *Social Forces, 73*(4), 1517–1551.

Braxton, J. M., Doyle, W. R., Hartley, H. V., III, Hirschy, A. S., Jones, W. A., & McLendon, M. K. (2013). *Rethinking College Student Retention.* San Francisco: Jossey-Bass.

Braxton, J. M., Hirschy, A. S., & McClendon, S. A. (2004). Understanding and Reducing College Student Departure. *ASHE-ERIC Higher Education Report, 30*(3).

Capps, R. (2012). Supporting adult-student persistence in community colleges. *Change: The Magazine of Higher Learning, 44*(2), 38–44.

Cavote, S., & Kopera-Frye, K. (2006). Non-traditional student persistence and first year experience courses. *Journal of College Student Retention: Research, Theory, & Practice, 8*(4), 477–489.

Chao, R., & Good, G. (2004). Nontraditional students' perspectives on college education: A qualitative study. *Journal of College Counseling, 7*(1), 5–12.

Chartrand, J. M. (1990). A causal analysis to predict the personal and academic adjustment of nontraditional students. *Journal of Counseling Psychology, 37*(1), 65–73.

Chartrand, J. M. (1992). An empirical test of a model of nontraditional student adjustment. *Journal of Counseling Psychology, 39*(2), 193–202.

Choy, S. (2002). *Nontraditional Undergraduates.* (NCES 2002–012). Washington, DC: U.S. Department of Education, National Center for Education Statistics.

Compton, J. I., & Cox, E. (2006). Adult learners in transition. *New Directions for Student Services, 2006*(114), 73–80.

Deutsch, N. L., & Schmertz, B. (2011). "Starting from ground zero:" Constraints and experiences of adult women returning to college. *The Review of Higher Education, 34*(3), 477–504.

Donaldson, J. F., & Graham, S. (1999). A model of college outcomes for adults. *Adult Education Quarterly*, *50*(1), 24–40.

Edwards, R., & Person, D. (1997). Retaining the Adult Student: The Role of Admission Counselors. *Journal of College Admission*, *154*, 18–21.

Eppler, M. A., & Harju, B. L. (1997). Achievement motivation goals in relation to academic performance in traditional and nontraditional college students. *Research in Higher Education*, *38*(5), 557–573.

Fairchild, E. E. (2003). Multiple Roles of Adult Learners. *New Directions for Student Services*, *2003*(102), 11–16.

Fincher, M. (2010). Adult student retention: A practical approach to retention improvement through learning enhancement. *The Journal of Continuing Higher Education*, *58*(1), 12–18.

Forbus, P., Newbold, J. J., & Mehta, S. S. (2010). A study of non-traditional and traditional students in terms of their time management behaviors, stress factors, and coping strategies. *Proceedings of the Academy of Educational Leadership* (Vol. 15, pp. 67–72). Las Vegas.

Gerson, J. M. (1985). Women returning to school: The consequences of multiple roles. *Sex Roles*, *13*(1/2), 77–92.

Graham, S. W. (1998). Adult growth in college: The effects of age and educational ethos. *Journal of College Student Development*, *39*(3), 239–250.

Hagedorn, L. S. (2005). Square pegs: Adult students and their "fit" in postsecondary institutions. *Change*, *37*(1), 22–29.

Hart, N. K. (2003). Best practices in providing nontraditional students with both academic and financial support. *New Directions for Higher Education*, *2003*(121), 99–106.

Horn, L. J., & Carroll, C. D. (1996). *Nontraditional Undergraduates: Trends in Enrollment from 1986 to 1992 and Persistence and Attainment Among 1989–90 Beginning Postsecondary Students*. Statistical Analysis Report. Washington, DC: National Center for Education Statistics.

Jacobs, J. A., & King, R. B. (2002). Age and college completion: Life-history analysis of women aged 15–44. *Sociology of Education*, *75*(3), 211–230.

Jacoby, B. (1989). The Student as Commuter: Developing a Comprehensive Institutional Response. *ASHE-ERIC Higher Education Report, 7*. Washington, DC: School of Education and Human Development, The George Washington University.

Jacoby, B. (2000a). Why involve commuter students in learning? *New Directions for Higher Education*, 109, 3–12.

Jacoby, B. (2000b). Involving commuter students in learning: Moving from rhetoric to reality. *New Directions for Higher Education*, 109, 81–87.

Kasworm, C. E. (2005). Adult student identity in an intergenerational community college classroom. *Adult Education Quarterly*, *56*(1), 3–20.

Kasworm, C. E. (2010). Adult learners in a research university: Negotiating undergraduate student identity. *Adult Education Quarterly*, *60*(2), 143–160.

Kasworm, C. E., & Pike, G. R. (1994). Adult undergraduate students: Evaluating the appropriateness of a traditional model of academic performance. *Research in Higher Education, 35*(6), 689–710.

Kerka, S. (1995). *Adult Learner Retention Revisited.* ERIC Digest No. 166. Columbus, OH: ERIC Clearinghouse on Adult Career and Vocational Education.

Kim, K. (2002). ERIC review: Exploring the meaning of "nontraditional" at the community college. *Community College Review, 30*(1), 74–89.

Klein, J. D. (1990). An analysis of the motivational characteristics of college reentry students. *College Student Journal, 24,* 281–286.

Laird, T. F. N., & Cruce, T. M. (2009). Individual and environmental effects of part-time enrollment status on student-faculty interaction and self-reported gains. *The Journal of Higher Education, 80*(3), 290–314.

Lucas, A. P. (2009). *Measuring the perception of mattering for adult students at California State University, Sacramento.* (Unpublished master's thesis), Sacramento, CA: California State University.

Metzner, B. S., & Bean, J. P. (1987). The estimation of a conceptual model of nontraditional undergraduate student attrition. *Research in Higher Education, 27*(1), 15–38.

Monks, J. (1997). The impact of college timing on earnings. *Economics of Education Review, 16*(4), 419–423.

Morris, E. A., Brooks, P. R., & May, J. L. (2003). The relationship between achievement goal orientation and coping style: Traditional vs. nontraditional college students. *College Student Journal, 37*(1), 3–8.

Ogren, C. A. (2003). Rethinking the "nontraditional" student from a historical perspective: State normal schools in the late nineteenth and early twentieth centuries. *The Journal of Higher Education, 74*(6), 640–664.

Pascarella, E. T., & Terenzini, P. T. (1998). Studying college students in the 21st century: Meeting new challenges. *The Review of Higher Education, 21*(2), 151–165.

Phillip, L., & Iris, M. (1997). Adults who do it all. *Adult Learning, 8*(5/6), 17–31.

Roksa, J., & Velez, M. (2012). A late start: Delayed entry, life course transitions and bachelor's degree completion. *Social Forces, 90*(3), 769–794.

Shields, N. (1993). Attribution processes and stages of adult life development among adult university students. *Journal of Applied Social Psychology, 23*(16), 1321–1336.

Sissel, P., Hansman, C., & Kasworm, C. (2001). The politics of neglect: Adult learners in higher education. *New Directions for Adult and Continuing Education, 2001*(91), 17–28.

Spanard, J. M. A. (1990). Beyond intent: Reentering college to complete the degree. *Review of Educational Research, 60*(3), 309–344.

Tan, D. L., & Pope, M. I. (2007). Participation in co-curricular activities: Nontraditional student perspectives. *College and University, 83*(1), 2–9.

Taniguchi, H., & Kaufman, G. (2005). Degree completion among nontraditional college students. *Social Science Quarterly*, *86*(4), 912–927.

White, J. (2002). Adult women in community colleges. *Catalyst*, *31*(2), 19–21.

Whitt, E. J. (1994). Encouraging Adult Learner Involvement. *NASPA Journal*, *31*(4), 309–318.

Wolfgang, M. E., & Dowling, W. D. (1981). Differences in motivation of adult and younger undergraduates. *The Journal of Higher Education*, *52*(6), 640–648.

CHAPTER 18

The Role of the Institution in Increasing College Student Persistence

Mary Ziskin
Jerome A. Lucido
Jacob P. K. Gross
Donald Hossler
Emily Chung, and
Vasti Torres

Over the years, and certainly with vigor for the past forty years, scholars have considered economic, psychological, sociological, and organizational theories to craft explanations for why students depart from higher education institutions (Braxton, 2000; Tinto, 2005). Vincent Tinto's groundbreaking Interactionalist Theory (2005), with its focus on student integration, is perhaps the most foundational work, and one that helped to launch a rich and continuous examination of personal, institutional, economic, and academic factors that influence student departure (Tinto, 1975, 1987, 1993). Often this work depicted the institution as a static entity within which the student either integrated or did not fit. This focus on the student has not yielded increased student success rates; therefore, it is important to consider the role that institutional policies and programs play in the student persistence equation.

One effort to capture the breadth of research identified a compendium of eight themes of student retention: intentions and attitudes, institutional fit and commitment, academics, social factors, bureaucratic factors, the external environment, the student's background, and money and finance (Bean, 2005). Further, John Braxton's (2000) edited volume offers a thorough examination of the "student departure puzzle." Beginning with a re-examination of Tinto's theory and moving to new theoretical directions, Braxton (2000) drew upon numerous scholars to call for expanded approaches to the Tinto model and for investigation beyond the constructs and weaknesses of that framework.

Current interest in student persistence remains high, and this led us, as co-authors on a recent College Board funded research report, to observe the following:

> Facing ever-increasing budgetary challenges, colleges and universities have sought to stabilize revenue streams by improving student retention on campus. More and more states are tying funding for institutions to retention and graduation rates. Furthermore, these same measures are key criterion for the widely followed national rankings of colleges and universities published by *U.S. News & World Report.* These and other developments demonstrate—for institutions as well as for policymakers—the importance of student persistence and the need for reliable, research-based information about it (College Board, 2011, p. 2).

Unfortunately, the attention paid to student persistence by researchers, policy makers, and institutions has not translated to increases in student progress. Nationally, completion rates among first-time enrollees at public four-year institutions remain modestly above 50 percent, while the comparable figure for those enrolling in public two-year institutions is just above 25 percent (Knapp et al., 2005).Overall, less than a third of the U.S. adult population hold a bachelor's degree (U.S. Census Bureau, 2009), and graduation rates for both public and private postsecondary institutions have declined in recent decades (ACT, 2009).

As Tinto (2005) noted, "The facts are unavoidable. Though access to higher education has increased and gaps in access between groups decreased, rates of college completion generally and gaps in completion between high- and low-income students have not followed suit" (p. 12). The picture is clear then. Despite decades of research that has identified and clarified reasons for student departure, the student success needle has not moved appreciably forward. It is time, as Tinto and others noted (Kalsbeek, 2013; Seidman, 2012; Tinto, 2010), to move beyond current theories and to formulate institutional actions.

Unfortunately, existing literature on research and practice provides little guidance on the role of institutional policies and practices in student persistence. Nor does the literature address efforts at improvement (Braxton, Hirschy, & McClendon, 2004; College Board, 2011). Specifically, research is needed on the extent to which institutions organize themselves to address student progress and the nature of those efforts. Are there formal mechanisms in place for planning, executing, and evaluating strategies and tactics aimed at increasing student progress? Moreover, what levels of intensity characterize institutions' efforts to improve student persistence, and how does this critical intensity of effort play a role in improving student outcomes? (College Board, 2011)

In response to this gap, this chapter presents the results of three studies directed at institutional organization and efforts to promote student academic success. The first two of these studies are national in scope, one aimed at four-year institutions and the other at two-year institutions. They examine how and to what degree two- and four-year institutions organize to promote student persistence. In doing so, these studies provide a foundation for additional research on institutional effort, intensity, and efficacy, and they provide a useful guide for institutional benchmarking. Following our presentation of these results, we provide two brief case study examinations of policy implementation, which demonstrate that variation in implementation can make a difference in how policies and practices affect student success.

THE COLLEGE BOARD STUDY ON STUDENT RETENTION: TWO NATIONAL SURVEYS

As a part of the larger College Board Study on Student Retention conducted from 2005 through 2012, researchers at the Indiana University Project on Academic Success (PAS) and the University of Southern California Center for Enrollment Research, Policy, and Practice (CERPP) collaborated on two national surveys focused on postsecondary institutions' efforts to increase student retention and other student success outcomes. One survey, the Survey of Community College Structures for Student Success (SCCSSS), focused on policies, practices, and organizational structures in place at community colleges throughout the United States (College Board, 2012), while the other survey, entitled the Survey of Student Retention Practices (SSRP), focused on four-year institutions across the country (College Board, 2011). These studies offer insight into the question of how institutions play a role in student success, as they were predicated on two central goals: (1) to understand the extent to which institutions were engaging in selected policies and practices, and (2) to explore whether these practices were associated with improved student success outcomes. The surveys were administered via e-mail to 1,064 community colleges (SCCSSS) and 1,484 four-year institutions (SSRP) nationwide. SCCSSS yielded a 22 percent response rate (237 institutions), while the SSRP response rate was 30 percent, with 441 institutions responding. Survey responses were supplemented with secondary data drawn from the Integrated Postsecondary Education Data System (IPEDS). These data included information on the institutions' retention rates, demographics, and financial aid from federal sources.

CONCEPTUAL FRAMEWORKS

The SCCSSS and SSRP surveys consider the role of the institution in the student persistence equation. Although this type of research is not meant to abandon the focus on student characteristics, it does illustrate that research is incomplete if it does not consider the synergistic nature of persistence as encompassing both the student and the institution.

In this line of inquiry, we drew on established research, theory, and practice-oriented literature to propose a framework of institutional structures, policies, and practices for further investigation via the surveys. For the national survey of four-year institutions (SSRP), we drew primarily on the policy levers outlined by Braxton and colleagues (Braxton, Hirschy, & McClendon, 2004; Braxton & McClendon, 2001–2002; Braxton & Mundy, 2001–2002). Accordingly, the survey's framework included the following policy levers for student retention:

- Coordination and intensity of institutional efforts
- Structures and practices that have been shown to reduce racial discrimination and prejudice on campus
- Fair implementation of administrative and academic regulations
- Directing students, through academic advising, toward satisfactory course experiences
- Support and development of active and collaborative learning strategies in the classroom
- Orientation and residential life practices that support frequent and significant student interactions with peers
- Provision of need-based financial aid

For the survey of two-year institutions (SCCSSS), we took a similar approach but focused on the contexts in which community colleges operate. Recently, discussions about the strain on community colleges' institutional capacity has come to the fore as they fulfill multiple missions and, in particular, grapple with rising enrollments in the context of significant budget cuts (Dundar et al., 2011; Mullin, 2010). Specifically in terms of retention, transfer, and degree completion, community colleges in comparison to four-year institutions serve a broad range of student populations and face challenges specific to their multifaceted roles as institutions. These include enrolling relatively high proportions of academically underprepared students, part-time students, and adult learners. At the same time, many students enter community colleges with the aim of completing a bachelor's degree, and many successful two-to-four-year transfer students leave community colleges without first completing a two-year credential (Shapiro et al., 2012). These complexities affect community colleges' outcomes, and within a context of increasing scrutiny on institutional account-ability and the national college completion agenda, researchers and policy makers are obligated to do a better job of taking these realities into account. Community colleges implement a great array of student success programs and support services given the higher rates of part-time enrollment, lower academic preparation, limited student financial resources, and the need to cultivate deep-er student engagement and faculty and peer interaction (Crisp & Taggart, 2013).

We based the framework primarily on the national-scale efforts of Achiev-ing the Dream and the Community College Survey of Student Engagement (CCSSE), and we adapted Braxton and colleagues' policy levers to fit the insti-tutional roles and conditions informing community college practice and policy (see Figure 18.1).

In this chapter, we focus on a subset of our results from the two survey studies, comparing findings on four key practices selected from the surveys' conceptual frameworks. In the following section we highlight results that were common for both SCCSSS and SSRP and are also consistent with the literature used in the frameworks for the surveys: (1) student orientation, and (2) early alert practices, as well as on two more broadly informed areas: (3) fostering a positive climate for diversity, and (4) coordination of student success efforts. We look at results in these four areas as examples that speak to the multiple levels that institutions must operate within simultaneously, in order to "move

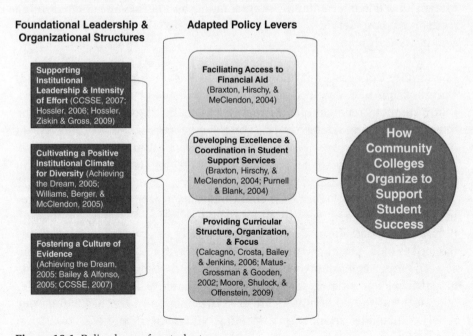

Figure 18.1 Policy levers for student success

the needle" on student success outcomes (McClenney, 2013). Although these four practices do not represent the full collection of findings from the studies, we include them here as a set of examples for discussion. These four practices figure prominently in the literature on institutional student success efforts and were selected to provide an overview of the two studies' findings. In addition, examining these practices will help to illustrate a central point of this chapter— that is, that there is variation in implementation as shown in the survey results.

In the discussion that follows, we present the collected findings from both studies regarding each practice in turn. By highlighting findings on community college practices found from the SCCSSS study first, followed by the SSRP study findings from four-year institutions, in each section, our aim is to illustrate (1) the range of practices and structures in place at institutions nationally, and (2) the variation in how these efforts are implemented.

Orientation

Student orientation programs are often a vehicle for institutions to help students make the transition to college, form a strong relationship with the institution, and gain an understanding of how to succeed and complete a degree at the institution (Braxton, McKinney, & Reynolds, 2006; Hossler, 2006; Mayhew, Vanderlinden, & Kim, 2010; Overland & Rentz, 2004; Patton, Morelon, Whitehead, & Hossler, 2006; Upcraft, Gardner, & Barefoot, 2005). Moreover, community colleges have in recent years brought increased attention to student orientation programming as one avenue for providing student support services through a multifaceted approach (Zeidenberg, Jenkins, & Calcagno, 2007).

Community Colleges Confirming findings from earlier studies (CCSSE, 2012; Upcraft, Gardner, & Barefoot, 2005), nearly all responding two-year and four-year institutions reported offering student orientation programs. However, the intensity of these programs varied in terms of being required for students and including a meeting an advisor. Figure 18.2 shows results from the SCCSSS survey of community colleges, highlighting responses on student orientation programs at participating community colleges.

Results shown in Figure 18.2 confirmed that nearly all responding community colleges, regardless of enrollment size, offered student orientation programs in some form. Looking more closely at the structures defining the orientation programs, however, we noted that less than 60 percent of responding community colleges required first-time, first-year students to participate in student orientation programming. Likewise, just under 60 percent of the community colleges participating in the SCCSSS survey reported including an individual meeting with an academic advisor as part of orientation.

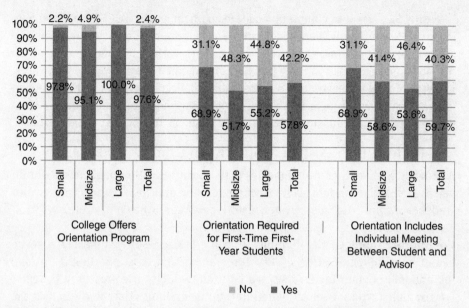

Figure 18.2 Community college orientation offerings, displayed by enrollment size[1]

[1] Note that in the SCCSSS study, institutional enrollment size was defined as the number of FTE (twelve-month full-time equivalent enrollment: 2008–2009); small: 1,999 or less (36.4 percent of the population, or 24.6 percent of the sample); midsize: 2,000–4,499 (30.7 percent of the population, 36.9 percent of the sample); large: 4,500 or above (33.0 percent of the population, 38.6 percent of the sample).

Four-Year Institutions Results of the SSRP study of four-year institutions similarly showed that although four-year institutions almost universally offered orientation programs, the details of implementation varied more widely. Among responding four-year institutions, for example, 37 percent reported having an orientation program lasting through the end of the first semester, while nearly half (47.1 percent) reported shorter orientation programs lasting two days or less. Although guidance is missing from the literature showing the optimal length of orientation programs, it may be reasonable to conclude that longer programs may cover topics in more depth.

Early Alert and Advising Practices

Early alert practices can aid in retention and student success efforts by systematically identifying students who are at greater risk of dropping out. The collection and examination of midterm grades, for example, in order to intervene and provide students with appropriate advising and academic support can be an effective early alert mechanism (Beck & Davidson, 2001; CCSSE, 2007; Gardenhire-Crooks, Collado, & Ray, 2006; Jenkins, Ellwein, Wachen, Kerrigan, & Cho, 2009; Reisberg, 1999).

Nearly 52 percent of community colleges participating in SCCSSS reported having some form of early alert system in place. Importantly, however, the depth of follow-through built into the early alert practices varied, with 30 percent of the respondents indicating that they had not implemented these early alert practices. Results from the survey of four-year institutions reflect less variation in implementation, with about 60 percent collecting midterm grades, and all of these implementing follow-up contact with students identified as having low midterm grades.

Cultivating a Positive Institutional Climate for Diversity

A growing body of literature indicates that a positive institutional climate for diversity is linked to student achievement, retention, and completion, especially for students of color (Hurtado, Alvarez, Guillermo-Wann, Cuellar, & Arellano, 2012).

Community Colleges Key findings from the SCCSSS study indicated that the extent and implementation of structures and practices supporting a positive institutional climate for diversity varied quite widely in community colleges. For example, across a set of related questions we found that about half of the responding colleges were engaged with practices supporting a positive climate for diversity. As shown in Figure 18.3, 49 percent offered faculty development programming focused on racial and cultural diversity on campus. Similarly, just under half (46 percent) reported having a campus committee charged with assessing campus climate for racial and cultural diversity. Forty-nine percent of responding institutions indicated they had conducted a formal assessment of campus climate for racial and cultural diversity in the past ten years.

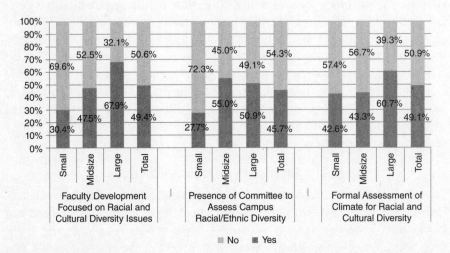

Figure 18.3 Community colleges' practices for cultural and racial diversity, displayed by enrollment size

Four-Year Institutions SSRP survey findings indicated that institutional efforts to create a positive climate for diversity also varied widely among four-year institutions. Of the 441 institutions participating in the SSRP survey, 38.7 percent rated their institution's structures for support of the retention of students of color as "more extensive than similar institutions," while 20.1 percent rated these efforts as lower than those found at similar institutions. Results from a parallel question asking respondents to rate their institution's structures in place to improve the campus racial climate showed a similar pattern, with 38.3 percent rating their institution higher than similar institutions and 17.7 percent estimating campus efforts as less extensive than those at peer institutions. Moreover, in a logistic regression analysis focused on whether structures were associated with higher student success outcomes, we found that survey responses on the structures in place to support the retention of students of color were significantly and positively associated with higher than predicted retention rate at the institutional level (see Table 18.1).

The significant and positive relationship between support for the retention of students of color and a higher than predicted retention rate suggests that institutions benefit from efforts to serve the multiple needs of a diverse student body. Other findings—results related to the retention coordinator's authority, for example—also hold important campus policy implications and are discussed further in the next section. Another result shows semester-length orientation courses to be a negative and significant factor predicting higher than predicted retention. This result is counterintuitive but may suggest that students' experiences in these course-length programs may not always match with program goals. This finding could imply the need for institutions to consider the many ways first-year students interact with, and potentially find support from, multiple aspects of their experience.

Coordination and Intensity of Institutional Effort

Finally, both studies of institutional practices designed to bolster student success provided a view of how colleges and universities organize themselves to improve student retention, completion, and transfer outcomes. One important part of this question centers on the intensity of effort, or the extent of structures and resources dedicated to efforts across campus. Another key aspect lies in the intentionality and coordination of these efforts (Hossler, 2006).

Community Colleges In the SCCSSS study, community college results showed that 68 percent of responding institutions reported having a coordinator, but the majority of these (64.6 percent) had little to no authority to fund new initiatives. We also examined the extent to which a culture of evidence was present at community colleges by assessing the experiences of those working directly with student success efforts. Study findings suggested that the majority

Table 18.1: Effects of institutional variables on likelihood of having a higher than predicted retention rate (four-year institutions)

Variable	β	Sig.	Odds ratio
Availability of a retention coordinator	-1.622	**	0.197
Authority to implement new initiatives	0.409	*	1.505
Availability of a formal, written plan at institutional level	-0.231		0.794
Availability of an orientation program that extends through first semester of classes	-1.057	***	0.347
Institution flags courses with high percent of Ds, Fs, or withdrawals	-0.487		0.615
Availability of academic support programs	0.130		1.139
Having structures in place to support retention of students of color	0.412	**	1.510
Constant	-1.906		
Nagelkerke	0.133		
N = 188			

$p < 0.01$*** $p < 0.05$** $p < 0.10$*

of community colleges are cultivating regular engagement with data. For example, 83 percent of SCCSSS respondents indicated that their administration prompted campus-wide discussions focused on student success "several times or more per year." However, only about 52 percent reported these discussions included data "to a great extent." Basing decisions and discussions in data can be understood as an indication of a pervasive culture of evidence on campus. These results suggest that although explicit campus-wide discussions centered on improving student success occur, frequently at a large majority of the participating community colleges (83 percent), a much smaller proportion (52 percent) reported this kind of culture-of-evidence use of data.

Four-Year Institutions In the study of four-year institutions, 74 percent of responding institutions reported having a student retention coordinator. However, the reported FTE dedicated for the position was often low. Only 18.5 percent of institutions with a coordinator dedicated more than 0.5 FTE to the role. Furthermore, few institutions indicated that retention coordinators had programmatic or funding authority associated with the position (15.0 and 5.4 percent, respectively). In addition, as shown in the logistic regression results discussed earlier, higher levels of authority and resources in the hands of a retention coordinator were associated with higher than predicted retention rates.

CONCLUSIONS AND IMPLICATIONS OF THE COLLEGE BOARD STUDIES

These studies' findings show that community colleges and four-year institutions are actively organizing for student success. Sizable majorities of participating community colleges and four-year colleges and universities offer orientation programs, while smaller majorities of institutions reported engaging in early warning practices. Among community colleges participating in SCCSSS, just under half reported that they engaged in faculty development and assessment practices associated with fostering a positive climate for diversity. Large majorities of two- and four-year institutions in both studies reported having a retention coordinator on campus. Even more important than these points, however, is the fact that the results from these studies reflect variation in the quality and depth of these structures and practices. Given this variation and the complexity of the issues, it remains unclear whether institutions' current efforts as implemented are equal to the task of increasing student retention and other student success outcomes. Consequently, we believe that this research points to the need for more in-depth understanding of the variation in the quality of implementation at the institutional level, and also of whether practices "work" (that is, to what extent are they associated with increased outcomes).

In the next section, we consider two case studies that explore implementation of institutional efforts for student success in further detail to show how this kind of information on programs and institutional practices can help to further our understanding of how institutions can make a difference in student success.

FINDINGS FROM THE IPAS IMPLEMENTATION STUDIES

Jeffrey L. Pressman and Aaron Wildavsky (1984), in their important study *Implementation* wrote, "A policy's value therefore must be measured not only in terms of its appeal, but also in light of its implementability" (p. xv). Their study was guided by their desire to understand how policies and programs conceived at the federal level differed in practice when implemented at the *street level*. Likewise, variation in implementing student success efforts impacts whether policies and practices succeed in improving student outcomes.

As demonstrated in the SSRP and SCCSSS survey studies, there is variation in the quality of implementation of student success efforts. It follows, then, that understanding the complexity of implementation is central to learning more about the institution's role in improving student success.

In the following sections, we present two examples of institutional actions on policy levers relevant to student retention (that is, orientation and advising) implemented and evaluated as a part of the statewide, Lumina-funded Indiana Project on Academic Success (IPAS) study. Through these examples, we explore how variation in implementation can make a difference in whether policies and practices effectively improve student success outcomes. Two case studies are presented as policy and practice exemplars. Both are positive exemplars but distinct in the context for implementation: (1) A discussion of an orientation program developed as a result of several concerns about student success at Ivy Tech Community College of Indiana (ITCCI) in Richmond, Indiana and (2) a major choice program developed as part of a Life Calling initiative at a small, religiously affiliated Midwestern university. Extant research points to the potential relationships between orientation as well as major choice and retention, which we discuss briefly next.

As noted earlier, in our discussion of the College Board survey studies, student orientation is a widely practiced programmatic structure through which institutions aim to support students' transition to college. Evidence of student orientation programs' link to retention has long been cited in research studies (see, for example, Boudreau & Kromrey, 1994; Glass & Garrett, 1995; Jenkins, Bailey, Crosta, Leinbach, Marshall, Soonachan, & Van Noy, 2006; Murtaugh, Burns, & Schuster, 1999). Moreover, orientation programs can provide a vehicle through which students can meet with faculty, practitioners, and each other and form bonds outside of the classroom.

The findings are mixed with respect to major choice and retention. Rick Kroc, Rich Howard, Pat Hull, and Doug Woodard (1997) found that institutional climate rather than individual programs appeared to be more important to success and adamantly stressed that the "mythology" surrounding undeclared students and lack of success was erroneous, as undeclared students graduated at the same rate as their declared peers. By contrast, Linda Serra Hagedorn, William Maxwell, and Preston Hampton's (2001) work on the retention of African-American men at a community college found that early identification of a major was a factor that predicted success. Similarly, white students who were undeclared were found by Edward St. John and colleagues (2004) to be less likely to persist.

Orientation at Ivy Tech Richmond

IPAS collaborated with Ivy Tech Community College of Indiana (ITCCI) to facilitate and evaluate a new mandatory orientation program for all students new to the ITCCI Richmond campus. The orientation content revolved around three challenges identified by staff and faculty as barriers to retention: the needs of first-generation students, the provision and reinforcement of academic support, and students' knowledge about vital aspects of financial aid.

The orientation program was seen as a means to increase students' academic literacy, thereby addressing needs in the three preceding areas. The campus team defined academic literacy as practical knowledge about college processes and services. With greater levels of academic literacy, the team believed, students would have more success—broadly defined as the achievement of students' academic goals, whatever they may be, at ITCCI Richmond—and that this would lead to increased persistence.

Requiring a full-day orientation was a matter of some disagreement among administrators and faculty at ITCCI Richmond. Conventional wisdom holds that community college students, many of whom are adults who work full-time, will not attend a mandatory orientation. In sum, an orientation, especially one that was a full day in length, was not considered within the realm of possibilities among some at the campus. Data indicated that although 95 percent of responding community colleges had an orientation program, only 38 percent reported requiring it for all first-time students (CCSSE, 2012). Nonetheless, ITCCI Richmond decided that for its pilot effort, it would make the orientation mandatory and a full day.

For the full-day orientation, all new students (first-time and transfer, full time and part-time) were required to attend a program that covered logistical aspects (such as financial aid, registration) of being a student and helped students connect with faculty and other students. Family and significant others were not invited to attend. Key faculty, such as those who taught gatekeeper courses or served as academic advisors, were invited to attend and in some cases help present material to the incoming students. In addition, current students were on hand to help answer questions as needed. From the beginning, evaluation of the initiative was a priority for the campus team overseeing its implementation.

Evaluation data came from institutional databases, programmatic information collected by staff, and focus groups with faculty and students. Institutional data included 2,007 students who registered for fall 2005, including the 402 new students who participated in orientation. Regression analysis was used to examine what factors, including students' background characteristics, academic preparation, college experiences, and financial aid status, were helpful in predicting persistence. Participation in the program was coded as a dichotomous variable and included in the logistic regression analysis (our outcome was year-to-year persistence). Although a number of limitations existed with respect to the analysis (for example, there was no true comparison group), the regression analysis provided partial evidence of the efficacy of the orientation program, enabling us to compare the likelihood of participants persisting compared to continuing students.

Overall, we found modest evidence that the program was helping students' academic success. In our regression analysis predicting likelihood of persisting, we found that orientation participants were neither more nor less likely to persist than continuing students, after controlling for orientation participation, race/ethnicity, and college enrollment characteristics (such as credit hours attempted, participation in developmental education). This was a difference from prior cohorts of new and transfer students, who were less likely to persist. At face value, we might conclude the orientation program was having no effect. However, findings from focus group discussions with students who participated in the orientation point toward the positive impact of orientation on participants. The students expressed an increased confidence and awareness that they gained from their attendance. Having all the faculty and staff at orientation helped establish positive communication from the start and made them feel a part of the college community, according to several students. Analysis of the interviews with the faculty showed that they sensed their first-year students were more informed and able to take more initiative than in previous years when no orientation was available.

Implementation of the orientation was intentional and focused on the persistence challenges identified by the campus work team. Given team members' beliefs in the need to address multiple student concerns (such as registration logistics and financial literacy), it was designed to be a full day, it was required of students new to the campus (first-time entrants as well as transfers), many key faculty were asked to attend, and serious evaluation efforts with consistent feedback loops were built into the process. This intentional and deliberate process of implementation helped the fidelity of the effort with respect to its intended outcomes: Faculty and staff consistently reinforced the message to students that they were welcomed and that staff could help answer questions and address concerns of the new matriculants. Moreover, faculty experienced positive direct (such as connecting with new students) and indirect (such as spending less time covering logistics in class) benefits. All of this, arguably, contributed to success in addressing persistence concerns.

Finally, and perhaps most importantly, implementation was done in a context-dependent way with consistent feedback to those implementing the program. For example, although initially it was believed that a full-day orientation was the best approach, feedback from students and faculty led the campus work team to shorten the orientation to half a day in subsequent semesters, balancing the competing demands on participants' times with the goal of integrating them into the institution. This is an important point, because traditional wisdom had held that students would not attend any orientation on the one hand, and, on the other hand, that more comprehensive orientations (similar to those at baccalaureate degree granting institutions) were inherently better. The campus work team remained focused on the specific needs of their institution and students in initially designing the orientation to be one day, and then reducing that time commitment even further.

Advising and Choice of Major at Religiously Affiliated Midwestern University (RAMU)

In fall 2000, Religiously Affiliated Midwestern University (RAMU) began an advising program aimed at helping undeclared students move toward a declared major. The launch of the program was based in part on the experience of administrators and faculty who noted differences in academic success between students with a declared major and those who were undeclared. These students became institutionally relabeled as *undeclared,* because administrators felt the *undecided* label carried negative connotations. Undeclared students arriving at RAMU in fall 2000 were encouraged to take a class designed specifically for them, entitled "Life Calling, Work, and Leadership." The course was grounded in the religious tradition of the institution, and students were encouraged to develop an understanding of the concept of *life calling* with the help of a *life coach.* Students were led through a facilitated process of trying to understand how the worlds of work, leadership, identity, and religious beliefs could be brought together in choosing a program of study. In addition to the course, students had access to an advising and mentoring center staffed with professional and paraprofessional advisors. Students could take inventories of their professional interests, gather information about majors and internships, and obtain career counseling. RAMU was able to invest significant institutional resources into developing the program, including the creation of a center devoted to life coaching and life calling. Moreover, the program had high-level support from institutional leadership.

Evaluation of the program employed a mixed-methods design for purposes of triangulation and complementarity. Data were collected via group interviews as well as institutional and programmatic databases. Logistic regression analysis was used to determine what effects, if any, participation in the program had on student persistence, controlling for student background, academic preparation, college enrollment characteristics, and student finances. We followed several cohorts of program participants. In addition, group interviews enabled us to gain insights into the relationships between program content and the observed program effects—in other words, the *why* and *how* of our evaluation. The evaluation was conducted early in the implementation of the program in order to provide a feedback loop to the practitioners that would enable them to make changes to the program as they felt necessary.

Overall, we found a strong positive relationship between program participation and persistence. For example, students in the 2001 cohort of course participants (n = 98) persisted at a rate of about 99 percent compared to an overall persistence rate of about 93 percent. (It is important to note that RAMU's retention rates overall are exceptionally high compared to other institutions.) Similarly, students in the 2002 leadership class cohort (n = 196) persisted at a higher rate year-to-year than the overall institutional rate, 97 percent versus 93 percent. Findings from the logistic regression analysis indicate that students who participated in the course in fall 2001 were nearly six times as likely to persist year-to-year as students who did not participate in the course, all other things being equal. Those students who enrolled in the course in fall 2002 were just under three times as likely to persist as students who did not take the course, again controlling for all else.

Analysis of the group interviews indicates three ways in which students may have benefited from the class. According to the students' perceptions shared in the interviews, the class helped students to lead more intentional lives and to come to terms with expectations (for example, from parents and peers) about having a declared major, and it provided them with the support necessary for them to be successful. As one example, several students expressed concern about coming to college without a clear choice of major. They expressed feeling "abnormal" and "displaced." The class provided these students with some perspective (that is, that discerning a major and potential career path was part of the collegiate process at RAMU) while also giving them tools (such as skills and interest inventories) for intentionally reflecting on their interests and aptitudes. Overall, the combination of quantitative analyses and the interviews led us to conclude that the Life Calling course had a strong positive effect on student retention at RAMU. Given the high level of investment in the implementation of the program, this is not surprising.

Lessons Learned

In sum, these case studies reveal important lessons about implementation of student success initiatives. First, evaluation of the programs with clear feedback loops was a common feature. Both institutions were intentional and deliberate in investing resources in evaluating program implementation and outcomes. This is a significant point, because evaluation requires resources and commitment. Consider, for example, that one of the recurring problems we encountered as we worked with other institutions in IPAS was that many lacked student databases or they did not track program participation among students, therefore making it impossible to compare participants to nonparticipants in terms of important outcomes (such as persistence). Moreover, collecting new data can be a significant undertaking. For example, collecting interview data is time consuming, many institutions lack the resources to commit scarce staff time to undertake studies like these two cases, or the staff lacks the training to undertake them. IPAS was asked to undertake these studies because the institutions themselves lacked sufficient staff and organizational slack to take on this kind of program evaluation.

Second, intensity of effort in implementation was an important factor for both institutions. This is evidenced in the resources dedicated to evaluation as well as program design and implementation. RAMU and ITCCI Richmond are illustrative of the ways in which two institutions with very different levels of resources invest in student success program implementation. In the case of RAMU, with relatively greater institutional resources, staff with particular expertise was hired, classes were developed, and money was allocated to their efforts. ITCCI, with relatively fewer resources, allocated staff time (thereby incurring a significant opportunity cost to the institution) as well as some money (for example, to pay for refreshments at the orientation) for students. No new resources were allocated at ITCCI. In both cases, however, resources were focused and institutional commitment was high. For example, ITCCI decided to do one thing (orientation), rather than implement multiple programs, which would likely have been unsustainable.

Third, implementation of the efforts was local and context-aware. Both institutions drew on national research and models of programs at other institutions. However, neither institution adopted models from other institutions wholesale. Rather, program implementation began with careful design and thought. For example, at RAMU, major choice and academic advising were framed in mission-centered (religious) ways. At ITCCI, despite concerns about asking busy commuter students to spend a full day on campus, the decision to cover multiple topics (such as financial literacy, how to register, and meeting faculty) in one day was actually a more efficient way to utilize student time than covering those topics repeatedly in classes or in a one-on-one setting.

Finally, these studies illustrate what can be learned about institutional retention initiatives if they are undertaken with rigor. Too often, campus policy makers say they cannot afford to undertake good programmatic research such as these two examples. Nevertheless, they can elect to spend (or not spend) thousands of dollars on programs and sustain these expenditures with little sense of the efficacy.

CONCLUSION

We began this chapter with the observation that decades of research and theorizing on student persistence have not led to advances nationally in college completion rates. Nevertheless, the research conducted has not been without fruit or impact. Indeed, scholars have helped us to understand the root causes for student attrition and given us strong theoretical foundations on which to build models of student success. We contend that directed institutional action—action that is grounded in this body of research and rigorous evaluation of the nature and intensity of institutional actions—shows promise in boosting student progress. We believe several questions are foundational to deeper inquiry into institutional action. These include whether or not institutions have embraced student progress as a goal, if and how they have structured themselves to do so, and what is the level of intensity of their effort. These are the issues that compelled our investigations.

The studies reported here make contributions in several areas. The 2011 College Board Study, "How Four-Year Colleges and Universities Organize Themselves to Promote Student Persistence: The Emerging National Picture," identifies practices and organizational structures that are now used to promote student success, and it also sheds light on institutional intensity of effort and emphasis at America's four-year institutions. The Study of Community College Structures for Student Success (SCCSSS) tracks the prevalence of the student success efforts in different forms in America's community colleges. Finally, the examples provided from the Indiana Project on Academic Success (Ivy Tech-Richmond and RAMU) suggest that when programs have organization, funding, administrative oversight, and favorable campus policies, they can move the needle.

The scope of our studies was large and space limitations permit us to provide only examples of our inquiry in this chapter. Even from a limited view of the studies, however, it is clear that there is large variation in the scope of student persistence organizations and in the delivery of student persistence activities and interventions across both two- and four-year institutions. In particular, we identified variations in the formality of organizational structure and in the intensity of efforts and resources across both sectors. These variations were observed across institutional size and were visible whether we looked at orientation, commitment to diversity, early alert systems, or coordination of institutional efforts.

Our studies suggest that institutions are, indeed, organizing to address student progress. However, the findings also suggest that institutional commitment in the form of budget and authority, rigorous follow-through, and regular assessment of results is often lacking. To illustrate, although 68 percent of participating two-year institutions indicated that they had a retention coordinator, 65 percent of those with coordinators reported little to no authority to fund retention initiatives. Similarly, 74 percent of four-year institutions in our study reported having a retention coordinator. Of those with coordinators, however, only 18.5 percent devoted more than one-half FTE of their time to the endeavor, and few had programmatic or budget authority to initiate action. Turning to programmatic responses, two-year institutions reported nearly universally that they offer orientation, for example, but less than 60 percent required that students attend the program. Similarly, less than 60 percent included an individual meeting between a student and an academic advisor. Further, early alert systems are in place at only 52 percent of two-year institutions, and less than 30 percent have directed follow-up with the information they gather. At four-year institutions, follow-up is more consistent, yet only 60 percent have early warning systems.

These findings offer two fundamental insights into organizational structures and practices designed to increase student retention in two- and four-year institutions. First, organizational focus and intensity is lacking across both sectors. Retention coordinators exist, for example, but few have the authority or budget to be effective. Second, institutional practices can be characterized as inconsistent and highly variable. Orientation programs, for instance, vary from nonexistent to lasting full semesters, some require students to attend and some do not, and some offer no mandated meetings with academic advisors, while this is a key feature of others. Similarly, early warning systems often exist, but only sometimes is the gathered information acted upon to aid students. On one hand, we can despair of the lack of commitment and focus we have observed; on the other, we can suggest that the elements of better results appear to be in place and improvement can result if greater attention and rigor can be applied.

Finally, we can offer several guiding principles to aid institutions toward achieving better results. First, our findings suggest that organizational structures such as coordinators and committees should have institutional backing in the form of visibility, budget, and authority to initiate retention-oriented policies and practices. Next, policies and practices designed to promote student progress should be evaluated regularly, and the information gathered from evaluations must be fed back into the programs for improvement. Both of these recommendations address the general lack of focus and rigor that, as shown in our studies, may characterize programs on many campuses. Enrollment management professionals can use these findings to support their advocacy for improved institutional practice surrounding student success. This kind of research can strengthen enrollment managers' position as they use their professional voice to urge leaders to adopt a more deliberate focus at the institutional level, for example. Moreover, findings from these studies can support enrollment management professionals in participating knowledgeably in campus discussions on student success. Supported by growing research in this area, enrollment managers can help push for institutional practices that reach across divisions and that support student success. Finally, the body of research on student retention serves as a strong foundation for institutional progress, and institutions should adapt the research to their local contexts to design effective policies and practices. Combined, these three recommendations portend better results. Moreover, acting on these recommendations would promote more incisive research into institutional practices across the system.

The results of these surveys offer insight into the current state of institutional structures, actions, and intensity of effort directed at promoting student progress in U.S. two- and four-year institutions. However, considerable work needs to be done. Lessons learned from our studies suggest that further research on the efficacy of particular organizational structures and levels of authority, responsibility, and budget would bear fruit in the form of clearer directions and implications for institutions. Further, these studies also suggest that work needs to be done to establish a culture of evidence on many campuses, a culture that would identify effective practices from those that are ineffective. Indeed, we use the term "promising practices" instead of "best practices" for institutional efforts that are now becoming normative. They are "promising" because they are grounded in research, theory, and practice-oriented literature. They are not "best," because they are as yet unproven in rigorous study to yield results for student outcomes. Scholars, institutional researchers, and administrators would do well to create and implement tools to evaluate their practice and review data points to determine how institutions can influence student persistence.

References

ACT. (2009). National Collegiate Retention and Persistence to Degree Rates; Retention and Degree Rates Tables 1–8. Iowa City, IA: ACT. Retrieved from http://www.act .org/research/policymakers/pdf/retain_2009.pdf.

Bailey, T. R., & Alfonso, M. (2005). Paths to Persistence: An Analysis of Research on Program Effectiveness at Community Colleges. *New Agenda Series*, 6(1). Indianapolis, IN: Lumina Foundation for Education.

Bean, J. P. (2005). Nine themes of college student retention. In A.Seidman (Ed.), *College Student Retention: Formula for Student Success* (pp. 215–243). Westport, CN: Praeger Publishers.

Beck, H. P., & Davidson, W. D. (2001). Establishing an early warning system: Predicting low grades in college students from survey of academic orientations scores. *Research in Higher Education*, 42(6), 709–723.

Boudreau, C. A., & Kromrey, J. D. (1994). A longitudinal study of the retention and academic performance of participants in a freshman orientation course. *Journal of College Student Development* 35(6), 444–449.

Braxton, J. M. (Ed.). (2000). *Reworking the Student Departure Puzzle*. Nashville, TN: Vanderbilt University Press.

Braxton, J. M., Hirschy, A. S., & McClendon, S. A. (2004). Understanding and Reducing College Student Departure. *ASHE-ERIC Higher Education Report*, 30(3).

Braxton, J. M., & McClendon, S. A. (2001–2002). The fostering of social integration through institutional practice. *Journal of College Student Retention*, 3(1), 57–71.

Braxton, J. M., McKinney, J., & Reynolds, P. (2006). Cataloging institutional efforts to understand and reduce college student departure. In E. P. St. John & M. Wilkerson

(Eds.), Reframing persistence research to improve academic success. *New Directions for Institutional Research*, 2006(130), 25–32.

Braxton, J. M., & Mundy, M. M. (2001–2002). Powerful institutional levers to reduce college student departure. *Journal of College Student Retention*, *3*(1), 91–118.

Calcagno, J. C., Crosta, P., Bailey, T., & Jenkins, D. (2006). *Stepping stones to a degree: The impact of enrollment pathways and milestones on older community college student outcomes*. (The Community College Research Brief No. 32.) New York: Columbia University, Teachers College, Community College Research Center. Retrieved from http://www.inpathways.net/SteppingStonestoaDegree.pdf.

Center for Community College Student Engagement (CCSSE). (2012). *A Matter of Degrees: Promising Practices for Community College Student Success (A First Look)*. Austin, TX: The University of Texas at Austin, Community College Leadership Program.

College Board. (2011). *How Four-Year Colleges and Universities Organize Themselves to Promote Student Persistence: The emerging National Picture*. New York: College Board.

College Board. (2012). *Securing the Future: Retention Models in Community Colleges*. Study of Community College Structures for Student Success (SCCSSS). New York: College Board.

Community College Survey of Student Engagement (CCSSE). (2007). Building relationships for student success. *CCSSE Highlights*, *6*(3), 4.

Crisp, G., & Taggart, A. (2013). Community college student success programs: A synthesis, critique, and research agenda. *Community College Journal of Research and Practice*, *37*(2), 114–130.

Dundar, A., Hossler, D., Shapiro, D., Chen, J., Martin, S., Torres, V., Zerquera, D., & Ziskin, M. (2011). *National Postsecondary Enrollment Trends: Before, During, and After the Great Recession*. (Signature Report No.1) Herndon, VA: National Student Clearinghouse Research Center.

Gardenhire-Crooks, A., Collado, H., & Ray, B. (2006). *A Whole 'Nother World: Students Navigating Community College* (Opening Doors Project Report). New York: Manpower Demonstration Research Corporation (MDRC).

Glass, J. C., & Garrett, M. S. (1995). Student participation in a college orientation course, retention, and grade point average. *Community College Journal of Research and Practice 19*(2), 117–132.

Hagedorn, L. S., Maxwell, W., & Hampton, P. (2001). Correlates of retention for African-American males in community colleges. *Journal of College Student Retention*, *3*(3), 243–261.

Hossler, D. (2006). Managing student retention: Is the glass half full, half empty, or simply empty? *College & University*, *81*(2), 11–14.

Hossler, D., Ziskin, M., & Gross, J. P. K. (2009). Getting serious about institutional performance in student retention: Research-based lessons on effective policies and practices. *About Campus*, *13*(6), 2–11.

Hurtado, S., Alvarez, C., Guillermo-Wann, C., Cuellar, M., & Arellano, L. (2012). A model for diverse learning environments. In J. C.Smart & M. B.Paulsen (Eds.), *Higher Education: Handbook of Theory and Research*, 27 (pp. 41–122). The Netherlands: Springer.

Jenkins, D., Bailey, T. R., Crosta, P., Leinbach, T., Marshall, J., Soonachan, A., & Van Noy, M. (2006).*What community college policies and practices are effective in promoting student success? A study of high- and low-impact institutions.* New York: Community College Research Center, Teachers College, Columbia University.

Jenkins, D., Ellwein, T., Wachen, J., Kerrigan, M. R., & Cho, S. (2009). *Achieving the Dream Colleges in Pennsylvania and Washington State: Early Progress Toward Building a Culture of Evidence.* New York: Community College Research Center, Teachers College, Columbia University.

Kalsbeek, D. H. (2013). Reframing retention strategy for institutional improvement. *New Directions for Higher Education, 2013*(161), 20–105.

Knapp, L. G., Kelly-Reid, J. E., Whitmore, R. W., Huh, S., Levine, B., Berzofsky, M., & Broyles, S. G. (2005). Enrollment in Postsecondary Institutions, Fall 2003; Graduation Rates 1997 & 2000 Cohorts; and Financial Statistics, Fiscal Year 2003 (NCES 2005–177). U.S. Department of Education. Washington, DC: National Center for Education Statistics.

Kroc, R., Howard, R., Hull, P., & Woodard, D. (1997). *Graduation rates: Do students' academic program choices make a difference?* Paper presented at the Annual Forum of the Association for Institutional Research, Orlando, FL.

Matus-Grossman, L., & Gooden, S. (2002). *Opening Doors: Students' Perspectives on Juggling Work, Family, and College.* New York: Manpower Demonstration Research Corporation (MDRC).

Mayhew, M. J., Vanderlinden, K., & Kim, E. (2010). A multi-level assessment of the impact of orientation programs on student learning. *Research in Higher Education, 51*(4), 320–345.

McClenney, K. (2013). Community colleges: Choosing change. *Change: The Magazine of Higher Learning, 45*(4), 26–35.

Moore, C., Shulock, N., & Offenstein, J. (2009). *Steps to success: Analyzing milestone achievement to improve community college student outcomes.* Sacramento, CA: Institute for Higher Education Leadership & Policy.

Mullin, C. M. (2010). *Rebalancing the mission: The community college completion challenge.* (Policy Brief 2010–02PBL). Washington, DC: American Association of Community Colleges.

Murtaugh, P. A., Burns, L. D., Schuster, J. (1999). Predicting the retention of university students. *Research in Higher Education, 40*(3), 355–371.

Overland, W. I., & Rentz, A. L. (2004). Orientation. In F. J. D.MacKinnon & Associates (Eds.), *Rentz's Student Affairs Practice in Higher Education* (3rd Edition) (pp. 239–267). Springfield, IL: Charles C. Thomas.

Patton, L. D., Morelon, C., Whitehead, D. M., & Hossler, D. (2006). Campus-based retention initiatives: Does the emperor have clothes? In E. P. St. John & M. Wilkerson

(Eds.), Reframing persistence research to improve academic success. *New Directions for Institutional Research, 2006*(130), 9–24.

Pressman J. L., & Wildavsky, A. (1984). *Implementation: How Great Expectations in Washington Are Dashed in Oakland; or Why It's Amazing that Federal Programs Work at All. . . .* Los Angeles: University of California Press.

Purnell, R., & Blank, S. (2004). *Opening doors. Support success: Services that may help low-income students succeed in community college.* New York: Manpower Demonstration Research Corporation (MDRC).

Reisberg, L. (1999). Colleges struggle to keep would-be dropouts enrolled. *The Chronicle of Higher Education, 46*(7), A54–56.

St. John, E. P., Hu, S., Simmons, A. B., Carter, D. F., & Weber, J. (2004). What difference does a major make? The influence of college major field on persistence by African American and White students. *Research in Higher Education, 45*(3), 209–232.

Seidman, A. (Ed.) (2012). *College Student Retention: Formula for Student Success* (2nd Edition). New York: ACE/Rowman & Littlefield.

Shapiro, D., Dundar, A., Chen, J., Ziskin, M., Park, E., Torres, V., & Chiang, Y. (2012). *Completing college: A national view of student attainment rates.* Herndon, VA: National Student Clearinghouse Research Center.

Tinto, V. (1975). Dropout from higher education: A theoretical synthesis of recent research. *Review of Educational Research, 45*(1), 89–125.

Tinto, V. (1987). *Leaving College: Rethinking the Causes and Cures of Student Attrition* (1st Edition). Chicago: University of Chicago Press.

Tinto, V. (1993). *Leaving College: Rethinking the Causes and Cures of Student Attrition* (2nd Edition). Chicago: University of Chicago Press.

Tinto, V. (2005). Reflections on student retention and persistence: Moving to a theory of institutional action on behalf of student success. *Studies in Learning, Evaluation, Innovation, and Development, 2*(3), 89–97.

Tinto, V. (2010). From theory to action: Exploring the institutional conditions for student retention. In J. C.Smart (Ed.), *Higher Education: Handbook of Theory and Research* (Vol. *25*) (pp. 51–89). New York: Springer.

U.S. Census Bureau. (2009). *Educational attainment in the United States: 2007.* Washington, DC: U.S. Census Bureau.

Upcraft, M. L., Gardner, J. N., & Barefoot, B. O. (2005). *Challenging and Supporting the First-Year Student: A Handbook for Improving the First Year of College.* San Francisco: Jossey-Bass.

Williams, D. A., Berger, J. B., & McClendon, S. A. (2005). *Toward a Model of Inclusive Excellence and Change in Postsecondary Institutions.* Washington, DC: Association of American Colleges and Universities.

Zeidenberg, M., Jenkins, D., & Calcagno, J. C. (2007). *Do Student Success Courses Actually Help Community College Students Succeed?* New York: Columbia University, Teachers College, Community College Research Center.

PART FIVE

THE IMPORTANT BACK ROOM

The Preface to this handbook speaks to a gap that has existed in the Strategic Enrollment Management literature between pieces written from an academic, research-based perspective and those reflecting a practitioner, functional view. This part of the book breaks new ground in the SEM literature by discussing core backroom enrollment functions alongside the preceding chapters written primarily from the broader academic and research-based perspective. The implications of bringing these perspectives together to a greater degree are significant. Programs and initiatives aimed at improving student access, attainment, and completion may be well intentioned, elegantly stated, and amply funded. However, if they do not adequately account for the policies, procedures, staffing, and technology required for efficient and effective delivery, those programs and initiatives are likely to fall short of their goals. This is more than mere supposition. As discussed in Chapter 2, significant gaps exist between societal-level enrollment goals and programs targeted to specific groups of students, especially those traditionally underserved by higher education, and the actual outcomes achieved. This despite countless meetings among blue-ribbon task forces and millions of dollars having been allocated to the problem, but perhaps with too little attention to the mechanics of program delivery. Later, in Chapter 27, we bring together calls for change in higher education and the need for more strategic planning. In the SEM planning model described there, we reference the need for adequate infrastructure to support the achievement of enrollment goals. Hence the need for the chapters in this Part V.

The first three chapters focus on the functional offices most directly connected to SEM—admissions, registrar, and financial aid. In Chapter 19, Jennifer DeHaemers and Michele Sandlin offer a look at the role of the admissions office in supporting SEM, providing a necessary link between the admission policy discussion in Chapter 8 with the SEM planning content of Chapter 27. This chapter illuminates the issues that define effective admissions operations ranging from structures and staffing to campus relations and student assessment. In Chapter 20, David Sauter and Howard Shanken follow by describing the new role of the registrar within institutions and how that role is important to the practice of SEM. Within the broader change scenario represented by SEM, registrar's offices face as much change as any one campus unit, as their historic role is expanded, making them key players in SEM organizations. Similarly, in Chapter 21, Tom Green delineates the functions of the financial aid office through the lens of SEM, building on the more policy-oriented discussions in Part III to outline the functional elements of effective aid delivery.

The concluding chapter in Part V addresses a topic that spans the previous three chapters—and virtually the entirety of higher education operations—in terms of relevance and importance: the use of technology. Here again, Wendy Kilgore and Brent Gage fill a gap in existing literature, which lacks coverage of an area of vital and growing importance in the delivery of higher education. Collectively these four chapters provide an operational foundation for SEM practice.

CHAPTER 19

Delivering Effective
Admissions Operations

Jennifer DeHaemers and
Michele Sandlin

T he admissions office plays a key role in an institution's overall Strategic Enrollment Management planning and operations. As the primary "front door" to the college or university, this department builds external relationships with high school and community college counselors, with prospective students and their families, and with the community at large. This chapter is an appropriate opener to this Part V because it focuses on the core operational components of SEM with regard to admissions. In this chapter, we discuss the role of the admissions office, organizational structure, staffing, space necessary for optimal efficiency, policies and procedures, technology, communications, and assessment. The extent to which these elements are employed efficiently, minimizing financial and staffing resources while achieving institutional goals for the number of students enrolled, will define the overall effectiveness of an admissions office. Whereas we focus primarily on the functions of undergraduate admissions offices at both baccalaureate institutions and community colleges, we also briefly consider graduate admissions. All are important components of an efficient and effective admissions office that can support university goals. Finally, we discuss the importance of cross-campus collaboration, the role admissions plays in retention, the impact of changes in the political and legal landscape, and technological advancements. Each of these topical areas is important in ensuring that the admissions office fulfills its role in meeting the university's SEM plan.

The admissions office is one of many key offices at a college or university that are integral to the overall enrollment management organization (Hossler, 1986; Huddleston, 2000). This office is charged with recruiting a pool of applicants, processing applications, and carrying out the institution's admission policy, while simultaneously collaborating with academic units across campus to ensure that university enrollment goals and budgetary requirements are realized. Generally, the offices with which admissions will most closely collaborate are those carrying out institutional research, assessment and planning, marketing and public relations, financial aid and scholarships, registration and records, new student orientation programs, and academic advising (Hossler, 1986; Jonas & Popovics, 2000). Although each of these offices functions separately, each must also work collaboratively so all can be successful.

Admissions is responsible for a great deal of activity that is intended to generate interest in the university, move prospective students through the enrollment funnel, and provide leadership on campus yield activities and best practices for faculty engagement with prospective students (Jonas & Popovics, 2000). Another function of an admissions office is to process applications according to admissions criteria as quickly as possible, all the while providing a high degree of excellent customer service. And all of these activities and functions are conducted with the express purpose of fulfilling the mission as well as college and university enrollment priorities.

ORGANIZATIONAL STRUCTURE

The organizational structure in the admissions office must support and promote operational efficiency and service to future students, families, the campus, and the public. If the office structure is not clearly articulated and aligned to the needs of future students, families, visitors, faculty, administration, and staff, it can create confusion, poor customer service, delays, workload duplication, and frustrated staff. "The close alignment of structure and tasks leads to a high level of performance" (Bolman & Deal, 2013, p. 96). Organizing the unit based on the order in which the work will be done will greatly enhance workflow efficiencies and will help achieve the unit and institutional enrollment goals, ensuring that the tasks within the unit are accomplished efficiently.

Depending on the type of institution, its mission, and the population of students it serves, the admissions office may encompass multiple functions, such as recruitment, outreach, pre-college programming, or other areas. However, the core operational function of processing applications for admission to the institution is almost universal: to streamline business processes and provide excellent service to external and internal stakeholders. The admissions office's scope of responsibilities begins with any initial contact with a prospective student, continues through the recruitment, application, admission stages, and ends when the student has matriculated to the institution.

Undergraduate admission is usually a centralized function from a recruitment and operations perspective. The criteria are standardized, and any exceptions to the policy are typically made by the chief admissions officer or an appointed admissions committee. Admission criteria typically fall into two categories: those based on objective criteria that measure a student's academic achievement or those based on both objective and subjective criteria that also consider the student's life skills and ability to succeed at the institution. This holistic review process has been used by highly selective institutions to shape their classes for many years. Highly competitive universities and academic programs may rely on an interview conducted by staff, faculty, or alumni to determine whether a student is prepared for the program and will be a good fit at the university. Interviews also help determine an applicant's readiness to undertake the rigors of the university or program.

Admission to graduate and professional programs is often decentralized, although it is also based on standardized criteria. Students in these programs typically make up a smaller percentage of the college or university's overall enrollment, and the recruitment approach is much more specialized. In Chapter 26, the admission of graduate, professional, and international students is discussed in more detail.

It is important that the admissions office be flexible and adapt its organizational structure to the priorities of the institution. It is advisable to review the organizational structure of the office and benchmark it against comparable institutions at least once every ten years. "Effective structures fit an organization's current circumstances (goals, technology, workforce, and environment) . . . and emphasize flexibility, participation and quality" (Bolman & Deal, 2013, pp. 99, 105).

The admissions unit should have a strong leadership team that is cohesive, united, and engaged. Members of the leadership team are the principals for the practical implementation of the strategic recruitment and admissions goals. As supervisors of the admissions staff, these leaders have two key duties: to allocate work and to coordinate team efforts (Bolman & Deal, 2013).

The admissions leadership team of a midsize to large four-year institution comprises a director, associate and assistant directors, team leads, administrative assistant, and technical and data leads (Figure 19.1). Smaller institutions will not be able to support or need this level of leadership depth but typically have a director and an assistant director or manager over the operational areas. The core units within the admissions office are usually headed up at the associate or assistant director level. Many campuses in North America also have added additional core unit(s) to manage communications, marketing, on-campus programming, social media, and/or data analysis. These units are also headed up by an associate or assistant director (Figure 19.2) and are a part of the leadership unit.

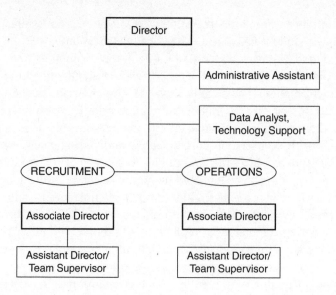

Figure 19.1 Admissions leadership team

The leadership structure at many institutions in a blended model may have admissions and registration functions combined, capitalizing on the "one-stop-shop" concept. For institutions that have open admissions, where all applicants are accepted, a blended model can provide greater flexibility when the depth in leadership depicted in Figure 19.1 is not necessary based on the less complex

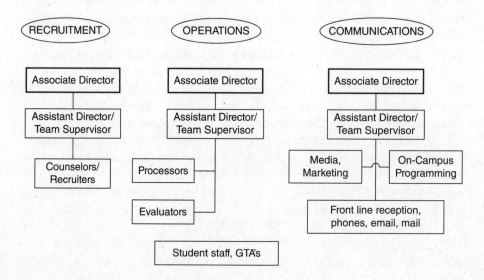

Figure 19.2 Members of the leadership unit

admission process. This helps to serve a greater number of future and current students at the same time, while providing increased efficiency for staffing. This has been a common model historically in community colleges, though that is changing significantly as many of these institutions are adopting more selective admission practices (Figure 19.3). At some private institutions, admissions operational functions are viewed as part of the responsibilities of the registrar's office, separate from recruitment, and thus admissions operations may be led by an associate or assistant director reporting to the registrar.

Aligning teams according to functional task areas creates synergy and results. Functional teams are able to capitalize and streamline cross training, backup support, technology, communication, and business processes within the team. "With the right structure, an organization can achieve its goals, and individuals can see their role in the big picture" (Bolman & Deal, 2013, p. 515).

STAFFING OPPORTUNITIES

The success of an institution in fulfilling its SEM plan is dependent upon having the right staff in the right positions. Without this, it will not matter what kind of academic programs the institution offers, how great the campus looks, or even how many games and championships the football or basketball team wins (Higgs & Westman, 2005). Having a staff that possesses the skills (self-directed, friendly, and outgoing) to market the university as well as recruit students

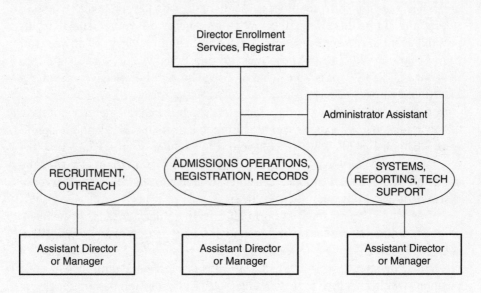

Figure 19.3 Blended community college model

to attend will ensure the likelihood of meeting enrollment goals. Further, staff who pay attention to detail, and who offer excellent customer service and follow-through, is important to get students admitted in a timely manner. Having the right number of staff to accomplish the work is also important.

As John Schuh and Lee Upcraft (2001) point out, the leadership and staffing in an admissions office is critical to success and affects the entire campus. Many times, individuals are selected for these management positions based on knowledge and expertise, whereas their actual ability to provide staff leadership, supervision, and management is a secondary consideration (Belker, McCormick, & Topchik, 2012). Supervision of employees is demanding; therefore, the people holding these positions must possess the necessary skills or be given professional development and coaching to achieve them.

The questions asked during staff interviews are important in determining whether the candidates have the right experience and education but, more importantly, the right attitude for the job (Belker et al., 2012). To assess a candidate's attitude, the hiring manager might ask a question such as this: "What did/do you like best about your last/current job?" A good answer will focus on how well that job challenged the candidate to grow, develop, and contribute more to the operation. If the applicant answers that the best thing was the free football tickets or the generous vacation policy, perhaps the candidate's priorities and those of the institution do not match (Belker et al., 2012). By asking questions about how the candidate behaved in the past, a hiring manger will get some idea of future performance potential. For example, the hiring manager may ask, "Tell us about a time you were confronted with a complex problem and what was your thinking process as you addressed that problem?" Another question might be this: "Describe a situation where you worked effectively as part of a team to accomplish a goal on time and within budget. What was your role? What did you learn?" These types of questions will provide insight into how the candidate works and if his or her style will be effective within the institution.

For entry level positions in the office, for which the candidate may not have as much related work experience, the hiring manager should ask about significant accomplishments while in college or high school or at previous employment (paid or volunteer). Questions about the most important decision the candidate was required to make can offer insight into the candidate's level of maturity and self-reflection (Stone, 2003).

For an admissions team to perform effectively to meet goals, staff members should be willing to put the institution and unit needs ahead of their own (Higgs & Westman, 2005). When, for example, the University of Missouri–Kansas City created a one-stop shop in 2012, it was with the understanding that no new positions would be added to the staffing table. Thus, new job descriptions were created and, in one case, an admissions counselor position in the admissions office was repurposed to fulfill the new job description and function. The admissions office lost a position to the new one-stop shop, but this new service center also relieved a portion of the admissions staff's work. Positions were also repurposed from financial aid and scholarships and registration and records offices to staff the new service center. These offices were not flush with staff to begin with, but the new center and new approach to staffing required everyone to put aside their fears about the impact on the workload and focus on providing improved service to students. That was the beneficial outcome of this initiative.

A director or associate director in admissions needs to build a team that is highly committed to the goals of the office and that is accountable for achieving results. With clearly defined roles and expectations, measurable goals, and a purpose to unite around, the team can focus on the task (Stone, 2003). The leader needs to build trust and confidence within the team, and helping them achieve successes (big or small) will build confidence and skills. When things go wrong—and they will—how the manager responds will either strengthen the trust or damage it. Focusing on behaviors that lead to the breakdown rather than focusing on the perceived shortcomings of team members will build confidence and trust (Belker et al., 2012) in the manager. Pairing a new team member with a more seasoned employee who is a strong member of the team to mentor is also a great way to build the team (Stone, 2003).

When a new team member comes on board, the hiring supervisor (director or associate director) should very quickly set clear expectations, share unit goals and individual goals, and clearly outline accountabilities. If a supervisor leaves this to chance, he or she is making an error in judgment that nearly always results in poor communication as well as unmet goals and expectations. It is difficult to hold staff accountable for their work if they have not been told for what they will be held accountable (Higgs & Westman, 2005). Because staff who work in admissions offices are relational and usually like working with people, they may have challenges with the managerial tasks that are required that sometimes call for direct and/or difficult conversations.

It takes time to train employees well, but training is a vitally important part of bringing a new staff person on board. A clear training checklist should be available to the manager to ensure that all topics and skills have been covered. These range from training the new employees on the work culture of the office and university to the nuts and bolts of their specific job function. For well-seasoned employees, the nuts and bolts might include working with the institution's student information system or purchasing policies, for example.

Ongoing professional development is another key component to training and is instrumental in helping exceptional staff enhance their skill set. This is a critical foundational piece of an admissions and enrollment management operation and will improve the whole team (Higgs & Westman, 2005). Managers need to help staff look beyond the national conferences, which are appealing and can indeed can be a terrific source of professional development, to find other, lower cost methods of obtaining professional skills. Some excellent professional development sources are online offerings through webinars, readings, on-campus classes, software programs, mentors, and other opportunities that may be presented on campus.

SPACE MANAGEMENT

The location of the "first face" office is crucial. It must offer potential students a strong, memorable first impression of the institution—a contributing factor in a future student's decision to attend or not. "The quality of the space affects people's attitudes and behaviors" (Blanchette, 2012, p. 67). Many campuses do not pay enough attention to or understand the importance of the admissions space in achieving enrollment goals. The following questions should be considered when planning for admissions space:

- How easy is it to find the admissions office?
- Is parking relatively close? Is it convenient? Is it free, or are students charged to park there?
- Does the institution's physical appearance instill that oh-so-important anticipation of college and create excitement?
- Is the admissions entrance and office attractive, open, and welcoming?
- Are the front desk staff positioned, present, and able to meet and greet those who enter the space?
- Is staff friendly, engaging, knowledgeable, and helpful?
- Are other key offices, such as financial aid, scholarships, bursar, registration, and housing, easily accessible?
- Does the space allow for a future student and his or her family to meet confidentially with an admissions counselor?
- Is there a media room where students can view information about the institution?
- Does the configuration of the space for the units within the office support workflow, and enhance and promote communication and collaboration within the unit?

These and other questions should be considered in assessing the utilization, presentation, and effectiveness of the admissions space. The optimal space for the admissions office should provide strong visibility on and off campus. This space should showcase the institution by being open, inviting, and attractive.

It should also support and enhance the unit's work and reaffirm or confirm the future student's college decision.

It is also important for admissions leadership to view the allocation of space according to the organizational structure—that is, the order in which a student needs to accomplish the required tasks to become enrolled, or the operational workflow of the unit. Joseph Gustin (2003) provides the following quick checklist to consider when developing new admissions space or re-engineering existing space:

- The space needs to support workflow and service to students.
- The space should provide for private conversations with staff, students, and families.
- The space needs to encourage teamwork, an open flow of information, and a sharing of resources.
- The space should be aesthetically pleasant, provide ergonomic considerations, and provide a workspace that is comfortable, productive, and invokes pride in the office and the institution.
- There must be adequate conference, planning, and meeting space.
- The space must encourage efficient processing.
- The space should be organized in workflow order.
- The space needs to present an accurate and strong first impression.
- The space must enhance communication.
- The lighting, air quality, and noise levels must be adequate and appropriate.
- The space must be safe and secure for staff and for visiting students and families.

When developing an admissions unit, officials must plan and provide space according to the functional area alignments within the greater central admissions unit. For most campuses, real estate is a scarce commodity that is extremely valuable and a politically charged issue. Teams should be co-located and able to communicate and work together easily to enhance team relationships, synergy, and productivity, and still support staffing coverage. When planning space, officials must consider current as well as future space needs. "Space needs to be configured for work being done today, not a relic of past processes" (Quinet, 2011, p. 45). Officials should review the SEM plan for the institution and plan for future enrollment growth (or decline) in the space management strategy. They must consider how the enrollment plan will impact staffing levels, new technology, or other areas, with regard to space needs for the future. One must always consider future growth, because the opportunity or availability for additional space in the future, more times than not, won't be an option.

POLICY AND PROCEDURES

Although Chapter 8 discusses admission policy in greater depth, a few words are relevant here as well. Admissions officials must always consider university-wide admissions policies and procedures, and policies may also be in place for individual academic programs; familiarity with these is not only important for those who are making admissions decisions but for the recruitment staff as well. Is the mission of the university to provide open access (open admission), or does it serve a very select group of students? All colleges and universities fall on a continuum between these two extremes, and admission policies reflect this.

In addition to institutional mission and enrollment goals, admissions offices must also be mindful of an increasing number of external expectations and policy implications. For example, there is a push nationally to increase the number of college graduates in the United States. This trend has led to the emergence of several organizations such as Complete College America, established in 2009, as well as multiple initiatives of the U.S. Department of Education (Walters, 2012), to cite two examples. Whereas the SEM team will set the institution's agenda, the admissions office can lead the discussion around accessibility and partner with other areas of the university to conduct market research to attract nontraditional student markets needed to meet this agenda. Leaders in admissions are poised to ask if there are unnecessary barriers to students who historically have not participated in higher education or those who leave and then seek to reenter colleges and universities. Addressing such issues requires that admissions officers exert leadership in analyzing institutional policies and procedures and recommending changes to support desired enrollment outcomes.

TECHNOLOGY AND THE ADMISSIONS OFFICE

The effective application of technology and student systems are addressed more fully in Chapter 22, but it is worth mentioning to admissions leaders to pause and consider the importance of being technologically current, not only for effective recruiting with current and future student markets, but also in back-office admissions functions that have a significant impact on yield. Many institutions struggle with the difficulties of bringing staff along to embrace, engage, implement, and take ownership of new technology. When considering new technology, training and professional development on business process and technology implementation must be a priority. For too many institutions, training and development end up on the cutting room floor during the budget battles of purchasing a new technology. "The budgetary erosion slowly and imperceptibly reduces the probability of a successful implementation" (Gorr &

Hossler, 2006, p. 16). This is the last activity that should be cut from a technology implementation process, however, because it directly impacts the success of that implementation. If training and development are neglected, the results can be disastrous—delayed implementations, unnecessary modifications, incorrect use or application of the technology, and untrained staff. In too many cases, institutions "dump," or significantly cut, the training budget to save funds after purchasing expensive new technology. Doing this, however, costs much more in the long run as opposed to investing in training to ensure success and make the solution viable.

"When implementing new technology, it is important to engage the staff, even though they are not enthusiastic about the new solution. These are the people who will be the face and voice of the new service environment. Staff determine the extent to which new technology solutions will be successful. Technology is key to modernizing the service environment, but it is not the whole solution" (Quinet, 2011, p. 44). When staff are included at the beginning of the process, they have a greater understanding of the product and the efficiencies that can be gained in their own work along with the students they serve. When staff are directly involved, they buy in, are more invested, and will provide a better outcome for the office and the institution. During the Request for Proposal (RFP) process, admissions officials can invite the staff to attend the vendor presentations so they can see firsthand what efficiencies will be achieved and what the technology does and does not do; this improves the business process and helps staff become more valuable employees.

When admissions officials consider new solutions that automate workflow and expedite processing, they must start by mapping or drafting what the current process is. They should identify what is working and not working, and what are the glitches, gaps, delays, and work stoppage issues. By being proactive and mapping the business process and workflow prior to any new technology search, the unit will be able to make a more informed technology selection decision. This will also help to jumpstart the RFP process and will result in a much better solution for the campus. Staff must be involved in this process: they are the ones who will be key to ensuring that the new technology is successful.

COMMUNICATIONS

Communication plans are commonplace in today's admissions offices. Customer relationship management (CRM) technology solutions automate, organize, and synchronize an institution's communication strategy, and they improve how admissions offices communicate on a more personalized level. When staff are developing and updating the communication strategy for the next recruitment cycle it is imperative that they base any and all decisions on strategy, methods, and delivery on data. Data is essential to building and keeping a communication plan on track (Higgs, 2005). Staff must assess the communication plan based on data that is qualitative (student, family, counselor feedback, and surveys) as well as quantitative.

By surveying students frequently and listening to how they prefer to receive communication, institutions can expand their reach to potential students who may have been overlooked. For example, implementing texting into the communication strategy may prove a successful plan. With the global surge in texting, CRM solutions are including the possibility for texting communication solutions. Researchers at Harvard University, for example, found that text messaging outreach increased college enrollment at some of their experiment sites, and the biggest differences in enrollments occurred in locations where students were the most underserved. In fact, at those experiment texting locations, students were 7.1 percentage points more likely to attend college than those in the control group (Supiano, 2013).

In an October 2009 study by St. Mary's University, the institution found that prospective applicants who opted in for text updates were seven times more likely to convert to an applicant. Of those applicants, St. Mary's also found that nearly half enrolled and were active text update subscribers. After all, virtually 100 percent of all text messages are read (Marshall, 2010). What was important from the St. Mary's study was that text messages should be "relevant, valuable, and important" to the student (p. 57). To launch an effective texting communication strategy, enrollment officials must be sure to request prospective students' mobile numbers in all online and print collateral and allow the applicant to opt-out easily. Most campuses solicit mobile phone numbers in all communications. The next stop is to execute a meaningful texting relationship via the CRM and communications strategy. Officials must stay true to the technology medium and keep text messages short, sweet, and important. Examples would be upcoming deadlines, needed documentation, upcoming events, updates, reminders, and so on.

Parents and families are the secondary audience in the college decision-making process. "Building an exemplary prospective parent communication strategy is paramount. Parents can be effective partners, reinforcing the messages that schools are attempting to deliver" (Wartman & Savage, 2008, p. 4). Building a track within the communication strategy based on parent and family feedback, as well as data on effectiveness, will have a positive impact on this important and influential market in the recruitment process. "Data from studies conducted in 2005 and 2007 show that schools that provide parent services are expanding their efforts beyond one or two annual events to include regular communications, dispersal of student development information, and inclusion of parents as members of advisory groups and as volunteers or mentors, and solicitation of funds" (Wartman & Savage, 2008, p. 2).

As the admissions team plans the communication strategy, they must remember that campus staff, faculty, and administration are a part of strategy. Key staff, faculty, and administration need to be informed of the following:

- Recruitment efforts
- Admissions funnel and enrollment numbers
- Application processing and turnaround times
- New technologies
- Workflow

These key contributors not only help to recruit the class and prepare for the upcoming year, they also encourage and reinforce the campus's role in recruitment and create buy-in. "Communication is the single most important component in ensuring buy-in" (Quinet, 2011, p. 45). It is also helpful to have multiple stakeholder perspectives and an understanding of the impact across campus when evaluating trade-off decisions in the recruitment communication strategy. Many admissions offices are having to make difficult changes to their communication strategies because of budget reductions or based on new student feedback. Changes can include reducing print promotions and focusing more on e-communications, social media, and/or texting.

The admissions office must lead by example and reach out to the campus by openly sharing information, soliciting feedback, and partnering. "Sharing department, enrollment and other annual reports . . . help them understand aspects of the enterprise and inspire points of pride" (Cramer, 2012, p. 55). Many years ago at an AACRAO SEM Conference, Richard Whiteside, who at the time was the head of Enrollment Management at Tulane University, shared a personal strategy during a workshop. He discussed how to inform the campus, build partners, and create buy-in. His was a simple idea but a difficult task to accomplish that takes a bit of courage and faith in one's colleagues: Whiteside (2005) recommended that at the end of each recruitment cycle, admissions should conduct an open forum and invite the entire campus. At the forum, the admissions staff would report on everything the office did during the past year to bring in the new class, including the following:

- All travel locations and results of those visits
- All admission and recruitment numbers
- Impressions by students, families, counselors, and other institutions
- What the communication strategy is and why
- Technologies used
- Status of application processing, volume, and workflow
- On-campus tours and programming

This strategy works for admissions professionals who are struggling with buy-in, building partners on campus, and engaging staff, or for those receiving negative feedback or campus criticism. Hosting a similar forum may help to open the doors of the admissions office to the rest of the campus, change minds, and build campus support.

ASSESSMENT

Admissions offices have long been about the business of assessing efforts, especially as they pertain to recruitment initiatives. It is through the type of SEM research described in Chapter 23 that the impact and effectiveness of an admissions office is measured. A primary and basic area of assessment is counting inquiries, applications, admissions, denials, and enrollees. The admissions office is on the front line when it comes to meeting the university's enrollment goals, and this often determines whether the office is on target to meet these goals by counting how many students are represented in each stage of the enrollment funnel. By drilling down to a specific high school or community college level, the office may determine how many students are inquiring or applying from a specific school in any given year compared to the previous year. This allows for mid-year adjustments to recruitment efforts. A number of programs are developed to drive interest and applications to the university. These range from campus visits, to preview days, special programs for high school students around specific majors, and collaboration with community-based organizations that support higher education, among others. Admissions leaders can gather information from program participants to determine how well the program is meeting the participants' needs. Steps taken to assess the effectiveness of recruitment or efficiency in processing applications are important for a number of reasons: they are useful in resource allocation, in building a case for a new or consistent course of action, and in understanding the position of the college or university in the market (Salomonson, 2005).

Beyond counting and satisfaction surveys, an emerging area for assessment has to do with learning outcomes. Outcomes assessment as well as program self-assessment provide an important cornerstone in an enrollment management organization (Jonas & Popovics, 2000) and are often undertaken on a scheduled, rotating basis. Initiatives undertaken by admissions should be purposeful with a clear outcome for learning about the university. The learning outcome may be as simple as "participants will be able to identify the university's scholarship application deadline" or "participants will be able to identify success strategies that will positively impact their educational experience." In either case, the admissions office will have identified that these are critical pieces of information that prospective students need to know and will obtain through the program. Admissions will ensure that answers are provided during the program. The survey or evaluation of the program must include questions about these specific items in order to assess whether the student actually learned this information. Each institution has key message points that should be assessed to ensure that participants are walking away from their interaction knowing what those points are.

Schuh and Upcraft (2001) identified difficulties in assessing an admissions office. On many college and university campuses, there can be more than one admissions office and admissions process (domestic versus international, undergraduate versus graduate and professional, and competitive admission degree programs versus noncompetitive admission degree programs), and a thorough review of all admissions processes would be complex. Of even greater complexity is the fact that many offices may impact a student's decision to enroll, over which the admissions office has no control. Campus housing, financial aid and scholarships, faculty interactions, academic support services, and the quality of labs and libraries are all factors that may help or hinder the efforts of the admissions office (Schuh & Upcraft, 2001). This means collaboration with offices of assessment and institutional research on formulating learning outcome statements and the assessment of these are critically important.

BEYOND THE ADMISSIONS OFFICE

For any admissions office to be successful in fulfilling its role in an enrollment management organization and in guiding staff and academic partners to reaching enrollment goals, the director and leadership team must look beyond the office itself. It is often said that it requires the efforts of the entire campus to bring in a class.

Further political, economic, and cultural changes have an impact on the admissions office and the university. The director can be especially valuable by keeping a watchful eye to external forces that may cause a change in policy, process, and planning. As we conclude this chapter, we consider a few of these issues with a broader lens.

Collaboration with Key Partners

To ensure a greater likelihood of success, the admissions office leadership must be a collaborative partner with other key offices on campus. Although one individual at the university is likely charged with overall enrollment management responsibility, the director of admissions plays a vital role in setting the tone to help other offices appreciate their role in meeting enrollment levels at the university. Students consider a number of factors when deciding to which institutions they will apply and at which they will enroll (Schuh & Upcraft, 2001).

They evaluate the safety of the campus, its location, the type and amount of scholarships available, the quality and quantity of campus housing, and the quality of the faculty and advisors. Therefore, it is important that admissions collaborate with these offices and functions. Based on the close interaction with prospective students and their families, admissions staff are the conduit to relate back to the campus the perceptions and expectations of the future alumni and their families.

Role in Student Success and Retention

Admissions does and should play a role in retention. It is, after all, their mission each year to bring in the new class of future alumni. On a global scale, more and more institutions are exploring how admissions can have a positive impact on student success and retention. They are doing so by considering more than just academic preparation, but life preparation. Areas such as life skills and noncognitive attributes are proving to be strong predictors of student academic success, improved persistence, and graduation rates. Kalsbeek, Sandlin, and Sedlacek (2013) wrote that "while grade point average (GPA) is the most significant factor for predicting first-year academic success," (p. 17) there is increasing evidence of the predictive value of adding noncognitive measures to academic admissions requirements to increase student success. This is particularly evident for nontraditional populations that are disadvantaged by traditional admissions practices (Kalsbeek, Sandlin, & Sedlacek, 2013). The foremost researcher in this area, William Sedlacek, University of Maryland College Park, has conducted a multitude of studies with diverse student types for more than thirty years. His studies bear out the retention predicting value of adding noncognitive measures to admission requirements. The measures developed by Sedlacek are a fair, practical, ethical, and legal assessment of a students' ability to succeed in college, regardless of his or her background.

The term "noncognitive variables" is used to refer to variables relating to adjustment, motivation, and student perception, which can be incorporated into any admissions process (Sedlacek, 2004). These variables reflect race, culture, gender, and knowledge that is learned and demonstrated in nontraditional ways, which "can reduce subgroup differences and . . . achieve the goal of predicting alternate measures of students' success" (Schmitt et al., 2013, p. 6). For institutions considering the use of noncognitive variables, there is precedence supported by case law for employing these variables within the admission process that is narrowly tailored, sophisticated, and research-based, and can achieve greater diversity in the student body and aid in the identification of successful students (Kalsbeek, Sandlin, & Sedlacek, 2013).

Colleges and universities that have added noncognitive variables to their admissions requirements are finding that these variables are associated with improved outcomes and higher retention, particularly for certain populations.

DePaul University's DIAMOND project, for example, which implemented non-cognitive variables into the admissions process, found this to be true. DePaul's preliminary results showed that their variables were predictive of first-year retention, particularly for students of color, and suggestive of second-year success (Kalsbeek, Sandlin, & Sedlacek, 2013). The application of noncognitive variables is allowing for earlier intervention methods because admissions officials can gather information on a student's needs before the student even arrives on campus. The end result is stronger preparation, better orientation programs, and mentoring and coaching programs that start on day one.

Looking Ahead

Admissions officers must stay abreast of the changing political and legal landscape. Challenges to affirmative action will continue to impact admission policies and practices and scholarship programs. From a political perspective, state legislators are questioning the cost of higher education as well as the preparation provided by colleges and universities. These questions have resulted in measures to limit the rate at which tuition may be raised (see *Missouri Senate Bill 389*, for example) as well implement performance-based funding models.

As the economies of many states try to recover from the 2008 recession, state allocations are declining. Public institutions are becoming more tuition-driven, similar to the way private institutions have always been. This necessitates efforts for greater efficiencies, more assessment, and greater accountability. Stagnant staffing levels in admissions and other offices creates environments in which employees are called upon to do more to meet enrollment goals at the same staffing levels, thus placing a greater value on technology. These conditions point even more to the necessity for competent, well-trained staff and ongoing assessment of initiatives.

CONCLUSION

The impact of an admissions office is far-reaching for institutions and the practice of SEM. From the relationships formed with high schools and community colleges, to communications with prospective students and families, to internal and external partnerships, the admissions office is one of the primary determiners of an institution's image. Moreover, from a SEM perspective, the effective and efficient functioning of this office is critical to meeting enrollment goals. How the office is staffed and organized is vital to ensuring optimal performance. Technology provides tools to help gain efficiencies and overcome limited staffing budgets. Collaborating with key offices across campus is also essential to the success of the admissions office. Not only will those partners assist in the improvement of admission communications and services, but they can help the admissions staff see how they fit into the big picture of institutional mission and student success. Ultimately, the admissions office is pivotal to future enrollments and institutional viability.

References

Belker, L. B., McCormick, J., & Topchik, G. S. (2012). *The First-Time Manager*. Retrieved from http://www.eblib.com.

Blanchette, S. (2012). Space & power in the ivory tower. *Planning for Higher Education, 41*(1), 64–74.

Bolman, L., & Deal, T. (2013). *Reframing Organizations: Artistry, Choice and Leadership*. San Francisco: Jossey-Bass.

Cramer, S. (2012). Mentoring the next generation of AACRAO leaders: Taking advantage of routines, exceptions, and challenges for developing leadership skills. *College & University, 87*(3), 53–58.

Gorr, W., & Hossler, D. (2006). Why all the fuss about information systems? Or information systems as golden anchors in higher education. *New Directions for Higher Education, 136*, 7–20.

Gustin, J. (2003). *The Facility Manager's Handbook*. Lilburn, GA: The Fairmont Press, Inc.

Higgs, R., & Westman, C. (2005). Coaching a winning enrollment management team. In C.Westman & P. Bouman (Eds.), *AACRAO's Basic Guide to Enrollment Management*. Washington DC: American Association of Collegiate Registrars and Admissions Officers.

Hossler, D. (1986). *Creating Effective Enrollment Management Systems*. New York: College Entrance Examination Board.

Hossler, D. (2009). Admissions testing & institutional admissions processes. *College & University, 84*(4), 2–11.

Huddleston, T., Jr. (2000). Enrollment management. *New Directions for Higher Education, 2000*(111). San Francisco: Jossey-Bass.

Hutt, C. D. (2010). Enrolling the tide: A case study of purposeful campus enrollment increases. *College & University, 85*(4), 10–17.

Johnson, A. (2000). The evolution of enrollment management: A historical perspective. *Journal of College Admission, 166*, 4–11.

Jonas, P., & Popovics, A. (2000). Beyond the enrollment management division: The enrollment management organization. *College & University, 76*(2), 3–8.

Kalsbeek, D., Sandlin, M., & Sedlacek, W. (2013). Employing noncognitive variables to improve admissions, and increase student diversity and retention. *SEMQ Strategic Enrollment Management Quarterly, 1*(2), 132–150.

Marshall, D. W. (2010). Incorporating texting into your communications mix. *College & University, 2*, 57–62.

Missouri Senate Bill 389. (2007). Retrieved from http://www.senate.mo.gov/07info/BTS_Web/Bill.aspx?SessionType = R&BillID = 8645.

Pugh, S. L. (2008). The influence of affordability in strategic enrollment management. *College & University*, *84*(2), 40–47.

Quinet, B. (2011). Customer service in the self-service era. *College & University*, *87*(1), 41–46.

Salomonson, K. (2005). Assessment. In C. Westman & P. Bouman (Eds.), *AACRAO's Basic Guide to Enrollment Management*. Washington DC: American Association of Collegiate Registrars and Admissions Officer.

Schmitt, N., Billington, A., Keeney, J., Reeder, M., Pleskac, T., Sinha, R., & Zorzie, M. (2012). *Development and Validation of Measures of Noncognitive College Student Potential*. Research report 2011–1. New York: The College Board. Retrieved July 14, 2014, from http://research.collegeboard.org/sites/default/files/publications/2012/7/researchreport-2011–1-validation-measures-noncognitive-college-student-potential.pdf.

Schuh, J., & Upcraft, L. (2001). *Assessment Practice in Student Affairs: An Applications Manual*. San Francisco: Jossey-Bass.

Sedlacek, W. (2004). *Beyond the Big Test: Noncognitive Assessment in Higher Education*. San Francisco: Jossey-Bass.

Stone, F. M. (2003). *The Manager's Question and Answer Book*. New York: AMACOM.

Supiano, B. (2013). Text messages can increase enrollment of low-income students. *The Chronicle of Higher Education*. Retrieved from http://chronicle.com/blogs/headcount/text-messages-can-increase-enrollment-of-low-income-students/34411.

Walters, G. (2012). It's not so easy: The completion agenda. *Liberal Education*, *98*(1).

Wartman, K., & Savage, M. (2008). Parental involvement in higher education: Understanding the relationship among students, parents, and the institution. *ASHE Higher Education Report*, *33*(6), 1–6.

Whiteside, R. (2005). Strategic enrollment management & strategic direct marketing. Presentation at the 15th annual AACRAO Strategic Enrollment Management Conference.

CHAPTER 20

The Registrar of the Future

David M. Sauter and
Howard E. Shanken

Strategic Enrollment Management seeks to enhance experiences and outcomes for students, faculty, and staff, as well as an institution's many external stakeholders. From an enhanced focus on student success (as described in the chapters in Part IV in this book), to reengineering backroom processes to deliver top quality services (Part V), to setting mission-driven goals (Chapter 27), SEM represents a fundamental change in the ways that institutions do business (Bontrager, 2004a). Critical to this change scenario is the idea that each individual working in the college or university setting performs a key role to help ignite the SEM transformation within the institution (Bontrager, 2004b). In no instance is this truer than with the role of the registrar.

The importance of the registrar role in SEM has not been well documented. Commonly under-acknowledged as a backroom function focused on routine processing tasks, relatively little has been written about the registrar role, aside from books and articles published by the American Association of Collegiate Registrars and Admissions Officers (AACRAO), the sole professional association directly affiliated with the work of registrars. Even within AACRAO circles, little has been written or presented on the role of registrars in SEM. This chapter is an initial effort to fill that gap.

This chapter addresses the evolving role of the registrar to be a primary SEM colleague and attempts to inspire readers to have institutional conversations about forming or strengthening strategic partnerships with registrars and their staffs within SEM structures. Among our theses is that there is need for added effort and sensitivity from both sides of this partnership. Registrars must be ready for further evolution of their role in a changing higher education landscape. Those outside registrar's offices will be required to bring registrar functions more fully into the mainstream of SEM practice, taking advantage of the registrar's close ties to academics to achieve new levels of institutional collaboration and student success. In short, this redefining of the registrar role is a prime example of the type of collaboration required between enrollment managers, their staffs, and a wide range of institutional colleagues to improve student retention and achieve institutional enrollment goals (Bontrager, 2004a).

DO WE EVEN NEED A REGISTRAR?

In these times of resource reductions and scrutiny of expenditures by various publics, along with process reengineering driven by technology and SEM itself, some institutions are asking, "Do we even need a registrar?" Gone are the days of registrar staff members sitting in their offices or behind a service window, disconnected from other departments, operating within a silo. In this chapter, we ask that you "think anew," especially if you have neither thought about the future of the registrar role generally nor thought specifically how it fits within a SEM framework. Registrars and their colleagues must move forward with fresh thinking about traditional registration and records functions in order for registrars to fulfill their promise of fully supporting SEM (Kisling, 2010).

This rethinking of the registrar role comes at a time of significant challenges. These challenges include staff reductions in the wake of technology enhancements and downsizing due to budget cuts, as well as retirements and the associated loss of professional and institutional knowledge. As a result there are fewer "hands on deck" in registrar's offices, and those staff members that remain face a steep learning curve. At the same time, there is a growing list of registrar responsibilities related to compliance and assessment. Finally, there is the very real issue of registrars who may be feeling a loss of status.

The reality is that the emergence of SEM itself has contributed to the perceived loss of status among registrars. The registrar was among the few original administrative positions on campuses, in many cases the "number two" administrator, and virtually always in the top five (Quann, 1979). As recently as the mid-1970s, when the term "enrollment management" first emerged, the registrar virtually always reported to the academic division of institutions, often directly to the chief academic officer. In contrast to this history, at institutions with SEM structures, the registrar now often reports to the chief enrollment officer (Bontrager, 2004a). Even when SEM structures do not exist, many registrars now report to a position such as assistant or associate vice president for academics. In either case, registrars today often operate at a level a step or two below their prior status in terms of reporting lines (Young, 2006).

Whatever their position on the organizational chart, registrars continue to perform tasks that are foundational to institutional operations. Ronder Young (2006) observed that the registrar's central mission has remained remarkably the same throughout the history of higher education: "to preserve the integrity, accuracy, and privacy of all academic records; to interpret institutional and governmental policies to the academic community and general community; and to efficiently distribute these records in full compliance with applicable policies, laws, and regulations" (p. 2). With the emergence of new emphases such as SEM and student success, the role of the registrar's office as a student service provider throughout the student life cycle has been accentuated. Depending on the institution, these functions range from transcript evaluation for prospective transfer admits, to verifying enrollment for financial aid and billing purposes, to term-by-term course registrations, to certification of graduation or other program completion, to providing official transcripts as the student becomes an alumnus—to name just a few. In recent decades and increasingly so, underlying these responsibilities are the technology capabilities required to complete transactions and deliver services efficiently and effectively. As a result, registrar staff members collaborate with information technology staff and third-party database vendors, both of whom rely heavily on registrar expertise. This typically results in the registrar's office having the largest group of technical experts on a campus, who are essential to implementing and maintaining student information systems. A complete discussion of the registrar's many responsibilities can be found in Barbara Lauren's 2006 compilation, *The Registrar's Guide: Evolving Best Practices in Records and Registration*.

Because many aspects of the historic registrar's role remain, and have been augmented by increased emphasis by initiatives such as SEM and student success, a quick answer to the question "Do we even need a registrar?" is a resounding "Yes!" At the same time, the registrar of the future is a different type of administrator than was previously the case, particularly when viewed through a SEM lens. The authors envision the contemporary registrar as a "connector position," a key professional whose overarching purpose is "connecting the dots" between institutional functions and organizational divisions. Registrars link the functions of course registration, academic record-keeping and transcript distribution, faculty grade submission, student services, financial aid eligibility, student information system deployment, and enrollment reporting, among others. In association with these functions, the registrar's office is an important bridge between the organizational divisions and functions of academic affairs, student affairs, institutional research, and enrollment management, regardless of how the latter may be named or organized on a particular campus.

Ultimately, what matters most is maintaining an "open systems environment," characterized by an institutional culture and climate that promotes collaboration across divisions and departments, especially academic units. (Henderson, 2012; Hossler & Kalsbeek, 2008; Pace, 2013).

This link to an institution's academic mission is inherent to SEM but is often difficult to achieve, making the registrar's office a preferred component of enrollment management organizational structures where such structures exist. When the registrar's office falls outside the enrollment management division, or is otherwise disconnected organizationally from other enrollment-related departments, it is imperative that the chief enrollment officer finds other means of creating dialogue and decision-making opportunities that involve registrar staff, utilizing organizational structures described elsewhere in this book.

As noted previously, not all registrars readily embrace these changes, lamenting the loss of direct connection to a high-ranking academic officer that often was the case previously. The fact that registrar reporting lines have often moved from an academic administrator to the institutions' chief enrollment officer has at times exacerbated registrars' perception of lost prominence. However, we believe that by embracing the perspectives proposed in this chapter, registrars can not only retain their institutional status, but actually raise the collective campus perception of their role as a key player in meeting student and institutional goals.

REGISTRARS' SEM EXPERTISE

The prior section described the basics of the registrar's historic role in higher education administration. Beyond those basics, registrars possess policy and process expertise that underpin academics, as well as a number of other vital campus functions, and thus are of vital importance to SEM. Registrar's policy expertise includes enforcing academic policy, monitoring student academic progress, and complying with federal and state regulations, including often being the chief institutional officer for adherence with the Federal Educational Rights and Privacy Act (FERPA). They also oversee long-standing program initiatives such as veteran's affairs, study abroad, and transfer articulation, as well as emerging ones such as the incorporation of massively open online course (MOOCs) into curricula. In the process realm, registrars oversee preservation of institutional records and their integrity, catalog production, degree and program certification, course and program curricular development, course registration, transfer evaluation, document imaging, transcript production, athletic certification, and graduation. In addition to the policies and processes with which they are directly involved, registrars provide vital support in other areas

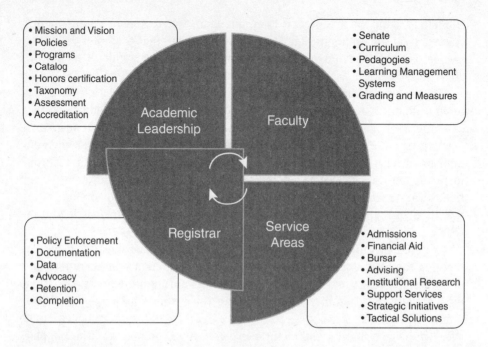

Figure 20.1 Registrar leadership connections

such as academic advising and enrollment reporting. The scope of registrars' influence is illustrated in Figure 20.1.

These cross-institutional responsibilities and the connections they foster position registrars to provide leadership in policy formation and process reengineering, enabling efficiencies and effectiveness that are of great benefit to SEM operations. Registrars create "bridges" from SEM units and concepts to other parts of the institution, often providing a "voice at the table" that may not otherwise exist.

As examples, the registrar's offices at Duke University and Miami University in Ohio have developed class scheduling systems that maximize student course selection and space utilization, not only to streamline both of these processes and deliver better services, but also to provide class demand data for academic units that aids in planning. Similarly, in Michigan, registrars have played key roles in working across departmental lines within institutions as well as among colleges and universities to develop policies and maintain systems supporting state and/or regional transfer agreements, a course equivalency exchange (Michigan Transfer Network, 2014), reverse articulations for two-year engineering degrees, and co-designing structures that support collaborative learning models. These efforts include the co-design and implementation of the

Michigan Community College Virtual Learning Collaborative (2014), where, in conjunction with the participating community colleges, an exchange was formed to allow students to take online course work from participating institutions in the state. Policies and procedures were implemented to set standards and enable the functions of admissions, registration, transcripting, financial aid, veterans' benefits, testing, and learning support. These types of broad collaborative efforts illuminate the vital role of registrars in institutional operations generally, with particular applicability to the activities and goals of SEM.

SEM organizations vary by the type, circumstances, culture, and historic precedent of institutions (Bontrager, 2004b; Hossler & Kalsbeek, 2008). Whatever form the registrar role takes on a particular campus, however it is named and to whomever it reports, the authors promote the concept of registrars working in close collaboration with other SEM-related departments and functions. Forward-thinking registrars find ways to build, sustain, and effectively demonstrate their significance and influence. A byproduct is that registrar staff members become immersed in their institution's SEM programs and activities, directly in terms of line authority, operationally as members of committees that support SEM, or both.

"Connecting the dots" to the stakeholders they serve, both within our physical institutions and virtually across the globe, is a core competency of registrars and all SEM practitioners, with an ever-increasing emphasis on student success and retention. Registrar activities in support of attracting and retaining students may not be as visible as an admission brochure, orientation website, or financial aid strategy. Activities and transactions such as those carried out by registrars are often less visible "backroom" functions. These include developing integrated academic exchange systems such as transcripts, transfer credit, and consortia agreements. Especially at community colleges, registrars help facilitate community-based programs focused on areas such as job training, reentry into higher education, and human resource management. Add the coordination of reporting, data collection and complying with various regulatory mechanisms, as well as connecting to community-based professional development recognition such as continuing education units (CEUs), and the registrar is again a key connector between enrollment services and academics, delivering on SEM's emphasis on student success.

In *Lean Higher Education* (2010), William Balzer asserted that processes have an indirect but important impact on institutional success, noting that student persistence and success is tied to their level of satisfaction with critical processes, including those provided by the registrar's office. In addition to the processes they facilitate, registrars usually play a primary role in identifying at-risk students who then receive attention in early-warning programs. Furthermore, Pikowsky (2012) outlined how the registrar's office can impact student learning. Pikowsky defined student learning as "changes in students themselves due to their college experiences" (p. 53), including their transactions with the registrar's office. She went on to note that the registrar's office impacts student learning both directly through activities such as committee involvement and indirectly in the teachable moments when a student interacts with the registrar's office either virtually or in-person. It is in these direct interactions that she believes the registrar's office can help students "hone essential skills and develop useful practical knowledge" (p. 54). On a macro level, by tying registrar process and service performance indicators to institutional level learning outcomes and/or general education outcomes, the office comes full circle in supporting SEM initiatives through efficient services, providing accurate data for decision-making, maintaining collaborative relationships with other departments, and advancing the student learning outcomes of the institution.

THE REGISTRAR'S LEGAL ROLE

Among the many collaborative relationships they maintain, registrars typically are the lead campus administrators for several vital functions. One, as has already been discussed, is maintaining the integrity of student academic records. Another is as one of the institution's primary legal protectors. Complexities arising from a litigious society, state and federal laws, and mandates—both direct and implied—from internal and external constituencies, all merge to require registrars to be legally savvy. Registrars receive legal requests on a routine basis, balancing individual and campus security with the benefits of an open society. All of these merge for registrar professionals within the SEM umbrella to be not only stewards of the law, but also a resource for internal and external stakeholders regarding laws such as FERPA, the Health Insurance Portability and Accountability Act of 1996 (HIPAA), and the Student and Exchange Visitor Information System (SEVIS).

Internally, registrars collaborate closely with general counsel and other institutional departments as the front line of defense against academically related legal challenges. Registrars must be aware of subpoena-compliance, coordinate record gathering in response to legal challenges, conduct FERPA training and management, oversee compliance and record security, and be attentive to privacy laws involving health and data security. Establishing clear procedures and exercising sound judgment to keep inquiries from escalating, requiring attention of general counsel, or becoming public serves the institution and SEM team very well. Externally, the registrar must maintain working relationships with governing agencies and professional associations such as AACRAO and the National Association of Foreign Student Advisors

(NAFSA) to stay abreast of legal mandates. In doing so, registrars contribute more than simply avoiding legal problems. By keeping smaller legal questions from becoming larger, more public ones, registrars help improve the student experience and void negative press that could adversely affect both recruitment and retention.

Registrars who play an active role in these institutional legal matters will emerge as a champion of the institution, reflecting well on both themselves and the enrollment management division when the registrar's officer is part of that structure. This is a prime example of the broader influence and credibility of mature SEM organizations, which bring together issues of policy and practice that previously had been thought of as disconnected.

KNOWLEDGE MANAGEMENT AND LEADERSHIP

In other chapters of this book and elsewhere in the literature, SEM is commonly described as a data-driven enterprise, with a prominent trend being the growth of enrollment research and data specialist roles (Bontrager, 2004a; Hossler & Bean, 1990; Lingrell, 2012; Wilkinson & Peterson, 2001). As stated by Scot Lingrell (2012), "The enrollment manager has the unique role of being a connecting link between the 'art' of collaboration among many offices and the coordination of many functions, and the 'science' of data analyses resulting in prediction, projection, and decision making" (p. 157). As noted previously in this chapter, registrars have historically played a primary role in creating and maintaining student records, as well as compiling enrollment reports for the Integrated Postsecondary Education Data System (IPEDS) and other data collection agencies. At smaller institutions registrars sometimes are the sole institutional researchers, while at larger institutions they typically coordinate closely with a separate enrollment or institutional research department. This aspect of the registrar's role can be expected to play an even greater role in the future, driven generally by the growth of institutional and student outcomes assessment requirements. More specifically, as registrars are increasingly drawn into the SEM arena with its focus on data-driven decision-making, they will be called on to play an enhanced role in helping manage all facets of recruitment and retention data collection and assessment. As noted recently by Archie George (2006), "all studies of the effects of college on students require data from systems maintained by the registrar. From registration to classroom assignments through grading and graduation, tracking students and their learning experiences is a higher priority now than ever before" (p. 361).

In addition to enrollment management and institutional research units, academic deans and department heads, finance divisions, as well as other campus offices, also collect data and at times maintain separate databases. While registrars tend to promote a "single system and one-source data" approach, this rarely is entirely achievable, especially at larger institutions. Examples of the multifaceted databases that typically exist include unit-level enrollment statistics, projections, and dashboards, data warehouses, and business intelligence initiatives. In this environment, registrars provide oversight for accuracy and security, attempting to mitigate the errors that inevitably occur when the same or similar information is maintained in more than one location. This often involves data validation and correction of errors to ensure the downstream accuracy of both internal and external reports. In this way, the traditional registrar role will move from data collection and reporting to an enhanced future role as knowledge managers for their institutions.

To an ever-increasing level, these knowledge management tasks are supported by technology. Chuck Hurley (2009) suggested that the successful contemporary registrar is an ambassador of data, "One who collaboratively brings forward the fruit of student-faculty data thanks to a combined knowledge of records and information technology" (p. 51). Registrars are critical players in planning, testing, implementing, documenting, and training staff in the use of newly deployed technology as well as with upgrades to existing systems (Krogh, 2006). Often they are called to play a project management role with regard to technology selection and implementation that includes the following (Adapted from Allen, 2006, p. 63):

- Writing a technology project charter
- Developing functional specifications for the project
- Writing technical specifications based on the functional specifications
- Creating mock-ups of the system
- Creating a task list
- Developing prototypes
- Testing the prototypes
- Demonstrating the system to campus user groups for feedback
- Developing a beta version of the system
- Testing the beta version
- Making the system operational
- Doing a postmortem on the initial project to determine how it could have been managed better
- Developing a plan for implementing future system upgrades

This requires understanding of the relationships with information technology departments as well as the impacts on others involved with student and enterprise-wide systems. The value of these relationships extends well beyond implementation of the technology itself. Technology systems are merely tools, not ends in themselves. Rather, the value of systems is realized only as they improve the efficiency and effectiveness of transaction processing and service delivery. Registrars' combination of experiences and relationships, bringing together knowledge of policies, procedures, and data from across the campus, makes registrars uniquely qualified to deploy technology to streamline institutional operations.

Registrars typically utilize their knowledge and technology expertise to provide campus leadership in following ways:

- Eliminating or reducing manual processes, paper forms, the number of steps required to complete transactions, and unnecessary student data bases or ancillary (bolt-on) systems.

- Determining whether to outsource or develop in-house capabilities for document imaging, document workflow, classroom scheduling software, foreign transfer credit evaluation, early alert strategies, and student life cycle communication plans.

- Developing or improving registration processes, campus-wide staff training, standard operating procedures, self-service opportunities for all members of the institutional community, physical or virtual one-stop student services, and management dashboards.

CONCLUSION

The core premise of this chapter is that the registrar is a key player in the success of SEM organizations and the institutions they serve. Building on the registrar's status as one of the original higher education administrators, successful registrars of the future have the potential to exert even greater influence. Their cross-campus connections and policy, process, and technology expertise provide vital infrastructure and services that contribute significantly to student and institutional success. In coordination with their institutions' legal counsel and given their roles as keepers of the student academic record and lead arbiters of directives such as FERPA, registrars are important players in maintaining sound legal footing. Similarly, owing to their engagement with student records and enrollment data, registrars support institutional research functions and the data-driven requirements of SEM and other aspects of strategic planning. As their combined tasks integrate with technology systems, registrars are significant contributors to the selection, testing, implementation, training, and maintenance of those systems. As a result, they typically lead campus efforts to deliver student services more efficiently and effectively.

This vision for the registrar role will be realized only as SEM practitioners and registrars themselves embrace it. As stated by Reid Kisling (2010), "A shift must occur where registrar staffs see themselves as peers of academics and partners in the delivery of educational programs" (p. 3). Ultimately, we must ask ourselves a series of questions: How will the registrar role be redefined for both new and seasoned professionals from a SEM perspective? How do we strategically embrace these changes? How do we actively use technology for student success and what will be the registrar's role? What does this mean for registrars' continued interaction with faculty and students? How will they balance the historically personal relationships across campuses (the "high touch"), while taking full advantage of new technologies available to make continuous improvements (the "high tech")?

As registrars seek to answer these questions, students, faculty, staff, and administrators will continue to rely on the registrar as a vital member of the SEM team. Indeed, SEM opens the door for rethinking the registrar role as a primary player in transforming institutions to face current and emerging changes in the higher education landscape. It is our hope that the concepts and questions we have raised will inspire you to have further conversations at your own institution about the role of the registrar as a key contributor to Strategic Enrollment Management.

References

Allen, M. D. (2006). Project management. In B. Lauren (Ed.), *The Registrar's Guide: Evolving Best Practices in Records and Registration* (pp. 57–64). Washington, DC: American Association of Collegiate Registrars and Admissions Officers.

Balzer, W. K. (2010). *Lean Higher Education: Increasing the Value and Performance of University Processes.* New York: Productivity Press Taylor and Francis Group.

Bontrager, B. (2004a). Enrollment management: An introduction to concepts and structures. *College & University, 79*(3), 11–16.

Bontrager, B. (2004b). Strategic enrollment management: Core strategies and best practices. *College & University, 79*(4), 9–15.

George, A. (2006). The registrar and institutional research. In B. Lauren (Ed.), *The Registrar's Guide: Evolving Best Practices in Records and Registration* (pp. 351–361). Washington, DC: American Association of Collegiate Registrars and Admissions Officers.

Henderson, S. E. (2012). Integrating evolving perspectives: The roots and wings of strategic enrollment management. In B. Bontrager, D. Ingersoll, & R. Ingersoll (Eds.), *Strategic Enrollment Management: Transforming Higher Education.* Washington, DC: American Association of Collegiate Registrars and Admissions Officers.

Hossler, D., Bean, J. P., & Associates. (1990). *The Strategic Management of College Enrollments.* San Francisco: Jossey-Bass.

Hossler, D., & Kalsbeek, D. H. (2008). Enrollment management and managing enrollment: Setting the context for dialogue. *College & University*, *83*(4), 2–9.

Hurley, C. (2009). Do not "fear" a strong registrar. *College & University*, *85*(2), 51–52.

Kisling, R. (2010). The strategic role of the registrar: Changing responsibilities in light of technology. *AC Solutions* (*1116*), 1–4.

Krogh, N. (2006). Implementation of student information systems. In B. Lauren (Ed.), *The Registrar's Guide: Evolving Best Practices in Records and Registration* (pp. 65–77). Washington, DC: American Association of Collegiate Registrars and Admissions Officers.

Lingrell, S. (2012). Getting it right: Data and good decisions. In B. Bontrager, D. Ingersoll, & R. Ingersoll (Eds.), *Strategic Enrollment Management: Transforming Higher Education*. Washington, DC: American Association of Collegiate Registrars and Admissions Officers.

Pace, H. L. (2013). Evolving the office of the registrar. *College & University*, *86*(3), 2–7.

Michigan Community College Virtual Learning Collaborative (2014). Home page. Retrieved April 2, 2014, from https://vcampus.mccvlc.org.

Michigan Transfer Network (2014). Home page. Retrieved April 2, 2014, from http://www.michigantransfernetwork.org/.

Pikowsky, R. (2012). Student learning outcomes: The role of the registrar. *College & University*, *88*(2), 53–56.

Quann, C. J. (1979). *Admissions, Academic Records, and Registrar Services: A Handbook of Policies and Procedures*. San Francisco: Jossey-Bass.

Wilkinson, R. B., & Peterson, A. (2001). Information of the realm. In J. Black (Ed.), *The Strategic Enrollment Management Revolution* (pp. 239–252). Washington, DC: American Association of Collegiate Registrars and Admissions Officers.

Young, R. (2006). The role of the registrar: Origins, evolution, and scope. In B. Lauren (Ed.), *The Registrar's Guide: Evolving Best Practices in Records and Registration* (pp. 1–7). Washington, DC: American Association of Collegiate Registrars and Admissions Officers.

CHAPTER 21

The Role of Financial Aid Operations in Fostering Student and Institutional Success

Tom Green

T he effective delivery of financial aid to students plays a critical role in Strategic Enrollment Management. The importance of financial aid to SEM was in initially discussed in Chapters 9 and 12 of this volume, providing an overview of the complex financial aid picture in the United States and the interplay of student aid with institutional budgeting and enrollment outcomes. This chapter will focus on the operational dynamics of financial aid. This includes the timing of award notices, effective policies in the review of student aid data, deployment of staff to meet institutional and student needs, and services to students and those who provide them financial support. Many enrollment managers, however, lack a fundamental understanding of financial aid operations—the services and processes that underpin the delivery of financial aid to students and the mechanisms by which financial aid professionals help educate prospective and current students, as well as the larger public.

Financial aid delivery plays an increasingly important role in overall institutional health. As more students and parents rely on aid to close the gap between student resources and educational costs, it represents an increased share of institutional revenues. Aid administrators must navigate a complex web of federal and state regulatory requirements to assure that the institution maintains compliance within aid programs, as well as institutional policies outside the aid office (nondiscrimination, gainful employment, Constitution Day, and so on) tied to institutional eligibility for aid participation. The stakes for noncompliance are high and mandate that enrollment managers gain and maintain a strong working knowledge of financial aid policy and how operations intersect with compliance.

Financial aid operations make up a key aspect of SEM infrastructure, where deployment and utilization of financial aid staffing, services, and awards are aligned with institutional mission, vision, and overall enrollment goals (Bontrager & Green, 2012). An institution's success in creating and sustaining the infrastructure for financial aid operations has a direct impact on its ability to influence student enrollment behaviors for both new and continuing students. Its relationship to the strategic use of institutional aid discussed in Chapter 11 is in the delivery of those awards in a timely and clear manner. Aid administrators must balance efficiency in operations to contain costs with the need to meet an ever-increasing roster of reporting requirements and compliance.

The integration of effective administrative systems is a key part of SEM (Kerlin, 2008). For entering students, evidence of this can be seen in both the clarity of initial information on student aid options and the timing of aid award delivery. For continuing students, it represents the degree to which the institution can simplify and facilitate persistence and degree completion.

FINANCIAL AID OPERATIONS AND SEM

The ability of the institution's aid operations to provide clear and timely information to prospective students and those who support them is complicated by the number of aid sources available, especially in the United States. The aid office must coordinate and explain the relationships between federal, state, institutional, and outside resources. This becomes especially important for students who are under-represented in higher education in regard to low-income (Bettinger, Long, Oreopoulos, & Sanbonmatsu, 2009) and especially Hispanic/Latino families and students whose parents have not attended college (College Board Advocacy and Policy Center, 2010). The aid office must integrate its efforts with admissions/recruitment, the bursar, and others to assure that the institution speaks to prospective students and others in a singular and clear voice.

Clear information on college costs and how to afford them starts well before a student is admitted to an institution. Community outreach and raising the financial literacy of students and their families are essential parts of increasing student participation and improving degree completion. Some of this outreach is initiated by secondary schools; other work is done by universities themselves in an effort to reach students and families outside the normal confines of education.

As students and their parents (if the students are dependent) consider the options for college, accurate information on costs and means to afford them play an important factor. For at least three decades, we have seen evidence that the cost of college (real or perceived) can act as a deterrent to students considering filing an application for admission (Manski & Wise, 1983). The dynamics of family on college attendance and costs are intertwined with the student's perception of herself/himself as being "college bound" or having aspirations of college attendance. Both socioeconomic status and financial aid policy impact the predisposition of students toward college-going behaviors, influenced by family educational and economic factors (Hossler, Schmit, & Vesper, 1999).

Interactions with the financial aid office can include community outreach activities undertaken by the office, and these inform both students and parents of accurate college costs and the availability of resources under federal, state, and institutional financial aid policies. The level of involvement by parents in this process is one indicator of their support for college attendance and can be an important determinant in whether or not the student's aspirations for college will manifest in actual applications (Hossler, Schmit, & Vesper, 1999).

As students move from college search activities to selection, the financial aid operation plays a pivotal role in assisting the student (and family) in determining the specific costs that may apply to the individual. The strategy for determining the aid package is variable, based upon the availability of discretionary funds at the institution. In some systems, such as many U.S. community colleges, regional public universities, and several national systems outside the United States, student funding is limited to the amounts provided through governmental programs, and the student's eligibility for these is determined through a formula outside the institution's control. In these systems, there is little or no discretionary aid and, therefore, no strategy for varying the amounts to be offered to students. The efficiency of the financial aid office in providing a timely aid package to students becomes the variable in how the student perceives the institution's affordability.

When discretionary aid exists at a level where offering it strategically to students can impact enrollment decisions, the financial aid office becomes a strategic partner with admissions (Hossler & Bean, 1990). The delivery of strategy through consistent information on opportunities to receive aid by the financial aid office is often a missed opportunity in operations. Too often, the work of attracting students to the institution is remanded to the admissions office, and communications with prospective students and their families is inconsistent from an institutional (and SEM) perspective.

Once students have enrolled at the institution and started toward their degree objectives, the role of financial aid operations becomes more direct. Although the level of partnership with admissions during the student choice phase may vary from institution to institution, the financial aid operations area and its student service team no longer have any buffer that may have existed through the admissions and recruitment efforts with prospective students and any financial supporters. The financial aid office's services to students are evident in the manner in which they provide information on aid award opportunities, comply with aid policies, respond to student/parent questions and concerns, and deliver timely aid packages.

As the student considers continued enrollment at the institution, the amount and type of aid offered shows some statistically significant relationships to retention and persistence (Gross, Hossler, & Ziskin, 2007). Perceived or real reductions in aid can influence students' decisions to apply for continued aid and/or return to college (Bettinger, 2004). Thus, the effectiveness of the financial aid office to provide accurate and timely information to current students has the potential to impact student decisions on persistence to degree positively or negatively. Aid policies matter as well. Some American aid offices fear financial aid fraud from students who may receive excess aid and then disappear, holding some funds until after the census date for the term. Although delaying the disbursement of aid may mitigate some (and very small) instances of these actions, it places stress on the majority of students who are attempting to balance work, family, and school commitments and expenses without the resources designed to facilitate enrollment.

Figure 21.1 shows the relationship between financial aid operations and an enrollment model of student aspiration, choice, and persistence to degree. This model blends attributes of several choice and persistence models, including

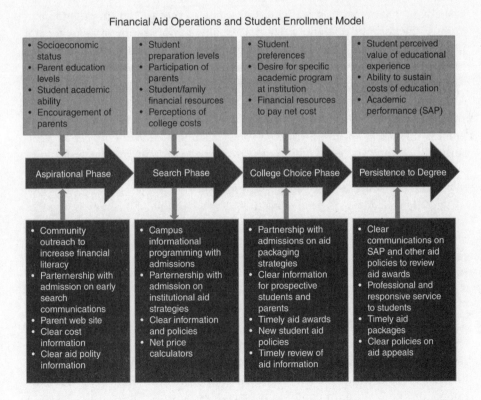

Figure 21.1 Interactions of student/parent backgrounds and financial aid operations

those by Katharine Hanson and Larry Litten (1982), Don Hossler and Karen Gallagher (1987), and Vincent Tinto (1993).

THE IMPORTANCE OF OPERATIONAL EFFECTIVENESS

Three areas of financial aid operations demand the attention of enrollment managers. Cost containment, scalability of operations, and an ever-changing compliance environment are key drivers in creating an effective and efficient financial aid office.

Costs of education outpace family income in the United States and have for the past several decades (College Board Advocacy and Policy Center, 2012). Although there are many reasons why college costs have outpaced family income (Ehrenberg, 2002), rising costs have caused financial aid operations to attempt to contain operational costs in a time when regulatory requirements and applications for financial aid in the United States have increased consistently each quarter since 2008, according to data compiled from the U.S. Department of Education quarterly processing volume reports (2013). As demands on financial aid staff have increased, actual staff increases mean increased institutional costs that, at some level, must be passed along to the student. In private institutions, the costs of operations are not usually subsidized by state or federal funding and therefore have a direct impact on student costs. At public institutions, tuition revenue has grown as a share of institutional revenue since 2008, where it represented 31.6 percent of revenues, to 2012, where it represented 42.2 percent of revenues, nationally (State Higher Education Executive Officers, 2013). In both private and public sectors, increased administrative costs to process financial aid and provide services to students and others create pressure on tuition costs, generally. As the pressure to contain costs collides with increased demand for services, enrollment managers are pressed to seek ways to contain costs through more efficient processes.

The identification of processes that can be refined or re-engineered to contain costs relies upon the ability of the organization to scale operations, where possible. Examples of scalable operations include the processing of financial aid applications or the electronic dissemination of financial aid awards through a batch communication system. Non-scalable operations involve counseling of students and their financial supporters.

Maintaining compliance with federal, state/province, or other regulatory agencies is of paramount importance to the institution. Regulations are constantly changing, and staying current with regulatory changes is a significant responsibility of the financial aid office. Should the institution become unable to receive funds because of its failure to comply with these regulations, the impact on the institution could be as severe as closure. These high stakes in institutional compliance can lead to overly restrictive policies and processes, however. These, in turn, can clog processing with unnecessary steps and restrictions on disbursement of aid that impinge on student success when they delay the awarding and distribution of funds to students.

Operational Effectiveness Defined

Although there are numerous aspects and nuances to the effective and efficient operation of a financial aid office, six key areas may be viewed as highly important:

- Analyses of data to understand the effect of aid on initial enrollment and persistence
- Identification and maximization of scalable and non-scalable functions and services
- Assessment and leveraging of available technologies
- Integration with government information and systems
- Supportive and responsive student (and parent) services
- Continuous training environment

Data analyses are discussed in other chapters. Their relationship to operations is the manner in which those analyses are created and used to change awarding patterns. In many cases, the results of analyses are developed after the fall census date. At this point, it is possible to assess both initial enrollment (matriculation) patterns from admitted students, as well as persistence patterns of students enrolled the prior term or year. Fund types vary and may be numerous. Aid data is typically calculated annually and divided into the enrollment terms for each student in that academic year. Once the data are extracted and prepared, the analysis should be performed with an informed perspective on aid types and sources. The experience and knowledge of aid administrators is critical to this work.

The extraction of data, preparation for analysis, and review of analyses are complex and often take weeks or months to complete. This leaves the aid administrator little time to model possible changes to aid and then implement the recommended changes for the next awarding cycle. Enrollment managers and aid administrators must jointly plan for the work required to perform these processes prior to fall census, rather than inserting the work into an already crowded agenda of work in the aid office and possibly missing critical timelines for the following year's aid awards.

In the preceding section, processes and services were identified as operations that fall into either scalable or non-scalable categories. Most areas of the financial aid office are scalable with the exception of student counseling, which includes face-to-face, phone, email, web forms, and other means of direct contact with students. Although this can be mitigated by strong web and other information services (which will be discussed later in this chapter), funding a higher education degree or credential can cause great stress for students, parents, and others who are helping to provide financial support and advice. Timely operations can also minimize the need for students to inquire about their status in being awarded and receiving aid, but cannot completely eliminate them.

Technology to assist in aid processing is another realm where the landscape is rapidly shifting. Selecting and leveraging technologies that can improve service to students, while improving the business processes in financial aid, requires both regular scanning of emerging solutions and critical evaluation skills to determine which of these options may be worth the investment of time and resources to implement and utilize. Tied to technology is business process review (BPR) and redesign. This is most commonly practiced during technology implementations but should be a regular part of all practices in the financial aid office. BPR is a key element of leveraging the existing technologies of an institution. Many institutions fail to utilize fully the technologies they have already purchased and installed. This most often occurs when the institution attempts to replicate old or outmoded business practices with newer technologies.

Because government support for students plays such a major and growing part of institutional revenues, institutions must efficiently integrate with these systems to ensure the accurate and timely transmission of information and funds. In Canada, this integration is with the provincial system within which the institution is located. In the United States, institutions must integrate with federal systems (Common Origination and Disbursement, Direct Loans, G5, and so on), as well as process information from one or more state systems.

Developing responsive and supportive systems to help students and those who financially support and advise them is challenging in any higher education environment. In 2012, more than two-thirds of all entering freshmen surveyed through the Cooperative Institutional Research Program (CIRP) reported that they had some major concerns about having enough funds to complete their college degrees (Pryor, Eagan, Palucki Blake, Hurtado, Berdan, & Case, 2012). More than half of all college seniors expressed concerns about having enough funds to pay college expenses and roughly one-third of all students surveyed reported investigating increased borrowing to meet costs (National Survey of Student Engagement, 2012). These concerns place a direct strain on the service systems of the financial aid offices, if for no other reason than to provide options and respond to questions.

The financial aid office must stay abreast of information to assure that it is both compliant with government and other funding regulations. The financial aid office must have a strong training and continuing education plan. Utilizing professional association networks, government training programs, and internal training options helps the financial aid office stay current with changing expectations and regulations for its operations. A failure to follow federal and state regulations cannot only disadvantage students, but can result in financial penalties being assessed against the institution.

OPERATIONAL CONCEPTS

A limitation of this chapter and its information is the American-centric view of financial aid that it presents. Although many concepts are common to any national system that provides aid directly to its students, the American system is uniquely complex. Its lattice of federal, state, and institutional aid programs that overlap and at times conflict with each other requires greater attention in this work.

One of the prime functions of financial aid support in any setting is to enable and sustain enrollment for students who cannot otherwise afford to do so. This must be done within the constraints of institutional resources and capacity; hence, the need for SEM planning and clear enrollment goals. The financial aid office must assure that students apply for and receive the maximum amount of government resources for which they qualify, while at the same targeting institutional resources to meet enrollment goals, including student retention and persistence.

Increasing financial aid literacy, as noted earlier, starts well before students enter the institution. In the United States, our focus on methodology to determine eligibility for aid can confuse the basic questions that most students and parents have about affordability. Figure 21.2 represents the calculation performed by American financial aid offices when determining eligibility for need-based federal aid. Most state aid programs utilize the data assembled from the Free

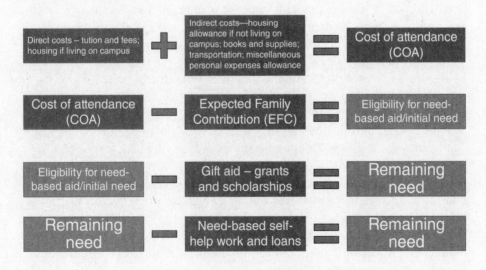

Figure 21.2 Federal calculation of eligibility for need-based aid

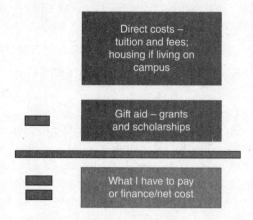

Figure 21.3 Student perspective on costs and aid

Application for Federal Student Aid (FAFSA) and aid in the form of grants or scholarships. The calculation of resources available to pay for college expenses through the FAFSA is based upon a formula approved by the U.S. Congress. The resulting figure is the Expected (or Estimated) Family Contribution (EFC), which is applied against the total estimated costs of attending (COA) one year of higher education at that institution.

Disclosure of this formula and the costs associated with attending the specific institution are regulatory requirements. However, aid offices often use this to answer the simple questions most people ask, "How much does it cost?" and "How can I pay for it?" This concept is illustrated in Figure 21.3 as the perspective of most students and parents or other financial supporters. This simplified perspective does not account for important costs, such as books and supplies (which vary widely by the courses taken by the student), or some variable costs, such as transportation to and from campus and personal expenses. However, it does focus on the student account or bill, which is one end result of the enrollment and financial aid processes.

Finding clear information on gross and net costs on an institutional website can be very challenging. The more complex federal calculation is often found on the financial aid site, a detailed listing of every possible charge and fee is found on the student accounts/bursar website, and there is little help to translate these into student costs. Net tuition calculators are a recent attempt to bridge these information gaps, but most (including the federal shopping sheet) use the broad, estimated COA as the basis for cost. This often leads students to assume that the amount owed the institution includes the estimates for books, transportation, and personal expenses.

CAMPUS-WIDE COLLABORATION AND PARTNERSHIPS

Like other aspects of SEM as discussed in this book, financial aid offices are dependent upon collaborative relationships across the institution. They must collect information from and provide information to a variety of departments and collegiate units. Student funding often comes from a development (in private institutions) or foundation (in public institutions) area, and many of these gifts come with donor restrictions. These restrictions require that the financial aid office find matching students and provide the awards to them, reporting the results back to the fundraising arm of the institution, which in turn reports results to donors. Similarly, academic and athletic departments may have funds under their control that are available to students. The financial aid office must coordinate these to ensure that the student's overall eligibility for need-based aid falls within the parameters shown in Figure 21.2.

Collaboration with the admissions/recruitment office has been previously noted in this chapter. Collaboration with an institutional retention/progression committee is equally important. Analysis of retention/persistence in relationship to financial aid can help guide institutional aid policy and inform faculty and administrative partners on such a committee of the parameters and dynamics of financial aid awards.

Academic areas are not equipped to answer complex financial aid questions from students, yet they are often a point of contact for instruction and academic advising. As a result, students express concerns about finances to academic personnel. Understanding some of the complexities of aid, as well as their ability to guide students to the financial aid office for assistance, can determine how effectively the institution, overall, supports the financial needs of its students.

Compliance in financial aid is the adherence to regulations that govern the administration of aid program, funds, determination of eligibility, reporting, and policies that align with federal education policies for higher education, such as non-discrimination, gender equity, FERPA, and observance of Constitution Day. This can also mean alignment with state/provincial policies as well. Although governmental compliance is the most specific of the ways in which we conceive of this term, following policies on institutional and outside funds also falls under compliance within the institution. Athletic compliance often requires participation of the aid office to provide data and closely liaise with the athletic departments to ensure that student awards fall within the parameters of the athletic association to which the institution belongs.

There are numerous other examples of collaboration between the aid office and its institutional partners. These include but are not limited to the registrar for attendance and related withdrawal information, academic affairs for term definitions, instructional locations, grading and policies for satisfactory academic progress, finance for application of payments, reconciliation of accounts and drawdown of funds from external sources, and fundraising/development for the stewardship of existing gifts and shaping of new gifts to meet student needs. This brief listing reflects the breadth of interactions that the aid office must develop and maintain to ensure that the resulting funds to students meet regulatory requirements and foster successful educational outcomes.

USING DATA TO MEASURE FINANCIAL AID OPERATIONS

The use of data to inform decision-making is a fundamental concept in SEM. In Chapter 3, data are used to analyze performance of aid awards for enrollment. Within the financial aid office, several measures can be implemented to assess the efficiency of operations.

Tracking the receipt of Individual Student Information Record (ISIR) files downloaded from the federal processor reflects the volume of processing that will be performed, overall. Although FAFSA filing volume has steadily increased since 2008, the institution may or may not see its volume of ISIR records increasing as well. This could indicate that students are not acting in a timely manner to file the FAFSA, that fewer students plan to register at the institution, or that students are unaware of the benefits of completing the FAFSA and its resulting aid options (that is, the student perceives that he or she may not qualify for grant assistance and does not understand state aid requirements or low-interest loan options). The financial aid office can assess the specific groups of students (new, continuing, undergraduate, graduate, and so on) to determine what pockets of students may or may not be submitting ISIR files to the institution. Appropriate interventions can be developed as a result. In this way, ISIR volume can act as a bellwether for enrollment trends at the institution. It may also indicate that a greater proportion of students need financial assistance in the coming year. The institution may therefore need to plan for institutional aid expenditures, as possible, to provide greater levels of assistance and increase student retention and persistence.

During the application process, the financial aid office is required to verify a certain amount of information provided by the student/parent during submission of the FAFSA. Measuring the number of files identified by the federal processor or the financial aid staff for review of possibly discrepant data is required to know the volume of review required. This allows the office's leadership to deploy staff to review the information, as well as project the timeline for file review to be completed and any resulting funds to be available to students.

Leading practices in this area promote two actions by students and parents (if the student is dependent). First, the IRS Data Retrieval process expedites the completion of the form and eliminates the need for the financial aid office to gather student/parent tax transcripts and compare them to the ISIR/FAFSA data. Aid offices that have aggressively marketed this feature to new and continuing students have seen significant reductions in staff time required to verify data. Second, the office uses its prior years' data on processing time to set a priority date for verification materials to be provided to the office. Information provided by this date is then reviewed prior to the start of the coming term, so that any possible funds may be available for the start of the term. Although these reviews can be complex, and some will result in students being found ineligible, the overall result is materials being received and reviews being completed earlier, so that funds are available to students for the coming term. The data on review times is continuously assessed, so that the priority document filing date can be adjusted accordingly.

Tracking the receipt and processing of documents for review is another way in which the financial aid office uses data to improve operations. Establishing processing codes within the student information system for records requiring verification and within those incomplete, complete, and reviewed designations allows staff to view the queue of records in real time. Management can adjust staffing deployment levels when queues are longer. Strategically, this can be used to determine times when the office may need to deploy temporary help to complete file review, which is discussed later in this chapter.

STUDENT SERVICE

Back-office processing is not the only area where data plays an important role in financial aid operations. The service provided to students and others is also an important area for measurement and information collection. A direct relationship exists between these services and information provided to students online.

Service-oriented financial aid offices gather data on service requests at their points of contact. Most modern phone systems can produce reports of call volumes by hour, by staff member, and with details on the time spent on the call, number of calls abandoned (not answered), and so on. These data can be used to plan staffing patterns in the office's call center or to plan the number of staff who need to be manning the phones at any given hour of the day. Beyond the volume of calls, the reasons for the calls should also be gathered.

Whether the financial aid office employs an email address or a web information request form to provide online services, measuring volume provides administrators with accurate information to deploy staff and to inform them of the issues that students and others may be having in the aid process. The web information request form provides benefits beyond an office email link. Requests can be categorized and routed to specialists who may be best equipped to answer them.

Walk-in traffic must also be measured, and there are two common measurement methods. Some institutions use the student's identification card and its magnetic strip to have the student "swipe in" when coming to the financial aid office. This can track the student on a unit level, if desired, to understand the contact pattern with that individual. Within the institutions deploying this technology, some also ask the student to identify his or her primary reason for the visit when entering. Technology resources are often limited at most institutions. Those institutions with fewer resources do not have to deploy sophisticated technology to take these measurements. They may use paper-and-pencil methods to "tick" the in-person visits along categories or reasons for the visit. Both methods allow the institution to understand the main issues or information needs that students have at that time.

The information gathered from student requests from phone, online, and walk-in services are used to feed automated phone and online information for students. Automated phone messages can be updated to reflect timely information, such as start dates for classes or dates for refund check distribution. The institutional website should be updated regularly with information that responds to the information students seek or with guidance on process and forms or other links. These can significantly reduce the inbound service levels and provide information to students at times when the office is not open for services. As the information is added to the institution's website under frequently asked questions or in other prominent locations, the measurement of the incoming topics should correspondingly drop. If not, the information being presented is not adequately addressing student needs.

STAFF DEPLOYMENT AND TRAINING

In this section, a paradigm for financial aid staffing is proposed, using three teams to cover most aid functions. The actual number of staff, the size of these teams, and the variety of arrangements of functions inside and outside the financial aid office in higher education will alter this paradigm to fit each institution's particular type, size, and scope.

The first of the three teams is focused on document and information processing. This team receives information from outside providers, such as federal application processors and state agencies. It also receives and processes information and documents directly from students or parents of dependent students. The team processes the information in preparation for its use by the two other teams in the financial aid office. This team typically comprises staff who perform clerical-level tasks and would include any number of student employees who assist in the receipt, sorting, recording, scanning, indexing, and routing of information to staff members.

The second team of the financial aid office is the program management and case review team. These are typically financial aid counselors or specialists with a higher level of complex analysis skills. They manage specific financial aid programs, such as the federal Pell grant program, federal direct loan programs, athletic grant programs, state grant programs, and so on. It is common for one team member to manage at least one and perhaps several of these programs at once.

The specialists review student cases and information, including verification cases, appeals for exceptional circumstances, appeals for continued aid beyond normal policy limits (such as Satisfactory Academic Progress), and other student requests that go beyond the expertise of the service team. These staff are frequently called upon to provide public information sessions to prospective and current students. These may include presentations at local high school financial aid nights or community gatherings, institutional open houses, and current student aid application drives.

Specialists also meet and communicate directly with students. Their level of engagement varies significantly by institutional type and size. At a small institution, these specialists may have significant direct contact with students, as their overlap with service teams is greater. In larger institutions, specialists may have little daily contact with students and focus more intently on case processing based on information submitted to other teams. Although almost all financial aid staff have contact with students at one time or another, the level of contact is not consistent across higher education.

The service team, our third of the three, provides direct interface with students and the public on a regular basis. Much of their work has been previously described in this chapter. This team may also be augmented with student employees, deployed to answer routine questions from students and others. One of the more effective uses of students is to help other students navigate online services. This can be especially helpful with rural or adult learner populations that are less frequently engaged with self-service technologies. Student employees in the service team may help fellow students as peer mentors, assisting them with initial FAFSA and PIN setup, student account initialization, portal navigation, and other self-service mechanisms the institution has deployed.

Management and leadership of these teams should be focused on continuous training and communication. At every level, the financial aid director should have a clear plan for professional development and training. Although the daily tasks of any office can overwhelm its communication pathways internally, the financial aid teams require regular communication and clear goals for the work to be performed. During the height of information processing for a coming term, the teams should have weekly updates and (even brief) meetings to set targets for information processing. Sharing data on current status of applications received, aid awarded, pending and completed reviews, and call-in, walk-in, and online traffic volume keeps the staff engaged with their partner teams within the office.

Training for all teams that have student contact should include interpersonal relations training. Financial issues can be emotionally charged, and having students and parents who are distraught over financial pressures to pay college costs is not uncommon. Student and parent aspiration often collide with reality in the financial aid and student accounts offices. Because students and parents may not make rational or sound financial choices, even with strong information systems and outreach from the institution, these offices are often charged with enforcing policies that are unpopular among students and parents. Learning to say "no" in a way that leaves the student and parent with dignity and hope for higher education options requires training, tact, and practice. Selection of staff is important, as well, because this is not a job that some people can perform day after day or with the empathy required.

Staffing efficiency includes the degree to which staff members are flexible enough to work across teams, as possible within their skill levels. Although it may not be feasible for a document imaging specialists to fill in and run the direct loan program, for example, specialists filling gaps in the service team or assuring that information processing continues when one team member is out requires cross-training and an understanding of how each business process integrates into the greater information-processing scheme. Using the business process guides mentioned earlier in this chapter as a basis for staff training reinforces the integration of information across all teams and functions of the financial aid operation.

Professional development is not limited to internal training. In the United States, the state-level associations of the National Association of Student Financial Aid Administrators (NASFAA) are key resources for training. Free federal training sessions are offered for both new and continuing professionals. A growing number of training sessions are available online, reducing travel costs and time away from the institution. Many state higher education systems offer training and regular communications among staff through annual meetings, conference calls, and other networking channels.

It is important for financial aid leaders to establish networks of other financial aid professionals through state and national associations and local outreach. These allow leaders to check on unusual circumstances quickly, varying approaches to common issues and establishing contacts for consortium agreements for aid when students cross-enroll at local institutions (an increasingly popular trend).

SPECIAL ISSUES WITH STUDENT INFORMATION

The financial aid office receives and reviews a great deal of personal student and parent information. In the United States, this includes the student's Social Security number (SSN), which is used as the linking unique identifier between the institutional student information system and external data sources, such as ISIR and state grant systems. Unique personal information is not limited to just the SSN. Student and parent income and asset information is also received and stored by the financial aid office.

The protection of student information in financial aid operations extends to other personnel at the institution. Although an academic adviser may have an appropriate need to know that a student has a financial hold that prevents registration, he or she does not need to know a student's personal financial background. The financial aid office must assure that it protects this unique student's information from any other area of the institution that does not have a demonstrated reason to see or access it.

Providing seamless financial service to students requires collaboration between the student accounts and financial aid offices. Both areas require viewing access to student account balances and financial aid awards. Extending view-only access to admissions team members for documents that may be outstanding in financial aid or award packages helps the institution communicate with students about their status in the financial aid process in a much more cohesive manner. Access to tax transcripts or other information that contains student and parent income and SSN information should be sequestered in the document imaging system to ensure that it is not viewed beyond the intended scope or intent, in the same way that an institution would restrict access to paper financial aid files.

TECHNOLOGY

As detailed elsewhere in this book, technology is a critical element in SEM today. Earlier in the chapter, technology was mentioned as one of many guiding concepts in financial aid operations. Two additional areas will receive additional investigation here.

First, document imaging allows the aid office to reduce or eliminate paper files. Recent changes in mechanisms to join student aid applications to tax data (IRS Data Retrieval) have reduced the need to collect tax returns, the largest paper data source in the financial aid office. However, additional documentation is still required for many students, and financial aid operations receive thousands of pieces of paper each year.

Imaging aid documents and indexing them to student records allows all student information to be processed without the creation and management of paper aid files. Like all areas of student records, the greatest efficiency and cost savings is realized when the imaging and indexing is done at the point of receipt. Students and staff can then see that documentation is on file without manually checking files or answering status questions via phones and email. Financial aid operations that image the documents after processing the information add work and student contacts to the process, rather than reduce them. Like student records, financial aid utilizes a myriad of forms. Creating and routing these through workflow (often enabled through document imaging systems) further reduces reliance on tracking and maintaining paper.

The second area of technology in financial aid that merits special consideration is communications through technology. The challenge for financial aid operations is staying abreast of multichannel communications with students, parents, guidance personnel, faculty, and institutional partners. Although colleagues may read email, this is effective with only a small portion of students. Social media channels and SMS texts may be more effective for additional portions of the student population, as well as parents and others. One important aspect of communications is that they are continuing to change, and preferences today may not be preferences tomorrow.

Financial aid operations must be prepared to communicate along multiple platforms with the same messages. At the same time, staff must be cognizant that they cannot share personal or sensitive information through channels that may be seen publicly or broadly. Letting a student know that he or she has been flagged for verification on the institution's Facebook page would be highly inappropriate. However, a note on the Facebook page about the importance of checking the status of your aid application in a secure portal with a link to the login site is completely appropriate, and some institutions find this to be effective. A companion Twitter message, a posting on the financial aid office web page, and postcards during processing season can all add to the effectiveness of communications.

CONCLUSION

Financial aid is a key collaborator in institutional SEM. Its reach spans nearly every department and touches nearly every person at an institution. The financial aid office's ability to communicate clearly and collaborate with its institutional partners often determines its effectiveness in meeting student needs as well as the needs and requests of those who financially support them.

Financial aid engages with students and their supporters across the enrollment cycle. From early outreach and community engagement to increase literacy, to college search and choices stages, financial aid operations play a key role in helping students make smart decisions about funding their degrees, while helping the institution reach its strategic enrollment goals. Financial aid continues to engage with students throughout their collegiate enrollment to foster retention and persistence to degree. After the student leaves the institution, financial aid continues to play a key role in minimizing loan defaults and helping students select the most advantageous repayment options for their student loans. Few areas of the institution have such a wide timeline of influence over student enrollment.

Containing costs at a time when demand is growing for financial aid services and resources are scarce or shrinking requires that operations are highly efficient. They must leverage existing technologies and wisely evaluate emerging technologies. This allows the operation to scale up in areas where that is possible and devote human resources to those areas that are not scalable and require human interaction.

Although the field of financial aid is technically complex, aid and enrollment leaders need to be careful to keep concepts and language simple when working with the public, students, parents, and colleagues who are not immersed in financial aid regulations and methods. Answering the simple questions that most people have about affording a college degree allows the financial aid office to engage them and bring them slowly into the intricate web of financial aid resources and programs that may help them access and attain higher education.

Strategy in financial aid can too often be viewed narrowly, as the application of institutional aid to drive enrollment outcomes. Although an important resource, institutional aid strategies can be seriously impaired if not supported by the effective delivery of those funds. For institutions in which institutional aid is a small or negligible percentage of overall aid, the effective delivery of national/federal and state/provincial funds plays an even greater role in an institution's financial and enrollment health, as well as the most important outcome, student success.

References

Bettinger, E. (2004). *How Financial Aid Affects Persistence*. Cambridge, MA: National Bureau of Economic Research.

Bettinger, E., Long, B., Oreopoulos, P., & Sanbonmatsu, L. (2009). *The Role of Simplification and Information in College Decisions: Results from the H&R Block FAFSA Experiment*. Cambridge, MA: National Bureau of Economic Research.

Bontrager, B., & Green, T. (2012). A structure for SEM planning. In B. Bontrager, R. Ingersoll, & D. Ingersoll (Eds.), *SEM: Transforming Higher Education* (pp. 271–284). Washington, DC: American Association of Collegiate Registrars and Admissions Officers.

College Board Advocacy and Policy Center. (2010). *Cracking the Student Aid Code: Parent and Student Perspectives on Paying for College.* New York: College Board.

College Board Advocacy and Policy Center. (2012). *Trends in College Pricing*. New York: College Board.

Ehrenberg, R. (2002). *Tuition Rising: Why College Costs So Much*. Cambridge, MA: Harvard University Press.

Gross, J., Hossler, D., & Ziskin, M. (2007). Institutional aid and student persistence: An analysis of the effects of campus-based financial aid at public four-year institutions. *NASFAA Journal of Student Financial Aid, 37*(1), 29–39.

Hanson, K. H., & Litten, L. H. (1982). Mapping the road to academe: A review of research on women, men, and the college selection process. In P. Rerun (Ed.), *The Undergraduate Woman: Issues in Educational Equity* (pp. 73–97). Lexington, MA: D.C. Health.

Hoover, E. (2013). NYU announces $1-billion campaign for financial aid. *The Chronicle of Higher Education*. Retrieved from http://chronicle.com/article/nyu-announces-1-billion/142503.

Hossler, D., & Bean, J., Eds. (1990). *The Strategic Management of College Enrollments*. San Francisco: Jossey-Bass.

Hossler, D., & Gallagher, K. (1987). Studying college choice: A three-phase model and the implications for policymakers. *College & University, 62*(3), 207–221.

Hossler, D., Schmit, J., & Vesper, N. (1999). *Going to College: How Social, Economic, and Educational Factors Influence the Decisions Students Make*. Baltimore, MD: The John Hopkins University Press.

Kerlin, C. (2008). A community college roadmap for the enrollment management journey. *College & University, 4*(83), 10–14.

Manski, C., & Wise, D. (1983). *College Choice in America*. Cambridge, MA: Harvard University Press.

National Survey of Student Engagement. (2012). *Promoting Student Learning and Institutional Improvement: Lessons from NSSE at 13*. Bloomington, IN: Indiana University Center for Postsecondary Research.

Pryor, J. H., Eagan, K., Palucki Blake, L., Hurtado, S., Berdan, J., & Case, M. H. (2012). *The American Freshman: National Norms Fall 2012*. Los Angeles: Higher Education Research Institute, UCLA.

State Higher Education Executive Officers. (2013). State higher education finance FY 2012. Washington, DC: SHEEO.

Tinto, V. (1993). *Leaving College: Rethinking the Causes and Cures of Student Attrition* (2nd Edition). Chicago: University of Chicago Press.

Troop, D. (2013). On Her Way Out, U. of Mich. Chief Gives $1-Million for Scholarships. Retrieved from http://chronicle.com/blogs/bottomline/on-her-way-out-u-of-michigans-president-gives-1-million-for-study-abroad-scholarships.

U.S. Department of Education. (2013). Quarterly volume reports by the National Association of Student Financial Aid Administrators (NASFAA). Retrieved November 2, 2013, from http://www.finaid.org/fafsa/fafsastatistics.phtml.

CHAPTER 22

The Role of Technology in Supporting SEM

Wendy Kilgore and Brent Gage

The chapters in this part of the SEM handbook make a compelling case for the importance of the functions delivered by enrollment service offices—admissions, registrars, and financial aid in particular—in providing the necessary infrastructure for the practice of Strategic Enrollment Management. Indeed, SEM has become dependent on evolving technology to manage these and other critical operations within complex college and university organizations. Technology has transformed business processes and the way in which institutions interact with both internal and external stakeholders. To wrap up this section on "backroom" functions, this chapter reviews the rapid growth of technology within institutions and in direct support of SEM, and the manner in which it has impacted institutions of all type and size. This transformation has also resulted in an evolution in SEM processes and professional skill sets, as well as expectations of internal and external stakeholders. Although technology has created tremendous efficiencies and opportunities for in-depth analysis, realizing its potential requires that the implementation and management of systems be thoughtfully managed and developed over time. The topics covered in this chapter provide context and guidance for how technology can impact institutional SEM efforts.

HISTORY

A. W. "Tony" Bates and Albert Sangra (2011) stated that "Technology is an essential component of any modern post-secondary educational institution, not only for supporting administrative activities, but also increasingly for the core activities of teach and learning" (p. XIX). This is, however, a relatively recent development. In the last twenty-five years, the application of technology at institutions of higher education has evolved quickly from eighty-column punch cards distributed to lines of students at registration and used to feed a student's course choice, to a mainframe computer, to 100 percent web-based student self-service for curricular and co-curricular experiences. Much of this change in technology can be attributed to the relatively recent widespread adoption of enterprise resource planning (ERP) systems, or comprehensive student information systems (SIS) and self-service functionality. William Gorr and Don Hossler (2006) posited that concerns about Y2K led many organizations, including higher education, to replace stand-alone systems with ERPs. They further stated that at the system level, the adoption of ERPs helped eliminate redundancy in data, standardize interfaces, and approach data standardization. ERPs opened the door for easy data sharing and consistent data sources for institutional users. Externally, recent technology also introduced global competition through the ability to deliver online learning content and services in a 24/7 environment. In the not-so-distant past, enrollment managers were primarily concerned with remaining competitive with a few key institutions. These competitors were often within a certain geographic boundary or identified by defined peer groups. However, now that prospective and current students are able to access services and learning content almost anywhere at any time, enrollment managers and institutional administrators must contend with a broader spectrum of institutional competition in their SEM efforts.

Although there is a rapidly growing pool of scholarly resources about online pedagogy and several resources on how to ensure effective ERP implementation, little has been written about the systemic application of technology to support SEM (see, for example, Bates & Sangra, 2011; de-la-Fuente-Valentín, Pardo, & Delgado Kloos, 2013; Gorr & Hossler, 2006; Wagner & Newell, 2004, 2006). Much available literature on the application of technology to support SEM is either produced as a marketing piece by technology vendors or published by non-profit membership organizations such as the American Association of Collegiate Registrars and Admissions Officers, National Association for College Admissions Counseling, and EDUCAUSE. This gap in scholarly literature leaves administrators and enrollment managers applying technology in a patchwork-quilt manner rather than approaching technology systemically and with a sound practice-based foundation.

CONTEXT

Understanding that some contextual references to 2013 technology included in this chapter may already be obsolete by 2014, the conceptual recommendations and considerations for the successful application of technology to SEM have been written in such a manner as to remain cogent for the foreseeable future. Even in this age of disruptive technology, some core functions will likely remain constant for the relatively near future (for example, ERPs, SISs, database structure, network structures, and so on), while much of the user interface will continue to change rapidly. For example, just in the last few years the preferred student-facing interface has evolved from a personal computer–based web platform to mobile platform compatibility for smartphones, tablets, and phablets, which are devices that combine smart phone and tablet functionality. Institutions must balance the need for a stable technology infrastructure with leading-edge interfaces. As such databases should be resilient and slow to adopt new technology, the way systems manage processes should be highly configurable to meet the institution's evolving process needs, and the access technologies (user interfaces) should be high-moving and fast-adopting of new solutions (for example, learning management systems [LMS], self-service systems, staff interfaces, and so on) (S. Hope, personal communication, October 2, 2013).

Although Stanley Henderson (2012) stated that there are two distinct goals of institutional SEM, one in which "institutions are working to determine and reach their optimum enrollments" (p. 3) and another in which institutions are more concerned with "maintaining their position and profile" (p. 3), the thoughtful application of technology is necessary to support either of these goals, as well as a variety of other institutional interests. In general, technology serves three overarching purposes when applied in higher education: (1) as a means to store data, (2) as a means to provide effective service, and (3) as a resource for business intelligence. Alternatively, Bates and Sangra (2011) viewed technology as one of the key factors in balancing three competing institutional forces: access, quality, and cost. Robert Jacobs and Ted Weston (2007) asserted that ERPs also provide "an information rich environment that is ripe for very intelligent planning and execution logic" (p. 363). They further provided administrators with a resource of good data from which to make viable decisions (Lingrell, 2012). Recently the 2013 EDUCAUSE "Top-ten IT issues" ranked three technology issues related to SEM as the numbers two, nine, and ten issues on the list. Respectively, these issues are "Improving student outcomes through an approach that leverages technology"," transforming the institution's business with information technology", and "using analytics to support critical institutional outcomes" (Grajek, 2013, p. 34). The ability to apply technology effectively to meet these at once synergistic and competing institutional purposes is further complicated by the heterogeneous nature of the end users at each institution.

The ideal environment for an easy and successful application of technology is a homogeneous one—that is, one in which the goals and needs of all end users are the same. In any system, homogeneity is unlikely, and in higher education in particular, Erica Wagner and Sue Newell (2004) posited that there is a different cultural context among the various technology user groups across an institution. These user groups often maintain unique goals and approaches to practice. Similarly, in a chapter of *The Tower and the Cloud*,

Jim Davis (2008) used the analogy of the institution as a global corporation, and within this analogy stated that "each frontline unit has its own unique interests, competing among, state national, and/or international peers much like a line of business"(p. 120). In practice, this means that if each administrative and academic unit were asked what the primary role of technology is for institutional SEM efforts, their answers would vary based on the area of expertise of the practitioner, his or her goals (assigned or personal), and the institutional/departmental culture and structure of the organization. For example, although the administrative group seeks to remain competitive in the global educational marketplace, staff are often focused on providing better service to students; faculty, on the other hand, are focused on ways to provide a viable technology platform to deliver subject content, improve student success, and assess learning outcomes and/or to assist with research. Students expect that institutions will accept and adopt new and emerging technologies (Ingerman & Yang, 2010; Wagner & Newell, 2004). William Balzer (2010) specifically tied student learning, persistence, success, and satisfaction to students' experiences with critical processes, of which most are supported and delivered by technology.

Figure 22.1 represents just some of the many technologies that prospects, applicants, and students may be expected to use throughout their tenure at an

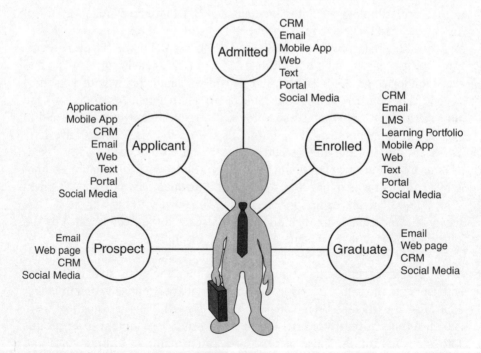

Figure 22.1 Technology in the student lifecycle

institution and as alumni. Each technology must be effective in its own right as well as collectively. Each may be part of a comprehensive ERP or a collection of distinct solutions tied together through data sharing. Less often, they are stand-alone solutions. The back office processes of the ERP/SIS are typically invisible to students, and they interact with the many technologies assuming they are all part of the same system and operated collectively by the institution.

Viewed within the context of these varied goals and needs, technology is a fulcrum for many SEM initiatives and student persistence, and, as such, should be considered holistically in the context of SEM planning. Doing this effectively is no small feat. To provide further context, one must consider the varied technology goals, needs, and expertise for the following user group examples.

Example User Groups

A vice president for enrollment management (VPEM) at a small private college is familiar with the need for clean and accurate data to make effective enrollment planning decisions. The VPEM is comfortable with the PC platform and likely proficient with the various tablet platforms. However, the laptop is the primary tool for accessing and manipulating data from reports. Although the VPEM is proficient in these areas, she usually defers to other staff to make technology recommendations, implement new technology to support SEM initiatives, and ensure that the data is accurate and timely. The VPEM is unlikely to be a day-to-day user of the ERP.

Comparatively, a faculty member with extensive online teaching experience may enjoy the new technology platforms for online learning. A typical experienced online faculty member is proficient with basic document uploading and manipulation in the LMS system as well as grading, chatting with students, supporting offline discussion groups, and developing measures of learning. Faculty members often have not received any formal training on any of the LMS software. They often prefer to communicate with students through the LMS platform instead of the institution email accounts. They are likely never to use the operational client interface for the ERP and access what they need through the self-service module.

A director of enrollment services at a large community college is a system power user and responsible for leading others in the effective daily use of the ERP and other ancillary system functions related to admissions, records, and registration. He is often part of the technology team and meets with this team regularly to discuss upgrades, issues, and new technology projects.

An academic advisor at a highly selective mid-size university may use the web portal functions in the SIS only to provide advising recommendations to advisees and to run degree audit checks. She may also require familiarity with the LMS for delivery of advising content or ongoing personal education.

On the other hand, a typical millennial student at a large state university may not even own a desktop PC and use only a laptop, phablet, or tablet for his coursework. This student is unlikely to use the institution-issued email regularly, and as such may miss key communications from the institution and from instructors. He often prefers texting as a means of communicating that some action is needed. This student also tends to drift from one emerging and trendy social media platform to another, and then quickly move on when the next best thing is released and popularized. To communicate effectively with students through electronic means, institutions must be agile in adopting new means of communication and consult students regularly on their preferred means of communication (Kilgore, 2012).

The preceding examples consider just a few of the many users of institutional technology. The holistic consideration, application, and adoption of new technology within the broader context of SEM plans and initiatives quickly becomes a large portion of what needs to be considered to remain competitive in the education marketplace.

TECHNOLOGY AND A SEM ENVIRONMENT SCAN

In the higher education marketplace, students have more options and more access to greater amounts of information than ever before. In addition, the way prospective students and parents are consuming information has changed dramatically, as institutions are one voice among many in their recruitment and marketing efforts. Students expect anytime access to information in an easy-to-use format in one location. From the point at which a prospective student is identified through each phase of the institution's outreach efforts, technology plays a critical role in recruitment, retention, reporting, and measurements of SEM efforts.

It is now the norm for multiple systems with high levels of functionality to be interwoven to meet the needs of SEM and student expectations. Recruitment software that is utilized at varying levels of sophistication is now commonplace, as intricate communication plans are developed for various segments of the prospective population. This software tracks and monitors student progress through the funnel as students move through various stages leading to the application for admission. Systems are then connected through complex interface protocols with a centralized student information system serving as the ultimate home of the student record. From this hub of student information, additional connections are created to facilitate degree audit functions, classroom space management tools, document imaging systems, retention tracking, student engagement efforts, development strategies, and data warehouse tools that enable complex institutional reporting mechanisms.

Effective enrollment management hinges upon the ability to achieve successfully five core functions dependent upon the technological tools in place to affect enrollment based upon established institutional goals:

- Effective reporting capabilities at multiple stages of the student life cycle
- Appropriate recording mechanisms that allow for measured effect to be determined as a means of assessment
- Increased efficiency in processing and automation that increases responsiveness and reduces operational costs
- Simplification of processes and access to information for students, parents, faculty, and staff
- Creation of tools that empower campus officials to access information readily to create a culture of data-driven decision-making

Although the needs and priorities vary greatly by institution, the core functions managed by SEM organizations depend upon the ability to leverage technology to inform decision-making while enhancing the student experience. Accurate, accessible information allows for ongoing alignment of resources to institutional priorities and provides a means of assessing the effectiveness of recruitment and retention efforts in meeting the institution's overarching goals.

As institutions scan the internal higher education environment, it is also essential that they stay aware of how technology in evolving externally to meet potential institutional demands and student needs. Enrollment managers must stay abreast of new technology and how students are consuming information, but they must also align technology with institutional goals and external demands. The ability to remain informed of current technological trends is critical as enrollment management leaders look to achieve institutional goals. Engagement in discussions at the national level can help to make sense out of a crowded landscape of opportunities. Although new solutions and upgraded tools are readily available, a strategic approach is critical in embracing new technology. A clearly defined institutional plan can guide priorities as new solutions are sought to solve existing problems and create new opportunities. The linkages between institutional goals and technology are essential as the senior enrollment officer attempts to manage competing priorities with limited resources.

The increasing demands for institutional accountability at the local, state, and federal levels have forced institutions to record and track essential data carefully. These reporting requirements come from a variety of sources and may be mandated with little time to implement. This requires that institutions respond quickly and adapt existing technology to manage new functions and record essential data throughout the student life cycle. New mandates in the areas of retention, graduation, financial aid, student indebtedness, student access, learning outcomes, and job placement are just a few of the areas in which systems must be able to respond to increasing demands.

Technology has an increasing role in state, regional, and national accreditation processes in which institutions must demonstrate that they have the tools in place to meet educational expectations. The demonstration of educational outcomes must now be articulated through data analysis as part of these periodic reviews. It is critical that the technology be in place to meet these expectations through the collection of data at key points in time.

Another challenge for the enrollment manager is to understand the expectation of students as they interact with their institutions. Students have an increasing expectation that access to information and assistance should be readily available in the manner in which they expect it to be delivered. Websites, student portals, and communication channels need to be designed with the user in mind. New technology that enables anytime access to information is now the expectation of students, and higher education must continue to be responsive in engaging its students. Continually evolving current technology and moving to new channels are important, as the ways in which students choose to consume information are constantly changing.

As the higher education market becomes increasingly competitive, enrollment management staff must be up-to-date with how best to reach their target audience. Traditional recruitment efforts now serve as a means to augment a multifaceted approach to marketing and outreach. With multiple channels available to students and parents, in which they can acquire information as part of the college search process, enrollment managers must continually find new ways to engage and connect with prospective students.

Leading practices can provide an essential roadmap for enrollment managers as they determine which tools, strategies, and analyses can help to inform their efforts as part of their overall plan. Professional development through state, regional, and national organizations is critical as creative uses of technology are being employed all over the world. The ability to learn from colleagues and adapt new technology to the primary needs of the institution is fundamental to the role of the enrollment manager.

Institutions must develop thoughtful and inclusive ways to prioritize technological needs relative to institutional goals. With multiple priorities competing for limited resources, institutions must be thoughtful as they embrace new technology. They should consider a number of issues when assessing technological needs and investment in new tools. Functional items that allow for effective course registration, delivery of financial aid, processing of admission, and maintenance of effective records are essential and must be addressed as primary concerns. Other solutions, such as document imaging and degree audit systems, must have champions who can articulate how these additional systems will help improve enrollment outcomes, address workload issues, and reduce costs.

An analysis of institutional goals can help guide technological priorities and lead to a more thoughtful process of assessing the current marketplace. Clearly established internal goals can serve as a blueprint for determining which efforts are most critical if enrollment management has specific targets or benchmarks in student recruitment. Technology can play a vital role in helping to mitigate increasing student recruitment costs through utilization of new communication channels and increasing the level of prospect qualification. Based on the institutional enrollment goals, many tools can help the institution shape the class and emphasize efforts at particular segments. If retention efforts are a priority, technological solutions can help identify and direct resources to at-risk students in a timely fashion. Capacity issues can be handled much more efficiently through an enterprise classroom management system that provides a global view of space utilization. The development of a well-articulated enrollment management plan will serve as an essential guide in leading the campus evolution of technology.

Opportunities for efficiency are another essential internal consideration for the implementation of new technology. The ability to automate manual processes and create more opportunities for student self-service can significantly impact the ability of SEM units to redirect resources. Implementation of technology that enables institutions to become more responsive, while requiring fewer processing staff, can offset costs and create new opportunities.

The adaptation to a new technology also requires a willingness within the campus culture to embrace change. Institutions should assess a new technology with regard to who will utilize the new tool on a daily basis. Thoughtful initial assessment, ongoing communication, and a clearly articulated rationale for the transition to new technology can greatly increase the impact of evolving technology.

Institutions must be realistic when considering technological advances given their existing infrastructure within the information technology domain. If sufficient resources are not available to manage new technology and leverage its features, little will be gained through new applications. In addition, the partnership with enrollment management and the information technology staff must evolve in a manner that maintains a high level of understanding of the business processes in place to implement the technology. This partnership will play a large part in determining the impact of the technology on the students and staff.

Although vendor-developed ERPs and SISs are still the most common core software used to support institutions of higher education, they are often too rigid in their configurability to meet unique institutional needs without modifications, they often do not provide functionality for all business needs, and institutions are tied to the vendor's enhancement schedule (Gorr & Hossler, 2006). On the other hand, these programs do provide a stable core for primary business functions and a single source for data, and they offer more supportable data sharing with third-party solutions than in the recent past. More recently, institutions are choosing "best-of-breed" solutions to support the dynamic environment of student front-end services and learning management systems as well as other specialty functions, and these solutions are networked through a data interface to the ERP/SIS. By adopting best-of-breed vendor solutions, institutions are able to take advantage of emerging technology in a manner that is not often supported within the traditional comprehensive ERP/SIS development timeline. Smaller focused solution vendors rely on client contract renewals to stay in business, so they tend to be more responsive to the needs and wants of both the institutional client and the emerging trends in user interfaces and delivery platforms.

Several models of system solutions are available in today's marketplace, including home-grown systems, open-source systems, vendor-developed comprehensive client-hosted ERP/SISs, Software as a Service (SaaS) solutions, and cloud/client-hosted hybrid solutions. Gartner, Inc. (2014) further defines SaaS as software that is owned, delivered, and managed remotely by one or more providers that deliver software based on a single set of common code and data definitions. This software is consumed in a one-to-many model by all customers at any time on a pay-for-use basis or as a subscription based on use metrics. As mentioned, the vendor-developed ERP/SIS is currently the most common solution, and these solutions tend to be client hosted and require a great deal of institutional infrastructure and human capital to support. Although this model can be supported at large institutions with sufficient IT staff, it is more difficult for smaller institutions to take full advantage of the functionality of these large ERPs. Vendors are more recently offering SaaS, which enables institutions to adopt scalable, externally supported ERP/SISs or single-purpose products (such as customer relationship management [CRM] software, LMS, alumni services, reporting, and so on) with fewer financial and human resources than client-hosted solutions. Cloud computing was included as number 3 in the EDUCAUSE (2013) "Top-Ten IT Issues" because it "can enable institutions to be more agile and deliver new services faster and with fewer or lower up-front costs" (p. 39). Ideally, any technology solution selected to support SEM efforts should be scalable, best-of-breed, and highly configurable by the end user with minimal programming expertise, and it should support an easy-to-use user interface that includes mobile platform compatibility. Measuring these attributes across the wide variety of technology options and selecting the right solution for today and for the future can be a challenge at an institution-wide level. This endeavor requires both strategic and operational leadership to assess and understand the current and future technology needs of the institution.

EFFECTIVE TECHNOLOGY REQUIRES SELF-ASSESSMENT

To address the technology needs of a complex organization, it is critical that the institution clearly define that its primary needs are being served by SEM. Key functions in admissions require a vastly different set of technology and tools that those required by the registrar, for example. Beyond function, institutions must ask, What is the ideal mode of delivery and output that is required to enable students and staff to meet their needs effectively?

To conduct a thorough technology self-assessment, each unit must determine how current processes interact with policy and the required output. This assessment will allow technology to serve core functions in a meaningful way, rather than changing business practices and needs to adapt to the system in place. To begin a technology needs self-assessment, each unit must address several key questions to establish the foundation for leveraging technology:

- Does the institution's policies reflect practice?
  - The effective use of technology is closely tied to how well policy, practice, and technology align with one another.
  - Policy, practice, and technology should be evaluated simultaneously.
- Has the institution adopted new technology and kept old processes as well?
- How often are students, staff, and others using existing technology?
- Is all of the functionality being used?
- Does a change in policy always coincide with a review of the affected technology, and vice versa?
- Do institutional practices reflect "best practices"?
  - What are the current leading practices?

The accurate interpretation of the results of each analysis is vital to effective decision-making regarding how to address the gaps in technology relative to the institution's needs. Institutions must further evaluate the technology solution within the context of how the technology will be used, by whom, and within other institutional contexts such as enrollment goals, applicable policy, and the culture and values of the institution or service unit. Kilgore (2011) identifies five additional evaluation activities and considerations:

- Aim to select a solution that "off the shelf" most closely meets the operational needs of the institution, retains or enables the ability of the institution to remain competitive with other institutions, and limits the number of non-value-added activities associated with the process.

- Differentiate and define required versus desired functionality.

- Conduct in-depth examination of the pros and cons of potential technology solutions such as purchase price, the timeline for implementation, internal and external human resource requirements, ongoing maintenance costs, and the company's track record of ongoing system development to meet continuously emerging needs.

- Measure and document the gap between the solution and required functionality and decide whether or not that gap is acceptable to the institution. If not, also document what would need to be done to close the gap, and the associated costs.

- Invite stakeholders to provide their input on the options.

A completed self-assessment serves as a blueprint for the selection and implementation of technology.

SUCCESSFUL SELECTION AND IMPLEMENTATION OF TECHNOLOGY

Susan Grajek (2013) stated that "the boundaries between academia and the rest of the world have never been more porous. These external forces are shaping the strategic priorities of higher education institutions" (p. 32). She further asserted that institutions, and particularly the information technology units of those institutions, need to implement and support systems that keep pace with innovations in e-learning, must use e-learning as a competitive advantage, and must meet students' and faculty members' expectations of current consumer technologies and communications (p. 32). The expectations of all stakeholders, including institutional administrators and staff as well as external parties seeking various forms of online information, represent a moving target in the midst of a technology environment that is quickly and constantly evolving. Reflecting these realities, sound technology decisions are inherently tied to institutional success. In a 2008 survey on institutions' strategic success factors, the ERP and its associated issues of cost, staff development, user training, business process modifications, and regulatory compliance ranked second in importance (Allison, DeBlois, & EDUCAUSE, 2008).

Furthermore, technology purchases and implementations must be planned to minimize any perceived or real impacts on front-line staff and daily operations. Kilgore (2009) asserts that implementation success "hinges on factors similar to managing any significant organizational change, such as a clear vision of the end goals, a champion for the effort, systemic buy-in from cross functional areas and the development of a realistic timeline to name a few" (pg. 1). The change management process requires that these questions be addressed (Fui-Hoon Nah & Delgado, 2006; Kilgore, 2009):

- How will this technology enhance the institution's ability to fulfill its enrollment goals?
- Are the institution's governance structures supportive of the change, and is the team leadership for the project given an appropriate level of authority and responsibility to get the job done?
- Is the institution's level of preparedness for the operational and cultural changes that will result from the implementation adequate?
- What functional areas are going to be impacted by this change in technology (such as admissions, records, registration, institutional research, finance), and are they involved in the decision-making?
- What business processes are we trying to change and improve with this new technology, and why and what other business processes will be affected?
- Are our current processes relevant to the end goal and the new technology?
- What is our expected level of customization or end user configuration?
- How much training is needed for staff, and is there adequate technical expertise (both in the operational unit and in the information technology unit) and infrastructure to support the new technology?
- Is the data needed for operational and regulatory purposes available to the institution?
- Does the proposed implementation timeline conflict with any operational business cycles?
- Is there a clear communication plan regarding the implementation with all stakeholders?
- Is there a clearly defined scope and timeline for the project?

The overall success or failure of a technology needs self-assessment and technology implementation rests almost entirely on the appropriateness and effectiveness of the administrative structure in place to support the institution's technology portfolio. There are several models of IT administrative models. Some models are more successful than others, and like a technology self-assessment, the right model depends on correctly understanding the institution's internal management needs, future aspirations, and the technology skills of staff.

ADMINISTRATIVE STRUCTURES

Bates and Sangra (2011) noted that "the decision to integrate technology within an institution is clearly a strategic issue, as it implies substantial investment, and at least implicitly, significant change in base operations" (p. 85). Institutions have come to rely on technology to facilitate the operation of complex, multidimensional operations in which student and internal customer expectations are ever-increasing. The EDUCAUSE Center for Applied Research found that the perceived effectiveness of technology varied very little by type of institution, and the linkages between technology use and institutional goals were highly correlated (Katz & Salaway, 2004).

Development of a clearly defined plan for SEM that connects key benchmarks and measures to the implementation and use of technology is critical. Institutional leaders must develop primary goals in areas such as enrollment and retention and then direct resources to provide the technology to achieve and measure the desired outcomes. Clearly articulated institutional goals serve as the roadmap on which strategies can be developed to achieve these goals. To serve these strategies, tactics rooted in the technology serve as the tools and measures on which SEM operates.

Creating meaningful linkages between the use of technology and desired outcomes within a SEM plan are critical, because they create the connection between the daily efforts of staff members to the larger institutional goals. If a primary goal of the institution is to increase the retention of part-time students enrolled at the graduate level, for example, efforts and measures can be implemented to ensure that progress toward these goals is achieved. This also creates priorities for the funding of initiatives within an array of competing priorities. SEM is dependent on a clearly defined set of institutional goals, and these goals also lead the direction in which technology is developed and implemented to meet those goals.

According to Bates and Sangra (2011), successfully integrating technology into the organization requires a systemic, ongoing, and regular focus, with daily and continuous attention throughout the organization. The technology resides in a dynamic environment where the competing needs of daily operations and preparation for future enhancements and advancements must be supported simultaneously. Recently, these concurrent responsibilities have begun to shift at many institutions from a centralized information technology control model to one of shared responsibility with the operational leadership and staff.

More traditional models of technology ownership rely on a centralized information technology (IT) infrastructure to make decisions about what technology will be supported, who will have access (security), and who is responsible for training and procedure development. The proliferation of applications above, beyond, and in addition to the core ERP/SIS have made it nearly impossible for IT staff and leadership to be responsible for all aspects of technology within the institution. A fully centralized model is also often more difficult to support at large, complex institutions, because vendor-provided solutions may not be easily configurable or customizable to meet the unique needs of each unit within the institution. Although one could assert that a decentralized model of technology management would be best to support SEM initiatives, a decentralized model where most IT services are controlled by subunits across the institution does not support a central tenant of this chapter, which states that technology to support SEM initiatives needs to be viewed holistically. On the other hand, decentralization reinforces the dissimilarities in needs and goals of individual units and often results in redundant and competing technology solutions residing in individual departments. For example, a CRM solution is often first selected by either admissions or alumni services. In a decentralized model, both units could select and implement two separate CRMs that require unique skills sets to support. Then again, centralization often limits the scope and type of end user input considered during operational decision-making regarding technology. Davis (2008) introduced the idea of a "layered model" of technology support, whereby a "marriage of autonomy and connectedness" supports joint responsibility and coordinated accountability across the institution's end users. Another way to look at this model is to think of IT as institutionalized, where technology services are centrally coordinated while supporting individual unit needs within the larger context of institution-wide strategic goals and initiatives (Organizational Models for Information Technology). This model seems best suited to support SEM initiatives because of the holistic approach. Whichever model is applied, institutions must develop a clear governance structure to support and control institution-wide technology decisions.

Within any organization, the balance between functional users and IT staff must be carefully managed. From the SEM standpoint, maximizing the level of functionality within a system is the desired outcome. To achieve this result, cooperation and the dedication of IT resources are required. To achieve a level of synergy between SEM practitioners and IT staff, it is critical that the institution create an understanding of the underlying business process being enabled by the technology. Through the development of a greater sense of understanding, IT staff can better meet the expectations and needs of SEM operations. As with any partnership, development of priorities and working in collaboration to help IT staff manage competing priorities is vital.

Leveraging technology effectively may be linked to financial limitations, and these are important considerations when determining the adoption of new technology. Heavily modified systems require significant, ongoing technical resources, and this must be a consideration when institutions evaluate change or new functionality. Having collegial relationships, including IT staff, at each phase of the process and having realistic expectations are critical when the role of technology is assessed within any SEM function.

For a moment, imagine all of the various sources of data production in institutions of higher education, which include but are not limited to the SIS/ERP, LMS, research, and social media. Today, electronic data is created 24/7/365 to support nearly all operational efforts, from email trails about donuts in the coffee room, to human resource payroll processing, IPEDS reporting, registration transactions, enrollment tracking reports, facilities repair tickets, and everything in between. As such, institutions operate in the age of Big Data. Recent thought identifies four dimensions of Big Data: volume, variety, velocity, and veracity (Mobertz, 2013). Volume is the scale of the data, variety reflects the different forms of data, velocity is the rate of data streaming, and veracity addresses the uncertainty of the data. All of this Big Data needs to be managed at an institution-wide level. "Managing" the data includes identifying how it is created, who creates it, assigning responsibility for the accuracy and integrity of the data, identifying the purpose of the data, creating a definition for the data, securing the data, tracking the data, and ultimately disposing of a vast majority of the data. Ronald Yanosky (2009) further defined institutional data management as "the policies and practices by which higher education institutions effectively collect, protect and use digital information assets to meet academic and business needs" (p. 2). Yanosky further stated the following:

> Our capacity to produce data and expose it over networks has far outstripped our ability to reform or replace the business, legal, and cultural practices that defined out relationship to information in the era before data superabundance. As a result, requirements relating to new forms of data are piled onto ongoing challenges from more familiar forms, while government and institutional leadership subject data to new kinds of regulation often in a reactive way not very well informed by an appreciation of data management principles (p. 2).

In the context of SEM initiatives, data needs to be available in a format that is easily interpreted, accurate, and timely. Data stewards must be actively engaged in identifying data integrity issues, creating and updating data dictionaries, and developing/modifying SEM-related analytic and strategic reports. Due to the interrelatedness of the data in relational databases, none of these activities can be successful if undertaken in silos. Silos often lead to different units across the institution reporting different values for what should be the same data, because each unit is using a slightly different definition and often a different field in the database from which data is drawn.

Within the context of supporting SEM, the IT infrastructure model described by Davis (2008), where IT is institutionalized and provides centrally coordinated services, is, at present, ideal to support institutional SEM efforts. Combining this organizational model with strong project management, functional power users, well-documented data definitions, and data mining resources provides institutions with infrastructure, service, a knowledge base, and data needed to support SEM effectively.

CONCLUSION

As the needs of higher education evolve to meet the demands of students, institutional operations, the workplace, and society at large, the technology required to meet these demands continues to change. Over the past twenty-five years, core functions of the university have been entirely transformed. Although it may be unimaginable to consider admissions, registration, and financial aid as entirely paper-based, manual processes, that was indeed the case not too long ago. As we look back at the transformation that new technology has brought to the workplace and our lives, it is important to look forward and embrace the advances that lie ahead.

Thus far, the implementation and utilization of technology in higher education has been inconsistent due to a variety of key factors, including "adoption and integration approaches, resistance, budget allocations, institutional priorities, shifting student demographics, organizational cultures, leadership issues, and failure to apply systemic approaches to adoption, among others" (Nworie, 2010, p. 308). Those inconsistencies notwithstanding, technology utilization represents perhaps the single most influential factor in higher education operations. As such, it is critical to SEM not only as is evident from the function-oriented chapters in this part of the handbook, but also as an element of the SEM planning process described in Chapter 27. As posited there, SEM planning must account for the campus infrastructure required to support successful recruitment and retention operations and initiatives, of which technology availability and utilization are primary components.

References

Allison, D., DeBlois, P., & EDUCAUSE Current Issues Committee (2008). *EDUCAUSE Review Online.* Current Issues Survey Report, 2008. Retrieved September 15, 2013, from http://www.educause.edu/ero/article/current-issues-survey-report-2008.

Balzer, W. K. (2010). *Lean Higher Education: Increasing the Value and Performance of University Processes.* New York: Productivity Press, Taylor and Francis Group.

Bates, A. W., & Sangra, A. (2011). *Managing Technology in Higher Education: Strategies for Transforming Teaching and Learning.* San Francisco: Jossey-Bass.

California State University, Sacramento. (n.d.). *Organizational Models for Information Technology.* Retrieved September 23, 2013, from http://www.csus.edu/irt/cio/strategicplanning/Documents/Organizational_Model_for_IT.pdf.

Davis, J. (2008). Beyond the false dichotomy of centralized and decentralized it deployment. In R. N.Katz (Ed.), *The Tower and the Cloud: Higher Education in the Age of Cloud Computing*. Washington, DC: EDUCAUSE.

de-la-Fuente-Valentín, L., Pardo, A., & Delgado Kloos, C. (2013). Addressing drop-out and sustained effort issues with large practical groups using and automated delivery and assessment system. *Computers & Education, 61*, 33–42.

Fui-Hoon Nah, F., & Delgado, S. (2006). Critical success factors for enterprise resource planning implementation and upgrade. *Journal of Computer Information Systems, 46*(5), 99–113.

Gartner, Inc. (2014). IT Glossary. Retrieved April 11, 2014, from http://blogs.gartner.com/it-glossary/.

Gorr, W., & Hossler, D. (2006). Why all the fuss about information systems? or Information systems as golden anchors in higher education. *New Directions for Higher Education, 2006*(136), 7–20.

Grajek, S. (2013). Top-ten IT issues, 2013: Welcome to the connected age. *EDUCAUSE Review Online.* Retrieved September 20, 2013, from http://www.educause.edu/ero/article/top-ten-it-issues-2013-welcome-connected-age.

Henderson, S. (2012). Integrating evolving perspectives: The roots and wings of enrollment management. In B. D. Bontrager (Ed.), *Strategic Enrollment Management: Transforming Higher Education* (pp. 157–171). Washington DC: American Association of Collegiate Registrars and Admissions Officers.

Ingerman, B., Yang, C., & 2010 EDUCAUSE Current Issues Committee. (2010). Top-ten IT issues, 2010. *EDUCAUSE Review Online.* Retrieved September 13, 2013, from http://www.educause.edu/ero/article/top-ten-it-issues-2010.

Ingerman, B., Yang, C., & the 2011 EDUCAUSE Current Issues Committee. (2011). Top-ten IT issues 2011. *EDUCAUSE Review Online.* Retrieved October 13, 2013, from http://net.educause.edu/ir/library/pdf/ERM1131.pdf.

Jacobs, F. R., & Weston, F. C., Jr. (2007). Enterprise resource planning (ERP)—A brief history. *Journal of Operations Management, 25*(2), 357–363.

Katz, R., & Salaway, G. (2004). *Information technology leadership in higher education: The condition of the community.* EDUCAUSE Center for Applied Research (ECAR). Retrieved October 13, 2013, from http://net.educause.edu/ir/library/pdf/ekf/ekf0401.pdf.

Kilgore, W. (2009). E*nsuring a Successful enrollment-related technology implementation.* AACRAO Consulting. Retrieved April 16, 2014, from http://consulting.aacrao.org/wp-content/uploads/2014/04/AACRAO_EnsuringSucessfulEnrollment_Final.pdf.

Kilgore, W. (2011). Managing evolving technology needs. AACRAO Consulting. Retrieved April 17, 2014, from http://consulting.aacrao.org/wpcontent/uploads/2014/04/AACRAO_Evolving-TechnoloyNeeds_Final.pdf.

Kilgore, W. (2012). Talk to me: Communicating effectively with your prospect, applicants, students and alumni. AACRAO Consulting. Retrieved April 11, 2014, from http://consulting.aacrao.org/talk-to-me/.

Lingrell, S. (2012). Getting it right: Data and good decisions. In B. D. Bontrager (Ed.), *STRATEGIC Enrollment Management: Transforming Higher Education* (pp. 157–171). Washington DC: American Association of Collegiate Registrars and Admissions Officers.

Mobertz, L. (2013). The four V's of big data. DashBurst. Retrieved October 8, 2013, from http://cdn.dashburst.com/wp-content/uploads/2013/07/the-four-v-s-of-big-data.jpg.

Nworie, J. (2010). Adoption of technologies in higher education: Trends and issues. In D. W. Surry, R. M. Gray, Jr., & J. R. Stefurak (Eds.), *Technology Integration in Higher Education: Social and Organizational Aspects* (pp. 307–325). Hershey, PA: Information Science Reference.

Phelps, J., & Busby, B. (2007). Service-Oriented architecture—What is it, and how to we get one? *EDUCAUSE Review Online.* Retrieved September 20, 2013, from http://www.educause.edu/ero/article/service-oriented-architecture%E2%80%94what-it-and-how-do-we-get-one.

Scientific American editors. (2013). Learning in the Digital Age. *Scientific American Special Report, 309*(2), 48–73. Retrieved from http://www.scientificamerican.com/report/learning-digital-age/.

Wagner, E. L., & Newell, S. (2004). "Best" for whom?: The tension between "best practice" ERP packages and diverse epistemic cultures in a university context. *Journal of Strategic Information Systems, 13*(4), 305–328.

Wagner, E. L., & Newell, S. (2006). Repairing ERP: Producing social order to create a working information system. *The Journal of Applied Behavioral Science, 42*(1), 40–57.

Yanosky, R. (2009). Institutional data management in higher education. EDUCAUSE Center for Applied Research (ECAR). Retrieved September 25, 2013, from https://net.educause.edu/ir/library/pdf/ers0908/rs/ers0908w.pdf.

PART SIX

DATA, POLICY, AND STRUCTURES

A mong the ways of thinking about Strategic Enrollment Management is to view it as an organizing construct that facilitates coordination and alignment among goals, strategies, and functions that otherwise tend to be addressed separately. This can occur at the institutional and societal level. As a result, threads of thought and practice extend across the many components of SEM. They have been mentioned throughout the chapters of this handbook. Several of the more prominent ones are addressed more fully in the chapters in this section.

In Chapter 23, Darin Wohlgemuth discusses campus-based research to support SEM goals, strategies, and tactics. This is especially pertinent, because SEM often is described as a data-driven enterprise. With the advent of increasingly robust technology, the generation of data has become much easier. At the same time, the resulting high volume of data has resulted in its own set of issues. Institutions often feel buried by data with inadequate direction on how to use it productively. The ability to distinguish between data that is merely interesting and data that actually makes a difference in decision-making is more important than ever. Through an analysis of general concepts followed by a case study, Wohlgemuth provides useful insights into structuring research efforts to gain focus and input to more effective decision-making.

Another challenge of SEM is managing internal enrollment goals and pressures with outside influences, prominently including policy setting at the national and state levels. That influence takes two major forms: It can dictate what institutions do in key areas such as allocating financial aid and reporting enrollment figures in ways that have significant funding consequences. But more than just setting externally imposed mandates, public policy also can inform and inspire institutions to set enrollment goals beyond what they might otherwise seek to achieve. In Chapter 24, Mike Reilly and Michelle Mott provide a valuable overview of the public policy landscape with important considerations for the future.

A common reaction to SEM is to wonder how any individual or organization can realistically manage such a broad and varied enterprise. Creating new levels of strategic thinking is vitally important and is well documented and analyzed by Adam Herman in Chapter 25. Tapping into streams of thought from outside SEM ranks, Herman provides fresh perspectives on how SEM organizations might position themselves to think differently about their planning and functions.

Concluding this section is Chapter 26 by Monique Snowden and Jay Goff, in which the authors speak to areas of growing interest, using SEM to improve enrollments and outcomes among graduate, professional, and international students. By combining an overview of recent trends that have prompted institutions to seek out SEM to improve enrollments of these students, along with the authors' own direct experience, this chapter provides guidance for applying SEM to these and other nontraditional student groups.

CHAPTER 23

Campus-Based SEM Research

Darin Wohlgemuth

Research is an important part of Strategic Enrollment Management. The existing body of both applied and academic work emphasizes the importance of data-driven or data-informed strategies (Henderson, 2005; Kalsbeek, 2006a; Sayers, 2006; Ward, 2006). This same theme is amply represented throughout this book, beginning in Chapter 3, where the authors assert that SEM is fueled by a comprehensive research agenda. The importance of data to SEM is also discussed in Chapter 27 on SEM planning. Tables and rows of data from student information systems, by themselves, however, are not helpful in informing SEM. The effective SEM researcher seeks to combine, transform, summarize, analyze, and synthesize the data to inform SEM decisions across the institution (Bontrager, 2004a, 2004b; Dolence, 1993; Jonas & Popovics, 2000; Moore, 2011). This chapter includes two main sections: SEM research structure and a case study of Iowa State University's Enrollment Research Team (ERT).

The first section consists of three main topics: staffing structures, data issues, and analytical tools. From a structural perspective, campus partnerships are critical to creating a culture of data-driven decision-making. This is true regardless of whether an institution has a designated individual who conducts SEM research, relies on the institution-wide institutional research department, or relies on a separate SEM research department. From a data perspective, SEM research includes both internal and external data. The first section concludes with a discussion of the analytical tools most helpful in conducting high-quality SEM research.

The second part of the chapter offers a case study of a SEM research unit at Iowa State University: the Enrollment Research Team (ERT). Several examples of the ERT's work are presented, including selected components of an environmental scan, enrollment projections with special attention to demographic shifts, a model of aggregate demand to help inform pricing discussions, and a project identifying students at risk of earning less than a 2.0 GPA during their first term.

In general, as discussed in this chapter, SEM research addresses the "3 R's" of SEM: recruitment, retention, and revenue. *Recruitment* research deals primarily with raw numbers and yield rates as students move through the admission funnel from prospect, to applicant, to deposited student, to enrolled student, as well as predetermined measureable outcomes from specific recruitment programs and activities. *Retention* research examines the progression of students by term and year using data available from the registrar's or institutional research office, including predetermined measureable outcomes from specific retention programs and activities. *Revenue* research accounts for the interplay of sticker price, financial aid, and net tuition revenue, or NTR. NTR is the revenue an institution takes in from tuition and fees, net of all institutionally funded grant aid provided to students (College Board, 2011).

As commonly noted in the SEM literature, significant overlap exists between these three areas of research (Bontrager, 2004a; Ward, 2006; Wohlgemuth, Gansemer-Topf, Forbes, & Compton, 2008; Wohlgemuth, Gansemer-Topf, Compton, Forbes, & Sullivan, 2009). Data from each area allow enrollment managers to answer questions from the points of intersection or overlap. For example, revenue research focused on the net price an individual student is willing to pay intersects with recruitment data to inform the institution's offer of admission and financial aid. Enrollment projections that consider the differences in retention rates by incoming academic characteristics represent the intersection of recruitment and retention data. Furthermore, projecting net tuition revenue for the next four years based on entering academic characteristics, the financial aid offered, and the residency of the students would consider all three of the aforementioned research areas (Ward, 2006). Many of the most interesting and important questions in SEM research are addressed by these types of intersections and, as this chapter will point out, a SEM research unit must have a grasp of all three to be effective.

SEM RESEARCH STRUCTURE

The existence and facilitation of an effective SEM research unit is affected by a variety of factors. Although the unit structure will depend on the size of the institution, the resources allocated to SEM, and the organizational structure of college or university (Kalsbeek, 2006a), the issues of staffing, data, and necessary analytical tools should be considered, regardless of the structure and size.

Staff

The staff structure required to support SEM research will depend on many factors. Some institutions may have a single position (or portion of a position) dedicated to SEM research, while others may have a team. If resources permit, forming a team of analysts who specialize in each of the key areas (such as admissions, registrar, financial aid) and collaborate on research projects in the intersections allows both gains from specialization and synergy that maximize expertise and effectiveness (Goff & Lane, 2008; Goff, Gragg, & Montgomery, 2009; Lingrell, 2012; Ward, 2006).

SEM researchers can come from a variety of academic backgrounds: economics, statistics, marketing research, psychology, sociology, and research and evaluation, to name a few. Individuals must be comfortable working with a variety of methodologies and complex data sets, have an understanding of basic statistics, and, ideally, perform advanced statistical analysis, such as simple and multivariate regressions (Ordinary Least Squares, Probit, or Logit), path or structural equation models, propensity score matching, or other data mining techniques (Kalsbeek, 2006b).

The "home" of a SEM research unit within an organizational chart will vary depending on the institution. In some cases, it may fit under the Office of Institutional Research, while in others, it may be housed within enrollment management, which could report directly to the president or operate through the student affairs or academic administration. Regardless of the physical and administrative location, the staff must have a clear understanding of the enrollment goals, access to data, and access to tools available to conduct empirical analysis to inform decision-making (Babey, 2002; Goff, Gragg, & Montgomery, 2009; Goff & Lane, 2008; Lingrell, 2012; Vander Schee, 2007).

The SEM researcher will benefit from creating partnerships with collaborators across campus, such as the institutional research office, university marketing, academic departments, and faculty members (Pollock, 2012; Schulties, 2013). Creating such partnerships and regularly presenting the results of the research will help build trust across campus. Based on experience, as tuition revenue becomes a larger portion of the budget, especially at public institutions, there is increased interest in understanding factors that influence enrollment, which makes building trust even more important.

Data

Many types of data are required to perform effective SEM research (Cornell and Lingrell, 2011; Hundrieser, 2012; Lingrell, 2012; Ward, 2006, 2007). Data that assist in creating an environmental scan are often external to the institution. Data drawn from the student information system at regular intervals provide point-in-time history used to benchmark current circumstances and forecast the end result. When the research unit consists of more than one individual, data may come from multiple sources, and additional coordination efforts are necessary to maintain consistency, integrity, and usability of the data. Finally, issues of confidentiality and accessibility of electronic files present an extra challenge that must be considered when a multiple-person unit is created.

External Data To be effective and accurate, SEM researchers must assess continuous changes in the environment, which requires access to economic, policy, and demographic forecasts for primary, secondary, and tertiary recruiting markets. Access to such external resources as Bureau of Labor Statistics, U.S. Census Bureau, U.S. Department of Education, ACT, College Board, and other such entities is vital (Lingrell, 2012). *Knocking on the College Door*, compiled by the Western Interstate Commission on Higher Education (Prescott & Bransberger, 2012), provides state-specific forecasts of high school graduates by ethnic background. The College Board's reports of Trends in Higher Education (College Board, 2013) and ACT's reports on college readiness (ACT, 2013) provide the national context of academic preparation for higher education as well as many key overviews of current practices in higher education across the nation.

The National Student Clearinghouse (NSC) provides nationwide analyses of major trends in higher education. The NSC's Sixth Signature Report, "Completing College," captures not only completion rates at the same institution, but also students who received their degrees after transferring to another institution (Shapiro & Dundar, 2013).

The U.S. Bureau of Labor Statistics (BLS) compiles and reports earnings and unemployment rates by educational attainment. The 2012 data reported average weekly earnings and unemployment rates by educational attainment (BLS, 2013). Triangulating these data with the institutional information from career services on student placement allows SEM research units to help shape messages on both the monetary benefits of higher education in general and the value of their academic institution in particular. Jim Black (2008) lists many additional sources of external data that are useful including the Cooperative Institutional Research Program Freshmen survey (CIRP), U.S. Census Bureau Population projections, Association of Institutional Research, National Survey of Student Engagement, and the National Student Clearinghouse, among others.

Thomas Davenport, Jeanne Harris, and Robert Morison (2010) noted that the type and source of data are determined by the question/issue at hand and the level of answer it requires. Therefore, in some instances, external data that can be customized to match specific institutional characteristics (such as academic entrance requirements) are especially important. For example, understanding the recruiting market requires tailoring external data to focus on admissible students rather than the general population of high school graduates. Both the College Board's Enrollment Planning Service and ACT's Enrollment Information Service provide access to customized aggregated counts of test-takers by many individual characteristics. These tools provide a SEM researcher with the ability to generate counts of test-takers at very detailed levels. An example is discussed in the upcoming case study.

Internal Data Many different data points and data sets are important for SEM research generated in-house (Cornell & Lingrell, 2011; Davenport, Harris, & Morison, 2010; Lingrell, 2012). Aggregate or non–student-specific data become valuable in creating the context to understand the individual-level data analysis. For example, the history of tuition and room and board rates is useful in understanding the changes in price-related decision-making. Similarly valuable are the aggregate counts of inquiries, applications, offers, and deposits for various groups gathered at regular intervals over time. Using past ratios to forecast the enrolling class of nonresident students in a particular college provides a mathematically based projection to start a discussion (Ward, 2007, Wohlgemuth, Compton, & Forbes, 2012).

Aggregate data within the registrar's domain include cohort retention rates and year-to-year progression rates. Since the cohort retention rates are widely reported, they are useful for nationwide or cross-institutional comparisons. First semester and year-to-year progression rates are also helpful. Amanda Yale (2010) suggests that to increase student success, rather than persistence, institutions can benefit from not only monitoring performance and retention earlier, but also creating meaningful student engagement with advisors and faculty. For example, tracking the percent of first-time, full-time freshmen entering the College of Engineering who are still enrolled in that same college does not fully capture the intricacies of individual behavior and institutional support. For example, helping a student struggling with the curriculum find his or her passion in a different major serves the student better, while bringing down the "within college" retention rate. This provides a challenge regarding cohort retention rates that only look at entering characteristics.

One possible solution, tested and used at Iowa State University, is to monitor yearly progress. This tracks students from one year to the next, rather than from their entering characteristics. To account completely for all students, the following second-year groups are examined: enrolled within the same college, enrolled in another college, graduated, and not enrolled. NSC data also allow counting some of the "not enrolled" as enrolled at another institution. This methodology is consistent with ideas expressed by David Kalsbeek and Don Hossler (2010), who emphasize the importance of academic progress toward a degree, rather than sole persistence or "simple year-to-year retention as a primary metric of success" (p. 8), and Yale (2010). Another alternative to traditional cohort retention rates is to look back at the characteristics of students who were successful (graduated) and find common factors that help explain differences in their academic paths to success (Forbes, Compton, Wohlgemuth, & Ralston, 2013).

The SEM researcher can also match institutional student-level data with external sources. For example, the NSC data on college enrollment and degree attainment can be used to augment the retention and graduation rate institutional data. Looking at the 3-R's, when NSC data are added to institutional data, the SEM researcher can identify primary competitor institutions for students who applied but did not enroll, report the college completion rates for students that transferred out, and begin to examine common factors (financial, academic, demographic, and so on) of students transferring out and completing their degrees at other schools.

The importance of historical data is noted in a variety of current studies, as it is viewed as one of the pivotal sources of information for enrollment (Lingrell, 2012), retention (Kalsbeek and Hossler, 2010) and collaborative SEM overall (Ward, 2006; Yale, 2010). It is also important to collect a complete set of individual-level characteristics that will allow the researcher to segment the populations recruited through similar strategies. For example, student athletes experience a completely different recruitment process than non-athletes. Geographic location of prospective students presents another example, especially for institutions that have tiered tuition structures or differences in scholarships. In these cases, resident/nonresident, in-district/out-of-district, athlete/non-athlete student groups should be analyzed separately. Generally, when the recruitment process and student decisions are significantly different, the populations should be analyzed separately, especially when enrollment probabilities are calculated.

One method of collecting individual-level data is to take snapshots of the key tables from the institution's student information system (SIS) at regular intervals—for instance, on the first of each month within the recruiting cycle. Each of these files will have to be stored on a shared server that other members of the SEM research team can access. Depending on the table structure of the data stored in the SIS, it may be possible to query the tables directly. An alternative method is to build a "flat record" query (such as one record per application, per semester) that includes data from multiple tables in the SIS. Exporting and storing this "flat file" regularly provides access to historical data when required. Because it is not possible to know what data/factors will be important in the future, the method of taking snapshots of SIS data tables directly may be helpful. It is critical that the SEM research team works closely with the central IT team to make sure these data files are kept secure. Finally, in a multiple-person unit, a common naming convention for the regular snapshot files is important for accessing historical data quickly and efficiently.

Analytical Tool Kit

SEM research continues to emphasize a collaborative approach to data management and utilization. Data in a useable form that are accessible and can be easily converted into meaning for the institution can be empowering, while an overwhelming amount of data that require a variety of additional manipulation do not create additional institutional value (Ward, 2006; Yale, 2010). To maximize the value of the available data, a SEM researcher must have tools to transform and merge data files into unit records or specific aggregation that are appropriate for analysis. As software tools vary in their complexity, scope, and purpose, a combination of tools is appropriate for effective and efficient work. Microsoft Excel is a valuable tool that has a wide range of functions and features that are useful in SEM research. Excel's "pivot tables" and graphing features are quick ways to summarize and aggregate data according to key characteristics. Excel also has the ability to connect directly to some institutional SIS. Combining this SIS connectivity with recorded macros that repeats a series of steps (such as refresh queries, perform calculations, update pivot tables using the queried data, and export summarized data to a different spreadsheet) creates a low-cost and straightforward way to generate off-line counts of data, such as number of applications, offers, or enrolled students regularly. Effectively, such systems can produce a low-cost functional data warehouse (Lingrell, 2012; Wohlgemuth, Compton, & Sullivan, 2011).

However, as a SEM researcher's work is not limited to frequency counts, more advanced statistical tools are necessary. As suggested by Davenport, Harris, and Morison (2010) and Scott Lingrell (2012), the variation in appropriate methodology and required software is determined by a many factors, such as the nature of the question, intended purpose of the solution, level of application, timeline, and such. Although Excel includes a variety of suitable data analysis tools, more robust statistical software tools may prove valuable for SEM researchers. SAS, SPSS, and Stata are only a few of the software tools that can perform complex, cutting edge statistical analysis. Another benefit of using more robust statistical tools is they can be used for data management, such as flattening and combining large data tables queried from the SIS into a record ready for regression or other analysis.

If SEM research is done by a team, the productivity of the team is increased when members agree to use a common software for statistical analysis. They can create parts of programs that can be updated and rerun to replicate the same set of output data at different points in time as well as cross-train each other in handling area-specific data. Cross-training provides backup support when one of the team is out of the office or when team members advance to the next step up in their careers.

Having a central place to store lines of code also enables the members of the team to create a "clean" data set using each iteration of the analysis. Note, however, that *clean* may not mean *accurate* based on the end of the term when errors in data entry are corrected. If a correction is made, it should be done in the SIS, not in the snapshot files.

CASE STUDY: IOWA STATE UNIVERSITY'S ENROLLMENT RESEARCH TEAM

The Enrollment Research Team (ERT) at Iowa State University has been fully operational in its current form since 2006. ERT comprises the director of enrollment research and research staff from admissions, student financial aid, and the registrar's office. Enrollment management at Iowa State reports to the senior vice president of student affairs. The director of the enrollment research reports to the associate vice president of student affairs and enrollment. The members of ERT have dual reporting lines, each having a direct line to his or her respective supervisor (director of admissions, director of student financial aid, or registrar), as well as reporting to the director of research. The ERT members focus on one area (admissions, registrar, or financial aid) and work together on projects that intersect. In terms of educational background, ERT has three individuals with Ph.D.'s (economics, education leadership and policy studies, and sociology), and two with master's degrees (public administration, and an MBA).

ERT meets twice per month to discuss projects each member is working on in his or her own area, and they work together on overlapping projects. Each team member is responsible for creating snapshots of critical data files from his or her area at regular intervals; the files are saved to a secure folder on central IT servers housing all data snapshots. ERT has developed a file-naming convention that allows all team members to know the source of the file, term, and date the snapshot was taken. ERT uses Stata as the primary software for statistical analysis and has created thousands of lines of code useable for a broad array of projects.

To achieve its primary purpose, SEM must be a collaborative process involving sharing, support, and trust within and across participating organizational units (Davenport, Harris, & Morison, 2010; Yale, 2010). Over the years, ERT members have developed a very strong level of mutual trust and data sharing, while maintaining the sovereignty of using and reporting data relevant to their own domains. For example, the registrar's researcher would never report financial aid information or admissions counts without first vetting it with the other ERT members. Given the academic background of the members of ERT and the existing relationships within the team, the members share credit for assistance with projects.

In addition, the ERT members are continuously receiving professional development training comparable to other staff, which enables them to remain current on trends and techniques through webinars as well as traveling to various professional conferences (Bontrager, 2004). As a result, the ERT has presented regularly at professional conferences, such as the AACRAO Annual Meeting, AACRAO SEM Conference, Association of Institutional Research, ACT's Enrollment Planners Conference, and others, allowing for a fluid exchange of experience and expertise within the ERT members and fellow SEM researchers from other institutions.

Many institutions may not have the luxury of resources for a team of researchers to work on SEM. Alternatives could include hiring upper-division undergraduate or graduate students, buying out a portion of a faculty member's time, or creating a SEM research committee that could help conduct, review research, and create action steps based on the research (Kalsbeek, 2006a; Moore, 2011). When this is the case, the responsibility to collect regular snapshots of data and provide the analytical tools would have to be taken on by the enrollment manager or in partnership with central IT.

SEM Research Projects

Over the years, ERT members have worked on a variety of projects that helped inform an array of decisions across campus. The last section of this chapter includes four of these projects to showcase the benefits having a functional SEM unit as a part of the institutions SEM process.

An Environmental Scan The environmental scans that ERT has worked on include a look back at recent enrollment history to frame the forecasted trends that will impact future enrollment. The sections that follow present a few components to consider when developing an environmental scan. The goal is to engage the campus audience in a planning discussion for SEM. As shown in Figure 23.1, Iowa State University is fulfilling the Land Grant mission of access to quality education by continuing to enroll more students. The most recent entering class set records for both new direct from high school (NDHS) and new transfer students (measured on the left axis), with no changes in the average academic ability of the enrolling students (not shown here for brevity).

Fall 2013 was the third consecutive year of record NDHS enrollment, with a 13.4 percent increase in NDHS that year alone. The increase in NDHS and new transfer enrollment since 2010 has resulted in record enrollment of undergraduates—27,659 (measured on the right axis)—and the total enrollment of 33,241. Notice in the figure that the graduate and professional enrollment, shown in the difference between the undergraduate and total enrollment, remains relatively constant over the time.

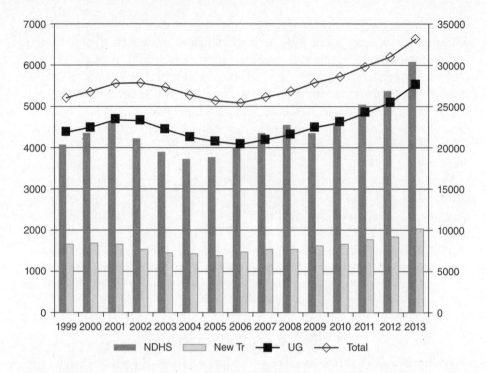

Figure 23.1 New direct from high school, new transfer, undergraduate, and total enrollment, 1999–2013

The graph also shows the decline in NDHS from 2001 to 2004, and from 2001 to 2005—for new transfer enrollment, which were leading indicators of the larger declines in undergraduate enrollment in 2003–2006. Two of the many factors that explain this decline are tuition increases and demographic shifts.

First, the reductions in state appropriations during that time period led to a dramatic increase in tuition. Figure 23.2 shows the NDHS enrollment (left axis) and the percentage change in tuition (right axis). Notice that the steep increase in tuition in 2002 and 2003 (18.5 percent and 17.6 percent, respectively) is clearly correlated with the downturn in new freshmen enrollment. This follows the "Law of Demand," which says there is an inverse relationship between the price and the quantity demanded, holding other factors constant. It is important to note that this graph does not "hold other factors constant," however; this issue will be addressed later using regression analysis.

Second, the change in population coincided with the decline in NDHS enrollment in 2003. Similar to the situation in surrounding states, the number of Iowa high school graduates, shown in Figure 23.3, fell 1.8 percent in 2003 and another 2.4 percent in 2004 (Prescott & Bransberger, 2012). Therefore, both the

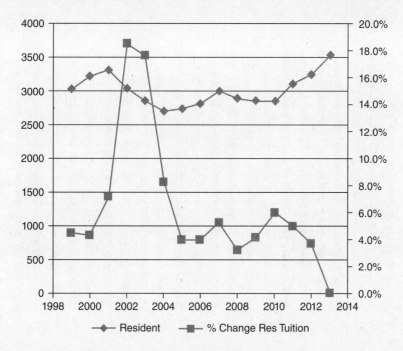

Figure 23.2 Resident NDHS enrollment and annual percentage change in resident tuition

large tuition increases and the declining high school graduates contributed to the decreased NDHS enrollment from 2003 to 2004.

Figure 23.3 also provides a look forward into the demographic shifts, which are often seen as drivers of enrollment. Iowa experienced another period of declines in the number of high school graduates from 2009 to 2013. However, looking back at Figure 23.2, the institution had record enrollment of NDHS resident students during these years. If the enrollment was a direct function of only the number of high school graduates, then rather than setting records, enrollment should have declined. The aggregate demand curve discussed next will separate and quantify the impact of many of these factors that influence enrollment.

The institution has also experienced a period of significant declines in state appropriations, more than 20 percent from 2009 to 2012. The simultaneous growth in enrollment and decline in state appropriations changed the overall revenue profile of Iowa State University to be more tuition dependent. Figure 23.4 shows the general state appropriations and tuition and fee revenue from 1965 to 2013, adjusted for inflation. There was a slight increase in state appropriations in the most recent year, but, adjusting for inflation, the institution is funded at levels comparable to the mid-1970s. Over that same period, the tuition revenue increased by nearly six times. Tuition and fees revenue now makes up more than 60 percent of the general university revenue.

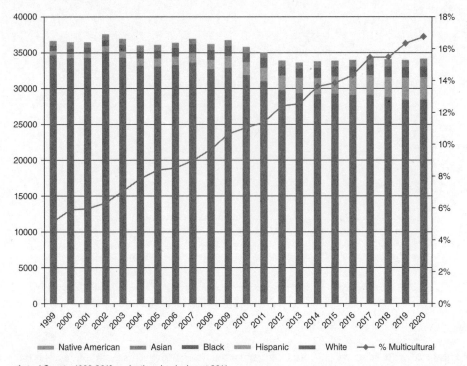

Actual Counts: 1999-2010, projectios sbeginning at 2011.
Source: Western interstate Commission for Higher Education, Knocking at the College Door: Projections of High School Graduate, 2012.

Figure 23.3 Public and private Iowa high school graduate (actual and projected) by ethnic group and percent of multicultural high school graduates, 1999–2020

Source: Iowa State University Budget Books

This decrease in state funding is a good example of the national trend in public higher education that is switching it from a public good to a private good. The State Higher Education Executive Officer Association's "State Higher Education Finance" report for fiscal year 2012 (2013) indicates that on a per-FTE enrollment basis, forty-eight of the fifty states have seen declines in state appropriations between 2007 and 2012. North Dakota and Wyoming are the exceptions. Many states have cut their funding of higher education, and students and families now pay a much larger share of the cost (burden) of education.

Projections and Demographic Shifts In thinking about enrollment projections, the WICHE high school graduate data, Figure 23.3 becomes valuable. The data provide estimates of the projected high school graduates from 2014 and out to 2020. The good news is that the number of high school graduates is projected to level off. However, notice a significant shift in the ethnic composition of Iowa high school graduates. Similar trends are also occurring in the key recruiting

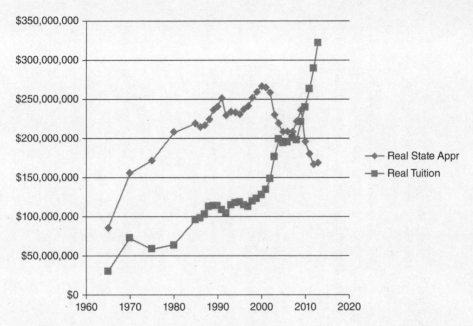

Figure 23.4 Budgeted real general fund state appropriations and tuition and fee revenue, 1965–2013 (adjusted to 2013 constant dollars)

states. The number of white high school graduates is expected to fall slightly and the number of multicultural high school graduates is expected to increase. Using the axis on the right side and the line plot, the percentage of multicultural high school graduates is projected to increase from 13 percent in 2013 to 17 percent in 2020. This demographic shift toward more ethnic minorities has implications for undergraduate enrollment at Iowa State (Table 23.1).

Both the Iowa Department of Education and WICHE report high school graduates by ethnic background. According to statistics, 3,996 multicultural and 30,999 white students graduated from Iowa high schools in 2011 (Prescott & Bransberger, 2012). Using ACT's Enrollment Information Services (EIS) software, the ACT tested the 2011 high school graduating class by the same ethnic backgrounds, which is helpful since more than 90 percent of the students at Iowa State take the ACT test.

Notice that about half of the multicultural students took the ACT, while about two-thirds of the white students took the test. Using EIS, we find the number of test-takers who meet minimum academic criteria for admission to define an approximate population of the high school graduates generally admissible. Of the high school graduates, about one in four multicultural students and one in two of the white students met minimum admissions requirements.

Table 23.1: Iowa State University market share of high school graduates by ethnic background

	Fall 2011				Fall 2020 projections			
	Multicultural	White & no response	Total	% MC	Multicultural	White & no response	Total	% MC
Iowa high school graduates (WICHE)	3,996	30,999	34,995	11.4	5,741	28,459	34,200	16.8
ACT test-takers (EPS)	2,116	20,852	22,968	9.2	3,040	19,143	22,183	13.7
Admissible (ACT EPS)	1,072	13,126	14,198	7.6	1,540	12,050	13,591	11.3
% of HS grad	27.0%	42.0%						
Applied	691	4,666	5,357	12.9	993	4,284	5,276	18.8
% of admissible	64.0%	36.0%						
Offered	563	4,297	4,860	11.6	809	3,945	4,754	17.0
Offer rate (offered/applied)	81.0%	92.0%						
Enrolled	353	2,752	3,105	11.4	507	2,527	3,034	16.7
Yield (enrolled/offered)	63.0%	64.0%						
Market share (% of admissible)	33.0%	21.0%						
% of population enrolled at ISU	8.8%	8.9%						

The data point to an issue for the entire higher education and K–12 community to address. It will take many groups working together to help communicate the value of higher education and to help students and families prepare for college while they are in elementary and middle school. Institutions of higher education will need to create partnerships between their faculty and K–12 educators, community groups, and others who will share in the effort to build up the academic preparation of multicultural students. It is important to inform campus that increasing the pipeline of academically prepared multicultural students will require long-term investments. Additionally, looking at these demographic shifts in light of projected enrollment in the next few years may mean an enrollment decline, since a smaller share of the growing population is academically prepared to enroll directly from high school.

WICHE projects that the 2020 high school graduating class will include 5,741 ethnically diverse graduates and 28,459 white graduates, as shown in Table 23.1. Using the same ratios as 2011, the enrolling class is projected to decrease by about seventy students if nothing else changes to help more diverse students become college ready (Ward, 2006; Wohlgemuth, Compton, & Forbes, 2012).

Notice that of the students eligible for admission in the state, 64 percent of the multicultural students applied and only 36 percent of the white group applied for admission, comparing aggregate counts. The recruitment efforts for multicultural students are strong. It is important to note that the yield of multicultural students surpasses the yield of majority students (33 percent versus 21 percent). There are many reasons for this difference, including general mobility and ability to pay, which can be examined in future research.

Finally, the table shows that the percentage of each population enrolled at Iowa State is nearly identical. It is safe to say that at least some recruitment strategies are working well for the multicultural students who meet academic credentials for admission.

Aggregate Demand Model It is also necessary to understand how each factor influences enrollment of NDHS students. Regression analysis separates the relationship of each factor with enrollment. It also helps estimate the own-price elasticity of demand, which measures the responsiveness of enrollment to a change in tuition. The own-price elasticity is the percentage change in enrollment for each 1 percent increase in tuition. Two methods of computing own-price elasticity have been used by the ERT, and both produced comparable results.

The aggregate model uses data from each county within the state for each of the past fifteen years as an observation to guide SEM strategies (Wohlgemuth, 1993, 1997, 2013). A few of the coefficients from the Ordinary Least Squares regression model are shown in the following equation, an aggregate demand curve for new freshmen:

$$\ln(\text{NDHS}) = \beta_0 - 0.75 \ln(\text{real ISU Tuition}) + 0.84 \ln(\text{real Income}) + 0.98 \ln(\text{HS\_Grad})$$

One of the useful features of the log-log regression (taking the log transformation of dependent and independent variables) is that the regression coefficients are also the elasticity estimates (Baye, 2010).

The own-price elasticity is the ratio of the percentage change in enrollment for a given percentage change in tuition, holding all other factors constant. The own-price elasticity is divided into three categories: elastic, unit elastic, and inelastic. The following table summarizes what each category means for policy discussions.

Elastic	Unit elastic	Inelastic
Range $(-\infty, -1)$	$= -1$	Range $(-1, 0)$
Enrollment is more responsive to price	Enrollment responds proportionately	Enrollment is less responsive to price
Revenue up if price falls	Revenue is maximized	Revenue up if price goes up

The own-price elasticity of demand is −0.75; this is in the inelastic range. If tuition were the only factor that changed, a 1 percent increase in tuition will lead to a 0.75 percent decrease in NDHS enrollment, according to the model. Since the demand for enrollment of NDHS students is in the inelastic range, or relatively less responsive, tuition revenue is expected to increase as tuition rates are increased. When the coefficient falls within the elastic range, an increase in the tuition rate would decrease in tuition revenue.

The aggregate demand curve also provides additional information to project enrollment for the next year. The state's economic conditions have been relatively stable this past year and, hypothetically speaking, the economic forecasts for next year are for income to increase by about 2.0 percent above inflation. The income elasticity is estimated to be 0.84. If per-capita income goes up by 2.0 percent next year, then there would be an expected increase in enrollment of 1.68 percent, holding all else constant. The WICHE high school graduate projections call for Iowa's high school graduates to increase by 0.5 percent. Using the coefficient, 0.98, the 0.5 percent increase in high school graduates should lead to a proportional increase in enrollment (0.5 percent × 0.95 = 0.475 percent). According to the model, enrollment and the number of high school graduates move the same direction and with a similar percentage change, when we control for other factors.

These two changes added up could be responsible for about a 2.2 percent increase in enrollment next year. If tuition went up by 3.0 percent, the new enrollment would fall by 2.25 percent = 3.0 percent × 0.75. If all three changes happened, enrollment would be projected to be nearly flat. It is important to remember that these regressions are estimates.

ERT also built a model of the individual probability of enrolling this year. The model is built on three years of individual records, specifically, NDHS offers of admission. ERT members in admissions and financial aid built the new model that looks at how factors in admissions information and financial aid influence the student's decision to enroll. The probit model estimates the probability of each person enrolling (Wohlgemuth, 1997).

The probit model was used to examine the impact of price on the probability of enrolling by computing expected enrollment under various tuition increase scenarios. This allows ERT to compute the percentage change in enrollment for each simulated percentage increase in price. The ratio of these two percentages is the own-price elasticity. The results of the probit model are very similar to the aggregate demand model: the own-price elasticity from the probit model is estimated to be –0.8, which is consistent with the coefficient derived from the aggregate model (–0.75). Both models indicate that demand is relatively less sensitive to price increases, so the optimal policy would be to increase tuition rates modestly.

Improving Retention Rates The final example of an ERT project involved all three of the R's (admissions, registrar, and revenue—student financial aid). ERT has been predicting the first-term GPA of all NDHS U.S. residents since fall 2007 (Gansemer-Topf & Forbes, 2012). A regression model was developed that used data from the admissions and financial aid application processes as predictors of a student's first-term GPA at Iowa State University. Each year, it is generally the case that the bottom 10 percent of predicted GPAs fall below a 2.0 GPA. The retention rates by first-term GPA, submitted to the Board of Regents, show that students who earn below a 2.0 GPA their first semester graduate at much lower rates; therefore, predicted first-term GPA serves as an early warning indicator. Thomas Miller and Charlene Herreid (2008) reported on a comparable project using logistic regression analysis at the University of South Florida.

Additionally, a nationally reported trend demonstrates that certain ethnic groups have lower graduation rates (Bowen, Chingos, & McPherson, 2009). The regression model takes all factors into consideration at the same time and computes the predicted first-term GPA. The names of the students with predicted first-term GPAs below 2.0 are shared with their academic advisors. Since the advisors can see most of the information used in the model and most have years of experience to understand that lower test scores are indicators of possible academic difficulty, such sharing is appropriate and in the best interest of the students. The goal would be to shape their advising appointments toward extra focus on getting the students to participate in some of the academic success programs and not to take an overly rigorous first-semester course load.

The model coefficients are shown in Table 23.2. This model used first-term GPA as the dependent variable. The coefficients and *t*-statistics from selected

Table 23.2:   Selected regressions results for first-term GPA regression 2011–2012

	Coeff	t	Significant
HS GPA	1.0511	46.19	***
ACT_SAT	0.0395	16.42	***
STEM Major	−0.2912	−12.12	***
Undecided	0.0324	1.08	
Female	0.0065	0.4	
Multicultural	−0.0976	−4.17	
Low Income	−0.0524	−2.21	***
Resident	−0.0812	−4.96	***
R-Sq	0.40		
N	10442		

variables are listed as well. As Table 23.2 shows, high school GPA and first-term college GPA move in nearly lockstep (1.05), meaning that, all else equal, comparing a student with a 3.3 and another with a 3.4 high school GPA, their college GPAs would also different by about 0.1.

ERT tested a few majors and found that students enrolled in the STEM (science, technology, engineering, and mathematics) majors have lower GPAs. Additionally, when the "undecided majors" were tested, their coefficient was not statistically significant. Existing retention tables show that multicultural students have lower retention rates, which is confirmed by the derived coefficients.

ERT also conducts analyses on the accuracy of the predicted GPAs. For example, of the 4,387 students predicted to earn a GPA above a 2.0, 3,887 did, indicating 89 percent accuracy. When used to forecast students likely to earn less than 2.0 GPA, the model's accuracy declined from 58 percent in 2007 to 40 percent most recently. The model correctly predicted 40 percent of the selected cases in the "less than 2.0 group" (438 predicted, 174 of those actually earned less than 2.0). The decline in accuracy of the "less than 2.0 group" can in part be attributed to the increased efforts in early warning and intervention implemented across campus since the inception of the model.

As demonstrated by these examples, Iowa State's ERT has worked on many projects over the years. ERT has combined internal and external data to measure the effectiveness of recruiting efforts. ERT has used basic ratio analysis to forecast enrollment in light of the changing demographics. Finally, the team has used regression analysis to inform tuition rate discussions and help identify students who are academically at risk. The examples included here are intended to illustrate the breadth and depth of SEM research.

CONCLUSION

SEM, as discussed in this book and many other presentations and publications, covers the entire college student experience, from the prospective student search process, through first enrollment, to graduation, to giving back as engaged alumni. When applying that perspective to SEM research, it is apparent that it is critical to have the right people, data, and analytical tools to inform programs and decisions throughout the student experience. Addressing this data agenda is more important than the administrative home of the research function to support SEM. In all structures, SEM research units need to reach out to build relationships and establish trust across campus. This can be done by sharing the work and collaborating with individuals across campus. As enrollment and net tuition revenue become more important to the institution, having a SEM research unit whose work is trusted becomes even more valuable.

The chapter highlighted that SEM research will accumulate a large amount of data from internal and external sources. Having historical data available allows the SEM researcher to develop data-driven and data-informed answers to questions about policy and strategy changes. The SEM researcher uses external data to benchmark institutional behavior in light of the larger context of higher education. The internal, student record–level snapshots of the student information system will allow the SEM researcher to develop and track summary statistics over time to forecast future enrollment. The individual-level records are the foundational for building predictive models for recruitment and retention, which are useful for forecasting revenue.

The case study at the end of the chapter offered an example of a SEM research team that has worked well for the structure and environment at Iowa State University. Whatever its structure, an institutional research effort to support SEM needs data, software, and resources to conduct high-quality empirical work. Also needed are investments in staff skill sets through professional development and other training opportunities.

When dedicated researchers have the data, the analytical tools, and the research skills, they can make important contributions toward SEM goals. These investments in people and resources can result in high-quality SEM research. When this research is shared with key stakeholders on campus, the enhanced decision-making that results will benefit not only SEM, but will set the institution on the path to accomplishing its broader mission and goals more efficiently and effectively.

References

ACT. (2013). *The Condition of College & Career Readiness 2013: How college and career ready are the 2013 ACT-tested high school graduates?* Iowa City, IA: ACT. Retrieved on December 20, 2013, from http://www.act.org/research/policymakers/cccr13/index.html.

Babey, E. R. (2002). *Strategic enrollment management: Creating a responsive, student-centered institution.* Retrieved from http://www.resccu.com/respaper3.html.

Baye, M. (2010). *Managerial Economics and Business Strategies.* Boston: McGraw-Hill Irwin.

Black, J. (2008) *The art and science of enrollment planning.* Retrieved from http://www.semworks.net/papers/the-art-and-science-of-enrollment-planning.pdf.

Bontrager, B. (2004a). Enrollment management: An introduction to concepts and structures. *College & University.* 79(3), 11–16.

Bontrager, B. (2004b). Strategic enrollment management: Core strategies and best practices. *College & University.* 79(4), 9–15.

Bowen, W. G., Chingos, M., & McPherson, M. S. (2009). *Crossing the Finish Line: Completing College at America's Public Universities.* Princeton, NJ: Princeton University Press.

Bureau of Labor Statistics, U.S. Department of Labor. (2013). Employment Projections: Earnings and unemployment rates by educational attainment. Retrieved October 5, 2013, from http://www.bls.gov/emp/ep_chart_001.htm.

College Board. (2011). Trends in Higher Education: Net tuition revenues, subsidies, and education expenditures per FTE student over time at private nonprofit institutions. College Board Report. Retrieved from http://trends.collegeboard.org/college-pricing/figures-tables/net-tuition-revenues-subsidies-and-educational-expenditures-fte-student-over-time-private.

College Board. (2013). Trends in Higher Education. Retrieved on December 20, 2013, from http://trends.collegeboard.org/.

Cornell, C., & Lingrell, S. A. (2011). *Managing up: Leading your executive council or board on enrollment issues.* General Session presentation for the Annual Meeting of the American Association of Collegiate Registrars and Admissions, March 15, 2011, Seattle.

Davenport, T. H., Harris, J. G., & Morison, R. (2010). *Analytics at Work: Smarter Decisions, Better Results.* Boston: Harvard Business School Publishing Corporation.

Dolence, M. G. (1993). *Strategic Enrollment Management: A Primer for Campus Administrators.* Washington, DC: American Association of Collegiate Registrars and Admissions Officers.

Forbes, G., Compton, J., Wohlgemuth, D., & Ralston, E. (2013). Dissecting the end: Factors that explain differences in time to degree and debt at graduation. Paper presented at the annual meeting of AACRAO SEM, November 11, 2013, Chicago.

Gansemer-Topf, A., & Forbes, G. (2012). *Using pre-enrollment data to develop and implement an analytical model to predict and retain academically at-risk students.* Association for Institutional Research Annual Meeting, New Orleans.

Goff, J., & Lane, J. (2008). Building a SEM organization: The internal consultant approach. *College & University. 83*(3), 20–27.

Goff, J. W., Gragg, L., & Montgomery, R. (2009). *Building a SEM organization as a data driven consultant.* Paper presented at the Annual Enrollment Planners Conference, Chicago, July 15, 2009.

Henderson, S. E. (2005). Refocusing enrollment management: Losing structure and finding the academic context. *College & University, 80*(3), 3–8.

Hossler, D. (1986). *Creating Effective Enrollment Management Systems.* New York: College Board.

Hundrieser, J. (2012). *Strategic Enrollment Planning: A Dynamic Collaboration.* Iowa City, IA: Noel-Levitz.

Jonas, P., & Popovics, A. (2000). Beyond the enrollment management division: The enrollment management organization. *College & University, 76*(2), 3–8.

Kalsbeek, D. H. (2006a). Some reflections on SEM structures and strategies (part 1). *College & University, 81*(3), 3–10.

Kalsbeek, D. H. (2006b). Some reflections on SEM structures and strategies (part 2). *College & University, 81*(4), 3–10.

Kalsbeek, D. H., & Hossler, D. (2010). Enrollment management perspectives on student retention (part 1). *College & University, 85*(3), 2–11.

Lingrell, S. (2012). Getting it right: Data and good decisions. In B. Bontrager, D. Ingersoll, & R. Ingersoll (Eds.), *Strategic Enrollment Management: Transforming Higher Education* (pp.155–171). Washington, DC: American Association of Collegiate Registrars and Admissions Officers.

Miller, T. E., & Herreid, C. H. (2008). Analysis of variables to predict first-year persistence using logistic regression analysis at the University of South Florida. *College & University, 83*(3), 2–11.

Moore, A. (2011). Keeping the dream alive: Gaining (and maintaining) cross-campus participation in SEM. *SEM Source.* Retrieved from http://www4.aacrao.org/semsource/sem/index57e0.html?fa = my&themonth = 10&theyear = 2011.

Pollock, K. (2012). SEM leadership. *College & University, 87*(3), 24–34.

Prescott, B., & Bransberger, P. (2012). *Knocking at the College Door: Projections of High School Graduates* (8th Edition). Boulder, CO: Western Interstate Commission on Higher Education.

Sayers, K. (2006). Information and inattentiveness in higher education planning. *College & University, 81*(3), 45–50.

Schulties, L. (2013). Strategic university partnerships for enrollment management. *Strategic Enrollment Management Quarterly, 1*(3), 194–203

Shapiro, D., & Dundar, A. (2013). *Completing College: A National View of Student Attainment Rates, Fall 2007 Cohort*. Herndon, VA: National Student Clearinghouse Research Center.

State Higher Education Executive Officers Association. (2013) State higher education finance, FY2012. Retrieved from http://sheeo.org/sites/default/files/publications/All percent20States percent20Wavechart percent202012 percent20REV20130322.xlsx.

Vander Schee, B. A. (2007). Organizational models for enrollment management at small colleges. *College & University*, *82*(3), 13–18.

Ward, J. (2006). Data-driven decisions: Using data to inform and influence decision-makers. *College & University*, *81*(3), 51–54.

Ward, J. (2007). Forecasting enrollment to achieve institutional goals. *College & University*, *82*(3), 41–46.

Whiteside, R. (2001). Models for successful change. In J. Black (Ed.), *The SEM Revolution*. Washington, DC: American Association of Collegiate Registrars and Admissions Officers.

Wohlgemuth, D. (1993). *Empirical analysis of the demand for higher education, 1966–1990*. (Unpublished master's thesis). Iowa State University.

Wohlgemuth, D. (1997). *Individual and aggregate demand for higher education: The role of strategic scholarships*. (Unpublished doctoral dissertation). Iowa State University, Ames, Iowa.

Wohlgemuth, D. (2013). Estimating the market demand and elasticity for enrollment at an institution. *Strategic Enrollment Management Quarterly*, *1*(1), 67–74.

Wohlgemuth D., Compton J., & Forbes G. (2012). *Projections when projections matter most*. American Association of Collegiate Registrar's and Admissions Officers, Strategic Enrollment Management Conference, Orlando, FL, November 2012.

Wohlgemuth D., Compton, J., & Sullivan J. (2011). *Dashboards without a business intelligence (BI) tool*. American Association of Collegiate Registrar's and Admissions Officers 97th Annual Meeting, Seattle, March 14, 2011.

Wohlgemuth, D., Gansemer-Topf, A., Compton, J., Forbes, G, & Sullivan, J. (2009). The enrollment research team: An example of collaborative strategic enrollment management research. *SEM Source*. Retrieved from http://www4.aacrao.org/semsource/sem/index884d.html?fa = view&id = 4249.

Wohlgemuth, D., Gansemer-Topf, A., Forbes, G., & Compton, J. (2008). *Iron SEM: Collaboration as the secret ingredient in creating practical SEM research*. American Association of Collegiate Registrar's and Admissions Officers, Strategic Enrollment Management Conference, Anaheim, CA, November 2008.

Yale, A. (2010). Expanding the conversation about SEM: Advancing SEM efforts to improve student learning and persistence (part 2). *College & University*, *85*(4), 29–38.

CHAPTER 24

Tracking SEM Policy Trends

Mike Reilly and Michelle Mott

The public policy landscape for strategic enrollment managers has shifted rapidly over the last decade as both state and federal governments have inserted themselves more deeply into the workings of higher education institutions. SEM practitioners and the institutions at which they work must now navigate an increasingly complex set of policy and regulatory directives as they seek to meet the goals of their institutions. The influence of public policy on SEM is evident throughout this book. Chapter 2 describes the demographic and economic bases for that influence. Chapters in Part III on pricing and financial aid repeatedly reference public policy, as do the chapters in Part IV dealing with student retention and the interplay of institutional goals with the growing degree-completion agenda at the state and national levels. In this chapter, we provide an overview of the development of federal and state policies impacting the work of enrollment managers, examine the current higher education policy framework, and identify trends moving forward.

Historically, the federal role in higher education has revolved around the democratization of college access and opportunities. The national discourse on higher education has shifted in recent years from increasing educational access to improving educational attainment. Spurred by global competitiveness and economic instability, the federal government has realigned its educational goals and prioritized programmatic funding to develop a new higher education agenda based on college affordability, performance metrics, and, ultimately, college completion. This realignment will have a significant impact on the work of SEM practitioners.

471

HISTORY OF THE FEDERAL ROLE IN HIGHER EDUCATION

From colonial times through the Revolutionary War, American higher education consisted mainly of privately chartered, degree-granting colleges with small, exclusive enrollments and religious affiliations (Trow, 1988). After the war, states slowly began to organize universities as publicly controlled institutions, but the federal government remained largely uninvolved. The institutions provided similar academic pathways to the established privately controlled colleges, which set the pace for the development of college education at the time (APLU, 2012).

By the early nineteenth century, numerous forces were combining to support federal interest in higher education and the American national state, but the origins lie within the Morrill Land Act of 1862 (Nemec, 2006). At the time, the United States was becoming a more established society with an economy based primarily on agriculture. Few institutions moved beyond the traditional classical curriculum, making higher education widely unavailable to workers seeking agricultural and technical education. Passage of the First Morrill Act reflected a growing demand to provide a broader segment of the population with the practical education needed in their daily lives (APLU, 2012).

Vermont Senator Justin Smith Morrill championed legislation to set aside public lands to states to establish colleges with the specific purpose of teaching agriculture, military tactics, mechanic arts, and industrial education. The First Morrill Act, also known as the Land Grant Act, greatly expanded the number and reach of colleges and universities throughout the country. Beyond that, many existing institutions expanded their programs, built new colleges, and ventured into the new disciplines of science and technology.

The Morrill Act successfully developed a system of land-grant colleges and universities managed by each state, but subject to broader federal policies based on the law. These modest beginnings formed the base of the federal government's expanded interest and involvement in higher education. Following the passage of the landmark law, Congress approved the Hatch Act in 1887. Recognizing the need for research to further agricultural development, the enacted legislation authorized federal funding for each state to establish an agricultural experiment station in association with each land-grant college (APLU, 2012).

With the Second Morrill Act of 1890, Congress began to make regular appropriations to support land-grant institutions. Its passage gave the federal Office of Education, established in 1867, responsibility for administering support for the original system of land-grant colleges and universities. Additionally, the act withheld funds from states that made distinctions of race in admissions. However, states that designated a "separate but equal" land-grant college for black students were eligible to receive the money. The institutions that were founded in the then-segregated southern states became known as the "1890 land-grants." The Native American tribal colleges are sometimes called the "1994 land-grants," in reference to the year they were issued land-grant status (APLU, 2012).

The Morrill Acts, coupled with the funding provided by the Hatch Act, laid the foundation for the rapid growth of American higher education and the establishment of state flagship research universities (Nemec, 2006). The laws eventually led to the creation of sixty-nine higher education institutions, though some with private support, and many not strictly devoted to agricultural purposes (Archibald, 2002).

The nineteenth century also gave rise to American community colleges, as we now know them. Many of the early community colleges began as normal schools—teacher preparation programs that extended from local high schools. By the 1920s and 1930s, the purpose of community colleges shifted to accommodate a developing workforce, heavily influenced by wide unemployment during the Great Depression (Phillippe & Patton, 2000).

The weak economy at the turn of the twentieth century through World War I proved financially crippling for some colleges and universities, and the period saw a decline in enrollment (Newfield, 2003). Post-war prosperity led to a brief spike in college attendance between 1920 and 1930, but the next great leap came after World War II (Archibald, 2002). In 1944, Congress approved the Servicemen's Readjustment Act, also known as the G.I. Bill, authorizing a range of benefits for returning veterans. The law significantly expanded federal support to higher education by providing tuition assistance that ultimately sent nearly 8 million WWII veterans to college.

The G.I. Bill created a new drive for more higher education options. Prompted by the popularity of the 1942 G.I. Bill, Congress approved similar measures in subsequent years to later generations of veterans. The Veterans' Adjustment Assistance Act of 1952 (P.L. 82–550) provided educational benefits to veterans of the Korean War. The Veterans Readjustment Benefits Act of 1966 (P.L. 89–358) extended benefits to active duty service members to encourage retention in the armed forces. Similar legislation was subsequently passed for Vietnam and more recently for veterans from the two Gulf Wars and the post-9/11 era.

The 1947 President's Commission on Higher Education suggested the creation of a network of public, community-based colleges to serve growing local needs. Community colleges became a national network by the 1960s with the opening of 457 public community colleges—more than the total in existence before that decade (Phillippe & Patton, 2000). The 1947 Truman Commission, the first federally charged study on higher education, also made sweeping recommendations to restructure and expand the government's involvement in higher education, calling for increased spending in the form of scholarships, fellowships, and general aid. Although many of the Commission's recommendations failed to come to fruition, the report sparked the first national rhetoric on higher education (Hutcheson, 2002) and undeniably set the stage for subsequent federal policy initiatives (Hutcheson, 2007). The Truman Commission Report proved to be the beginning of a number of presidential efforts to influence the direction of American higher education.

A few years later, the Cold War stimulated the first example of comprehensive federal education legislation. In 1958, Congress passed the National Defense Education Act (NDEA) in response to the Soviet launch of Sputnik. Triggered by the government's belief in the need for highly trained individuals to compete with the Soviet Union in scientific and technical fields, the law included support for loans to college students (Archibald, 2002). It also provided funds for the improvement of science, mathematics, and foreign language instruction in elementary and secondary schools; graduate fellowships; foreign language and area studies; and vocational-technical training (U.S. Department of Education, 2012). Congress expanded its educational interests with the Elementary and Secondary Education Act in 1965, launching a far-reaching set of programs, including the Title I program of federal aid to disadvantaged children to address the problems of poor urban and rural areas. That same year, the landmark Higher Education Act authorized assistance for postsecondary education, including financial aid programs for needy college students.

The Higher Education Act of 1965 (HEA) developed the essential components of the federal student aid programs in existence today, which helped 42 percent of undergraduates pay for higher education in 2011–2012 (Radwin, Wine, Siegel, & Bryan, 2013). The original law contained eight sections: Title I made federal grants available to states for the purpose of strengthening community service programs, focusing mainly on research and continuing education. Title II authorized funding for institutional library resources including books and materials, training to develop new techniques and to encourage more individuals to join the profession, and cataloging services for the Library of Congress. Title III provided aid to developing institutions, primarily southern institutions serving African American students, community colleges, and technical institutions. Later reauthorizations of the HEA largely changed the intent of these sections, shifting Title I to more general provisions and Title II to teacher quality enhancement. Additionally, the institutional aid authorized under Title III expanded to serve other minority and underrepresented student populations.

Title IV authorized federal aid to students attending higher education institutions. This section drastically broadened the scope and access of student aid for higher education, making it generally available to postsecondary students. Prior to the HEA, federal aid for students in higher education was available only to specific students, such as G.I. Bill benefits for veterans, or through specific areas of study, such as loans to students in the scientific and mathematical fields through the National Defense Education Act. Title VI expanded work-study programs; established Education Opportunity Grants, later renamed Supplemental

Educational Opportunity Grants (SEOG); and created federally insured loans with subsidies on interest for eligible full-time students. At the time the HEA was enacted, grants were primarily intended for low-income students, while loans were targeted toward the middle class (Cervantes et al., 2005).

Title V established a National Teacher Corps and provided grants and fellowships to improve teacher education programs. Successive reauthorizations funded teacher quality enhancement through Title II, and the focus of Title V moneys moved toward developing institutions. Title VI originally authorized funds to improve undergraduate instruction through technological upgrades. The Education Amendments of 1972 incorporated aspects of the National Defense Education Act of 1958, providing support for programs considered critical to national security (Cervantes et al., 2005). The amended legislation established grants for foreign language and area studies, national research centers, language resource centers, foreign language instruction, and foreign travel.

The Higher Education Facilities Act of 1963 amended Title VII of the HEA to provide funding for the construction of educational facilities. The section also changed during reauthorization to establish grants for graduate and postsecondary improvement programs. Title VIII originally outlined general terms and definitions used throughout the legislation.

The Higher Education Act of 1965 established the federal government as a major player in higher education policy. Since its enactment, subsequent amendments and reauthorizations have only deepened and expanded that federal role (Cervantes et al., 2005). Changes to the authorizing legislation resulted in the proliferation of aid programs and beneficiaries; the development of new aid programs, such as Pell Grants and Parent Loans for Undergraduate Students (PLUS); the addition of educational tax credits; the commissioning of federal studies and reports; and, eventually, the incorporation of program integrity measures to protect borrowers and taxpayer investments.

During the 1960s and 1970s, the nation's interests and the federal government's focus shifted to anti-poverty and civil rights issues. The passage of laws such as Title VI of the Civil Rights Act of 1964, Title IX of the Education Amendments of 1972, and Section 504 of the Rehabilitation Act of 1973, which prohibited discrimination based on race, sex, and disability, led to the dramatic emergence of the U.S. Department of Education's equal access mission, making civil rights enforcement a fundamental and long-lasting focus of the agency (U.S. Department of Education, 2012).

RACE-BASED ADMISSIONS IN THE COURTS

In 1978, the U.S. Supreme Court issued a landmark decision in the *Regents of the University of California v. Bakke* case (438 U.S. 265), declaring that race-conscious admissions programs were constitutional. At the time, the medical school at the University of California at Davis operated a special admissions program that reserved 16 percent of its placements for minority applicants. Allan Bakke, a white male twice-denied admission to the medical school, filed a reverse discrimination suit against the university, citing evidence that his grades and test scores surpassed those of many minority students who had been accepted for admission.

In a highly fractured ruling, the Supreme Court found that the university's use of strict racial quotas violated the Civil Rights Act of 1964 and the equal protection clause of the U.S. Constitution's Fourteenth Amendment. Although the court invalidated quotas, it held that race could be one of the factors considered in choosing a diverse student body in admissions decisions of institutions of higher education. The pivotal opinion of Justice Lewis F. Powell, Jr., stated that a university's interest in promoting diversity within its student body was compelling and that a "properly devised admissions program involving the competitive consideration of race and ethnic origin" would be constitutional (*Regents of the University of California v. Bakke*, 1978). Rooted in academic freedoms arising out of the First Amendment, an institution's interest in promoting educational diversity encompasses not just racial diversity, but an array of elements, such as sex, religion, geography, social or economic backgrounds, talents, and interests, that can contribute to the overall diversity of the student body and can promote the exchange of ideas central to a university's basic mission (Ancheta, 2003).

The *Bakke* decision also contains a ruling regarding legal standards for colleges and universities that receive federal funding. Under Title VI of the Civil Rights Act of 1964 (42 U.S.C. § 2000d et seq., 28 C.F.R. § 42.101 et seq.), institutions that participate in any program or activity that received federal financial assistance are prohibited from discriminating on the basis of race, color, and national origin. The Court held that, in cases of intentional discrimination, these institutions are subject to the same standards mandated under the equal protection clause of the Constitution. Therefore, the admissions policies of both public and private universities that receive federal funds are subject to the same legal requirements of "strict scrutiny" when race is taken into account in admissions decisions (Ancheta, 2003). Ultimately, the *Bakke* ruling set the precedent for the legal use of race-conscious programs on a number of levels, altering the way admissions and financial aid offices considered race.

By the late 1980s, the issue of affirmative action was widely debated and, in many cases, hotly contested. Some portions of the American public felt that job advancement and college admissions should be based solely on merit rather than on a system that considered race and gender (Hadley, 2005). As this opposition grew, the Supreme Court started to impose significant restrictions on race-based affirmative action with several decisions that gave greater weight to claims of reverse discrimination and outlawed the use of minority set-asides in cases where prior racial discrimination could not be proved. Then, the state of California approved the California Civil Rights Initiative (Proposition 209) in 1995, prohibiting all state agencies and institutions from giving preferential treatment to individuals based on their race, sex, color, or national origin. The Supreme Court effectively upheld the constitutionality of California's ban in 1997 by refusing to hear a challenge to its enforcement. Similar legislation was subsequently proposed in a number of other states and approved in Washington, Michigan, Nebraska, Arizona, Oklahoma, and New Hampshire. Following the passage of these affirmative-action bans, institutions in those states shifted gears to remove the components of their admissions policies to comply with their new state laws, despite some concerns the consequences.

Around that same time, the U.S. Court of Appeals for the Fifth Circuit considered a case challenging the race-conscious admissions policies at the University of Texas on the grounds of equal protection. The 1996 decision in *Hopwood v. Texas* (518 U.S. 1033) argued that there was no compelling state interest to warrant using race as a factor in admissions decisions. Due to jurisdictional issues, the Supreme Court denied *certiorari* on the case, leaving the lower court ruling intact. As a result, the *Hopwood* decision stood at odds with the judicial precedent set by the *Bakke* case, weakening the already embattled status of affirmative action in higher education (Scanlan, 1996).

Over the years, questions about whether the *Bakke* case served as a plurality opinion or a binding precedent arose. In 2003, the Supreme Court ruled on a pair of cases regarding admissions policies at the University of Michigan. Both decisions reaffirmed that the consideration of race in college admissions decisions serves a compelling state interest in "the educational benefits that flow from a diverse student body." Both decisions also narrowed the scope of when and how race may be considered. The *Grutter v. Bollinger* (539 U.S. 306) case examined the process employed by the university's law school to determine admission. In an effort to achieve diversity, the process took into consideration a host of subjective factors including test scores, undergraduate performance, and race and ethnicity, among other things. The Supreme Court ruled that the law school's admissions policy did not violate the equal protection clause or Title VI because it used race in a "narrowly tailored" manner, employing a "highly individualized, holistic review of each applicant's file," as recommended by Justice Powell in his concurring opinion in *Bakke* (*Regents of the University of California v. Bakke*, 1978).

Gratz v. Bollinger et al. (539 U.S. 244) challenged the institution's undergraduate admissions policy that awarded points to students on the basis of race. The University of Michigan used a 150-point scale to rank applicants, with 100 points needed to guarantee admission. The system automatically awarded a 20 point bonus to candidates from underrepresented ethnic groups, including

African Americans, Hispanics, and Native Americans. The Supreme Court ruled that the undergraduate admissions program's use of race or ethnicity was not "narrowly tailored" and thus violated the equal protection clause. The Court argued that because the university's ranking system gave an automatic point increase to all racial minorities rather than making individual determinations, it made "race a decisive factor for virtually every minimally qualified under-represented minority applicant" (*Gratz v.Bollinger*, 2003).

Ten years later, the Supreme Court vacated and remanded an appeals court decision that upheld a race-conscious admissions program—modeled on the standards set forth in *Grutter* and *Gratz*—at the University of Texas at Austin, finding that the lower court had not subjected the program to "strict scrutiny." The *Fisher v. The University of Texas at Austin* case did not directly revisit the constitutionality of race-conscious admissions decisions. Instead, the Supreme Court held that the appeals court had misinterpreted *Grutter* in giving deference to the university's judgment that each applicant was evaluated as an individual and that its consideration of race was "necessary" to achieve the educational benefits of diversity.

Although the decision does not substantially alter the legal landscape for colleges and universities, it does place the burden on institutions to demonstrate that their race-conscious policies are narrowly tailored to the goal of diversity and that race-neutral policies would not create a sufficiently diverse student body.

The Supreme Court returned to the issue of race-conscious admissions policies in the spring of 2014 (*Schuette v. Coalition to Defend Affirmative Action* (No. 12–682). Unlike *Fisher*, the *Schuette* case challenges the constitutionality of state affirmative-action bans. In November 2006, Michigan voters approved the Michigan Civil Rights Initiative, modeled on California's Proposition 209, prohibiting discrimination or preferential treatment in public education, government contracting, and public employment. The Coalition to Defend Affirmative Action, Integration and Immigrant Rights, and Fight for Equality By Any Means Necessary, also known as BAMN, filed suit to block the portion of the law concerning higher education, arguing that it violates the U.S. Constitution's equal protection clause by disadvantaging racial and ethnic minority groups in the political process. The Supreme Court upheld the constitutionality of Michigan's voter-approved ban on racial preferences in college admissions, noting the right of states to vote on policies that have an impact on minority citizens. The ruling not only left the Michigan measure in place, but also made clear that the court would reject any similarly argued challenge to the bans on race-conscious admissions adopted by voters in Arizona, California, Nebraska, Oklahoma, Washington, Florida, and New Hampshire. Although this decision may have a major impact on SEM practitioners, as additional legislative and electoral challenges to affirmative action arise in other states throughout the country, it leaves intact the court's prior holdings recognizing that institutions of higher education may use all legally permissible methods to achieve their diversity goals.

NATIONAL EDUCATION COMMISSIONS

In 1983, the *Nation at Risk: The Imperative for Educational Reform* report from the Reagan-appointed National Commission on Excellence in Education, was significant in that for the first time a federal commission explicitly concluded that higher education was "failing" in its effort to meet the educational needs of the country. The report was critical of nearly every dimension of student preparation, teaching at the secondary and postsecondary level, and alignment with the workforce. It also focused on America's declining position relative to other industrialized nations, a comparison that still serves as a major impetus for critiques of higher education and the benchmarks for national degree attainment (Gardner, 1983).

Maintaining the theme of critically assessing the performance of higher education was the 2006 "The Test of Leadership: Charting the Future of American Higher Education," more commonly known as the Spelling Commission Report led by President George W. Bush's Secretary of Education, Margaret Spelling. The Spellings Commission report generated considerable debate among legislators, academic leaders, higher education associations, and the media. It also highlighted the complex relationship between policy makers and higher education leaders in developing a constructive approach to addressing the challenges of educating citizens (Oldham, 2006).

TRACKING SEM-RELATED POLICY TRENDS

Federal critiques of performance have not only persisted, but permeated the policy discussions in recent years regarding American higher education. The United States currently ranks seventh in the world for the proportion of young adults enrolled in college, but the country lags in the attainment of baccalaureate and sub-baccalaureate degrees and certificates (OECD, 2013). Studies have indicated that employment in jobs demanding high-level knowledge and skills beyond high school diploma will grow more rapidly over the next decade (Carnevale, 2013). Obtaining a postsecondary credential has arguably become the clearest pathway for students to achieve middle-class status and for the country to compete in the global economy (U.S. Bureau of Labor Statistics, 2010).

Armed with that information, the public discourse surrounding higher education has shifted to reflect the growing belief that higher education is necessary for success (Immerwahr et al., 2010). At the national level, the Obama administration adopted college completion as the centerpiece of its federal education policy agenda. In February 2009, President Barack Obama addressed a joint session of Congress declaring that, "by 2020, America will once again have the highest proportion of college graduates in the world" (Obama, 2009). With the administration's goals focused on increasing the number of college graduates, Obama challenged every American to commit to at least one year of higher education or postsecondary training. The president's 2020 goals, which were incorporated into the American Graduation Initiative, included measuring progress on five indicators: college costs, graduation, student loan repayment, student loan debt, and earnings potential (Kanter, 2012).

As policy makers increasingly focused on performance and productivity measures to improve college completion rates, the economic recession forced them to scale back public funding for higher education (SHEEO, 2012). Coupled with rapid enrollment growth—due in part to the stagnant economic environment—these funding cuts left institutions financially strapped. Many colleges and universities responded by raising tuition in an effort to offset the reductions in state appropriations. This shift in the burden of educational costs to students and their families made it more difficult for students to identify and enroll at institutions that best met their needs to earn a degree or credential successfully (Prescott & Bransberger, 2012).

In recent years, the number of students borrowing to cover college costs, as well as the amount of money that they borrow through both federal and private loans, has increased consistently. By 2011, two-thirds of college seniors who graduated had student loan debt, with an average of $26,600 for those with loans (Reed & Cochrane, 2012). These recent college graduates have also entered a disappointing job market, still facing high unemployment rates. The unemployment rate for young college graduates in 2011 remained high at 8.8 percent, a slight decrease from 2010, which saw the highest annual rate on record for this group at 9.1 percent (Reed & Cochrane, 2012). As a result, many students struggle to find well-paying jobs that allowed them to repay their student loans.

Throughout the recession, student loan default rates have risen consistently, with the national two-year cohort default rate on federal loans at 10 percent for the 2011 fiscal year and the three-year rate at nearly 15 percent for the 2010 fiscal year (U.S. Department of Education, 2013a, 2013b). Borrowers who default on federal loans face severe consequences, including additional collection fees, loss of federal aid eligibility, loss of deferment or forbearance options, and seizure of Social Security, disability income, and state and federal tax refunds. Additionally, the federal government does not fully recover monies when a borrower defaults, resulting in a net loss for the government and taxpayers. Unsurprisingly, as rates rose, taxpayers and policy makers began to scrutinize the return on those higher education investments.

The growing concern surrounding rising tuition prices and student loan debt resulted in a range of new policies aimed at reining in college costs, providing value for students and their families, and preparing students with a high-quality education to succeed in their careers. Proposals to reform student aid programs, expand education tax credits, adjust student loan interest rates, and expand relief for debt-ridden borrowers emerged from the Obama administration, federal and state lawmakers, higher education organizations and foundations, and other interested parties. SEM practitioners should expect additional scrutiny of institutional efforts to contain costs and student debt.

Policy makers also focused on transparency and accountability measures to provide students and families with more accurate and relevant information to help them make sound financial decisions in pursuing their higher education goals. The Obama administration launched the "Know Before You Owe" campaign in an attempt to simplify and centralize information to compare colleges by cost, graduation rate, loan default rate, amount borrowed, employment, and financial aid packages awarded (Obama, 2011).

The administration targeted institutional accountability through a number of methods. In 2010, the U.S. Department of Education adopted a new set of rules governing the financial aid system that had major implications for colleges and universities. Fueled specifically by dismal reports of for-profit institutions failing to provide students with degrees but leaving them saddled with significant debt, the regulations aimed to rein in abuses within student aid programs. The program integrity rules tightened institutional eligibility, adding restrictions on incentive compensation and misrepresentation, and established a wide range of compliance requirements for campus administrators.

Transparency and accountability efforts spilled over into Congress as well, with both the U.S. Senate and the House of Representatives conducting research, holding hearings, and constructing legislation to increase federal oversight of colleges and universities. The Education Department pushed forward on additional regulations to require for-profit and technical institutions to provide more evidence that they are preparing their students for the work force. At the same time, President Obama issued an executive order to protect veterans and service members and their families from aggressive and deceptive recruiting by institutions, namely proprietary, seeking their military benefits (Executive Order No. 13607, 2012). The order established new standards for how institutions that receive military and veterans' education benefits recruit students, disclose financial information, and track student-learning outcomes. SEM practitioners need to pay close attention to these efforts to insure that they are in compliance and remain eligible for participation in programs to assist veterans and service members.

The administration's most recent and ambitious proposal to promote college affordability and improve educational outcomes combines numerous aspects of the established 2020 completion goals. In August 2013, President Obama announced plans to create a new rating system for colleges in which they would be evaluated based on measures of access, affordability, and outcomes. The proposal calls on Congress to tie federal student aid to college performance, such that students who enroll at high-performing colleges would receive larger Pell Grants and more favorable rates on student loans. It challenges institutions to offer students a greater range of affordable, high-quality options, such as competency-based learning, course redesign, the use of technology for student services, and more efforts to recognize prior learning. The proposal also plans to expand programs and options in an effort to help struggling borrowers repay their debt (The White House, Office of the Press Secretary, 2013).

The president's proposals represent one of most extensive and far-reaching efforts of the federal government's involvement in higher education policy to date. Much of the national discourse in the coming years will likely revolve around the proposed college ratings system, but the road toward public approval and implementation will not be smooth.

THE ROLE OF STATES

Although the Tenth Amendment deferred to the states the primary responsibility for the management of higher education, the states' impact on the goals and practices of higher education was limited for many years. The California Master plan was one example of a state taking an active role in the shaping of higher education, the makeup of institutions, and the distribution of state resources (Callan, 2009). It offered a bold plan for reaching the education attainment goals for a rapidly growing state by managing and funding enrollments at its community colleges and four-year systems. For many states, however, the primary state role was to provide funding for enrollments at public institutions and financial aid in the form of grants and work-study (in many cases state-supported financial aid was available to students attending private institutions as well).

The state funding formula for higher education enrollments was largely an incremental, full-time equivalent (FTE) student model based on the enrollments at an institution at a particular point in time, usually the average FTE over the course of a year. States provided a substantial portion of a student's cost of instruction, while the student contributed more modestly to that cost in the form of tuition. Institutions would project anticipated increases in FTE enrollment and build that into their budget requests to the state. Enrollment managers and admissions officers were then tasked with reaching those enrollment targets, making sure not to fall below the funded enrollment levels but also not over-enrolling to the point of straining institutional resources.

Critics of this "access" funding model argued that it encouraged institutions to maintain high enrollments with little regard to the success or graduation of those students. The Student Right To Know Act, passed in 1990, required institutions to report graduation rates for their full-time, degree- or certificate-seeking entering students, but these rates were often overlooked and seldom factored into state funding decisions. The confluence of state finance structural imbalances, a global recession, and a national shift in focus from "access" in higher education to "success" fundamentally changed the role of the state in the financing and managing of higher education.

As the recession began in 2007–2008, states found themselves short of operating revenue required to finance state operations fully. State funding for higher education, often the largest portion of discretionary spending in a state budget, saw significant declines. In fiscal year 2013, only twelve states provided more funding for higher education than they did in 2008. Some states, such as Arizona and New Hampshire, have seen declines in state funding of more than 35 percent during this period (Palmer, 2013). At the same time, states and public institutions in particular raised tuition rates rapidly in an attempt to backfill state funding cuts. This shift in the proportion of the cost of student instruction from the state to the student had been happening since the early 1980s, but the pace of the shift from 2008 to 2012 was unprecedented.

Reliance on tuition for operating revenue has been a characteristic of independent institutions since their beginnings, but now many state institutions receive substantially more of their operating revenue from tuition than from state support. Enrollment managers at all types of higher education institutions now must consider tuition revenue as part of their student enrollment mix. Institutions that never actively recruited nonresident or international students now consider these students an essential part of their enrollment and financing strategy.

In response to the changing financial landscape, increased scrutiny of the return on state investments, and the success or lack thereof of students at their institutions, states have taken an increasingly active, and in many cases aggressive, role in the management of higher education institutions. A number of states have started to experiment with new initiatives to boost college attainment, driven in part by funding from major philanthropic foundations and at the behest of gubernatorial and legislative leadership from all political backgrounds. Some initiatives have been broad-based, covering the wide spectrum of higher education. Others have had a more specific focus, concentrating on subgroups such as community colleges and adult populations or on disparities among low-income and minority students (Russell, 2011).

Performance-based funding, where state support for higher education institutions is determined at least in part on metrics such as retention and graduation rates, have been around since the late 1970s but gained little traction.

Early models focused on outcome indicators, such as graduation rates, number of degrees/certificates awarded, job placement rates, or student success on licensing exams. More current systems evolved to encompass intermediate progress measures, alignment with states' higher education and workforce priorities, greater portions of state funds distributed on performance, and stakeholder input (Harnisch, 2011). As of spring 2014, thirty states are implementing or in discussions to implement some version of performance-based funding (NCSL, 2014).

This shift is significant for SEM practitioners who previously focused much of their attention on the enrollment portion of a student life cycle. With the shift to performance-based funding models, as much attention must be paid to retention and graduation of students as enrolling them. In a performance-based funding scheme, poor retention and graduation rates cannot be overcome by bolstering the enrollment of new students, something that was possible in an incremental FTE funding approach. Despite recent attention, there is no compelling evidence of the link between performance-based funding models and improved student outcomes at this time (Friedel, Thornton, D'Amico, & Katsinas, 2013). SEM practitioners are only beginning to understand the implications of these new funding models and impacts on practices.

State legislatures are also becoming increasingly active in the management of institutions beyond the traditional funding role. States' reach into the management of institutions include dictating the mix of students, including the percentage of transfer students at baccalaureates, the number or percentage of resident students, and limits on the number of international students. Legislatures have passed laws dictating which courses must transfer from community colleges, what class standing must be given to transfer students with associate degrees, the amounts and types of credit that must be awarded for Advanced Placement exam scores, and how courses shall be numbered (Education Commission for the States, 2013).

States have mandated how remediation and developmental education will be conducted and funded at public institutions. In Iowa and other states, institutions have been instructed that they may no longer use tuition from students as a source of financial aid for other students, something tuition discounting routinely does. In other states, institutions are required to devote a certain percentage of their tuition revenue to financial aid for students, a process often referred to as "return to aid." Waivers of tuition are often required by state legislatures for certain categories of students such as dependents of veterans or children of deceased police officers or firefighters. Some states require institutions to eliminate low-enrollment programs. A number of states are directing institutions to recognize and award prior learning assessment. Others specifically ban the consideration of race or ethnicity in admissions decisions.

Another public policy challenge for SEM practitioners is the growing achievement gap in college attainment among students of different ethnic and economic backgrounds. This gap in attainment has been part of the public policy conversation for many years, yet there is little evidence that efforts at closing the gap have been successful. Although degree and certificate production has increased substantially over the last decade, with overall college degree attainment increasing in every state, the disparity in degree attainment between white students and ethnic minorities has grown in all but a few states (Jones & Kelly, 2013). In some states, the gap in degree attainment is more than 30 percent.

At the same time, the demographics of the college-age population are changing rapidly in many parts of the country, leading state officials and policy leaders to conclude that the difference in college participation rates among ethnic and low-income populations could impact their ability to meet the skill and employment needs of their economies in the future. All states will see significant increases in the number of jobs that will require some postsecondary education, with most of the jobs requiring associate degrees or above (Carnevale, 2013). The Western Interstate Commission for Higher Education (WICHE) projects that Hispanic high school graduates will grow by 68 percent by 2025, while the number of white high school graduates will decline by 13 percent over the same period. By 2020, at least nine states are projected to have a majority of their high school graduates from ethnic minority backgrounds (Prescott & Bransberger, 2013). The need to close the achievement gaps and increase degree attainment among diverse populations is now seen as an economic imperative as well as a moral one.

MOVING FORWARD

The definition of success in the world of SEM is no longer based simply on achieving institutional enrollment targets. The public policy and regulatory landscape now requires that successful SEM practitioners consider a broader range of factors than those that contribute to the student decision-making process and what competing institutions are doing. Increasingly, success will be determined both by the institution and its specific goals as well as by those of the broader public agenda.

Within this context, enrollment managers should consider the following questions as they develop their enrollment strategies:

- Does your institution's funding formula include student success metrics? If so, how does this funding formula impact your decisions about which students to admit to your institution?

- What are the characteristics of students who are successful at your institution? Are there segments of your student population who consistently underperform? Is your institution prepared to provide the resources and services to all students who enter your institution? What are the policy tradeoffs between selecting students who will be successful versus providing access and opportunity?

- Does your state have specific public policy initiatives and goals (number or percentage of in-state students, priorities or requirements for the number of transfer students, and so on) that must be met? Do you have a means of providing input and information to policy makers in your state who are making decisions that will impact your management of enrollments?

- What are the socioeconomic characteristics of your student body? Do your institutional aid practices impact this profile? What are your student debt levels and have these increased substantially over time?

- Has your institution evaluated its goals for diversity in the context of the institutional mission (a necessary process to meet the requirements of Supreme Court guidance on establishing diversity as a "compelling interest")? Does your institution consider race or ethnicity in admissions decisions and, if so, is your practice "narrowly tailored"? Has your institution documented the results of race-neutral admissions strategies before adopting a race-conscience approach?

- How successful are students at your institution who began their studies elsewhere? Are there gaps in completion rates for transfer students who enter with associate degrees and those who do not (Shapiro et al., 2013)? Do you have institutional practices in place, such as credit for military experience and prior learning assessment, to serve veterans and returning adult students?

- How is your institution organized to comply with federal regulation? Is regulatory compliance coordinated or do individual units manage different components of federal regulation?

CONCLUSION

In this chapter we have examined the history of the federal role in higher education and the development of the public policy and regulatory framework impacting the work of SEM practitioners. We also looked at how states are playing an increasing role in determining the outcomes of higher education and raising their expectations about what they are getting for their investments. And we offered a series of framing questions to help SEM practitioners examine their activities in the context of those public policy issues that we anticipate will be most prominent in the years to come.

SEM has been an evolving practice since its inception, requiring practitioners to stay abreast of new theories and developments as they seek to meet their institutional goals. With the growing complexity of the public policy and regulatory landscape, enrollment managers now must also navigate a rapidly changing set of directives from both the state and federal levels and evaluate their strategies both in terms of institutional goals and priorities as well as the broader public framework. SEM practitioners who are cognizant of the public policy and regulatory landscape will be well positioned to serve their institutions and communities better.

References

Ancheta, A. (2003). *Revisiting Bakke and Diversity-Based Admissions: Constitutional Law, Social Science Research, and the University of Michigan Affirmative Action Cases.* Cambridge, MA: The Civil Rights Project at Harvard University.

Archibald. R. B. (2002). *Redesigning the Financial Aid System: Why Colleges and Universities Should Switch Roles with the Federal Government.* Baltimore, MD: The Johns Hopkins University Press.

Association of Public and Land-Grant Universities (APLU). (2012). *The Land-Grant Tradition.* Washington, DC: Association of Public and Land-Grant Universities.

Callan, P. M. (2009). *California Higher Education, the Master Plan, and the Erosion of College Opportunity.* National Center for Public Policy and Higher Education.

Carnevale, A. P. (2013). *Recovery: Job Growth and Education Requirements Through 2020.* Georgetown University Center on Education and the Workforce.

Cervantes, A., Creusere, M., McMillion, R., McQueen, C., Short, M., Steiner, M., & Webster, J. (2005). *Opening the Doors to Higher Education: Perspectives on the Higher Education Act 40 Years Later.* Round Rock, TX: TG Research and Analytical Services, November.

Education Commission for the States. (2013). State Education Policy Database. Retrieved from http://www.ecs.org/html/statesTerritories/state_policy_developments.htm.

Executive Order No. 13607, 3 C.F.R. 248–252 (2013).

Friedel, J. N., Thornton, Z. M., D'Amico, M. M., & Katsinas, S. G. (2013). *Performance-Based Funding: The National Landscape.* Tuscaloosa, AL: The University of Alabama Education Policy Center.

Gardner, D. P. (1983). *A Nation at Risk: The Imperative for Educational Reform.* Report from the National Commission on Excellence in Education.

Gratz v. Bollinger, 539 U.S. 244 (2003).

Grutter v. Bollinger, 539 U.S. 306 (2003).

Hadley E. (2005). Did the sky really fall? Ten years after California's Proposition 209. *BYU Journal of Public Law*, *20*(103), 103–107.

Harnisch, T. L. (2011). *Performance-Based Funding: A Re-emerging Strategy in Public Higher Education Financing*. Washington, DC: American Association of State Colleges and Universities.

Hopwood v. Texas, 518 U.S. 1033 (1996).

Hutcheson, P. (2002). The 1947 President's Commission on Higher Education and the National Rhetoric on Higher Education Policy. *History of Higher Education Annual*, 22, 91–109.

Hutcheson, P.A. (2007). Setting the Nation's Agenda for Higher Education: A Review of Selected National Commission Reports, 1947–2006. *History of Education Quarterly*, 47(3), 359–367.

Immerwahr, J., Johnson, J., Ott, A., & Rochking, J. (2010). *Squeeze Play 2010: Continued Public Anxiety on Cost, Harsher Judgments on How Colleges Are Run*. San Jose, CA: Public Agenda and the National Center for Public Policy and Higher Education.

Jones, D., & Kelly, P. (2013). *Getting to 2025—A Status Report on Degree-Attainment Goals . . . and What We Need to do to Reach the 2025 Target*. Presentation at State Higher Education Executive Officers Policy Conference, August 2013,Orlando, FL.

Kanter, M. (2012). *An America Built to Last*. Remarks of the Undersecretary for Postsecondary Education to the National Council of State Directors of Community Colleges, Spring 2012 meeting, Orlando, FL.

National Conference of State Legislatures (NCSL). (2014). *Performance-Based Funding for Higher Education*. Retrieved from http://www.ncsl.org/research/education/performance-funding.aspx.

Nemec, M. R. (2006). *Ivory Towers and Nationalist Minds: Universities, Leadership, and the Development of the American State*. Ann Arbor: The University of Michigan Press.

Newfield, C. (2003). *Ivy and Industry: Business and the Making of the American University, 1890–1980*. Durham, NC: Duke University Press.

Obama, B. H. (2009). Remarks of President Barack Obama. Address to Joint Session of Congress, Washington, DC, February 24, 2009.

Obama, B. H. (2011). Remarks by the President on College Affordability. Speech at the University of Colorado Denver Campus, October 26, 2011.

Oldham, C. (2006). *A Test of Leadership: Charting the Future of U.S. Higher Education*. Report from the Secretary of Education's Commission on the Future of Higher Education.

Organisation for Economic Co-operation and Development (OECD). (2013). Education at a Glance 2013: OECD Indicators. OECD Publishing.

Palmer, J. C., Ed. (2013). Grapevine: An Annual Compilation of Data on State Support for Higher Education. Illinois State University. Retrieved from http://grapevine.illinoisstate.edu/index.shtml.

Phillippe, K. A., & Patton, M. (2000). *National Profile of Community Colleges: Trends and Statistics* (3rd Edition). Washington, DC: Community College Press, American Association of Community Colleges.

Prescott, B. T., & Bransberger, P. (2012). *Knocking at the College Door: Projections of High School Graduates* (8th Edition). Boulder, CO: Western Interstate Commission on Higher Education.

Radwin, D., Wine, J., Siegel, P., & Bryan, M. (2013). 2011–12 National Postsecondary Student Aid Study (NPSAS:12): Student Financial Aid Estimates for 2011–12 (NCES 2013–165). Institute of Education Sciences, U.S. Department of Education. Washington, DC: National Center for Education Statistics.

Reed, M., & Cochrane, D. (2012). *Student Debt and the Class of 2011*. Oakland, CA: The Institute for College Access & Success.

Regents of the University of California v. Bakke, 438 U.S. 265 (1978).

Russell, A. (2011). *A Guide to Major U.S. College Completion Initiatives*. Washington, DC: American Association of State Colleges and Universities.

Scanlan, L.C. (1996). *Hopwood v. Texas*: A Backward Look at Affirmative Action in Education. *NYU Law Review*, 71(6), 1580–1584.

Shapiro, D., Dundar, A., Ziskin, M, Yuan, X., & Harrell, A. (2013). *Completing College: A National View of Student Attainment Rates-Fall 2007 Cohort*. Signature Report 6. Herndon, VA: National Student Clearinghouse.

Smole, D. P. (2012). *Campus-Based Student Financial Aid Programs Under the Higher Education Act*. Congressional Research Service Report RL31618. Washington, DC: Congressional Research Service.

State Higher Education Executive Officers (SHEEO). (2012). *State Higher Education Finance FY 2011*. Boulder, CO: SHEEO. Retrieved from http://www.sheeo.org/sites/default/files/publications/SHEF_FY11.pdf.

Trow, M. (1988). American higher education: Past, present, and future. *Educational Researcher*, 17(3), 13–23.

U.S. Bureau of Labor Statistics. (2010). Education pays: More education leads to higher earnings, lower unemployment. *Occupational Outlook Quarterly*, Summer 2010, 32.

U.S. Department of Education. (2012). The Federal Role in Education. Retrieved from http://www2.ed.gov/about/overview/fed/role.html.

U.S. Department of Education. (2013a). *Official FY 2011 Two-Year Cohort Default Rate Briefing*. Washington, DC: U.S. Department of Education Office of Federal Student Aid.

U.S. Department of Education. (2013b). *Official FY 2010 Three-Year Cohort Default Rate Briefing*. Washington, DC: U.S. Department of Education Office of Federal Student Aid.

The White House, Office of the Press Secretary. (2013). *FACT SHEET on the President's Plan to Make College More Affordable: A Better Bargain for the Middle Class*. (Press Release). Retrieved from http://www.whitehouse.gov/the-press-office/2013/08/22/fact-sheet-president-s-plan-make-college-more-affordable-better-bargain-.

CHAPTER 25

Strategic Thinking
Enrollment Organizations

Adam J. Herman

S trategic Enrollment Management organizations and their operations within institutions of higher education are influenced—even pressured—by multiple forces, as considered at length in Part I of this volume. These influences include competing institution-level strategic priorities, consumers (which include prospective and current students and their parents), alumni, and internal constituents. Some internal constituents, including senior organizational leaders, often recognize the SEM organization's role in promoting the institution brand, increasing the prestige associated with the institution itself, and strengthening the value of the degrees the institution confers. Although SEM organizations engage in strategic planning to address short- and long-term goals, as addressed in Chapter 27, all chapters in Part V speak to the daily enrollment-related operations (which, in turn, affect the execution of strategies) that often are affected by multifarious simultaneous concerns and shifting priorities. In light of the dynamic marketplace and shifting concerns, which literature and frameworks can SEM organizations draw on to best leverage relevant information from within their institutions (compared to the marketplace) as well as professional associations, peer institutions, and internal colleagues?

This chapter introduces two key frameworks—resource-based view (Barney, 1991) and attention-based view (Ocasio, 1997)—that can be used to assess internal resources and the distribution of attention. This chapter also presents additional frameworks that specifically relate to the absorption and exploitation of external information (Cohen & Levinthal, 1990) and entrepreneurial orientation (Covin & Slevin, 1989; Lumpkin & Dess, 1996). In addition to introducing key conceptual frameworks, this chapter provides examples of how one can leverage these frameworks and lenses within the SEM organization while being sensitive to a variety of forces. Some of these forces include campus climate, norms, and values; collaboration practices; and the structure of the SEM office and other campus units. This chapter provides examples of practices that build upon the frameworks, but practitioners should take care to use the frameworks as lenses for analyzing their own organization, SEM strategies, institutional context, and environment.

The reader will note that strategic theories and frameworks are introduced, some of them more foundational than contemporary, to guide operational analysis within institutions of higher education. These frameworks and diagnostic tools are introduced not as a replacement for contemporary management and leadership literature (a category of volumes that has no lack of titles) but, rather, to introduce chief enrollment officers and SEM leaders to frameworks and theoretical lenses than are absent from the contemporary conversation in enrollment management.

UNDERSTANDING THE RESOURCE-BASED VIEW

Whereas organizations frequently give substantial attention to external analysis of opportunities and threats outside the organization, and how these opportunities and threats relate to competitive advantages, organizational leaders must also pay attention to the internal factors that provide competitive advantages as well (Barney, 1991). Barney's resource-based view provides a framework in which managers can analyze the "assets, capabilities, organizational processes, [organizational] attributes, information, knowledge, etc." (p. 101) that lead to a competitive advantage. The foregoing are known collectively as an organization's *resources*, and Barney further groups resources into three categories: *human capital*, *physical capital*, and *organizational capital*. Barney is quick to observe that not all of the resources an organization possesses in each category of capital contribute to competitive advantages for the organization, but some of the resources contribute specifically to *sustained competitive advantage*, the conditions that enable an organization to "[implement] a value-creating strategy not being implemented by any current or potential competitors" (p. 102) and which is also difficult for competitors to duplicate.

In identifying resources within their organizations, SEM leaders can brainstorm resources that fall under each category. For *human capital*, leaders can assess the specific talents and strengths of individuals within SEM organizations that give the SEM unit strengths that are difficult to duplicate and contribute significantly to competitive advantages. For *physical capital*, leaders can consider specialized equipment (or even technology) that the SEM organization leverages, which competitors do not. Finally, leaders should consider *organizational capital*, specific processes, routines, customs, or rituals that make an individual SEM organization distinctly competitive.

Leaders may find it easy to overlook the organizational capital that makes particular SEM organizations distinct. For example, leaders can consider whether there are specialized decision-making routines that allow their SEM leadership team to make decisions more quickly (or with better operational intelligence) than competitor institutions. In some organizations, the existence of more data, and specific decision rules, allow better decisions to be made more quickly than if those capabilities were not in place (Eisenhardt, 1989). SEM leaders can also consider specific processes in place to identify when existing processes are not working and need to be adjusted. *Dynamic capabilities,* processes to change existing routines and processes, are resources themselves than can help keep an organization competitive (Eisenhardt & Martin, 2000).

Analysis by SEM leaders should not be limited only to the SEM organization, though. As a component of a larger entity (the university, state system, or branch campus), the SEM organization is both a specific resource within the larger organization and made up of other resources, including specific physical, human, and organizational assets.

IN PRACTICE: IDENTIFYING AN ORGANIZATION'S RESOURCES

SEM leaders are advised to utilize the resource-based view as a lens for evaluating the resources that keep both their institutions and their particular SEM organizations competitive. Considering the human, organizational, and physical capital within the institution that serves as a competitive advantage can help SEM leaders identify specific assets that would be difficult for others to duplicate easily.

Human capital can include both individuals inside the SEM organization and individuals across the campus. Within the SEM operation, a number of individuals can be considered strategic human capital resources. For example, leaders can identify the admissions counselors who are particularly adept at helping prospects considering multiple destinations assess the value of their specific campus from a field of competitors and enroll there. Examples of such valuable human assets include the following:

- The financial aid counselor who (perhaps even to the dismay of her colleagues and superiors) is often highly sought after by families experiencing difficult financial situations or that have unusually complex financial aid difficulties

- The information technology specialist or data analyst who goes beyond just delivering reports and information but is capable of anticipating the needs of senior leadership and offering advice, constructive criticism, or additional perspectives on reporting and analysis

- The associate registrar who has been at the institution for more than twenty-five years, presents at state and national conferences, and always has her pulse on what other institutions are doing to stay ahead in records and registration management

As leaders identify the individuals (or groups of individuals) who contribute to a SEM organization's competitive advantage, they can formulate a list of who these individuals are, what they do, and how they serve as a value-creating resource that leads to a competitive advantage.

Organizational capital within the SEM unit can include specialized processes, protocols, or routines that provide a competitive advantage. Leaders creating a map or inventory of the various processes within their SEM organizations should be able to identify some processes and practices that are done very well and would be difficult for others to duplicate easily. Physical capital within the SEM organization would include physical assets or technological equipment that gives a specific SEM unit a competitive advantage over SEM units at peer institutions in the marketplace.

It can be helpful to think about resources that enable a competitive advantage through the lens of branding. Especially in the United States, brand equity and brand value assist organizations in defining and promoting the value they deliver to customers, while also helping customers mitigate against risks in decision-making. Brands are incredibly powerful, because "they are an effective way to secure a sustainable competitive advantage. The brand allows improved identification of the product . . . [and] are a real way to build customer loyalty" (Campbell, 2002, p. 210). The resources that make up an organization, in many cases, are either explicit components of the brand's value proposition or are internal constituent parts that enable a brand to stay competitive.

COMPETITIVE RESOURCES OUTSIDE OF SEM ORGANIZATIONS

In addition to a chief enrollment officer completing such an inventory of their entire SEM operation, heads of organizational sub-units can also complete resource inventories and share them both with their direct reports and their supervisors, providing an opportunity for multiple levels of organizational leadership to see not just the strategic priorities their colleagues are pursuing but also the strategic assets (or resources) available to achieve those goals.

Enrollment management serves dual roles, leading the SEM functions of their institutions while also serving as senior managers (and often senior promoters) of the institution to a variety of constituencies, which gives chief enrollment officers a uniquely valuable vantage point from which to identify and evaluate the institution's resources as a whole. Although such resources are often less within the locus of control of the chief enrollment officer, SEM officers can help identify and leverage institution-wide resources in a variety of ways. For example, stories of individual faculty or key administrators are often deeply intertwined into the organizational sagas and narratives of distinctiveness institutions share both internally (as part of the organizational cultural mythology) and externally (in marketing pitches or on campus tours) (Clark, 1972). As part of an evaluation of key competitive resources, SEM leaders should include human capital unique to the institution that serves to set the college or university apart in the marketplace. This could include the award-winning physicist, the American studies professor whom every student loves because of his effective story-telling techniques and his unwavering commitment to students, or the beloved basketball coach who takes time to talk to any student about their academic progress.

Organizational capital outside of the SEM organization can, again, include processes or practices, but it could also include features, rituals, and customs that give the organization a competitive edge (perhaps a robust career services office that maintains rich ties to alumni willing to hire students, or an homecoming celebration that brings the campus together for an entire weekend). In this case, the career services office can provide a tangible benefit directly tied to the value proposition for which students are attending the institution; the career services office helps students find a job. But an annual celebration can be equally important, demonstrating to prospective students and families that the campus contains a rich, vibrant community where students are valued as individuals. Physical capital outside of the SEM organization can include aspects of the campus's physical plant, distinct features of campus architecture or buildings, or the city or town in which the institution is situated. Whereas the resources within the SEM division may be easier for the SEM leadership to control, all of an institution's resources can be leveraged in SEM planning.

This section of the chapter introduced the resource-based view and given guidance on identifying human, physical, and organizational capital within and outside the SEM organization. The next chapter introduces conditions that influence the allocation of attention within organizations and discusses how understanding the allocation of attention can lead to better SEM decisions and results.

ALLOCATING ATTENTION IN THE SEM ORGANIZATION

Even in organizations with well-defined, valuable resources that keep them competitive, demands on decision makers' time often exceed the attention decision-makers can pay to the variety of areas that need attention. Regardless of institution size, control, setting, or type, decision-makers cannot realistically focus on every aspect of the organization. Research shows that individual decision-makers are likely to *satisfice*, or meet a decision acceptability threshold, when faced with large amounts of information (Simon, 1947). Building on the notion of satisficing, Ocasio (1997) proposes three principles for distribution of attention within organizations: (1) the focus of attention, (2) situated attention, and (3) structural distribution of attention.

Leveraging Ocasio's attention-based view, SEM leaders can and should analyze the heuristics and decision rules within their organizations that tell employees (from receptionists, to admissions counselors, to processing staff, to senior managers) when to stop satisficing and start maximizing. Imagining a typical admissions office, a director of admissions could be faced with multiple internal and external demands in the same day: a major news magazine releases the results of its annual rankings survey on the same day that the president's office sends a high-profile visitor to receive a personal tour; or, the weekly application tracking meeting occurs at the same time an irate prospective parent is yelling in the lobby in front of twenty other prospective students and their families. For the most part, these are easy quandaries to respond to and are familiar to professionals. It is not difficult to put the rankings report down and give a VIP tour or to pause the weekly meeting to help resolve a parent issue.

What can be challenging for seniors leaders is allocating attention among typical, routine, mundane, and otherwise ordinary processes in the office. It is impossible for an admissions director or chief enrollment officer to pay attention to all of the processes and practices occurring in the office (nor should one person be expected to know every detail of the office's operation), but sometimes it is easy for the precursors of urgent situations to get lost among routine processes. In his principle of situated attention, Ocasio (1997) observes that "what decision-makers focus on, and what they do, depends on the particular context they are located in" (p. 190). In other words, some signals or data points could be the equivalent of an organizational "fire alarm" sounding, but only if practices and processes are in place for senior leaders to be attentive to the alarm.

In Practice: Allocating Attention in the SEM Organization

Because chief enrollment officers cannot see and hear everything that is going on in their organizations at all times, it is important that they empower staff to provide critical feedback and even sound euphemistic "alarm bells." Although many senior managers have "open doors" to direct reports, leaders would do well to remind individuals at all levels of the organization that reasonable decisions, and reasonable communications, are welcomed and encouraged. The admissions application processor who notices anomalies in a report comparing applications-to-this-week-last-year might just brace herself for a rise in applications in the future, or wonder about the downtick, but what if this employee were encouraged to go a step further, and alert her supervisor, or formulate hypotheses, or ask additional questions?

Leveraging Ocasio's (1997) attention-based view in SEM organizations ensures that these organizations can meet strategic objectives through "shared collaboration":

> Because [higher education organizations] are organizationally complex and pride themselves on high degrees of decentralization, an ethos of collaboration must be cultivated among administrative and student support units and faculty, academic administrators, and student life professionals. This is necessary in order to blur the boundaries between academic affairs, student affairs, business affairs, and other functional units. This kind of cooperation is needed to improve the undergraduate experience. (Hossler, Kuh, & Olsen, 2001, p. 212)

Following are specific examples of how SEM organizations could leverage the attention-based view to offer better service.

Decreasing Satisficing to Promote Ease of Organizational Navigation As Ocasio (1997) argues, attention is a finite resource. Decision-makers within a higher education organization, for example, cannot possibly devote equal levels of attention to all areas. The idea of attentional distribution suggests weighty demands on any given decision-maker or staff member: they are asked to make numerous decisions, each with potential implications for student satisfaction, success, and retention.

Because individuals cannot possibly treat every decision equally, they must instead use cues from a given decision context to determine whether they should *maximize* (conduct the most thorough information search possible of all implications and choice option to determine the best one) or *satisfice* (select the first most appropriate choice) (Lutz, 1982). As demands on time increase, Lutz argues, higher education staff are asked to satisfice on many decisions rather than maximize on one. A critical choice within an organization involves assessing which types of cues staff will use to determine whether to maximize or satisfice on a decision.

This idea of maximizing and satisficing relates, for example, to the ease with which students can navigate higher education.

Let's consider the case of a student who walks into the registrar's office, wearing a heavy backpack and looking like she just walked several miles to solve an administrative problem she is having. (Perhaps she is even late for class!) Unfortunately for this student, whereas she has come to discuss the late registration fee she noticed on her bill, this sort of request is actually handled by the bursar's office or the office of student accounts, and not the registrar's office.

At the satisficing end of the response continuum, a staff member could report that there is nothing that can be done for them. "Our office doesn't handle that issue," a staff member might say. "Go see the bursar." A senior might be grateful for the advice, and walk down the hall to the correct office. A freshman, however, might wonder, "What's a bursar? How will I find the bursar?" and then realize, "I'm late to class. I better get going." and feel disgruntled by, or confused by, the experience altogether.

At the maximizing end of the response continuum, the same staff member might say, "Oh, it might seem logical to come here to inquire about that charge, but this type of inquiry is actually handled by the bursar's office, down the hall. I can walk you there!" A senior might consider the response unnecessarily generous, and a freshman might be very grateful for the assistance.

It is, of course, unreasonable to expect that staff members will maximize at all times. Yet the proposition that satisficing is consistently necessitated by the demands of the university environment is worthy of some healthy skepticism. It is important to empower employees—especially those in student service positions—to respond with significant discretion. SEM leaders can encourage employees to ask follow-up questions, "Do you know where the bursar's office is? Can I help you get there?" or to locate additional data on the students they encounter (such as recognizing whether the student is a freshman new to campus or an experienced senior).

Research on group decision-making suggests that individuals are distinctly less likely to listen to those within a group who are perceived as having a lower status (Kaplan & Martin 1999). Further, these lower status individuals are less likely to speak in group-decision conditions. This situation persists even when these individuals are experimentally assigned information valuable to the decision scenario. Thus, when lower status individuals are ignored, groups produce poorer overall decisions. When there was a high perception of a status differential, individuals within a group were less likely to bring all available information to bear on their decision-making.

For senior enrollment managers, having processes in place to communicate with line staff, and encouraging communication, is not just about having an approachable leadership style or being seen as possessing humility. Rather, open communication between all levels of the organization can lead to key information-holders sharing important information. An application processor who notices a drop in application counts year over year should feel empowered to alert someone. The registrar's office front-line employee who redirects twenty students a day who really need to see the bursar can request that better signage be placed in the building or ask that the student billing website better indicates where students can go to solve such problems.

For its part, senior management should be prepared to respond to concerns brought forth by a number of individuals, whether those individuals are direct reports to the chief enrollment officer or individuals lower down the organizational hierarchy or in another unit. This is not to suggest that organization charts and protocols do not matter, but to suggest that a culture of open communication across organizational sub-units, which leads to greater information sharing, can promote organizational performance.

Leaders can be particularly alert for scenarios where phrases such as, "That's not how *we* do it here," or "That financial award letter? *They* will never fix it." In these scenarios, who is "we"? Who is "they"? Leaders should foster an environment in which staff are empowered to provide feedback and can use both formal and informal systems to provide feedback, even for employees not in traditional "leadership" roles.

Following are some key practical questions to consider:

- What kinds of attention are rewarded within the SEM organization?
- Which metrics get talked about the most? The least?
- Who are the key decision-makers?
- How do "line" employers in the SEM organization provide feedback that gets noticed by key decision-makers?
- How do faculty or other campus constituents provide input or feedback regarding SEM practices? Does this impact the goals of key individuals in the SEM organization, or where their attention and efforts are placed?

The issue of valuing all statuses of information-holders becomes even more critical in the next sections of this chapter, which look at how to leverage information from outside the organization and exploit it to drive performance.

Bringing Outside Information In: Leveraging Absorptive Capacity

Among the key resources Barney (1991) identifies are "capabilities" that organizations possess, which enable them to have sustained competitive advantages. Cohen & Levinthal (1990) define *absorptive capacity* (AC) as a capability that helps organizations (1) *recognize* information outside the organization, (2) *assimilate* that information into the organization, and (3) *exploit* the information to improve performance or outcomes.

Organizations with AC are able to take stock of the knowledge within the organization as well as information that exists outside the institution and enact policies and processes that cause knowledge "transfers . . . across and within sub-units that may be quite removed from the original point of entry," and then exploit that knowledge for competitive purposes (Cohen & Levinthal, 1990, p. 131). This applies to a variety of information, but in this case it applies especially to information or data that may exist within the marketplace that will allow an institution of higher education (IHE) to have knowledge—about either competitors or itself—that will help the IHE develop a stronger connection within the context of SEM. Further, Lane, Koka, and Pathak (2006) suggest the importance of AC when they offer that, "developing and maintaining absorptive capacity is critical to an [organization's] long-term survival and success because absorptive capacity can reinforce, complement, or refocus the [organization's] knowledge base" (p. 833). When the information enables a college or university to connect more purposefully or effectively with a prospective student or family, or an enrolled student, or alumnus, that information can be crucial.

It is worth noting, however, that the information gained through AC activities may not be about specific prospective students but, rather, may be about competitor institutions. Perhaps two associate directors of undergraduate recruitment units are out at lunch—just two colleagues sharing a meal together—when one of them shares that a lot of new students are applying from a given geographic region because a prominent alumnus had recently endowed a scholarship in her hometown for students who attend the institution in question.

At least three distinct types of processes must be engaged to transform an ordinary lunchtime conversation to one in which an admissions staff member could leverage absorptive capacity: *recognition, assimilation*, and *exploitation*. Each of these steps can be important on its own, but each is necessary and required for absorptive capacity to be fully leveraged.

Recognition of Information as Valuable First, the staff member must *recognize* the value of the information and operate in a context in which recognition of such information is a valued activity. (In other words, someone has to tell staff to be on the lookout for information that can be useful to sustain competitive advantages.) Cohen and Levinthal (1990) specifically observe that the recognition stage results from "interactions across individuals who each possess diverse and different knowledge structures [that] will augment the organization's capacity for making novel linkages and associations—innovating—beyond what any one individual can achieve" (p. 133). In this case, an attentive admissions officer might simply recognize the value of knowing about this new scholarship opportunity for students at another school and can make reasonable assumptions about ways this new scholarship could impact students who are cross-shopping the two institutions.

Assimilating Information into the Organization In a SEM context with absorptive capacity activities, recognition is only the first step. After recognizing the value of the information, the enrollment officer next needs to *assimilate* the information within the institution to various stakeholders who—by virtue of having the information—could be in a position to utilize it in a way that may enhance the market position or brand equity of the institution in the eyes of certain prospective students or their families. According to Lyles & Schwenk (1992), the ability of an organization to leverage recognized external information depends, at least in part, on the existing structures and processes within the organization for assimilating the knowledge.

Exploiting Information for Competitive Purposes Cohen and Levinthal (1990) observed that, "absorptive capacity refers not only to the acquisition or assimilation of information by an organization but also to the organization's ability to exploit it" (p. 131). Thus, we now turn to the final process that must occur in a SEM unit where AC activities are present: *exploitation*. In the case of the endowed scholarship, *exploitation* of the information might include the institution matching the scholarship funds for students who have received the scholarship at the competing university. Or, even before the application phase, the institution might advertise highly generous merit or need-based aid to counter the effects of the new scholarship. If the enrollment management unit works closely with the development office, the admissions office might work to reallocate unrestricted donated funds to a similar scholarship, or begin looking into donors of its own (either to compete directly in the market where the new scholarship was created or to create in a different market where that competition does not exist).

In sum, an undergraduate recruitment apparatus with absorptive capacity would have processes in place that enable the enrollment management unit to recognize valuable external information, assimilate it within the organization, and exploit it for performance-oriented gains. Spending time crafting an information-sharing culture, or system, is crucial, because, as Ocasio (1997) observed, attention is a finite resource in organizations. This is especially true in higher education where the "allocation of issues, answers and decision-makers within specific . . . activities, communications and procedures" is controlled in a variety of manners at different institutions (Ocasio, 1997, p. 191). In short, there's no single method for organizing an admissions office or enrollment management division, so it's important that if AC is to be leveraged, time and attention are given to the process of doing so.

LEVERAGING AN ENTREPRENEURIAL ORIENTATION

Entrepreneurial activities involve individuals, business units, or organizations making a "new entry as an essential act" of entrepreneurship (Lumpkin & Dess, 1996, p. 138). Although there are popular conceptions of entrepreneurship that focus on individuals or small businesses (or, for example, franchises), Lumpkin and Dess conceive of entrepreneurship in such a manner that individual units within organizations can engage in entrepreneurial activities to the benefit of the entire organization. Thus, an admissions office (or other SEM function) can behave with an entrepreneurial orientation, and engage in entrepreneurial activities, and have those activities benefit the entire IHE. In this section, we consider how SEM organizations that have the latitude to behave entrepreneurially can be more effective in the undergraduate recruitment process.

Building on seminal work in defining entrepreneurial orientation (such as Miller, 1983; Covin and Slevin, 1989), the work of Lumpkin and Dess (1996) identified "five dimensions—autonomy, innovativeness, risk taking, proactiveness and competitive aggressiveness—[which] have been useful for characterizing and distinguishing key entrepreneurial processes" (p. 136). These dimensions will not apply to each and every SEM organization within an institution of higher education, but the ability of an SEM unit, such as admissions, to possess an entrepreneurial orientation is closely linked to the structure and culture of an organization. For example, an organization with lots of role conflict may inhibit risk taking or autonomy because "the degree of incongruity or incompatibility of expectations communicated" from the central administration to the enrollment management units may lessen the degree to which enrollment management staff feel freedom to act autonomously or take risks (Bess & Dee, 2008, p. 262).

In this section, each of the elements of entrepreneurial orientation are considered in turn, with a focus on how they may be enacted within an admissions or recruitment operation. SEM leaders can utilize the following elements, and consider their own institutional context, to determine how to leverage entrepreneurial orientation appropriately within their SEM organizations.

Autonomy

Lumpkin and Dess (1996) describe autonomy as "the independent action of an individual or a team in bringing forth an idea or a vision and carrying it through to completion . . . In an organizational context, it refers to action taken free of stifling organizational constraints" (p. 140). For an admissions office, the chief enrollment officer would want to ensure that the admissions office has the ability to pursue key activities, such as setting the recruitment fair participation calendar or choosing which high schools to visit, as long as these activities fit into strategies set by the president or provost, and the chief enrollment officer. If the admissions office does not have the autonomy to plan and execute its own recruitment activities, this could create two problems: (1) inefficiency when the admissions office must seek permission from a higher level authority to modify the recruitment schedule, or, worse, (2) lost opportunities when the admissions office wants to visit a particular territory or engage in a specific activity, and the institution loses potential customers because of organizational constraints. If the admissions office has autonomy in this case, it can responsibly pursue recruitment activities that make sense in the context of its broader strategies.

Innovativeness and Risk Taking

According to Lumpkin and Dess (1996), innovativeness "reflects an [organization's] tendency to engage in and support new ideas, novelty, experimentation, and creative processes that may result in new products, services, or technological processes" (p. 142). In the case of admissions offices, it may be difficult to forge ahead with new ways of conceiving core admissions services or modifying deeply entrenched application or technological processes because they have existed at an institution for such a long time. To measure the innovativeness of a particular admissions office for the purposes of this study, the chief enrollment officer may look at processes that have changed and have had a net positive impact on students.

Risk-taking behaviors are related to innovativeness, especially in IHEs whose structures are well established over time, as Lumpkin and Dess (1996) highlight potential risks, including "personal risk, social risk and psychological risk" (p. 145). Individual actors in a SEM unit may shy away from new ideas or innovation, specifically because of risk, whether that takes the form of organizational risk or social risk within the structure of the IHE.

Proactiveness

Lumpkin and Dess (1996) observed that "by exploiting asymmetries in the marketplace, the first mover can capture unusually high profits and get a head start on establishing brand recognition. Thus, taking initiative by anticipating and pursuing new opportunities . . . also has become associated with entrepreneurship" (p. 146). It logically follows, then, that in markets in which an IHE is seeking students, the admissions office should be empowered to pursue new opportunities and take initiatives, especially when it comes to recruitment activities. In addition, the admissions office, and more broadly the enrollment management unit, should be a stakeholder "at the table" when the institution makes decisions on packaging new degree programs or unveiling new off-campus satellite centers, because the admissions office may be able to provide important data or decision insights related to the target markets in those areas.

Competitive Aggressiveness

Competitive aggressiveness refers to the "propensity to directly and intensely challenge its competitors to achieve entry or improve position, that is, to outperform industry rivals in the marketplace" (Lumpkin & Dess, 1996,

p. 149). Whereas universities do not ordinarily challenge rivals explicitly in advertising or print materials, there are several manifestations of competitive aggressiveness that can help IHEs as a whole and specifically admissions offices. First, institutions can look at competitors in given markets and bolster messaging and advertising that specifically differentiates (for the better) their IHE against competitors. This may include, for example, a university touting the number of students from a particular recruiting market or comparing itself to academic programs for which a rival university is specifically well known.

IN PRACTICE: MEASURING ENTREPRENEURIAL ORIENTATION IN THE ADMISSIONS OFFICE

The preceding descriptions provide a sense of what entrepreneurial orientation is, but measuring does not simply involve looking at an admissions office or a university structure and determining whether it is entrepreneurial. For future scholarship, for example, Lumpkin and Dess's (1996) instrument could be adapted to admissions offices in order to detect the presence of entrepreneurial orientation and help determine possible areas in which entrepreneurial orientation could lead to more effective outcomes.

It is worth noting, too, that the effectiveness of entrepreneurial activities also depends on the decision-making style and environment within the organization (whether "organization" here is the IHE itself or the sub-unit of enrollment management or admissions). By combining capabilities of absorptive capacity (AC) with entrepreneurial orientation, IHEs can leverage the synergistic benefits of fast, strategic decision-making coupled with real-time information. Eisenhardt (1989) observed in one study that to speed up decision making "executive teams making fast decisions used extensive information—often more information that the slower decision makers used. However that information was not forecasted information. Rather it was *real-time information,* especially on an [organization's] competitive environment and operations" (emphasis in original) (p. 549). Thus, being able to act on real-time information is crucial in decision-making situations. For entrepreneurial orientation to reap maximum benefit in an admissions office, the office would have to have processes in place to make real-time market information quickly available to key decision-makers (whether through absorptive capacity or other mechanisms). It is this kind of synergy that, for example, would allow an IHE to adjust tuition discounting or merit scholarship offers for specific geographic markets based on information it learns about how much aid competitor institutions are offering.

INSIDE THE STRATEGIC-THINKING SEM UNIT

This chapter introduced two key business theories, resource-based view and attention-based view, to help the reader think strategically about assets within the SEM organization and within their colleges and universities that lead to competitive advantages. In addition, readers were introduced to two capabilities, absorptive capacity (AC) and entrepreneurial orientation (EO). In this section, we consider what life looks like in the strategic thinking SEM unit by considering some key questions that apply to the concepts covered thus far.

Strategic Resources That Lead to a Competitive Advantage

- *Who* are the key *human assets* in the SEM unit who add significant value to the organization? This includes not just the named "leaders" but also specialists, technologically-savvy individuals, or key relationship-builders for the unit.

- *Who* are the key *human assets* outside of the SEM unit who keep the top-level organization (college/university/system) competitive?

- *What* are the key *organizational* processes, internal advantages, protocols, or norms that allow the institution (or the SEM unit) to stay competitive?

- *What* are the key *physical assets* that allow the institution to stay competitive? Are there special technologies or tools that enable the staff to do their jobs better than competitors?

Allocation of Attention

- Which issues do chief enrollment officers pay attention to within the organization? Which issues do middle-managers pay attention to?

- Are there key issues, because of the context of their work (or institutional context), that chief enrollment officers or middle managers *should* pay attention to, but currently do not?

- Is the organization truly one that works to minimize power distance and status differentials so that information flows throughout the organization? Are there key individuals the SEM leadership should be meeting with, but do not see regularly, so that decisions can benefit from enhanced knowledge/expertise/relationships?

Absorptive Capacity

- What guidelines are in place within the SEM unit to help *identify* valuable external information? Are staff able to *identify* information that may be valuable in the external environment?

- Which *informal* processes are in place to *assimilate* information? What is shared at staff meetings? Are there regular opportunities for staff to reflect and share with each other information they are learning at conferences, from professional colleagues, from news publications, and from informal networks? Having regular opportunities to share can facilitate the flow of information across organizational networks.

- Which *formal* processes are in place to *assimilate* information? Is there a knowledge database or internal intranet available for staff to post, share, and retrieve information from other organizational sub-units? Or are there silos that keep information shuttered within respective enclaves?

- How are staff encouraged to *exploit* external information? Is there a culture that promotes taking risks and not being afraid of failure?

Entrepreneurial Orientation

- How often are staff encouraged to *proactively* identify new ways of doing things?

- Are staff encouraged to be autonomous and *try new ideas?*

- How does the SEM organization assess *risks* of new initiatives and decide which risks are worth taking?

- Are there social norms that dictate the difference between thoughtful calculated risks with probabilities for positive outcomes, versus risks that may not pay off? (McGrath, 1999)

CONCLUSION

This chapter is not intended to provide prescriptive advice but, rather, to illuminate possibilities for identifying strategic resources, understanding how educational leaders allocate their attention, and identifying where absorptive capacity and entrepreneurial orientation may fit into a specific SEM organization as capabilities worth leveraging. Taking this longer view of SEM practice also requires the incorporation of *dynamic capabilities*; in other words, and as further discussed in Chapter 27, SEM organizations must have structures in place that help them refine processes over time to keep the organization competitive and strategic (Eisenhardt & Martin, 2000; Zollo & Winter, 2002). These dynamic capabilities may require the implementation of new reporting routines or regular meetings to discuss key indicators, but what is important is that the processes in place that result from enhanced strategies should be continually assessed and updated.

Dynamic capabilities also have the effect of giving organizations permission to fix processes rather pointing fingers at people. Updating processes using real-time data and strategic indicators can help leaders respond to with organizational politics and silos and unite SEM organizational members with a shared sense of purpose, leading to shared goals and collaboration to turn weaknesses into opportunities, rather than ascribing blame to an individual.

Chief enrollment officers who are students of organizational theory will be familiar with the various organizational dynamics that influence decision-making, process management, interpersonal relationships, and bureaucracy on their own campuses. It is worth noting that a keen sense of an individual institution's culture, norms, political forces, and bureaucracy is a prerequisite for creating a strategic thinking enrollment management organization where one has not previously existed. In discussing the individualism of campuses, Birnbaum (1988) observed that "institutions can share similar core cultural elements and organizational subsystems and still not function in the same way. Although organizational patterns appear to systematically differ among institutional types, no two institutions are identical" (p. 176). Considering Birnbaum's observations about a campus's individual culture, it logically follows that not all of the foregoing tactics and strategies can be implemented in the same way on one campus as on another. Chief enrollment officers can utilize the frameworks in this chapter as tools for analysis, and determine which ones will be most effective on their own campuses.

References

Barney, J. B. (1991) Firm Resources and Sustained Competitive Advantage. *Journal of Management*, 17(1), 99–120. Retrieved from http://jom.sagepub.com/content/17/1/99.full.pdf.

Bess, J. L., & Dee, J. R. (2008). *Understanding College and University Organization: Theories for Effective Policy and Practice*, Vol. 1. Sterling, VA: Stylus Publishing.

Birnbaum, R. (1988). *How Colleges Work: The Cybernetics of Academic Organization and Leadership*. San Francisco: Jossey-Bass.

Campbell, M. C. (2002). Building brand equity. *International Journal of Medical Marketing*, 2(3), 208–218.

Clark, B. R. (1972). The organizational saga in higher education. *Administrative Science Quarterly*, 17(2), 178–184.

Cohen, W. M., & Levinthal, D. A. (1990). Absorptive Capacity: A New Perspective on Learning and Innovation. *Administrative Science Quarterly*, 35(1), 128–152. Retrieved from http://www.jstor.org/stable/10.2307/2393553.

Covin, J. G., & Slevin, D. P. (1989). Strategic management of small firms in hostile and benign environments. *Strategic Management Journal*, 10(1), 75–87. (Reprinted in 2006 special issue.) Retrieved from http://onlinelibrary.wiley.com/doi/10.1002/smj.4250100107/abstract.

Eisenhardt, K. M. (1989). Making Fast Strategic Decisions in High-Velocity Environments. *Academy of Management Journal*, *23*(3), 543–576. Retrieved from http://www.jstor.org/stable/256434.

Eisenhardt, K. M., & Martin, J. A. (2000). Dynamic capabilities: What are they? *Strategic Management Journal*, *21*, 1105–1121. Retrieved from https://noppa.aalto.fi/noppa/kurssi/23e23000/harjoitustyot/23E23000_eisenhardt___martin__2000_.pdf.

Hossler, D., Kuh, G. D., & Olsen, D. (2001). Finding (More) Fruit on the Vines: Using Higher Education Research and Institutional Research to guide Institutional Policies and Strategies (Parts I & II). *Research in Higher Education*, *42*(2), 223–235. Retrieved from http://www.springerlink.com/content/jr2473pm4g723338/fulltext.pdf.

Kaplan, M. F., & Martin, A. M. (1999). Effects of Differential Status of Group Members on Process and Outcome of Deliberation. *Group Processes and Intergroup Relations*, *2*(4), 347–364. Retrieved from http://gpi.sagepub.com/content/2/4/347.abstract.

Lane, P. J., Koka, B. R., & Pathak, S. (2006). The Reification of Absorptive Capacity: A Critical Review and Rejuvenation of the Construct. *Academy of Management Review*, *31*(4), 833–863. Retrieved from http://www.unilu.ch/files/the_reification_of_absorptive_capacity.pdf.

Lumpkin, G. T., & Dess, G. G. (1996). Clarifying the Entrepreneurial Orientation Construct and Linking It to Performance. *Academy of Management Review*, *21*(1), 135–172. Retrieved from http://www.jstor.org/stable/258632.

Lutz, F. W. (1982). Tightening up Loose Coupling in Organizations of Higher Education. *Administrative Science Quarterly*, *27*(4): 653–669. Retrieved from http://www.jstor.org/discover/10.2307/2392536?uid = 3739656&uid = 2&uid = 4&uid = 3739256&sid = 21101372700457.

Lyles, M. A., & Schwenk, C. R. (1992). Top management, strategy, and organizational knowledge structures. *Journal of Management Studies*, *29*(2), 155–174. Retrieved from http://onlinelibrary.wiley.com/doi/10.1111/j.1467--6486.1992.tb00658.x/abstract.

McGrath, R. (1999). Falling forward: Real options reasoning and entrepreneurial failure. *Academy of Management Review*, *24*(1), 13–30.

Miller, D. (1983). The correlates of entrepreneurship in three types of firms. *Management Science*, *29*(7), 770–791. Retrieved from http://dx.doi.org/10.1287/mnsc.29.7.770.

Ocasio, W. (1997). Towards an attention-based view of the firm. *Strategic Management Journal*, *18*(S1), 187–206.

Simon, H. A. (1947). *Administrative Behavior: A Study of Decision-Making Processes in Administrative Organizations.* Chicago: Macmillan.

Zollo, M., & Winter S. G. (2002). Deliberate Learning and the Evolution of Dynamic Capabilities. *Organization Science*, *13*(3), 339–351. Retrieved from http://www.jstor.org/stable/3086025.

CHAPTER 26

Emerging SEM Organizations for Graduate and International Students

Jay Goff and
Monique Snowden

In this final chapter of Part VI, we turn our attention to the emerging use of Strategic Enrollment Management approaches for more specialized areas of student enrollment such as international students and students enrolled in graduate programs. Increasingly, academic leaders who are accountable for strengthening graduate, professional, and international enrollment are leveraging SEM philosophies, structures, and practices that have been successfully implemented to achieve undergraduate enrollment goals at two-year and four-year colleges and universities. The potential of SEM adoption and adaptation in deeply entrenched academic domains with "loosely coupled" academic and enrollment services gives import to SEM development, in theory and praxis. To that end, this chapter focuses on emerging SEM organizations in pursuit of strong and sustainable graduate, professional, and international student enrollment.

The chapter is organized into three sections followed by a summative outlook for the future. The first section highlights graduate and professional education enrollment imperatives and SEM structures for graduate education. In the second section, we focus on the global competition for international students. This is followed by a discussion of the emerging SEM organizations that are necessary to grow and support the enrollment of international graduate and undergraduate students. Finally, we offer concluding remarks about the practical viability of using SEM toward meeting the demand for graduate, professional, and international student enrollment.

THE EMERGENCE OF SEM ORGANIZATIONS IN GRADUATE AND PROFESSIONAL EDUCATION

Perhaps there are no better examples of the complex and diverse nature of graduate and professional education in the United States than the trends in law and medical school enrollments. Both of the well-established fields are experiencing dramatic changes in the numbers of students seeking professional law and medical education, respectively. On one side, first-year law student enrollment has been declining since 2010. According to the American Bar Association (ABA), first-year law student enrollment for the 2013–2014 academic year fell 11 percent to *39,675*—the lowest since 1977—compared to *44,481* for 2012–2013, *48,697* for 2011–2012, and *52,488* for 2010–2011 (American Bar Association, 2012, 2013; McDonald, 2013). On the other side, first-year medical student enrollment has been increasing since 2009. The Association of American Medical Colleges (AAMC) recently reported that "total number of applicants to medical school grew by 6.1 percent to 48,014, surpassing the previous record set in 1996 by 1,049 students" (AAMC, 2013).

Partly in response to the downward enrollment trend of first-year law students, the ABA is undertaking a project to revitalize law education and address the high costs associated with attaining a professional law degree. In contrast, the combined effects of an anticipated and significant shortage of physicians by 2020 and the increasing number of individuals gaining access to health insurance are driving forces behind an enrollment growth imperative for U.S. medical schools. The AAMC (2013) pointed out, "overall growth in medical student enrollment can be attributed, in part, to the creation of new medical schools as well as existing schools' efforts to expand their class sizes after the AAMC, in 2006, called for a 30 percent increase in enrollment to avert future doctor shortages" (para. 4).

More generally, the Commission on the Future of Graduate Education in the United States concluded, "the global competitiveness of the US and capacity for innovation hinges fundamentally on a strong system of graduate education" (Wendler et al., 2010). Strong stakeholder (such as policy makers, business leaders, and higher education administrators) responses to the commission's proclamation coincide with new, emerging, and expanding education markets, competency-based curricula, unbundled academic roles, and technological advances that are being reconceptualized as intentional design in service of education, rather than merely disruptive to education.

The need for a stronger U.S. workforce with advanced degrees and global perspectives is essential to national, organizational, and personal vitality. At national and organizational levels, it is estimated in *Pathways Through Graduate School and into Careers* that new jobs in the United States requiring an advanced degree will grow to 2.5 million positions by 2018 (Wendler et al., 2012). To meet projected labor force demands for more highly educated workers, U.S. colleges and universities will need to increase current annual master's degrees awarded by 18 percent and doctorate degrees awarded by 17 percent (Wendler et al., 2012). At the personal level, labor earnings data show that individuals possessing earned graduate and professional degrees have the highest earning potential and lowest unemployment rates (see Figure 26.1). It has long been evidenced that postsecondary educational credentials are prerequisites for holding the vast majority of high-rewarding jobs in America (Brown, 1995, p. 2). Kay Kohl (2000) emphasized that "people need continuous learning to stay occupationally relevant" and "to ensure employment stability" (p.19). So, for many individuals in the U.S. workforce, post-baccalaureate education is more than a self-enriching endeavor; it is an absolute necessity.

Administered annually since 1986, a survey of graduate enrollment and degree attainment is jointly sponsored by the Council of Graduate Schools (CGS) and the Graduate Record Examinations (GRE) Board. The survey gathers data

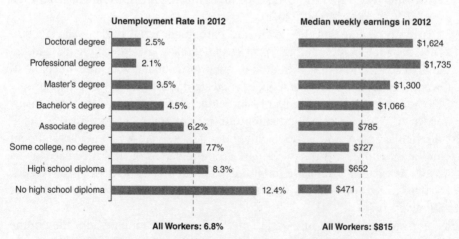

Source: Adapted from Bureau of Labor Statistics, Current Poplulation Survey, 2013
Note: Data are for persons age 25 and over. Earnings are for full-time wage and salary workers.

Figure 26.1 Employment value of earning graduate and professional degrees

about applications to U.S. graduate schools, graduate student enrollment, and graduate degrees and certificates conferred. The enrollment data trends reported in *Graduate Enrollment and Degrees: 2002 to 2012* (Gonzales, Allum, & Sowell, 2013) support the following conclusions:

- **Graduate student enrollment growth is stronger for international vs. domestic students.** Over the past one- and five-year periods, growth in total graduate enrollment was greater for international graduate students than domestic graduate students. Between fall 2011 and fall 2012, total graduate enrollment increased 2.8 percent for international students but fell 3.2 percent for domestic students. Between fall 2007 and fall 2012, total graduate enrollment increased 2.2 percent annually on average for international students, compared with 1.3 percent for domestic students (p. 59).

- **Prospective graduate students are more likely to enroll in master's degree and graduate certificate programs.** Institutions responding to the survey enrolled a total of nearly 1.74 million students in graduate certificate, education specialist, master's, or doctoral programs in fall 2012 (p. 11). About three-quarters (74.1 percent) of graduate students in fall 2012 were enrolled in programs leading to a master's degree or a graduate certificate. The remaining quarter (25.9 percent) were enrolled in doctoral programs (p. 12).

- **Graduate student enrollment at private, not-for profit institutions has stronger growth than graduate student enrollment at public institutions.** Between fall 2007 and fall 2012, the average total graduate enrollment increased 1.1 percent annually. Average annual growth was 1.2 percent at public institutions and 1.7 percent at private, not-for-profit institutions. Between fall 2002 and fall 2012, the average total graduate enrollment increased 1.8 percent annually, with stronger growth at private, not-for-profit institutions than at public institutions: 2.2 percent versus 1.5 percent (p. 59).

- **International students are more likely to enroll in U.S. research universities for graduate study.** The overall distribution of graduate students varied considerably by institutions' Carnegie classification, with temporary residents (that is, international students) more highly represented in research universities than at other types of institutions. At research universities with very high research activity (RU/VH) and those with high research activity (RU/H), respectively, 24.9 percent and 16.2 percent of all graduate students were international. In contrast, merely 6.9 percent of graduate students at doctoral/research universities and 6.1 percent of those at master's colleges and universities were international (p. 13). According to the National Science Foundation

(National Association for College Admission Counseling, 2012), during the same reporting period, 84 percent of all international doctoral students were enrolled in science, technology, engineering, or mathematics (STEM) fields of study.

- **Domestic graduate students are more likely to enroll in regional college and universities for graduate study.** Overall, more than half (60.3 percent) of all international graduate students were enrolled at research universities with very high research activity (RU/VH), while only 32.4 percent of all U.S. citizen and permanent resident graduate students (that is, domestic students) were at these institutions. In contrast, 29.7 percent of all domestic graduate students, but only 10.9 percent of all international graduate students, were at master's colleges and universities (p. 13).

- **Graduate students enrolled at regional colleges and universities are more likely to enroll part-time.** Among total enrollments for which enrollment status was known, nearly six out of ten (57.5 percent) graduate students were enrolled full time in fall 2012, and 42.5 percent were enrolled part-time. Research universities with very high research activity (RU/VH) had the highest percentage of full-time students (73.0 percent), and master's colleges and universities had the lowest percentage (37.1 percent) (p. 11).

The enrollment trends reported by CGS/ETS suggest a compelling need for emerging SEM organizations that attend to graduate and international enrollment. Further, the trends and associated conclusions are guiding context for this chapter.

EMERGING GRADUATE AND PROFESSIONAL SEM ORGANIZATIONS

Renowned architect Louis Sullivan is credited with coining the phrase, "Form ever follows function." Similarly, Don Hossler and David Kalsbeek (2008) posit that SEM "structure should follow strategy and so should reflect the particular, idiosyncratic institutional culture, climate, and character" (p. 7). Within colleges and universities, the form and function of *academic units* (such as decentralized schools and distributed departments/programs) differs from that of *administrative units* (such as centralized admissions and financial aid offices). Moreover, the structural forces in a particular institutional context influence the extent to which graduate program SEM units are centralized, decentralized, or distributed.

Possessing knowledge about how graduate and professional schools, departments, and programs are structured and operate—in respect to organization, leadership, and decision-making—is salient when planning and assessing the application of SEM in those particular contexts. Once again, ideally, enrollment strategy should precede establishing SEM structures. However, long-standing and persistent organizational forces in a particular institution can impede SEM strategy and structures. Furthermore, organizational characteristics and history can shape SEM organizational possibilities for graduate programs at institutional, school/college, or department/program levels.

The degree of SEM functional interdependence, integration, and coordination depends on leadership design and the structural forces at play. Prominent factors that guide SEM organization and characteristics include, but are not limited to, institutional type and size. The prestige, brand strength, wealth, and markets that academic programs appeal to also play important roles in determining the structure and focus of SEM organizations at the graduate level. For example, graduate programs that serve working adults, that are not highly ranked, and that offer courses on evenings, weekends, or via asynchronous online delivery models commonly will have most SEM activities managed by a centralized unit. Further, graduate programs with these particular characteristics often have strong administrative leadership, while many of the classes are delivered by adjunct (full-time and/or part-time) faculty.

In some cases, graduate SEM activities will report to the same senior enrollment officer who is responsible for undergraduate enrollments. However, for graduate programs that are highly ranked, well-funded, primarily rely upon full-time faculty and enroll full-time students, SEM units are often developed at the program level (for each program) and the full-time faculty will have a strong say in SEM structure and efforts. Another way to frame these distinctions is to conclude with the summary that institutions, schools, departments and/or programs that *compete on ranking and prestige* tend to have local and decentralized SEM units, while those institutions and program that *compete on cost, location, and convenience* tend to have more centralized SEM organizations. These centralized units may report through an associate dean at the school or college level, or they may be centralized at the institutional level and report to the senior enrollment officer or to the dean of graduate studies.

A key to SEM success is developing a strong understanding of an institution's academic environment—particularly faculty's role in recruiting and retaining students. As previously suggested, faculty composition, roles, and involvement in recruitment and retention activities influence how SEM is perceived among academicians and impacts how SEM is operationalized in graduate and professional schools, departments, and programs. A few pervasive factors that can impact how SEM is regarded and implemented in the academic setting of a particular institution are (1) academic perspectives that significantly differ from administrative standpoints on matters of enrollment, (2) shared governance structures that can protract enrollment-related decisions, and (3) strong

Table 26.1: SEM organization and characteristics

Characteristics	Centralized	Decentralized
Institutional appeal	Regional	National
Institutional brand	Weak	Strong
Program selectivity	Low	High
Program rank	Unranked	High
Program faculty composition	Part-time/adjunct	Full time/tenured
Student demand	Low	High
Student enrollment	Part-time	Full time
Student performance	Low	High
Graduate placement/licensure	Low	High

disciplinary alliances that may constrict new program development and the discontinuance of underperforming programs. These factors can drive and influence SEM structure—for example, centralized or decentralized.

Institutional, program, and student characteristics impact whether graduate SEM organizations are more or less centralized (see Table 26.1). There may be perceived correlations between the characteristics listed; however, they are not mutually exclusive. For example, there are obviously graduate programs with regional appeal and high student demand. The consideration of whether centralized or decentralized SEM structure is more or less desirable (and possible) for a similarly situated graduate program depends on the enrollment strategy and established enrollment goals for that particular program. In some instances, these characteristics run along a continuum. For example, as programs become more highly ranked and/or the proportion of full-time students increases, graduate programs are more likely to move toward becoming more decentralized.

Between centralized and decentralized SEM structure is distributed organization, which is a "middle ground" structural configuration. Distributed graduate SEM organizations typically operate within decentralized structures that reflect self-contained centralized features (such as a decentralized department within a centralized school, where the program operates in a distributed manner). Decentralized and distributed SEM organizations' leaders use institutional and unit-level policies, overarching and programmatic regulations, legislative mandates, judicial rulings, and various laws to guide obligatory enrollment practices and sustain the highest degree of operational autonomy that may be possible in a particular college or university setting.

The composition of an institution's student body also factors into the development of a decentralized, centralized, or distributed SEM organization. This often is driven by the nature and number of cross-institutional services needed to attract, enroll, and support distinct student populations. For example, CGS/ ETS graduate enrollment trends reported in this chapter indicate that domestic graduate students are more likely to enroll in programs at U.S. regional colleges and universities, in comparison to their international graduate student counterparts who are more likely to enroll in programs at national institutions. It is therefore conceivable that colleges and universities with a substantive number of international graduate students, given the large number of related compliance and specialized services needed, may be better situated to consider centralized SEM organizations that integrate international programs and services.

INTERNATIONAL STUDENT GROWTH AND SEM ORGANIZATIONS

Every year, nearly 3 million post-secondary students study outside their home countries (Lasanowski, 2009). It is estimated that by 2025, up to 7.2 million of the world's college-bound students are likely to have the resources to be globally mobile and will be searching throughout the world for their college or university of choice (Bohm et al., 2004). Analysts have speculated that the worldwide total number of post-secondary students could rise to 250 million by 2025 (Bohm et al., 2004; Ruby, 2009).

For the past fifty years, the United States has remained one of the primary destinations for students desiring to study outside their home country. Currently, around 800,000 non-U.S. residents are enrolled in U.S. colleges and universities, contributing an estimated $24.7 billion to the nation's economy (Institute of International Education, 2012). The fairly consistent annual growth rates have been a notable phenomenon. Surprisingly, until the last decade, only a few U.S. institutions had been proactive in making substantial investments in resources and enrollment systems to develop and nurture the international populations (Choudaha & Chang, 2012).

Today, most U.S. college or university executive leaders commonly address the need for their institutions to cultivate a nonresident student population. As demonstrated in strategic plans and vast numbers of new global initiatives, these leaders articulate how the presence of global students provide the entire campus community with a more in-depth understanding of our internationalized society, culture, and economy. Higher education's internationalization efforts are widely supported by societal and business leaders who have recognized the deep and long-lasting benefits of providing today's students and workforce with strong global perspectives and understandings (Donohue & Brilliant, 2012). In addition to enhancing the learning environment, most college and university presidents also recognize international students' capability to fill available capacity in classrooms and residential facilities, while providing significant new tuition and fee revenues.

Although it is estimated the U.S. market share of the 2.9 million mobile international students (IIE, 2012) remains the highest in the world, many countries have been overt in their intentions to attract a larger share of these student populations. The Observatory on Borderless Higher Education estimates that in 2009 the United States attracted 22 percent of globally mobile students, while the United Kingdom followed with a 12 percent share, and Australia was third with 11 percent of the market (Lasanowski, 2009).

The worldwide competition for attracting international students has grown considerably. Over the past decade, government-sponsored student recruitment activities have had positive impacts for a number nations. Between 1999 and 2005, U.K. universities' international student enrollments grew by 29 percent, Australia's by 42 percent, Germany's by 46 percent, and France's by 81 percent. By 2009, Australia's government-sponsored recruiting efforts had helped attract nearly one-third as many international students as the United States (Wildavsky, 2010). Overseas students now account for 20 percent of Australia's total university enrollments, making higher education the country's third largest export after coal and iron ore (Wildavsky, 2010).

In response to these trends, it is no surprise that more and more colleges and universities are moving toward SEM structures and strategies to maintain or increase their ability to attract and retain international undergraduate and graduate students. Key SEM considerations include the role of rankings (which appear to be more important to international students), organizational structures, pedagogical changes, and the use of transfer and recruitment partnerships. Each of the strategies is equally important to enrolling international students. These are examined in the next section.

RANKINGS IMPACT ON INTERNATIONAL STUDENT CHOICE

Similar to institutions' leveraging of name recognition or brand strength in graduate and professional programs, a significant element of most international student recruitment efforts is validating an institution's quality and the value of its degree. Institutional reputation, or prestige, has commonly been cited as a compelling influence on prospective students' college choice factors (Schoenherr, 2009).

Prospective student questions about institutional and program quality are not unusual in any recruitment effort. As most experienced international admissions officers know, foreign students and parents are quick to ask about the availability of degree programs—and just as quick to inquire about a college's "rankings." Knowledgeable students will specifically ask about the Times Higher Education World University Rankings; Quacquarelli, Symonds, or QS World University Rankings; *US News* "Best Colleges" rankings; and the Academic Ranking of World Universities or Shanghai Consultancy rankings. Under the pretext of quality management, a number of government agencies and foreign universities also use the college rankings to limit the number and types of U.S. universities approved for partnerships or exchange programs (Hazelkorn, 2011).

Given the large financial investment needed to attend a U.S. university, the heavy interest in rankings should not be surprising. Most students and their families have limited knowledge of U.S. schools and often assume rankings and selectivity to represent institutional quality. They are likely unaware of the ranking methodologies and their heavy focus on peer reputation, research output, and levels of admission selectivity, rather than measuring institution's effectiveness in boosting student learning, personal growth, and persistence to a desired degree and career path.

The influence of university rankings on international student decisions is difficult to gauge. Students in a global college search process are seeking direct and comparative information. It is natural for them to rely on external sources claiming to verify a school's attributes and value. Many institutions have responded to these inquiries by creating detailed home pages and publications emphasizing a wide variety of honors, awards, and external ratings. To align better with the Asian and European Union education and workforce development standards, some U.S. universities have started to promote their learning objectives and student mastery levels in their recruitment communications.

Although SEM efforts are intended to help institutions continually improve their overall student and academic environments, the direct impact of rankings is often discussed and argued, but it is still difficult to measure. To complicate further the wide variety of ranking methodologies and use of sometimes murky data, ranking organizations regularly change the evaluation criteria and weighting of various inputs, thus making a formal pursuit of improving rankings a precarious enrollment strategy. Only a very few U.S. institutions have accomplished managing their institutional position and achieving significant improvements in their ranking positions. Generally these efforts included long-term, systematic, strategic and quality-focused planning to target resources, reshape the student profile, and improve student performance and research levels. Unfortunately, pressures to improve, or even maintain, rankings have also encouraged ethical lapses among institutions in the United States and throughout the world.

SEM ORGANIZATIONS FOR INTERNATIONAL STUDENTS

As discussed previously, structural forces at the institutional level have typically driven whether graduate and professional programs have employed centralized, distributed, or decentralized SEM organizations. Traditionally, graduate faculty composition, institutional type, and strength of brand have been the driving factors in the level of SEM integration attempted. Successful international enrollment efforts at U.S. colleges and universities without a strong brand or rankings have commonly depended on a wide variety of institutional student service collaborations, from global outreach activities, to immigration support and new student orientation, to intensive language tutoring.

Before examining some of the emerging strategies and tactics, there are several key structural questions that need to be considered when designing a SEM organization for international students. They include the following:

- Should such an international focused unit be part of the campus-level domestic undergraduate SEM organization?

- Because of the expertise of Offices of International Student Services (OISS organizations) should international SEM units be housed within OISS organizations?

- Where should international graduate student SEM units be located?

There are no standard answers to these questions, nor is there empirical evidence to support the efficacy of any particular organizational structure.

There are several advantages in locating undergraduate recruitment, financial aid, orientation, and student success initiatives within a comprehensive campus-wide undergraduate SEM organization: it provides economies of scale with respect to the organization of targeted communication and recruitment efforts, it centralizes maintenance of recruitment databases, and it integrates international students into campus-funded scholarship programs, orientation efforts, and student retention initiatives. A critical determinant can also be the location of the office that evaluates the academic credential of international undergraduates. If this office is located in the undergraduate SEM organization, then it is even more efficient and effective to locate international undergraduate SEM operations in the broader campus organization.

However, a strong argument can also be made for locating this international unit within an Office of International Student Services (OISS). Such offices usually have members who are trained and experienced in working with international students. On some campuses, OISS units are staffed with professionals who have a deep and abiding interest in international students, which may or may not be the case in the SEM unit that works with domestic students. OISS professionals are more likely to have had experiences with a wide range of cultures and understand the nuances in a wide variety of students' needs. These attributes can make OISS units ideal organizations to be responsible for managing undergraduate international student enrollments. The one downside can be that the institution has to create two units with CRM access, two sets of recruitment staffs, and so forth. Integration and collaboration with other institutional units becomes more complicated and time-consuming.

The best approach to organizing SEM activities for international graduate students is dependent upon the level of centralization or decentralization of graduate student SEM efforts. If, as discussed earlier in this chapter, the recruitment of graduate students is housed within a centralized graduate SEM unit, then the most sensible way to organize the recruitment and retention support of international graduate students is to locate these activities within a centralized office. If the recruitment of graduate students is decentralized in departments, or programs within departments, then working with international graduate students will likely be part of the recruitment and success efforts of each of these individual academic units. In either case, it is likely that a centralized office will provide analysis of academic credentials from other countries. As with domestic graduate students, the extent of the involvement of faculty in the admission of international graduate students will also influence the functioning of SEM units for international graduate students.

What is not analogous to graduate SEM organizations, however, are the enrollment strategies and collaboration levels intrinsically needed to support substantial international student enrollments. Where the organizational drivers for graduate SEM organizations may be more flexible and autonomous depending on a school's brand strength and student performance levels, if the efforts are to be successful, international enrollment services generally should not be afforded the same level of organizational elasticity. In other words, the range of unique services needed to support this population (immigration and legal compliance, language and writing support, cultural guidance, special approval for employment and training, and so on) is unlikely to be provided by a single graduate academic unit but can be supported by a broader SEM organization.

As discussed in previous chapters, ideally the SEM organizational framework is steered by senior-level leaders who, together, form SEM planning structures such as councils, committees, and teams (Bontrager & Green, 2012). By using a SEM structure to directly involve individuals responsible for the internationalization efforts with the other key recruitment and retention focused stakeholders and decision-makers, the resulting SEM structure would support the desired levels of cross-campus collaboration needed to drive a substantial international enrollment effort.

In closing this section, it is worthwhile noting that it is entirely possible that organizational structures for international students will change over time. A new vice-president or provost can arrive with a strong preference for locating SEM efforts for international undergraduate and/or graduate students in OISS units. Eight years later, a consulting group charged with looking for efficiencies in administrative units may recommend locating all SEM efforts within the campus-wide SEM organization. Regardless of the organizational location of SEM organizational efforts for international students, one concept that should not be lost is the ongoing need for collaboration across SEM units, academic units, and OISS units. Finally, it is important to note that in addition to marketing, recruitment, orientation, and retention efforts, there are also academic initiatives that can positively influence international student enrollments. These are examined next.

CHANGES TO EXPAND GLOBAL ENROLLMENTS: FOCUS ON ENGLISH INSTRUCTION

Other countries and aspiring global universities see the great opportunities in expanding their nonresident student bases as well. Many are embracing SEM strategies better to meet globally mobile students' needs and interests.

To attract more students traditionally drawn to English-speaking countries and universities, many schools throughout the world are restructuring degree programs by forgoing course instruction in their native languages. In 2013, just over 6,600 English-taught master's programs were offered in European countries where English is not the primary language of instruction. The change in language instruction included universities in the Netherlands, Germany, Spain, and France (Brenn-White & Faethe, 2013). Sweden and other Scandinavian countries have also changed the instructional language for most of their graduate-level programs. The increase was ten times higher than the overall number of English-taught programs offered in 2002. The number of English-instructed degrees in Sweden alone increased by 38 percent over 2011 (Brenn-White & Faethe, 2013).

Saudi Arabia's well-known 2009 science, technology, engineering, and mathematics (STEM) enrollment initiative involved investing in a $20 billion endowment to build and support the King Abdullah University for Science and Technology (KAUST). The school uses English as its official language of instruction and focuses on graduate STEM research degrees. KAUST aims to attract and enroll 800 of the most promising graduate students from around the world with outstanding facilities and well-funded assistantships (Lindsey, 2011).

China has also groomed this SEM approach. In 1995, the Chinese Ministry of Education launched Project 211, a nationwide program to promote the quality and international competence of more than 100 selected Chinese research universities. Project 211 universities actively seek Western faculty and enroll 50 percent of all foreign, English-speaking undergraduate and graduate students in China. Under this effort, a number of Chinese universities initiated English-taught classes and degree programs to ensure the institutions could attract and support non-Chinese foreign student populations. By 2012, the Chinese Ministry of Education reported thirty-four Chinese universities were approved to offer sixty English-taught university degrees (Ministry of Education of the People's Republic of China, 2013).

In the United States and the United Kingdom, a growing number of colleges have used a variety of English as Second Language (ESL) or Intensive English programs to attract university-bound, international students needing English training prior to starting degree credit courses. In 2012, almost 39,000 international students, or about 6 percent of the total nonresident students studying in the United States, were enrolled in intensive English programs at U.S. postsecondary institutions (IIE, 2012).

PARTNERSHIPS TO DEVELOP STRONGER STUDENT PIPELINES AND AFFILIATIONS

The proliferation of international partnerships among colleges and universities has created a new sustainability issue for SEM practitioners. As U.S. and foreign higher education institutions seek ways to build stronger collaborations, dual and joint degree programs have been a cornerstone project. NAFSA defines dual degrees as "degrees in which a U.S. and a foreign institution grant concurrent, independent degrees" (Tobenkin, n.d., p. 38). Joint degrees are defined as official arrangements in which "two institutions collaborate to award a single degree" (p. 38). Both programs provide a formal structure for students and faculty to build stronger global awareness and have rich educational and cultural exchange experiences.

CGS has estimated that more than 50 percent of U.S. graduate schools had established collaborative graduate degree programs with one or more international higher education institutions by 2008 (Denecke, 2012). Many undergraduate departments have embarked on similar dual-degree programs. It is relatively common for colleges to maintain a series of "2 + 2" articulated partner transfer degree programs with a variety of international college and universities, although the maintenance and management of the programs often becomes a conundrum for the enrollment management leaders to track and support.

Often the dual and joint degree is used as a formal tool to bind institutions and create stronger academic and faculty-based relationships. The CGS survey indicated that "attracting international students" and building on faculty interests were among the most cited motivations for establishing and maintaining the programs (Denecke, 2011). Kris Olds (2011) outlines the major modes of current enrollment collaboration programs that include international dual and joint degrees:

- Study abroad
- Student exchange agreements
- Course-to-course transfer agreements

- Articulation agreements (2 + 2, 1 + 3, 3 + 1)
- Third-party contracts for educational delivery
- Off-campus program or course location
- Distance education and online delivery of educational programs
- Collaborative course or program sharing
- Sequential degrees

Although each of these efforts has proven to be helpful in integrating academic units with the enrollment activities, the broad scope of needed planning and constituent collaboration is often underestimated. Organizations in the European Union (such as the Bologna Process), Canada (such as Imagine Education in Canada) and Australia (such as Study in Australia) have embarked on a number of developing programs that intend to balance the best interests of students, faculty, host communities, government and immigration agencies, and the partnering institutions, while providing ethical and reliable services. These coordinated partnerships are designed to attract overseas students and integrate assistance from the college selection process through arrival on campus.

No discussion of SEM structures and strategies for international students would be replete without a discussion of one of the most pressing issues in international admissions: the use of third-party recruitment organizations. This topic has received a great deal of attention in recent years and is briefly examined in this chapter.

NEED TO MANAGE RECRUITING AGENCIES AND COMMISSION-BASED SERVICES

Most units at U.S. colleges and universities have become engaged in a wide range of activities to promote their global experiences and opportunities for international students. A number of schools have elected to use commission-based international recruiting agencies or local agents to expand their recruitment and matriculation abilities. The practice is commonly accepted in many countries and is sometimes an expected protocol. Outsourcing worldwide student search and outreach activities can be daunting, but many schools have found agents to be a particularly effective service in Asia, the Middle East, Latin America, and far eastern Europe (Shay, Molony, & Mittal, 2013).

A 2012 *Inside Higher Ed* survey indicated about 20 percent of U.S. colleges and universities were currently using commissioned agents for international student outreach, recruitment, and matriculation support (Jaschik, 2012). This survey summary noted that many more schools were considering the practice.

In most situations, international applicants seeking admission to U.S. universities pay agents to guide them through the admissions, visa, insurance, college deposit, and travel processes. The number of students who choose to employ agents is difficult to measure and appears to vary from country to country. Agents will often serve as a cultural liaison between the student, his or her parents, and the university admissions officers. Considering the expensive and often complicated bureaucracies of some countries, an agent's work, if done properly, can be extremely beneficial to both the student and the universities involved.

The practice of using agents also has detractors. Stories of unscrupulous agents have been widely discussed, as has the ethics of using incentive-based enrollment services—which is not permitted with domestic student recruitment in the United States. The National Association for College Admissions Counselors (NACAC) examined the practice and concluded that students do find value in agent services, but the practice must be closely monitored by the sponsoring college or university (NACAC, 2013). In September 2013, NACAC elected to amend its statement of principles of good practice to stipulate that "member institutions who choose to use incentive-based agents outside of the United States will ensure accountability, transparency and integrity" (Redden, 2013).

New agent compliance standards are developing in the United States. In response to the ethical concerns, the American International Recruitment Council (AIRC) has generated a series of certification standards for both international recruitment agencies and agents. Similar to multistep certification processes used in the United Kingdom and Australia, AIRC certification stages include external reviews, self-studies, and the development of improvement plans (Stripling, 2009). U.S. institutions choosing to continue the practice will be encouraged to amend their agent agreements to reflect similar practices.

CONCLUSION

As more U.S. institutions consider and realize the benefits of strategic enrollment planning throughout the academic enterprise, the emergence of SEM organizations and strategies that can effectively manage and serve graduate, professional, and international student populations will continue. Colleges and universities without strong market positions, or rankings, will aim to stay competitive in a growing international environment by altering and innovating many of higher education's time-honored structures and practices. To date, extant strategic transformations in the academy include significant changes in pedagogical stances, instructional design, mobility of academic credentials, and formal partnership alliances with government and for-profit organizations. Many of these laudable efforts, and those on the horizon, are positioning colleges and universities to answer societal needs for higher education and to meet the global demand for a more robust workforce with advanced degrees and strong global sensitivities, by way of growing enrollments, while also diversifying student bodies and internationalizing campuses (physical and virtual). SEM approaches will further develop pragmatic institutional goals in the areas of enrollment optimization, expansion of graduate programs, the internationalization of the student body, and the achievement of revenue targets. Thus, from a broader organizational development perspective, SEM is arguably the nexus between many important public policy initiatives in postsecondary education and institutions' mission-driven objectives and aspirations.

This chapter examines ways in which SEM strategies and structures are increasingly being employed in graduate education and to achieve international student enrollment goals. Although this chapter demonstrates some of the unique attributes of working with these student populations, the underlying concepts that make up SEM can be employed not only to domestic undergraduate students but also to most other student populations. The information presented here argues that precisely where SEM units are located (within a central campus SEM division, within decentralized professional schools, in graduate programs, or in international student services organizations) is not important; what is valuable is the utilization of SEM principles and strategies to achieve enrollment-related goals. The same student life-cycle planning that is discussed in Part VI of this volume are equally relevant for graduate programs and the recruitment and support of international undergraduate and graduate students. Focusing planning around the SEM philosophy will initially encourage firmer coordination, and eventually full integration, of the best practices for supporting a college's or university's optimal international and graduate student profiles and success rates.

In the final part of this handbook, Part VII, chapters focus on the planning process for SEM units, current trends in SEM, and ethical issues in SEM. Chapter 30, the final chapter, considers the future of SEM.

References

American Bar Association. (2012). Enrollment and Degrees Awarded 1963–2012 Academic Years. Retrieved from http://www.americanbar.org/content/dam/aba/ administrative/legal_education_and_admissions_to_the_bar/statistics/enrollment_ degrees_awarded.authcheckdam.pdf.

American Bar Association. (2013). ABA Section of Legal Education reports 2013 law school enrollment data. Retrieved from http://www.americanbar.org/news/ abanews/aba-news-archives/2013/12/aba_section_of_legal.html.

Association of American Medical Colleges (AAMC). (2011). *Results of the 2010 medical school enrollment survey.* AAMC Center for Workforce Studies. Retrieved from https://www.aamc.org/download/251636/data/enrollment2011.pdf.

Association of American Medical Colleges (AAMC). (2013). *Medical School Applicants, Enrollment Reach All-time Highs.* Retrieved from https://www.aamc.org/newsroom/newsreleases/358410/20131024.html.

Bohm, A., Follari, M., Hewett, A., Jones, S., Kemp, N., Meares, D., Pearce, D., Van Cauter, K. (2004). *Vision 2020: Forecasting international student mobility: A UK perspective.* The British Council. Retrieved from http://www.britishcouncil.org/eumd_-_vision_2020.pdf.

Bontrager, B., & Green, T. (2012). A structure for SEM planning. In B. Bontrager, D. Ingersoll, and R. Ingersoll (Eds.), *Strategic Enrollment Management: Transforming Higher Education* (pp. 273–284). Washington, DC: American Association of Collegiate Registrars and Admissions Officers.

Brenn-White, M. & Faethe, E. (2013). *English-Taught Master's Programs in Europe: A 2013 Update.* New York: Institute of International Education (IIE). Retrieved from http://www.iie.org/Research-and-Publications/Publications-and-Reports/IIE-Bookstore/English-Language-Masters-Briefing-Paper-2013-Update.

Brown, D. K. (1995). *Degrees of Control: A Sociology of Educational Expansion and Occupational Credentialism.* New York: Teachers College Press.

Bureau of Labor Statistics. (2013). Current Population Survey. Retrieved from http://www.bls.gov/emp/ep_chart_001.htm.

Choudaha, R., & Chang, L. (2012). *Trends in International Student Mobility.* New York: World Education Services. Retrieved from http://www.wes.org/RAS.

Council of Graduate Schools (CGS). (2012). *An Essential Guide to Graduate Admissions.* Washington, DC: Council of Graduate Schools.

Denecke, D. (2011). *The Graduate Collaboration Project: Some Findings that Suggest Directions for Outcomes Measurement.* A presentation to the National Science Foundation (NSF). Washington, DC: Council of Graduate Schools. Retrieved from http://depts.washington.edu/cirgeweb/wordpress/wp-content/uploads/2012/11/Daniel-FINAL-Denecke-NSF-2011-Workshop-on-Intl-Outcomes.pdf.

Donohue, T. J. & Brilliant, M. (2012). *International Agenda: The U.S. Chamber's Plan to Help Americans Compete and Win in the Worldwide Economy.* U.S. Chamber of Commerce Retrieved from http://www.uschamber.com/international/agenda.

European Higher Education Area (EHEA). (2013). *The Bologna Process.* Retrieved from http://www.ehea.info/article-details.aspx?ArticleId = 3.

Gonzales, L. M., Allum, J. R., & Sowell, R. S. (2013). *Graduate Enrollment and Degrees: 2002 to 2012.* Washington DC: Council of Graduate Schools.

Hazelkorn, E. (2011). Questions Abound as the College-Rankings Race Goes Global. *The Chronicle of Higher Education.* Retrieved from http://chronicle.com/article/Questions-Abound-as-the/126699/.

Hendrickson, M., Lane, J. E., Harris, J. T., & Dorman, R. H. (2012). *Academic Leadership and Governance of Higher Education: A Guide for Trustees, Leaders, and Aspiring Leaders of Higher Education.* Sterling, VA: Stylus Publishing.

Higher Education Research Institute. (2007). *College Rankings and College Choice: How Important Are College Rankings in Students' College Choice Process?* HERI Research Brief. Retrieved from http://www.heri.ucla.edu/PDFs/pubs/briefs/brief-081707-CollegeRankings.pdf.

Hossler, D., & Kalsbeek, D. (2008). Enrollment management & managing enrollment: Setting the context for dialogue. *College & University, 83*(4), 2–11.

Hudzik, J. K. (2011). *Comprehensive Internationalization: From Concept to Action.* Washington, DC: NAFSA: Association of International Educators.

Institute of International Education. (2012). *Open Doors 2012: Report on International Educational Exchange.* Institute of International Education (IIE).

Jaschik, S. (2012). Debt, Job, Diversity and Who Gets It: A Survey of Admissions Directors. *Inside Higher Ed.* Retrieved from http://www.insidehighered.com/news/survey/debt-jobs-diversity-and-who-gets-survey-admissions-directors#ixzz2hERvejA9.

Jaschik, S. (2013). Rigging the Rankings? *Inside Higher Ed.* Retrieved from http://www.insidehighered.com/news/2013/04/08/irish-university-tries-recruit-voters-improve-its-international-ranking.

Kohl. K. J. (2000). The Postbaccalaureate learning imperative. In K. J. Kohl & J. B. Lapidus (Eds.), *Postbaccalaureate Futures: New Markets, Resources, and Credentials* (pp. 10–30). Washington, DC: Oryx Press.

Lane, J., & Kinser, K. (2012). Oversight of Internationalization—Who's Responsible? *The Chronicle of Higher Education.* Retrieved from http://chronicle.com/blogs/worldwise/oversight-of-internationalization%E2%80%94who%E2%80%99s-responsible/29170.

Lasanowski, V. (2009). *International Student Mobility: Status Report 2009.* Surrey, UK: The Observatory on Borderless Higher Education.

Lindsey, U. (2011). Saudi Arabia's $10-Billion Experiment Is Ready for Results. *The Chronicle of Higher Education.* Retrieved from http://chronicle.com/article/Saudi-Arabias-10-Billion/128041/?sid = gn&utm_source = gn&utm_medium = en.

McDonald, M. (2013). *First-Year Law School Enrollment Drops to 36-Year Low.* Retrieved from http://www.bloomberg.com/news/2013–12–17/first-year-law-school-enrollment-declines-to-lowest-in-36-years.html.

Ministry of Education of the People's Republic of China. (2013). List for English-taught Programmes in Chinese Higher Education Institutions. Retrieved from http://www.moe.gov.cn/publicfiles/business/htmlfiles/moe/moe_2812/200906/48835.html.

National Association for College Admission Counseling. (2012). Summary of Best Practices: Comprehensive Strategic International Enrollment Management: Recruitment, Retention, and Reentry. Washington, DC: National Association for College Admission Counseling. Retrieved from http://www.nafsa.org/_/File/_/mr_best_practices.pdf.

National Association for College Admission Counseling. (2013). Report of the Commission on International Student Recruitment. Washington, DC: National

Association for College Admission Counseling. Retrieved from http://www.
insidehighered.com/sites/default/server_files/files/NACAC%20International%20
Commission%20Report_Pre-Pub%20Draft.pdf.

National Association for College Admission Counseling. (2014). *Doctorate Recipients
from U.S. Universities: 2012*. Washington DC: National Science Foundation.
Retrieved from http://www.nsf.gov/statistics/sed/digest/2012/nsf14305.pdf.

O'Banion, T., & Wilson, C. D. (2011). *Focus on Learning: A Learning College Reader*.
Chandler, AZ.: League for Innovation in the Community College.

Olds, K. (2011). What are international dual & joint degrees? *GlobalHigherEd*. Retrieved
from http://globalhighered.wordpress.com/2011/02/10/what-are-international-dual-
joint-degrees/.

Redden, E. (2013). Giving Agents the OK. *Inside Higher Ed*. Retrieved from http://
www.insidehighered.com/news/2013/09/23/admissions-association-lifts-ban-
commissioned-agents-international-recruiting.

Ruby, A. (2009). *The uncertain future for international higher education in the Asia-
Pacific region*. Paper presented at NAFSA Annual Conference, May 2009, Los
Angeles, CA.

Schoenherr, H. J. (2009). *Beyond academic reputation: Factors that influence the college
of first choice for high achieving students*. Dissertation, University of South Florida.
Retrieved from http://scholarcommons.usf.edu/etd/8.

Shay, M., Molony, J., & Mittal, G. (2013). *Best Practices in the Use of Student Recruiting
Agents by Graduate Schools and Programs*. QS – Quacquarelli, Symonds, Ltd.
Retrieved from http://ajcunet.edu/Assets/Conference/File/Best%20practices%20
in%20the%20use%20ofstudent%20recruiting%20agents%20by%20graduate%20
programs.pdf.

Stripling, J. (2009). Sunshine for International Recruiting. *Inside Higher
Ed*. Retrieved from http://www.insidehighered.com/news/2009/12/04/
international#ixzz2hE0bQxBA.

Tobenkin, D. (n.d.). Web Extra! The European Model for Joint and Dual Degrees.
National Association of Foreign Student Advisors. Retrieved from http://www
.nafsa.org/Find_Resources/Publications/Periodicals/International_Educator/Web_
Extra!_The_European_Model_for_Joint_and_Dual_Degrees/.

Wildavsky, B. (2010). *The Great Brain Race: How Global Universities are Reshaping the
World*. Princeton, NJ: Princeton University Press.

Wendler, C., Bridgeman, B., Cline, F., Millett, C., Rock, J., Bell, N., & McAllister,
P. (2010). *The Path Forward: The Future of Graduate Education in the United States*.
Princeton, NJ: Educational Testing Service.

Wendler, C., Bridgeman, B., Markle, R., Cline. F., Bell, N., McAllister, P., & Kent,
J. (2012). *Pathways Through Graduate School and into Careers*. Princeton,
NJ: Educational Testing Service.

PART SEVEN

PUTTING THE PIECES TOGETHER

Part VII brings this book to an end. Chapter 27 provides a summative look at strategic enrollment planning. Bob Bontrager and Tom Green speak to the challenge of SEM planning as it takes into account the many and varied enrollment considerations and influences addressed throughout this handbook. Because SEM is one of the newer constructs related to the structure and management of higher education, the recasting of institutions around SEM principles represents an exercise in change management. To achieve the required level of change, institutions must move from traditional planning to strategic planning. Chapter 27 describes a SEM planning model made up of three frameworks: the SEM Organizational Framework, the SEM Process Framework, and the SEM Planning Framework. Reflecting the variability of institutional types and circumstances, these frameworks are not intended to be overly proscriptive or rigid. Rather, they are malleable and may be modified to meet the needs of each institution. The chapter concludes with discussions of each stage of the SEM Planning Framework, adding details to the steps required to achieve sustainable enrollment outcomes.

Chapter 28 covers current issues in SEM, beginning with an overview of the implications of demographic trends and perspectives on how U.S. higher education institutions will accommodate the increasing number of first-generation Latino students. The growing importance of tuition rate increases at public-sector institutions and student debt among the many students enrolled in both public and private colleges and universities are addressed in this chapter, as are the calls for public institutions to find ways to reduce these costs. Though discussed to some extent in other chapters, Chapter 28 presents a brief discussion of the potential impact of affirmative action lawsuits going forward. It also includes some analysis of the growing role of states in setting goals for public institutions associated with enrollment outcomes through the use of performance budget funding. In addition, it discusses the growing level of competitiveness among postsecondary institutions for not only U.S. students but also for many affluent international students. In addition, many universities and colleges in Canada, the European Union, and elsewhere are also seeking to enroll more American students to help increase their tuition coffers. This chapter closes with a discussion of the changing structure of SEM organizations and the pressures experienced by many senior enrollment managers who must decide whether the institution should hold steady or increase tuition revenue.

Chapter 29 examines ethical issues in SEM. The author asks whether the marketization and privatization of postsecondary education has gone too far. Have too many institutions adopted unethical admissions marketing approaches? What is the right balance between need- and merit-based financial aid to meet student and societal needs? This chapter raises interesting questions regarding how institutions might start lowering their costs and how they might help reduce the amount of ever-growing student debt. It also discusses ethical issues around the College Completion Agenda and the negative impact it could have on educational access for low-income students. SEM practitioners find themselves traversing contested terrain, and it is too soon to say how they will eventually navigate the many upcoming challenges. Nevertheless, Chapter 29 asks important ethical questions about policies and practices associated with SEM.

Chapter 30 summarizes the purpose and foci of the previous chapters in this handbook. In particular, it highlights the value of the three types of chapters included in this volume: chapters that draw heavily on academic research to inform the strategies and practices of SEM units, chapters regarding relevant campus-based research to guide campus strategies and practices, and chapters that examine the organizational structures and operational activities of SEM organizations. These chapters also focused on technology, the effects of public policy, and connections between SEM and higher education finance and campus budgeting.

The second part of Chapter 30 briefly covers the likely future of SEM in the United States and abroad. The future will include shifts in accountability and funding and continued pressures on senior enrollment officers, increased pressures on the uses of public and institutional sources of financial aid, the appropriate role of admissions tests and affirmative action, and demographic shifts that will drive many of the goals of SEM organizations. Overall, we believe that the importance of SEM at colleges and universities is likely to continue for the foreseeable future.

CHAPTER 27

Strategic Enrollment Planning

Bob Bontrager and
Tom Green

T hroughout the many chapters of this handbook, perhaps the most prominent point made is that Strategic Enrollment Management is a complex, multifaceted enterprise. Thus, conducting SEM planning is a significant challenge. In this first chapter of the summative Part VII, we offer a structure for organizing the various elements of the SEM landscape into actionable plans for achieving desired recruitment and retention outcomes.

Along with the myriad, actively changing forces that affect American higher education, the nature of strategic enrollment planning has changed as well. SEM plans historically have been conceived as comprehensive treatises addressing every facet of institutional operations and data that impact recruitment, student success, and completion. The resulting documents are exhaustive, both in terms of length as well as the efforts required to compile them. Institutional personnel often expend so much time creating such plans that there is little energy left to carry out the enhanced enrollment activities specified in the plan. In such cases, the prospect of creating the proverbial "report that sits on the shelf collecting dust" is all too real. Indeed, during their consulting work, the authors have the repeated experience of sitting in the office a senior enrollment officer for the opening meeting of a SEM consultation, only to look over at a bookshelf to see multiple reports from prior SEM consultations, including reports compiled within the past six months. The current context of SEM practice calls for a new approach to planning that is more nimble, process-oriented, and actionable.

STRATEGIC PLANNING AND CHANGE MANAGEMENT

As addressed by multiple chapters in this handbook, in recent decades, higher education has been marked by increased complexity and challenge. Within this context, the ability of institutions to manage change effectively and plan strategically is at once more important and more daunting than ever (Drucker, 1997; Gumport & Sporn, 1999; Rowley, Lujan, & Dolence, 2001; Zemsky, 2013). In 1997, Peter Drucker observed that "the most important area for developing new concepts, methods, and practices will be in the management of society's knowledge resources—specifically education and health care, both of which are today over-administered and undermanaged" (p. 21), presaging the situation in which higher education finds itself today. With roots dating to medieval Europe, colleges and universities have developed into cumbersome institutions marked by tradition, inertia, and a potent political structure. As noted by Daniel Rowley, Herman Lujan, and Michael Dolence (2001), "the power of campus politics lies in the group's ability to veto change directly or to surround it with procedure and ritual that confounds, dilutes, or smothers it" (p. 6).

The need to create and effectively manage change is one of the defining themes of higher education practice generally, and SEM specifically. In a self-described summing up of his long career critiquing higher education, Robert Zemsky (2013) not only reasserts his contention that change is needed but offers this pointed analysis: "The notion that American higher education changes slowly but purposefully is wrong. The nation's colleges and universities are not slowly evolving. They are, in fact, pretty much stuck where they were in the 1980s—largely unable to control their costs [and] locked in a competition for students" (p. 16). Zemsky goes on to describe four primary forces that explain this tendency toward change-avoidance: a disengaged faculty, a federalized market for higher education, an untenable regulatory system, and an increasingly fractured learning environment in which there are many voices but no evidence of what undergraduates are actually learning (pp. 92–93). He offers a checklist of initiatives required to bring about change in American higher education. Included are institutionally focused items, such as making the academic department the unit of instructional production, to nationally focused items, such as making students enrolled in remedial education programs eligible for Pell grants (p. 203ff).

If Zemsky's analysis is useful in calling out the systemic issues to be addressed in bringing about change, his prescriptions may lack adequate specificity at the operational level. In addition to the broader types of initiatives advocated by Zemsky—many to be engaged from outside the academy—SEM requires a wide range of functional changes from within institutions that suggest new planning processes and structures. Again, this runs counter to the organizational nature of colleges and universities, which are prone to engage in "traditional planning," when what is needed is a higher level of "strategic planning" (Rowley, Lujan, & Dolence, 2001). Traditional planning engages in setting goals and developing steps to achieve them, while strategic planning seeks to align the institution with its environment. Additionally, traditional planning specifies activities and associated time frames for completing them, whereas strategic planning concerns itself with broader vision, mission, and directional issues. As such, strategic planning results in "living" documents that are subject to periodic reevaluation and revision (p. 36ff).

THE NATURE OF SEM PLANNING

Within this context of strategic planning generally, there are two overarching points to be made about the specifics of SEM planning (Bean, 1990). First, the creation of a SEM plan is among the most critical planning tasks for most institutions. A case could always have been made that colleges or universities would not exist without students. That fundamental point is made more compelling by current financial realities. This book includes multiple references to the changing funding dynamics in higher education, such that the vast majority of institutions both in the United States and abroad are now tuition-dependent to a significant degree. Today, more than ever, institutions would not survive—or would be far less robust—without adequate numbers of students.

Second, creating a viable SEM plan requires a combination of traditional and strategic planning. As will be discussed more fully later in this chapter, effective SEM planning emanates from a foundation of strong institutional strategic planning. A pervasive shortfall of SEM plans is an overreliance on traditional planning in the form of strategies and tactics intended to boost recruitment or retention rates. Many institutions find themselves locked into a short-term planning cycle that is focused on meeting the coming year's budget expectations, attempting daily to respond to a steady stream of anecdotes of recruitment or retention shortcomings, along with a virtually endless list of proposed initiatives for correcting them. The result often is a conglomeration of activities, each of which has some merit, but lack coordination and alignment. This leads to staff overload, limited return on investments, and failure to meet enrollment goals (Bontrager & Green, 2012). Ultimately, in the absence of clarity regarding institutional vision, mission, and direction, as specifically manifested in detailed enrollment goals, SEM plans developed under the traditional model will yield limited results.

Reflecting the breadth, complexity, and multiperspective nature of SEM, Kalsbeek (2006) delineates four SEM orientations that are relevant to SEM planning. The *administrative orientation* focuses on the coordination, integration, and often the co-location of varied enrollment-related processes at an institution. The *academic orientation* focuses on the development of curricula and academic support programs that provide relevant content and credentials; that are accessible in terms of time, location, and delivery mode; and that facilitate student persistence and educational goal attainment. The *market-centered orientation* focuses on the institution's market position relative to other institutions of higher education, with the goal of ensuring competitiveness of its academic programs and elevating its position within its targeted audiences or markets. The *student-focused orientation* focuses on caring for the students who benefit from or participate in enrollment-related processes and initiatives.

Achieving higher levels of coordination among these related but disparate orientations within an institution is the defining challenge of SEM planning (Bontrager & Green, 2012). Of particular importance is balancing institutional and student interests. In most cases, this involves shifting the focus of campus personnel from institutional best interests to those of students—what Rowley, Lujan, and Dolence (2001) refer to as changing the paradigm from "provider-driven to consumer-driven higher education" (p. 52).

A SEM PLANNING MODEL

Effective SEM planning is elusive for many institutions. Although it is akin to the strategic planning done on most campuses, the knowledge required to create a plan for enrollment that aligns mission, vision, market position, opportunities, and challenges is outside the scope of many institutional leaders' skill sets. Enrollment planning models are often incomplete, and when institutions attempt to create a single, comprehensive SEM plan, the result is an unwieldy planning process with limited benefit. Other institutions fail to use a planning model at all, engaging in a series of meetings marked by the anecdotal exchange of student experiences and strategies gleaned from other institutions, and resulting in sketchy plans lacking measurable outcomes. A more formal approach is required to bring the right people to the table addressing the right questions in a manner that is coordinated, based on hard data, establishes predefined measurable outcomes, and meets enrollment goals consistently over time.

As presented here, effective SEM planning derives from a set of frameworks that, as a whole, seek to align the institution with its environment and mission (Bontrager & Green, 2012). The frameworks are designed to achieve greater harmony among an institution's SEM processes, the organizational structure for decision-making and continuous improvement, and the development of recruitment and retention initiatives with cross-campus input, integration, and buy-in. They set a path for the institution to move toward becoming a fully functional and integrated SEM organization. Although the specific application of these frameworks will vary according to the specific needs of each institution, they offer a conceptual basis and roadmap for creating a SEM planning process that leads to sustainable enrollment outcomes.

The frameworks lay out the who, the how, and the what of SEM planning and transformation into a SEM organization. They are tightly interlaced, such that a description of any one will rely upon some elements of another. Readers are encouraged to read through all three frameworks, and then return to them to understand fully the relationship among them.

The SEM Organizational Framework

The first framework focuses on the "who" of SEM planning, describing personnel deployment. Figure 27.1 displays a set of linked teams. Some campuses may already have these teams assembled under different names, such as "president's cabinet" for the Executive Leadership group or "student success committee" for the Retention Council. Others may have developed "enrollment committees" that combine recruitment and retention council efforts. The least common group to find on any campus is the data team that is focused on enrollment information.

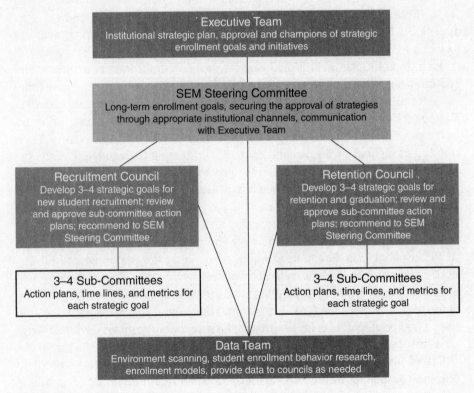

Figure 27.1 SEM Organizational Framework

Achieving campus-wide buy-in on any initiative requires broad-based participation. Striking the balance between soliciting opinions from everyone at the institution and gaining forward momentum in developing SEM plans is specific to each institution. However, the SEM Organizational Framework provides guidance on how the interaction and separation of teams into distinct roles can facilitate the plan's development.

Senior leadership is key to the development and execution of the SEM planning and effective SEM systems in the organization. Composition of the SEM Steering Committee needs to include personnel at a sufficiently high level to reflect the importance of SEM at the institution. Membership should include those with broad authority for policy and budget, such that faculty, staff, and administrators clearly identify this group with decision-making status, institutional understanding, and the ability to weigh competing institutional interests objectively. Appointing co-chairs of the SEM Steering Committee demonstrates the shared governance of the group and is recommended. It is common to see one of these co-chairs emerge as the practical leader of the group, but the assignment of two or more co-chairs (that is, leadership from academic affairs, student affairs, and enrollment management) sets a clear tone of collaboration across the units. The chairs of the Recruitment and Retention Councils, as well as the Data Team, are added here to provide linkage between all teams.

The SEM Steering Committee fulfills three major roles: First, it provides a key link between the working teams below it and the Executive Team above. It must interpret broad institutional policies, mission, budgetary constraints, and culture when considering SEM initiatives. Second, it reviews the recommendations for SEM goals, strategies, and tactics that are detailed in the SEM Process Framework. It must balance these against those broad institutional priorities and realities. Communicating concerns or information to the Executive Team about these is part of this second duty of the Steering Committee. Finally, the SEM Steering Committee must keep the process on track and on time. Although Recruitment, Retention, and Data team leaders must also bear this responsibility, the SEM Steering Committee must assure that all teams are completing the steps in the planning process thoroughly and in a timely manner.

The SEM Organizational Framework shows the inclusion and segregation of Recruitment and Retention Councils. Separating the planning for and discussion of recruitment and retention efforts avoids a classic conundrum in SEM planning, where retention discussions inevitably turn to issues of entering student quality. Because most institutional data show general associations between higher preparation levels (that is, high school or transfer GPA, standardized test scores) and one-year retention rates (Fernald, 2011; Ohio University Office of Institutional Research, 2012), it is common for retention groups to place the burden for improved outcomes on better recruitment. Correspondingly, personnel charged with recruitment and admission note that high retention rates make it easier for them to attract students with higher preparation levels. There is truth in both statements, however, and the result is often a détente between the areas that paralyzes true change in strategies and practices.

The balance between recruitment and retention varies at most institutions at any given time. At one institution, new student size and quality may meet institutional needs but the subsequent retention, persistence, and graduation rates fall short of expected or desired outcomes. Another institution may have strong retention results but lack the number of students it needs to meet its enrollment and financial goals. The relative focus on SEM planning and the roles of these two teams may vary, as a result. One institution may place more emphasis on enrollment strategies for new student enrollment and another may have greater needs for improved retention and graduation rates.

All institutions should deploy both Recruitment and Retention Councils, regardless of their perceptions of current enrollment health. The opportunity to review institutional and environmental data, evaluate current strategies and tactics, and broaden institutional participation in enrollment conversations should not be underestimated, nor should it be passed over because the institution believes its current levels can be maintained in perpetuity. The factors that impact both new and continuing student enrollment can change too quickly to allow for complacence.

There may be some existing teams that fill the roles outlined in the SEM Organization Framework, while other teams need to be constructed. Selection of institutional personnel should be considered with two primary factors in mind: First, the co-chair principle suggested for the Steering Committee should be considered. Appointing one staff and one faculty member to head each reinforces the institutional collaboration required to achieve strong SEM planning results. Second, the size of the councils should be as small as possible while still achieving a reasonable level of inclusion. Some selections may be required to assure the process has legitimacy among the institution's community. Opinion leaders and/or trusted members of the institutional community may need to serve in order for others to believe that the council has achieved the status needed to drive change. Others may have a vested stake in the outcomes of the process or their voices may be important to informing strong decisions about goals, strategies, and tactics. Largely, these groups need to be populated by those who will execute a crisp planning process, rather than those who may serve solely to share their opinions. Each institution's selection of council members will differ slightly and should be sensitive to institutional culture and political needs, while not becoming enslaved to them at the expense of strong, timely planning.

Setting clear expectations for the roles of members of the Recruitment and Retention Councils is key. These councils are charged with developing recommendations. However, they likely cannot see the larger implications of their work against institutional priorities. Therefore, they must clearly understand that they are not empowered to chart the institution's enrollment future without the response and approval of the Steering Committee. This arrangement also allows the Steering Committee to coordinate the recruitment and retention efforts across the planning team structure, eliminating duplicative or conflicting strategies.

Underpinning the Steering Committee and Recruitment and Retention Councils is the Data Team. Figure 27.1 reflects the importance and role of enrollment data to SEM, which is detailed later in this chapter. The co-chair principle applies across the SEM Organizational Framework; a faculty and a staff member should also head the Data Team jointly. There may be a range of disciplines from which to choose a faculty member for this role. Economists, higher education researchers, social scientists, and others may be strong choices for inclusion on the Data Team. Their understanding of environmental scanning, statistical methods in social sciences, student choice factors, and student retention research, along with a strong interest in participation and work on this team, can guide the selection process.

Data teams are typically small in size and include staff members at the institution with the skills and access to retrieve student records data from institutional information systems. Institutional researchers should be joined with practitioners in admission, financial aid, and student records. Although the raw data elements may be accessible through one skilled institutional researcher, the context for the data in the larger enrollment environment typically requires the inclusion of admissions, financial aid, and student records personnel on the Data Team.

The Data Team's role in planning is further described in both the SEM Process Framework and the SEM Planning Framework that follow. Generally, however, the role can be summarized as assembling both external and internal data and information to frame the environment in which the institution exists and the behaviors of students, once enrolled, through degree or credential attainment. Following this initial work, the team builds enrollment models to test the assumptions of the enrollment goals and strategies. The team responds to additional requests for information and data during the development of SEM plans and creates or assures the existence of reporting mechanisms to track the progress of expected outcomes against actual results.

The SEM Process Framework

The Organizational Framework is also closely related to the SEM Process Framework (Figure 27.2) in sustaining enrollment outcomes. This arrangement of teams is required to monitor and maintain ongoing SEM planning at the institution. Throughout the planning process, teams should be reviewed to assure that the personnel required to create the plan are equally valuable in its

Process steps   Performed by

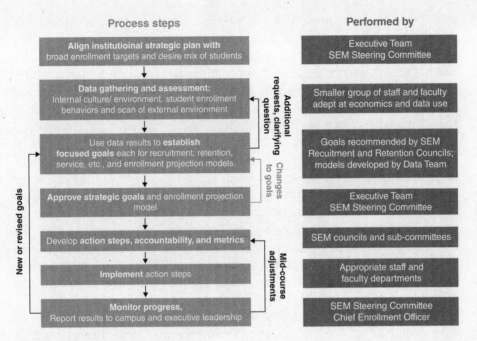

Figure 27.2 SEM Process Framework

monitoring and continued adjustments. In short, the institution should not make long-term commitments to membership on a council to accommodate for changes required to its composition.

The second planning framework examines how these groups perform their roles and duties in the SEM planning process, as well as ongoing monitoring and improvement of SEM results. The SEM Organizational Framework is tied to the SEM Process Framework in two ways. The description of each team's role can now be seen as a step in the process for development and ongoing monitoring of SEM plans.

The SEM Process Framework is a series of steps, each having several processes embedded within it. Working from the top of Figure 27.2 to the bottom, the plan develops from the broadest institutional goals to detailed action plans and specific measurements of those plans. The SEM Process Framework emanates from continuous improvement concepts. The feedback loop of gathering data, including and sharing governance, monitoring of results, and adjusting course will be familiar to those who have worked with similar processes in the past, such as accreditation self-studies and strategic plan development. One such example of a continuous quality improvement process in higher education is the Higher Learning Commission's Academic Quality Improvement program.

Within the process steps illustrated in Figure 27.2, several crucial concepts are embedded. First, the framework places the setting of enrollment goals within the broader strategic planning framework of the institution. Although it is not uncommon to find some reference to an institution's strategic plan in a SEM planning document, or conversely a reference to enrollment in an institution's overall strategic plan, it is far less common to find strategic plan goals defined sufficiently to allow for sound enrollment planning. The linkage between the institution's strategic plan and the SEM plan must then rest at the Executive Leadership level, where the broad vision of the institution is formed and/or translated into operational plans. The addition of the SEM Steering Committee broadens the discussion beyond the executive team and adds the enrollment focus to it.

The challenge of defining the institution's future in terms of enrollment size and student profile becomes the work of the Executive Team and sometimes the Steering Committee, depending on the amount of executive overlap between them. It is at this highest organizational level that the institution must not only create long-range institutional goals but challenge itself to know how the size and profile of students enable the institution to realize its mission and fill its niche in the higher education landscape.

This first step in the process enables the institution to chart the course of SEM planning to understand the ways in which it may go about meeting that challenge over the next five to ten years. Second, the broad student enrollment goals and profiles are researched and supported by data and information that test the goals against internal and external constraints and opportunities. This assures the institution that its decisions are based on sound and thorough research, avoiding planning by anecdote or decisions that are insulated from demographic and market trends. The Data Team's role here is broad, looking for evidence in external or internal information and data that address these broad goals and aspirations for the institution's future. Is the pipeline of potential new students growing, or shrinking, the same within the current areas where students have been drawn for the past five years? Do labor statistics support the growth of current programs through increased demand for graduates? What are the retention benchmarks of institutions with similar profiles and how could meeting these improve overall enrollment? If the institution desires to grow, does it have the programmatic, faculty, and physical plant capacity to handle more students?

The Data Team at this point may build enrollment projection models to test the broad enrollment goals developed in the prior stage. These models look at new and continuing student enrollments to show the combined effects of changes to recruitment and retention. As most recruitment and retention goals tend to be developed in isolation from one another, the model can serve as a profound "reality check" for the institution at this point. Institutions that have used such models in the SEM planning processes have learned that some of their original aspirations were lofty, with unrealistically high improvements to recruitment and retention required to achieve the broad goals. Others have found that their assumptions were too conservative and that the combination of some additional new students and moderate improvement in retention would achieve the desired results much sooner than planned.

Third, the process framework assumes broad involvement of persons across campus, from different administrative levels, departments, and roles, including faculty. This is important in several respects. The perspectives of faculty and staff outside the enrollment management offices expand the understanding of recruitment and student success with the specific culture and context of the institution. It is also important to ensure that the campus broadly embraces the implementation of the plan, participating appropriately and seeking to know its outcomes because involvement enabled their interests to be piqued. The plan is grown from both the top (executive leadership) and the institution's grass roots (its staff and faculty), so that implementation of the plan has the greatest possible chance of being successful.

The SEM Planning Framework

The SEM Planning Framework (Figure 27.3) augments the process and organizational frameworks by identifying the primary phases of SEM planning. It adds the "what" to SEM planning, thus completing a comprehensive planning model.

Effective SEM planning happens as an institution works from the bottom up of the pyramid shown in Figure 27.3, with planning efforts at lower levels

Figure 27.3 SEM Planning Framework

forming the foundation for those efforts above them. This provides an architecture for developing SEM plans that will achieve long-term results. The following narrative provides further description of SEM planning phases (Bontrager & Green, 2012).

Link to the Institutional Strategic Plan To be effective, enrollment planning must be viewed as an extension of the institution's mission and strategic plan. This point warrants special emphasis. In our institutional and consulting work, we have seen many instances in which institutional strategic plans were poorly aligned with the goals and programs being carried out by those charged with operational responsibility for recruitment and retention. In these cases, the main link between institutional and enrollment planning often is financial—that is, it is based on how many students are required to achieve budget goals for the coming year. Typically, such planning is primarily focused on the past, with expectations of what may be achievable being based on enrollment results of the past few years.

By contrast, linking enrollment planning to the institutional strategic plan has a number of advantages. It connects enrollment planning to the full scope of institutional mission, vision, and operations. Beyond just financial outcomes, this approach addresses other critical areas such as academics, student life, advancement, and community engagement. It also extends the enrollment planning horizon, because institutional strategic plans are typically developed for time frames of five years or more. The longer time frame enables prioritization of enrollment efforts rather than attempting to address every recruitment and retention goal for every target group of students at the same time. It also facilitates longer range planning for all campus departments. Even more importantly, it shifts the institutional mindset from a "rearview mirror" perspective to the much more powerful and energizing concept of planning toward the institutions' desired future.

Key Enrollment Indicators Identifying the metrics by which you will measure success is critical to any planning process. For strategic enrollment planning, key enrollment indicators, or KEIs, provide the first component of a two-stage bridge between aggregate enrollment goals typically included in institutional strategic plans and the more specific goals required of SEM planning (Bontrager & Green, 2012).

Depending on institutional type, KEIs will include enrollment goals across a broad scope of student and institutional attributes, as well as performance metrics. Common KEIs include the following:

- Student attributes
  - Academic ability

- Academic program interest
- Special skills (such as fine arts, leadership, athletics)
- Race/ethnicity
- Undergraduate/graduate/certificate
- Financial means
- Geographic origin
- Institutional attributes
  - Program capacities
  - Facility capacities
  - Course delivery mode (on-campus, satellite campus, online)
- External factors
  - Demographics in target student markets
  - Economic trends
  - External mandates (such as federal or state governments, governing entities, accreditors)
- Performance metrics
  - Recruitment yield rates (such as prospect-admit, admit-deposit, deposit-enroll)
  - Retention rates (such as first-to-second year, four- to six-year graduation)
  - Selectivity measures (such as average high school GPA, average standardized test scores, percentage of applicants admitted and enrolled)
- Measurable outcomes for specific recruitment and retention initiatives
- Aggregate tuition revenue
- Net revenue resulting from specific enrollment initiatives

Data Collection and Analysis The second component of the bridge between aggregate enrollment goals and specific SEM goals is provided through data collection and analysis. Building on points made earlier in this chapter related to the Organizational Framework, this phase of the SEM planning process includes the following steps.

Benchmarking Benchmarking involves compiling statistics on an institution's performance on key enrollment indicators over the past three to five years. Reviewing earlier data is rarely useful given the speed and degree of change in the factors influencing enrollment from year to year.

Compiling New Information The transition to a SEM planning approach nearly always involves gathering information that has not existed in the past or that may have existed but was not previously included in enrollment planning. Information on KEIs may not have been collected previously, maintained consistently over time, or directly linked to SEM plans. Filling these data gaps is critical to the SEM planning process. Where historical data simply does not exist, the SEM Steering Committee will recommend protocols and staff assignments to begin collecting it.

Environmental Scanning Institutions operate in environments with myriad external factors that influence campus aspirations and operations. Effective enrollment planning requires that institutions account for the factors that exist today and, to the extent possible, future trends. Such information is relatively easy to obtain from a number of governmental and higher education agencies. Usually, various campus departments have been monitoring some of the desired data. SEM planning provides a framework for bringing that information together into a comprehensive data package, in the context of focused enrollment discussions that will enable the data to be utilized for more effective decision-making.

As addressed fully in Chapter 23, it bears emphasis here that an institution's data agenda should be addressed with focus, restraint, and a long-term view of enrollment planning. The goal of well-informed SEM decision-making can quickly devolve into an endless attempt to parse out every datum that has some bearing on enrollment, or into some "interesting" but insignificant data mined by a player in the SEM planning process. Institutions may spend copious amounts of time analyzing and reanalyzing increasing amounts of data, trapped in the proverbial "paralysis by analysis," while readily apparent opportunities to improve recruitment or retention outcomes pass them by. Neither this stage of the planning process nor the SEM planning model as a whole should be allowed to supersede day-to-day enrollment decisions. Near-term decisions will gradually and increasingly be informed by the SEM plans that result from the longer-term planning process. Therefore, there is no need to pursue the unattainable ideal of answering every potential question before establishing plans and moving forward.

Setting Strategic Enrollment Goals This phase of SEM planning is a direct outgrowth of an institution's strategic plan, with delineation of key enrollment indicators and data analysis as intervening process steps (Bontrager & Green, 2012). Again, to the extent institutional strategic plans identify enrollment targets, they generally do so at a macro level, lacking the specificity required of SEM plans. Such specificity is provided as SEM planners develop KEIs, although simply identifying KEIs is inadequate. KEIs take on meaning as they are benchmarked and examined for future trends in the data collection and analysis phase.

Thus, the next phase of SEM planning is to set enrollment goals for each KEI that are strategic in their linkage to the institutional strategic plan and informed by data. This includes two important components: One is setting "x-by-y" targets for each KEI, where "x" is the desired change in the KEI and "y" is a specified time frame. The other is prioritizing which KEIs and associated goals will receive primary attention at the beginning, in the middle, and toward the end of the SEM planning schedule. A common pitfall of institutional strategic plans and many SEM plans is to seek to address every enrollment goal at the same time. Such plans often say "we want to enroll more first-year students *and* increase their academic credentials *and* increase diversity *and* increase international enrollment *and* improve retention rates *and* reduce the discount rate *and* increase net tuition revenue"—implying that all of these goals will be achieved at the same time.

The reality, however, is that few institutions have the capacity to launch initiatives across a large range of enrollment goals concurrently. Or, perhaps more to the point, rarely can they do so successfully and cost-effectively. As with all other types of planning, when institutional resources are spread too thinly across multiple initiatives, outcomes tend to be diminished. It is better to begin with three or four initiatives aimed at specific target student groups that are deemed to be of highest priority, spend two or three years refining and establishing them, and then move on to other enrollment goals. This is where the earlier reference to extending the enrollment planning horizon becomes important. Advocates for a particular group of students may not be happy that their group is not among those to receive focused attention in years one to three of a ten-year enrollment plan. However, if they can see that such attention will be given in years three to five of the plan, with clear rationale for focusing on other groups ahead of theirs, they generally will be more satisfied than they would be in the absence of detailed enrollment goals for the longer term.

Developing Strategies and Tactics With the preceding planning phases completed, an institution will be well positioned for implementing enrollment strategies and tactics that have a significantly greater likelihood of being successful generally, as well as utilizing staff and financial resources more efficiently and effectively. This point runs counter to the prevalent temptation to begin enrollment planning at the tactical stage. Where enrollment goals are not being met, campus conversations tend to be dominated by rapid-fire tactical ideas. Common examples include appointing a director of retention, expanding use of social media, acquiring new technology systems, improving the institution's website, adding academic support programs, offering more financial aid, increasing advertising, or sending a recruiter to international locations—to name just a few. The list of potential strategies and tactics is virtually endless, leading many institutions to add initiatives continually. The result often is an unwieldy mix of disjointed recruitment and retention efforts that drain staff and financial resources. Such efforts may in fact result in increased enrollment over the short-term. However, absent the comprehensive planning process being outlined here, enrollment gains usually will fade after a year or two, or they will be much more costly than necessary.

Achieving Sustainable Enrollment Outcomes The ultimate goal of the SEM planning model is to position an institution for sustained achievement of its enrollment goals over the long term. This is not a quick or easy process. Institutions may believe that their enrollment goals are too urgent to engage in a process that may take two or three years to complete. Developing KEIs and enrollment goals can be a challenge in itself, as doing so typically elicits strong disagreements about institutional mission and direction. Additionally, there often is reluctance to establish the ambitious committee structure specified by the SEM Organizational Framework, given the common observation that "we already have too many committees."

Despite those views, institutions experiencing subpar enrollment results—whether in relation to the desired number or profile of students—typically have been in that situation for a number of years. In that context, it is not realistic to think they will be able to reverse those results in short order. As previously discussed in this chapter, higher education needs to make fundamental changes to long-standing patterns. Changing those patterns will require time and adjustment of existing organizational structures. Certainly this SEM planning model requires multiple committees that consume significant staff time. Whatever the forces that argue against implementing such a structure, an institution should ask itself this: "Where does enrollment rank on the list of institutional priorities?" In our experience, the response to that question is nearly always that enrollment is the top priority. With that being the case, it may not be unreasonable to devote the substantial time and staff resources required of the planning process described here.

Finally, for developing long-term plans, it is critical that an overall planning schedule and deadlines are set, with clarity of the points at which decisions will be made and acted upon. This is where the link to the SEM Process Framework, Figure 27.2, is especially important, particularly as an institution augments the process steps delineated there with an annual timeline for SEM planning. At that point, and as another contrast to traditional SEM plans, the SEM planning model described here is an ongoing, organic process. Plans are continuously refined as additional data are gathered and outcomes are assessed term-by-term.

CONCLUSION

This chapter began by noting the challenging strategic enrollment planning in today's higher education environment. Improving enrollment outcomes requires fundamental changes in how institutions plan and operate. The SEM planning model we describe offers clear steps for organizing the *who*, *how*, and *what* of effective SEM planning. The Organizational Framework describes who is involved, representing various levels of the institutional structure addressing different components of the plan. The process framework specifies how planning proceeds through distinct points of engagement by persons throughout the institutional structure. The planning framework delineates what actually is addressed by those involved at the stages of the planning process. Taken together, these three frameworks constitute a model for effective SEM planning.

The planning frameworks presented here are not intended to be proscriptive. Rather, they are malleable to the needs, history, and culture of each institution. Composition of SEM planning committees will vary, the order and timing of process steps are subject to revision, and each stage of the planning framework will play out differently to suit each campus in the best way.

However it unfolds at an institution, SEM planning has two defining characteristics, urgency and complexity, which lead to two concluding points of emphasis. First, SEM is not a quick fix. Given the impact of enrollment on institutional finances and general sense of well-being, it is understandable that when desired enrollment outcomes are not being met, campus leaders seek to "turn things around" as quickly as possible. However, that very urgency can be the bane of the long-term planning process that is required to achieve sustainable, positive results. Fortunately, the desire for short-term gains and positioning for long-term enrollment success are not mutually exclusive. As an institution begins the longer term SEM planning process, opportunities for immediate improvement of recruitment and retention results will become apparent and should be deployed. In doing so, SEM planners should give attention to the planning principles described in this chapter, such as using hard data to determine how an initiative can best be enacted and specifying the measureable outcomes to be achieved, and then incorporating the initiative into longer-term planning.

Second, any complex, long-term process is enacted one step at a time. It is not unusual for institutions to view the planning process described in this chapter and conclude that they cannot marshal the required staff time and attention, and thus continue to muddle along with minor adjustments to the ineffective efforts that led to their enrollment concerns in the first place. The point is to get started, implementing initial organizational, process, and planning steps, and then building on them over time. In doing so, institutions will soon begin to achieve more robust enrollment outcomes.

References

Bean, J. P. (1990). Strategic planning and enrollment management. In D. Hossler, J. P. Bean, & Associates (Eds.), *The Strategic Management of College Enrollments* (pp. 21–43). San Francisco: Jossey-Bass.

Bontrager, B. (2004). Enrollment management: An introduction to concepts and structures. *College & University. 79*(3), 11–16.

Bontrager, B. (Ed.) (2008). *SEM and Institutional Success: Integrating Enrollment, Finance, and Student Access.* Washington, DC: American Association of Collegiate Registrars and Admissions Officers.

Bontrager, B., & Clemetsen, B. (2009). *Applying SEM at the Community College.* Washington, DC: American Association of Collegiate Registrars and Admissions Officers.

Bontrager, B., & Green, T. (2012). A structure for SEM planning. In B. Bontrager, R. Ingersoll, & D. Ingersoll (Eds.), *Strategic Enrollment Management: Transforming Higher Education* (pp. 271–284). Washington, DC: American Association of Collegiate Registrars and Admissions Officers.

Drucker, P. F. (1997). The future that has already happened. *Harvard Business Review, 75*(5), 20–24.

Fernald, J. L. (2011). *Who Leaves UC Santa Cruz and When? Retention and Graduation Among Freshman Cohorts.* UC Santa Cruz Institutional Research and Policy Studies. Retrieved from http://planning.ucsc.edu/irps/Enrollmt/retain/RetentionStudy(Dec2011).pdf.

Gumport, P. J., & Sporn, B. (1999). Institutional adaptation: Demands for management reform and university administration. In J. C. Smart & W. G. Tierney (Eds.), *Higher Education: Handbook of Theory and Research,* Vol. XIV (pp. 103–145). New York: Agathon Press.

Hossler, D., & Kalsbeek, D. (2008). Enrollment management & managing enrollment: Setting the context for dialogue. *College & University, 83*(4), 2–11.

Kalsbeek, D. (2006). Some reflections on SEM structures and strategies (part 1). *College & University, 81*(3), 3–10.

Kalsbeek, D. (2007). Reflections on SEM structures and strategies (part 3). *College & University, 82*(3), 3–12.

Ohio University Office of Institutional Research. (2012). *Factors Associated with First-Year Students Attrition and Retention at Ohio University Athens Campus.* Athens, OH: Ohio University.

Rowley, D. J., Lujan, H. D., & Dolence, M. G. (2001). *Strategic Change in Colleges and Universities: Planning to Survive and Prosper.* San Francisco: Jossey-Bass.

Zemsky, R. (2013). *Checklist for Change: Making American Higher Education a Sustainable Enterprise.* New Brunswick, NJ: Rutgers University Press.

CHAPTER 28

Trends in Strategic
Enrollment Management

Don Hossler

In this chapter, an examination of trends in Strategic Enrollment Management focuses on a range of public and institutional policies and practices that have been discussed in previous chapters and identifies some trends that did not fit topically into earlier chapters but are relevant to the possible of future directions for the field of SEM. Don Hossler, Larry Hoezee, and Daniel J. Rogalski (2007), in *Enrollment Management Review*, included this quote from Hossler:

> When asked to describe my job toward the end of my eight-year tenure as Vice Chancellor for Enrollment Services at Indiana University Bloomington, I offered the following description: "It is my job to manage the nexus of revenue, prestige, diversity, and access for the campus." This nexus mirrors conditions and trends in the larger society. (p. 2)

Hossler's observation is still relevant today, and at a macro level, it captures the topics considered in this chapter: the demographic trends that will continue to affect SEM; the focus on college costs, financial aid, and debt load; the future of affirmative action and its connections with access; growing scrutiny, regulation, and legislative action at the federal and state levels; growing competition and its impact on institutions; and changes in the SEM organizational structure, financial choices, and priorities.

DEMOGRAPHIC CHANGES AND THEIR EFFECTS ON INSTITUTIONS

Although the changing characteristics of students were discussed in Chapter 2, the issue of demographics did not receive a complete discussion so are considered more fully in this chapter.

Research has indicated that, in the world of higher education, student demographics are changing. For example, as early as 1998, the Western Interstate Commission on Higher Education projected a declining number of white high school graduates and an increasing number of first-generation, low-income Latino students (WICHE, 1998). The Educational Testing Service (ETS) released a well-crafted report on emerging trends for postsecondary education entitled *America's Perfect Storm: Three Forces Changing Our Nation's Future* (Kirsch, Braun, Yamamoto, & Sum, 2007) that also called attention to the changing demographics in the United States and the implication for postsecondary institutions. In 2008, the book *SEM and Institutional Success: Integrating Enrollment, Finance and Student Access,* edited by Robert Bontrager, also addressed these concerns and outlined some of the potential impacts for colleges and universities:

- Fewer students entering postsecondary education because first-generation Latino students had lower postsecondary participation rates
- More price sensitivity because more students would be coming from lower income families
- Fewer students with high ACT and/or SAT scores, which would increase competition for a smaller pool of high-ability students
- Pressure on four-year residential institutions because they cost more to attend, and first-generation Latino students are more likely to live at home and commute and to start their postsecondary careers at community colleges

Hossler mused as to whether these trends might reduce the sway of rankings publications, because postsecondary leaders would discover that in order to maintain fiscal health, they would have to enroll more low-income students with lower academic indicators.

Despite the demographic trends identified in research, leadership at many colleges and universities, including senior enrollment officers, has failed to consider and plan seriously for the pending changes in the demographic make-up of recent high school graduates. Despite the demographic realities facing postsecondary leaders, their actions largely ignored these trends. Indeed, in 2010, Hossler, Jacob Gross, and Brandi Beck authored a study funded by the

National Association for College Admission Counseling, *Putting the College Admission "Arms Race" into Context*. The authors of this study were surprised to find that, despite the warnings about demographic shifts that had been known for some time, between 2001 and 2008 virtually every sector of four-year institutions, from regional public institutions to the most selective private institutions, had been increasing the size of their entering first-year classes. Thus, at a the very time when many colleges and universities should have been planning for either steady state or declining enrollments, institutions had been increasing their class sizes.

The reasons for this are understandable, however. Public institutions were seeking more tuition revenue to offset declining state support. Private institutions were enrolling more students either to offset the rising costs of providing healthcare and faculty salaries, improving their technological infrastructure, and, among at least some elite institutions, they were responding to critiques of not enrolling more high-ability, low-income students by increasing the number of students they were admitting. Nevertheless, at a time when most postsecondary institutions in the United States should have been planning for fewer students and a larger percentage of more price-sensitive students, they were instead expanding capacity with all of the attendant costs—more support staff, more faculty, and perhaps even expanding the size of their physical plant capacity. And then the Great Recession hit in 2008, which exacerbated all of these factors.

Although published empirical research that links these trends has yet to appear, there can be little doubt that the Great Recession further intensified the impact of these demographic trends. This simultaneously caused most of the public sector and the less affluent private institutions to seek to enroll even more students to offset further reductions in state support, reductions in some state scholarship programs, and a decline in the value of endowments. The projected declines started to manifest in fall 2012 and continued into fall 2013. Reports from the National Student Clearinghouse Research Center documented an enrollment decline in the United States of 1.8 percent in 2012 and another drop of 1.5 percent in the fall of 2013 (National Student Clearinghouse Research Center, 2013).

The longer-term effects of all of these factors upon tertiary education in the United States remains to be seen, but, to date, the effects of these changes have been most pronounced in community colleges and for-profit institutions. The private sector appears to have maintained or even slightly increased their share of postsecondary enrollments. However, this may have happened because of the increases in campus discount rates, as discussed in previous chapters of this volume, which may not be sustainable. For some public and private two- and four-year schools, enrollments have remained or increased as a result of a growing number of international students. The percentage of international students enrolled in U.S. institutions increased by 7 percent between 2012 and 2013 (Institute of International Education, 2012). However, international student enrollments can be volatile and subject to political, economic, and demographic trends in other countries. In addition, the number of domestic high school graduates is expected to reach and exceed the number of high school graduates that the United States experienced from 2008 to 2021 (Prescott & Bransberger, 2012).

TUITION COSTS, FINANCIAL AID, AND STUDENT DEBT

Synthesizing across all of the chapters in Part III as well Chapter 24 by Reilly and Mott brings into focus an important trend for senior enrollment officers: to track and assess the ongoing effects of rising college costs, growing concerns about student debt levels, and a complex mix of federal, state, and institutional aid policies. Although the effects of these pressures are similar across public and private institutions, there are also differences. As noted in Chapters 10, 11, and 24, public institutions face two cross-cutting issues of pressure: holding down tuition costs, while states are simultaneously reducing funding per FTE student enrolled. In addition, community colleges and regional public institutions are more likely to enroll larger numbers of low-income students who are more likely to accrue high levels of debt and are at greater risk of not graduating. Less selective private colleges and universities, which typically also have smaller endowments, face rising levels of sensitivity to price and to accruing higher levels of debt. President Obama's proposal to create a college ratings system is clearly intended to draw more attention to college costs and student debt levels. As noted in *SEM and Institutional Success: Integrating Enrollment, Finance and Student Access* (Bontrager, 2008), these demographic trends have resulted in a multifaceted set of concerns for senior enrollment officers. As documented in Chapter 10, for private colleges and universities, student debt issues have resulted in high discount rates for many institutions, and questions are being raised as to whether we have reached the limits of the efficacy of discounting as an effective SEM strategy. Robert Zemsky has suggested that the postsecondary education industry has entered the *post-discounting era* (Kalsbeek & Zucker, 2012). For institutions that have relied heavily on merit aid to enroll a more academically able student body, more and more critiques are being voiced and published (see, for example, Heller, 2006; Pusser, 2002). Recently, several small, regional, private institutions have announced that they are rolling back and reducing their tuition (Rivard, 2013).

The Association of Governing Boards and the National Association of College and University Business Officers are collaborating on a grant from the Robert J. Woodruff Foundation to develop a benchmarking tool that is used by both public and private sector institutions to compare their financial aid allocations against those of peer institutions (Hossler and Price, 2014; Price and Hossler, 2014). Although it is too soon to ascertain the impact of this new tool, the two sponsoring organizations believe that it may lead to more scrutiny of the efficacy and fairness of large institutional investments in merit aid. President Obama has also launched an effort to enroll more low-income students and help them complete their degrees. This is likely to result in a greater investment in need-based financial aid (Calmes, 2014).

Finally, as already been noted, the U.S. Department of Education has changed the number of years used in calculating student loan default rates. As a result, loan default rates are now higher, and the penalties for high default rates to institutions have increased. Senior enrollment officers at two- and four-year colleges that enroll higher numbers of low-income students who are at greater risk of default will now be carefully monitoring student default levels and possibly more carefully evaluating how many students who are at risk of default they can admit.

The combination of all of these factors suggests that SEM organizations are entering a period of significant uncertainty. How senior enrollment officers work through these issues will likely vary by state and region; because state policies, demographic characteristics, and the economic conditions in various regions of the country are sufficiently varied, it is unlikely that all institutions in the various postsecondary sectors will respond in similar ways. It will be interesting to see how a discussion of these issues will be written ten years from now. As the saying goes, *time will tell.*

AFFIRMATIVE ACTION AND ACCESS FOR WHOM?

In Chapter 24, Mike Reilly and Michelle Mott devote considerable attention to the history of court cases on affirmative action. As they demonstrate, the pattern in recent years has been increasingly to reduce the conditions under which affirmative action is legal. Carnevale and Rose (2003) have been among several scholars and observers of higher education who have posited that race-based affirmative action no longer has broad societal support, but there is strong support for income-based affirmative action. Other higher education scholars and observers have made similar arguments (Astin & Oseguera, 2004; Heller, 2002). Although scholars have demonstrated that income-based affirmative action plans will not lead to equality of representation in postsecondary education across all races (see, for example Karen, 2002; Trent, Owens-Nicholson, Eatman, Burke, Daugherty, & Norman, 2003), it nevertheless seems likely that, increasingly, senior enrollment officers will be directing their staffs to focus on strategies to help their institutions achieve equality of access based on measures of socioeconomic status.

GROWING GOVERNMENT REGULATION

One of the most significant changes to affect tertiary education in the United States is the growing level of federal and state regulation and oversight. Interestingly, these same trends are evident in Europe and other parts of the world (Jacobs & Van der Ploeg, 2006). Traditionally, education has been primarily the domain of the state; however, the federal government is attempting to increase its regulatory oversight of postsecondary education.

At the state level, governors, legislators, and state higher education executive officers (SHEEOs) have been turning to performance-based budgeting models to try to create incentives for public institutions to focus more on containing tuition costs, on areas of research that could enhance the state's economy, and on college completion. Research on the efficacy of performance-based budgeting to influence these outcomes is mixed (Dougherty & Reddy, 2013; Tandberg & Hillman, 2014). Kevin Dougherty and Vikash Reddy (2013), however, suggest that performance-based budgeting has failed for the following reasons:

- Officials developing these policies don't know how to affect campus performance.

- Campuses have capacity constraints (such as time, analytical infrastructure, and so on) that affect their response to these efforts.

- Performance goals are unclearly defined and even more ambiguous in terms of how to achieve these goals.

These authors have also focused on the fact that state incentive budgets are changed too often, and thus colleges and universities lack the time horizons to react to one set of incentives before another set of incentives are in place.

It can be difficult to tease out the effects of state performance-based budgeting and federal- and foundation-funded projects. Both the second Bush and the Obama administrations have made college success (matriculation, persistence, and graduation) their educational priorities (Anderson, 2013; U.S. Department of Education, 2006)). In addition, influential foundations such at the Bill and Melinda Gates Foundation and the Lumina Foundation have similar priorities. Although these efforts may not have had the level of impact hoped for by policy makers, most senior college administrators, including senior enrollment officers, have made college completion an important institutional goal (Callan, Finney, Kirst, Usdan, & Venezia, 2006; Hossler, Ziskin, Lucido, Schulz, Dadashova, & Zerquera, 2011; Ziskin, Lucido, Torres, Chung, & Hossler, 2012).

Part of the dilemma institutions face in trying to respond to these policy goals is that, simply put, *achieving these goals is more easily said than done.* As Kalsbeek and Zucker assert in Chapter 5, the profile of an admitted class of students, and the market structures in which they compete, can explain most of the variance in persistence and graduation rates. The complexities of trying to control costs or limit student borrowing have already been discussed in that chapter.

A final area of increasing state, and even multistate, regulation is in the area of articulation and transfer agreements. Only fourteen states have not enacted some type of legislation that seeks to govern transfer and articulation agreements among two- and four-year public institutions (Bautsch, 2013). The goal of policy makers is to increase the number of students who move seamlessly from two- to four-year institutions. Thus far, scant empirical evidence has shown that these policies have had any effect (Anderson, Sun, & Alfonso, 2006; Roksa & Calcagno, 2008). The lack of evidence of effectiveness, however, is not likely to sway policy makers for several reasons. First, it is less expensive to deliver the first two years of college at a two-year institution. Second, many policies have not been in effect long enough to be certain about the extent of their effectiveness. As researchers identify more factors associated with successful or unsuccessful policies, state policy makers continue to refine state policies and regulations. The key takeaways for SEM personnel are as follows:

- For both public and private postsecondary institutions, having sound transfer and articulation policies in place are likely to be important, because they are significant to state policy makers and because colleges and universities are likely to see more and more students enrolling in at least some classes at two-year colleges.

- Senior enrollment officers are likely to find themselves in conversations in which campus leaders are trying to identify ways to offset the revenue loss from 100- and 200-level classes that are used to subsidize 300- and 400-level classes as well as graduate-level courses.

INCREASED COMPETITION

With the demographic changes that have already been examined in this chapter, there are more students starting their collegiate careers at community colleges, more competition from for-profit institutions (though this has subsided some in the last two years), and some competition for U.S. institutions from institutions in Canada, Europe, and Australia (Kingsbury, 2013; Schoof, 2012).

Evaluating the competition is more complex than simply indicating which institution a student attends. As noted, more students attending community colleges erode the cross-subsidies that have been used to maintain a wide range of majors at both private and public institutions. In addition, as David Breneman and Brian Pusser (2006) note, for-profit institutions typically offer only majors that are relatively low cost to deliver and that attract large numbers of students, such as education, public administration, or business. This undermines the ability of a college or university to support majors that are in lower demand, such as classics, archaeology, or expensive majors in STEM fields.

This kind of competition requires that SEM organizations not only compete with a wider range of institutions but also that they be well-informed about campus budgeting schemes. As discussed in Chapter 10, an understanding of the budget drivers of a college or university can be valuable information when, for example, the provost asks the senior enrollment officer to try to increase enrollments in under-enrolled foreign language programs, or is expressing concerns about the university's inability to subsidize a major in the history of science. One of the ways senior enrollment mangers demonstrate the range of their knowledge, and why they should have a seat at the cabinet of the president or provost, is that they understand all of these financial complexities.

The next few years are likely to be difficult ones for postsecondary institutions and for SEM units. Demographic trends, more competition, greater price sensitivity, concerns about the erosion of the financial model for colleges and universities, and uncertainty about the future directions of campus financial aid discounting can result in a good deal of stress and ambiguity for SEM units.

CHANGES, CHANGES, AND THE EVOLUTION OF SEM ORGANIZATIONS

Considering all of these ongoing trends, it should come as no surprise that SEM organizations are seemingly always in the midst of change, and there is a dearth of research on this topic. Thus, this chapter draws upon both the scarce empirical research that is available as well as upon approximately twenty-five years of consulting, shop talk with seasoned enrollment officers, and eight years as a senior enrollment officer. In this section, organizational factors that have not yet been discussed are examined.

It is overly simplistic in some ways to divide the discussion into two categories—small colleges and midsize to large institutions, because factors other than size influence the scope of SEM organizations. For example, selectivity and institutional wealth increase the odds that an institution either will not have a SEM unit or that enrollment management will be more decentralized (Goff & Lane, 2008). This is consistent with the work of Hossler and Larry Hoezee (2001), who posit that resource dependency theory can provide a good explanation of the types of institutions where SEM structures have become more common.

Small Colleges

Small institutions are increasingly making marketing part of the SEM organization. In many ways, it is surprising that this did not happen sooner. It is difficult to get accurate information on the amount of tuition revenue received by an average small private college that is neither highly selective nor well known. In 2001, Robert Toutkoushian reported that in 1995, 55 percent of the revenue earned by private colleges came from tuition, and that reliance on tuition had increased by 8 percent over the preceding twenty years. If we extrapolate to 2014, we can postulate that the average revenue earned by tuition for all private institutions (including large private research universities, Ivy League institutions, and so forth) is up to 60 percent. Though speculative, it is not a reach to suggest that for many small, less visible, and less well-endowed colleges, an excess of 70 or even 80% percent of their revenue comes from tuition. With this information in hand, it is easy to see why many presidents and boards of trustees now realize that focusing upon students, and their families, are their most important constituent groups. Chapter 23 details the types of research required to create successful SEM programs. Most small private institutions cannot afford to retain a staff capable of undertaking all of this research, however. John Lawlor (2013) and David Kalsbeek (2013) have both suggested that most small private institutions rely upon consulting groups to undertake the bulk of their enrollment research activities. It has also become commonplace at many small private institutions to merge student affairs divisions and SEM divisions. Often, the senior enrollment officer is also the chief student affairs officer. This is in part the result of the competitive salaries offered to seasoned enrollment managers who oversee both student affairs and enrollment management. Additionally, at small colleges and universities, managing SEM organizations is less likely to be encumbered by organizational silos. Often, decisions are made at small institutions informally in face-to-face conversations. Senior enrollment officers typically report directly to the president (Schulz & Lucido, 2010) and are actively involved with the board of trustees. Unlike their larger public institution counterparts, private institutions commonly have a board committee that is focused upon enrollment issues (AGB, 2010).

Finally, it is axiomatic that SEM organizations at small, private, regional institutions face a difficult task in attracting students. Hossler (1999) notes that institutional size, proximity to large population bases, and level of visibility influence the task of admissions recruitment. The more regional the market for an institution, the lower its overall visibility and the more difficult its task of attracting students. Unfortunately, although the very same institutions typically have fewer financial resources, because they are private, they are also more costly to run. Regional public institutions also struggle with some of the same limitations and often have even fewer resources to allocate to SEM activities. Nevertheless, small institutions can be great training grounds for SEM professionals, because they get to do a little bit of everything, and staff often has to be more creative than they need to be at larger institutions with more resources.

Midsize and Large Universities

As the size of an institution increases, so does its visibility, and the levels of complexity and decentralization increase for institutions with SEM organizations. Discussions on where to locate international student SEM efforts and graduate student SEM activities are illustrative of complexities that increase as universities increase in size and in the number of programs they offer. Additionally, although senior enrollment officers at small regional institutions may face the largest challenges with respect to building awareness and a strong student applicant pool, enrollment managers at midsize and large universities face other challenges. The lack of centralization and a less personal environment, coupled with contexts that are likely to be more political, result in more organizational silos and a more diverse set of enrollment goals that can be challenging.

Differences between public and private institutions are likely to remain noticeable. For example, private institutions are likely to spend more than their public counterparts to recruit students. A 2011 report from the consulting firm Noel-Levitz reported that median expenditure to recruit a student at four-year private colleges and universities was $2,185. In addition, the ratio of FTE staff to students recruited was 1:33. For public institutions, the median for four-year institutions was $457 per student, while the median for community colleges was $108. The median FTE staff per student enrolled at community colleges was 1:108 (Noel-Levitz, 2011).

To whom the senior enrollment officer reports is also more varied at larger institutions. Schulz and Lucido (2010) found that at most research universities, the senior enrollment officer reports to the provost, while at most master's institutions, the reporting line was to the president. As noted in previous chapters, with greater institutional size comes more complexity and often more decentralized SEM activities. In both large and small institutions, the offices of the registrar and financial aid report to the senior enrollment officer. Interestingly, in the Schulz and Lucido study, the researchers found that most consultants recommended that institutions adopt more centralized enrollment structures.

As institutions increase in size, they are more likely to have a centralized research group within the SEM division and more likely to be less reliant on external consultants. In addition, larger institutions are more likely to produce marketing materials in-house. As institutional size and complexity increase, Jay Goff and Jason Lane (2008) observed that the senior enrollment officer often acts more like a consultant to various departments, programs, and so on, because he or she often lacks the authority to enact desired changes. As the size of the institution increases, the greater the likelihood that enrollment managers will spend more time with internal stakeholders (the president/provost's cabinet, deans of the various schools, international student service offices, vice-presidents for diversity, and so forth), trying to build support for the plans of the SEM organization and trying to head off bad ideas that could consume large amounts of time and money. At universities with large enrollments, each college and school may admit students directly into their respective schools; this means that the undergraduate SEM organization may have to develop separate enrollment plans for each college and/or school. In some case, these schools may even compete with one another for students, which, of course, complicates the task of the senior enrollment officer even further.

AND, OF COURSE, MONEY, MONEY, MONEY

The 2011 Noel-Levitz survey of enrollment management practices reported that many colleges and universities have seen reductions in funding in recent years. Even prior to the Great Recession, SEM organizations have competed with other campus units for funding and struggled with how to allocate funds within the SEM unit. As noted earlier, senior enrollment officers need to understand the budgeting process and priorities employed at their institutions so they know how to *play the game.* This is particularly true in times of financial duress, when there are no easy answers. Staff in SEM units need to understand the drivers and politics of campus budgeting decisions and must have the internal financial infrastructure to demonstrate the return-on-investment for the programs being funded.

Ongoing assessment of SEM programs and operations is not only necessary in order for senior enrollment officers to justify their budget requests in hard times, but perhaps more important is the role assessment can play in allocating funds internally. SEM units need to have at least some idea of whether an investment in a staff member to manage chat functions and tweets for the admissions office, for example, is more important than hiring an admissions officer who will live in Los Angeles and help recruit students to attend a college in Minnesota. Other considerations compete for funding as well. For example, should the admissions office go completely paperless in its communication with students and parents? Will moving to a one-stop-shop for the offices of financial aid, registrar, and the bursar save enough money to fund the acquisition of new software for course-level enrollment planning without sacrificing student satisfaction with the services provided by these offices?

Senior enrollment officers also need to gather evidence regarding the efficacy of campus-based financial aid expenditures. Are the aid packages for international students achieving their desired goals? Is the organization providing too little need-based financial aid for low-income students, and is this one of the reasons that their persistence and degree completion rates are low? Once an institution decides to use campus aid to shape the class, this also raises other interesting questions. Because all of these dollars are fungible, SEM units can consider funding trade-offs. Would the campus be better off using some of the campus aid dollars to invest in more academic support staff to assist students who are underperforming academically? Would some campus aid dollars yield a greater return on investment if they were spent on expanding the Honor's College so that more high-ability students could be admitted?

These questions are illustrative of the decisions that must be made regularly within a SEM organization. Given our difficult financial times, senior enrollment officers must grapple with these questions and decisions daily, and there are no signs that these pressures are going to abate in the near future. Indeed, if Zemsky is correct and we have entered the post-discounting era (Kalsbeek & Zucker, 2012), we may see not only a diminution of campus dollars being used to help craft the class, but we may also see more acceptance of where each institution falls in various college ranking schemes and some de-emphasis on the importance of rankings to campus policy makers. This is not a prediction, but it is also not entirely out the realm of possibilities.

CONCLUSION

Those involved with SEM sit at the intersection of some of the most pressing and contested public and institutional education policy issues in many parts of the world. The pressure for accountability and for institutional prestige are global phenomena that are unlikely to abate in the foreseeable future, as both will continue to put pressure on SEM organizations. Demographic changes will continue to have an important impact on many institutions in the United States as well as in other parts of the world. Much of Europe, Russia, Japan, and other countries face demographic issues and enrollment-related concerns. In some instances, birth rates have declined, meaning fewer potential college-age students (Faruqee & Mühleisen, 2003; Goldstein, Lutz, & Testa, 2003; Philipov & Kohler, 2001).

In the United States, SEM organization leaders must be knowledgeable about developments in federal and state public policies. Any state that adopts aggressive transfer and articulation policies between public two- and four-year institutions will impact the enrollment patterns at regional private institutions located within the state. Federal efforts to hold down the costs of college will affect all sectors of postsecondary education. States that have generous merit scholarships may cause public and private colleges and universities to invest more in need-based financial aid, since merit aid may not be a concern.

Finally, the offices and activities that make up a SEM division will continue to change and evolve. Seasoned enrollment managers need to be students of the organizational culture in the institutions at which they work. With changes in presidents and provosts may come changes in organizational structure. The most important element of successful SEM strategies is the application of planning frames such as those discussed in Part VI of this volume and a commitment to be data-driven with regard to decisions affecting admissions, financial aid, orientation, and student success efforts.

References

Anderson, G., Sun, J. C., & Alfonso, M. (2006). Effectiveness of statewide articulation agreements on the probability of transfer: A preliminary policy analysis. *Review of Higher Education*, 29(3), 261–291.

Anderson, N. (2013). College presidents on Obama's rating plan. *Washington Post*. Retrieved from http://www.washingtonpost.com/local/education/ college-presidents-on-obamas-rating-plan/2013/08/30/b3cebc38-10cf-11e3-b4cb-fd7ce041d814_story.html.

Association of Governing Boards (AGB). (2010). *2010 Policies, Practices, and Composition of Governing Boards of Independent Colleges and Universities*. Washington, DC: Association of Governing Boards.

Astin, A. W., & Oseguera, L. (2004). The declining "equity" of American higher education. *Review of Higher Education*, 27(3), 321–341.

Bautsch, B. (2013). State Policies to Improve Student Transfer. *Hot Topics in Higher Education*. Retrieved from http://www.ncsl.org/documents/educ/student-transfer .pdf.

Beck, H. P., & Davidson, W. D. (2001). Establishing an early warning system: Predicting low grades in college students from survey of academic orientations scores. *Research in Higher Education*, 42(6), 709–723.

Bontrager, B. (Ed.). (2008). *SEM and Institutional Success: Integrating Enrollment, Finance and Student Access*. Washington, DC: American Association of Collegiate Registrars and Admissions Officers.

Bontrager, B. (2014, January 22). Personal conversation.

Breneman, D. W., Pusser, B., & Turner, S. E. (Eds.). (2012). *Earnings from Learning: The Rise of For-Profit Universities*. SUNY Press.

Callan, P. M., Finney, J. E., Kirst, M. W., Usdan, M. D., & Venezia, A. (2006). *Claiming Common Ground: State Policymaking for Improving College Readiness and Success*. San Jose, CA: National Center for Public Policy and Higher Education.

Calmes, J. (2014). Obama Lauds Pledges to Expand College Opportunities. *The New York Times*, New York, January 16, 2016. Retrieved from http://www.nytimes. com/2014/01/17/us/politics/obama-lauds-pledges-to-expand-college-opportunities .html?_r=0.

Carnevale, A. P., & Rose, S. J. (2003). *Socioeconomic Status, Race/Ethnicity, and Selective College Admissions*. New York: Century Foundation.

Dougherty, K. J., & Reddy, V. (Eds.). (2013). Performance Funding for Higher Education: What Are the Mechanisms? What Are the Impacts? *American Higher Education Report*, 39(2). San Francisco: Jossey-Bass.

Faruqee, H., & Mühleisen, M. (2003). Population aging in Japan: Demographic shock and fiscal sustainability. *Japan and the World Economy*, 15(2), 185–210.

Goff, J. W., & Lane, J. E. (2008). Building a SEM Organization: The Internal Consultant Approach. *College & University*, 83(3), 20–27.

Goldstein, J., Lutz, W., & Testa, M. R. (2003). The emergence of sub-replacement family size ideals in Europe. *Population Research and Policy Review*, 22(5–6), 479–496.

Heller, D. (2006). *Merit aid and college access*. Paper prepared for the Symposium on the Consequences of Merit-based Student Aid, Wisconsin Center for the Advancement of Postsecondary Education, University of Wisconsin, Madison.

Heller, D. E. (Ed.). (2002). *Condition of Access: Higher Education for Lower Income Students*. Westport, CT: American Council on Education/Praeger Publishing.

Hossler, D. (1999). Effective admissions recruitment. *New Directions for Higher Education*, 1999(108), 15–30.

Hossler, D., Gross, J. P. K., & Beck, B. M. (2010). *Putting the College Admission "Arms Race" into Context*. Alexandria, VA: National Association for College Admission Counseling.

Hossler, D., & Hoezee, L. (2001). Conceptual and theoretical thinking about enrollment management. In. J. Black (Ed.), *The Strategic Enrollment Management Revolution* (pp. 57–76). Washington, DC: American Association of Collegiate Registrars and Admissions Officers.

Hossler, D. & Price, D. (2014, March/April). Tuition discounting in an era of accountability and scarcity. *Association of Governing Boards Reports.*, 2(22), 35-39.

Hossler, D., Hoezee, L, & Rogalski. (2007, Fall). *The Enrollment Management Review, Issue 1*. New York: The College Board.

Hossler, D., Ziskin, M., Lucido, J., Schulz, S., Dadashova, A., & Zerquera, D. (2011, March). *How Four-Year Colleges and Universities Organize Themselves to Promote Student Persistence: The emerging national picture*. New York: College Board.

Institute of International Education. (2013). *Open Doors 2013: International Students in the United States and Study Abroad by American Students are at All-Time High*. Press release. Retrieved from http://www.iie.org/Who-We-Are/News-and-Events/Press-Center/Press-Releases/2013/2013-11-11-Open-Doors-Data#.UtwVrWco4id.

Jacobs, B., & Van der Ploeg, F. (2006). Guide to reform of higher education: A European perspective. *Economic Policy*, 21(47), 535–592.

Kalsbeek, D. (June 7, 2013). Personal conversation.

Kalsbeek, D., & Zucker, B. (2012). *Sustainable SEM: An integrated perspective*. Paper presented at the AACRAO SEM Conference, Orlando, FL.

Karen, D. (2002). Changes in access to higher education in the United States: 1980–1992. *Sociology of Education, 75*(3), 191–210.

Kingsbury, K. (2013). Low costs lure U.S. college students abroad. *Reuters*, U. S. Edition. From Retrieved from http://www.reuters.com/article/2013/05/13/us-college-abroad-options-idUSBRE94C0V420130513.

Kirsch, I., Braun, H., Yamamoto, K., & Sum, A. (2007). *America's Perfect Storm: Three Forces Changing Our Nation's Future.* Princeton, N J: Educational Testing Service.

Lawlor, J. (March 5, 2013). Personal conversation.

The National Student Clearinghouse Research Center. (2013). *REPORT: Current Term Enrollment Report – Fall 2013.* Retrieved from http://nscresearchcenter .org/currenttermenrollmentestimate-fall2013/http://nscresearchcenter.org/ currenttermenrollmentestimate-fall2013/.

Noel-Levitz. (2011). *2011 Cost of Recruiting an Undergraduate Student Benchmarks for Four-Year and Two-Year Institutions: What Is a Typical Budget and Staff Size for Admissions and Recruitment?* Higher education benchmarks: Noel-Levitz report on undergraduate enrollment trends. Retrieved from https://www.noellevitz. com/documents/shared/Papers_and_Research/2011/2011%20Cost%20of%20 Recruiting%20Undergraduate%20Students.pdf.

Philipov, D., & Kohler, H. P. (2001). Tempo effects in the fertility decline in eastern Europe: Evidence from Bulgaria, the Czech Republic, Hungary, Poland, and Russia. *European Journal of Population/Revue Européenne de Démographie, 17*(1), 37–60.

Prescott, B. T., & Bransberger, P. (2012). *Knocking at the College Door: Projections of High School Graduates.* Boulder, CO: Western Interstate Commission for Higher Education.

Price, D. & Hossler, D. (2014, April). Matching grants. *Business Officer Magazine,* pp. 24–32.

Pusser, B. (2002). Higher education, the emerging market, and the public good. In P. A. Graham & N. G. Stacey (Eds.), *The Knowledge Economy and Postsecondary Education: Report of a Workshop* (pp. 105–125). Washington, DC: National Academies Press.

Rivard, R. (2013) Tuition (Paper) Cuts. *Inside Higher Ed.* Retrieved from http://www .insidehighered.com/news/2013/09/16/small-private-colleges-steeply-cut-their-sticker-price-will-it-drive-down-college.

Roksa, J., & Calcagno, J. C. (2008). *Making the Transition to Four-Year Institutions: Academic Preparation and Transfer.* Retrieved from http://scholar.google.com/ scholar?q=Roksa%2C+J.%2C+%26+Calcagno%2C+J.+C.+%282008%29.+& btnG=&hl=en&as_sdt=0%2C15.

Schoof, R. (2012). U.S. college students lured by lower costs to Canada, U.K. *The Seattle Times*, November 4, 2012. Retrieved from http://seattletimes.com/html/ nationworld/2019608278_canadacollege15.html.

Schulz, S., & Lucido, J. (2010). *Who We Are: An In-Depth Look at Enrollment Professionals, the Movement to Centralize Enrollment Systems and External Influences on Our Practice.* Paper presented at College Board Western Regional Forum, San Diego, CA.

Tandberg, D. A., & Hillman, N. W. (2014). State higher education performance funding: Data, outcomes, and policy implications. *Journal of Education Finance, 39*(3), 222–243.

Toutkoushian, R. K. (2001). Trends in revenues and expenditures for public and private higher education. In M. B. Paulsen & J. C. Smart (Eds.), *The Finance of Higher Education: Theory, Research, Policy, and Practice* (pp. 11–38). New York: Agathon Press.

Trent, W., Owens-Nicholson, D., Eatman, T. K., Burke, M., Daugherty, J., & Norman, K. (2003). Justice, Equality of Educational Opportunity, and Affirmative Action in Higher Education. In M. Chang, D. Witt, J. Jones, & K. Haukta (Eds.), *Compelling Interest: Examining the Evidence on Racial Dynamics in Higher Education.* Report of the American Educational Research Association Panel on Racial Dynamics in Colleges and Universities. Stanford, CA: Stanford University.

U.S. Department of Education. (2006). A National Dialogue: The Secretary of Education's Commission on the Future of Higher Education. Retrieved from http://www2.ed.gov/about/bdscomm/list/hiedfuture/index.html?exp = 0.

Western Interstate Commission for Higher Education. (1998). Policy Indicators for Higher Education: WICHE States. *Regional Fact Book for Higher Education in the West.* Boulder, CO: Western Interstate Commission for Higher Education.

Ziskin, M., Lucido, J., Torres, V., Chung, E., & Hossler, D. (2012). *Securing the Future Retention Models in Community Colleges.* New York: College Board. Retrieved from http://advocacy.collegeboard.org/sites/default/files/community-college-security-future-retention-models-5875.pdf.

CHAPTER 29

Ethics and Strategic Enrollment Management

Marc M. Camille

"College Recruiting: Salesmanship or Guidance?"

Read again the quotation above. It is not the title of this chapter. Is it the title of an article from a recent issue of *Journal of College Admission* or a presentation at the American Association of Collegiate Registrars and Admissions Officers (AACRAO) SEM Conference? Is it the ponderings of a dean of admission or a director of college counseling, wondering about the tension that exists today between colleges seeking to meet enrollment goals and guidance and college counselors seeking to help students enroll at good-fit institutions? Could it be the title from a recent newspaper article? Although the answer to all of these questions could conceivably be yes, this simple, yet provocative statement is indeed the title of a journal article. The article was written by R. E. Blackwell and published in *The School Review* in 1936.

Three-quarters of a century later, the issues and observations raised by Blackwell (1936) are eerily similar and perhaps even prophetic to those that characterize the ethical dilemmas facing today's Strategic Enrollment Management professionals. Blackwell's opening paragraph reads, "College recruiting is one of the most significant problems in the education field today" (p. 417). Among his numerous concerns raised, Blackwell leveled his most cutting criticism toward what he deems to be the inappropriate behavior of "field representatives," now referred to as admission counselors:

The college field representative has possibilities of becoming the most important liaison officer of higher educational institutions. However, as the work of the field representative is handled in a large number of institutions, it represents, in the opinion of the writer, the most deadly curse of American higher education. . . . The subject of this discussion . . . distinguishes between desirable and undesirable recruiting methods and practices, between constructive and destructive work with prospective students. The writer can see no place in a self-respecting institution of higher education for a salesman. . . . The salesman is interested in an individual student only to the extent of the income gained from the prospective student if the salesman is successful in "landing him" (p. 420).

Although Blackwell's prose and pan toward the behaviors of his period's "college field representatives" today refers singularly to the admission work of SEM professionals, it nonetheless points us in the right direction to examine modern-day ethical dilemmas. Perhaps it is mere coincidence that today's National Association for College Admission Counseling (NACAC) organization was founded in 1937, a year after Blackwell's article, and in its inaugural year the association established a "code of ethics" (NACAC, 2013).

Before we consider the ethical implications of SEM, it will be beneficial to establish working definitions of ethics and of SEM. Ethics is defined as "moral principles that govern a person's or group's behavior" (Oxford Dictionaries, n.d., a) and moral is "concerned with the principles of right and wrong behavior and the goodness or badness of human character" and "holding or manifesting high principles for proper conduct" (Oxford Dictionaries, n.d., b). For the purposes of this chapter, references to ethics and ethical behavior will be applied through a lens of the set of right and wrong principles and behaviors that involve SEM decision-making, policies, and practices, with a concern for the potential impact on human beings.

Previous chapters of this handbook have provided historical context and the evolving definitions of SEM, and the various elements, offices, policies, and procedures of a SEM organization should now be familiar. Individual SEM practitioners may endorse or put into practice SEM definitions that appeal to their preferences or institutional circumstances, and common across all definitions of SEM is a comprehensive approach to managing student enrollments, from prospective students through alumni. However, given the current conditions affecting higher education and SEM practitioners within the United States and abroad, an argument can be made for the relevance and appropriateness of applying a market-centered orientation and definition to SEM.

Modern higher education is rife with increased scrutiny and skepticism, from the general public as well as local and national governments. Among the defining concerns and influences facing higher education today are calls for greater accountability and cost containment; questions regarding the value of postsecondary degrees; demand for broader access and increased degree completions; curricular reform and delivery mode innovation that challenge the traditional, residential, defined timeline experience; changing demographics in which the nation's college-going population is growing at uneven rates nationally and with increased racial and socioeconomic diversity; and a continued decline in financial support for higher education at the local and national government levels, which has resulted in increased competition for resources and students, and notably, students (and their parents) who have the ability to pay. In short, the environment that defines modern-day higher education, and thus, that of today's SEM practitioners, is impacted by market forces that suggest, and perhaps require, that postsecondary institutions become more market oriented than was historically the case. With these conditions in mind, consider a relevant definition of SEM by David Kalsbeek (2006):

> Strategic Enrollment Management is the systematic evaluation of an institution's competitive market position, the development of a research-based definition of the desired or preferred strategic market position relative to key competitors, and then marshaling and managing institutional plans, priorities, processes, and resources to either strengthen or shift that market position in pursuit of the institution's optimal enrollment, academic, and financial profile (p. 4).

The presence of market forces in higher education, or said differently, the view of higher education as a market place, necessitates the consideration of the impact of those market forces on postsecondary institutions' missions, visions, and values. Enrollment management professionals often are at the front lines of responsibility for acquiring the financial resources necessary to fund institutional budget priorities, and the balance struck between mission and market challenges SEM practitioners with issues of ethical decision-making, policies, practices, and tactics.

This chapter provides a synopsis of the key historical and present ethical issues faced by enrollment management professionals, including highlights of previous literature that has addressed SEM ethics issues. It is important to note that the purposes and constraints of this overview chapter necessitate a cursory review of the literature, and unquestionably additional issues exist that over the years have garnered attention. Nonetheless, in reviewing historical and present issues, including case studies and opportunities for reflection, the intent is to provide SEM practitioners with context for use in their future decision-making around policy and practice issues.

SYNOPSIS OF PREVIOUS LITERATURE

Since the onset of the twenty-first century, higher education leaders, researchers, and wonks have increasingly observed that over the course of the past four decades, higher education in the United States has become commercialized and marketized. As a result, the nation's colleges and universities have increasingly become more responsible for and dependent on institutional sources for annual operating revenues versus the historical funding that came from state and federal government allocations (Bok, 2003, 2013a; Zemsky, 2009, 2013; Zemsky, Shaman, & Shapiro, 2001; Zemsky, Wegner, & Massy, 2005). Common among the themes of Derek Bok, Robert Zemsky, and their contemporaries in assessing the shifting of higher education's funding to institutional sources is the resulting presence of a heightened competition for those resources and the student tuition dollars that are the primary funding source for most institutions. Commencing with the introduction in the mid-1980s of the first college rankings issue by *US News & World Report*, the decades that followed have seen the nation's populace beguiled into accepting as truths the definitions of educational quality prescribed by prestige-based rankings such as those published by *US News*. Postsecondary institutions' resulting relentless pursuit of higher rankings, or said differently, institutional prestige, has triggered an admissions arms race and further fueled the fire that feeds higher education's chase for ever increasing resources (Bok, 2003; Hossler, 2000a; Zemsky, 2009; Zemsky et al., 2001; Zemsky et al., 2005).

Additional research argues that the core values within the country's higher education system have shifted from those that are mission-centric to those that are more market-driven (Bloom, Hartley, & Rosovsky, 2006; Bok, 2003; Zemsky, 2009; Zemsky et al., 2001; Zemsky et al., 2005). Market influences and commercialization, through their influences on the U.S. system of higher education, have replaced public-oriented benefits with those based on individual or private gain. Higher education today is seen primarily as a private benefit, one that advances an individual's opportunities for success in society and, more specifically, for getting a good job with a higher salary (Astin, 1997; Zemsky et al., 2005).

To summarize, higher education's purpose has evolved (or perhaps deteriorated) to that of being seen primarily as a private versus public benefit, providing individuals with a means to career opportunity and success, and the influence of commercialization and market forces has pushed colleges and universities down a path in pursuit of ever greater resource demands, which when coupled with the pursuit of greater prestige associated with institutional positioning in annual, ordinal rankings that dominate perceptions of institutional quality, result in ever increasing pressure on SEM professionals to meet elusive enrollment goals and objectives. Today's SEM professionals often are faced with competing and unrealistic priorities; it is not uncommon for campus SEM leaders to be tasked with achieving a triad of student body characteristics that typically are unlikely, if not impossible, to realize: increase academic quality, increase access for underrepresented and underserved populations, and lower the discount rate and increase net tuition revenue. Don Hossler (2007) summarized these tensions:

The pressure to hit an exact enrollment target, to increase enrollment for additional revenue, to raise the average SAT score for an entering class, or to increase the proportion of enrolling African American students can present difficult challenges, and in this context, discerning what is best for students is not always easy. In addition, on many campuses the admissions office may be charged with achieving two or three of these goals simultaneously, increasing the pressure and difficulty. It is easier, for example, to increase quality if a smaller class can be recruited. It is easier to be selective when fewer students need to be admitted (p. 103).

The past decade has seen a rise in media reports of examples within the enrollment management profession of compromised ethical decision-making, practices, and behaviors. Although the current set of market influence observations are more recent to higher education, questions regarding student recruitment practices and their ethical soundness, or lack thereof, appear in literature dating back nearly a half century.

As early as the 1970s, evidence exists of questionable admission and financial aid practices similar to those identified by Blackwell (1936), that when examined through an ethical lens and with little imagination might easily be applicable to today's issues. A number of NACAC journal articles from the 1970s included themes that associated admissions recruitment practices with salesmanship and gimmicks, called to question the use of merit versus need-based scholarships, and suggested the need for a review of the ethics of the admissions profession; also noteworthy were speculations that the questioned admissions practices were stemming from the decade's demographic projections of declining numbers of future high school graduates causing excess supply versus demand (Haines, 1975; Johnson & Sline, 1973; McKenna, 1976). In his analyses of a recruitment practices survey conducted by the Admissions Practices and Procedures Committee of the Pennsylvania Association of College Admissions Counselors (PACAC) in the spring of 1974, R. W. Haines (1975) noted that although need-based financial aid was almost unanimously approved, only one-third of respondents approved the use of merit-based scholarships. Haines also noted that although 83 percent of respondents approved the use of direct mail to students who had released their names and addresses for that purpose through providers such as the College Board, only 7 percent approved the direct mail outreach to students who had not released their names, and 82 percent disapproved or strongly disapproved direct requests from admission officers to guidance/college counselors for contact information for their school's top students. In a 2012 opinion-editorial, Esther Hugo (2012) found the issues raised by Haines (1975) to be similar and instructive to those of today, such as a need for clarity and transparency in student recruitment and admission policies, pressures on enrollment management professionals to constantly deliver better results with less resources, and a call for ethics to inform decision-making.

Numerous themes emerged during the 1980s, and a review of the literature reveals a variety of enrollment management ethical issues still relevant to today's SEM practitioners. In a *Change* magazine article, Maureen Mackey (1980) noted a variety of concerns regarding the use of marketing techniques by college admission office personnel in their student recruitment efforts, questioning the use of films and marketing tactics:

> A product of big-ticket audiovisual talent, the film is an impressive display, selling a collegiate fantasy like a Disneyland package. . . . As higher education turns from a seller's to a buyer's market, colleges are beginning to study their "customers." Though embarrassed administrators prefer terms like "academic evaluation" to the unscholarly "marketing," the activity is essentially the same (pp. 51–52).

In a speech delivered at the Annual Meeting of the American Council on Education in 1979 and later adapted for an article in *The National ACAC Journal*, then Boston University President John Silber (1980) addressed a variety of admission and enrollment management issues. Silber provided his observations on topics such as the increased presence of marketing tactics and the changing goals of admission officers as they sought to enroll a broader representation of students beyond only the highest achievers.

The sentiments and concerns expressed by Mackey (1980) and Silber (1980), and later echoed by Larry Litten (1981) and Edward Fiske (1981) could easily be found among the concerns of the current decade, and few of today's enrollment management professionals, if any, would argue their legitimacy. Fiske (1981) identified a number of areas in which he perceived abuses were occurring in college admission, grouping them into themes that included gimmickry, deception, payment for enrollees, no-need scholarships, early deadlines, and over-admission. Johnson (1989) made similar observations: "commissions are paid, many publications do exaggerate reality, recruitment strategies often coerce, and financial aid awarding is sometimes analogous to poker betting strategies" (p. 27).

The decade of the 1990s saw enrollment management issues continuing to be questioned through an ethical lens. Topics such as need-aware versus need-blind admission practices and the cultivation of parents as donors faced increased scrutiny (Jump, 1995; Nicklin, 1994). James Jump (1995) addressed the topic of need-blind versus need-aware financial aid practices, noting the increased use of need-aware admission and its potential impact on lower income students' admission options, but his greatest angst about the need-aware practices was directed toward those institutions that did so without transparency. Conversely, Jump (1995) and Sandy Baum (1998) observed that some institutions use need-aware admission to be able to afford to fund adequately with financial aid the students they do end up admitting. Nonetheless, further criticism toward the use of applicants' family income data to identify potential future donors was voiced by Julie Nicklin (1994) in a *Chronicle of Higher Education* article, in which she cited a number of cases of deceptive tactics employed by admission personnel in capturing parental income data for need-aware admission and potential donor cultivation purposes. Like Jump (1995) and Baum (1998), Nicklin expressed her greatest concern with the lack of transparency in the employed tactics, versus the actual gathering of information regarding potential donors whose philanthropy could make it possible for deserving students with high financial need to attend the institutions. Themes of deceptive admission and financial aid practices were common in the 1990s, as noted in a *Journal of College Admission* article by Victoria Gallagher (1992), in which she addressed financial aid tactics such as bait-and-switch. Gallagher cited Ernest Boyer's 1987 report, *College: The Undergraduate Experience in America*, to help reinforce concerns over misrepresented facts, referring to Boyer's observation that only a small number of colleges providing misrepresentative information could lead to widespread public mistrust toward admission professionals. Concerns about misrepresentation of data and deceiving communication practices on the part of admission officers date back to the 1930s (Blackwell, 1936) and continue to be present today (Hossler, 2007; Strauss, 2013).

PRESENT AND FUTURE ISSUES

Admittedly, the themes outlined so far in this chapter are samples of the literature and ethical concerns raised over the years with regard to enrollment management practices. Today, more than a decade into the twenty-first century, enrollment management professionals work in an environment still marked by many of the same challenges from the past, including demands to generate ever larger proportions of institutional revenues, issues regarding changing demographics, and competing enrollment composition goals. The temptation to sacrifice ethics to achieve desired enrollment outcomes still exists, and as Robert Hodum (2012) found, numerous higher education organizations that are involved directly or indirectly with elements of enrollment management have made public and organization-wide commitments toward ethical practices through the creation of various codes of conduct, including Association for Continuing Higher Education's *Code of Ethics*; National Association of Foreign Student Advisers' *Statement of Ethics*; National Association of Student Financial Aid Administrators' *Statement of Ethical Principles*; Council for Advancement and Support of Education's *Statement of Ethics*; and National Association of Student Personnel Administrators' *Standards of Professional Practice.* Of course, missing from the list are the more commonly known NACAC *Statement of Principles of Good Practice* and AACRAO *Statement of Professional Ethics and*

Practice. Whether viewed as proactive or reactive attempts at shaping profes-sional behavior, the myriad organizations' professions to ethical conduct have not eliminated the occurrence of SEM professionals continuing to fall victim to temptation, with resulting accusations around questionable practices. What follows is a sampling of current issues and headlines.

Student Recruitment Issues

The work of admission officers still garners attention and scrutiny among the higher education and media communities. Many of today's concerning issues and practices of enrollment management work are of a similar ilk to those of the past, and current critiques of enrollment managers strike a similar tone to those of the past. Bok (2013a) wrote

> In the fierce competition for students, more than a few admissions offices engage in recruitment practices that are more akin to those of a used car salesman than to methods appropriate to a profession ostensibly seeking to help students choose the right college. For-profit universities are the worst offenders. Yet many nonprofit colleges, under pressure from above to produce more applicants and higher SAT scores, engage in inflated advertising, early decision programs, and unseemly public relations campaigns to "rebrand" their institution, not to mention the shady methods employed by some colleges to manipulate the data that go into determining a college's place in the media rankings. Such tactics, even by a minority of institutions, chip away at the trust and respect with which the public views higher education (p. 143).

A more recent issue is the practice of test-optional admission policies. Today more than 800 four-year colleges and universities have some type of standard-ized test-optional admission policy (Fairtest, 2013). Although the increased ac-cess rationale for implementing test-optional admission policies can easily be justified through an ethical lens, test-optional admission has yielded additional ethical quandaries, such as institutions requiring test scores for scholarship consideration but not admission purposes and then proceeding to include the test scores of all scholarship recipients in profile data, regardless of whether they applied for admission as test-optional candidates. It is likely a majority of institutions may in fact be doing the right thing in terms of how they report standardized test score profiles; Jonathan Epstein (2009) nonetheless found inconsistency with how test-optional admission is being practiced and reported the following:

> How can an ethical institution that distrusts the SAT's validity or perceives it to be biased continue to evaluate any applicants using the test? How can scores be meaningful in evaluating a student's abilities when they are submitted, but irrelevant when they are withheld? . . . But, what institutions do with scores

that are submitted and how they account for the scores that are not is still an unanswered question. Do colleges use these policies to artificially inflate their SAT averages by reporting only the scores of self-selected students that choose to submit test scores? (p. 17)

Student Funding Issues

The literature reminds us that throughout the history of U.S. higher education, financial aid's purpose has primarily been a means to achieving institutional enrollment goals and, oftentimes, individual donor objectives (Hossler, 2000b). It wasn't until the 1960s that financial aid's access and equity agenda first gained traction (Baum, 1998; Hossler, 2000b). Today, the same issues continue, as Hossler (2000b) wrote:

> Critics argue that campus-based aid should be used to assure access and equity for all students. They note that tuition discounting and financial aid leveraging strategies are also leading to higher tuition rates so that colleges and universities can use the additional revenue to fund merit scholarships for students who might otherwise qualify for additional need-based financial aid in order to be able to afford to attend a college or university of their choice. These assertions are correct. No current observer of financial aid policy would disagree with these observations (p. 87).

More recently, Bok (2013a) concurred with Hossler's (2000b) observations regarding the negative impact of tuition discounting and aid leveraging on access and equity goals:

> Some colleges admit certain students . . . because their parents are alumni or possess the wealth to make a substantial gift. Others allocate large parts of their scholarship funds on the basis of athletic prowess, academic ability, or other grounds unrelated to financial need, leaving too little aid to allow poor but worthy applicants to enroll. Such practices, together with the sharp increase in strategic tuition discounting, have struck especially hard at students from low-income families (p. 143).

The use of tuition discounting and financial-aid leveraging has not been limited to private institutions. In recent years, larger numbers of public institutions have been using financial-aid leveraging tactics to enroll larger numbers of low-need, higher quality students (Baum & Lapovsky, 2006; Wang, 2013). Marian Wang (2013) wrote

> Attention has long been focused on the lack of economic diversity at private colleges, especially at the most elite institutions. What has been little discussed, by contrast, is how public universities, which enroll far more students, have gradually shifted their priorities—and a growing portion of their aid dollars— away from low-income students (para. 15).

Zemsky (2013) affirmed the trend of public institutions, notably the "flag-ships," in their shifting financial aid expenditures away from need-based and access agendas to those that are merit- or prestige-based:

> Less well understood, and less often commented on, has been a parallel shift in the undergraduate profiles of the nation's public flagship universities. . . . Like their private research counterparts, public flagship universities now enroll substantially fewer recipients of Pell Grants. . . . Though these flagship institutions substantially increased the amount of institutionally funded aid they awarded, much more of these funds went to recruit students from families with a $100,000-plus income than to recruit students from low-income families (p. 50).

In addition to identifying his concerns about current financial aid practices, Bok (2013a) also offered an appealing, yet unlikely solution:

> If groups of competing colleges could agree to give up tuition discounts and merit aid, and allocate scholarship funds in strict accordance with need, they might have more to give the neediest applicants. . . . However, persuading all or nearly all competing colleges to accept such an arrangement would be a tall order. Moreover, such agreements would run a substantial risk of violating the antitrust laws (p. 140).

The idea of reprioritizing need-based versus merit-based financial aid is of personal interest. A number of years ago, I convened a meeting of the presidents and chief enrollment officers from a number of Catholic, comprehensive institutions located between Washington, DC, and Boston, with similar admission and rankings profiles, to discuss the topic of merit aid, its proliferation, and whether our missions, as Catholic institutions, called upon us to emphasize access and equity over the pursuit of prestige. The day's discussion led to universal agreement that ideally our financial aid strategies and policies would dramatically change, from the use of merit-based scholarships and the futile pursuit of higher rankings and prestige to need-based assistance, designed to provide greater access and opportunity, a value inherent in our collective institutions' missions. Alas, there also was unanimous agreement with Bok's (2013a) observations that without wide endorsement and implementation of that type of change in financial aid strategy across a large swath of institutions, it would likely be unfeasible to execute alone or even among a small but similar group of institutions. Clearly an example of *the Prisoner's Dilemma* (McPherson & Schapiro, 1994), the topic has not been raised since.

With decreased federal and state financial aid support, notably in the form of gift aid, many private institutions have been packaging larger amounts of self-help sources to meet demonstrated need, including private and institutional loans and larger student-employment awards. Of concern, research has shown that students who work more than manageable amounts of hours on a weekly basis while enrolled in college tend to face greater challenge in integrating into college life, earn lower grades, and complete degree programs at lower rates; likewise, research also has shown that increased borrowing as a larger source for funding higher education has not led to higher completion rates across all types of colleges or specifically for low-income and first-generation students (Gladieux & Perna, 2005; Perna, 2010).

Another issue that originated in the admission world but more recently has emerged in financial aid circles is demonstrated interest, with enrollment managers seeking to identify student qualities and characteristics that predict greater likelihood of enrollment, thus increasing yield rates with these admits versus those that lack the predictive modeling statistical power. In a recent *Chronicle of Higher Education* article, Ry Rivard (2013) revealed that enrollment professionals and consultants have identified that the position where an institution is listed on the Free Application for Federal Student Aid (FAFSA) correlates to where the institution is ranked as a preference by the student completing the form; a higher spot on the list equates to higher desire to attend. Specific questions were raised regarding the ethical implications of using that information to determine how much gift aid to award and/or whether or not to admit a student based on his or her estimated interest (Rivard, 2013).

College Persistence and Completion Issues

The college completion agenda continues to be a dominant priority in higher education and among public policy makers. Nonetheless, over the course of the two most recent decades, the percentage of students attending four-year public universities that graduate with bachelor's degrees in five years has declined from 47 percent to 43 percent, while the equivalent statistic for students at four-year private institutions has held relatively steady at 58 percent, and the rate for both private and public institutions combined has decreased from 54 percent to 53 percent (ACT, 2013). With regard to first-to-second-year retention rates, since 1992 the rate for students attending four-year public institutions has remain unchanged, at 72 percent; the equivalent statistic for students attending four-year private institutions has decreased from 76 percent to 72 percent, and the rate for public and private institutions combined has decreased from 75 percent to 72 percent (ACT, 2013). Although the above rates are aggregate and differences exist across institutions by Carnegie classification and admission selectivity, neither retention nor degree completion rates at four-year institutions have notably improved since 1992. In addition, a drill-down into either retention or completion rates beyond the aggregate measures provided above reveals that for groups of institutions within Carnegie classification category or within admission selectivity groups, rates are notably lower than the aggregate means. Systemic improvements in retention and completion rates have not occurred, as observed by Vincent Tinto (2006):

> Substantial gains in student retention have been hard to come by. Though some institutions have been able to make substantial improvements in the rate at which their students graduate, many have not. Indeed the national rate of student persistence and graduation has shown disappointingly little change (p. 2).

With regard to the role that enrollment management practices have or have not contributed to stalled retention and graduate rates, arguments can be made that some admission and financial aid policies have been impediments to progress. In more recent years, the increased practice of tuition discounting, financial aid leveraging, and the packaging of greater proportions of self-help aid (loans and student employment) have garnered negative press. Matthew Quirk (2005) wrote

> Others will intentionally gap poor students so severely that they decide not to attend in the first place—or, if they enroll, the long hours of work-study and mounting debts eventually force them to drop out. Called "admit-deny," this practice allows a college to keep poor students out while publicly claiming that it doesn't consider a student's finances when making admissions decisions (para. 18).

Quirk's (2005) observations are supported by research as well. Hossler, Mary Ziskin, Jacob Gross, Sooyeon Kim, and Osman Cekic (2009), after reviewing relevant literature, concluded that loans as a source of financial aid do not tend to enhance student persistence and loan debt has a negative impact on student persistence.

CASE STUDIES AND OPPORTUNITIES FOR REFLECTION

Unfortunately, the examples of ethical compromises related to enrollment management issues and professionals appear to be occurring with more frequency in recent years. The intent in this section is not to single out any particular institutions or individuals. Rather, the examples provided highlight some of the more common issues, and of more importance, provide opportunities for SEM professionals to reflect upon the cases and to think critically and deeply about future implications.

For the first example, we turn to a well-regarded, mid-Atlantic, private, research institution, in the headlines in recent years for a number of enrollment management ethical shortcomings. In 2012, an article by Eric Hoover in *The Chronicle of Higher Education* discussed the discovery by the institution during an internal review of its admission statistics, that for more than ten years it had been misreporting class rank data to *US News* for its annual rankings issues.

> A little less than a year after the *US News* data issues, the same institution was singled out in another *Chronicle* article, in which Beckie Supiano (2013) addressed the institution's recent confession to using need-aware admission tactics despite years of public declarations, including prominently on its website, that the university was fully need-blind in rendering all admission decisions. Supiano did note that the new senior enrollment manager at the institution, hired after the *US News* incident, was adamant in stating they were working toward a fully transparent admission process. Although this particular institution appears to have lapsed in ethical judgment on more than one occasion in its enrollment management practices, numerous examples exist of other institutions that have had ethical issues related to enrollment management result in public reveals. Sadly, in a recent twelve-month span, five institutions were cited for misreporting admissions data to *U.S. News*, as reported in *The Washington Post* by Nick Anderson (2013). Higher education media outlets such as *The Chronicle of Higher Education* and *Inside Higher Ed* continue to report, with seeming increased frequency, on instances of senior enrollment management professionals resigning or being terminated as a result of ethics missteps (DeSantis, 2014; Jaschik, 2014).

Without question, market forces, changed demographics, and the financial impact from the nation's latest economic crises are triggering increased pressure on SEM professionals, and the combination of these forces and the pressure to succeed seems to be taking its toll on adherence to ethical standards and principles. Reflecting upon the ethical lapses of others, SEM professionals need to keep front and center the implications of their own policy practices and decisions. All of us who work as SEM leaders are well served to consider moral obligations and institutional mission imperatives over personal advancement and institutional ambitions.

CONCLUSION AND IMPLICATIONS

Based on the information presented so far in this chapter, it would be tempting to conclude that SEM and ethics seem to be competing forces. For nearly a century, a variety of admission and financial aid practices, and now the enrollment management profession at large, have been questioned for their ethical decisions and implications by the general public, the media, the government, and those who work and research in higher education. Undeniably, much of the research findings and questions of concern have been justified. And clearly the pressure on SEM practitioners to achieve elusive, ever-increasing goals, which often times are competing and nearly impossible to achieve, is contributing to the proliferation of ethical lapses. Arguably, the pressures on today's SEM practitioners are at peak intensity and complexity, as suggested by Hossler and Kalsbeek (2013):

> What has changed—and changed dramatically—in the past five years is the external environment within which enrollment management leaders are called to steer their institution's enrollment strategy. The stakes are now higher than ever for doing so effectively. Because of these new challenges, SEM leaders are increasingly being asked to speak to the *sustainability* of the institution's enrollment strategy, which includes the viability of pricing and discount strategies, the high reliance on federal and state aid, the rising levels of student debt burdens and default rates, demographic shifts in the institution's primary market, its rates of student success and completion, the competitiveness of its market position, and so on (p. 23).

Nonetheless, despite the increased pressures and complexities of the job, and despite the compromised ethics of some SEM professionals and their resulting practices, there also is ample evidence, empirically and anecdotally, of the positive impact of SEM practices and policies on myriad higher education outcomes. Rather than questioning whether SEM and ethics can coexist for the greater good, one can argue that they are inherently interwoven, and when viewed as such, offer a framework for SEM practitioners to be successful in meeting prescribed goals and objectives, and equally significant, to do so in a manner that is proportionately grounded in institutional mission and responsive to the market.

The inclusion of mission-related goals in SEM practice is not a new idea. Goals such as increased opportunity for underserved populations have been among institutional priorities for decades. The opportunity for difference in the future, however, rests in how those mission-related goals are balanced with market-related goals and pressures in informing SEM strategy. By way of example, Hossler (2007) juxtaposed the differences in mission-related enrollment management goals for elite, private institutions from those of community colleges, which he previously described as fulfilling regional needs for degree attainment or individual courses, and accordingly providing open access to higher education:

> At the other end of the continuum are highly selective, elite private institutions such as Yale, Stanford, Williams, and Amherst—institutions that expend extraordinary amounts of time and effort to select an entering class of students they believe will fit, be successful, make positive contributions to the campus community, and find their educational experience satisfying (p. 103).

If one applies an ethical lens to SEM and utilizes the prescribed mission and market balance as a compass, it is reasonable to conclude that the described enrollment goals of the elite, private institutions mentioned previously are inherently ethical—students who fit, are successful, contribute positively to the campus community, and are satisfied with their experiences. Perhaps the ideals of student fit, success, positive contributions, and satisfying experiences are SEM goals that can and should be applied regardless of an institution's stated mission, or its admission selectivity, Carnegie classification, or prestige.

If we refer back to Quirk's (2005) "The Best Class Money Can Buy" article, arguably the most scathing criticism of enrollment management to date, in addition to numerous accusations, the article also includes suggestions that point SEM practitioners toward a more balanced mission and market approach:

> Indeed, the sophisticated methods of enrollment management may be the only way for schools to hang on to their principles while surviving in a cutthroat marketplace (para. 7). . . . And although competition increasingly threatens a university's principles, the most innovative work in the profession comes from enrollment managers who attempt to align market with mission (para. 39).

It is suggested that achieving an intentional balance between mission and market that elevates the importance of mission more than has been the norm offers SEM practitioners the potential for enrollment success and ethical harmony. Kalsbeek (2009) wrote

The functions and responsibilities of EM require us to have one eye on market-based realities and one eye on mission-based aspirations and manage the tensions between them in a way that moves our institutions forward. I believe that . . . EM is not the root of the problem but rather the only way that the tensions between market and mission can be effectively, strategically and intentionally balanced, choosing among the inevitable tradeoffs considered with purpose and with principle (p. 15).

Kalsbeek has walked the walk in addition to talking the talk, hosting in 2009 and 2011 symposia titled, "Balancing Market and Mission," which gathered "enrollment and mission leaders to discuss the balance between mission aspirations and market realities as they shape enrollment strategies and outcomes" (DePaul University, n.d., para. 1). In recent years at a number of enrollment management conferences, I've given presentations titled *Market Realities vs. Mission Statements: Achieving Balance in Enrollment Strategy and Communications*. The intent in the presentations was to offer an example of how the SEM strategies at Loyola University Maryland have balanced mission and market, offering examples of admission, financial aid, and marketing strategies and subsequent enrollment results over time that offer evidence of success from both the mission and market perspectives.

Although the onus falls upon SEM practitioners for more intentional reflection on issues of ethics and the prominence of mission in addition to market in policies and practice, there is a parallel need and role for presidential and trustee leadership on the issue. Chief SEM officers ultimately receive direction from presidents and trustees, and the old adage of leadership starting at the top applies. Former president of Harvard University, Bok (2013b) wrote, "Presidents and trustees would thus be well advised to examine their existing policies and try to eliminate practices that seek immediate financial benefit at the cost of compromising important academic values" (last para). Trinity Washington University president, Patricia McGuire (2007), also is compelling when she suggested the following:

> Trustees can help presidents keep rankings in perspective. Rather than demanding to know why your university dropped several places in the rankings, or rather than celebrating an increase of a few notches, ask more meaningful questions about the data collected and reported in these magazines: What student achievements best represent our values? What are the typical questions families and prospective students ask of the admissions office? Are we providing the clearest, most effective information possible to them? . . . Do we track our year-to-year retention rates effectively? . . . Rankings may be inevitable parts of higher education's reality today, but they need not be determinative of our reputations and purposes (p.21).

The sentiments raised by Bok (2013b) and McGuire (2007) echoed the suggestions championed by Kalsbeek (2009). Hossler and Kalsbeek (2013) offered their prescription for shared leadership and responsibility between trustees/presidents and SEM leaders:

> As we noted in 2008, it ultimately falls to the board of trustees, executive administrators, and governance structures to set appropriate priorities and directions to ensure that both short-and long-term institutional and societal goals are effectively kept in balance. Senior enrollment management leaders have the opportunity and the obligation to help those senior policymakers understand the tensions and trade-offs and the context and consequence of the decisions they make. Having a disciplined and intentional process and an organizational structure for effectively managing the pursuit of multiple—and often competing—enrollment goals is increasingly critical to institutional viability and vitality (p. 23).

This handbook is intentional in its choice of "strategic" enrollment management as its subject matter, which suggests an approach to managing enrollments with a long-term or comprehensive philosophy. Bob Bontrager (2004) argued "SEM is not a quick-fix approach. To the contrary, SEM involves a series of carefully-deployed strategies and processes that are implemented, evaluated, and readjusted over time" (p. 15). If a SEM practitioner is by definition one who employs a strategic, or long-term, comprehensive perspective, then isolated goals or perspectives seen strictly through a singular lens should not exist. I suggested earlier that for the purposes of exploring the topic of ethics and SEM, references to ethics and ethical behavior will be applied through the lens of the set of right and wrong principles and behaviors, concerning potential impact on human beings that involve SEM decision-making, policies, and practices. To be a "strategic" enrollment manager is to be long-term and comprehensive in approach. To be an "ethical" strategic enrollment manager is to approach the work with care for what is right and what is wrong, and for principles and behaviors and their potential impact on human beings. Perhaps the mission and market compass is a necessary balance for ethical decision-making in enrollment management, and absent ethical decision-making, "strategic" enrollment management may not be possible.

QUESTIONS FOR REFLECTION

Ethics is a complicated subject, and applying ethics to the work of SEM necessitates reflection upon right and wrong, considering potential impact on human beings. How often does your own SEM organization conduct staff retreats or meetings in which the ethical implications of SEM practices and policies are considered? As a possible path toward ethical reflection in practicing SEM, the following questions are offered:

- With regard to your institution's SEM goals and priorities and resulting practices and policies, how clearly are they articulated from the board/president/supervisor? Have you engaged in meaningful dialogue with the board/president/supervisor regarding the ethical implications of these practices and policies?

- In assessing your SEM practices and policies, what is the balance between mission and market? Are you comfortable with that balance?

- Are your current SEM practices and policies designed to benefit all of your institution's students? Are there any unintended consequences that negatively impact a subset(s) of students? If so, what might you be able to do to change these outcomes?

References

ACT. (2013). 2013 Retention/completion summary tables. Retrieved November 2, 2013, from http://www.act.org/research/policymakers/pdf/13retain_trends.pdf.

Anderson, N. (2013). Five colleges misreported data to U.S. News, raising concerns about rankings, reputation. *The Washington Post*. Retrieved October 8, 2013, from http://articles.washingtonpost.com/2013--02--06/local/36940782_1_scott-jaschik-admissions-data-rankings.

Astin, A. W. (1997). Liberal education & democracy: The case for pragmatism. *Liberal Education*, *83*(4), 4.

Baum, S. (1998). Balancing act: Can colleges achieve equal access and survive in a competitive market? *College Board Review, 186*, 12–17.

Baum, S., & Lapovsky, L. (2006). *Tuition Discounting: Not Just a Private College Practice*. New York: College Board.

Blackwell, R. E. (1936). College Recruiting: Salesmanship or Guidance? *The School Review, 44*(6), 417–424.

Bloom, D., Hartley, M., & Rosovsky, H. (2006). Beyond private gain: The public benefits of higher education. In P. G. Altbach & J. Forrest (Eds.), *International Handbook of Higher Education* (pp. 293–308). The Netherlands: Kluwer Press.

Bok, D. C. (2003). *Universities in the Marketplace: The Commercialization of Higher Education*. Princeton, NJ: Princeton University Press.

Bok, D. C. (2013a). *Higher Education in America*. Princeton, NJ: Princeton University Press.

Bok, D. C. (2013b). The ambiguous role of money in higher education. *The Chronicle of Higher Education*. Retrieved September 12, 2013, from http://chronicle.com/article/The-Ambiguous-Role-of-Money-in/141035/.

Bontrager, B. (2004). Strategic enrollment management: Core strategies and best practices. *College & University, 79*(4), 9–15.

DePaul University. (n.d.). Balancing market and mission symposium. Retrieved October 28, 2013, from http://www.depaul.edu/emm/caa/symposium/.

DeSantis, N. (2014). Flagler College Official Resigns over Inflated Admissions Data. *The Chronicle of Higher Education*. Retrieved February 19, 2014, from http://chronicle.com/blogs/ticker/flagler-college-official-resigns-over-inflated-admissions-data/73031.

Epstein, J. (2009). Behind the SAT-optional movement: Context and controversy. *Journal of College Admission, 204*, 8–19.

Fairtest. (2013). National Center for Fair and Open Testing: SAT/ACT optional 4-year universities. Retrieved October 20, 2013, from http://www.fairtest.org/university/optional.

Fiske, E. B. (1981). Ethical issues in recruiting students. *New Directions for Higher Education, 1981*(33), 41–48.

Gallagher, V. (1992). Ethical considerations in college admission practices: A proposal for dialogic involvement. *Journal of College Admission, 137*, 8–12.

Gladieux, L., & Perna, L. (2005). *Borrowers Who Drop Out: A Neglected Aspect of the College Student Loan Trend*. San Jose, CA: National Center for Public Policy and Higher Education.

Haines, R. W. (1975). Student recruitment practices: A survey yields some surprises. *The National ACAC Journal, 20*(1), 35–37.

Hodum, R. L. (2012). A normative code of conduct for admissions officers. *New Directions for Higher Education, 160*, 29–39.

Hoover, E. (2012). George Washington U. Inflated Class-Rank Data for More Than a Decade. *The Chronicle of Higher Education*. Retrieved November 22, 2013, from http://chronicle.com/blogs/headcount/george-washington-u-inflated-class-rank-data-for-more-than-a-decade/32828.

Hossler, D. (2000a). The problem with college rankings. *About Campus*, *5*(1), 20.

Hossler, D. (2000b). The role of financial aid in enrollment management. *New Directions for Student Services*, *89*, 77–90.

Hossler, D. (2007). Putting students first in college admissions and enrollment management. In J. G. Kramer (Ed.), *Fostering Student Success in the Campus Community* (pp. 101–119). San Francisco: Jossey-Bass.

Hossler, D., & Kalsbeek, D. (2013). Enrollment management and managing enrollments: Revisiting the context for institutional strategy. *Strategic Enrollment Management Quarterly*, *1*(1), 5–25.

Hossler, D., Ziskin, M., Gross, J., Kim, S., & Cekic, O. (2009). Student aid and its role in encouraging persistence. In J. C. Smart (Ed.), *Higher Education: Handbook of Theory and Research* (pp. 389–425). The Netherlands: Springer.

Hugo, E. (2012). Recruitment practices change, but issues remain the same. *Journal of College Admission*, *214*, 38–39.

Jaschik, S. (2014). College VP Inflated Stats. *Inside Higher Ed.* Retrieved February 19, 2014, from http://www.insidehighered.com/news/2014/02/18/flagler-college-admits-vice-president-changed-admissions-statistics#sthash.ulndMH9o.dpbs.

Johnson, B. (1989). Student recruitment: Have we gone too far? *Journal of College Admission*, *125*, 25–28.

Johnson, J. J. & Sline, R. W. (1973). Ethics: Recruitment and matriculation techniques. *The National ACAC Journal*, *17*(3), 6–7.

Jump, J. W. (1995). The ethics of need-blind admission. *Journal of College Admission*, *147*, 12–15.

Kalsbeek, D. (2006). Some reflections on SEM structures and strategies (part 1). *College & University*, *81*(3), 4.

Kalsbeek, D. (2009). Opening address. Balancing Market and Mission: Enrollment Management Strategies in Catholic Higher Education Symposium. Retrieved October 28, 2013, from http://www.depaul.edu/emm/_downloads/caa/2009_MarketMissionSymposium_KalsbeekOpeningAddress.pdf.

Litten, L. H. (1981). Avoiding and stemming abuses in academic marketing. *College & University*, *56*(2), 105–122.

Mackey, M. (1980). The selling of the sheepskin. *Change*, *12*(3), 28–33.

McGuire, P. (2007). Outflanking the rankings industry. *Trusteeship*, *15*(1), 18–21.

McKenna, D. L. (1976). Ethics for earthquakes and other emergencies. *The National ACAC Journal*, *21*(2), 26–28, 34.

McPherson, M. S., & Schapiro, M. O. (1994). *Merit Aid: Students, Institutions, and Society.* New Brunswick, NJ: Consortium for Policy Research in Education, Report 30.

National Association for College Admission Counseling (NACAC). (2013). NACAC history: 1937. Retrieved October 27, 2013, from http://www.nacacnet.org/about/history/Pages/1937.aspx.

Nicklin, J. (1994). Cultivating parents: Colleges see them as potential contributors; critics decry some tactics used. *The Chronicle of Higher Education.* Retrieved October 16, 2013, from https://chronicle.com/article/Cultivating-Parents/84603/.

Oxford Dictionaries. (n.d., a). Retrieved October 12, 2013, from http://www.oxforddictionaries.com/us/definition/american_english/ethics.

Oxford Dictionaries. (n.d., b). Retrieved October 12, 2013, from http://www.oxforddictionaries.com/us/definition/american_english/moral?q=morals#moral__9.

Perna, L. W. (2010). *Understanding the Working College Student.* Sterling, VA: Stylus.

Quirk, M. (2005). The best class money can buy. *The Atlantic.* Retrieved October 12, 2013, from http://www.theatlantic.com/magazine/archive/2005/11/the-best-class-money-can-buy/304307/.

Rivard, R. (2013). Using FAFSA Against Students. *Inside Higher Ed.* Retrieved October 28, 2013, from http://www.insidehighered.com/news/2013/10/28/colleges-use-fafsa-information-reject-students-and-potentially-lower-financial-aid.

Silber, J. R. (1980). Marketing higher education: The survival value of integrity. *The National ACAC Journal, 24*(3), 6–9.

Strauss, V. (2013). Should colleges consider financial aid in admissions decisions? *The Washington Post.* Retrieved October 25, 2013, from http://www.washingtonpost.com/blogs/answer-sheet/wp/2013/10/25/should-colleges-consider-financial-aid-in-admissions-decisions//.

Supiano, B. (2013). George Washington U. now admits it considers financial need in admissions. *The Chronicle of Higher Education.* Retrieved November 22, 2013, from http://chronicle.com/article/George-Washington-U-Now/142527/.

Tinto, V. (2006). Research and practice of student retention: What next? *Journal of College Student Retention: Research, Theory & Practice, 8*(1), 1–19.

Wang, M. (2013). Public colleges' quest for revenue and prestige squeezes needy students. *The Chronicle of Higher Education.* Retrieved September 12, 2013, from http://chronicle.com/article/Public-Colleges-Quest-for/141541/.

Zemsky, R. (2009). *Making Reform Work: The Case for Transforming American Higher Education.* New Brunswick, NJ: Rutgers University Press.

Zemsky, R. (2013). *Checklist for Change: Making American Higher Education a Sustainable Enterprise.* New Brunswick, NJ: Rutgers University Press.

Zemsky, R., Shaman, S., & Shapiro, D. (2001). *Higher Education as Competitive Enterprise: When Markets Matter.* San Francisco: Jossey-Bass.

Zemsky, R., Wegner, G. R., & Massy, W. F. (2005). *Remaking the American University: Market-Smart and Mission-Centered.* New Brunswick, NJ: Rutgers University Press.

CHAPTER 30

Summing Up: The Present and Future Tense for SEM

Don Hossler and Bob Bontrager

U sing the word "tense" in a title may, upon first read, seem an odd choice for inclusion in a summary chapter of any book, but in this case the term fits. Definitions of the word include such phrases as "taut," "characterized by strain," "a state of nervousness." All of these phrases capture the lived lives of Strategic Enrollment Management organizations and many of the individuals who work in these organizations. SEM sits at the intersection of some of the most pressing public and institutional policy issues in the United States. Concerns about access, equity, affirmative action, affordability, student debt, and postsecondary education quality both inform public policy debates and create substantive cross pressures on SEM organizations. In addition, they face concerns about equity and diversity, the use of SAT and ACT test scores, the insatiable press for additional tuition revenue, institutional financial aid discount rates, and greater prestige (often simplified for four-year institutions as their numeric ranking in the *US News & World Report* "America's Best Colleges" series). This is no small group of expectations and pressures to juggle. It does, like all important administrative functions, create a modicum of tension and leads us to the conclusion that working within SEM organizations is never dull and often presents more interesting opportunities (or challenges) than any individual or organization might rationally wish for. We offer these observations in both a tongue-and-cheek fashion and also with a focus on the realities of holding senior leadership positions in SEM organizations.

PRESENT TENSE

It should be clear by the end of this volume that the factors and challenges that shape SEM divisions within postsecondary institutions are both complex and varied. Recall the information presented in Chapter 28, which examines the growing trend of having separate SEM organizations for graduate and professional schools, as well as applying SEM concepts to the recruitment of international students. These are important developments for two reasons. First, they demonstrate the extent to which SEM has become a normative administrative function that goes beyond traditional undergraduate enrollment management efforts. Second, these developments have created new career opportunities for higher education professionals who are interested in a career in SEM.

The first part of this volume provided a context for the remainder of this handbook, which is its primary focus. By the time readers have reached this ending chapter, it should be evident that SEM is a blend of using the latest research on areas such as college choice, financial aid, student retention, student success, and higher education finance, along with research conducted for individual campuses on market position, the effects of campus-based aid, and studies of student engagement, the effects of diversity, and academic support. These bodies of research help guide SEM strategies, policies, and practices. The amount of campus dollars being spent on SEM has grown dramatically as has the staff of admissions, financial aid, registration and records; research units housed within SEM; the costs of acquiring student information system software; and the increasing amount of campus-based financial aid dollars that are being spent on efforts that *shape the class.* Don Hossler and Derek Price (2014) have documented this increase:

> Recent studies conducted by the National Association of College and University Business Officers (NACUBO) show that the average discount rate at private institutions in 2012 was 39.7 percent for all students and 45 percent for first-year students. More recently, tuition discounting has become increasingly common among public colleges and universities, with research showing that the average tuition discount rate (that is, the ratio of total institutional grant aid relative to gross tuition revenues) has been steadily rising since 2002, to 12.3 percent in 2008 (p. 36).

Articles about pressures of finding, supporting, and retaining high quality IT staff in SEM divisions has become an important consideration. Collectively, these rising costs have not gone unnoticed, and SEM divisions find themselves increasingly under pressure to reduce their costs, while of course still achieving all of the objectives.

In this volume, we have tried to show the linkages between what might be thought of as *academic research* and practice across the offices of admissions, financial aid, registration and records, and, although the organizational home is more varied, the coordination of efforts to enhance student retention and graduation. Other recurring themes have been presented in this handbook, such as the role of technology. Technology has become so important that it underpins virtually every office in educational institutions. Thus the role of technology has merited its own chapter but is also discussed extensively in chapters that cover offices and functions in the areas of admissions, financial aid, registration and records, and student retention. Technology has become so important that many offices within SEM organizations routinely face difficult decisions about replacing traveling admissions professionals or whether to eliminate two support staff positions in order to fund a new technology-focused position or to retain well-trained technology professionals (Wolff & Bryant, 1999; Waters, 2012).

In this volume we have devoted considerable attention to the utility of research and technology for successful SEM efforts. SEM units cannot be successful if they do not have access to institutional research efforts that focus on admissions and recruitment, financial aid, and student retention. As already noted, most large universities now have their own internal SEM staff, while many smaller colleges and universities rely on consultants. Regardless of the source of research, it is critical to the successful SEM efforts. We also emphasize, however, that the importance of careful attention to the organization and management of the various functional units that make up SEM divisions should not be lost. Several chapters in Part V emphasize the importance of hiring good staff and of finding the right organizational structure for offices such as admissions or financial aid, and the value of training and professional development. One of the potential risks within a SEM division is that senior management will get so enamored with strategy, enrollment and financial aid modeling, and technology that they will forget about some of the basic elements of running any successful organization. Having the right mix of experts in the various specialty areas within admissions, financial aid, and registrar's offices, along with a robust information technology environment and the staff to support both the functional requirements of each office and to support the systems is essential. These chapters also emphasize the importance of speed and timeliness of decisions and communication, space management, implementation of policies that protect student privacy, assessment of programs and policies, and connection with important divisions on campus such as academic affairs, the office of the CFO, and so on. Sometimes it is so easy to get caught up in the in the more exotic and visible aspects of SEM that these important backroom elements can be overlooked and their value underestimated.

Strategic planning and thinking are also discussed in this volume and play and important role. Strategic enrollment plans have several benefits. They bring both internal (staff within the SEM organization) and external stakeholders (other university stakeholders) together to help create a joint vision for SEM divisions. The importance of creating this joint vision of the near-term goals of a SEM organization should not be underestimated. Involving this range of stakeholders can build support for a plan that will energize internal stakeholders and create greater understanding and buy-in among external campus stakeholders. Chapter 27 provides an excellent insight into the enrollment planning process in which both SEM units and the larger campus should be engaged. Chapter 26 provides a thoughtful discussion of the steps and SEM division can take so that the entire unit becomes a strategic sensing unit, where staff within the unit realize that they may attend internal or external meetings to obtain information that can be very useful to one or more of the offices within a SEM organization. We also emphasize the importance of a good understanding of public policy and demographic trends as part of any ongoing planning process. Future demographic projections and public policy trends are essential as they shape the context for SEM planning.

Collectively, this volume offers a comprehensive understanding of the roles and responsibilities of senior leader in SEM organizations. It also provides a broad overview of the research, management, and planning functions and the critical role they play in successful SEM divisions.

THE FUTURE TENSE

Although the chapters in this handbook have not focused heavily on the future, several chapters have noted trends that are affecting SEM, ranging from challenging demographic developments and public policy directions, to the growing influence of technology and the race for prestige and how it influences institutional enrollment goals. There is little to suggest that the demands and challenges on SEM divisions and their senior leaders are going to abate. The list of pressure points is extensive:

- Societal and public policy pressures institutions to keep tuition costs low while institutional policy makers increasingly look to SEM organizations to enroll enough students at the right price to balance campus budgets (Johnson, n.d.; Wolff & Bryant, 1998; Waters, 2012).

- There are growing societal and public policy concerns over rising costs and the merit arms race: how much should institutions spend on merit-based financial aid (Kirp, 2005; Luzer, 2010)?

- Pressures on college admissions include the appropriate role for standardized tests such as the ACT or SAT exams. Do non-cognitive measures and holistic review represent a better approach? And what is the future affirmative action in college admissions (Wright, 2000; Zwick, 2004)?

- The ever-present pressures to improve institutional prestige, which are even strong among community colleges, where federal and state policy makers pressure to improve their retention rates, transfer rates, and their production of certificates and degrees (Frank, 2012; O'Meara & Bloomgarden, 2011).

- Although public policy pressures are in tension with those delineated in point 3, pressure from federal and state policy makers asks institutions to increase access and completion among low-income, first-generation college students, but as pointed out in Chapter 5 by David Kalsbeek and Brian Zucker, student academic indicators at time of entrance are very good predictors of who will eventually earn a degree or certificate.

- Budget reductions within postsecondary institutions make it more difficult for SEM units to achieve institutional objectives (Archibald & Feldman, 2010; Martin, 2011). This is particularly vexing because of the constantly rising costs of technology—both software and the staff to maintain and use software.

- Virtually all of the concerns we have delineated are true for many parts of the world. Concerns about how to pay for tertiary education are relevant to almost every nation around the globe. Demographic trends of growth or contraction are driving enrollment policies in many countries. China is expanding postsecondary access, while Japan and Russia, for example, face environments where there may not be enough recent high school graduates to fill the current capacity of their tertiary education systems. The press for colleges and universities to be more efficient is a global phenomenon (Guimarães, 2013; Lesthaeghe, 2010; Peng, 2011).

In Chapter 1, we started with the observation that SEM was arguably one of the newest major administrative functions to emerge in postsecondary education. The rise of new organizational functions always begs the question, Is this an administrative fad or does it represent a change that will persist and remain part of the postsecondary education administrative landscape? We posit that given the pressures we have outlined in this chapter and throughout the handbook, SEM is here to stay.

References

Archibald, R. B., & Feldman, D. H. (2010). *Why Does College Cost so Much?* New York: Oxford University Press.

Frank, R. H. (2012). The prestige chase is raising college costs. *The New York Times*, March 10, 2012.

Guimarães, R. R. (2013). The future of higher education in BRIC countries: A demographic perspective. *Revista Brasileira de Estudos de População*, *30*(2), 549–566.

Johnson, N. (n.d.). *College Costs and Prices:* Some Key Facts for Policymakers. Lumina Foundation Issue Papers. Retrieved from http://www.luminafoundation.org/publications/issue_papers/College_Costs_and_Prices.pdf.

Hossler, D., & Price, D. (2014). Tuition discounting in an era of accountability and scarcity. *Association of Governing Boards Reports*, *2*(22), 35–39.

Kirp, D. L. (2005). This little student went to market. In R. Hersh & J. Merrow (Eds.), *Declining by Degrees: Higher Education at Risk* (pp. 113–120). New York: Palgrave Macmillan.

Lesthaeghe, R. (2010). The unfolding story of the second demographic transition. *Population and Development Review*, *36*(2), 211–251.

Luzer, D. (2010). The Problem with Financial Aid. *Washington Monthly.* Retrieved from http://www.washingtonmonthly.com/college_guide/blog/the_problem_with_financial_aid.php.

Martin, R. E. (2011). *The College Cost Disease: Higher Cost and Lower Quality.* Northampton, MA: Edward Elgar Publishing.

O'Meara, K., & Bloomgarden, A. (2011). The pursuit of prestige: The experience of institutional striving from a faculty perspective. *Journal of the Professoriate*, *4*(1).

Peng, X. (2011). China's demographic history and future challenges. *Science*, *333*(6042), 581–587.

Waters, J. K. (2012). The High Cost of College: Is Tech Part of the Problem or the Solution? *Campus Technology.* Retrieved from http://campustechnology.com/articles/2012/06/25/the-high-cost-of-college.aspx.

Wolff, T. L., and Bryant, P. S. (1999). *Top Ten Trends in Enrollment Management.* Retrieved from http://www.luminafoundation.org/publications/synopsis/enrollment99.pdf.

Wright, L. F. (2000). The role of standardized admission tests in the debate about merit, academic standards, and affirmative action. *Psychology, Public Policy, and Law*, *6*(1), 9.

Zwick, R. (Ed.). (2004). *Rethinking the SAT: The Future of Standardized Testing in University Admissions.* New York: Routledge.

NAME INDEX

591

SUBJECT INDEX

603

Eduventures, 21
EFC. *See* Estimated family contribution
Efficiency: of advertising, 117; electronic
  transcript and, 141; inefficiency, 501;
  operational, 378; outcomes-based funding
  and, 251; staffing, 422; system, 136;
  technology and, 405, 435
1890 land-grants, 473
EIS. *See* Enrollment Information Services
El Paso Community College (EPCC), 139
Elasticity: cross-elasticities, 182; own-price,
  464; pricing and, 181–184
Electronic transcript, 141
Elementary and Secondary Education Act, 474
Eligibility: for financial aid, 415; model of
  admissions, 149, 150, 152, 160–161
Email, 424
Emotional skills, 166
Empirical support, 277–279, 282–283
Empirically based models, 271, 274–276
Engineering schools, 152
English as Second Language (ESL), 521
English instruction, 520–521
Enhanced recruiting models, 316
Enhancement model, of admissions, 150
Enrollment: admission and enrollment
  partnership models, 137–139; analysis
  models for, 225–227; behavior, 220–222;
  co-enrollment programs, 137–138; cross-
  enrollment, 422; decline in, 551; demand,
  81–82; funnel, 131; goals for, 375, 386, 390,
  544–545; growth of, 385, 480; key indicators,
  542–543; measures of, 88, 90; new transfer,
  457–459; nontraditional patterns of, 128;
  part-time, 512; projection models for, 540;
  sustainable outcomes, 546; at two-year
  institutions, 32
Enrollment Information Services (EIS), 461
*Enrollment Management: An Integrated
  Approach* (Hossler), 8
Enrollment Management Review, 549
Enrollment Planning Service, 453
Enrollment Research Team (ERT), 449–450; of
  Iowa State University, 456–467
Enrollment-based budgeting, 35
Enterprise resource planning (ERP), 428–429,
  431, 435–436, 438, 441
Entitlement model, of admissions, 150
Entrepreneurial orientation (EO), 491, 500–503,
  505; autonomy and, 501–502; competitive
  aggressiveness and, 502–503; innovativeness
  and, 502; measuring, 503; proactiveness and,
  502; risk-taking and, 502
Entrepreneurship, 500–501

Entry characteristics, 292, 293, 294–296, 299,
  302–304
Entry level positions, in admissions office, 382
Environment: academic, 515; of campus, 280;
  open systems, 33, 399
Environmental change, in demand, 179
Environmental model, of admissions, 150
Environmental scan, 544; at Iowa State
  University, 457–460; technology and,
  432–437
EO. *See* Entrepreneurial orientation
EPCC. *See* El Paso Community College
Equilibrium, 320
Equity: admissions and, 156–160; brands, 493;
  social, 25
ERP. *See* Enterprise resource planning
ERT. *See* Enrollment Research Team
ESL. *See* English as Second Language
Essays, 153
Estimated family contribution (EFC), 226, 416
Ethical issues, 530, 565–567; case studies
  of, 576–577; completion and, 575–576;
  conclusion to, 577–581; future issues of,
  571–576; persistence and, 575–576; present
  issues of, 571–576; previous literature on,
  567–571; reflection on, 576–577, 581; student
  funding and, 573–575; student recruitment
  and, 572–573
Ethnicity, 23–25, 295, 461–462; college
  choice by, 55–62; completion rates and, 24;
  persistence and, 246. *See also* Students of
  color; *specific ethnic groups*
ETS. *See* Educational Testing Service
Europe, 10, 554–555, 560. *See also specific
  countries*
European Union, 522, 530
Excel (Microsoft), 455
Exchange process, marketing as, 104–105
Executive leadership, 535, 540
Executive Team, 540
Expected costs, 51
Exploitation, 505; of information, 491, 500
External changes, in demand, 179
External data, 452–453
External factors, 543
External information, absorption and
  exploitation of, 491
External stakeholders, 114, 378, 427, 587

F
Facebook, 118, 424
FAFSA. *See* Free Application for Federal
  Student Aid
Fairness, admissions and, 156–160

If you found this book useful, take a look at these subscriptions.

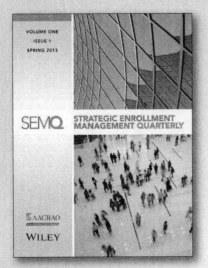

Strategic Enrollment Management Quarterly

Quarterly subscription

wileyonlinelibrary.com/journal/semq

Enrollment Management Report

Monthly subscription

www.enrollmentmanagementreport.com

The Successful Registrar

Monthly subscription

www.thesuccessfulregistrar.com